Contents

List of Illustrations — *vii*

Preface — *xi*

Acknowledgments — *xv*

Transcribers' / Editors' Notes — *xvii*

Prologue — 3

Introduction — 4

First Chronicle — Attending High School in Tennessee, January 1, 1885–November 27, 1886 — *29*

    Chapter 1 — A Student's Dilemma, January 1, 1885–September 14, 1886 — *33*

    Chapter 2 — Deciding on a Vocation, September 15, 1886–November 27, 1886 — *57*

Second Chronicle — Living among Big Jim's Band, November 22, 1891–January 22, 1892 — *87*

    Chapter 3 — Clerking for Big Jim's Business Council, November 22, 1891–December 2, 1891 — *91*

    Chapter 4 — Reflecting on Traditional Absentee Shawnee Culture, December 6, 1891–January 22, 1892 — *109*

Third Chronicle — Making a Living in Oklahoma Territory, March 14, 1892–November 28, 1897 — *127*

    Chapter 5 — Translating at Big Jim's Crossing, March 14, 1892–April 12, 1893 — *130*

    Chapter 6 — Interpreting at the Indian Missions, February 2, 1895–October 2, 1895 — *157*

    Chapter 7 — Teaching at Choctaw City, October 3, 1895–March 6, 1896 — *231*

Chapter 8	Teaching at Shawnee, March 9, 1896—April 24, 1897		*261*
Chapter 9	Living on His Own, May 1, 1897—November 28, 1897		*318*

Epilogue *361*

Appendix *375*
Notes *433*
Bibliography *443*
Index *453*

Illustrations

Map

I.1. Oklahoma tribal land division, 1866–1889 9

Figures

I.1. William Shawnee Sr., before 1871 7
I.2. Elizabeth Jane (Wright) Shawnee, before 1871 7
I.3. Thomas Wildcat Alford 20
I.4. Farm that may have belonged to William Shawnee Sr., before 1900 24
I.5. Possible portrait of Walter Homer Shawnee and Dudley Joseph Shawnee 26
1.1. Page 89 of William Ellsworth Shawnee's First Chronicle 30
2.1. Page 16 of William Ellsworth Shawnee's Second Chronicle 88
3.1. Page 10 of William Ellsworth Shawnee's Third Chronicle 128
E.1. Eva Estella Shawnee 367
E.2. Rebecca Shawnee 368
E.3. Lydia Shawnee 368
E.4. Marquis Lafayette Shawnee 369
E.5. Emeline Shawnee 369
E.6. Julia Inez Shawnee 370
A.1.1. Page 1 of Big Jim's memorial 379
A.1.2. Page 2 of Big Jim's memorial 380
A.1.3. Page 3 of Big Jim's memorial 381
A.1.4. Page 4 of Big Jim's memorial 382

A.1.5.   Page 5 of Big Jim's memorial *383*
A.1.6.   Page 6 of Big Jim's memorial *384*
A.1.7.   Page 7 of Big Jim's memorial *385*
A.1.8.   Page 8 of Big Jim's memorial *386*
A.1.9.   Page 9 of Big Jim's memorial *387*
A.1.10. Page 10 of Big Jim's memorial *388*
A.1.11. Page 11 of Big Jim's memorial (missing) *389*
A.1.12. Page 12 of Big Jim's memorial *390*
A.1.13. Page 13 of Big Jim's memorial *391*
A.1.14. Page 14 of Big Jim's memorial *392*
A.1.15. Page 15 of Big Jim's memorial *393*
A.2.1.   Emeline Shawnee's lease, April 19, 1913 *395*
A.2.2.   Notary page of Emeline Shawnee's lease *396*
A.2.3.   *William Shawnee v. John Marshal* petition, Oct. 11, 1897, page 1 with cover sheet *397*
A.2.4.   *William Shawnee v. John Marshal* petition, page 1 without cover sheet *398*
A.2.5.   *Shawnee v. Marshal* petition, page 2 *399*
A.2.6.   William E. Shawnee land allotment, June 11, 1890 *400*
A.2.7.   William E. Shawnee land allotment cover page *401*
A.2.8.   William Shawnee Sr. land allotment document, Jan. 25, 1890 *402*
A.2.9.   William Shawnee Sr. land allotment cover page *403*
A.3.1.   Julia Shawnee account statement, Oct. 31, 1911 *405*
A.3.2.   Julia Shawnee account statement, Nov. 30, 1911 *405*
A.3.3.   Julia Shawnee account statement, Dec. 31, 1911 *406*
A.3.4.   Julia Shawnee account statement, Jan. 31, 1912 *406*
A.3.5.   Julia Shawnee account statement, Feb. 29, 1912 *407*
A.3.6.   William E. Shawnee bank note, April 12, 1898 *407*
A.3.7.   Accounting scratch paper *408*
A.3.8.   Miscellaneous addition scratch pad *408*

A.3.9.   William E. Shawnee's signature card *409*

A.4.1.   Beginning of Carrie Warrior letter, second copy *411*

A.4.2.   Carrie Warrior letter, continued *412*

A.4.3.   Page 9 of letter from Walter H. Shawnee to George Shawnee *413*

A.4.4.   Page 10 of Walter H. Shawnee's letter *414*

A.4.5.   Page 1 of letter from Asst. Comm. regarding lease to Asa Walls *415*

A.4.6.   Page 2 of letter from Asst. Comm. *416*

A.4.7.   Dept. of Interior letter, July 22, 1912, regarding W. Shawnee Sr. estate *417*

A.4.8.   Letter from Burt & Shaha attorneys to Emeline Shawnee, Dec. 3, 1912 *418*

A.5.1.   William Shawnee Sr. *420*

A.5.2.   Back of William Shawnee Sr. photo *421*

A.5.3.   Unidentified infant *422*

A.5.4.   Elizabeth Jane Shawnee *423*

A.5.5.   Back of Elizabeth Jane Shawnee photo *424*

A.5.6.   Possible photo of William Shawnee's farm *425*

A.5.7.   William E. Shawnee *426*

A.5.8.   Back of William E. Shawnee photo with signature and studio hallmark *427*

A.5.9.   Walter and Dudley Shawnee, 1883 *428*

A.5.10. Back of Walter and Dudley Shawnee photo *429*

A.5.11. Walter or Dudley Shawnee *430*

A.5.12. Back of Walter or Dudley Shawnee photo *431*

A.5.13. Back of envelope in which documents and photos were stored, with inscription *432*

Preface

William Ellsworth Shawnee was a young man of black and Native American ancestry who was adopted by, and grew up among, the Absentee Shawnees in what is now central Oklahoma after the Civil War, and kept a diary. This book includes a transcribed, annotated version of Shawnee's handwritten diary from that era, as well as copies of other documents that were filed with his diary in the Pottawatomie County Historical Society archives in Shawnee, Oklahoma. His diary, which is not presented in chronological order, was previously transcribed and published, as it had been written, in the *Autobiography of William Ellsworth Shawnee*.[1] This version of Shawnee's diary before you is presented in chronological order and couched in context. Background is provided on Shawnee's environment and some of the people he identifies in his diary; this volume also connects Shawnee's life with the lives of those in his immediate family. The intent is to help the reader understand the era during which Shawnee and his family lived among the Absentee Shawnees, not to detail already well-documented Oklahoma, Absentee Shawnee, or African American history.

According to Shawnee's diary, he, his father, and some of his brothers served as interpreters for the Absentee Shawnees, Kickapoos, Society of Friends (Quakers), and federal Indian agents. Shawnee's diary reveals that his family lived in central Indian Territory before the land runs of the 1880s and 1890s and afterward in Oklahoma Territory. They interacted with other central Oklahoma tribes, which included the Iowa, Citizen Potawatomi, and Sac and Fox, and with the nearby Seminole, Creek, Cherokee, Choctaw, and Chickasaw Nations. Shawnee wrote entries in his diary in both English and Absentee Shawnee. In addition to entries describing his daily activities, Shawnee peppered his diary with Absentee Shawnee language lessons, biblical lessons, school lessons, and Quaker lessons on morality.

We heard about William Ellsworth Shawnee several years ago during our research on Pottawatomie County schools. Local newspaper articles written about him suggested that he had been the first teacher in the first high school that Betty attended. An excerpt from his journal included the surname of a family in

Betty's high school. That intrigued us. Articles written about Shawnee also suggested that he was a friend of Thomas Wildcat Alford, an Absentee Shawnee who had attended Virginia's Hampton Normal and Industrial Institute. Hampton had been built for former slaves in 1868, and ten years later had accepted Native American students. We found Alford's attendance at Hampton and his friendship with Shawnee intriguing. Even more intriguing was an essay that we read about Shawnee's eight siblings who had also attended Hampton Institute as Indian students, not as black students. The essay revealed that Hampton school officials identified students as black or Indian and segregated them on campus accordingly. Yet there was nothing in the essay that connected Shawnee to his siblings who attended Hampton. We wanted to learn more about Shawnee's education and about the education of Shawnee's siblings and their connection with the Absentee Shawnees. We also wanted to better understand the relationships of Native Americans, blacks, and whites in early Pottawatomie County to determine whether the information would be useful in our research on Pottawatomie County schools.

Several Pottawatomie County Historical Society members noticed our interest in William Ellsworth Shawnee and asked us if we would consider transcribing his diary after we finished our project on the Pottawatomie County schools. They informed us that multiple efforts at transcribing his diary had been started and then abandoned. After we agreed to their request, one of the historical society's members arranged a meeting for us with the Absentee Shawnee cultural director. After more inquiry, we learned that Shawnee's original handwritten diary was still located in the Santa Fe Depot Museum—now the Pottawatomie County Museum—in Shawnee, Oklahoma, and that the daily entries in the diary were not presented in chronological order. Although Shawnee's handwritten diary had been in the Historical Society archives for several years, it is uncertain who donated the diary to the Historical Society or when it came into the society's possession. The diary consists of three separate journals dating from January 1, 1885, through August 30, 1897. The dates December 1, 1886, through September 1891, and the dates May 1893 through December 1894, are not covered in any of the journals.

After unsuccessfully attempting to contact the previous transcribers to determine how much of his journals they had completed, we transcribed exact replicas of the journals and published them for the Pottawatomie County Historical Society. The annotated chronicles before you highlight Native American, black, and white relationships over time. Because William Ellsworth Shawnee was an adopted Absentee Shawnee citizen, our effort at transcription began only after we consulted with the Absentee Shawnee cultural director, Joseph Blanchard. He asked why we were writing about one of their citizens and what our sources of information were. We told him about the diary and identified some of our sources. Among other sources, we obtained information about Absentee Shawnee history from the University of Oklahoma Western History Collection. It was outlined in a course developed by the American Indian Institute at the University of Oklahoma in the spring of 1969 and presented by Julia Jordan to the Absentee Shawnees in Little Axe, Oklahoma.[2] In addition, we obtained photographs of and data about Shawnee's siblings from Hampton University with the assistance and permission of the Absentee Shawnee tribe. The greatest difficulties we faced in obtaining sources were paucity of written records about Shawnee during his era, conflicting names and conflicting birthdates for the same individual, and conflicting dates for the same event.

What can one tell about Shawnee from his journals? After the Civil War, Shawnee had spent the bulk of his life among Native Americans in the area that is now central Oklahoma, particularly among the Absentee Shawnee tribe. He was a devout Quaker. The Absentee Shawnees, though divided into two bands in Shawnee's era, were a close-knit group regardless of whether they were deemed "traditional" or "progressive." The role of the interpreter, regardless of race, was important in providing a cultural bridge between the tribe and the traders, government agents, lawyers, missionaries, and ordinary citizens around it. Shawnee's family was intimately involved with and interpreted for both Absentee Shawnee traditional and progressive groups.

William Ellsworth Shawnee's journals are important for many reasons. They include highlights of Absentee Shawnee history; they preserve some features of the Absentee Shawnee language and culture during the latter part of the nineteenth century; they preserve lessons from the Quaker manuals of the time; they provide a first-person view of the work of interpreters among the Native peoples in early central Oklahoma; they provide little-known insights into black history in early central Oklahoma; they include little-known history about relationships among Native Americans, blacks, and whites in the area; and finally, the heart of these journals reveals what it was like to be a young adopted Absentee Shawnee man of mixed black and Native American heritage, who lived among both bands of the Absentee Shawnees, and navigated the worlds of Native Americans, whites, and blacks in early central Oklahoma.

Acknowledgments

The assistance and advice of the following people were instrumental in transcribing and producing this annotated, chronological version of William Ellsworth Shawnee's journals: Ken Landry, director of the Pottawatomie County Museum, and his staff; Tom Terry, president of the Pottawatomie County Historical Society; Ken Fullbright, past executive director of the Santa Fe Depot Museum; Dr. Robert Barnard, Pottawatomie County historian; Joseph H. Blanchard, former cultural director of the Absentee Shawnee Tribe; Leonard Longhorn, former cultural director of the Absentee Shawnee Tribe; Kelli Mosteller, director of the Citizen Potawatomi Nation Cultural Heritage Center; Second Chief Ben Barnes of the Shawnee Tribe; Mosiah Bluecloud, Native language translator; staff of the Oklahoma History Center; the late Hon. Glenn Dale Carter; attorney James T. Stuart; Donzella Maupin, archives manager, and Andreese Scott staff member, Hampton University Archives; Absentee Shawnee tribal representative Anthony Johnson, oversight official of the Cultural Preservation Department, and other officials Andrew Warrior and Suzie Newport Nease; and Emily and Neal Schuster, copyeditors.

Transcribers' / Editors' Notes

In transcribing William Ellsworth Shawnee's journals, we followed the guidelines of the National Archives and Records Administration (available at www.archives.gov/citizen-archivist/trancribe/citizen-archivist/transcribe/tips) and the Association for Documentary Editing, as indicated in *A Guide to Documentary Editing—Online Edition* by Mary-Jo Kline and Susan Holbrook Perdue (available at http://gde.upress.virginia.edu).

As noted in the preface, Shawnee's original, handwritten journals are not in chronological order. This version of his journals presents his daily activities in chronological order.

Shawnee's journals include English, Absentee Shawnee, Kickapoo, and Greek words.

His original, often phonetic, spelling of words has been retained (e.g., cannot, can not, to-day, sepulchre, corallary, Lă-loú-wē-pĕă, and Κυριάκος). For clarity, the spelling of some words has been suggested in square brackets (e.g., remeny [remedy?]).

Letters of the alphabet that were illegible in the original entries but that appeared in partially clear words have been suggested and enclosed in square brackets (e.g., tinep[i]wei).

Obscured or missing words and letters that could be determined by context have been suggested in square brackets for the sake of clarity (e.g., thru[st] or send [them?]).

Words and phrases that were completely illegible are indicated with [. . .] in square brackets.

In some instances, a note to the reader is inserted in [*square brackets*] where ink blots and other flaws affected the legibility of the original document.

Text added by the transcribers for clarity is provided in italic type and enclosed in square brackets (e.g., [*page 55, missing page*] or per mentem [*mensem—month*]).

Unrecognizable words and phrases are flagged with the letters "sp" and a question mark in square brackets to indicate possible spelling errors (e.g., "Maly [*sp?*] outfit of marshalls").

Names have been transcribed as written (e.g., Miss Kessel, Miss Kessell, or W^m. P. Hastings).

Dates have been transcribed as written (e.g., January 25th 1897); journal entry dates have been italicized and placed on the left-hand side of the page, (e.g., *Jan. 24th 1897, written today*).

Punctuation has been transcribed as written with one exception: equals signs that Shawnee used to hyphenate words have been replaced by hyphens.

Underlined text has been transcribed with the underlining retained rather than converted to italic type (e.g., "together again").

Crossed-out text has been transcribed as crossed out (e.g., ~~Hereafter~~ Elsewhere).

The original paragraphing has been retained. When Shawnee's paragraphing was unclear, the transcribers inserted paragraph breaks as needed for clarity.

Pagination in the original journals is indicated in italic type in square brackets (e.g., [*page 12*]). Page numbers refer only to the original documents and not to the chronological version of the files we created.

Double square brackets indicate Shawnee's use of square brackets in the original text (e.g., [[Moce henoke mike . . . .]]).

The names of newspapers and titles of books that could be identified as such have been placed in italic type (e.g., the *New York Independent*).

Accounting sheets for bookkeeping exercises have been placed in table format to ensure the entries appear aligned here as they appear in the original journal.

Accounting scratch pad entries for bookkeeping exercises have been reproduced here in similar size and placement on the page as they appear in the journal.

Other entries (e.g., lines of poetry) are also presented here to resemble how they appear in the journals.

Black Interpreters Living Among the Absentee Shawnee Indians in Early Central Oklahoma

Prologue

Life on the frontier was constantly changing, and early central Oklahoma was no exception. A land run in 1889 created six new counties, including current Oklahoma and Cleveland Counties, and established the beginning of Oklahoma Territory in what is now central Oklahoma. After the land run, beginning with the Oklahoma Organic Act in 1890, new laws were ushered into the area by the Oklahoma Territorial Legislature. The laws were interpreted and implemented by the local governments. In 1891 at Big Jim's Crossing in Cleveland County, William Ellsworth Shawnee, a young Quaker, wrote in his journal: "The whites are supreme here now, and they are opposed to any marriage between a partial colored person and one of themselves, even to the extent of enacting and enforcing laws against this thing. These laws, though unjust and unfair, do not violate anything that is our positive duty toward God. So there is no adequate cause for disobeying them, . . . But there is no law forbidding colored and Indian from marrying. . . . Consequently no objection can be raised against a marriage between myself and Carrie." Shawnee entered those words in his journal after Oklahoma's second land run, which established Pottawatomie and Lincoln Counties in Oklahoma Territory. The second land run had opened Indian lands in central Oklahoma to non-Indians and subjected everyone to the new laws, such as the marriage laws Shawnee wrote about. Shawnee was a passionate young man who wanted to marry Carrie Warrior, the woman of his choice: however, he was bound to obey the new territorial laws even though he believed some of them were unfair. Shawnee was also bound to obey divine law. He wrote: "Passion is very strong in men; this is a veritable fact. The divine law forbids all indulgence in passion except in matrimony, . . ." If Caroline Warrior would not consent to be his wife, Shawnee planned to ask Emma Valentine, a young black woman whom he had met in the East. He wrote: "The first choice would please both me and my brothers; the second choice pleases, not them but me. . . . Time alone can tell what to do."

Introduction

American Indians in central Oklahoma today face the same issues that Native people faced during the latter part of the nineteenth century when William Ellsworth Shawnee lived among them: What does it mean to be a citizen of my tribe? What does it mean to be a U.S. citizen at the same time? What cultural traditions do I want to keep? What technology and changes in U.S. culture am I willing to embrace? Who am I willing to invite into my tribe as a marriage partner? How do I want my children to be educated? And just as important for some individuals, who can I trust, be they friends, educators, or government officials?

One difference between American Indian lives today and during the era in which Shawnee lived is that the great effort to rid Native peoples of their cultures and to assimilate them into U.S. culture other than on their own terms has passed. Tribal governments were restored in the twentieth century, facilitating their making other U.S. citizens aware of their relationships with their neighbors and aware of their contributions to U.S. culture. Histories that describe the radical changes that took place in the relationships among American Indians, blacks, and whites in Indian Territory after the Civil War depict Indian-black-white relationships in eastern and western Indian Territory, but only Indian-white relations in central Indian Territory, if at all. William Ellsworth Shawnee, who lived in central Indian Territory after the Civil War, wrote in his diary about ordinary people there and provides glimpses of the relationships among Indians, blacks, and whites under both Indian governments and the Oklahoma territorial government.

Who Was William Ellsworth Shawnee?

Shawnee was an educated man of black and Indian ancestry who lived with his family in central Indian Territory (known today as central Oklahoma) among the Absentee Shawnees after the Civil War. He was a prolific writer and kept a diary, consisting of three journals, which describe his day-to-day activities, his education, and his finances. Among his other pursuits, he interpreted for the Absentee Shawnees as his father, William Shawnee Sr., had done before him. William Ellsworth Shawnee's journals document the important roles of interpreters in the Indian community in early central Oklahoma. The journals also reveal the changes in the lives of, and in the interrelations among, Indians, blacks, and whites in early central Oklahoma as land became the "must have" commodity, and new laws that came with the land runs dictated the behavior of Indian and non-Indian alike.

To make more sense of William Ellsworth Shawnee's journals, it is important to put the time of his birth in perspective. Although he lived in central Oklahoma most of his life, Shawnee was born in Lawrence, Douglas County, Kansas, on December 23, 1868, three years after the end of the Civil War. By this point, most blacks who set foot in what we now call the United States of America had been stripped of much of their African culture and assimilated, as some would contend, into American culture, except as slaves—not as U.S. citizens. They performed some of the same jobs, used the same language, and practiced the same religion as whites. Even free blacks were not citizens until the adoption of the Fourteenth Amendment in July 1868, just five months before Shawnee was born. Some American Indians were also citizens of the United States, but only those who had been forced or volunteered to take allotments of land on which they were taxed. Others who lived on reservations were not taxed and were not considered citizens. Shawnee and his family, when they moved to central Oklahoma with the Absentee Shawnees after the Civil War, first lived among, and were adopted by, Indians who were not U.S. citizens. Natives in Indian Territory were citizens of their own tribes. Moreover, they wanted to live on their own reservations in communal groups, to govern themselves, and to maintain their own cultures. Becoming U.S. citizens was neither important nor desirable to them.

William Ellsworth Shawnee's Ancestry

We don't know when William Shawnee started using Ellsworth as his middle name. His name is listed in William Shawnee Sr.'s family records as William Ivery Shawnee. Most of Shawnee's ancestry is sketchy; however, he provides some clues about his family in his journals. His parents, William Shawnee Sr. and Elizabeth Jane (née Wright) Shawnee, were wed in Lawrence,

Kansas, on December 7, 1867, in the African Methodist Episcopal (AME) Zion Church. He was thirty and she was nineteen.[1] They were identified as U.S. citizens in 1870. The 1870 U.S. census reported that William Shawnee Sr. lived on a farm in Eudora Township in Douglas County, Kansas, with his wife, Lizzie, and his son, William.[2] The census listed their race as mulatto and the races of their closest neighbors as whites and blacks. The 1870 agricultural census for Eudora listed Shawnee Sr. as having a forty-acre farm where he raised grain and kept horses and swine.[3] Shawnee Sr. and Elizabeth also had a daughter, Cora Anner, who was born in Lawrence on September 3, 1870, after the census was taken. Her name is also listed in Shawnee Sr.'s family records.

Shawnee wrote passionately about his father at times, both revering and criticizing him. About his father's heritage, he wrote: "He is a mixture of races. It is apparent that he is not a full blooded colored person from sight. His complexion is yellow or copper-colored, his hair curly but not kinky." Shawnee Sr. had five siblings. William Ellsworth Shawnee writes two different accounts of his father's ancestry. One was that William Shawnee Sr. was the son of a Cherokee slaveholder, in North Carolina, and a mulatto girl about seventeen or eighteen years old. It is unclear whether Shawnee claims that Shawnee Sr.'s father was born in North Carolina or whether Shawnee Sr. was born there. In Shawnee's story, his grandfather morphs into Shawnee Sr. The second account of Shawnee Sr.'s ancestry was that Shawnee Sr. was born in the Cherokee Nation in Webbers Falls, Indian Territory, and that Shawnee Sr.'s father's ancestry was Cherokee and Mexican, while his mother's ancestry was Cherokee, Shawnee, and colored. Shawnee Sr. and Hester Chisholm (wife of William Chisholm, who was the son of Jesse Chisholm for whom the Chisholm Trail was named) were cousins, the children of two sisters. Shawnee Sr. once lived with the father of Jack Girty, a colored man in Cherokee country in Indian Territory. As a youth Shawnee Sr. was captured with some other Indians by a band of Indians who would become known as Absentee Shawnee, and was adopted into the tribe. Shawnee Sr. lived among the Absentee Shawnee as one of them. Having a faculty for languages, he was valuable to the tribe as an interpreter and translator. He was fluent in English, Cherokee, and Shawnee languages, and had "a passing acquaintance" with the

Creek, Kickapoo, Delaware, Sac, and Seminole languages. Shawnee Sr. taught himself to read and write after he became an adult, and he wrote his own letters.

William Ellsworth Shawnee's mother, Elizabeth, was born in 1849 in Arkansas.[4] Shawnee wrote that her skin was as white as a white woman's and her hair just as straight, and that she was half Cherokee and half colored. Elizabeth could barely read and write; Shawnee wrote letters to Elizabeth's mother for her. Elizabeth had a sister, Martha Lacy, who was born in Arkansas and moved to Kansas.[5] Martha had a daughter, Enola. Shawnee and his Aunt Martha exchanged letters about his cousin "Nollie."

above Fig. I.1. William Shawnee Sr. before 1871, when he migrated to Indian Territory. Courtesy of the Pottawatomie County Museum, Shawnee, Oklahoma.

William Ellsworth Shawnee's Journals
Shawnee authored three journals from 1885 through 1897, parts of which are written in the Absentee Shawnee language of his era. Other parts contain language lessons with Absentee Shawnee to English translations. According to members of the Absentee Shawnee tribe who are aware of those portions of his journals, Shawnee used phonetic spellings for the Absentee Shawnee words.

Equally important to their value in preserving the sound of some of the Absentee Shawnee language, Shawnee's journals begin to fill a void in early central Oklahoma history. They

above Fig. I.2. Elizabeth Jane (Wright) Shawnee, before 1871. Courtesy of the Pottawatomie County Museum, Shawnee, Oklahoma.

highlight the interrelations among central Oklahoma Indians, blacks, and whites after the Civil War. Most histories that document the radical changes that took place in the relationships among Indians, blacks, and whites in Oklahoma during the post-Civil War period are silent about blacks and their relationships with Indians and whites in central Oklahoma. In contrast, Shawnee's journals reflect the world through the lens of a young, black Quaker of that time and place. His journals prove that blacks lived among the Indians and whites in central Oklahoma after the Civil War. Moreover, Shawnee's journals reveal that the Absentee Shawnees in central Oklahoma treated his family as citizens with the same rights and privileges as other tribal citizens. Shawnee's journals further provide a window into the interrelations among the Indians, blacks, and whites after the land runs in central Oklahoma.

Shawnee paints a picture of the world around him and exposes his innermost thoughts and feelings as he records his activities, observations, desires, and prayers. His journals are historic records of the times and reveal that, as an interpreter, he stood at the intersection of several cultures and related easily to people of all races. His journals portray the lives of ordinary people who lived in early central Oklahoma, including his family, friends, and others with whom he came in contact. Many characters who jump out of the pages of his journals are American Indians and whites who worshipped at the Quaker missions in central Oklahoma. Others who skip across the pages of his journals are whites and blacks whom he met when he attended high school in Maryville, Tennessee, and immigrants who rushed to central Oklahoma during the first two land runs. Shawnee exposes notions about citizenship, race, culture, and self-identity. He provides insight into his own character as he reminisces about his education in Indian Territory and Tennessee; describes his duties as tribal clerk, laborer, surveyor, interpreter, translator, farmer, and teacher among the Indians; ponders his romantic interests; and blasts racial intolerance, including that within his own family.

Central Oklahoma Occupants through the Civil War
Where is central Oklahoma, and who lived there during the nineteenth century? What we consider central Oklahoma today was, for much of the nineteenth century, sandwiched between the

Cimarron River on the north, the South Canadian River on the south, Creek and Seminole countries on the east, and the "Unassigned Lands" on the west. The Unassigned Lands—unoccupied lands that had been ceded by the Creek and Seminole Nations to the federal government after the Civil War—are the lands that opened to settlement during the run of 1889. The North Canadian River, a principal feature of the terrain, meanders through the center of the area, northwest to southeast. Indians lived along the North Canadian. What would become central Oklahoma was before the land run home to the Absentee Shawnee, Citizen Potawatomi, Kickapoo, Iowa, and Sac and Fox Indians. The Deep Fork River crossed the land halfway between the Cimarron and North Canadian rivers and separated the Kickapoo and Iowa reservations. Whites in the area before the run included spouses of Indians, Indian agents, Christian missionaries, and traders. Blacks included William Shawnee Sr.'s family, who lived among the Absentee Shawnees in Indian Territory, and subsequently in Oklahoma Territory.

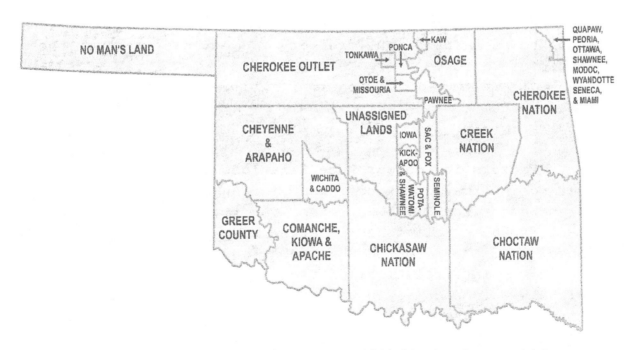

Map I.1. Federal division of tribal land, 1866-89, in what would become the state of Oklahoma. Courtesy of the Oklahoma Department of Transportation.

Thousands of indigenous peoples lived in Indian Territory before the Civil War. The history of the Indian groups who lived in Indian Territory, the removal of Indian groups to Indian

Territory before the war, and the roles of various Indian Territory groups in the war are well documented. Tribes in the western portion of Indian Territory before the war included the Apaches, Comanches, Caddoes, and Wichitas. Those who lived in the eastern portion after removal but before the war were the Cherokees, Chickasaws, Choctaws, Creeks, and Seminoles. While citizens of the various nations in eastern Indian Territory lived much like many U.S. citizens, they were not. As citizens of sovereign nations, they owned large tracts of land, and some owned slaves. Some joined the Confederates in the Civil War, while others joined the Union. Some attempted to flee to Kansas to evade the war.[6]

The land in central Oklahoma where William Ellsworth Shawnee eventually lived was owned by the Creeks and Seminoles before the war. After the war, five different tribes made the area home. Members of at least two of the five, however, had lived there before. Shawnee Indians who moved to the area between 1839 and 1859 thrived there before the war. Some had moved there from Texas and some from Kansas. They became known as the Absentee Shawnee tribe.[7] During the Civil War, the Absentee Shawnees in Indian Territory fled to Kansas under the leadership of Cherokee Jesse Chisholm, and some served in the Union army.[8] The Kickapoos had moved to central Oklahoma from Texas before the Civil War,[9] and some fled to Mexico during the war.[10]

Factors in Postwar Race Relations (1865–1887)

Conflicting information exists about Indian-black interactions before and after the Civil War. Less information exists about Indian-black-white relationships after the war. As previously mentioned, William Ellsworth Shawnee's journals provide a glimpse of the interrelations of these three groups after the war in what would become central Oklahoma. What influenced the relationships of these three groups after the Civil War? Several factors influenced Indian-black-white interrelations in the United States and its territories, including Indian Territory, after the Civil War. First, the attitudes among these groups in the United States and its territories toward each other had already been developed over a long period of slavery. Although some Indians owned slaves, whites believed that both blacks and Indians were inferior. Blacks and Indians each believed that the other was inferior and that whites were untrustworthy.[11] Second, Indians owned large tracts of land in the West that settlers wanted to occupy. Third, blacks were presumed to be assimilated into mainstream U.S. society already, albeit as slaves and not as citizens. Much of their African cultures had been stripped from them and replaced by American culture. Many American citizens did not believe that blacks should have equal social status. A fourth factor in postwar race relations was that the federal government took actions in dealing with American Indians and black Americans that had long-term consequences for both citizens and noncitizens alike. The government promoted homesteading in the West, oscillated in how it treated blacks and implemented Reconstruction, and made changes in Indian policy.

Promotion of homesteading meant that American Indians would have to give up most of their land. The Homestead Act was signed into law in 1862. It allowed a person to possess a homestead by filing an application for undeveloped federal government land, improving the land by building a structure on it, growing crops and living on it, and filing a deed for the land at a local land office by submitting proof of residency and improvements.[12] Over time this led to the transfer of land, once owned by Indians, to a majority of non-Indians.

The government's approach toward blacks oscillated from toleration of slavery to abolition of it, and from extension of U.S. citizenship and the right to vote to disenfranchisement and segregation. The government took several steps in abolishing slavery. It adopted the Thirteenth Amendment to the Constitution, which freed the slaves,[13] although the measure did not free the slaves in Indian Territory. The government established the Freedmen's Bureau in March 1865, which, among other things, aided in educating freedmen and others.[14] The government also defined U.S. citizenship and the rights of citizens in the Civil Rights Act of 1866. Citizenship extended to former slaves and free blacks but excluded Indians who were not taxed (i.e., those living on reservations).[15] After defining citizenship, the U.S. government adopted the Fourteenth Amendment to the Constitution, which addresses citizenship rights and equal protection under the laws.[16] The 1866 Civil Rights Act and the Fourteenth Amendment nullified the *Dred Scott v. Sanford*[17] decision that had been handed down by the Supreme

Court in 1857. The court had held that a black person, enslaved or free, was not a citizen. After nullifying the *Dred Scott* decision, the U.S. government adopted the Fifteenth Amendment, which prohibits the federal and state governments from denying a citizen the right to vote based on that citizen's race, color, or previous condition of servitude.[18] Following the amendments, three Enforcement Acts gave the president legal authority to protect citizens in their right to vote because of the violence that had been perpetrated against black citizens in the South when they tried to vote.[19] However, the government moved U.S. troops out of the South in 1877, leaving black voters without support.[20] Hostilities between some whites and blacks followed, and blacks soon became disenfranchised through Jim Crow laws.[21]

Changes in Indian policy were of paramount importance in Indian-black-white race interrelations after the Civil War and beyond. Since its beginning, the United States had established diplomatic relations with the various Indian nations through treaties. In March 1871, the U.S. Congress passed the Indian Appropriations Act, which provided that the government would no longer contract with Native peoples by treaty, although it would continue to honor treaties already in existence.[22] Another change in Indian policy was the implementation of Grant's Peace Policy to solve the perceived problems associated with American Indians. The reasons for Grant's policy were many and varied. Some Indians had become destitute and had lost much of their population because of warfare, disease, and other reasons. Settlers continued to push west and fought to open up reservation land for settlement by non-Indians. Some states wanted to get rid of all their reservations. The intrusion of non-Indians on Indians was breaking down Indian self-government. Relationships between Indians on reservations and their non-Indian neighbors were not good. Much public opinion was against legislative reform favoring American Indians. Indians were thought to be in the way of industrial development, such as the building of new railroads. Fraudulent activity in some Indian agencies drained away Indian appropriations. Some U.S. citizens wanted to change what they thought were inferior Indian cultures and religions to resemble those of the whites. As a result of these multifaceted reasons, Indian policy changed from one of isolating Indians on reservations to one of assimilating them into U.S. culture. Tribes were to be subject to U.S. laws, and their members converted to Christianity and educated. The communal reservation lands were to be broken up and Native peoples forced onto individual land allotments, and given U.S. citizenship.[23]

Postwar Central Oklahoma Native Reservations, 1867—1877

As previously noted, Shawnee's journals provide a firsthand view of Indian-black-white interrelations in what would become central Oklahoma during the era in which he wrote. Postwar life followed a different path for Indians and their slaves in Indian Territory, and for all other noncitizen Indians elsewhere, than it did in the rest of the country. The first attempt to contain each Indian group on a reservation with well-defined boundaries began before the policy change to assimilate all Indian groups into U.S. culture. Although each group of American Indians who went to Indian Territory after the Civil War had a different removal experience, their lives were intertwined with each other and with those who lived around them.

How Reconstruction was implemented with regard to tribes in what would become central Oklahoma was dependent on treaties the government had renegotiated with the eastern Indian Territory nations. In 1866 the government wrote new treaties with the tribes in Indian Territory that had sided with the Confederacy. Treaties for the Cherokee, Chickasaw, Choctaw, Creek, and Seminole peoples required that they cede part of their land to the United States to be used for the settlement of other Indians, abolish slavery and adopt their former slaves into their tribes, grant right of way for railroads to be built across their land, and accept land allotments by individual members of the tribes. All five nations complied with the treaties and gave their former slaves limited rights as citizens, though the Choctaws waited twenty years before they adopted their freedmen. The Chickasaw Nation never adopted its former slaves, and the government never removed them from the Chickasaw reservation. Therefore, the Chickasaw freedmen were left in an uncertain status for forty years, as they had no Chickasaw citizenship or U.S. citizenship until Oklahoma became a state in 1907.[24]

In central Oklahoma after the war, the federal government relocated the Absentee Shawnee, Kickapoo, Citizen Potawatomi, Iowa, and Sac and Fox Indians to the western part of the Creek and Seminole lands that had been ceded to the government. Except for the Unsettled Lands to their west, where no one lived, these five groups settled in an area bordered on all sides by other Indian groups, with whom they frequently interacted. Much of what we know about the Indians who inhabited what would become central Oklahoma comes from the reports of Indian agents. Indian agents, working on behalf of the federal government, and Christian missionaries aided in the settlement of and the administration of day-to-day affairs of these tribes. In addition to looking after the interests of the federal government, the agents supervised annuity payments to Native peoples and enforced various treaties. Christian missionaries strove to acculturate Native peoples by establishing missions and building schools and providing teachers. Others who played key roles among these groups were licensed traders and interpreters and translators. Licensed traders opened stores and stocked them with goods of interest to the tribes. Interpreters and translators, similar to their counterparts in other tribes, bridged cultural barriers between the Indians who could not speak English and the Indian agents, missionaries, and traders.

Although resettlement of these five new Indian groups has been generally thought of as easy, in comparison to removal of the western Indian Territory tribes, for whom settlement was peppered with warfare,[25] these resettlements were not without their issues, too. The federal government negotiated treaties with the Absentee Shawnee, Citizen Potawatomi, and Sac and Fox Indians in 1867, for reservations in Indian Territory. However, the treaty that the government negotiated with Absentee Shawnee chiefs John White and Samuel Hill on March 2, 1867, was never ratified. In 1867, therefore, the Absente Shawnees began returning to their homes in Indian Territory without titles to their lands. Moreover, the land making up the reservation covered by the treaty negotiated with the Citizen Potawatomi included the area already occupied by the Absentee Shawnee.[26]

The Absentee Shawnee moved to Indian Territory over a period of years, during which time William Shawnee Sr. moved with them. According to Quaker and Kansas historical records, William Shawnee Sr. appeared among the Absentee Shawnee Indians in 1870 in Indian Territory. In November 1870 Quaker Indian agent William Nicholson from Kansas, and his group, conducted a tour of the Indian agencies in Kansas and Indian Territory. They encountered Absentee Shawnee chief John White, Samuel Charley, Joseph Ellis, Robert Deer, and William Shawnee Sr. in Indian Territory, where they had lived before the Civil War. Nicholson reported that they spoke some English, lived in crude houses, and were rounding up their livestock and assessing the damage inflicted on their property during the war. Their total property damages amounted to about two hundred thousand dollars. Further, according to Nicholson's report, some Absentee Shawnees had already returned to Indian Territory, some were at Bird Creek, and more were planning to come from Kansas. Nicholson estimated that there were about seven hundred Absentee Shawnees in all. The Sac and Fox Agency was assisting them with their claims against the federal government for damages. At a conference several days later, Nicholson listed Robert Deer in the conference minutes as an Absentee Shawnee interpreter.[27] Since Shawnee Sr. lived on a farm in Douglas County, Kansas, as indicated by the 1870 U.S. census, one can only speculate as to whether he lived with the Absentee Shawnees in Indian Territory before the war and lost property there, or whether he was there with the others, when Nicholson saw them, assessing the property damage and acting, along with Robert Deer, as an interpreter.

The other four groups began moving to Indian Territory by 1869. When the Sac and Fox began moving from Kansas to Indian Territory in 1869, the Quakers established an Indian agency for them near what is present-day Stroud, Oklahoma.[28] The agency came to serve all of the tribes in the area. When the Citizen Potawatomi began moving to Indian Territory in 1870, they found the Absentee Shawnees living on their reservation. The federal government had made a mistake and had assigned both groups to the same area. The mistake had to be corrected without making new treaties with the two groups. As previously noted, the government abolished treaty making with the Indian nations in 1871. Therefore, the final settlements of these tribes in what would become central Oklahoma were made through other means. In 1872, by congressional action, the Absentee Shawnees were allowed to remain on the Citizen Potawatomi reservation where they had settled.[29] The Kickapoos were induced to move to Indian Territory by 1873,[30] and the Iowas began moving there in 1876.[31] Both were assigned reservations by executive order in 1883.[32]

After Chief White died, a split occurred among the Absentee Shawnees over land allotments. In 1872, after White's death, the

Absentee Shawnees elected John Sparney and Joe Ellis as chiefs. They served for ten years. During their administration, the federal government passed a law authorizing the Citizen Potawatomi reservation to be divided into allotments because many Citizen Potawatomi had become citizens in Kansas and could not hold land in common. When the Citizen Potawatomi reservation allotments began in 1875, some members of the Absentee Shawnee tribe who also lived on the Citizen Potawatomi reservation took them. Absentee Shawnee chiefs Big Jim and Sam Warrior refused to accept any land allotments in severalty.[33] Big Jim, the grandson of the famous chief Tecumseh, carried on his grandfather's tradition to oppose relinquishing Indian lands. In 1876, under the leadership of Big Jim and Sam Warrior, Big Jim's band, as it is known today, split from the Absentee Shawnee group led by John Sparney and Joe Ellis and moved north of the Absentee Shawnee lands to the Kickapoo Reservation. In 1883 the remaining group of Absentee Shawnee Indians, the White Turkey band as it is known today, elected White Turkey and William Littleaxe as chiefs following John Sparney and Joe Ellis. Not long after Sparney and Ellis served as chiefs, both died—Ellis in 1884 and Sparney in 1885.[34]

To meet their goals for Christianizing, civilizing, and assimilating the Indians into American society, the federal government sponsored schools. Both Quaker and Catholic missionaries worked among the tribes in what would become central Oklahoma. The Quakers worked among the Sac and Fox, Absentee Shawnee, Kickapoo, and Iowa settlements, and they also served the Citizen Potawatomi. In 1872 a Sac and Fox boarding school was opened near the Sac and Fox Indian agency,[35] and Quaker Joseph Newsom and his family built a mission and school for the Absentee Shawnees south of present-day Shawnee near the Shawneetown trading post. By 1875 the federal government had taken over the Quaker school but kept the Quakers as teachers. At first, the Quakers used the Bible, beginning with Genesis, to instruct Absentee Shawnee students, according to Thomas Wildcat Alford, one of the first students. Other early students included David Alford, John King, Martin Starr, Charley Starr, Jacob Tomahawk, Susie Tomahawk, Robert Conalas, Cooper Wilson, Annie Wilson, Isaac McCoy, and Bud Tyner. The advantage of this effort is that it began to provide the Absentee Shawnees with a cadre of English-speaking people who could relate to the Indian agents without an interpreter. Thomas Alford, along with John King, two of the first graduates of the Absentee Shawnee School, would later be sent to school in the East and become leaders in their tribe. Elkana Beard succeeded Joseph Newsom at the Absentee Shawnee mission in 1877, and Franklin Elliott succeeded Elkana Beard in 1879. Two of the first members to attend the Absentee Shawnee mission were a Citizen Potawatomi couple, Antoine and Mary Bourbonnais. Attempts had been made to establish a Kickapoo mission at the Kickapoo village in 1875, but they were unsuccessful.[36]

The Catholic Church established a mission and school on the Citizen Potawatomi reservation. Father Isidore Robot from France founded Sacred Heart Mission in 1876, and later built Sacred Heart Institute for boys and St. Mary's Academy for girls in the same vicinity. Some white children, along with the Indian children, attended these schools. Catholics also established missions in surrounding areas and aided in building and conducting a school for Choctaw and Chickasaw freedmen, who lived on the south bank of the South Canadian River, until the freedmen were able to settle on their allotments.[37] The Citizen Potawatomi also built four public day schools with the aid of the Sac and Fox Indian Agency.

Breaking Up Central Oklahoma Native Reservations, 1877—1887
Although education played a pivotal role in breaking up the Indian reservations in Indian Territory, Indian students who were both informally and formally educated shaped the future Indian communities in what would become central Oklahoma. After the Civil War, some Indian children who lived in the area never attended the local schools founded by the missionaries and never learned English. They participated in their traditional ceremonies and passed their various cultures on through informal and oral traditions. Some Indians who attended school embraced American culture as a means to save their own. They passed their various cultures, as well as American culture, on to future generations through both formal and informal methods.

Formal Indian education was influenced largely by two men with opposing views on race and on educating Indians. Both General Samuel Chapman Armstrong and Captain Richard Henry Pratt had fought in the war, spent time around Native Americans, and commanded black troops at one time or another. Their opposing views shaped Indian education and the results of their perspectives still reverberate today as Native American groups seek to reclaim their cultures.

With regard to race, Armstrong believed that whites were superior to Indians and blacks. As a young man, Armstrong had witnessed the inclusion of manual labor into the curriculum for Hawaiian students, which he noted forced them to work, unlike their parents whom he deemed lazy. He believed that former slaves should be educated like those Hawaiian students, and later believed the same for American Indians. In 1896 in Virginia, Armstrong founded Hampton Institute, a private boarding school for former slaves, with the aid of the Freedmen's Bureau. The curriculum included the liberal arts, and agriculture and mechanical subjects. He aimed to develop black leaders and teachers to take their place in American society as it was.

When it came to race, Pratt believed that whites had a superior culture to blacks and Indians but that there were no innate differences in the races. He believed that cultural differences stemmed from environmental differences. He had noticed that after two hundred years of association with whites, blacks had acquired their language, adopted their characteristics, and had become fellow citizens alongside them. He believed that Indian education should be built upon black experience and that Indians also needed to have constant and intimate contact with whites in order to be transformed into fellow citizens alongside them. In 1875 Pratt delivered several Indian prisoners to St. Marion Prison in Florida. There he taught the Indians English and self-support by putting them to work. After three years, they did not want to return to their tribes. Pratt then sought a school for them to attend. The "presumed need to educate Indians to white society" took Pratt and his prisoners to Hampton Institute. Pratt and Armstrong's meeting about Indian education led to the development of off-reservation boarding schools designed to assimilate Indians into American society. Local Indian schools built by the missionaries were ultimately supplemented by these Indian boarding schools. These schools appeared first in the eastern United States, then in the West, built on the model of the school conducted by Richard Henry Pratt in Fort Marion Prison in Florida.[38]

Hampton Institute was opened to Indian students in 1878 at the persuasion of Richard Henry Pratt. Once the Indian program at Hampton began, Armstrong and Pratt's opposing views on race and on education of Indians became obvious. Armstrong believed that it would take years to assimilate the Indians into white American society. His plan for Indian education was evolution. He believed that the Indians should be taught their culture in addition to the liberal arts and mechanical and industrial subjects and that they should return home and teach their own people. He also segregated the black and Indian students on the Hampton campus. Conversely, Pratt's plan for Indian education was revolution. He believed that Indians should be assimilated into white society quickly. He believed that the Indian students should not be taught their culture, that they should be taught English, and that they should not be allowed to speak their language at school. Pratt thought that the Indian and black students should not be segregated on campus. Both Armstrong and Pratt believed in an "outing system," a program in which the Indian students would go out and work for whites on farms and other places when school was not in session.[39] Several children from the Absentee Shawnee, Citizen Potawatomi, and Sac and Fox tribes in what would become central Oklahoma later attended Hampton. When Thomas Alford attended Hampton, he described the school as part military and part industrial because the students wore uniforms and marched and drilled.[40] Encouraged by the success of the first Indian students from Ft. Marion at Hampton, but dismayed by the manner in which the Indian program was implemented, Richard Henry Pratt started an off-reservation Indian school using the abandoned army barracks at Carlisle, Pennsylvania, in 1879, which the legendary central Oklahoma athlete Jim Thorpe attended.[41] Other boarding schools were built later that central Oklahoma Indian students attended, including Chilocco Indian School in north-central Oklahoma and Haskell Institute in Lawrence, Kansas.[42] Whereas the philosophy behind many black schools of that era was for students to return home and help their people, the philosophy behind the Indian schools was to dissuade Indian students from practicing their culture and to prepare them to assimilate into and compete in U.S. society.[43]

In 1882 Thomas Alford returned to Indian Territory from Hampton Institute and taught at one of the Potawatomi day

Fig. I.3. Thomas Wildcat Alford, teacher, interpreter, and member of the Absentee Shawnee tribe. Date unknown. Courtesy of the Pottawatomie County Museum, Pottawatomie County Oklahoma.

schools.[44] Later he taught at the Absentee Shawnee School.[45] John King returned from Hampton Institute and opened a store near current-day Dale, Oklahoma.

By 1883 the Native residents of what would become central Oklahoma were in various stages of "assimilation" into U.S. culture, with the aid of the missionaries. Many of these people were largely self-supporting, while some depended on annuity payments to make ends meet. Most of them planted gardens and owned horses, cattle, hogs, garden implements, and wagons. Some still hunted. Some held rigidly to their traditional customs, including religion, housing, and dress. Some lived in tents and bark houses. Others, for example the Citizen Potawatomi, dressed similarly to and built houses that looked like those of whites in the states. Many of the Indians were dissatisfied about the allotment of their land and refused to take it in severalty. They wanted to remain on a reservation, in which the land was held communally. Native peoples were divided about the government's plan for the education of their children. Many supported the schools, and others were adamantly opposed to them. Some were afraid that educating their children in the methods of the prevailing culture would make the children have hearts like white people.[46] In 1883 there were still no local schools for the Iowas and Kickapoos.[47] That year, William Ellsworth Shawnee was on his way to Maryville, Tennessee, to begin school at Freedmen's Institute. Also in 1883, those Absentee Shawnees who had fled to the Kickapoo Reservation under the leadership of Big Jim to avoid allotments were doing well economically but were considered intruders. Asked repeatedly by the government to move, they continued to refuse.[48] In 1886, the government forced Big Jim's band out of the Kickapoo Reservation, and the group eventually moved to a new home near current-day Little Axe in Cleveland County. By 1888 Big Jim's band began a claim against the government for losses sustained from its forced move from the Kickapoo Reservation.[49]

In 1883 Franklin Elliott was still at the Absentee Shawnee Mission near Shawneetown. In 1885, Elliott built a frame church building. The congregation of fifty included Indians, blacks, and whites. In 1885, Dr. Charles Kirk and his wife succeeded the Elliotts. Church membership reached sixty-three and remained at that number for eight years.[50] Other forces surrounding the Indians in what would become central Oklahoma would lead to major changes in their lifeways. Railroads were being built though Indian Territory, east, west, north, and south. Cattle were being driven through the territory. Would-be homesteaders pressured the government to open up the Unassigned Lands for settlement. On February 8, 1887, the General Allotment Act, also known as the Dawes Act, provided for the allotment of all lands in severalty to all Indian tribes except the eastern Indian Territory nations and attached U.S. citizenship to the act of taking an allotment.[51]

Postwar Central Oklahoma Non-Indian Settlements, 1888—1897
After years of agitating for land, non-Indians won the fight to settle in Indian Territory on former Indian lands. The Indian Appropriations Act of March 2, 1889,[52] paved the way to open the Unassigned Lands to homesteaders. On April 22, 1889, thousands of whites and blacks from all over the United States, but mainly the neighboring states of Kansas, Texas, and Arkansas, rushed into the Unassigned Lands and staked claims. Overnight, six counties were established, marking the beginning of Oklahoma Territory.[53]

In 1890 the Oklahoma Organic Act[54] was passed, which established a seventh county and created the boundary of Oklahoma Territory and reorganized the legal system of Indian Territory. The act prepared Oklahoma and Indian Territories for statehood. It established a government for Oklahoma Territory and provided a mechanism for Indian tribes in Indian Territory to allocate their communally held land to individual tribal members. Titles would be granted to tribal members who took allotments and to homesteaders who claimed and improved a parcel of land. To entice individual Indians to take allotments, the Indian Naturalization Act allowed Indians to apply for citizenship. In 1890, all of the Indians were enumerated. Also in that year, apart from the Kickapoo, the reservations in what would become central Oklahoma were surveyed and allotments were provided to the Indians. Chief Big Jim held out until the end. Those Absentee Shawnees who assisted the Indian agents in enumerating the Indians and surveying and allotting the Indian lands were the students who had been sent east to Hampton and other schools—students such as Thomas Alford, John King, and William Ellsworth Shawnee. The Absentee Shawnees, even though there were disagreements among them regarding allotments, exercised control over who was enumerated at that time. The second land run in the area took place on September 22, 1891, establishing the current Pottawatomie and Lincoln Counties. Before the government finished breaking up the Indian reservations, however, it changed its way of dealing with the Indians by establishing a simpler procedure for getting the Indians to agree to its decisions. In September 1893, an act of Congress abolished tribal governments and established business committees to conduct tribal business. The men named by the government for the first Absentee Shawnee business committee were Thomas Alford, Thomas Washington (Long Tom), John C. King, John Welch, Switch Little Axe, White Turkey, and Big Jim. Alford was selected to serve as the first chairman. When Big Jim and John Welch refused to serve on the committee, Thomas Rock and Walter Shawnee (William Ellsworth Shawnee's brother) served in their places. After abolishing tribal governments, the federal government continued to break up the reservations. The Kickapoo Reservation was broken up and opened to settlement in 1895.

Incoming migrants to Oklahoma Territory made new laws regarding marriage, burial, education, religion, and more; these measures were prone to adversely affect certain Indian customs and lifeways and would shape the interactions of all the races in the state to come. Laws were enacted and enforced at territorial, county, and city levels. The First Territorial Legislature, which met in August of 1890, used the term "colored" to designate anyone of African descent; it used the term "white" to designate all others, including Indians. One issue that proved to be contentious when establishing Oklahoma territorial laws was whether to establish mixed or separate schools for the two races. This was so contentious that no decision was made until December of that year, and it was a compromise. The counties had the option to establish mixed-race or separate schools, and both kinds were established in what would become central Oklahoma. There were some all-white schools established at first, but few for blacks. Some Indian children enrolled in the white public schools, and some remained in Indian schools.

Indian agents and Christian missionaries continued their work of "assimilating" the Indians between 1888 and 1897 as new people came into Oklahoma Territory to live alongside the Indians and to decide the laws for their new society there. While new laws were being decided, the Iowa mission was built in 1887 and a school was opened in 1890.[55] After unsuccessful attempts to establish a mission at the Kickapoo village beginning in 1875, a school was finally opened there in 1890.[56] During this time, more off-reservation boarding schools for Indian students were established.

The Quakers continued working at their missions and schools, and William Ellsworth Shawnee volunteered among them. Charles Kirk stayed at the Absentee Shawnee Mission until he died in 1893, and Rachel Kirk continued as superintendent until the following year, when she started teaching in the various missions throughout the area. In October 1894, George N. Hartley and L. Ella Hartley took over the work of the mission. By that time many Indian children had started to attend the local white district schools and government boarding schools.[57] In 1897 a mission was established among the Big Jim Band of Absentee Shawnees.[58] It was between 1894 and 1897 that William Ellsworth Shawnee volunteered at and described his activities at the area's Indian missions in his third journal.

In 1896 the *Plessy v. Ferguson* decision,[59] which allowed segregation on rail cars, dramatically impacted the lives of all Oklahoma Territory residents. Racial segregation became the law. In 1897, Oklahoma Territory repealed all previous school statutes and declared that only segregated schools would be established in Oklahoma Territory. Teachers were required to be of the same race as their pupils, which severely limited the interactions of Indians, blacks, and whites for years to come. However, the children of William Shawnee Sr., as adopted Absentee Shawnee citizens, continued to attend the Absentee Shawnee boarding school. While their relationships with the

Absentee Shawnees did not change, their relationships outside of the tribe did.

Black Interpreters among the Absentee Shawnees, 1867-1897

According to William Ellsworth Shawnee's journals, Shawnee Sr. moved his family to Shawneetown, Indian Territory, to live among the Absentee Shawnees in 1871. He built a house, planted peach and apple trees, started a farm, and sold goods that he had brought from Kansas. He also aided the Quakers in starting their Absentee Shawnee Indian School. After moving there, Shawnee Sr. and Elizabeth had three more sons, Dudley Joseph (1872), Walter Homer (1874), and George Eli (1876). The family lived there as adopted citizens of the Absentee Shawnee tribe.

Fig. I.4. Possible photograph of William Shawnee Sr.'s farm in Indian Territory before 1900. An unidentified farmer stands on the right. Photo courtesy of the Pottawatomie County Museum, Shawnee, Oklahoma.

William Ellsworth Shawnee attended the Absentee Shawnee Indian School for eight years, beginning in 1875 at the age of six. At that time the government had already taken over the school and retained the Quaker teachers. Quaker Joseph Newsom had a daughter, Emma, who also taught in the school, and a son whose name was Ellsworth. Because the Indians sometimes took English names, it is possible this is where William Ellsworth Shawnee acquired his middle name. Shawnee learned how to speak Absentee Shawnee at school "and used it much more than English." The instruction was not simply religious in nature at that time. Shawnee studied arithmetic, reading, geography, spelling, penmanship, language, grammar, history, and drawing. His sister, Cora Anner, attended the same school.

Between 1878 and 1887, Shawnee Sr.'s family suffered two tragedies. In 1879 both Shawnee Sr.'s daughter, Cora Anner, and his wife, Elizabeth, died. He continued to live and work among the Absentee Shawnees and maintain his home and farm. In spite of the difficult circumstances, Shawnee Sr. ensured that his sons were educated. His three sons—Dudley Joseph, Walter Homer, and George Eli—attended the Absentee Shawnee Indian School. William Ellsworth Shawnee continued at the school until 1883. Beginning in 1883, he attended four years at Freedmen's Normal Institute in Maryville, Tennessee, a school that had been established in 1872 by the Quakers for former slaves. Shawnee returned to Shawneetown, Indian Territory, in 1887.

After his wife Elizabeth died, Shawnee Sr. married Julia Andersen, a Creek freedwoman from Indian Territory. Their first three children were born between 1883 and 1887 when Shawnee was attending school at Maryville. Eva Estella was born in 1884, Rebecca in 1886, and Lydia in 1887. After 1887, Shawnee Sr. and Julia would have six more children, for a total of nine.

Shawnee Sr. worked among both bands of the Absentee Shawnee tribe. He supported Big Jim with legal claims and made trips to Washington, D.C., with him. As adopted members of the Absentee Shawnee tribe, in 1890 Shawnee Sr. and his children received annuity payments and allotments of land in present-day Pottawatomie County. Shawnee Sr. continued farming. He met and became involved with new Oklahoma Territory residents in Pottawatomie County and elsewhere, including the Reverend John W. Dunjee, a Baptist minister who migrated in from Minnesota. Rev. Dunjee was a missionary who traveled from place to place establishing Baptist churches. He was the father of Ella, Drusilla, and Roscoe Dunjee. Ella and Drusilla taught in Oklahoma Territory schools, and Roscoe later owned the *Black Dispatch*, a newspaper in Oklahoma City.

Shawnee Sr. continued to send his children to school. After leaving the Shawnee Indian School, Dudley Joseph, Walter Homer, and George Eli attended Haskell Institute in Lawrence, Kansas. Walter also attended the Chilocco Indian School. All of them returned to Shawneetown, Oklahoma Territory, at first and leased or worked on the property that had been allotted to them as part of the Absentee Shawnee settlements.

Fig. I.5. Two men presumed to be Walter Homer Shawnee and Dudley Joseph Shawnee, younger brothers of William Ellsworth Shawnee; date unknown. Courtesy of the Pottawatomie County Museum, Shawnee, Oklahoma.

Shawnee Sr. and Julia had five more children between 1888 and 1897. These were Marquis Lafayette (1890), Emeline (1891), Julia Inez (1892), Donna Fredonia (1895), and Myrtle (1897).[60] Some of the children began attending the Absentee Shawnee Indian School. Shawnee Sr. became a Baptist minister and a missionary to the Indians. He built a Baptist church in nearby Tecumseh. It is possible that he was influenced by Rev. John W. Dunjee. After about six years, Shawnee Sr.'s health began to decline, and he gave up his missionary work.

Between 1888 and 1897, the year of William Ellsworth Shawnee's last entry in his journal, he described how he made his living in various pursuits including farming, interpreting, building roads, translating, surveying, and clerking, but what he desired most was to teach. He had returned home from Maryville with the intent to lift up his people. He documented language lessons for the Absentee Shawnees and volunteered at the Quaker missions. He prayed that he would become a better Christian and tried to interest the Absentee Shawnees in Christianity and schooling. After the land runs, he met and leased land to settlers in Oklahoma Territory. He kept abreast of the latest laws and the latest news to determine how they might affect him and his friends. At last he married and started his own family. He mingled easily with Indians, whites, and blacks alike and in his journals provides glimpses of how they related to each other.

First Chronicle

Attending High School in Tennessee

January 1, 1885–November 27, 1886

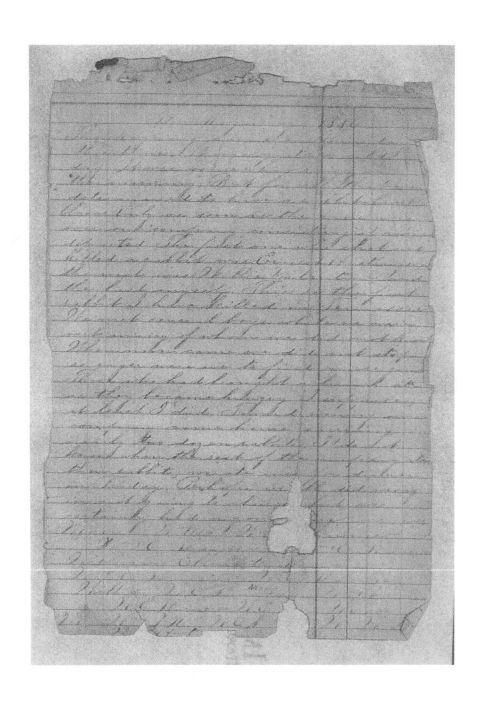

Fig. 1.1. Page 89 of William Ellsworth Shawnee's First Chronicle.

Overview of the First Chronicle

William Ellsworth Shawnee, age fourteen, arrived in Maryville, Tennessee, from Indian Territory in November 1883, after an anxious trip alone for the first time. He had travelled there by rail and steamboat to attend Freedmen's Normal Institute, a school established by Quakers for former slaves in 1872. Black schools were intended to develop black leaders and teachers who would take their place in American society as it was, not in a changed society in which everyone would be treated as equals as some hoped Reconstruction would accomplish. As at similar black schools such as Hampton Institute, students at Freedmen's Institute were taught to return home and encourage others of their race, respect labor, and lead by example. William P. Hastings, a Quaker and the first teacher at Freedmen's Institute, taught the first class in the old AME Zion church in Maryville. By 1874, Quaker Yardley Warner from Philadelphia, the Freedmen's Bureau, and William B. Scott, a black Tennessee newspaper owner, had secured funds and built a new school to replace the old church.[1]

In Maryville Shawnee experienced a cultural awakening. His exposure to the Quakers in Tennessee would have been familiar because they had been his teachers in Indian Territory; however, most of his student companions in Maryville would have been black as opposed to Indian, which described most of his companions in Indian Territory. Life in Maryville would introduce him to the southern black culture in the area. By Shawnee's third year in school, his experiences in Maryville and Knoxville had favorably disposed him toward living in Tennessee. He informed his father that he believed that black citizens could prosper in the state. At that time eastern Tennessee was more lenient toward its black citizens than many southern regions. Maryville had been pro-Union during the Civil War, as well as a base for abolitionist activity. The city also boasted Maryville College, a Presbyterian college where both black and white students were enrolled. Although he was in poverty, Shawnee thrived in this academic environment. Before he left Tennessee, Shawnee visited other parts of Tennessee and was exposed to pro-Confederate white culture.

Shawnee's first journal, dated January 1, 1885, through November 27, 1886, contains diverse types of entries that reveal his experiences as a student. The journal is a bound, legal-size document written mostly in ink, much of which is faded and difficult to read. It is written entirely in English. The journal contains pages 1-104, with additional writing on the inside front cover and the front flyleaf. Pages 97-100 are missing, and a few pages are blank. A letter from his brother Walter Shawnee is also tucked inside the front cover. The daily entries are not in chronological order. Shawnee wrote this entire journal while he was a student at the Freedmen's Normal Institute in Maryville, Tennessee. In it he wrote about his school friends, his family in Indian Territory, his finances, his religion, and his plans for the future. In addition to daily entries, the journal includes Shawnee's autobiography, lessons from the Quaker manuals, and homework exercises in subjects such as bookkeeping and penmanship. This version of the journal has been put in chronological order and is denoted as his "First Chronicle."

Chapter 1

A Student's Dilemma
January 1, 1885—September 14, 1886

By his third year, Freedmen's Normal Institute had changed William Ellsworth Shawnee's life. Hastings was still teaching at Freedmen's Institute when Shawnee arrived, and he sponsored and taught Shawnee for three years. Shawnee became a Quaker at age sixteen and started his first journal in Maryville at age seventeen, after his third year in school. At that point, Shawnee also became uncertain about his future.

In June 1886 Shawnee was in a precarious position at the end of the spring semester at school. He was uncertain whether Hastings would pay his expenses at Freedmen's Normal Institute the following year. On June 22, 1886, he wrote a letter to his father explaining his situation. On August 5, 1886, he elaborated in another letter to his father: "My expenses are not to be paid for another year[. . . .] Mr. William P. Hastings is no longer a teacher in our school. He resigned." Shawnee was left in a quandary. His father could not afford to pay his way home, and Mr. Hastings would no longer pay for his school scholarship. What could he do?

Although Shawnee's first journal entry is dated January 1, 1885, his first daily activity was recorded on June 3, 1886. It is a copy of a letter he had written to his friend Mary Sherman, a student who had gone home from Freedmen's Normal Institute at the end of the spring semester. In the first half of his first journal, Shawnee also recorded his impressions about religious meetings of the Quakers at Freedmen's Normal Institute and of meetings at Methodist and Presbyterian churches. On a regular basis he recorded school lessons such as bookkeeping and penmanship exercises, poetry, and lessons in logic, history, civics, and the classics. Other entries included lessons from the Quaker manuals, copies of letters Shawnee exchanged with his family and friends, and Sabbath school lessons.

[*Back of the front cover*]

      George E. Shawnee

        Shawneetown

          Ind[ian] Territory

[*The above scripted entry does not appear to be in William E. Shawnee's handwriting.*]

[*front page of flyleaf before page 1*]

      W. E. Shawnee,

        Maryville,

      Blount Co. <u>Tennessee</u>.

        Jan. 1, 1885.

[*back page of flyleaf before page 1*]

Arg. [*Argument*] If those that were baptized with the baptism of water, were not therefore baptized with the baptism of Christ; then the baptism of water is not the baptism of Christ.
    But the first is true;
    Therefore also the last.
And again,
    If he, that truly and really administered the baptism of water, did notwithstanding declare, that he neither could, nor did, baptize with the baptism of Christ; then the baptism of water is not the baptism of Christ.
    But the first is true;
    Therefore also the last.
If the baptism with water were the one baptism, i. e. the baptism of Christ, as many as were baptized with water would have put on Christ.
    But the last is false;
    Therefore also the last [*first?*].
And again.
    Since as many as are baptized into Christ, i. e. with the one baptism, which is the baptism of Christ, have put on Christ, then the water-baptism is not the one baptism, viz. the baptism of Christ.
    But the first is true,

Therefore also the last.

[*page 1*]

                    Williami Ellsworthi Shawnees
                    Tabula numeri arithimeticae.

```
1/2  = .5              20/32 = 5/8  = .625
1/4  = .25             21/32 = .65625
3/4  = .75             22/32 = 11/16 = .6875
1/8  = .125            23/32 = .71875
3/8  = .375
5/8  = .625
7/8  = .875
1/16 = .0625
3/16 = .1875
5/16 = .3125
7/16 = .4375
9/16 = .5625
11/16 = .6875
13/16 = .8125
15/16 = .9375
1/32 = .03125
2/32 = 1/16 = .0625
3/32 = .09375
4/32 = 1/8 = .125
5/32 = .15625
6/32 = 3/16 = .1875
7/32 = .21875
8/32 = 1/4 = .25
9/32 = .28125
10/32 = 5/16 = .3125
11/32 = .34375
12/32 = 3/8 = .375
13/32 = .40625
14/32 = 7/16 = .4375
15/32 = .46875
16/32 = 1/2 = .5
17/32 = .53125
18/32 = 9/16 = .5625
19/32 = .59375
```

[*page 2*] *The 3rd of June, 1886,*

A true copy of the letter to Miss Mary Eleanor Sherman.

                    Maryville, Tennessee,
                        June 3, 1886.

Miss Mary Sherman,

Dear Friend:—

As you desired and asked me to write to you, I will write a few words. I have, in truth, been very lonesome since you have all left. That morning I came back from the depot I did scarcely know what to do. I took a walk directly after reaching the dormitory, and after that I felt much better. I believe I shall stay and go to school here another year. At least, my father said that I might better stay because there were so many strikes and their consequent troubles going on, and he was somewhat afraid for me to come. He was somewhat afraid for me to come here, too; but I was so bent on coming that he readily consented as I had company as far as St. Louis, which as you remember, is the metropolis, or largest city, of Missouri. Last evening was Wednesday evening and we had a glorious meeting at seven o'clock at night instead of at eleven in the morning. There were only a few present, but we enjoyed ourselves for all that. I write to you and Maria, but tell the others that I have not forgotten them and I give my best [*page 3*] wishes to all. Tell them to put in a word or two when you write. I stay at Mr. Valentine's just now. I may stay there all summer, though, as the poet Longfellow rightly observes, "a boy's will is the mind's will," and I know not what I shall do. I was quite disappointed, as I had been sure that I would go home. I wanted to go, merely because my father wished it, not because I was home-sick. I am quite well at present, and trust you and Martha and the rest are the same. Is Martha coming to school next term? Of course, you are coming, and, besides, you have not graduated yet as (Martha) your sister has. You must study Algebra and Latin and oh, my! many other things yet. There are none of the boys here yet except John Hassler and his brother. Mr. and Mrs. Hastings are well. Willie Hastings graduated at college last week, and I did not get to hear him speak. Long letter and interesting next time. Please write. Hoping soon to receive a very long and interesting letter from "Little Mamie," I remain

      Your friend,
    William Ellsworth Shawnee,
The word in parenthesis is not in the original letter.

 A true copy of my compliment to Mary Boyd.
[*page 4*]

       Maryville, Tennessee
        June 11, 1886
Miss Mary Boyd,
I wish your company to school next Sabbath, at the Freedmen's Normal Institute. Sabbath School begins at two o'clock, afternoon. Will you be willing to come? Willie Valentine intends

Katie's company so there (is) no fear of our (being) alone, I suppose. If you accept, please say where we shall meet you, etc. etc.

      William Ellsworth Shawnee,

Instead of the words in parenthesis the original has "need be" and "going".

      Miscellaneous.

Dare to change your mind, confess your error, and altar [alter?] your conduct, when you are convinced you are wrong.

 A true copy of the answer to my letter of June 3, 1886 (on page 2).
      Athens, Tenn.
      June 7, 1886.
Mr. Willie Shawnee
      Dear Friend:—
Your kind letter is at hand after being wrote [[written]] some considerable time. I was glad to hear from you. We had a good time coming home we got here at three [[o'clock P.M.]] and the depot was crowded. We had a good time on the third Sunday in [*page 5*] last month. Martha has had the mumps and is now better. Mary Jackson has got the mumps. I have been very lonesome having departed from all of my school-mates. I am coming back to school and I don't know [[whether]] Martha may come back. I was sorry that you were disappointed. I am coming back up there in two or three weeks if my father will let me. I wrote [[have written]] to him about it. I want to start in [[at]] the first of the term. Mr. Nelson was here last week and we had a nice time. Give my best wishes to Miss Emma and Mrs. Valentine. Please excuse the short letter
    From Little Mamie,
     Your friend,
    Mary E. Sherman.

June 18/1886.
 I attended a picnic this afternoon at a grove beyond the depot, East Maryville. There were a considerable number present. They were of the Colored Presbyterian Sabbath school at Knoxville, Tennessee. Maud Brooks was there and she remained behind at Mr. Cansler's. She is a very nice and accomplished young girl. God, who has hitherto preserved my life and has shone mercy in a thousand ways, will, in due time, provide for [*page 6*] me and carry me through life nobly and wisely if I will

permit him. Lord, help that I may love Thee supremely, Amen, forever.

        William E. Shawnee.

June 18th, 1886 [*entry moved from page 69, top of page*]
    The Lord God of host answered my prayer this evening and I write this for my remembrance. He has answered my prayers before but I have been in doubt about it since then, but now it is true there is no doubt. The Lord shall be my life and my song henceforth and forever more. I need to study my Bible more and use my tongue less; but if any (be it much or little), let it be in a way far different than heretofore.

A true copy of my letter to my father, *June 22nd 1886*, W.E.S.

        Maryville, Tenne[s]see,
        June 22nd 1886,

My Dear Father:—
    As it is rainy to-day and I can do no work, I thought I might better write to you. I work when the weather is suitable, but it has been very rainy for the last three weeks. It is quite hard on me, my hands have been sore and blistered, but they are now becoming tough. PaPa, I am seventeen years old, but I wish I were twenty-one. I would like to earn money and support myself instead of being supported. But I have been able to do nothing except to earn my board. I could earn money by teaching school but I am not ready for that. The schools do not run very long and I would make very little because my expenses would be great. The truth is, the expense to be incurred by getting ready to teach keeps me from teaching school. Another still: I can not enter my class at the beginning of the term, because I would [*page 7*] be teaching and could not get away.
    It is not certain whether I can attend school next term, because I have not yet received assurance that my expenses will be paid another year. I went to Knoxville on the 20th of this month. I attended the Methodist meeting in the forenoon and the Presbyterian Sabbath-school in the afternoon. I have been in this school once before. Owing partly to the dedication of the new Methodist church which some had gone to see, and partly to the inclemency of the weather, but few were present. I like the school very well. Papa, there are some nice good looking young ladies, who live in Knoxville and attend here, too. And they are colored too. Then there are some handsome young gentlemen here, too. They have a very good church that must [cost?] perhaps a few thousand. I was the only stranger there present, I suppose. The Methodist church is said to have cost $20,000. It is also

said to have above 600 members. Wheat is quite light here this year and corn is generally about knee high. The following things I would like to have:—
1. A Business College education.
2. A College and a Musical education.
3. A good position, where I could make [*page 8*] an honest living. I would like very well to live in the states, and I would like to be in some business. I would like to be somebody in the world. But it is a difficult march to usefulness. I would not seek popularity, but would desire to do the right for right's sake. Fully confident that the promise is not that the path of life shall always be smooth, I desire to trust God at all times and in all places. I desire to do exactly right in all things to the best of my knowledge though there be many fiery furnaces through which I must pass. I am confident that if I do exactly right, I need entertain no fear. I am in good health at the present and trust you are all in like condition. I know what I shall do: I will bear whatever is my lot patiently and bravely. I wish we all lived here in Tennessee. I say this (and when I find I am wrong, I'll take it back), that in Tennessee, in Democratic Tennessee, the colored people have at least as good a chance to rise and be a crown of rejoicing to themselves and others as their kindred elsewhere and if they wish and if they want a better chance here, they ought not to have it. Let them go and improve the opportunity they have and all will be well. I say that there is "no cross" where [*page 9*] there is "no crown." We must work if we would prosper wherever we are. Honest labor is the tool that raised the universe and is not to be sneered at. Great men and women and good men and women have labored and do still labor, therefore labor is honorable. Whatever is right for us to have and just that we should have should be the product of our labor. We must not wish for something for nothing, for that would be Naboth-like. [*Naboth, a word used by Jewish scholars meaning a double injustice (1 Kings 21)*] Now I must not write an essay. I must close. I shall need another suit of clothes before school begins and I don't see how I can avoid having some clothes made. I am almost without clothing, should I attend school. I am indebted to Wm P. Hastings $5.00. I have a suit that cost me $9.00, then I bought a pair of shoes for $2.50. A straw hat for 55 cts. So recently I have spent $12.05, as I show above. I have a suit that cost $10.00, but it is now old, having been worn two years.

       Your son,
        Willie E. Shawnee.
To my father, William Shawnee,
    Shawneetown,
      Indian Territory.

[*page 10*]

        Quotations made by William Ellsworth Shawnee,
              Eight mo. 2nd, 1886.

Taken from the Friends' Review of 1st mo. 3, 1874. An address to the members of the Society of Friends and those professing with them.

"Dear Friends:—To everyone who feels desirous of the well-being of our Society, not only as concerns our own members, but also as regards the good of our fellow-beings at large, for the benefit and ingathering of whom we are justified in believing our Society was brought together and united as a compact whole, even to gather by precept and example from shadow to substance, from form to reality, to any one among us thus feeling and viewing things, it can be a matter of no small interest to view a Conference such as has just been held in London, with its representatives from all parts of the land."

                Demand Note
$2000.   Maryville, Tennessee,
                  Sept. 6, 1886.

On demand for value received. I promise to pay W. A. Miller, or [*on?*] order Two thousand dollars, with interest at 6 per cent.
                W. E. Shawnee

$750.   Maryville Tenn., Sept 6, 1886
     Two years after date I promise to pay [*text ends here*]

[*page 11*] [*only two lines inscribed on this page*]
    Willie Shawnee a good boy. a a a
    Carrie Warrior. Anna Redman

[*page 12*]

        Maryville, Tennessee, 8th mo. 5th, 1886.

Dear Father;
It has come for me to talk and write in the language of the truth. I regret only one thing, even that I am not yet a young man. Here I am, working for my board <u>alone</u>. But I want either to work for some compensation or to work as an apprentice, and under no other condition than either of these. My expenses are not to be paid for another year nor do I wish them to be paid now, since Mr. William P. Hastings is no longer a teacher in our school. He resigned. If I had my board paid (I have no chance to earn it), I could attend Maryville College.

[extraneous figures on the remainder of the page] 45
[-] 18
27

1886 12 31
1859 12 31

[*page 13*] [*All handwritten bookkeeping data are presented in tabular form here to preserve the alignment of the entries.*]

Date			Tobacco-Account		Dr.	Cr.
1859	Dec	31	To Tobacco 1 year		5.20	
1860	Dec	31	" Int on $5.20	.06%	.31	
"	"	"	" Tobacco 1 year		5.20	
1861	Dec	31	" Int on $10.71		.64	
"	"	"	" Tobacco 1 year		5.20	
1862	Dec	31	" Int on $16.55		.99	
"	"	"	" Tobacco 1 year		5.20	
1863	Dec	31	" Int. on $22.74		1.36	
"	"	"	" Tobacco 1 year		5.20	
1864	Dec	31	" Int on $29.30		1.76	
"	"	"	" Tobacco 1 year		5.20	
1865	Dec	31	" Int on $36.26		2.18	
"	"	"	" Tobacco 1 year		5.20	
1866	Dec	31	" Int. on $43.64		2.62	
"	"	"	" Tobacco 1 year		5.20	
1867	Dec	31	" Int on $51.46		3.09	
"	"	"	" Tobacco 1 year		5.20	
1868	Dec	31	" Int. on $59.75		3.60	
"	"	"	" Tobacco 1 year		5.20	
1869	Dec	31	" Int. on $68.55		4.11	
"	"	"	" Tobacco 1 year		5.20	
1870	Dec	31	" Int. on $77.86		4.67	
"	"	"	" Tobacco 1 year		5.20	
1871	Dec	31	" Int. on $87.73		5.26	
"	"	"	" Tobacco 1 year		5.20	
1872	Dec	31	" Int. on $98.19		5.89	
"	"	"	" Tobacco 1 year		5.20	
1873	Dec	31	" Int. on $109.28		6.56	
"	"	"	" Tobacco 1 year		5.20	
1874	Dec	31	" Int. on $121.04		7.26	
"	"	"	" Tobacco 1 year		5.20	
1875	Dec	31	" Int on $ 133.50		8.01	
"	"	"	" Tobacco 1 year		5.20	
"	"	"	By Amount to Balance			146.71
					146.71	146.71

[*page 14*]
1. The fallacy of begging the question consists in offering as proof that which is only a mere variation of the assertion to be proved.
2. When the assertion to be proved requires only the justification of the application of a term, any mere variation of the former expression will answer as a reason for proof.
3. A thesis is a proposition formally set forth to be sustained by proofs.
4. The six sources of argument are:
    (1) Proof from Explication or Analysis.
    (2)   "   " Antecedent Probability.
    (3)   "   " Signs of Consequences.
    (4)   "   " Instances or Examples.
    (5)   "   " Analogy.
    (6)   "   " Testimony or Authority.
5. The fives [*sic*] modes of Explication are:
    (1) Definition. (2) Enumeration. (3) Distinction.
    (4) Limitation. (5) Interpretation.
6. Every true definition is composed of two parts, the genus and the differentia.
7. By genus is meant king or class.
8. The differentia is that quality or those qualities which distinguish the object or kind of objects in question from all the others embraced in the genus.
9. The differentia must be positive, as opposed to negative; it must be intelligible; it must not contain a synonym or paronym of the word defined; and it must be expressed with the utmost precision. [*page 15*]
10. Enumeration. Sometimes a term can be explained by enumerating all that it includes or comprehends.
11. Distinction, this method of explication is by pointing out the difference or differences between the given term or topic and some other with which it might be confounded.

                      From Observation.

    A man should always have an account book and keep a true and correct account therein. First, to see whether, at the close of certain seasons, his business has yielded him a reasonable profit, or none at all. Secondly, to be posted as to the sum of his business and, in case disputes should occur concerning an account, to be able to settle the matter satisfactorily to himself and others. Thirdly, to avoid being cheated by him who would be so careless or dishonest as to do such a thing.

    Old persons are incompetent to raise children aright and should not ~~doe~~ ~~do~~ ~~so,~~ take upon themselves the responsibility therein. First, seeing the children are apt, as is too often the case, to be weak, sickly, old-looking, deformed, or diseased. Secondly, because they are often either too lenient or to strict, spare the rod, fail to instruct the child in that they ought, in short, they often leave the child to govern and teach itself.

[page 16] *Eight mo. 22, 1886.*
    The day was beautiful. In the even[ing] I went to Sabbath-school at the Freedmen's Normal Institute. The meeting, which was held after the Sabbath-school, was glorious. Two lady Friends were present, and strengthened us greatly. They were Mrs. Levering and Miss Blancher, both teachers in the Morristown Academy.
    Miss Blancher has a sweet voice; she can speak so very kindly that I believe that she is a gentle and kind teacher. She said that I ought to go to their school, that she would be glad to have me there, and that it would cost me only six and one-half dollars per month. Mrs. Levering always has something either to ask or tell me, when I see her. She told me that I ought to have some profession in view, that the school at the Morristown Academy commenced the second Second [*sic*] Day in the Ninth Month, that I should write to my father, to see if he could not pay my way in their school, and that I should, in case I should go home before the first of the Ninth month, come to see her. Both of the ladies paid much attention to the children in talking to them when the services were concluded. Miss Blancher selected to [two?] pieces for vocal praise—nos. 122 and 138, [*page 17*] Gospel Hymns. Miss Hattie Agnes Valentine has been sick during the past week, and is not much better yet. The laboring man and others need a Sabbath that he may rest. O how the weary worker hails his day of rest and praise to God! In the Sabbath school, he is instructed in the word of God, taught to sing nice songs that fairly teem with Bible truth, and therefore better qualified to travel the journey of life. Wherefore may none underrate the importance of the Sabbath-school. None who fully appreciate the importance of one day's rest to the laborer after six days of toil, who realize the value of the ~~value~~ Sabbath school as an handmaid of both morality and religion, and who desire to live up to the commands of God to his chosen people, ~~the Jews~~ confirmed by the practice of the disciples of Christ, the primitive Christians, and the Churches of the present day, can fail to appreciate the Sabbath.

[*page 18*]
                        Book Second of Caesar.
1. While Caesar was in hither Gaul in winter-quarters, as we have declared above, frequent rumors were brought to him, and

also he was made more certain by the letters of Labienus that all the Belgae, which we have said are ~~the~~ a third part of Gaul, ~~were con~~ are conspiring against the Roman people and giving hostages to one another; that these are the causes of conspiring: first, because they were fearing lest, all Gaul having been pacified, our army would be conducted to them; next, because they were incited by ~~some~~ certain Gauls, some of whom although they had been unwilling that the Germans should dwell longer in Gaul yet they were hearing it grievously that the army of the Roman people should winter and become settled in Gaul; others of whom were desiring new affairs because of their fickleness and levity of mind; they were incited by some also because that in Gaul the kingdoms ~~are~~ were generally occupied by the more powerful and by those who ~~had have~~ had the means for hiring men, who had been able less easily to follow that thing under our government. Caesar having been moved by these messages and letters enlisted two new legions in nearer Gaul and in the beginning of the summer sends Quintus Pedius a lieutenant into interior [*page 19*] Gaul who should lead it. He himself as soon as there began to be a supply of fodder, comes to the army; he gives the business to the Senones and other Gauls who were nearest to the Belgians that they should learn those things which are being carried on among them and th[ey] should make him more certain of those things. All these instantly announced that bands are being collected and the army being collected to one place. Then indeed the thought that he ought not to hesitate but should set out to them. A corn supply having been prepared he moves the camps and in about fifteen days comes to the territories of the Belgians. Therefore when he had come unexpectedly and sooner than all opinion the Remi who are the nearest of the Belgians to the Gauls sent to him the embassadors [*sic*] Iccius and Andecombrius the foremost of the state who should say that they commit themselves and their property into the protection and power of the Roman people that they ~~are~~ have not ~~conspired against the Roman people~~ agreed with the other Belgians and have not conspired against the Roman people that they are prepared both to give hostages to the commands, receive them to the cities and assist in corn and other supplies that the other Belgians are in arms [*remainder of text is missing*]

[*page 20*] [*penmanship exercise with various names and phrases*]
Quiet words quell angry passions. . . . Anna Wilson, Shawneetown, . . . Carrie Warrior, Shawneetown, . . . Willie Shawnee Indian Territory, . . . Gertrude Washington, . . . Madeline Toupan, . . . Ella Coltrain, . . . Bertha Coning, . . . Caroline Salyser, . . . Mary Chisholm, . . . Bessie Salyser, Louisa Johnson, . . . Annie King, . . . Debbie Ellis, . . .

Kittie Wilson, . . . Nannie Cansler, . . . Minnie Valentine, . . . Business University

[*page 21*] [*bookkeeping exercise; William E. Shawnee's school dates were 1883–87.*]

		Tobacco Account	Dr.	Cr.
1876 Dec 31		Amount from page 13	146.71	
"	"	" Int. on $146.71	8.80	
"	"	" Tobacco 1 year	5.20	
1877 Dec 31		" Int on $160.71	9.64	
"	"	" Tobacco 1 year	5.20	
1878 Dec 31		" Int. on $175.55	10.53	
"	"	" Tobacco 1 year	5.20	
1879 Dec 31		" Int. on $191.28	11.48	
"	"	" Tobacco 1 year	5.20	
1880 Dec 31		" Int. on $207.96	12.48	
"	"	" Tobacco 1 year	5.20	
1881 Dec 31		" Int on $225.64	13.54	
"	"	" Tobacco 1 year	5.20	
1882 Dec 31		" Int on $244.38	14.66	
"	"	" Tobacco 1 year	5.20	
1883 Dec 31		" Int on $264.24	15.85	
"	"	" Tobacco 1 year	5.20	
1884 Dec 31		" Int on $285.29	17.12	
"	"	" Tobacco 1 year	5.20	
1885 Dec 31		" Int. on $307.61	18.46	
"	"	" Tobacco 1 year	5.20	
"	"	By Amount to Balance		331.27
			331.27	331.27

[*page 22*] [*bookkeeping exercises*]

		Asa B. Leonard		Dr.
1886				
Jan. 4		To 1 Quarter Beef, 150 lbs	@ 5¢	7.50
Feb. 10		" 40 Lbs. Pork	.08	3.20
"	15	" 14 Bu. Corn	.45	6.30
May 10		" Plowing Garden		1.75
"	15	" 18 Bu. Potatoes	.35	6.30

June 12	" 250 Lbs. Wool		.40	100.00
July 12	" 2 Day's Work with Team		1.75	3.50
Nov. 1	" Pasturing Cow 14 wks.		.20	2.80
Dec. 4	" Hauling 24 Cds. Beech and Maple		1.50	36.00
				167.35

1886   O. D. Knowlton   Dr.

Jan 4	To 8 Bu. Potatoes	@ .35	2.80
" 4	" 4 " Corn	.42	1.68
Feb. 10	" 10 " Potatoes	.35	3.50
" "	" 12 " Wheat	.87½	10.50
May 1	" 16 Lbs. Butter	.12½	2.00
" 6	" 14 Bu. Corn	.45	6.30
June 10	" 14 " Potatoes	.35	1.40
July 10	" 10 Tons Hay	4.25	42.25
Sept. 25	" Pasturing 4 Cows, 10 Wks.	.20	8.00
" "	" " 1 Horse, 9 "	.25	2.25

[*page 23*] [*bookkeeping exercises*]

      Asa B. Leonard   Cr.

1886			
Jan. 4	By 2 Lbs. Black Tea	.70	1.40
" "	" 4 Lbs. Coffee	.14	.56
" "	" 25 Lbs. Brown Sugar	.10	2.50
" 25	" 3 Gals. Molasses	.44	1.32
Feb 10	" Cash		40.00
June 12	" 18 Yds. Calico	.15	2.70
" "	" 3 Papers Pins	.05	.15
Dec. 4	" 1 Pr. Kip Brogans		1.25
" "	" 18 Lbs. Rice	.06	1.08
" "	" 9 Lbs. Loaf Sugar	.14	1.26
" "	" 9 Yds. Merrimac Sheeting	.09	.81
" 29	" <u>Cash to Balance</u>		114.32
			167.35

1886   O. D. Knowlton Cr.

May 1	By 1 Set Double Harness	30.00
June 10	" 1 Brass Plated Single Harness	35.00
July 2	" 1 Saddle, Bridle, and Martingale	18.50

[*page 24*] [*bookkeeping and penmanship exercises*]

1880   O. D. Knowlton   Dr

Jan	4	To	8 Bu. Potatoes		.35
"	"	"	4 Bu. Corn		.42
Feb	10	"	10 Bu. Potatoes		.35
"	"	"	12 Bu. Wheat		.87½
May	1	"	16 lbs. Butter		.12½
"	6	"	14 Bu. Corn		.45
June	10	"	4 Bu. Potatoes		.35
July	2	"	1 Saddle, Bridle and Martingales		

[*The remainder of page 24 is an exercise in penmanship; extraneous practice letters have been omitted.*]

William David Irene Georgia Hattie Agnes Valentine West . . . Agnes . . . Xerxes Yea Spoils. Natal. John H. Hassler, . . . John Hassler . . . Valentine . . . George Benson, Nora . . . Ann Harbor Vernon. All men are not angels. Summer. United States of North America. Marble to sell. Learn of me. William Shawnee . . . Barnes. Wm P. Hastings, Maryville Tennessee. Maud R. Brooks Redfox Store, Anna, Maude R. Brooks, Knoxville Tenn. Knoxville . . . Maude R. Brooks God is eternal. Emma, Hepworth W. E. Shawnee

[*page 25 top of page*] [*bookkeeping exercise*]

1880		O. D. Knowlton	CR.
May	1	By 1 Set Double Harness	30.00
June	10	" 1 Brass Plated Harness	35.00

[*page 25, middle and bottom of page*] [*penmanship exercise—list of names, independent phrases, and passages of a letter*]

Hattie House. Indian Territory, M Wm Hannum, Wm E. Gladstone, Mary Mary A. Woolbridge. Emma Valentine George Washington. G. A. Toole. Mary Mary Magnolia McClure. Maryville.

    Miss Maude R. Brooks.
    Miss Mary Valentine
    Maude R Brooks, M M
    Maude R. Brooks, Maude
    W^m E Shawnee. W^m E Shawnee
    Maude R, Brooks.
    Maude R. Brooks,
    Maude R. Brooks,
    Henry Smith. Come and see,
    Dear Friend: I–

W^m E E Ellsworth.
William E. Shawnee

Knoxville, Tenn.

(Fiction) June 3, 1887

Maude R. Brooks.

With pleasure I ask your company to Sabbath School next Sabbath. Please grant it, and please [*end of text*]

Your friend,

William E. Shawnee

Mr. W. E. Gladstone. W^m
Maud R. Brooks, Carrie
Maud R. Brooks, Caroline

[*page 26*] [*Bookkeeping exercises. Page 22 has the identical account entry for O. D. Knowlton dated as 1886.*]

1880		O. D. Knowlton		Dr.	
Jan 4	To	8 Bu. Potatoes	[@].35		2.80
" "	"	4 Bu. Corn	.42		1.68
Feb. 10	"	10 Bu. Potatoes	.35		3.50
" "	"	12 Bu. Wheat	.87½		10.50
May 1	"	16 Lbs. Butter	.12½		2.00
" 6	"	14 Bu. Corn	.45		6.30
June 10	"	14 Potatoes	.35		1.40
July 10	"	10 Tons Hay	4.25		42.25
Sept.25	"	Pasturing 4 Cows, 10 Wks.	.20		8.00
" "	" "	1 Horse, 9 "	.25		2.25
" "	"	Cash to Balance			2.57
					83.50

1880		Isaac Mitchell		Dr.	
Jan 10	To	2½ Doz. Hen's Eggs	.14		.35
Feb 10	"	4 Lbs Butter	.15		.60
" "	"	2 Bu. Wheat	.75		1.50
Mar 4	"	1 Qr. Beef 175 lbs.	.05		8.75
May 14	"	18 lbs. Wool	.30		5.40
" "	"	14 " Butter	.11		1.54
June 10	"	Cash to Balance			8.91
					27.05

[*page 27*] [*bookkeeping exercises*]

1880		O. D. Knowlton		Cr.	
May 1	By	1 Set Double Harness			30.00
June 10	"	1 plated Single Harness			35.00
July 2	"	Saddle, Bridle & Martingale			18.50
					83.50

1880		Isaac Mitchell		Cr.	
Jan. 1	By	1 Pr. Kip Boots			3.00
" "	"	1 " Over Shoes			2.50
Feb. 10	"	1 Pr. Rubber Overshoes			1.25
" "	"	1 " Buckskin Mittens			.75
Mar. 4	"	1 Pr. Congress Gaiters			3.00
" "	"	2 pr. Misses' "	1.25		2.50
" "	"	2 Pr. Children's Gloves	.15		.30
May 14	"	2 Pr. R.R. Jenny Linds	1.25		2.50
" "	"	1 Pr. Enameled Gaiters			2.50
" "	"	6 Linen Handkerchiefs	.60		3.60
June 5	"	2 Pr. Boy's Suspenders	.15		.30
" "	"	3 Pr. Mixed Half Hose	.20		.60
" 10	"	1 Leghorn Hat			1.50
" "	"	2 Pr. Calf Buskins	1.00		2.00
" "	"	3 Pr. Black Hose	.25		.75
					27.05

[*page 28*] [*bookkeeping exercises*]

1879		Sheep & Wool Acct.		Dr.	
June 1	To	Cash for 160 Sheep	1.25		200.00
Dec 15	"	Pasturing 6½ mo. per 100	3.00		31.2o
Mar 15	"	Feed & Care 3 mo per 100	12.00		57.60
June 1	"	Pasturing 2½ mo. Per 100	3.00		12.00
" "	"	Washing & Shearing per 100	6.00		9.60
" "	"	Int. on $200 1 yr	.07		14.00
" "	"	Profit on Sheep			153.60
					478.00

1880		Henry Webster		Dr.	
Jan 1	To	15½ lbs. Butter	.14		2.17
" "	"	25 lbs. Cheese	.08		2.00
" 5	"	40 lbs. Butter	.14		5.60
June 4	"	10 lbs. Linen Rags	.04		.40
July 1	"	10 lbs. Butter	.10		1.00
" "	"	4 Doz. Eggs	.08		.32

		" Cash to Balance		.65
				12.14

[*page 29*] [*bookkeeping exercises*]

1879		Sheep & Wool Acct.	Cr.	
June 1		By 600 lbs. Wool	.40	240.00
"	"	" 152 Old Sheep	1.25	190.00
"	"	" 64 Lambs	.75	48.00
				478.00

1880		Henry Webster	Cr.	
Jan 1		By 1 Family Bible		3.00
"	"	" 1 Webster's Dictionary		3.50
"	"	" 1 Copy Meyhew on Education		1.00
" 10		" 1 Higher Arithmetic		.75
"	"	" 1 Smith's Arithmetic		.50
"	"	" 2 Intellectual Algebra	.37½	.75
June 4		" 4 Qrs. Writing Paper	.20	.80
"	"	" 2 Tower's Readers	.25	.50
"	"	" 2 Webster's Spellers	.10	.20
July 1		" 1 Well's Grammar		.38
"	"	" 2 Practical Arithmetics	.38	.76
				12.14

[*page 30*] [*bookkeeping exercises*]

1880		Henry Webster	Cr.	
Sept. 10		To 25 Bu. Tomatoes	.30	7.50
"	"	" 10 lbs. Butter	.12½	1.25
Dec. 12		" 20 Cords Wood	2.25	45.00
				53.75

1880		Pork Account	Dr.	
Sep. 10		To 45 Hogs, wt. 9856 lbs.	.03	295.68
"	"	" 17 Hogs. Wt. 4180 lbs.	.02¾	114.95
"	15	" 900 Bu. Corn	.40	360.00
Oct. 25		" Moving & Grinding 280 bu. Corn	.06	16.80
Dec. 10		" Slaughtering 62 Hogs	.75	46.50
"	12	" Marketing 62 Hogs	.20	12.40
"	"	" Profit on 62 Hogs		123.67
				970.00

[*page 31*] [*bookkeeping exercises*]

1880		Henry Webster		Cr.	
Sep. 10		By 2 Qrs. Writing Paper	.25		.50
"	"	" 1 History			.50
"	"	" 1 Day Book 5 Qrs.	.34		1.70
"	"	" 1 Ledger, 5 Qrs.	.34		1.70
Nov. 1		" 3 Higher Arithmetics	.75		2.25
"	10	" 1 Smith's Astronomy			.75
"	"	" 2 U.S. Histories	.62½		1.25
Dec. 15		" 4 Qrs. Writing Paper	.20		.80
"	"	" 1 Temperance Offering			2.25
"	20	" 1 American Reader			.50
"	"	" 1 Ivory Holder			.19
"	"	" 1 Box Wafers			.06
	"	" Cash to Balance			41.30
					53.75

1880		Pork Account		Cr.	
Dec. 11		By 750 lbs. Pork	.05		37.50
"	12	" 18,650 lbs. Pork	.05		932.50
					970.00

[*page 32*] [*bookkeeping exercises*]

1879		Beef Account		Dr.	
July 20		To 21 Yoke Oxen	68.00		1428.00
Aug. 4		" 12 Cows	15.00		180.00
"	10	" 22 Cows	12.50		275.00
"	20	" 23 Steers	20.00		460.00
Nov. 1		" Pasturing 78 Cattle, 11 wks	.12		130.64
"	"	" 100 Loads Pumpkins	.50		50.00
1880					
Feb. 1		" 100 Tons Hay	4.50		450.00
"	"	" 1800 Bu. Corn	.35		630.00
"	"	" Grinding 1800 Bu. Corn	.05		90.00

1879		Beef Account		Dr.	
July 20		To 42 Oxen	68.00		
		Mistake			

[*page 33, top of page*] [*bookkeeping exercise*]

1880		Beef Account		Cr.	
Feb. 1		By 21 Yoke Oxen, 41,160 lbs.	.05		2058.00
"	"	" 37 Cows Wt 22,200 lbs.	.04½		999.00
"	"	" 23 Steers, wt 16,100 lbs.	.05		805.00

1880			John Adams		Dr.	Cr.
Jan. 10		By 2 Axes		1.25		2.50
"	"	" 3 Ax Helves		.20		.60
Apr. 4		" 3 Hoes		.65		1.95
"	"	" 1 Hoe		.44		.44
June 10		" 3 Scythes		.88		2.64
"	"	" 2 Scythe Snaths		.75		1.50
"	20	" 1 Log Chain, 20 lbs.		.10		2.00
"	"	" 1 Bush Scythe				1.00
July 2		" 1 Grain Cradle				3.00
"	"	" 2 Hay Rakes		.15		.30
Sep. 10		To Cash to Balance			15.93	
					15.93	15.93

[page 33, bottom of page] [penmanship exercise]

W. E. Shawnee . . . Maud . . . Mars . . . Mary Boyd, Kittie B. Wilson, Sally Conalas, Annie Conalas, Julia Conalas, Mary Chisholm, Sallie Chisholm, Malinda Quinine Ira. Edith Ella Nellie Sallie Sabbath. Tenn . . .

[page 34] [penmanship exercise with three names, practice letters omitted]

    William P. Hastings . . . William E. Shawnee . . . Carrie Warrior

[page 35, top of page] [The top of this penmanship page is inverted. Practice letters have been omitted.]

8 months from Aug. 5, S E Gaskell & Co 8 months from date Note @ 8 months from Aug 5, Rosa G. Hastings . . . Anna . . . Angeline Carrie Caroline Chisholm.

[page 35, bottom of page] [penmanship exercise, practice letters omitted]

William E. Shawnee, Irene Benson, Nellie Shawnee, I Nellie Benson, Oscar, mind It is not by sleight . . . Kerr, John A . . . Angeline Carrie Warrior

[page 36] [penmanship exercise, practice letters omitted] . . . Come and see us once more, Come and see us Thy friend, Wm E. Shawnee
Harry B. White, the Grand Worthy Chief Templar of Ohio says, "'The Worst Foe' is, I believe, the best book on temperance that I have every read." Uxbridge Business College . . . Below we give a few of the many words of commendation and praise received

from those who have read "The Worst Foe." Below Business College
. . .

[*page 37*] [*penmanship exercise*]
      William E. Shawnee . . . Angeline, Carrie, Amelia . . .
Maryville, Tenn. . . . Practice makes perfect. . . .

[*The following two-page letter, dated Aug. 25, 1886, from Walter Shawnee is tucked inside this ledger before the flyleaf.*]

                Shawneetown Ind/Ter
                   Aug 25, 86

    Brother, my Brother
You must write Willie to me, I have not heard from you in a whole year, you don't write[.] I wrote to you when I was at Chilocco[.] I think I wrote to you before I started, if you don't write to ~~t~~me when you get this letter, I am not going to answer any more of any shuch [such] letters from that country, I say what I mean. There were many boys went home from Chilocco some that I will never see again perhaps. I kinder hated to leave because I had good many friends up there, there were five of them. Amos Tartleh, Edward Howard, Thomas Pratt, Ernest Lushboug and Johnson Lane. I don't know wheather [whether?] you know any of them or not, well they are the best boys in the whole 137, boys. They are different tribes too. Excuse me for bad writing I am in such a hurry because I think you won't write any way
        Lovingly your
           brother

        W. C. Shawnee [Walter Homer Shawnee?]
          or
        Walter Shawnee
  Oh bad writing but in a hurry.

Ninth Month 1st, 1886. [*text moved from page 74 to precede Sept. 11, 1886, entry*]
    Alf Taylor, The Republican candidate for governor, did speak something on prohibition like the following:—"Every prohibitionist should vote the Republican ticket this fall, because the Republican party favors the submission of the pending [[prohibitory]] amendment,—their favorite text and doctrine. I myself favor the submission ~~of~~, reserving my right either to reject or accept it at the polls."
    On the other hand Bob Taylor, the Democratic candidate for governor, spoke nothing concerning the amendment or prohibition

either directly or in directly. His speech was a failure; for I heard each candidate, and judge truly. Some Democrats are so partisan that they will not hear their party or its candidates vilified.

What did the partisans of Alf Taylor mean when they pinned the red ribbon to the lappets of their coats? What would the Republicans think if the Democratic or any other party should adopt the red flag? What should the Democrats think if the Republicans should continually wave a bloody shirt?

What I ask, should the Union party think when the Republicans adopt the red ribbon, the badge worn by the liquor oligarchy in the Atlanta [*page 75*] and Richmond struggles for temperance legislation? What do they think? Is it a compromise? It certainly looks like it.

Even in the social play room the left-lappet red ribbon, that liquor emblem, exhibit[s] itself. What is the moral depravity of young ladies when a young man should openly and boastingly declare that he is "drunk"? when his lips diffuse the fumes of liquor?

[*page 38*] [*This entire page is in tabular format due to the inscribed numerals in the two right hand columns. The text and its spacing are consistent with the columns of numbers.*]

Sept. 11, 1886

	Sept.	Oct.
I must practice daily	11	16
and seek to improve	12	17
This practice begun Sept. 10.	13	18
	14	19
The Public School	15	20
The Public School is the	16	21
poor man's college, for	17	22
very few people, at most,	18	23
are so fortunate as to	19	24
attend a higher institution	20	25
of learning. What culture,	21	26
therefore, the masses	22	2[7]
receive must be acquired	23	2[8]
in their own school. Education	24	2[9]
should be mental, physical,	25	[30]
moral and religious.	26	3[1]
The public school professes	27	
to deal with all except	28	
the physical. If Mental	29	
education be lacking, the	30	
masses will be utterly	1	

powerless to promote their
own interest. They will become
the dupes both of profligate
and unprincipled ringleaders
and of political demagogues.
The latter curse the world
of American politics today. In short
the unlearned or illiterate,
man is incompetent to exercise
the duty of sovereign voters
and ought to be disfranchised
for the benefit of himself, his
neighbors and his state.

[page 39]
Partyism may blind many a man so that he disregards his own interest, that of his neighbors, and that of his country. Men should be educated up to their duty as rulers as well as in other important matters. Boys are beginning to form habits of smoking and chewing tobacco. This, I believe arises chiefly from misconceived notions of its use upon the system. A course of study in physiology upon the subject would do enormous good. In like manner a thousand evil habits may be uprooted and as many good ones firmly established. I am prepared to say that all the evils that befall the human race chiefly result in consequence of ignorance.

Who fares best at table, who have the most neat and comfortable homes, who have the most money on hand, who are most successful and honest in business, who are more stable in matters of religion, business, and politics, who exercises the duty of man more completely than an intelligent citizen? The illiterate have nothing to talk of except some idle tale, some occurrence in their immediate neighborhood. They are frequently engaged in worthless and meaningless jangle, to tease one the other.

[page 40] *Second Day Ninth Month 13, 1886.*
The day was cloudy, but it did not rain. In the morning I cut some wood, in the evening I took the horses to water, and was pulling fodder the remainder of the day. The day was counted for Jesus.

Third Day 14th. [September 1886]
It was rainy. In the morning I fulfilled my duty by helping to haul a load of stove wood to town. Before the school bells had marked their hour of school, on the 14th of Ninth month,

might have been seen a colored boy riding through the rain and seated upon the hindmost part of a load of wood. Scoffed and despised by his friends, who clearly showed it by their actions, though their voice was unheard by him. Such are the trials and the poverty that oppressed Wm E. Shawnee in 1886! He felt miserable and longed for a better day and better times. But cheer up, poor one, the glory will be the brighter because of the great obstacles overcome. The best friends—those who should have been kind in word and action—openly scoffed at and despised him. Let God judge, I ask, and let time and eternity reveal the result. May I, at some time, be realizing pecuniary reward in some position where I may feel [*page 41*] satisfied, O God I pray. In the evening he watered and fed the horses. At night he sat up to study while others slept. The day was counted for Jesus.

[Sept. *14, 1886, letter to Shawnee's father moved from page 96*]

                    Maryville, Tennessee
                      Sept. 14, 1886.

Dear Father:

    I feel very well because I am enabled still to write to you. I am not to return home, and that hope is lost. You tell me to see whether my expenses would not be paid home: I cannot tell. I was told some time before you wrote last, that I would have to look out for myself. I cant yet see any way open for improvement. If I had enough money, I would attend a Business College; but that would cost more than my expenses here for three years. It would cost about Two hundred dollars for twelve months. It is in Indiana. I would like to attend there two years, or twenty four months. If I had Six hundred dollars I would become a business man of no uncertain sound. I would like to earn such an amount and go there. I cannot earn that amount on a farm, but I can by teaching school. And if I could do that, I would be content. Where is such a position I ask myself? Where, Where? [*The rest of this page is a penmanship exercise.*]

Chapter 2

Deciding on a Vocation
September 15, 1886-November 27, 1886

In June 1886, when Shawnee did not return home to Indian Territory, he lived with George and Nora Valentine and their eight children and worked as a farm laborer for his board. At night he stayed up late and practiced penmanship and bookkeeping while the others slept. He continued recording the same diverse types of entries in his journal, including information about his history. By the time September came around, Shawnee still had no means to return to school and remained with the Valentines. He wore tattered clothes to work and lamented being poor.

In his journal, Shawnee wrote about some of his other friends at Maryville as well as some friends and family from Indian Territory. One of his friends from the institute was Charles Cansler, a grandson of William B. Scott, who was one of the founders of the school. Cansler later became a prominent citizen in eastern Tennessee.[1] Shawnee also identified two future romantic interests—Carrie Warrior from Indian Territory and Emma Valentine from Maryville.

Shawnee was an avid reader and kept abreast of current affairs by subscribing to and reading the *Christian Nation*, a weekly Presbyterian newspaper. He constantly read the Bible and decided to read it from cover to cover. He prayed for divine guidance in seeking his vocation. He decided to become a teacher and a scholar and worked toward that end.

Shawnee ended his first journal in Tennessee. Before he left there, he also had the opportunity to learn about southern white culture. He tested for a teacher's certificate after graduating from Maryville, and he tested again and received a first-year certificate in Rhea County, Tennessee. Rhea County, unlike Blount County where Shawnee lived, had supported the Confederates during the Civil War. Shawnee's last entry is dated November 25, 1886, about a year before he returned to Indian Territory. There is some indication in his third journal, which was written years later, that he spent a year in Tennessee after he stopped recording in his first journal. He also wrote that he taught for two months in Spring City, Tennessee.

During Shawnee's last two years in Tennessee, major events took place in Indian Territory where he lived. In 1886 the federal government forced Big Jim and his followers to vacate the lands they were occupying in the Kickapoo village and to return to their own reservation.

Fourth Day 15th [*September 1886*]
    I was at work the whole day, and at night I attended meeting at the Freedmen's Normal Institute; at which but few were present. Talked too much in the day when there was no necessity. Trials great. Thought no short time concerning my present condition. If I could attend the Indianapolis Business University in a near future, I would feel better.

[*continuation of Fourth Day 15th*] Remain[ed] up to write this while others slept. Clouds hang overhead despair sneers and poverty oppresses.—
    O God, who art in heaven, forgive the sins of an unworthy servant, for Jesus' sake. Guide and teach me for thy sake, O Lord. Bless all as many as duty binds me to pray for. Sanctify me and concentrate me forever and let thy holy Spirit abide with me. Amen forever.
    The day was counted for Jesus.

    The Long Journey
When our feet become heavy and weary
On the valleys and mountains of life,
And the road has grown dusty and dreary
And we groan in the struggle and strife,
We halt on the difficult pathway,
Glance back over valley and plain,
And sigh with a sorrowful longing
To travel the journey again.

For we know in the past there are pleasures,
And seasons of joyful delight,
While before all is doubting and darkness,
And dread of the gloom and the night;
All bright sunny spots we remember
How little we thought of them then!
But now we are looking and longing
To rest in those places again. [*continued on page 52*]

[*page 42*] Don't wait for something to turn up but <u>turn</u> up something.
    Wm Ellsworth Shawnee [*writing in the third person*] was born Dec. 23rd, 1868, in Lawrence, Shawnee Co., Kansas. While [he was?] very young his parents removed to Shawneetown, Indian Territory, where resided the Shawnee Indians with whom his father had spent his younger days from time unknown. When [he was?] six years old his parents sent him to the Mission School established by the Friends and afterward supported by the [U.S.] Government. Before he had gone to school, he knew not what any

sort of bad language was, never having heard any. He could speak no language but English and his mother and father had previously taught him his alphabet. But there at school he fell into bad influences besides undergoing rough treatment from his fellows. He soon learned to speak the Shawnee language and used it much more than English. His fellows endeavored to use him as a tool in mischief but failing in that they taught filthy words both English and Indian. These have always been the source of all mischief to him. Whatever he has done of wickedness or spoken wickedly has been caused by the bad words taught by thoughtless school-mates. One of his early teachers was Miss Ella Coletrain. Another was Miss Eva Woodward, who deceased shortly after vacation. She was a good little lady.
[*page 43*] Attend to your own business.
He loved her much. He was told that she died while asleep. He remained under the teaching of Miss Coletrain for nearly four years. She was a good teacher. Once she gave him a long declamation to commit as soon as possible. It was evening and he left his books in the desk as was his custom, and went home. Next morning he rose early, went to the school-house, commit[ted] the piece (as he called it), and went up stairs to his teacher's room, to recite it to her. He met her leaving her room to ring the first bell and handed her the piece. Then he recited it to her so well that she patted him on the shoulder and embraced him in her arms, and told him that he was a smart boy. The last he heard of her was, that she had just graduated from a college in Kansas. He was under the instruction of Miss Della H. Davis about four years. She was a good teacher. She and her sister Margaret were my teachers for quite a while. Miss Della was taking a box of chalk from a shelf in the school room. But the chalk fell from the box to the floor, making quite a clatter. Della exclaimed. "Get out of the way, Margie!" Whereupon the pupils all laughed. Margaret in the course of times married and moved away, and Della departed to return no more. It was the custom then for the pupils to go to the states
[*page 44*] Nothing can suppress genius; it will rise.
to school. W^m wanted to go; but two giants lay to obstruct his way. They were: (1) he was too young; (2) he was colored and not Indian (as the supposition of some was as to the latter, but whether true he knows not nor cares nor even believes). His parents were poor and could in no wise afford to bear his expenses. He, however, was willing to go and learn. Finally after three years of trouble he found a position in the Freedmen's Normal Institute, where his expenses were duly borne for three years. He started hither only fourteen years of age, without any experience in traveling. He left home on the 14th of August, 1883, and reached the railroad station one hundred miles

distant in company with some friends of his, who were going to St. Louis, Mo. He arrived in St. Louis on the morning of the 22nd, and shortly departed for Nashville, Tenn. He arrived in Evansville, Ind. that evening and remained there overnight. Next morning he boarded the train, which ran down upon a barge drawn by a steamboat in the Ohio. The train was ferried 12 miles down the river to Henderson, Ky. Thence it resumed its journey. This then was his first steamboat rid~~ge~~. He reached Nashville late in the evening of the 23rd. A[l]most immediately he resumed his journey, departing for Chattanooga, Tennessee. He arrived at Chattanooga at 10 o'clock

[*page 45*] Don't wait for something to turn up, but <u>turn</u> up something.

at night. Here was a boy 14 years of age who but a week before knew nothing of a city except in the abstract, alighting from a train amid a crowd of total strangers! He made his way to the waiting room and remained expecting to sit there the rest of the night. But a porter came and led him to a hotel where he was comfortably provided for. Here he remained until noon of the 24th, when he took his departure for Knoxville, Tennessee. He arrived there late in the evening and remained at a hotel the next day. On the 25th, at half past 3 o'clock, he departed for Maryville, and in another hour or two was at his destination. He was well treated and graduated in English the first year. Afterwards he studied Geometry, Book-keeping, Greek, Latin, etc. for two years longer. As he had previously toiled for his support during former vacations, so he did after his third year. He was expecting soon to return home but his father informed him that he was sorry he could not bear his expenses home. He was informed by his teacher that his expenses would be paid no longer and that he should care for himself. He had neglected to answer his brother's letters and now he was informed that unless he wrote to his brother, he would receive no more letters of him. He could not secure employment as an apprentice.

[*page 46*] Diligent in duty, serving God.

He toiled daily for his board. Because of the hard times then reigning in the land, he had not asked his father for money. He had spent his money for Sunday clothes, that he might be decent in Church and Sabbath-school. He [His?] every day clothing was poor. His shoes were worn out, so that his toes were easily seen, yet he wore them. He did menial service, and [was] laughed at by children who knew him, as he passed along. Ladies turned up their noses as they passed him. Thus is the trial of him who left home under poverty's lash, who was compelled to seek aid from those who knew him not, or live in ignorance. There are giants still in his pathway. One of these—poverty—huge and tall, bids defiance to him. Now after 11 years of sin and toil supported by them who are God's ministers, he seeks God's guidance and pardon and deliverance. If he henceforth remains true to his God who has led him thus far, he will surely triump[h] and his joy will be brighter because of the darkness that is past. Here at seventeen he toils by day and reads and practices penmanship at the forepart of night while others sleep.

[*page 47*] [*bookkeeping exercises*]

Date	Time	Rate	Prin.	%	Payment	Inst.	Amt	New Princ.
1867-6-10 mo. da.								
1867 5-24	12-4	.029	$600.	6	$50.	$17.40	$617.40	$567.40
1868 3-21	3-25	.0185			$12.	$10.4969	$577.8969	565.8969
1868 3-14	7-9	.017⅓			$75.	9.8088796	$508.717063	
1868 3-6	10-15	.016				8.0112924		

[*The section below the table on page 47 is the "Scratch Pad" area for the preceding table entries. There are a variety of figures and arithmetical calculations from three to ten decimal places in disarray.*]

[*page 48*] [*bookkeeping exercises*]

1879		Beef Account		Dr.
July 20	To	21 Yoke Oxen	68.00	1428.00
Aug. 4	"	15 Cows	12.00	180.00
" 10	"	23 Steers	20.00	460.00
" 20	"	22 Cows	12.50	275.00
Nov. 1	"	Pasturing 102 Cattle 11 wks	.12	134.64
" "	"	100 Loads Pumpkins	.50	50.00
1880				
Feb. 1	"	100 Tons Hay	4.50	450.00
" "	"	1800 Bu. Corn	.35	630.00
" "	"	Grinding 1800 Bu. Corn	.05	90.00
" "	"	Amount to Balance (Gain)		164.36
				3862.00

{Note: This table offsets the credit (Cr.) Beef Account Table on page 49 for 1879.]

1880		F. M. Granger		Dr.
Jan. 10	To	10 Cords Wood	2.25	22.50

"	"	" 18 Bu. Potatoes		.30	5.40
"	25	" 20 lbs. Butter		.14	2.80
Feb.	10	" 18 Bu. Wheat		1.38	24.84
"	26	" 25 lbs. Butter		.15	3.75
Mar.	4	" 2 Tons Hay		4.50	9.00
"	22	" 10 Bu. Potatoes		.35	3.50
June	10	" 10 Bu. Wheat		1.40	14.00
July	2	" 4 Day's Work		2.00	8.00
"	24	" Pasturing 2 Cows, 12 wks		.20	4.80
Nov.	25	" 10 Bu. Wheat		1.38	13.80
"	"	" 80 lbs. Butter		.14	11.20
"	"	" 75 " Cheese		.07	5.25
Dec.	1	" 4 Tons Hay		5.00	20.00
"	30	" Cash			10.09
"	"	" my Note at 30 Days to Bal.			50.00

208.93

[*Note: In Dec. 30 entry, cash was made to balance what was sold to F. M. Granger to offset what was owed F. M. Granger for 1880. See table page 49, "1880   F. M. Granger   Cr."*]

[*page 49*] [*bookkeeping exercises*]

1880			Beef Account		Cr.
Feb	1	By	42 Oxen, wt 41,160 lbs.	.05	2058.00
"	"	"	37 Cows, 22,200 lbs.	.04½	999.00
"	"	"	23 Steers, 16,000 lbs.	.05	805.00
					3862.00

1880			F. M. Granger		Cr.
Jan.	4	By	1 Common Harness		16.00
"	"	"	3 " Halters	.75	2.25
"	"	"	2 " Bridles	.75	1.50
Apr.	10	"	1 Common Saddle		7.00
"	"	"	1 Quilted Saddle		25.00
"	"	"	1 Pr. Martingales		.75
June	6	"	1 Buggy Harness		20.00
"	"	"	1 Single Harness		13.00
"	"	"	2 Bridle Halters	1.20	2.40
July	2	"	1 Buggy Harness		25.00
"	"	"	1 Double "		30.00
Nov.	15	"	Repairing Collars		.38
"	"	"	1 Throatlatch		.20

"	25	" 1 Leather Trunk		20.00
Dec.	20	" Trimming Buggy		18.00
"	"	" Repairing Harness		2.25
"	"	" 1 Tug Harness		24.00
"	"	" 1 Bridle Halter		1.20
				208.93

[page 50, top of page] [bookkeeping exercises]

1880		Oat Field 5 Acres		Dr.
Apr.	20	To 5 Days Plowing	2.00	10.00
"	26	" 18 Bu. Seed Oats	.31	5.58
"	"	" 3/4 Days Sowing	1.00	.75
"	27	" 2 Days Harrowing	1.50	3.00
July	20	" 5 Days Harvesting	1.25	6.25
Sept.	22	" Threshing 200 Bu. Oats	.06	12.00
Oct.	26	" Marketing do. do.	.03	6.00
"	"	" Interest at $20 per Acre	.07	7.00
"	"	" Profit on Crop		7.42
				58.00

1879		Wheatfield, 60 Acres		Dr.
June	25	To Plowing 60 Acres	1.75	105.00
July	20	" Harrowing do.	.33$^{1/3}$	20.00
Sep.	10	Cross plowing do.	1.25	75.00
"	15	" 90 Bu. Seed Wheat	.75	67.50
"	"	" Sowing 60 Acres	.10	6.00
"	"	" Harrowing do.	.75	45.00
1880				
July	10	" Reaping 60 Acres	1.00	60.00
"	14	" Hauling Wheat to barn	.33$^{1/3}$	20.00
Aug	1	" Threshing 1500 Bu. Wheat	.10	150.00
"	15	" Marketing 1350 Bu. Wheat	.02	27.00
"	"	" Interest at $20 per Acre	.07	84.00
"	"	" Amount to Balance (Gain)		495.50
				1155.00

[page 50, bottom of page] [penmanship exercise that contains only one name]
Miss Maude R. Brooks.

[page 51, top of page] [bookkeeping exercises]

1880		Oat Field Acres		Cr.
Oct.	26	By 200 Bu. Oats	.25	50.00

			Straw for fodder		8.00
					58.00

1880			Wheatfield 60, Acres		Cr.
Aug. 15	By	100 Bu. Seed Wheat		.75	75.00
"	"	" 50 " Wheat		.75	37.50
"	"	" 1350 Bu. do.		.75	1012.50
"	"	" Straw			30.00
					1155.00

[*page 51, bottom of page*] [*penmanship exercise*]

[. . .] Hoping to see you at home, and clasp thee to my heart, I am as ever thy loving friend,

        Wm E. Shawnee

 Miss Maud R. Brooks.

[*page 52*][*continuation of "The Long Journey"*]
But vain of the vainest is sighing,
Our course must be forward and on;
We cannot turn back on the journey,
We cannot enjoy what is gone.
Let us hope, then, as onward we travel,
That oases may brighten the plain,
That our road be along the sweet waters,
Though we may not begin it again.

For existence forever goes upward—
From the hill to the mountain we rise,
On, on o'er invisible summits,
To a land in the limitless skies.
Strive on, then, with courage unshaken—
True labor is never in vain—
Nor glance with regret at the pathway
No mortal can travel again.

Fifth Day 16th [September 1886]
 Ellsworth was at work in the corn today. The weather was pleasant. It was painful to see others going to school and himself not. Work on [*page 53*] Ellsworth patiently and bravely;

the cloud will pass away by and by. Read some and sat up at night as usual. He made many mistakes. Trials were many.

"Let the words of my mouth and the meditation of my heart be acceptable in thy sight, ~~my~~ O Lord my Strength and my Redeemer. The day was counted for Jesus.

Sixth Day 17th [*September 1886*]

He was at work all day. He had trials and temptations to bear. He thought of his father; of his present condition; and of the future. The day was hot in the cornfield, where he was most of the day. He longed for manhood and prosperity. He meditated upon the home in heaven, and said that life was worth living. A boy's thoughts are many. Help, O holy Father a poor, weak, dependent creature for Jesus' sake. May he live hereafter more especially for thy glory. He read and wrote while others slept. He counted the day for Jesus.

Blessed be the name of the Father and of the Son and of the Holy Spirit.

Amen for ever,

Seventh Day 18th. [*September 1886*]

He was at work in the cornfield today. About 3 o'clock P.M. there came a heavy rain, which lasted about an hour and a half. He went to the mill [*continued on page 56*]

[*page 56*] [*continuation from page 53*] very late in the evening came home and ate supper went to town and returned with shopping. Shopping should be done in the morning. Trials and temptations. He thought of getting a business education and also of learning a trade, so that he might be able to make a living thereby if necessary. He would be very glad to have a home, where he could have everything comfortable and neat. Maude Idella Ganoung saluted him as he passed her this evening (a thing she almost always does). He weighed 114 lbs. today, last week 112. He labored while others slept. "Keep thy heart with all diligence; for out of it are the issues of life." The day was counted for Jesus. Geo. W. Valentine bought him a pair of shoes at $1.25. Hattie Valentine is quite sick yet.

[*page 54*] [*bookkeeping exercises*]

1880		Potato Field, 20 Acres		Dr.	
May	1	To Plowing 20 Acres	1.50		30.00
"	10	" 225 Bu. Seed Potatoes	.30		67.50
"	"	" Planting 20 Acres	1.50		30.00
June	25	" 10 Days Work	1.25		12.50

"	"	" 30 Days Hoeing	.75		22.50
Nov.	1	" 70 Days Digging	.75		52.50
"	"	" Marketing, 10 Days	2.00		20.00
"	"	" Interest at $30 per Acre	.07		42.00
"	"	" Amount Balance (Gain)			515.50
					792.50

1880		James Davidson		Dr.	Cr.
Jan.	2	By 18 lbs. Brown Sugar	.08		1.44
"	"	" 15 " Rice	.07		1.05
"	"	" 12 " Soft Sugar	.14		1.68
Feb.	10	To Cash		4.00	
"	"	By 10 lbs. Codfish	.06		.60
"	"	" 2 Gal. Molasses	.44		.88
Mar.	4	" 12 lbs. Butter	.15		1.80
"	"	" 10 " Cheese	.08		.80
"	24	" 8 " Corn Starch	.11		.88
"	"	" 2 " Saleratus	.09		.18
"	"	" 4 " Ginger	.10		.40
Apr.	12	" 4 Bu. Potatoes	.42		1.68
"	"	" 6 Doz. Eggs	.10		.60
"	"	To Cash		4.00	
May	1	By 1 Hay, 18lbs.	.09		1.62
"	"	" 14 lbs. Cornmeal	.01		.14
June	10	" 12 " Rice	.06		.72
July	2	" ½ Bu. Potatoes	.50		.25
Aug.	1	" 10 lbs. Mackerel	.09		.90
Aug.	1	To Cash to Balance		7.62	
				15.62	15.62

[page 55, top of page] [bookkeeping exercises]

1880		Potato Field, 20 Acres			Cr.
Nov.	1	By 2450 Bu. Potatoes	.25		612.50
"	"	" 200 do. do	.15		30.00
"	"	" 600 do. do.	.25		150.00
					782.50

1880		Henry Ingalls		Dr.	Cr.
Jan.	4	To 8 Cords Wood	1.50	12.00	
"	"	By 1 Pr. Kip Boots			4.00
"	"	" 3 " Children's Garters	.60		1.80

"	"	" 2 " Boy's Suspenders	.14		.28
Apr.	10	" ~~3 Pation~~ 3 Prs. Gloves	.15		.45
"	14	" 4 Linen Hdkfs.	.60		2.40
"	"	" 2 Pr. Misses' Gaiters	1.25		2.50
May	6	" 1 Seghorn Hat			1.50
"	"	" 2 Plam Leaf Hats	.30		.60
"	20	To 80 Lbs. Wool	.40	32.00	
"	"	By Cash to Balance			30.47
				44.00	44.00

[*page 55, bottom of page*] [*penmanship exercise with only three names*]
Maud Brooks, Mary Boyd, . . . Wm Ellsworth . . .

Sabbath Ninth Month 19. [*September 1886*]

Little Mary M. Valentine arranged the table on which ~~has~~ his books are. Thanks is due to her, she has wrought a good work. He attended Sabbath-school at the African Methodist Episcopal Zion Church. The day in the forenoon was fine. God has blessed me, I should be very thankful. Lord, I love thee more dearly than ever. May I live near thee forever and ever. Amen.

[*page 57*] In the afternoon he attended Sabbath School and church. At night he held some familiar words with his friend, Geo. Benson. He thought that if he got a chance to earn money, he would attend a Business College. I would to God I could. Thanks be to God for the Christian Sabbath. He thanked little Mary for her trouble. May I become an earnest and faithful worker for Christ. May I do his will O righteous Father, for Jesus' sake. He made many mistakes. Lord pardon them all. I pray thee. The day was counted for Jesus. Lord, I love thee. Amen.

Second Day 20th, 1886 [*September*]

He was beset of satan frequently during the day. He was occupied profitably, being at work. He thought of earning money; of attending Business College; of studying music; and of subsequent life. O that God would help him to lead a successful life! Let him do his past patiently and bravely, for Jesus, and all is well. He talked too much. Let those things which are not thy own alone. Know before judging. Princess Beatrice is a smart little girl, and shows it too. Though modest, yet bold in duty. The day was counted for Jesus. Glory and honor to Jesus Amen.

[*page 58*] *Ninth Month Third Day 21st* [*September*]

The day was profitable spent in toil. Mistakes were many. He thought of school. He is patiently waiting for further light. It is better to travel surely and slowly than to fall. Quit not that which is certain to enter into that which is doubtful. He read the first three chapters in Genesis. If the Lord will, he hopes to read the Bible through in a year. The day [was?] warm, but it was quite cool in the morning and the evening; and it did not rain. The day was counted for Jesus. Bless the Lord. Amen.

[page 62] 9/21/1886
   I have never seen a person who did not have faults of some kind. Hast thou? I have never seen and known a person who did not make mistakes. In fact, man is not infallible. Every thing that man invents is consequently not perfect. Yea even that which he does is not done right. In short, he never finds but what he could have done better. O the mistakes of my own life! How many! A parent tells a child that it should not and can not have a certain thing; the child cries, and the parent yields. Is not there a mistake made here? Does not the child here learn to bring the parent to terms by crying whenever its whim is not gratified? Is this teaching a child, or letting it teach itself? There are enough self taught, or rather devil-taught, ~~of~~ children already. Some parents believe and declare that dirt makes children strong, healthy, and beautiful. Children must either be governed or else they govern themselves. Early training is the best training, because the most effective. Self denial is taught best when very young, when such teaching is most needed, than after the passions *[page 63]* have either partially or fully mastered the individual. In this also preventive is better than cure. What a person says and does affects his whole life. Wisdom in speech is as important as wisdom in action. How much mischief may an idle word do! How often does an evil word spoken in company haunt the memory of our companions? Who can count the mischief done by evil words? All know their pernicious effect, for all have seen them. They are known among the inhabiters of all the earth. Well does the plalmist [psalmist?] say, "What man is he that desireth life, and that loveth many days, that he may see good? Keep thy tongue from evil, and thy lips from speaking guile.

Fourth Day 22nd, 1886.
   He was at work part of the day. He attended Preparative Meeting, after which satan hurled a severe dart at him, but in vain, for God delivered him. He afterwards read the 4th, 5th, & 6th chapters of Genesis. W. P. Hastings departed for Boston this morning. He made several mistakes. He longed for better times. He said that he would never make long visits. Mrs. L. S. B. Hastings committed a secret to him. Received a letter from J. W.

Pritchard, editor of the [*Presbyterian weekly journal*] *Christian Nation*, dated Sept. 7, 1886. The day was counted [*page 59*] for Jesus. He is yet in an unsettled state of affairs. He longed for many things which he could not get. O that God, for Jesus' sake; would forgive and pity him. Help, O Lord, I pray.

Fifth Day 23 [September 1886]
    Was not at work all day. Severe were temptations, but God's will was done. His friend Geo. Benson presented him a copy of the answers to Wentworth's Algebra. He read the 7th, 8th, and 9th chapters of Genesis. He read also nearly a whole copy of the *Christian Nation*—a weekly journal published in New York city—aloud to Mr. and Mrs. Valentine. A little girl said "Good evening" to him, as he was passing along the street, reading a copy of the *Christian Nation*. She was white. Next time children whom he does not know, salute him, he wishes to know their names. He received two copies of the *Christian*—one dated Sept. 15, the other Sept. 22. The day was counted for Jesus. "Bless the Lord, O my soul" Amen.

Sixth Day 24. [September 1886]
    Was at work all day. It was chopping wood that I was doing. I was quite tired when night came. He thought much concerning oaths. Temptations [*continued on page 60, bottom of page*]

[*page 60, top of page*] *New Orleans Dec. 1, 1875.*
    $19 Four months from date I promised to pay the order of E. D. Warner, Nineteen Dollars, value received, Ninety
    [*The second paragraph is a penmanship exercise.*] Dec. 19, 1886. William E. Shawnee . . . Ella, Maude R. C. Brooks, Mary, MC & Coning Jones & Co., Maude, Redman, Wm E. Shawnee. . . . Alcohol is a poison. Caroline Coning Jones & Co. Xerxes . . . Kansas, King of kings and lord of lords.

[*page 60, bottom of page*] *Sixth Day 24 [September 1886]*, continued [*from page 59*]
proved him, but God heard him. He longed to attend school, enter into some business, and perform the trust that might be laid upon him. After supper he took Mrs. L. S. B. Hastings' mail to her. He read the 10th, 11th, and 12th chapters of Genesis. He sat up at night for the sake of improvement. The day was won, and counted for Jesus. Amen.

Seventh Day 25th. [September 1886]
    He was busy at work part of the day, and also attended Monthly Meeting, which was held in the afternoon. He was beset with temptations, but God has delivered him therefrom. He [*page

61] counted the day for Jesus. Amen. He read the 13th, 14th, and 15th chapters of Genesis, and also the first 5 chapters of St. John.

Sabbath Ninth Month 26, 1886.
He read the 16th, 17th, 18th, 19th, and 20th chapters in Genesis. Thus in six consecutive days he has read twenty chapters in Genesis. He has sat up for several consecutive evenings for the sake of literary improvement. He has won and counted another week for Jesus. Hossanna [sic]; blessed is the King of Israel that cometh in the name of the Lord, to reign for ever and ever. Amen, forever.

The Sabbath School Sessions for the preceding three months. Golden Text—The Son of man must be delivered into the hands of sinful men, and be crucified. Luke 24:7.

Lesson 1. Jesus and the blind man. John 9:1-17.—Sabbath, Seventh Month 4th, 1886.

Golden Text—One thing I know, that, whereas I was blind, now I see. John 9:25.

[*page 64*]
A Journal of Wm E. Shawnee begun *10th Month 1, 1886. Sixth Day.*
He saw Charles Cansler, an old friend and school-mate of his near his home. Charley was milking a cow. He also saw Mary A. Boyd, a friend and school-mate of three years standing, who saluted him as he passed. Charley Boyd, father of Mary Boyd—the same who saluted him—asked him why he did not attend the Maryville College, and pressed him for an answer. He told Charley that it was because he could not bear his own expenses. Charley told him that it would not cost much. To which he replied that it would cost more—much more—than he could pay. He was at work helping to haul sugar-cane to mill. He has begun to read the Bible regularly each day. To-day he read the 6th, 7th, 8th, 9th, and 10th chapters in Exodus. Last month he finished reading Genesis and the first five chapters in Exodus. Wm H. Valentine, son of George and Nora Valentine, has arrived from Ebenezer, where he is teaching school. I am sojourning with George and Nora Valentine. They have eight children. In order of age, William, Sarah, Emma, Harriet, Mary, Minnie, Leo, Albert, and George. The day was counted for the Lord Jesus, Amen.

[*page 65*] [*blank page*]

[*page 66*]
．．．．．．．．．．．．．．．．．．．．Reflections of Wm E. Shawnee
Tenth Month 5, 1886

．．．．．．．．．．．．．．．．Maryville, Tenn., Oct. 5, 1886.
My Brother Walter:
．．．．．I received your letter a few days since, also I received Howard's letter.

[*page 67*]
．．．．．．．．．．．．．．．．Grecian History as translated by
．．．．．．．．．．．．．．．．．．．．Wm E. Shawnee,

．．．．．Many wars having been prosperously carried on in Asia, Darius waged war against the Scythians and entered Scythia with seven hundred thousand armed men, when the enemy would not give him the opportunity of a battle, fearing lest the bridge over the Ister having been broken down, his return to his own would be cut off eighty thousand men having been lost, he fled in terror. Thence he subdued Macedonia; and when he returned from Europe into Asia, his friends exhorting that he could reduce Greece into his power, he prepared a fleet of five hundred ships and placed over it Datis and Artaphernes; and he gave to them two hundred thousand foot soldiers and ten thousand cavalry. (215) [*continued at paragraph 215 on page 76*]

215. [*moved from page 76*]
Literal Latin Translation, with Latin mode of arrangement.

．．．．．Many in Asia prosperously having been carried on, Darius with [[the]] Scythians war waged, and with armed seven hundred thousands of men Scythia entered, when [[the]] enemy to him of [[a]] battle [[the]] power not would give, fearing, lest, having been broken down [[the]] bridge of [[the]] Ister, [[the]] return to his would be cut off, having been lost eighty thousands of men, having been alarmed he fled. Thence Macedonia he subdued: and when from Europe into Asia he had returned, exhorting [[his]] friends that Greece he could reduce into his power, [[a]] fleet of five hundred ships he prepared and over it Datis he placed and Artaphernes and to these two hundred of foot soldiers thousands, and ten of horsemen he gave.

[*page 68*]
．．．．．．．．．．．．．．．．Should I attend school after Christmas?

I am seventeen years old; after Christmas I shall have been eighteen. I intend a new era in my life. Before eighteen others have done all the thinking for me, which I suppose was not much,—after that time I shall seek direction and guidance from the Lord God, the Source of my instruction, he is my helper and my king.

Hitherto I have been supplied and advised by others; here after by and through God's help, I intend to attend unto mine own necessities. Since God is my Strength and Trust, why should I continue a burden to others? Cannot He that made me, keep me? Or lacketh he wisdom, that he can not guide?

Before eighteen, I trusted in man. I believed man. Here after I shall trust in God and believe Him only as toward myself. Hitherto I have erred grievously, here after I shall, by and through the Lord's mercy and grace live a Christian. I shall joy in trial, in tribulation. I shall seek and work for Jesus all the time. I shall work and study for Him only.

I shall not attend school after Christmas because I am meditating plans of which such a course would be subversive. I have chosen to be a teacher and a scholar for Jesus, to fulfil the purpose [continued on page 69, bottom of page]

[page 69, bottom of page] [continued from page 68] of my life, according to the Scriptures: Fear God, and keep his commandments; for this is the whole duty of man. How can I fear God, and keep his commandments if I have not a chosen and appointed place? If I ascertan not, nor fulfil, his appointment? I have an inclination to study and to teach. I like it, and I firmly believe I am engaged by duty to follow such a course. I intend to learn a useful trade also. I can not secure the means to enable me to attend school in so short a time. Therefore to enable me to command means necessary to pursue my qualification as a teacher and scholar and to as a part of such a qualification, I propose by and through the Lord's help to secure a thorough, practical, and complete Business College education.

[page 70] A journal of daily transactions, begun by Wm Ellsworth Shawnee

Tenth Month 21st, 1886.
1. The morning was rather cold, and it was cloudy most of the day. W^m was busy at work all day. He thought of learning to draw, to be able to paint nice pictures. He studied Caesar's Commentary some at night, and read some in a history of Rome, which George Benson, his friend, lent to him. He is engaged to write an essay for his friend, entitled "Tongues." He was

ridiculed by some youths as he passed through Maryville, Tenn., on horseback bringing two bushels of cornmeal from mill. The day was counted for Jesus.

Tenth Month Sixth day 22nd, 1886
　　The morning was somewhat cold, but there was no frost. He was busy, being engaged till late in the evening. He thought how pleasant it would be to have a home, where he might study and read as much as he desired. He went to the Post Office, where he met his old friend, Wm H. Hannum. After coming back he read through the *Christian Nation*; a Presbyterian journal of New-York-city of great merit, and at the same time assisted in shelling peas. Such is the early life of Wm Ellsworth Shawnee, and let him never forget his present state as contrasted with the glorious [*page 71*] future God the Lord will give him. Never let him forget or despise labor; but let him work with his own hand be of such conversations as becometh the Gospel of Christ, and effeminate in dress. Let him not despise or overlook the poor, seeing he himself was also poor and knows the mind of the poor. The day was counted for Jesus.

Tenth Month 23rd, Seventh Day, 1886.
　　The morning was cold as usual and it continued so until after 8 o'clock. He was occupied in the forenoon, in assisting in hauling wood.
　　Be loving, and thou will never want for love; be humble and thou will never want for guiding.
　　Self reverence, self knowledge, self control, These three alone lead life to sover[e]ign power.

[*page 72*] Query: Does a natural proclivity to crime diminish the guilt of the act?

Address.
　　~~Does~~ Should parents be compelled by law to send their children to school?
　　In proportion as the intelligence of a country is to be desired so is the importance of the right solution of this question.
　　But as our all wise Creator has made no two persons alike in facial expression so he has made no two alike in opinion. Therefore are we here in debate, Ladies and Gentlemen.
　　The fathers of our country in framing our institutions appealed to the judgement of the people of this country as to the correctness of their reasonings. The result, my friends, is the grandest experiment of free government upon the face of the globe. This proves the correctness, to some extent of their

theories. In a republic like ours the people must be educated so as to examine our principles, or they will despise ~~or desreg~~ and be ignorant of them. Now it is our boast that we have more schools and institutions of learning than any people on earth. But are the people well educated? Are they capable of understanding the principles of free government? Can they understand their responsibility? No! illiteracy is still great in our country, especially in the Southern [*page 73*] states. Statesmen proclaim, "Ignorance in our country is a crime." But that does no good. People are illiterate even yet. There are thousand[s] of voters—the crowned sovereigns of our land—totally illiterate! Young boys and girls, young men and women, in illiteracy can't read, can't take the responsibility of voters. What must be done? I answer: compel their parents to send them to school.

Again in many cases, the children wish to attend school. The schools are here but it may be they are not all properly maintained. The parents say; "No; we want you. You can go by and by: time enough yet." Years go by, and my friends, but 'by and by' never comes! Whose is the fault? What is the remedy? Parents sometimes sometimes [*sic*] send [them?] a week, a month or even two months, and the[n] desist. Who's at fault? The Affirmative solution of this question provides a remeny [remedy?]; is it not the true one?

I favor the affirmative answer because children have rights which should be respected. If a parent kills a child, does not the law consider it a murder? It is as much a murder as if he or she had killed the most grey-headed person on earth. Why in the name of truth, justice, and common sense ~~have~~ should parents be allowed to deny their children that which will benefit them in life, will made [make] them better men and women; yea more, ~~more~~ better citizens. [*Continued on the last half of page 75.*]

[*page 74, entry dated Sept. 1 moved to precede journal entry dated Sept. 11*]

[*page 75, top of page moved as part of Sept. 1 entry*]

[*page 75, last half*]   Better in church and State. No such right as the contrary can he claimed.

There are reasons why the state should enact such a law. 1. It will diminish crime. One reason why the liquor traffic raises its huge visage among the most intelligent communit[i]es and every where else is because people are ignorant of the effects of alcohol on the system. Here is the source of three fourths of all crime. Education will right this to a very great

extent. Education will act as a powerful agent in lessening other sources of crime.
2. It will lessen taxation. There will be less expense on account of jails, penitentiaries, poorhouses insane assylums, etc., because the masses will have a source of support that is true, noble, and laudable. Ambition will [*continued near the bottom of page 76*]

[*page 76, top of page*] *Eleventh Month 7, 1886 Sabbath.*

David in the sixth [*remainder of the sentence omitted*]

[*page 76, -bottom of page*] [*continued from page 75*] despise public support and correction.
3. It is necessary for the perpetuation of the state. We all despise the traitor, one who does not love his country but tries to destroy it. Look at the movements of the anarchist at Chicago. This is the class that filled Rome with terror in her last day. Every body says, [*page 77*] The anarchist must go. I say: prevent anarchy. The illiterate are the material of which this class is formed. Profligate and unprincipled leaders incite the masses and then none can control. Self-preservation is the state's first law. Education of the masses perpetuates the existence of the state by elevating them and making them intelligent to understand their duty as far as duty goes, in a word—Godward; by giving them honorable employment as so decreasing state burdens; and by making them patriots.

Therefore ladies and gentlemen, the state is competent and should provide for the education of the masses by compulsion.

Then will ignorance indeed be a crime[;] captivity will be led captive[;] the land will blossom as the rose[;] and our land and country the greatest wonder that the world has ever seen.

[*page 78*] *Eleventh Month.*
Every soul should be subject unto the higher powers, because rulers are not a terror to good works, but to the evil. Syllogistically arranged:
Every soul should be subject unto that which is not a terror to good works, but to the evil;
Rulers are not a terror to good works, but to the evil;
Therefore every soul should be subject unto rulers.

Question. Resolved. That the prosperity of the United States is greater than that of foreign countries. Is the prosperity of the United States greater than that of foreign countries?

F Providence

David, in the tenth psalm, saith, Why standest thou afar off, O Lord? why hidest thou thyself in times of trouble? It would seem from this that even David in his trouble was made to ask, Why, standest thou afar off, O Lord. Sometimes the Lord seems to us to be afar off. It is because we have not put our trust in him as we should. Sometimes when we seek the Lord we cannot feel him near, but we should trust him and say within ourselves, Though he slay me, yet will I trust in him. This is some of David's experience and we are confident when we read in his our own. The Christian will have trouble and vexation of spirit, but he should not be unmanned by [*page 79*] them, and will not as long as his trust is in his God.

A prayer of Wm E. Shawnee.

Lord, thou art God, who hast made the heavens, and the earth, and the sea, and all that is in them; hear my prayer and give ear unto my supplications. Cut me not off in thine anger, but have mercy upon me; for thou art merciful and gracious, longsuffering and abundant in goodness and truth. I have sinned, but thy blood applied can cleanse my wounds. If thou wilt, thou canst make me whole. Do thou be pleased to heal, guide, and protect me for thy own sake. Have mercy upon my friends, O Lord; be thou to them a shield; help them in their weaknesses. Grant that we may do thy will concerning us; and when thou seest meet, quicken us and fit us for thy home above, for Jesus' sake.
Amen.   131 words.

Prayer.

David saith in the fifth psalm, My voice shalt thou hear in the morning, O Lord; in the morning will I direct my prayer unto thee, and look up.

If David prayed unto the Lord every morning, certainly I should. My eyes should be directed toward heaven when I pray. Help me, Lord, to pray unto thee every morning, after the manner of thy servant David of old.

[*page 80*] *Begun Eleventh Month 11, 1886.*

He [*writing in third person*] worked over three hours for Joseph Broyles on the 9th at chopping wood. He weighs 116½ lbs and is 5 ft 2¾ inches high, and is 17 yrs 10 mo and 18 days old.

David saith in the fifty-fifth psalm, Evening, morning, and at noon will I pray, and cry aloud; and he shall hear my voice. I should pray regularly at evening, morning and noon, and cry aloud; my voice must be heard—cry aloud saith David. The Lord help me to observe this.

David saith in the eighty-sixth psalm, Be merciful unto me, for I cry unto thee daily. David's reason for God's mercy is, I cry unto thee daily. Certainly God will be merciful unto me if I cry unto him daily. Help me, Lord, to cry unto thee daily.

David in the one hundredth and sixty-fourth psalm saith, Seven times a day do I praise thee because of thy righteous judgements. Certainly I can praise the Lord seven times a day if David could and did. Lord, help me to praise thee seven times each day.

In the tenth chapter of Daniel, he saith: Now when Daniel knew that the writing was signed he went into his house, and his windows being open in his chamber toward Jerusalem, he kneeled upon his [*page 81*] knees three times a day, and prayed, and gave thanks before his God, as he did aforetime. Know the truth, and do it regardless of circumstances or consequences. Daniel prayed and gave thanks to God three times a day, and certainly I can do the same. Lord, help me to do likewise.

[*page 82*]
O Lord, in order to praise and give glory to thy name, to do what I believe thou hath given me to do, and to ease my conscience toward thee, I have seen fit to write this manuscript. I pray that thou by and through thy holy Spirit cleanse, purify, and sanctify me for the work; and guide me in thine own way to serve thee. Father do, for thy son's sake. Amen.

To all whom this may come and to whosoever readeth, whether Christian or not, William Ellsworth Shawnee wisheth grace, mercy, and peace from God our Father and the Lord Jesus Christ, to whom be all glory and honor, dominion, praise, and thanksgiving, now and ever. Amen.

Among all classes of men, there are none who deny the existence of some supreme Being while in their primitive state. But when they become wicked and depraved, they depart from this state, burning with lust one toward another, and forgetting God, have changed the manner of him into a lie, worshipping the stars and the sun and the moon and lusts of their own flesh.

[*page 83*] [*This page is blank except for incoherent scribbling that does not appear to be written by William Shawnee.*]

[*page 84*] Opion, Opinion, sentiment, purpose, decision, sentence, vote, question, sense, purport.
Opinion: sentiment, idea, notion, judgement, settled persuasion.
Character, reputation, mark, figure;

1. It should represent his justice among men, (that is, civil government as a divine ordinance should represent his (God's) justice among men.[)]
2. Individual character is the standard of the nation's strength. Work, therefore, for the regeneration of the individual. Christianize each voter.
3. The fear of public opinion in a free country, where character and motives are discussed without reserve, is strong enough to make converts of most men, but when it becomes a moral principle that a man if a representative owes it to his party to vote with it through thick and thin, and is bound, if only a private citizen to support the regular candidate, there is a turning of moral rules upside down that may corrupt the character of a whole country.

Conclusions:—
1. The whole country has a character, which may be corrupted.
2. The turning of moral rules upside down may corrupt this character.
3. Character and motives are capable [*page 85*] of being discussed.
4. That an individual posses[ses] character, which is the standard of the nation's strength.

IV. Allegiance is broken ~~off~~ if a man deserts his party, and the abuse is so strong when individuals do this that a vast amount of moral courage is needed to make the change. Only when numbers go over together will they help each other in combinations. This principle, which puts partisanship in the room of patriotism, and fear in that of conviction, only retards the death of a party, that is mortally wounded already. But it debases character more than almost any thing else.

Conclusions.
1. That character is capable of being corrupted, and of being debased.
2. That the application of an evil principle will debase the same.
3. That a principle or courage itself may be "moral."
4. That "moral courage" is what is sometimes required to do right.

V. As there are men who hang about courts of justice and who make their living by seeking places on juries, which places of all others they are the least competent to fill, so we have a class of men styled politicians, men of little moral character, of no culture, but skilled [*page 86*] in trickery, whose aim is not how to serve best the interest of the country, but how to secure their own selfish ends.

Conclusions.
1. That those styled politicians are men of little moral character, of no culture, skilled in trickery and that they seek their own selfish ends.
2. That a person may have little moral character.
3. That politicians should aim to serve the interest of their country.
4. That an "aim" may be good or bad.
5. That men have sought places they were the least competent to fill.
6. That skillfulness in trickery is bad.
Written Eleventh Month 23rd, 1886.

Writing of Wm Ellsworth Shawnee
Begun Eleventh Month 27th, 1886, Seventh Day

Today was one of perplexion in thought. My determination is to serve the Lord; for this alone is the Divine purpose and intention of my life. In accordance with this foregoing purpose and intention, I have chosen as I most firmly believe, under the Lord's guidance, to be a teacher and a scholar for Him. I have in like manner determined to secure a thorough, practical, and complete business education, at some reputable [*page 87*] school. I appeal to the Lord my Prophet, Priest, and King for guidance, strength, aid, and comfort and sanctification for my life work, for everything good, noble, and pure necessary or convenient in my work. The Day was counted for Jesus.

[*page 88*] I am going to be a teacher and a scholar. It shall be my life work, if the Lord God, who is the only wise, omnipotent, omniscient, and everlasting God forever, be willing. If He by his holy Spirit teach, cleanse, purify, and sanctify me for the work. Firmly believing that such a choice was made by and through His divine guidance, I am engaged not only to seek diligently and earnestly to qualify myself for his using and aiding, but also "to fear God, and keep [h]is commandments; for this is" my whole duty, both Godward and man ward. Written by Wm E. Shawnee *Eleventh Month 24, 1886.*

Is the service of an orator absolutely necessary?
People are very often not interested or solicitous enough to read what would be apt to come to their hands, to rightly instruct and guide them, or to give such consideration to a subject as to assure a right and timely solution. Others are not

able to read for themselves and must look to some other source for their supply of information.

[*page 89*] Thanksgiving 1886. [*November 25, 1886*] Thanksgiving came on Thursday this time. It was quite a cold day. It was somewhat rainy in the morning. But for all that we determined to have a rabbit-hunt. Accordin[g]ly as soon as the sun was over, our company, consisting of nine, departed. The first one who shot and killed a rabbit was Ernest Hastings; the next was Willie Valentine, and the last myself. This is the first rabbit I have killed in Tennessee. We met several boys while we were out, many of whom we did not know. When noon came we did not stop, so eager were we to find more game. Those who had brought a lunch ate as they became hungry, I suppose; at least I did. Toward evening our company came home carrying nearly two dozen rabbits. I do not know when the rest of the company ate their rabbits; we ate ours for dinner on Friday. Perhaps we [a]ll did wrong in not going to church[,] but we certainly had a good [ti]me. we. we. [*The rest of the page is a penmanship exercise of his name.*] . . . William E. Shawnee

[*page 90, blank page*]

[*page 91*] [*page contains a penmanship exercise with illegible scribbling*]

[*page 92, blank page*]

[*page 93*] [*The page number has been destroyed; the number was determined by its position in the original document.*]
1[.] The compiler of the First Class Reader, and of the Second Class Reader solicits the attention of teachers and of all persons interested in education to the present work which is <u>intended</u> for the use of children in the third class in our grammar schools of ages varying from nine or ten to twelve years.
2. A few lessons on moral subjects will be found toward the close which it is hoped, will not prove too dry to serve the purpose for which they are <u>intended</u>.
3. The following scheme of exercises in orthoepy is <u>intended</u> as a manual for the daily practice of those who use this volume, to secure correct habits of articulation and pronunciation.
4. They (the anti-Chinese outrages) ought to be suppressed, and must be if we <u>intend</u> to be true to our treaties with China.
5. [*There is no text for this number.*]

[*page 94, missing page number*] [*The top of the page has deteriorated so that only the bottom half of the first few letters of the first sentence is readable.*]

    A teacher is an [. . .] be a school master and orator, or a minister of the Lord Jesus. The profession is noble, in that God was the first instructor of man. He made garments for Adam and delivered to Moses the first written instrument—the decalogue. For it is in itself Godlike, since it seeks to elevate a fallen race to make the cultured useful to themselves and others and fits them for upbuilders of the people. The teacher's work will live after him and will materially affect whole communities for good.

    As a stone thrown into a pool of water will cause ripples that will hasten from the center to the brink, so will the influence of a teacher be great and powerful among the people, molding and refining their characters.

[*page 95, missing page number*] [*penmanship exercise with a few names and words*]

Alice Branner, Plain Facts, Wm E. Shawnee [. . .] Maud Brooks, Maude R. Brooks, R. Branner, Anna Alamanac, [. . .] Mrs. Rosa G. Hastings, [. . .] Commercial Current [. . .] Robert Redman, [Jo]hn C. Words.

[*page 96*] Alice Branner.

[*moved Shawnee's letter to his father, dated Sept. 14, from page 96 to precede journal entry dated Sept. 15*]

[*page 97, missing page*]

[*page 98, missing page*]

[*page 99, missing page*]

[*page 100, missing page*]

[*page 101*]
Sabbath School Lesson

Sabbath, Eleventh Month 21, 1886.
Subject of the lesson, John's vision of Christ.

Lesson.—Rev. 1:4:18.
Golden Text, I am he that liveth, and was dead; and, behold, I am alive forevermore. Rev. 1:18

Conclusions from the first verse:—
1. That this is the revelation of Jesus Christ.
2. That God gave this revelation unto Jesus Christ.
3. That the ~~intention and~~ design and purpose of this revelation was for Christ to show unto his servants things which must shortly come to pass, or happen.
4. That Christ sent and signified it by his angel into his servant John

2nd verse.
1. That John bare record of the word [of] God; That he bare record of the testimony of Jesus; That he bare rec[ord] of all things that he saw.

3rd verse.
1. That he that readeth the words of this prophecy is blessed
2. That they also are blessed who hear the words of this prophecy, and who keep those things which are written therein, or in it.
3. That he that readeth and they that hear~~eth~~ and keep the words of this [pro]phecy are blessed because the time [is at] hand or near. [*page 102*]

4th verse
1. That John is writing to seven churches, and salutes them.
2. That these seven churches were in Asia.
3. That John desires grace and peace to be [to?] them, the grace and peace which cometh from him who is, and who was, and who is to come.
4. That John desires that grace and peace to be to them, which comes from the seven Spirits.
5. That these seven Spirits are before the throne of him who ~~was~~ is, who was, and who is to come.

[5]th verse and 6th.
That John desires that grace and peace to be unto them, which is from Jesus Christ.
That Jesus Christ is the faithful witness; that Jesus Christ is the first begotten [of] the dead; that Jesus Christ is the [pr]ince of kings of the earth.
That John desires glory and dominion to be forever and ever unto him who loved us, and washed us from our sins in his own blood, and hath made us kings and priests unto God and his Father; that is, unto the Father of him who loved us, who washed us from our sins in his own blood, and who has made us kings and priests.

7th verse.
1. That he to whom John desireth glory and dominion forever and ever comes with clouds.
2. That ever[y o]ne shall [see] him [. . .] [*end of page frayed*]
[*page 103*] 7th verse
3. That all kindreds of the earth shall wail because of him to whom John desireth glory and dominion for ever and ever.
4. That John adds, Even so Amen; that is, even so let it be God's will be done.

8th verse
1. That the Lord saith, I am alpha and omega. I am the beginning and the ending.
2. That the Lord is he who is, and who was, and who is to come.
3. That the Lord is the Almighty.

9th verse.
1. That John was in the Isle that is called Patmos, for the word of God, and for the testimony of Jesus Christ.
[2.] That John was the brother of those to whom he was writing in tribulation and in the kingdom and patience of Jesus.

10th verse.
1. That John was in the Spirit on the Lord's day (I suppose that was either the Sabbath or the day of the vision).
[2.] That John heard behind him a great [vo]ice, as of a trumpet.

[11th ve]rse.
[1.] [T]hat this voice said, I am Alpha and [Om]ega the first and the last.
[2.] [That] it told John to write in a book what he saw, and send it to the seven Churches which are in Asia.
[3.] That these churches are: Ephesus, Smyrna, Pergamum, Thyatira, Sardis, Philadelphia, [and] Laodicea. [*page 104*]

12th verse.
1. That John turned to see the voice that spoke with him; 2. That while turned, he saw seven golden candlesticks.
verse 20. 1. That the seven stars and the seven candlesticks is a mystery. 2. That the seven stars are the angels of the seven churches, and the seven candlesticks are the seven churches.

verse 13. That in the midst of the seven candlesticks John saw one like [. . .] the Son of man, clothed with a garment down to the feet, and girt about the paps (nipples) with a gold girdle.

    What is grace? What is peace? Latin GRATTA, favor, gratitude, grace; favor; gratitude; thanks, grace; mercy; kindness; thankfulness; gratitude, gratefulness; thanks; acknowledgements.

Peace; quiet; tranquility, calm; ease, repose; concord. [*The first journal ends here.*

Second Chronicle

Living among Big Jim's Band

November 22, 1891-January 22, 1892

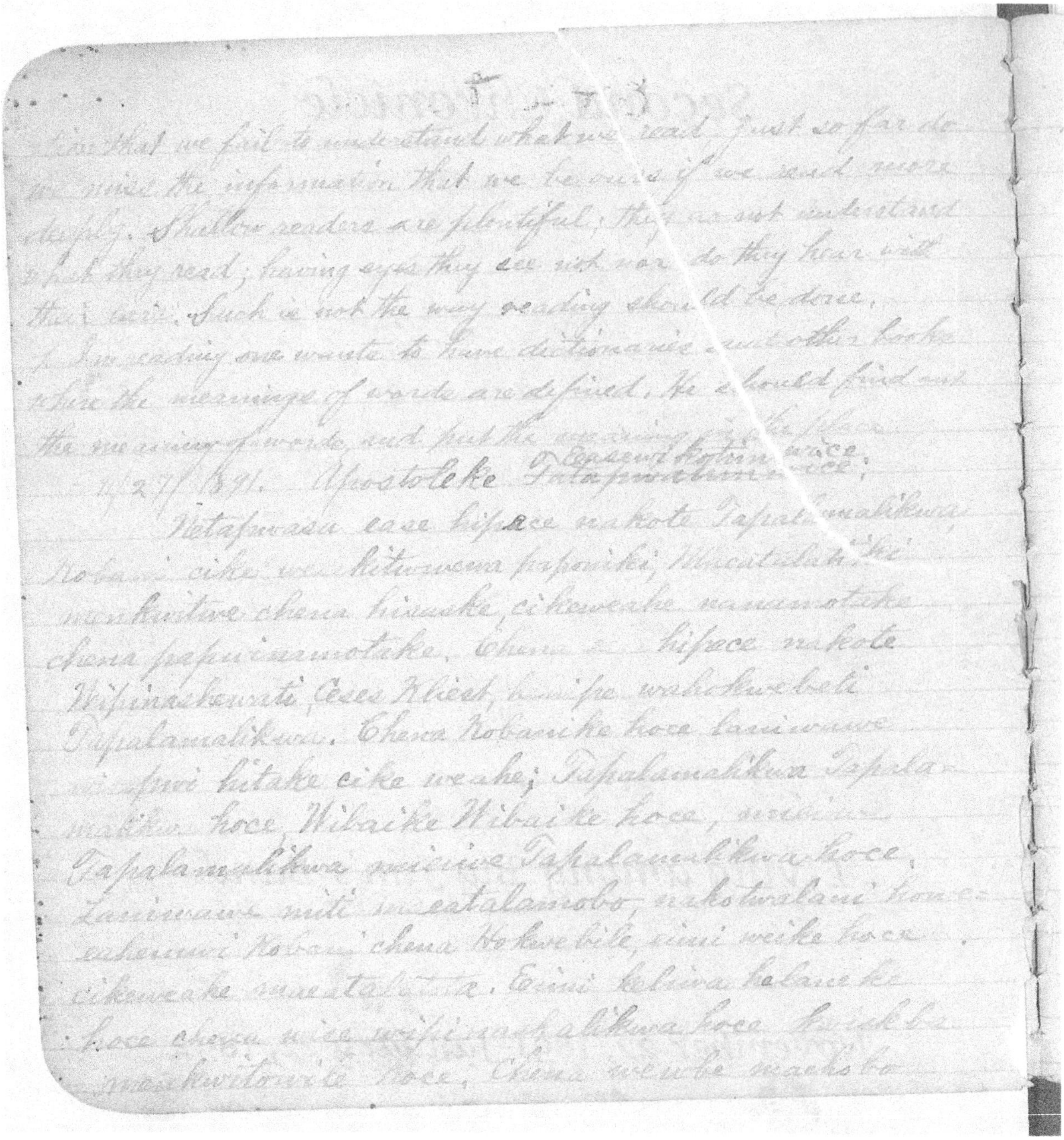

Fig. 2.1. Page 16 of William Ellsworth Shawnee's Second Chronicle.

Overview of the Second Chronicle

Several things happened in the life of William Ellsworth Shawnee before he began his second journal. Upon returning home from Maryville in 1887, the number of jobs he held nearly were as numerous as the changes in the world around him. In 1888 he worked for Alexander Crain, a notary public in Seminole County, and in 1888 and 1889 he farmed for his father. Also in 1889, the first land run took place on the Unassigned Lands, also known as the Oklahoma District, opening the area to non-Indians. The second land run, opening the central Oklahoma Indian lands to non-Indians, took place in central Oklahoma in September 1891. To prepare for the allotments and land runs, Shawnee worked with Thomas Wildcat Alford, John King, and others under the guidance of Indian agent Major N. S. Porter to survey the various Indian reservations.[1]

Shawnee served as a clerk for Big Jim's business council after he returned from Maryville. In a key move, the council met at Big Jim's Crossing on December 3, 1889, with John Welch as chairman. Its purpose was to prepare a memorial to submit to the Commissioner of Indian Affairs to seek assistance for damages and losses sustained by Big Jim's band when it was forcibly removed from the Kickapoo Reservation in 1886. Shawnee recorded the proceedings of the council and assisted in collecting the names of the claimants. Big Jim and William Shawnee Sr. were selected to act on behalf of Big Jim's band in pursuing their claims against the government. The claim was filed in Washington, D.C., on March 1, 1890, and was later allowed.[2]

Shawnee began his second journal in November 1891, almost four years after he returned to Indian Territory from Tennessee in November 1887. His second journal includes entries dated from November 22, 1891, through January 22, 1892. It is a bound, letter-sized document, written in ink, and faded. Although difficult to read, much of it is legible. It contains both English and Absentee Shawnee words. Illegible scribbling, possibly by Shawnee's younger siblings, appears on several pages. The original journal pages are unnumbered, with the first two pages missing. Daily entries of the journal are not in chronological order. For ease of transcribing and reading, the pages were numbered 3-72. In his second journal, Shawnee writes about his ancestry, his romantic interests, child rearing, the attitudes of the Absentee Shawnee youths among whom he lived, and his religious beliefs. This version of his journal has been put in chronological order and denoted as his "Second Chronicle."

Chapter 3

Clerking for Big Jim's Business Council
November 22, 1891—December 2, 1891

Shawnee's diverse entries in the first half of his second journal included daily activities, opinions, observations, romantic letters, information about his ancestry, and an essay about his early life—"The Autobiography of William E. Shawnee." His first entry was a list of books that he had either purchased or desired to read. His daily entries began on Sunday, November 22, 1891. Between that date and December 2, 1891, Shawnee lived at Big Jim's Crossing, or Little Axe, where Big Jim finally settled after he was forcibly removed from the Kickapoo Reservation. Shawnee lived in a dwelling with several young and middle-aged Indian males and tried unsuccessfully to steer the men away from gambling. He grew stronger in his Christian faith, but could not interest the others in it. He clerked for Big Jim's business council and performed manual labor for his keep. "I made myself tired with work today. I cut wood until my arms ached," he wrote. He also continued to correspond with Carrie Warrior, one of his romantic interests.

[*Pages 1 and 2 of the original journal are missing.*]
[*page 3*]
College, Author "Officer of the Holy Spirit," "Christ our Sanct[*ifi*]cation" etc., etc. Chicago: Publishing association of Friends 1889."
5. "A Latin Grammar for Schools and Colleges by Albert Harkness, Ph.D., LL.D., Professor in Brown University. Revised Standard Edition of 1881. New York: D. Appleton and Company, 1, 3, and 5 Bond Street, 1883."
6. "A Greek Grammar for School and Colleges by James Hadley, Late Professor in Yale College. Revised and in part rewritten by Frederic De Forest Allen, Professor in Harvard College. New York D. Appleton and Company 1,3, & 5 Bond Street. 1885"
7. "Self-Help with illustrations of Character and Conduct [by] Samuel Smiles, Author of "The Life of George Stephenson." A Revised and Enlarged Edition. New York: The American News Company, 39 and 41 Chambers Street.
8. "C. Lallusti Crispi Catilina et Jugurtha, with Explanatory Notes, Lexicon, etc, by George Stuarn, A.M., Professor of Latin Language in the Central High School of Philadelphia. Revised Edition. Philadelphia: Eldridge and Brother, No. 17 North Seventh Street, 1886."
9. "The Pious Remembrances, selected by Rebecca Collins. Second Edition. Philadelphia: Claxton, Remsen, and Haffelfinger,[*page 4*] 1869"
10. "The Harp of Religion. Christian Poetry. Original and Selected. Edited by Augustine J. H. Duganne. ~~Phl~~ Philadelphia: Henry Longstreth, No. 347 Market Street 1845."
11. "Howard the Philanthropist and his Friends, by John Stoughton, D.D., Author of "William Penn," "History of Religion in England," etc. London: Hodder and Stougton, 27 Paternoster Row. MDCCLXXXIV."
12. "Character by Samuel Smiles, author of "Self-Help," Life of the Stephensons," the Huguenots," etc., and Editor of "Round the World! Chicago and New York: Balford, Clarke, and Co. 1885."
13. "Cassel[l]'s Latin Dictionary. Latin-English and English-Latin, by J. R. Beard, D.D., and C. Beard, B.A. Fifty-third Thousand, Cassell & Company, Limited: London, Paris, New York, and Melbourne."
14. "The Morning Star: a Treatise on the Nature, Offices, and Work of the Lord Jesus Christ by Luke Woodard Minister of the Gospel of the (Orthodox) Society of Friends. New Vienna: O. Friend's Publishing House Press, 1875."
15. "Sadler's Counting House Arithmetic: a New and Improved Work on Business Calculations, with valuable [*page 5*] Reference Tables, by W. H. Sadler and A. J. Nugent. Tenth Edition: Baltimore, Md. 1886."

16. A Dictionary of the English Language. Academic Edition. Mainly abridged from the latest edition of the Quarto Dictionary of Noah Webster, LL.D., by William G. Webster and William A. Wheeler, New York and Chicago: Ivison, Blakeman & Company. Springfield, Mass.: G&C. Merriam & Co., Cincinnati, Ohio: Van Antwerp, Bragg, and Company.

17. "A Complete Concordance to the Holy Scriptures by Alexander Cruden, M.A. A New and Condensed Edition. Edited by John Eadie, D.D., LL.D., Professor of Biblical Literature; author of the "Analytical Concordance to the Holy Scriptures"; "Biblical Encyclopedia"; "Ecclesiastical Cyclopedia"; etc., with an Introduction by Rev. David King, LL.D., author of "Principles of Geology in relation to Religion"; "Treatise on the Lord's Supper, etc. etc. New York: Dodd, Mead, & Company, 751 Broadway.["]

18. "William Penn, the Founder of Pennsylvania by John Stoughton, D.D. London: Hodder and Stoughton, 27 Row, 1882.["]

First Day, Eleventh Month 22nd 1891. Night.

The night is cold, and a very cold north wind has been blowing all day. I have not cover enough, I sleep cold some. I have not clothing enough. I get cold when about my work, but I [*page 6*] praise the Lord I am yet in good Health. The council left off its clerical work for to-morrow on account of my observance of this day. This is usual in their acts, but yet they do not feel under obligation to observe likewise.

I do not get much reading or writing done to-night, for I run from the light to the fire to warm every few minutes. Some of the young and middle aged men were playing cards and betting to-day, and I told them they were doing the Devil's work, that it made the loser poor and miserable, and that it kept men idle; but all I could say had no visible effect. It did not exasperate.

I do not care for being made fun of for religion, God be thanked. Though the furnace be heated 100 times hotter, I would, by God's grace assisting, remain unmoved. Some of this was done to-day.

There is no person on earth too young or too old to be won for Christ and for his Gospel. Boys and girls are often full of sin, why can they not oftener be full of faith and of the Holy Ghost? Where are the boys and girls that pray daily, that are living good lives for Jesus' sake, that are going to be power on earth for God and his truth? Where are the fathers and mothers that ought to be raising such children, and teaching them [*page 7*] to know these things and to secure happiness by doing them? Boys and girls can exercise faith in Christ very young indeed.

It is easier to believe at an early age than after 21 when the person has been as long in sin and wrong training and influence. Why can not children be trained in Christ as soon as they are learning to talk. Care should always be taken to keep them aloof from all bad habits, such as swearing, profane language, tobacco using, drinking alcoholic liquor, unchastity or impurity, gambling, stealing, or associating with evil persons. Evil persons here means those who would teach evil habits, such as those just named. Such evil persons are infinite in number and do a vast amount of harm in the world.

It should be remembered that children acquire evil habits by bare imitation of others, but also by the persuasion and false representations of their associates. A child that acquires an evil habit may not be aware of the evil consequences. Care should always be taken to instruct children of the results consequent upon the devotion to any and all evil habits.

But more; children must be trained up in good habits. Care should be taken to secure such a desirable thing as this. Though this may cause [*page 8*] much study of books and of past personal experience and the experience of neighbors as received from conversation, and though it may cause such work and watchfulness, yet it is worth while. The child is immortal, and its training will affect its character to all eternity as well as here on earth. The study of biographical literature is to be especially commended to parents, on account that it shows how influences develop men or women.

It is well that the Lord's Prayer be learned by children very young; but parents are prone to have the children say it only while very small and gradually leave it off until it is entirely left off. Other prayers may be used as well as this, and will relieve the monotony. Besides the meaning of the Prayers should always be told, line upon line, and precept upon precept. Parents strangely neglect to explain the meaning of prayers or scripture passages. I am sorry to have to say that too often they themselves do not know the meaning; but nothing is more certain that if they do not know, it is their duty to find out as soon as possible.

But better. Teach the child how to find out the meaning for himself. Question him, and let him have [*page 9*] time and opportunity to find out the answers. If he can not, show him how, and let him learn the art. By this means his thinking and investigating powers will be developed, and gradually mental independence will be acquired.

It should not be forgotten that the school the child attends will have a great and lasting influence upon him. The books used and the competency of the teacher will be sure to have much—very great—influence. The direction the parent gives the child, the incentives he presents, the counsel he gives will also have an influence upon him.

School children are prone to indolence and flirtation is rife among boys and girls. These two things should be guarded against by word and by act. There are just two means to influence others, and they should never be forgotten. They are, 1[.] Words, 2. Acts. There are no other.

But school children have a vast influence over one another, especially for evil. Parents, teachers, guardians, ministers, should look out for evil influence from this source. One bad boy can do immense harm to his associates while at school. Moral harm is the kind here spoken of.

[page 10] If a bad boy is known to attend the same school be sure that he is exerting evil influence over some one. A bad boy is one who swears, or uses unchaste language, or uses tobacco, or drinks alcoholic liquor, or is unchaste or impure in any respect whatever, or who steals, or tells lies, or neglects to observe the Lord's Day, or makes light of religion, or who is impolite or rude, or who does not obey the teachers, or makes any disturbance in school, or who writes to or makes love to the girls, or who does not do right at all times and under all circumstances. A boy who does any or all these things may be imitated by another, or by persuasion, argument, conversation, or compulsion may induce another to act as he does.

A child wants to be taught labor is honorable and to learn all the labor it can. Show it the products of labor the house, wagons, grain, clothes, food, utensils, cars, cities, and thousands of other useful things and show that they are the products of noble labor.

A child wants to be taught the sinfulness and foolishness of gambling. This is a crying. Gambling is a form of stealing; it makes the loser poor and causes suffering; it occupies time that ought to be spent in labor; it makes men disdain [page 11] labor, for they say that work is a slow way to get money, and will tell of winning $5 in a little while; it leads to cheating, quarrelling, and sometimes to fighting; and it is difficult for one devoted to it to abstain therefrom.

Dr. J. H. Kellogg's "Plain Facts" contains advices that no parent, teacher, or guardian can afford to neglect, if he is interested in the welfare of children under his care.

It is not right to think that boys and girls should not be as highly educated as they are capable of. It is not wise to think that girls should not be as learned as boys. Does not a young man want a wife near as learned as himself as possible? Will a learned man want a wife of no education, or even of little education?

It is an error to think that boys should not be as morally good as girls. What man wants an impure woman? What woman wants a licencious man? Does not God want men to be just as chaste as men want women to be?

The use of tea, coffee, and tobacco should be put away and never be allowed to the rising generation. None of the three can be well spoken of, and the last is especially abominable. Do not use tea, coffee, or [*page* 12] tobacco, cocoa, or chocolate, opium, or any stimulant, except as a medicine.

Children should be taught to obey their parents in every thing, except when solicited to sin against God or Christ. They should be taught to obey civil government in all things except where allegiance to God is interfered with.

Father and mother should never quarrel either in the presence of children or elsewhere. Quarrels bring anger and ill-feeling; they cause one to say things he does not mean to say, or that he is sorry he said after. He is liable to make mistaken statements, for anger hinders the memory and perverts the judgment.

History—national and biographical—collected by others and collected by one's self is useful. Biblical history should be learned and taught to the children. Indeed, the Bible, both the Old and the New Testament, should be the text-book of every parent, teacher, guardian, and minister.

It is every man's duty to collect a library of useful volumes. One who is known to have a taste for books and reading matter will be presented with such by benevolent persons even without his request. [*page* 13] But he should buy books and papers, and use and consult them on different subjects. Go to some reliable person and get him to recommend good books to you. No one has any time to spend on bad books; life is too short for such a thing. One can not get too many of good books, but his means must put a limit to the number. It must be remembered that much is learned by flying from book to book that could not be learned readily otherwise. But one's own observing powers should be cultivated independently of books. One must do this in order to understand books. Go to wise counsellors to find out the hidden meaning. One can't follow all he reads in different books; and it will be absolutely impossible for him to believe all he reads, for he will read contradictory things or things incompatible with each other. Great care should be taken to understand the real meaning of what one reads. Make use of dictionaries, grammars, and philological works and common sense rules. A good imagination is of use in understanding books as well as the attention of the mind for the purpose of finding out things. But books and reading are not an end, but means to an end. The end is to secure happiness. [*page* 14] The end is to promote physical welfare and comfort and the moral and spiritual graces as well as the glory of God and the good of mankind. One's reading is quite sure to do others good as well as himself. It will surely do his children good and his wife good.

Conversation is also a means of knowledge and happiness What is read may be verified by the observation of others learned by us through conversing with them. Interrogation is salutary in its results. It brings out knowledge. The wider one's range of persons the better, if the persons are good, intelligent, and true. One should record the results for the information of others. This will not be labor lost. In conversation, as elsewhere, one should always distinguish matters of fact and matters of opinion; he should ascertan the opportunities his informer had for ascertaining the facts. He should be capable of reasoning on facts.

Personal observation and experiment is a means of knowledge. Travelling is favorable to this. Even working at a trade has its advantages. This is certain knowledge. Reading and conversation may begin, help, direct, or incite to further observation of a thing, or lead to experiments. It is important to study logic and metaphysics, as they aid one in [page 15] this department of activity. The people that are nearest and dearest to us will however influence us much unconsciously.

11/23/1891

There are difficulties and discouragements in the pathway of life, but there are also beautiful and delightful places. For the sake of the latter we ought to hear the former. Difficulties call forth our courage and our patience and develop us thereby. But for God's sake is a higher reason why we should do battle with difficulties and overcome them. Strong in faith we should rest assured that God will bring out all things well. Persevere in the paths of justice before God; sanctify him in your heart, let him be your fear and your dread, and ask him to sanctify you wholly by his Holy Spirit.

Laziness and indolence are evils among men. You will see a strong young man, who eats as much as any one, do very little work. Just as soon as one has no work to do, then he seeks to dress himself as neatly as possible. He has no honest way to make money, or else the honest way is difficult and consequently it is disliked.

11/23/1891.

On Reading.

We read that we may understand what we read. To acquire the meaning of what we read is our end. Hence if we do not understand what we read, just in the proportion [page 16] that

we fail to understand what we read, just so far do we miss the
information that we [would?] be ours if we read more deeply.
Shallow readers are plentiful; they do not understand what they
read; having eyes they see not nor do they hear with their ears.
Such is not the way reading should be done. 1. In reading one
wants to have dictionaries and other books where the meaning of
words are defined. He should find out the meaning of words, and
put the meaning in the place.

11/27/1891.

Apostoleke ~~Tatapwatimwice~~ Easewikotimwice.

Netapwasa ease hipace nakote Tapalamalikwa Kobani cike
wesekitwwewa paponiki, Maeatalatiki menkwitwe chena hisaske,
cikeweahe nanomotake chena papwinamotake. Chena ease hipece
nakote Wipinashewati, Ceses Kliest, henipe wahokwebeti
Tapalamalikwa. Chena Kobanike hoce laniwawe wise pwi hitake cike
weahe; Tapalamalikwa Tapalamalikwa hoce, Wibaike Wibaike hoce,
mieiwe Tapalamalikwa mieiwe Tapalamalikwa hoce, Laniwawe miti
maeatalamobo, nakotwalani howeeahemwi Kobani chena Hokwebile,
eimi weike hoce cikeweahe maeatlatota. Eimi keliwa halaneke hoce
chena wise wipinash alikwa hoce kwisk ba menkwitowile hoce.
Chena wewbe machobo [*page 17*] Wase Cacilikomi hoce chena Malwe
papwipiwetakati hoce; chena helane machobo. Bikhobo nabipe
keliwa hoce, hikwelaniwawe Pontius Pilateke, chena hobapsemobo,
chena honski miwenbokonikeke, ealicemoike mamatiwekitake. Chena
menkwitoke hawi, limitipewi Kobani howieiwenkeke milikwihe.
Chena noke wapeawi mselalamakobewaneke wisetapolwilice
laniwawelece chena napalece; heni hokemiwewa miti likwi
eihisauwele. Chena ease hipece Wase Cacilikomi, Talpalamalikwa
chena mimelewati laniwawewa; Kobanike chena Hokwebamike wamaki.
Heni mimimitominsobo chena mimselalamobo wece Kobani chena
Hokwbile eahoseliwilobowice: heni papekekiliweti
mimosekeekwalece hotiwihe. Chena ease hitake nakote, babibieike,
Kabileke chena Apostoleke Cherche.

Netasewa ease hitake nakote baptismawewa tihil hotakeke
pemeliwewani, chena netkiwipiti wisisehonskinobowice napakke,
chena kokwalikwise laniwawewa. Amen.

Wipinashewati Hominutomawa.

Kobani menkwitowile tise eapine, skiti wewasemimota kebowa.
Wepeae~~ike~~ skiti tihokemiweine; wenakitota easetahaine
hosketimkwa [*page 18*] pise mankwitoke easenakitotake. Melenika
henoke kisakeke nekisakekewe tikwhinemani. Chena hilhimiwenika
nemosanahekinani, pise kili easehilhimiwikece
mamosenewheimekecke. Chena take nkeswasepa witimicekocemobonika,
pieakwi kepikbanepa macike hoce. Keika keli hene tihokemiweke,

chena hene wesekitwwewa, chena hene mslelamakobewa kobewa, kokwalikwise. Amen.

Mimitomawani

1. Tapalameine, Maeatalameine, howanenama ease pemeliwei. Macetbana nepemeliwe, keposkonimola ~~easeta~~ ealalatimine. Pieakwi henoke eanamai ealakwe hikwalamice helaneke, chena easehotibi laskiwice heni Wipinashe wati wise wipinashe wace, nebakhakoni nemicelaniwawewani. Nemicelapwi we koce easepemelotoli, keli Wase Tapalameine. Pwi hilhimiweine nemicelaniwawewani kokwalikwise skwtake nanapobikwibo. Wipinashewaine, piwhelo kemskomeke kebanelo nepeine liwewani hoce. Howa nabibieikebe eomi limake. Wase Cacilikomi, melelo ~~ko~~ noke wise laniwawei, wise nsepecbiei tihokemiwece Tapalameti. Tapalamewati honecinile machelo. Ceses neli hoce hisanwi, wise wipinashece; [page 19] pieakwi homskwme miti netiwipinaehako pwi tapwasa, chena pwi paketimi nemicelaniwawewi; pwi kotike setahai, pwi macelapwiei ease macepemeliwei pwi macetahai wise piketimi kokwalikwise macike, chena weli wise nakilike. Npaniselo, Wase Caeihkomi wise macelapwiei, wise kotike setahai howi, wise hotinike litanimi cikeweahe macike, chena wise tapwatswike Ceses. Melelo wesekitwwewa, "Tapalameine, hilhimiwelo nepemeliwewani Ceses Kliesti hoce," wise heoi. Melelo wise tapwasai cikeweahe mamatiwekitake ketawekitameke. Ketao Tapalameine, "Tapwasalo weike Ceses Klieste chena kawipinashakope," Onetapwasa, hilhimiwelo, kebanelo Ceses homskwmake, kebowa hoce. Melelo wise tapwasai easemacekebaneine. O Tapalameine, chena kahoseliwilala ealikwise laniwawei. Amen.

11 Mo. 29, 1891 A.D. First day of the week.

The weather was fine, the sun shining and the sky cloudless. In the afternoon I made a short visit to my friend Nanapeaskiki and found him better and able to walk about the room. His sister was well also; she is now about 7 years old and is small. My friend's mother was sick with the ear-ache. I found his aunt [page 20] washing clothes, and asked her if she did not know what day it was. She said, Yes, I know. Afterwards I told her she had broken the will of God, and she said that she did not know it was the rest day until a little while ago, and that now she had gone into washing and the matter could not be recalled.

I am endeavoring, by the grace of God, to live a life worthy of him. But I freely confess that the sins of my life have been many, about 5000 to the best ability that my counting can attain. The past is dark, but I am not relying on God to keep me as never before. The reason I have not been fully kept heretofore is that I have had so little faith, and have so often neglected prayer. For a short time I was in infidelity, the result of reading "Volney's Ruins" [C. F. Volney, *The Ruins*]; but at school I remembered that I had read an answer to this book, and that set me to place no confidence in it, but there I was pretty well out of religion. But blessed be God, for he put it into the heart of Dr. Chas. W. Kirk to pray with and for me and I was healed again. Blessed be the name of the Lord. This was the result of neglecting the meetings of the Christians; first there was simply indifference, and after some time dislike and [*page 21*] aversion. O the sins that might have been prevented if I had been converted sooner: if I had been trained Godward from my mother's womb all the way to this very day! But I thank God for this experience that will enable me to bring up my children aright, if God should be pleased in [the] Future to grant me any. I can also now the better guide, direct, watch, advise and instruct those not my children, but those whom God may move me to speak unto or help.

See how bad men are aggressive in getting others to commit like sins as themselves! A whiskey peddler has no trouble in inducing Indians to purchase and use his merchandise. The very young men readily learn to curse and swear and use profane language from foul-mouthed citizens. All sins seem to be readily taken hold of, but not so good things. How hard to induce one young man to give up his bad habits! How hard to get blind ignorance and blind credulity asay [away?] from peoples' eyes so they can see the truth! How hard to uplift humanity! If evil workers are so aggressive, why may not good workers be just as aggressive. Evil workers try to influence any and every one their way, why should not good workers do likewise?

[*page 22*] There is no nobler thing than religion. There is no separation between morality and religion. What is called morality is only so much of religion as is necessary for the habitable condition of society. Religion should be made the chief thing in life. Intellectual training does not make a good man, but there is such a thing as a man's knowing what is right, but not doing it. But religion or rather God by His Holy Spirit does make a man holy and lovely. <u>Knowing</u> and <u>Doing</u> are two distinct things, and too often are not found together in the same person.

The parent is [who?] neglects the religious training of his child is making a very dangerous mistake. Do men and women act as if religion were the most important thing? No: they generally act as if it were the least importance. Some shallow pates [parents?] act and speak as if it were of no importance. In Oklahoma City, a few days ago a white man said that he believed that "all the hell there is, is here on earth." Of course this shows he did not believe all the Bible said, and if this man can believe just what he pleases Bible or no Bible, every other man can be allowed the same privilege, and then there would be opinions without number, and men could commit sin [*page 23*] without any fears of torment here after.

Penalties make laws; without penalties there could be no laws. When we obey a law we secure happiness; when we disobey a law we incur misery, a penalty. Happiness is an object desirable; misery is undesirable; hence we should be obedient to law. God has laws, and to these laws are attached rewards and penalties. Misery in this age, and eternal torment in the age to come is the penalty attached to unforgiven sins; while happiness and eternal bliss are the rewards attached to obedience to the will of God through Jesus Christ.

11th Mo. 30th, 1891 A.D.

I did not forget to pray this day, and I rejoiced at the prospect of some little success. I would bless the lord so much if he should really grant me success. A life of usefulness is a life of beauty. I am not well dressed, but, by the grace of my God, I am trying to put on the most beautiful garments of righteousness to the glory of His name.

I made myself tired with work to-day. I cut wood until my arms ached.

There is one male of 21 who does not assist. He does not even cut wood. He wears his best on his back. He plays cards, gambles, drinks alcohol, and is [*page 24*] foul-mouthed, and for a while was guilty of bigamy, and is no doubt of fornication.

Three of these companions used my lamp and bed to play cards upon to-day. I did not want to order them to desist for an elder was present but did not partake of the game, but I had positively forbade betting. So to-night they crowded around the light selfishly and I scarcely had room to read my book. One of them spat tobacco juice all around the wall, for the bed is in a corner. They pretended not to be betting but I believe they were all the same; for at the end of the game they would look at each other covertly in the face as if agreeing to something. But they turned the lamp over partially and broke the top part of the chimney. And at last set to make fun of me reading, for I would read somewhat in a whisper, as I was memorizing Cicero's first oration "in Catilinam." They went on with their fun about this and other things at my expense, but I paid no attention but of course could not keep from hearing. This rather grated on my feelings, for I deserved their thanks for bearing with their depriving me of the light so that I could not do what I wanted. Now this is what man is when he is [*page 25*] untrained. He considers his own interest only, not the interests of others also.

Card playing or other gaming is liable to objection independent of the sin of betting often connected with it. It is liable to be made the means of wasting many precious hours, that might be turned to better account. It is very liable to lead to betting. Gaming alone becomes dull soon, and betting is added to increase the interest in the game, if not for the purpose of gain. Hence it is that playing is liable to lead to betting. For my part I have no time to waste in gaming though I have played checkers just to interest others. But I carried it too far; it took up too much of my time, and I am glad we have no board now to play. It is the past time of shallow minds.

12th Mo. 1st, 1891 A.D. Third Day of the week.

At the beginning of a new month I am resolved to live nearer to God my God, and to abstain from every sin for Jesus' sake, who purchased me with his own precious blood. I love the Lord now, but I want to love him more constantly, more fervently, more faithfully. I now examine my conscience thus. Have I done any sins to-day? The answer is, Yes, at least three sins. In examining [*page 26*] for sins I am resolved to give all doubtful cases to God, and reckon them in the list of sins.

O that I had been brought up better from a child that I might never have committed so many sins! I was converted at about sixteen, I think; but I ought to have been converted in the cradle. At sixteen I was already old in sins through the influence of evil companions and through my own depravity, and also the influence of Satan. I am heartily sorry for all the sins I have ever committed, and wish I had not committed them; but by eating the flesh of the Son of man and by drinking his blood by faith, I have remission of my sins (Praise the Lord), and adoption into the family of God. I have been born again of the Holy Ghost and am a candidate for eternal salvation through Jesus Christ. I am trusting in that sacrifice offered by Christ on Calvary for the remission of my sins and for regeneration and sanctification by the Holy Ghost. I am not saved by my work but by the grace of God through faith in Jesus Christ, I believe all the Holy Scriptures both of the Old Testament and of the New. I believe they were written by men moved of the Holy Ghost, and they are [*page 27*] able to save the soul through faith in the Lord Jesus. I am ready to do whatever God requires at my hand; if it be to suffer death for Him, well; if persecution, well; if security and peace, well. I want to be the means of leading souls to the Lord Jesus that they may be washed from their sins in his blood. I want to be a reader and an expositer [*sic*] of Holy Scripture to others. In order to be the better able to do this I want to learn Latin, Greek, and Hebrew, so as to explain to others the hidden meaning. I want to be qualified for my work by an effusion of the Holy Ghost, so as to be made competent for the work and to bring glory to God through Jesus Christ.

12th Mo. 2nd 1891 A.D. Fourth Day.

I have been thinking much of late of making Carrie Warrior my choice *pro uxore* [L., *for a wife*]. Her sister Mary advised me to do that thing, promising her assistance. But her motive seems to be rather of a low order, for she said she would tell Carrie that I had plenty of stock. She advised me to write to her sister, which advise [sic] I followed, though I had not decided to follow her advice. Carrie answered my letters promptly, asking an early reply. Judging from her letters alone she is a good girl, and seems favorably inclined towards myself. A year or two ago she [*page 28*] asked me to write her, but it did not seem to me to be proper to comply with the request. She must think of me considerably for she wrote one letter 11 Mo. 7th, and another 11 Mo. 14.

The whites are supreme here now, and they are opposed to any marriage between a partial colored person and one of themselves, even to the extent of enacting and enforcing laws against this thing. These laws, though unjust and unfair, do not violate anything that is our positive duty toward God. So there is no adequate cause for disobeying them, because we are bound to obey all laws—good or bad—except those that interfere with our allegiance to God. Yet the white and the colored people are mixing, but it is the baser sort of whites, and the colored race is not benefited by this. This mixing is adulterous, for it is not by means of matrimony. Such laws ought to be abolished, and let all men marry whom they will. The case would then be better. The colored race would run out in a short time, and there would be no cause for further trouble.

But there is no law forbidding colored and Indian from marrying. Such marriages are sanctioned by Indian custom, as the cases of Robert Deer, Hester [*page 29*] Chisholm, Caroline Chisholm, and Shawniego, and others do show. Consequently no objection can be raised against a marriage between myself and Carrie. Even her sister Mary advises it. But of course the propriety of my marriage will be submitted to the Monthly Meeting of which I am a member. And my ecclesiastical superiors desire me not to marry without notififying [sic] them beforehand.

A good many times I have been asked whether I were married or not. Some have heard a rumor that I was married when nothing of the kind existed, for rumors are either true or false, and this was false.

Marriage imposes a burden upon a man—that of supporting a wife and children and of feeding a good many outsiders. A man before marriage can dispose of his property as he pleases; after marriage his wife and children have a share in his property as well as himself, consequently he can not do as he pleases with it.

An unmarried man can get a living easily and do an amount of work for Christ that a married man can not do, and can do it with the least expense. A married man must have money and property before he can be free to do other work. The unmarried man [*page 30*] always has the advantage over the married man.

If it were not for one thing celibacy were an easy matter, and that is passion. St. Paul says, "But on account of fornications let every man have his own wife and every woman her own husband." Passion undoubtedly exists for the purpose of compelling a person to propagate his species. All the way that fornications can be avoided by the generality of men is through marriage. Passion is very strong in men; this is a veritable fact. The divine law forbids all indulgence in passion except in matrimony, and even there man and wife are to nourish their bodies with utmost moderation and tolerance. According to most physicians who are authority not more than one indulgence is allowable per mentem [*mensem—month*] even in matrimony, while others contend that copulation should only be for the purpose of reproduction and then only when reproduction is possible.

All sexual intercourse should be abstained from during gestation and lactation. These are most salutary precepts, and happy would be mankind were they generally practiced.

Outside of matrimony nothing but continence can be lawful. Not even the one indulgence per Mentem [*mensem-month*] [*page 31*] is allowable. Continence is a most salutary habit. It gives a full face, while incontinence produces emaciation. The former gives high spirits and a clear head and a hand steady for writing; the later brings headache, languor of body and mind, and a trembling hand. The first is salutary and healthful every way to body and mind; the second is many ways injurious to the physical and mental constitution.

There is no virtue more important than chastity. Yet it is a scarce thing among mortal[s]. Many have a reputation of possessing it, who nevertheless have it not. Why this virtue is so scarce is a subject most worthy of serious inquiry. One reason it is so scarce is the influence of companions for evil. A companion will teach a pure-minded but ignorant little child filthy words and at the same time explain their meaning until they are well understood. Here then the child starts in the road of evil speaking. The child is taught by the companion to repeat the words after him, and this is the genesis of the habit of evil speaking, which erelong is continued without the effort or influence of companions. Companions also incite him to do evil things and here begins [*page 32*] the habit of overt sinning. Hence the necessity of finding good companions for children. All persons should not be trusted until proof of innocence has been established. Persons who are reputed to be good are too often unfit to be companions of children.

I have seen an Indian boy swear in English who could not speak English at all. He was about 12 or 13 years old, and he was merely repeating what he had often heard young men—some of them his own brothers—say.

On My Ancestry

My mother used to tell me when I was small of the war and the soldiers, but I was only ten years old when she died, consequently I do not remember. She was of medium h[e]ight, as white as a white woman and with hair just a straight, and was a woman beautiful to look upon. She could read and write only a little. She said her name was Elizabeth Jane Wright, that her father was named Wright, and that he and her mother parted, and that he went to California and was never heard of since. She used to use me to write to her mother, telling me what to write. I wish those letters could be found now. [*page 33*] My mother was nineteen years old when she married to William Shawnee in 1867 A.D. They were married in the city of Lawrence, Kansas. Aunt Martha tells me that William Shawnee was a Methodist while he was up there.

William Shawnee my father was born at Web[b]er's Fall[s], Indian Territory about the year 1834 A.D. Web[b]er's Fall[s] is in the Cherokee Nation. He is a mixture of races. It is apparent that he is not a full blooded colored person from sight. His complexion is yellow or copper-colored, his hair curly but not kinky. His stature was medium, rather heavy set. Converted to the Christian faith after he left the Shawnees, he was at first Methodist and afterward a Baptist. He learned to read after he was grown and also to write.

Those who are acquainted with the facts say that his father was part Cherokee and Mexican, and that his mother was part Shawnee and Cherokee. His mother was also part colored. Hester Chisholm and he are the children of two sisters so said my father.

My father has quite a faculty for languages. He can speak fluently the Cherokee, the Shawnee, and the English languages, and has a passing acquaintance [*page 34*] with the Creek, the Kickapoo, Delaware, Sac, and Seminole languages. He can write his own letters and is a frequent reader of the Bible in which he is well versed. He is not a singer, but yet is fond of vocal music; yet though he tries hard to sing, yet he can not skillfully. But in his reading he does not use a dictionary, and does not understand every thing he reads. He has strong faith in the doctrine of baptism by immersion and is quite diligent in having family prayer, singing, and Bible reading. He pays his debts, makes plenty of money, has a large orchard, and much stock, and sends his children to school, for all which deserves high honor. He has been for a long time an interpreter for the Shawnees, and has been to Washington, D.C. thrice on that errand. He is excessive in hospitality to white, colored and Indian. Prudent even to excess; he does not offend any man. Though high tempered, his anger endures only for a little while. A friend of industry, of schools of religion is he. The mistakes he makes are of the head rather than of the heart. Polite to others, but not to his own family. At times quarrelsome, but his children are also quarrelsome with him. If he had been better educated, it would [*page 35*] have faired better with himself and family. The education he has was not acquired in the school-room; but it would never the less have been better if it had been, other things remaining equal. A person can be more truly useful to himself and others who is well-educated. With all the dangers that accompany the highest civilization around his own children, no parent should neglect to render himself as intelligent as possible in order to defend his children against them. Though intelligence is a very important thing, yet alone it is dead. We must <u>do</u> what we <u>know</u> in order to acquire happiness and shun misery.

Andrew Barnett also said that when the U. S. troops were about to take away my mother's folks that the mistress had hidden my mother in the house but on being informed the soldiers rifled the house and brought forth the girl destined by Providence to be my mother. No wonder they hid her, for she was no doubt very beautiful.

There were five of us born of one mother and one father. 1. Willie Shawnee, the oldest. 2. Cora Shawnee, the next oldest, who died in school at the Shawnee Mission. 3. Dudley Shawnee, the next oldest, now (*12th/2/1891*) in school at Haskell Institute. 4. Walter Shawnee, [*page 36*] the next oldest, now in school at Haskell. 5. George Shawnee, the youngest. Now in school at Haskell.

Autobiography of William Ellsworth Shawnee

The subject of this sketch was born in the city of Lawrence, Douglas County, Kansas, Twelfth Month 23rd, 1868 A.D. His father's name was William Shawnee, and his mother's name was Elizabeth Jane Wright. They were married in Lawrence, Kansas, in 1867, and after their second child a daughter was born moved to Shawneetown, Indian Territory, and settled down there in the fall of 1871. Here William Shawnee soon built a house and set out a peach and apple orchard, which in after years proved to be a real benefit to him. He brought some goods with him from Kansas also, which he sold. He also opened a small farm at this home.

About this time the Friend's or Quakers were contemplating the establishment of a school at Shawneetown, and William Shawnee acted as interpreter for them. They succeeded in establishing a day-school, and Thomas Alford, David Alford, Martin Starr, Charley Starr, Jacob Tomahawk, Susie Tomahawk, Robert Conalas, Cooper Wilson, Annie Wilson, Isaac McCoy, [*page 37*] Bud Tyner, were among the first pupils. Joseph Newsom was the first teacher. The school was established about 1872 when I was only three years old, and was a day-school at first.

My father once asked mother at what age I should go to school, and she replied "At six", So I had to wait. I used to think that going to school was something like churning butter. But they taught me my letters before I ever set foot inside a school-house. I was taught also and memorized the 1st Psalm before I ever went to school. I was taught also the Lord's Prayer.

When I was six years old, I started to school, I had on a new cap, of which I may have been a little proud. When I reach[ed] the school limits, I went with the schoolboys, but they were rather unsocial. They pulled off my new cap, and threw it into the water, and they deceived me and caused me to eat a raw crawfish, and then impudently laughed at my simplicity.

I went to school and recited for a few times in the chart class, but they soon put me out of that into the First Reader. I regretted this, and did not understand why it was done. But I remembered I used to do all the answering, and they no doubt banished me [*page 38*] to give the others a chance. Martin Starr used to tell me that he used to teach me in school, but said that I repaid him afterwards by teaching him. I began to go to school in the year 1875. During my school career in this school I studied the following books, Ray's Arithmetic, Primary and Complete, McGuffey's Fourth Reader and Fifth Reader, Geography, Spelling, Penmanship, Harvey's Language Lessons, and also his Grammar, An elementary history of the United States[,] Appleton's Fourth Reader, and was a great consulter of Webster's Unabridged Dictionary when I could get a hold of it, for it was kept in the parlor instead of in the school room. I also memorized pieces that my teacher's assigned me, but never wrote a composition of any kind. We never studied anything outside of school hours. We always left our books in the school room. We studied Drawing some. I continued eight years in this school from 1875 to 7th Mo. 1883. My teachers during this period were many, Ella Coltrain, Della Davis, Margret Davis, Horace V. Easterling, and Eva Woodara, were among the number. They were all good teachers and won my esteem and affection. But it must be confessed that the Sunday Schools we had did not [page 39] do us much good. We had not the remotest idea that we were to become Christians; nor were there active efforts made to bring about these desirable results. We were often talked to by Elkano Beard, and later by Franklin Elliot, Friend's missionaries stationed at Shawneetown. We did not have the Ten Commandments taught and explained to us. Yet at collections at 7 P.M. songs were sung from the Gospel Hymns and sometimes prayers offered and the Bible read.

Tenth Month 9, 1891 A.D., while at Kansas Yearly Meeting I saw Della Davis, one of my former teachers. She had taught me for four years. She said, when she saw me, "This is the boy I have been wanting to see." She shook hands with me, and among other things she said I was not as tall as she had expected. I was glad indeed to see her. She was almost as good looking as formerly, with an appearance of gentleness and goodness.

Chapter 4

Reflecting on Traditional Absentee Shawnee Culture
December 6, 1891–January 22, 1892

Living with Big Jim's band at Big Jim's Crossing gave Shawnee the opportunity to observe traditional Absentee Shawnee culture. He adopted the attitude of some whites about traditional Indian culture and believed the manner in which the whites passed traditions on to their descendants in written form was superior to the oral methods used by the Indians. He tried to persuade the Indians to give up some of their superstitions. Besides describing the behavior and beliefs of his companions, he included in his journal lessons from the Quakers' manuals on morality, essays on the education of children, and copies of his letters to Carrie Warrior asking her to be his girl. He wrote several passages in the Absentee Shawnee language of his time using phonetic spellings. He decided to translate the Gospels into Absentee Shawnee and translated several passages. He ended the second journal on January 22, 1892.

First Day 12/6/1891 A.D.

Shawnee women go barefoot this day even when they have shoes. This day was a cold day, and yet all the girls were barefoot in the morning. The wife of Totomo [Totommo] [*Little Jim*] has been bare foot for some time. I saw her go out to the well to draw water early on a cold frosty morning. She was barefoot today, and did not put on her shoes when I told her and even though I kept [*page 40*] asking her to put on her shoes. I did not wonder at all that she had a bad cold and a cough.

I hear with sorrow that the Shawnee young men and even that their councilors drink whiskey and get drunk. And also that one young boy stole and sold a $35 or $40 mare for $15.

Several young men to-night kept up profane and sensual talk. They say any thing and every thing to raise a laugh among themselves. They would not desist at my exhortation. This had the effect of exciting them to foul-mouthery. How is it that in the presence of their Chief the young generation use such language. The answer is because he does not rebuke them, and occasionally uses such language himself.

How often are good men ashamed of their principles and neglect to make them known to others! I am guilty of this myself in regard to my principles in peace, etc., because I think it will only cause ridicule or amount to nothing. But we need to teach, line upon line, precept upon precept, and actively show our disapprobation of all wrong and our approbation of all right, and do this to the glory of God.

How evil men make evil propositions to others to [*page 41*] get them to do evil. Should not good men be as ready, just as ready, just as prompt, and just as active, in making good propositions to others to get them to do good? Can we not learn wholesome lessons from the conduct of evil men? Yes, we certainly can, and do unconsciously often. How prone are men to commit evil! They sin daily. Who can number the sins of men? How irreligious are men in these days! Should not other men be prone to do right as God shall assist them by his grace. Oh, the influence for good one single man or woman may exert if righteous and aggressive for God and his truth.

I must study Latin, Greek, and Hebrew, in order to read the Bible in the original. I do not want to obtain a smattering only of these languages but I want to be skillful in them, and thorough as thorough can be. I must expend some money in this direction as soon as possible, and I ask God to bless me in my endeavors. There is no use letting good opportunities go by unimproved. I am at work on Λúw with a [vim] as well as the declension of nouns, and I am memorizing the first oration against Catihric [*sp?*] as Cicero spoke and wrote it. I want more literature in Latin and more in all these languages. I have no Hebrew as yet.

[*page 42*] [*Dec. 14th?*] *1891 A.D.*
   Devoted to Recording of Days—Good Books for sale by P. Blakiston, Son, and Co.
   1. 12th Mo. 7th   1. *Action on the Reproduction Organs* $2.
   2. 12th Mo. 9th   2. Allingham, *Diseases of the Rectum* 1.25
   3. 12th Mo. 10th 3. Arthur, *Decay of the Teeth*   1.25
   4. 12th Mo. 11th 4. Aveling, *Influence of Posture in Gynecic and Obstetric Practice* 2.00
   5. 12th Mo. 13th 5. Barwell, *Curvature of the Spine* 1.75
   6. 12th Mo. 14th 6. Beard and Rockwell, *Medical Electricity*   6.50 Shup.

[*page 43*]
                    Wanted *12/30/1891*
   "Life of Tecumseh and his brother The Prophet, with a Historical Sketch of the Shawnee Indians["].
            By Benjamin Drake,
               Cincinnati 1852.

   My purpose is that in case I can not get Caroline Warrior to take Emma J. Valentine. The first choice would please both me and my brothers; the second choice pleases, not them but me. Emma is a good girl only fourteen months younger than myself, and is tall; I like a tall girl being of short stature myself. Emma is tolerably good looking, but is of a good heart and a good life. She is one of my admirers, and I think that I could live happy with her all my days. Carrie is a nice good girl of a good heart and life, and is a Christian. But I fear her folks may not want to give her to a person of colored extraction like myself, or whether she would really be willing to marry such a person. Time alone can tell what to do. I prefer Carrie for some reasons, and Emma for other reasons.

[*page 44*] *12th Mo. 7, 1891 A.D. Second Day of the week.*
   I love the Lord with all my heart, with all my mind, with all my soul, and with all my strength. By thy grace, O Lord, I want to leave undone every thing that is opposed to thy will, and I want to believe and do every thing that Thou would have me believe and do. O Lord, that I might be an instrument in thy hand to do some good to the honor and glory of thy name. Thy glory, O Lord Jesus Christ; let me seek; let me serve thee sincerely and fully as long as I have breath. Give me strong faith and perseverance and unchangeableness of purpose to serve

thee. Lord, I am heartily sorry for all my sins, and I ask Thee to wash me from my sins in Jesus' blood. O feed me by faith with the body and blood of Christ that it may remit all my sins and make me a child of thine now and unto the ages of ages. Lord, help me in my work for Thee, O help me, make me competent by the baptism of the Holy Ghost and thine shall be praise from this present time unto the ages of ages, Amen.

12th [Mo.] 9th, 1891.

Wrote a letter to Walter H. Shawnee, a student at Haskell Institute, and my brother.

One Shawnee boy, S. has stole recently one mare and colt and sold them for $15, one pony, nearly two years old and [*page 45*] sold it for six dollars, and one cow. He bought boots and things to wear and at once two gallons of whiskey for $6.20 cts. He is about 15 or 16 years old and has perhaps never been to school, yes, probably not. The cause of his thus acting is attributed by wise-acres to be his knowledge of the English language, obtained by association with an English speaking companion several years ago. As if the bare and superficial knowledge of the Anglo-Saxon tongue is the cause of the theft.

The inferences of uneducated men are not always to be trusted, and consequently their beliefs. Traditional beliefs are firmly held to by some people, and to hear them talk, they believed them as firmly as if they had been seen by themselves. Especially is this so in regard to the religious beliefs of Indians. Though they believe these things so strongly—indeed one would not hardly believe if told how strongly, yet these things are not to be relied on. They are things most unreasonable, and being pretended to be handed down from mouth to mouth since the creation of the world are indeed very unreliable. It is astonishing how men can believe such nonsense. But Indians are not acute thinkers in this regard; the race are easily de [*sic*] [*page 46*] deceived, even by one another. No dependance can be placed in oral tradition whatever. The first authors of it must be worthy of confidence and must have had ample means of knowing the facts of which they testify, and those who succeed them must not add to nor diminish from the testimony. There is no way to ascertain the credibility of the witnesses when the time is in the shadowy past; we must depend upon the mouth of men who are not acquainted with the facts but who have only heard these things.

Reason must decide upon these things. It may go to records, to present facts, to antecedent probability, and to whatever other means it can, to see whether these things are true or not.

The Gospel and the Bible facts must be received by faith. Argument alone can not convert the soul; there must be an assertion and the will must be persuaded to accept it, but argument may confirm faith. Faith, faith, faith; believe, belief,—this is what God requires. How good the moral code of the Bible, how true its statements as to the depravity of man, how it honors the Creator, not the creature, how it makes men and women good through the influence of the Holy Ghost!

[page 47] 12 Mo. 11th, 1891 Sixth Day.

At night made a little experiment to show the Chief that the steam arising from water is really water. I heated some water in a pot oven until it was boiling, then I took it away from the fire, and placed a cold slate into the steam rising out of the pot-oven. It condensed on the slate in fine shape. He had before denied that such steam was only water in another form. Remember this: people believe what they see with their eyes rather than what they are told or what they read.

May I not follow up this experiment by hundreds and thousands of others. It would not only instruct myself but also others. Among the first things I may fix a way by which to evaporate a quantity of water into steam and then condense that same steam back into water again in such quantity that the condensed water may be seen with the eye, felt with the hand, and tasted with the tongue. This would establish the fact beyond any possible doubt that steam is a form of water

First Day 12th Mo. 20th, 1891.

Before daylight I translated the first twenty-one verses of the sixth chapter of St. John. I am resolved, by the grace [*page 48*] of my God, to translate at all times that I can. I must learn at the same time the Greek and the Latin languages. I must also learn Hebrew. But the first parts of the Bible I translate should be the four gospels, and this end I should set my mind like a flint, and never swerve from it as long as I live, or until the work shall have been accomplished. There are great difficulties in the way of this, such as the paucity of language, the multitude of errors the trouble and labor of comparing with each other parallel passages, the weariness of the flesh, etc. But supported within by a conscience void of offence toward God and toward man, and seeking the aid of the Holy Ghost. I believe I can be made by Him competent to the task.

Many words will have to be retained and not translated, namely, 1. The names of persons and places, baptize, Pascha temple, church, etc.

First Day 12th Mo. 20th, 1891. Anno Domini mei.

I am firmly resolved and determined to master three languages of utmost importance, viz., the Latin, the Greek, and the Hebrew. I need literature and I am bound, by the help of God, to get it. I want to read the revealed [*page 49*] will of God to man in the original tongues as well as in ancient and modern translations. It is a matter that is admitted by the intelligent that the mere English reader is liable in many instances to fail of apprehending the true meaning of the Sacred Scriptures, but as my honored predecessor Robert Barclay observed, one who is well versed in the original may mistake the meaning in some instances. Robert Barclay agreed that there ought to be schools for teaching such pupils these languages as were "inclinable thereunto." I judge I am one of those so inclinable. Robert Barclay was versed in these languages.

Example is a powerful thing in life. One may be following the example of others though unconscious to himself that he is doing so. It consists in doing as others do under exactly similar circumstances just because they do so. For instance one should learn that the Apostle Paul never married a wife, but preached the gospel to the end of his life, and should decide in his mind to do exactly the same just because Paul did so and with Paul's motives would be following Paul's example so far.

Since the Apostle Paul abstained from marriage, [*page 50*] and was approved of God all the time, it follows that the act of abstaining from marriage is no sin. Paul also abstained from fornication, adultery, and all impurity, and one who would follow his example must do the same. If abstaining from marriage was no sin in Paul's day it is no sin now. This alone is not sin, but one sins in case he does not remain continent physically and mentally. This is a hard road, and yet it is possible by the grace of God to man, for it was possible with Paul. God assists men by his grace now well as he did in Paul's day, and continence must be possible to the Christian by the grace of God through Jesus Christ. The Holy Ghost is eternal and ever present with the children of God as their Sanctifier, and He will do all God's will yet as well as in Paul's day. He was to "abide" with Christians forever. What we need is more faith in God's revealed will, more prayerfulness, and more resistance to temptation. One who has fallen into evil habits may experience great difficulty in returning to the path of virtue. Hence the necessity of keeping free from evil habits. And as children often grow up in evil habits, it is the duty of parents or teachers or guardians to use the rod and to [*page 51*] keep the children out of vile habits. What use is it to pray God to keep the children out of vile habits when you do not go to work to keep them from vile habits yourself?

12th Mo. 21st, 1891.

O Lord I have sinned against heaven and in thy sight, and have need of being forgiven of my sins by thee. My sins do humble me, and give a sense of my own weakness. Lord, I am very weak and have too often yielded to Satan. Lord, thou knowest my whole heart and being; thou knowest more of me than I know myself. Thou hast separated me from my mother's womb and kept me unto this hour. Thou has showered down blessings upon me, for all which I give thee the most hearty thanks. O Lord I do not pray unto thee enough; I do not have faith enough. O do thou keep me from sin the remainder of this day. Do thou enable me to live for thee and to thee. Lord, care for me, help me, assist me in time of temptation. Feed me with the body and blood of Jesus Christ, that by so eating and drinking I may receive the remission of all my sins, adoption into thy family, and sanctification, and consequently eternal salvation. Lord, make me a co-worker of thine. I have put my hands to the plow," O Lord, keep me from ever looking back, and may all the glory and honor be thine. Amen and Amen.

[*page 52*]

Opinions, penned *12/20/1891*

J. C. said, "Weake sakimeki eakitemoce mieinekwa, neswib[e]vek kito easemace kitamoce chena piwetaka. Pieakwi henoke mieinekwa eakitamoce, walani wise miloboce seta ha. Winitabeke henoke mieinekwake; miti likwi howa papwi winitabeti hotise tilaniwaweikwa."
M. speaking of young woman about 16 or 18 said: "Ho, wasek kwawi wakhe, pieakwi homimilakoke helanehe. Miti skinoke eipiwetaka heneeataki; neli kili miti skiti netilalami hene eataki hekwawi."
J. T. said: "Mine easewikotike Siwinwi. Eapiwetakache hekwawa, heni wasece kikeki wewesihakole, heni miti weahe nseliweta. Pieakwi kotiki weabi wakesekiwile nale hipalobile. Minenoke easewikotike Siwinwi. Eamace laniwawece hipalobi, nakotwibe kesibo lakhe heni helane miti hotiwesihile nale hekwale. Hile kieacese waki miti weaki nseliweta." M. S. said in reference to her refusing to marry a certain man: "Pobe honinbihe hekwahe. Wakenike bipi miti setaha heni hekwawi, melwwen [*page 53*] nhawi, ksika hileki seweskitowe. Hene wace hisenalece likbwe wewhe. Honibihe bipi heni helane hekwahe." On another occasion she said to me, "Siwinnokwa kaponi, howa miti eimiti kwilisketapake kenecinike. Take mamkitawebeti hekwawi kewesiponi." On another occasion she aaid, on my saying, Kamele Kebemabi (in fun, ["] Wake, heni kaponi; kahiwekiwi tawihe, chena neli mace hotieahe mbobohe naheli, howa nakolapkiwi."

[page 54]
We are not as good as we know; we believe in good principles that we do not practice. One may be convinced that a thing is good and true and yet not practice that thing. This is because an evil habit has ensnared him. It is best to break off an evil habit at once, for it grows stronger the longer it is practiced, and inflicts more damage to a person if it is longer continued. One evil feature of an evil habit is that it weakens the will, and makes the individual a great amount of trouble if he tries to give it up. O guard the young against entering into evil habits; tell them the truth about the matter, and study up to the best of your ability that you may tell them if you do not know. Evil appetites grow stronger as they are indulged. O that I could live life over again with the knowledge and good disposition God has now given me! But thank God, that I can yet praise and glorify him, and can even now be made a co-worker with him. O how I do love the religion of Jesus and Jesus himself. Religion is the chief thing in life, and yet how we thrust it into the background! Jesus said: If ye love me, keep my commandments. I love him, and so I am bound to keep his commandments.

Third Day 12th Mo. 22nd, 1891. Anno Domini mei Jesu Christi.
Translated to the 33rd verse of the 6th chapter of St. [page 55] John, including that verse. The translation is teaching one more that I would otherwise know, and my heart's desire will be gratified if it should only teach one person the revealed will of God. There is work to be done, and I have set my eye on translating the four gospels. I have put my hand to the plow, and by God's grace shall never turn back. But the work is rather great but should be done.

Mat. 3:7 Pieakwi eamace nawice mace Pharisaeke hoce chena Sadducaeke hoce easepeilace milikwhe hobaptisma wewaneke, hotalihe.

Mat. 20:22. Pieakwi niseti kiliwe Jesus hotalihe, Miti kewikotiniwi nanitotimakwa: hiketapelabepwi wise manakwa heni tapheki neli wisimanai? chena hene baptismwewa wisi baptizimhoboi, wisebaptizimhoboeakwa, ? hiketapelabepwi.

12th Mo. 28, 1891 Second Day of the Week.
The beliefs of old men are hard to change. Big Jim is about 56 years old, and he believes in witchcraft, in sickness of certain kinds being caused by spirits of the deceased. He actually keeps a light burning all night so that the spirits of the deceased may be afraid to come near. One night we awoke and found the light out from some cause. It was then sitting where

there could not have been [*page 56*] much wind. He said to me, May be the spirit of some departed person put the lamp out. He also believes that it is no wrong to take human life under some circumstances, and that it is no sin to kill an enemy in battle. Also he believes it is not wrong to have more than one wife, or to divorce a wife if she should fight her husband, or quarrels with him if he comes home late. He believes fornication is no sin under certain circumstances. He also believes that the Creator of the Red Man is a woman, and that the Creator of the white man is the Evil God, the one who torments bad Indians with fire until they have paid for all their meanness, and then the evil God lets him go on to where all his good relatives are. That the Creator of the Indian has given him a law, and the Creator of the white man has given him a law, and the Indian will become miserable if he lives as does the white man. That the Indian was created on this continent, and the white man across the ocean. That when all the Indians give up their Indian ways, then the end of the world will come. That their woman-Creator will finally burn up all the white people and their God, and that they will never be any more. They lay the cause of all their poverty upon the white man. But they all have drank [*page 57*] whiskey some time or other of their lives. John Sloan was drunk once, and I saw him. All their young men drink whiskey, use tobacco, and use sensual and profane language, and are lazy, and with very little sense and no manners. When the parents have very little sense, what can be expected of the children. Many of the young women and girls use tobacco, and that for want of sense and training. The old are backward about correcting the young even when they see them doing what is wrong or impolite. Again, the Indians will not report one of their number to the whites even if he has stolen, but will answer they do not know, when questioned even if they strongly believe another to be guilty, as Mŭskōthà did in the Sēmotà case.

The women will be barefoot in cold weather, but they pay the penalty for their folly. They will not put on shoes when told to do so.

J. C. was the man that actually told me not to read to the young men out of my books. One of his sons is supposed to have died in the penitentiary, and two more have lately been stealing horses. The Indians say that he is afraid of his own sons, the reason he does not say anything to them, but [*page 58*] just lets them go ahead. They stole horses, bought whiskey, got drunk, and also bought some clothing.

B. J. [*Big Jim?*] says that as soon as an Indian boy can talk English he steals some one's horse, and goes and sells it. That if he could not talk English, he would not do so. But what can be said of him who does right simply because he is too ignorant to do wrong. B. J. seems to imply that the ability to speak English, even a little—is a cause for horse stealing. This simply shows his blind cynical disposition. Who is able to see a causal connection between talking English and horse stealing.

The Indian girls that can not talk English are long about getting breakfast, and in filling lamps grease up beds, and boxes. What do these girls know about things? If the parents know very little, what of the children. Such girls use tobacco on the sly. Doing what they know their parents would not approve of. They like play and sleep, and work just as little as they can. They like to have others do things for them but never think of returning the compliment.

There are young men that do not earn their board. They shun work. They will ask you to stop your employment and go help them, but they will [*page 59*] not help you when they are idle, if you ask them for a favor. This thing of ingratitude is in an Indian; he is a miserable, blind, distrustful, cynical creature. He is always afraid that someone is going to cheat or deceive him. He imagines he knows everything when, in fact, he is stuffed full of traditional nonsense. Quick to accept the evil, stubborn as a mule about accepting the good. O what can save the Red man? His Indian ways can't save him. He has had thirty-years rest from war, and is he improving. No; he is getting worse, and is decreasing in numbers.

Second [Third] Day 12/29/1891.
Looking at a little boy about eight years of age, I said to myself, What will this boy come to? Will he ever drink strong liquor or use sensual and profane language, or gamble, or will he ever steal, or commit murder? Will he marry, and bring up a family of children as God wills, or will he commit adultery or fornication or masturbation. Will he go to school and learn to read, write, count, and other useful things. Will he be taught holiness and purity and truth and righteousness in the fear of God, or will he be left without cultivation? Will he be taught to believe in Christ for the remission of his sins, or will he brought up in [*page 60*] the habit of ungodliness. Children need to be kept from all bad habits both by precept and example; they need to be led into all good habits both by precept and example. When I was in my teens, I looked upon labor as something disgracefull. I was ashamed to labor before my companions who had nothing to do. I looked upon exemption from labor as an honorable desideratum. I was ignorant, then, indeed, and foolish, as young people in their teens are. They lack knowledge and serious-mindedness. I will tell when I think an individual is in great danger, and that is from thirteen to twenty. The parents who neglect to carefully instruct and train his child

during this period is foolish and blind, and can not see afar off. Incompetency on the part of parents to properly instruct and train their children is one great reason that wickedness is so rife in this world of ours.

Many parents are themselves guilty of evil habits. Some parents even hide their evil habits from their children. I have known a father who used tobacco who did not want his children to know the fact, lest his child should follow his example. Children do imitate the example of their fellows and of their elders. Indeed they too often imitate the evil habits of their [*page 61*] elders, and not the good. There are many parents who would not tell their children of the sins of their past lives. One desirable thing is to keep the young out of all sin, and at the same time to bring them up in the faith and in the hope of the Gospel of Jesus Christ. Do not ever tell the children any lies or untruths, such as the Santa Claus fable which as a child I did long believe myself. If we tell such things to children, without likewise telling them of their falsity, do we not allow them to believe what we ourselves know to be absurdly, as that Santa Claus comes down the chimney, at the dead of night, and other such lies.

The companions of a child from cradle to twenty will have a very great and very important influence upon him. These will necessarily be hundreds in number, and they all contribute their amount of influence, some more, some less. One can tell the opinion of an ill[it]erate person if he knows his companions; the opinions of an educated person are not always influenced by his companions, as they may be and frequently are formed from the literature he peruses. An educated person has besides the testimony of those with whom he comes into contact the testimony of literature, often that of thousands of years standing. An educated person [*page 62*] is more liable to have correct beliefs and correct principles of morality and religion than the uneducated. There is no use in being ignorant in this age of opportunities for becoming well-informed. Yet no one person can guide himself correctly through life; he must be guided by the common sense and inferences of his friends. Many minds are more apt to look on all sides of a subject than a single mind. Yet the fact that the multitude allow a thing to be true is not necessarily to be sufficient warrant for believing it. There is a Book called the Book of Facts. These facts are either obtained by observation or experiment. <u>Whatever is not read in this book of facts, or is not clearly inferrible therefrom, is neither an item of knowledge nor an article to be believed</u>.

Starting with this position, that this Book of Facts is the ultimate authority on all matters of knowledge and belief, let every one who reads therein whatever he may, so long as he submits to the ultimate authority here mentioned. This Book of Facts is God's book, and is second in authority to the Holy Bible; the same principles that have so well been applied to the Bible may also be used in explaining the book of facts. The term facts is here used to mean all phenomena that are capable of being appreciated [*page 63*] by the senses.

Indians work very little, while the white man works all the time Spring, Summer, Autumn, and Winter. This is one reason why the white man is superior to the Indian, that is, because he works more, and works incessantly. Thus he makes acquisitions that descend to other generations, and the following generation hand down the same attainment improved to the succeeding generations, and thus the evolution is continued.

The same thing is to be said in regard to knowledge and belief. The white man is constantly changing his belief according to ever increasing evidence, and past ages have recorded facts which have descended to other generations to be used by them. Besides all this the whites have the Bible and Christianity, and this is the true spring of all their happiness and prosperity.

The Indian has no way of ascertaining past events except by tradition–Trash—with the color of facts told from father to son. Even facts that which actually did occur are mixed with fables, and the whole is believed by credulous red men. Even Chiefs and Councillors believe the whole of these fables. Thus Tecumseh, who was killed in 1813 is today 1891 believed by the Shawnee to be a god, even before 80 years had passed away extravagant [*page 64*] fables cluster around the ambitious warrior. They tell [how the warriors] were safe from bullets if near his person, but [. . .] apace the bullets flew thick and fast, how that the whites did not kill him but how an old Shawnee woman caused him to be killed, how that Tecumseh is to come again if a war should arise, to the Shawnees if they still held to their old Indian ways, to some other tribe, if they should not; how that Tecumseh, Tenskatawa and a sister in the other world were married, and that they were simply incarnated into this world, and that when they called the wife a sister, she blushed for shame, and went back to the other world, and such preposterous fables.

Third Day 12th Mo. 29, 1891, Night.

This night Webster Tyner, Totommo, John Sloan, and Tom Ellis' little boys kept making fun of me for a considerable time, saying a good many mean things. Among other things they got into sensuality in their talk, and made a good many to me unpleasant remarks, one of which was, that if I should come up in company with some boys one would think I was a boy that had his face blackened. Big Jim allowed all this, and once put in a remark of a sensual nature but not reflecting on me. These young [*page 65*] people positively have no manners, and the ancients among them seem determined that no one shall teach them any. To state the fact they have very little knowledge [. . .] sense, or at least they are corrupt, ungrateful and an ungodly race. I pen this to show what man is capable of doing. I am going to ask Big Jim if he thought I would let my brother's make fun of any body on earth as he has let his children make fun of me. The old folks are mostly to blame for this and other things. Why do they not give their children over to some one to teach them some sense. If this is Indian custom, we want none of it.

Any opposition to education or Christian religion, no matter from what source, is reprehensible. The opponents, if sincere, are making a lamentable mistake; if not, they are criminals and ought to be silenced by some means or other. Savage songs may captivate the ear, but in a greater degree do Christian songs captivate the whole soul. The trouble with many people is that they are highly educated enough. Every person ought to attain to acquisition of every item of knowledge he possibly can, but all the faculties ought to be symmetrically educated and developed. But more than this experimental religion is more to be desired than even education. The experience of the religion [*page 66*] of Jesus Christ is to be a present possession to everyone. It is of great benefit and vast importance to the individual and to the whole human race

The way to protest against evil is not to do it, as well as to speak against it, and, if necessary, to suffer for it. A child should be brought up as nearly free form all vices and sins as possible; but he should be brought up in all the virtues and in the religion of Jesus Christ, who saves people from their sins.

He is a virtuous and religious person who amid sin and vice abstains from vice and stands firm in righteousness. The man who is innocent from sin because of fortunate surroundings, but who could not stand amid temptations and the contrary example of others and even in the midst of ridicule or worse is not what he ought to be, to say the least.

I have seen little boys of seven and eight vomiting forth sensual talk. This is to be deplored and even this in the presence of persons 50 years of age. What must be the moral status of a person who should not rebuke such proceedings as this in the young.

Young red skins have lately rode off horses without the knowledge or consent of the owners. Lately two instances [*page 67*] have come to our knowledge in which this has happened. Both of these were young men. These things are the result in the ~~work~~

one case of the incapacity of a father and a grand mother. It was said that this young person has been serving the Devil for a long time by his wickedness. The other is a young fellow who has been a horse-thief in time past. When one has started on the downward road, it is hard to get back again to the path of virtue. This is the reason that children should be carefully taught and trained, that the very beginnings of sin may be cut off, and the children saved from evil habits. The surroundings of a child will be sure to exercise a most powerful influence over him; hence the necessity of the best surroundings during an early life that the habits may be firmly formed before the individual emerges into actual life. This is the best way: seeds of sin and vice will fall into the heart of the child sooner or later.

The secret of accomplishing results in this world is effort—repeated and continual effort on our part to do so. If we wish to bring up a child rightly, we should be constantly making vigorous efforts to do so. We should read books understandingly and gain information from them; we should learn from our own personal [*page 68*] experience and observation. We should record the results of our acquisitions for use of ourselves or others, and as books remain, our words may descend to other ages, and be the means of informing them. We should teach the children true principles in the place of the trash so often taught children; but more than this, we should constantly and perseveringly teach them, and besides we should superintend them, repressing every evil in them and cultivating every good thing in them. We should give our children every particle of education that they are capable of, but should care for the health of their bodies and their physical development. We should make them capable of transacting common business, and let them be taught the nobility of manual labor. Show them what things come by manual labor and do not be afraid of adding too much to the dignity of manual labor. It is a good thing if they be taught some trade or profession.

Desiderata for parents to secure for their children
1. Good physical development.
2. Capability of acquiring property.
3. Symmetrical and complete moral development. [*page 69*]
4. A thoroughly experimental religion—the religion of the Savior Jesus Christ. Regular prayer every day by the child or young person.
5. A symmetrical and general education. This can not be too complete or carefully acquired. The parents should still care for their children in school—warding off evils, securing good things for them, guiding, correcting, inciting them, and correcting [*sic*] them.

6. A knowledge of men—their superstitions and follies, and enough of these should be seen to give the student a correct knowledge of what a poor state barbarism is.
7. Some experience in real life so as to train them to perceive and endure the tempests of temptations that may attack a human being. Show them from observation and from literature the mistakes of others, show them how weak human nature is, and that their own natures are restrained from this by the grace of God.

Watch their companions—this is the source of vast influence and it may be for good or bad. The bad influence is what we desire should be avoided. No one wishes to avoid good influence—influence that is toward God, holiness, purity, charity, righteousness, and all the Christian graces.

[page 70] *First Day First Month 3rd, 1892 at home near Shawneetown.*

I went to Bible school in the morning and went and took dinner at Mary Spybuck's, and found her very sick with headache. I found Jennie here, and she left her sister and came into the other room to talk to me. Nellie was also there. Accompanied Jennie in the wagon to the Gov. Doctors, seeking medicine. On the way, she said in answer to questions concerning her younger sister. "Miti pise kawike maweahese micelaniwawe, pieakwi kokwa hotabhita. Wise nakimoi netasekikwi; henepahe wasi netakwi, chena wakenikwe miti ketakosawitowa, tape, netakwi." Again, ["]Ho kweline kawalalamakwi; sakimeki koce walalamakwi, eamicelobeine hoce, moce hena miti ketikitiwenosili~~kwi~~, melwwe keniswalamakwi."

                 Copy of the letter to Carrie Warrior.
"Norman, Okla. Ter. 12/28/1891.
    Miss Carrie Warrior,
        Haskell Institute,
            Lawrence, Kansas.
My Dear Friend:

It may be that I wrote you too long a letter [page 71] last time, so that you may have thought it was too long that you could by no means be able to answer it. I was looking for a letter from you soon, and would be quite glad to receive a letter from you.

The weather has been rather cold here but then we have had no snow at all this winter. I heard that you have already had three snows up there.

I will tell you one thing that I do not care to have you tell any one, because it pertains to no one except you. That is, I want you to be my girl, but I do not want to write any other kind of letters to you except letters of friendship. For I desire you to learn all you possibly can in school, and any other kind of letters might not be for the best. In case you should not desire to be my girl, we can still pen letters of friendship to one another.

Last Wednesday the 23rd of December was my birthday, and it was my twenty-third birthday. I spent the day in writing letters and studying.

How old do you suppose you are?

I do not believe I ought to write a very long letter to you; for it seems that when I do, I can get no answer. So I shall make this letter short, but hope you will write a long letter to me. I can answer a letter a mile [*page 72*] long as well as a short letter.

I hope you are still a Christian. The Christian warfare will not be over till one has passed out of this life into the future life. One has many things to learn after being born into the kingdom of God, hence attendance at church, sabbath school, religious reading, and prayer are indispensable to the young Christian.

Well, I shall close for this time, hoping to hear from you rather soon. If I did not care something for you, I would not do as I am doing. Now if you tell what I tell you not to tell, Carrie, remember it will be an almost unpardonable sin.

        Your true friend,
        William E. Shawnee.

P.S. At Shawneetown, Okla. Ter. 1/3/1891. [*1892?*]

Carrie, I have come home for a time and I attended Bible School and Church to-day, and I saw Jennie at Mary Spybuck's. Mary is sick with La Grippe and has a violent headache, but I hope she will be better soon. Many people have been sick around here. Jennie told me of your letter to her, and said that you asked her to become a Christian, and seemed much pleased with it. I explained to her quite fully what to do to become a Christian, [*page 73*] and she said she was willing. Do you not see what your missionary letter has been the means of doing under the blessing of God?

I wish I could see you for about two or three hours, because I would like to talk to you about school matters and a few other things. I want you to go to school more and not to come home and remain. You can not learn too much. You may come home on a visit, but must be sure to go back again. I want to tell you one thing, and if you please, do it. You can save $25 or more out of this money that will soon be paid to the Shawnees, and go back whenever you wish. If you do not do this, I do not see how you can go back. Write soon to your friend. William E. Shawnee. Direct your letter to Shawneetown.

1/3/1891 [*1892?*]
   Carrie, I want one of your pictures sometime. I hope it shall be just like you.
   I do not know whether you will like it about being my girl or not. I rather think you may. From all I can ~~learn~~ gather you have long thought well of me, even when I was small, and also yourself. However, I can not know anything till you write. If I am mistaken, you will doubtless correct all mistakes. [*page 74*]
           Your True Friend,
              William E. Shawnee

1/4/1891 [*1892?*] *Promises by the bride.*
   1. I will by the grace of God govern my temper and not get angry and not be easily provoked.
   2. I will not be too frequent in asking or expecting money from my husband. I will be a Christian wife. Loving, merciful, and just to my companion.
   3. I recognize the fact that my husband is the head of the family by divine appointment. When I and he differ, I will cheerfully submit without quarreling or unnecessary talking. I will obey him in all cases except those only which concern God and conscience. Yet as he is a Christian, I will look to him for Christian instruction, care, and guidance.
   4. I recognize the fact that my husband is nearer to me than any one else, and so I will not, before Almighty God, reveal his faults, but pray for him and help him to overcome them; and I ask him to do same toward me.
   5. I agree to obey all the precepts given to wives in the blessed Bible; and I ask and expect my husband to obey all the precepts given to husbands in the Bible. [*This completes the second journal.*]

1/13/1892 Fourth Day. [*moved from page 42*]
   According to Mary, Carrie wants a young man to abstain from writing to other girls, and when she finds out that a young man is writing to other girls, she quits ~~them~~ him. That when she is sick, she cries, and is most melancholy, easily despairing of recovery. She says that Carrie will marry me and that she will tell Carrie to do so. She agreed with me that Carrie's folks might oppose, but said that their folks always opposed them.
   [*1/22/1892*] According to Mary, Carrie came to puberty at thirteen years of age, and she attributed it to the frequent

arousing of the passions; that she matured at 15. This is written at Shawneetown 1/22/1892.

Third Chronicle

Making a Living in Oklahoma Territory

March 14, 1892–November 28, 1897

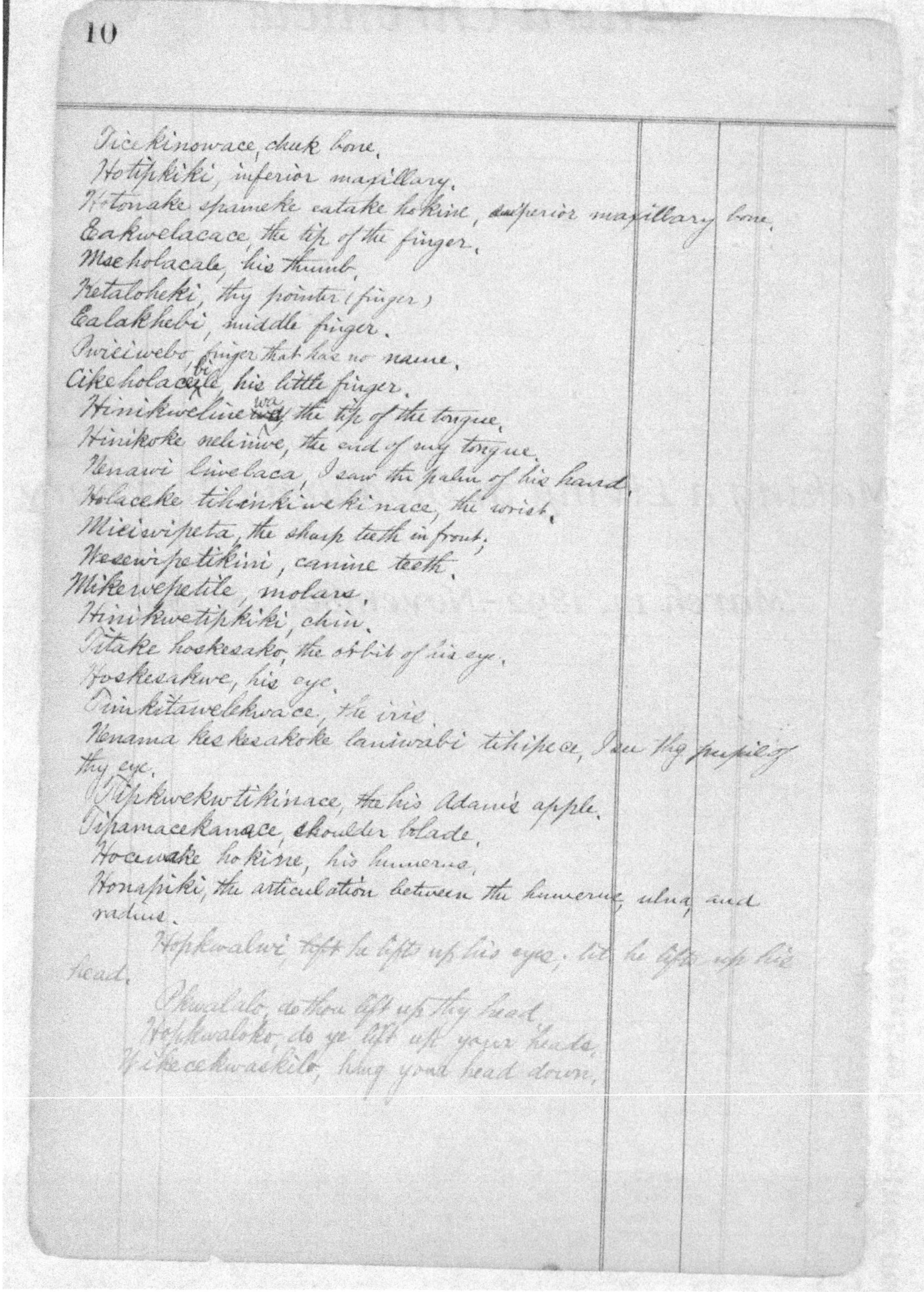

10

Ticekinowace, cheek bone.
Hotipkiki, inferior maxillary.
Wetonake spiuneke eatake hokine, superior maxillary bone.
Eakwelacace, the tip of the finger.
Mseholacale, his thumb.
Ketaloheki, thy pointer (finger).
Ealakhebi, middle finger.
Iwiciwebo, finger that has no name.
Cikeholacale, his little finger.
Hinikweline wa, the tip of the tongue.
Hinikoke nelinive, the end of my tongue.
Nenawi livelaca, I saw the palm of his hand.
Holaceke tihinkiwekinace, the wrist.
Miliswipeta, the sharp teeth in front.
Wesewipetikini, canine teeth.
Mikewepetile, molars.
Hinikwetipkiki, chin.
Titake hoskesako, the orbit of his eye.
Hoskesakwe, his eye.
Tinikitawelekwace, the iris.
Nenama heskesakoke laniwabi tihipeca, I see the pupil of thy eye.
Tipkwekwtikinace, the his Adam's apple.
Tipamacekanace, shoulder blade.
Hocawake hokine, his humerus.
Honapiki, the articulation between the humerus, ulna, and radius.
Hopkwalwi, tift he lifts up his eyes; let he lifts up his head.
Pkwalilo, do thou lift up thy head.
Hopkwaloko, do ye lift up your heads.
Wikecekwaskilo, hang your head down.

Fig. 3.1. Page 10 of William Ellsworth Shawnee's Third Chronicle.

Overview of the Third Chronicle

William Ellsworth Shawnee was still living at Big Jim's Crossing when he began recording in his third journal, only two months after he completed his second one. His third journal includes daily entries from March 14, 1892, through November 28, 1897. It is a legal-sized, bound document, written in both pencil and ink, much of which is difficult to read. It includes English, Absentee Shawnee, Kickapoo, and Greek words. The pages are numbered 1-264, with pages 1, 2, 175, 176, 215, and 216 missing. Daily entries of the original journal are not in chronological order.

    In this journal, Shawnee provides introductory Absentee Shawnee vocabulary lessons, translates part of the New Testament Gospels into Absentee Shawnee using phonetic spelling, and describes his interactions with well-known Absentee Shawnee tribal figures such as Chief Big Jim, Chief White Turkey, and artist Ernest Spybuck. He writes about his job interpreting among the Absentee Shawnees, Kickapoos, and others. He writes about the religious traditions of the Quakers and his interactions with them, and about the monthly meetings at Absentee Shawnee and Kickapoo missions established by the Quakers. Shawnee also writes about his ancestry; his farm, farming, and sharecroppers; his romantic interests and marriage; and social relations among the American Indians, blacks, and whites. He writes about his job as a schoolteacher, his interactions with black and white public school authorities, his attendance at all-white teachers' institutes, and his interactions with prominent black Oklahoma Territory citizens such as Rev. John W. Dunjee. This version of Shawnee's third journal is in chronological order and is denoted as his "Third Chronicle."

Chapter 5

Translating at Big Jim's Crossing
March 14, 1892—April 12, 1893

Between March 14, 1892, and April 12, 1893, Shawnee prepared to teach the Absentee Shawnees. In his journal he developed and recorded vocabulary lessons, with translations from Absentee Shawnee to English and from English to Absentee Shawnee. He used phonetic spellings and diacritical marks to indicate word pronunciation. Shawnee's journal also includes a transcription of a historical Absentee Shawnee document—the removal document of the Absentee Shawnees from Texas in 1836. Other entries include information he copied from the Quaker church manual on marriage and baptism, an essay he wrote on the Lord's Supper and the Lord's Day, and passages of the Gospels translated into Absentee Shawnee.

[*Pages 1 and 2 of the original journal are missing.*]
[*page 3*]
6 Hosketapea means on the surface of the water.
   Hosketbike " on the top of the log.
   Hosketimkwa " on the face of the earth.
   Limbike " under the log.
   Limapea " under the water.
   Limike " under the earth.
   ~~Hiwibike~~ Hiwibbike, beyond the log.
   Sepitikwa, on the under side.
   Sepitikwa kahocemimithi, hew the log on the under side.
   Pikitikwa, by the tree or close by the tree.
   Pikitikwa nepiwe, he is standing by the tree.
   Pikitikwa limitipewi, he is sitting by the tree.
7. Wipekwe, pumpkin.
   Bamkwi, striped pumpkin.
   Helane-wipekwe, man-pumpkin, very small pumpkin.
   Sketimake, water melon.
   Sinpokwike, mush-melon.
   Kisecaeike, cucumber; Kisecaei ksika nale, kiskwa hoskece.
   Mskocebike, beans.
   Laniwawe time, Indian corn.
   Takoseawe time, white man's corn (yellow corn).
   Limikabeke, peanuts.
   Hopaneake, sweet potatoes.
   Wiweapanei, turnip.
   Meisebike, Irish potatoes.
   Msaske papkwitapaeike, cabbage.
   Pkwitapaei, ksika; hene wace nsetotake.
   Msemenike, apples.
   Pokimike, peaches.
   Sakikowesi, onion.
   Sisketotake, lettuce.
8. Nanakikwi, cotton-wood tree, Plu.: Nanakikoke
   Mesemese, Burr oak. Plu. Mesemesa.
   Hinepe, elm tree. Hinepea, elm trees.
   Wipikomese, Post oak. Plu. Wipikomesa.
   Wipikomeseke, grove or place of Post oaks.
   P[abiki]kwemese, black jack, Plu. Pabikik[wemesa].
   [*page 4*] Pikikemese, white oak. Plu. Pikikemesa.
   Kwcamese, hickory. Plu. Kwcamesa.
   Hieipamese, Black oak. Plu. Hieipamesa.
   Metwikemesa, Willow. Plu. Metwikemesake.
   Timetwikemesekeke, where a grove of willows are.
   Micisemese, Persimmon, Micisemesa Plu.
   Timicisemesekeke, where persimmon trees are.
   Menewilomese, Black haw. Plu. Menewilomesa.

Timenewilomesekeke, where a grove of ~~willows~~ black haus [haws] are.
Pikinewese, Walnut[.] Plu. Pikinewesa.
Tipikinewesekeke, where a grove of walnuts are.
Kibamese Pecan. Plu. Kibamesa.
Tikibamesekeke, where a grove of pecans are.
Kikewamese [*blank space*]. Plu. Kikewamesa
Pskepemese, smooth hickory. Plu. Pskepemesa.
Kiselhikamese, Hackleberry tree. Plu. Kiselhikamesa.
Kwsakwikome, Hackleberries.
Meilikwi, Ash. Plu. Meilikoke.
Timeilikwekeke, in a grove of Ash trees.
Kesowikwitwi, Sycamore. Plu. Kesowikwitoke.
Tikesowikwitwekeke, in a grove of sycamores.
Mtakwipilwi, Mulberry. Plu. Mtakwipiloke.
Timtakwipilwekeke, in a grove of mulberries.

9. Hocapkikitwe, root. Plu. Hocapkikito, roots.
Tihocapkitwekeke, where plenty of roots are.
Tihocapkikitoweke, where its roots are.
Papkaeikke, branch. Plu. Likbana pkaeikwitwe.
Pikaeikwitwe, full of branches, giving off branches all along.
Pamecetakonike, a parallel branch.
Miletakonike, full of branches.
Mameceke, that which is many or plenty.
Matako, trees[.]

Mankwitwe, heaven. Mankwito, heavens.
[*lower corners of page 4 torn off*]
[Man]kwitoke, in the heaven. Mankwitokewile, heavens.
[Man]kwitowile, heavens.
[. . .]neke setahake Siwinwike neke hilikhe, kesake
[. . .]taske wikini kebeke; tapake wibeboke; pieakwi
[. . .]ke, hisaskek lakeloke. waki eapa[. . .]
[*page 5*] wice miekwebeke, nakote eakobetake likwi ei[e]ipeke limike [*sp?*] eamace pansenowice. Sakimeki laniwake hene easeniwiwice bipi.

Neke sakimeki laniwake minetoke bipi.
Minetoke easenobocke.
1. Sakimeki laniwake.
2. Nacepa minetoke.
3. Nanamkeke. Sing. Nanamke.
4. Kokombani.
5. Mice Mineto.
6. Matkwike.
7. Ketikekena.
8. Weniseke.

9. Kikelake.
10. Msepaseke.
11. Minetowe msepaseke.
12. Minetowe kikitilikwi.
13. Minetowe kikwi.
14. Minetowe msawa.
15. Minetowe mbobwi.
16. Minestowelaneke.
17. Hipockeliwabi.
18. Nisebake.
19. Tekimba. (Tecumseh) English [*written above* "Tecumseh"].
20. Msekenapekwi.
21. Kikcepesewabbe.
    Naskitalikwe, weighed down with a load.
    Keselikwe, hurt by something mashing one.
    Bikekwahowa, yoke, or collar.
Oksenewe bikekwahowa, ox yoke.
Eahisetabake, cross.
Nenieakwi msawa, a horse bore me, I rode a horse.
Msawa kanieakwa, let a horse bare thee, ride a horse.
    Pemenkwi, rope. Plu. Pemenkwini.
    Cekkapetiwa, he is plowing (in land plowed before).
    ~~Pws~~ Pwskwipetiwa, ~~break~~ he is breaking land. This word is used only for breaking land—new land.
Timiskipetiwa, he is howing with a plow, used for weeding

[*page 6*] out standing corn or any thing else with a plow.
Cikelelacaei, without form or shape.
Hotakwikobi, wooden bottle. Kepiskheki, stopper.
Tiwetabi, lamb [lamp] chimney.
Tiwata, chimney, Hotakwe tiweta, wooden chimney.
Sekone tiweta. stone chimney.
Skosaneki, wick roller of a lamp.
Saseliki, plate saselikini, plates.
Kibwewe likini, coffee cups. Sing. Kibwewe liki, coffee cup.
Tapheki, cup. Plu. Taphekinike.
Saswibeke, saucers. ~~Plu.~~ Sing. Saswibekewile.
Eisekwiphimeke, dish. Plu. Eisehikwihekoke.
Hobiwikkobi, brass kettle. Plu. Hobiwikkobike.
Hisaskewikkwi, jug. Plu. Hisaskewikkoke.
Sekonikkwi, stone jar. Plu. Sekonikkoke.
Kicewikkwi, ~~oven~~ skillet. Plu. Kicewikkoke, skillets.
Msewipeamkwi, long or big spoon. Plu. Msewipeamkwinike.
Wipeamkwi, spoon. Plu. Wipeamkwinike.
Wipeamkwibi, little spoon. Plu. Wipeamkwibike
Mamkitawike hiwekiceki, ink.
Hiwekiceki, pen holder, Plu. Hiwekicekini.

Pickewaei, too thick, said of ink.
Skwipeake, near the water, in close proximity to it.
Skwipeabeke, near the water.
Hilapepkwikime, water here and there, pools here and there.
Hilatetke kimeweei, springs here and there.
Peawi tinep[i]wei, he came to me.
Peawi tihipei, he came to where I was, to me.
Tihipei wieace peatba, he came toward me.
Bepeke wieace hawi, he went toward the river.
Mtakoke wieace peatba, he came toward the tree.
Henewieace netalicemo, I am speaking concerning (toward) that place.
Tipkwikimeke, nsenikekike, ~~wali~~ wali, nsepeake, they stopped or came to a hole or pool of water.
Hiwibewikho, outside the fence.
Hiwibehotawaneke, outside the city.
Tipwilewitake, outside the smoke; lit. where the smoke [*page* 7] is not.
Hiwibbe skwitake, outside the gate.
Hiwibe kime, behind the house.
Easkwitiwimeke, the side the door is on, in front of the house.
Hikwcekime, the roof of the house.
Hikwcekime limitipewi, he is sitting on the roof of the house.
Papametikbake, joists of a house.
~~Hiko~~ Hipwcepkwinabo, upstairs, in the second story.
Lilihoceki, bell. Plu. Lilihocekini.
Kikkwceki, drawer knife. Plu. Kikkwcekini.
~~M~~ Pskecewilikini, saddle bags.
Mtakwi eitipetikinbake, gun scabbard.
Mswibipei, Comforter. Plu. Mswibipeake.
Lakwisheki, chinking. Plu. Lakwishekini.
Lakwishota, to chink, or, it is chinked.
Tapeskewanota, daubed. Tapeskewaniwa, he is daubing.
Pocike, corner of the house.
Tipepocaeike, where the corners are.
Tbiceki, shelf. Plu. Tbicekini.
Eitipkilake, fire hearth.
Masekkike, wind.
Tatkike, air.
Nanekelanikwitwe, shaking motion in the air.
Mbiwinwe, fog. Membiwike fog.
Hiwininwe, ~~fog~~ misty rain.
Papekestake, mist.
Titoci, a hollow, or ravine.
Hosawike, ridge.
~~The~~ Bekaei, gradual decline of a hill.

Nkwimake; Bepeke hekwe spitanwe, an elevation reaching to a stream.
Wasatake, on top the hill.
Eapbitake, on the hill side.
[. . . at the foot of the hill where the . . . is] [*bottom of page cut off*]

[*page 8*] On the translation of "Within."
1. Within the camps.
   Peteka pipesaeiwekini wacehitake.
2. Within me, Limake neike.
3. Within him, Limake weike.
4. Within a hundred, Tapawa hotipe.
5. Within his fame, Easewalalamoboce hotipe.

Through.
1. Through the gate, Skwitake (hoce) wieace. (?)
2. Through fear, Kpanwi ksika.
3. through age, Kelanewe ksika.
4. Through sport, Wasepabewa hoce.
5. Through force, Wesekitwwewa hoce.
6. Through one's self, Neike hoce (out of me).

Behind.
1. Behind the mountain. Hiwibe pamitake.
2. Behind the dedication of the temple. Timace hobapelototake mimitomaweki noce.
3. Behind the memory of man. Helaneke witikitiwemkiwalatimwice hileki ~~wiacl.~~ wiace.

Beyond.
Beyond the river, Hileki eatiki bepeke.
Beyond the tree, Hiwibe mtakoke.
Beyond the house, Hiwibe kime.
Beyond the road, ~~Hileki eatikwa meawaneke~~, Hilekewe eackini.
Beyond the hill, Hiwibe makwikeke.
Beyond my belief, Miti moce easetahai.
Beyond my knowledge, Nenotkwewikoti.
Beyond my power, Nenotkwelabe.

Behind.
Behind me, Hotinike neike.
Behind thee, Hotinike ~~keli~~ keike.
Behind them, Hotinike weiwi.
Behind him, Hotinike weike.
Behind us, Hotinike keinike.
Behind you, Hotinike keiwike.

Sundry phrases.

In the beginning of our work. Hena ketaleme pekitabepa.
In the beginning of the morning. Hena waske wipinwe.
[page 9] In the beginning of our talk, Hena ketalame pakekiliwepa.

In the beginning of the morning may be translated, Hena helame wipinwe.

Or we may translate thus.

In the beginning of our work, Hena waske kepakitibepa.
In the beginning of the morning, Hena waske wipinwe.
In the beginning of our talk, Hena waske kepakekiliwepa.
In the beginning of his journey, Hena waske wapba.
In the beginning of Spring, Hena waske malokime.
In the beginning of summer, Hena waske ~~ma lo kime~~ paliwe.
In the beginning of autumn, Hena waske tikwike.

Netikwilati, I hold in my mouth, said of water or other substance.
Petiwepetaneki, coat. Plu. Petiwepetanekini.
Patikhowa, hat, Plu. Patikhowani.
Lilikekwanskwe, husk, Plu. Lilikekwansko.
Holikase, boat, Plu. Holikalile, boat[s].
Makebabi, lamb, Plu. Makebabike,
Limitibi, faetal lamb. Plu. Limitibike.
Pakelabi, an animal whose mother has died, for instance, cow or sheep. Plu. Pakelabike.
Kasenonice, his step son or daughter.
Sing. Kasenonoboti, Plu. Kasenonobocke.
Nobi, my father, Nobani, our father.
Kobi, thy father, Kobwi, your father.
Hobile, his father, Hobwile, their father.
Nobani is our father, and does not denote that the one spoken to has the same; kobani means that the one spoken to has a share in the father as his father.

Eitiwebanekeke eake, table. Eitiwebanekeke, dining table.
Hiwibikwa, on the other side of the tree; behind the tree.
Lilikwikwa, between the trees.
Lilikkini, between the road, in the middle of the road.
Sakopetiki, a sachel made of oiled cloth.
Hokeneke, in the forehead.
Mimiwanhe, eye-brows.
Lilikocila, the saeptum of the nose.
Howetoniwile, his wiskers or mustache.
[page 10] Ticekinowace, cheek bone.
Hotipikiki, inferior maxillary.

Hotonake spameke eatake hokine, superior maxillary bone.
Eakwelacace, the tip of the finger.
Mseholacale, his thumb.
Ketaloheki, thy pointer (finger).
Ealakhebi, middle finger.
Pwieiwebo, finger that has no name.
Cikeholaceabile, his little finger.
Hinikwelinewa, the tip of the tongue.
Hinikoke nelinwe, the end of my tongue.
Nenawi liwelaca, I saw the palm of his hand.
Holaceke tihinkiwckinace, the wrist.
Mieiwipeta, the sharp teeth in front;
Wesewipetikini, canine teeth.
Mikewepetile, molars.
Hinikwetipkiki, chin.
Titake hoskesako, the orbit of his eye.
Hoskesakwe, his eye.
Timkitawelekwace, the iris.
Nenama kes kesakoke laniwabi tihipece, I see the pupil of thy eye.

Tipkwekwtikinace, ~~the~~ his Adam's apple.
Tipamacekanace, shoulder blade.
Hocewake hokine, his humerus.
Honapiki, the articulation between the humerus, ulna, and radius.
Hopkwalwi, ~~lift~~ he lifts up his eyes; lit. he lifts up his head.
    Pkwalalo, do thou lift up thy head.
    Hopkwaloko, do ye lift up your heads.
    Wikecekwaskilo, hang your head down.

    [*page 11*] The word "Glory"—its Translation

Jno.1:14. Kenamapa <u>howiwaseli.</u>
Jno.2:1. Chena easematatatike <u>wiwaseli.</u>
Jno.12:41. Eanamake weli <u>howiwaseli.</u>
Jno.8:50. Nanitiwipiti miti pasakwe neli <u>wiwaseli.</u>
Jno.17:24. Wihese wanamaniwi <u>nawiwaseli</u> [nea]iiac[esu]eleine.
Jno.12:28. Nobahe <u>wiwaseli</u> easeboine. Namace wiwaseliwe, chena noke nawiwaseliwe.
Jno.13:32. Wiwaseli nele weike, pipeace wiwaseli nele oce weli pasakwe, chena wawiwaseliwe walani.
Jno.16:14. Pipeace wawiwaseli neli.
Jno.17:1. Hena kekwebi keli.
    17:5. Wiwaseli neli wece keli.
    21:19. Howikotalile wieace wihese napake wiwaseli T.
Jno. 7:39. Kesikea C. miti kawike mahowaseliwe.

An Academic Dictionary Says: C

"Glory, n. [[Lat. gloria.]] 1. High reputation. 2. An object of pride or boast. 3. Pride; boastfulness. 4.Celestial honor; heaven, 5 (Panit.) A circle of rays round a head of entire figure.

Syn. Renown; celebrity; distinction; grandeur; nobleness."

As a verb, 1. "to exult with joy["]. 2. To boast; to be proud of.

Glorify, v. [[Latin. glorificare; gloria, glory, and faccre, to make]]. 1. To make glorious or illustrious. 2. To render homage to; to adore.

Instances.

Gen 31:1. Chena kobani howeaheme hoce hoponi eomi mselalamakobewa.
Ex. 28:2 Kahostiwi kecaneni petanekini, wisem mselalatotake chena wise holabeike.
1 Sam. 2:8. Hipipewi wamoike mselalamakobewa.
1 Sam 4:21. Hisanwe mselalamakobewa.
1 Chron. 22:5. Hene wekewi pipeace wamaeititotota chena wamselalatota.
1 Chron. 29. Keike mselanewewa, chena wesekitowewa, chena mselalamakobewa.
Esther 5:11. Chena hotitoti homselalamakobewa hopiwwawaneke wamoike. (Mselalamakobewa hoponi ksika weabi eapiwace).
Job. 40. Kapetaneka mselalamakobewa chena holabewa. [*page 12*]
Mimiwobo, they took it for him.
Mimikwe, they took it away from him.
Nemimiwi, I took it for him, also, I took it from him.
Hotikalamile, he respects her or him. This word denotes that one does not use profane language in the presence of his sister or other relative or any person because of fear or respect. In the case the person spoken of is a female relative it denotes the absence of sexual intercourse. If one commits incest, it would be said of him: Miti hotikalamile nanhilwalamice.

Remark. That is one thing peculiar about Shawnee words, and that is their excessive meaning. For instance there is no word for "head"; but nese means my head; kese means thy head; and howese means his head. Necaneni means my brother, and he may be either older or younger than myself; but nebabi means any older brother; nemebi means any older sister, while nebemabi means my younger brother or sister, but the word does not denote the sex, consequently it is applied indiscriminately to male or female.
Nebemabi skwabibi means my younger sister.
Nebemabi skeliwabebi means my younger brother.

Kwekhinwe, holikase, the boat sank; This is the proper way of expressing this fact; though some say, Kokei holikase; this last expression is however universally intelligible.

Kwekhinno holikalile, the boats sank, the boats are thought of as performing the act.

Mike holikalile, ships, literally big boats.
Nekokeni means I dip it; that is, I put it into the water and raise it up again: but neketihi means I immerse it, that is, I put it under the water and let it remain without withdrawal. Hoketihi means he immersed it. Keketihi, thou immersed it. Kekokeni, thou dipt it. Hokokeni, he dipt it.

Nemoskepeani, I raise it out of the water. I withdraw that out of the water which is already there.
Lakwhiska, to jump belly foremost into the water.
Lakwhiska heni hinekwi, that squirrel jumbed [jumped] into the water. Lakwhiska is very connotative; it means to jump into the water, even when water is not mentioned.

[*page 13*] Ketisenwi heni hine kwi, the squirrel was immersed. This is the result of jumbing [jumping] into the water. The action is represented as that of the squirrel and hence <u>was immersed</u> is not precise. <u>The squirrel sunk himself in the water</u> is better. In this case, ketisenwi was used even though the squirrel was not completely covered, and the sinking lasted only a short time, as the creature was running away as fast as it could.

Likokwa pece kwikoke; ho likokwa ~~webikilimo~~ wesekilimo! These two exclamations were made by a companion speaking of a certain persons diving for a long time. Here the word <u>koke</u> must be rendered in English <u>dive</u>, while above I rendered it <u>dip</u>. From this it is evident that it is not the absolute equivalent of dip. <u>Put under water with the purpose of taking out again</u> is the exact meaning of <u>koke,</u> I believe. The translation of the above is, <u>he dives for a very long time, he holds his breath very long</u>.

Bwipahe kekokeni, you put it under water for a short time. Pece kekokeni, you put it in the water for a short time. Strange to say each of these expressions may be used while the person still has the thing under water; the first may be said to induce him to let it remain, the other to induce him to witdraw it.

Pece kekokeni netali, ca howa homoskepeani, I told him that he had kept it under water for a long time, and then he withdrew it.

The verb "Koke"

1. Nekoke, I dive   1. Nekokepa, we dive
2. Kekoke, thou divest   ~~Kokeke, the~~

3. Koke, he dives   2. Kekokepwi, you dive
                                                      3. Kokeke, they dive.

    Notice that koke is seen in all these six forms, yet alone it signifies <u>he dives</u>.

      Kokei holikase, the boat sinks.

      Kokei holikalile, the boats sink.

Notice that kokei takes either a singular or plural subject.

      Mbanimese, maple tree. Plural. Mbanimesa, maple trees.
Mbanimesa malise wihocehostota, Sugar is made from maple-trees.
Nakote pakekiweke, one drop (of anything).
[page 14] Miti moce nakote pakekiweke Laniwawem skwe hoponi, He has not even one drop of Indian blood (in him).

    There is no such word in Shawnee as wiwaseli; even an intelligent Shawnee can not guess what the word can be intended to mean.

Wiwase = he wears nice (good) clothes.
Wiwasekita = ornamented, said of a book, a house, a shirt, a knife, or any article that is ornamented.
Wiwasewa, ornamented clothes as a whole; whatever is worn as ornaments, nice clothes, handkerchiefs, etc.
Wiwaselo, Do thou put on nice clothes or articles[?]
Wiwaseko, Do ye put on nice clothes or articles[?]
Kewiwasepa, We have on nice clothes or articles.
Kewiwasepwi, you all have nice clothes or articles.
Wiwaseke, they have on nice clothes or articles.
Takiwehe newiwase, miti tapice, I have on some nice things, but not many.
Tapalo kewiwasepwi, You all are fully dressed, i.e. you have on nice clothes and ornaments.
Wekoce wiwase! He ~~has~~ is adorned to the utmost, is adorned to the highest extent.

    Hilieomi Kikiwba tipambace. Hekwawi bipi heni, chena kenwinkwa; howa bipi likwi eapambace neniketano welabi mtakoke, howa hene wace kiwaskike nale. Laniwake eatiwice milikwihe eapeice, howa molspe eisba, miti houinbakowile laniwake; pieakwi takoseike honinbakowile. Laniwa ksika heni, hene wacepwi laniwake nbice. Translation. This is where a kàkàwthĕ (tornado) has passed. This (kàkàwthĕ) is a woman, and she has long hair; so when she passes a place, her hair twines around the trees, and that is the reason they fall down. When she comes close to the houses of the Indians, she flies up high, she does not kill Indians, but she does kill white people. Because she is an Indian, therefore she does not kill Indians.

    Nacepa milakhe eakiwaskike mtako, Wiweibito senobo heni neaseliweti; pieakwi heni Kikiwba likwi eieawi, nacepa halakiwaski mtako eahice. Ninipe kili msakkea weli pakwe wiwiweitipaski, Wiweibito [page 15] macelobeti heni; heni pieakwi mamsekelaki wiweibito likwi eahice mieilakhe mtako kikiwaski. Translation, When trees are fallen down in one place alone, Hà-wē-yà'-thà-to is he that has done work, But Kàkàẃthĕ travels scattering trees along his path. Sometimes it happens that leaves or dust whirl round and round, that is a little Wà-wē-yà thà-tī, but when a great wà-wē-yà-thà-tō goes anywhere, trees fall in a certain place (as if around in a circle). The gesture with the hand would show that this <u>mieilakhe</u> is in the form of a circle (say 100 yards or 50 yards in diameter[)], in which area all or nearly all the trees have fallen down.

    Nanamkeke howiwetbatiniwi pibkwike, hopipimwatoniwi kamowike. Kemas sombanike neke nanamkeke. Eawinasatimwice nanamkewin we ketieopa. Helanilo hoponiniwi, chena hopipamotiniwi mtako, holile kitaliniwi. Eapamotimwice mtako papike easeliweike ketiopa, nekeeo hopamotiniwi, nalocen ketiopa. Takoseike mtilikwi easeniwice Nanamkehe, miti ksika howikomiwihe.

    Nakote Siwinwi helane sakime ki mine easece. "Pise matkwike hetoke neke nanamkeke. Howa kiketisenoke likwi napeke, chena eomi milaspeke pipambake hopipipiwitainniwi weiwi pise kilipalawi eas kihokwece, howaca homekonameke wihoce panbanwe nape eoni sikeke, howaca kehiwa ktalinwe ketieopa."

Pokinwe, rising in waves, said of the sea, or ocean.
Wiweitinwe, it flows in a circle (or circles) said of the water of a river or other stream.
Nanapeaei, it ripples, said of ripples made on the surface of still water by throwing a stone into it. These rip[p]les move toward the shore.
Kebekwi, he is washing his (or if a woman, her) face.
Kebelaca he is washing his hands.
Kebilbetano, he is washing his feet.
Kehetońwi, he holds his mouth closed.
Benskékománo, he holds his nostrils closed.
Patakwelacaski, he doubles his hands into a fist.
[page 16] Kepeteeape, he or she holds his or her arms closed by sitting.
Kepeteeakwibowani, pants; from their doing this are probably so called.
Mitatiwile, leggings.
Hokoti, her dress; a woman's garment.
Pbewa, a handkerchief, Nepbewa, my handkerchief; kepbewa, thy handkerchief; hopbewa, his handkerchief; nepbewani, our handkerchief; kepbewanwi, your handkerchief; hopbewanwi, their handkerchief.

    Pbewa—a handkerchief.
    Ne-pbewa—my handkerchief.
    Ke-pbewa—thy handkerchief.

Ho-pbewa—his handkerchief.
Ne-pbewa-ni, our handkerchief.
Ke-pbewa-nwi, your handkerchief.
Ho-pbewa-nwi, their handkerchief.

1. Ne- prefixed to a word denotes my, I.
2. Ke- " " " " " thy, thou.
3. Ho " " " " " his, him.

In the plural notice that, Ne, ke, and ho are also prefixed, but that in addition <u>ni</u>, nwi, and nwi, are affixed to the word.

Hi'kwta, blacked by smoke, as a lamp or its chimney.

On the origin of a Shawnee name. <u>Nánapea</u>.
[*page 17*] *Shawneetown, Okla. Ter. 3/14/1892. Second Day.*
Kickapoo Tradition in regard to the migration of the Shawnee to the south in the Kickapoo language, as taken verbatim from the lips of Pakotahi by the writer:—

["]Nabipei hobemamihi easesinace hobabahine; hiene eamecece mikokice; hiene eahipesesice hobabami, hena eamatiwace mikokice; hena eawapobace eahikwace; wace sitake neahice; hene wace Siwinowi hence.["}

The same rendered into Shawnee language:— Noteka hobemami eahehiliwelace hobabile; hena eanotekace homece mkwi hobetile; hena eahipiliwece hobabami hena matiwa mkwi hokitile; hena wapba eaweikowace; wace liwikwake hawi; hene wace Siwinwi senoboce.

Again the following story is told by the Kickapoos but is here given only in Shawnee:—

Hena eawapbace Siwinwi wace hwik[iw]ake hawi, chena mskakwe homki; hene eamacemkike hene tihipece. Howace netise mesime homki, pieakwi howa homiceloti hene homesime mamkike, Henoke eanitiokeice hene timicelotike.

Mine eieowice Kekipoke; "Hena waske timaeatalamobowice laniwake cieiki Kekipoke bipi; howa hotibilikwi pkawi heni hobabami; howa chebani noke eaniotewice ca kotike litowake; chena Siwinwi Siwinwi hotasatiwes, pieakwi Kekipo hene eiski easetike wei."

Siwinwike niseti hobemami pkawi eiwike.
Neswebip[. . .]neke wacanenitecke, howa heni hobemami [h]ikwi pikani, howa heni holabami labalo, howa eamacelabaloce hocikitini mkwi hokitile, nale holacewile pieakwi hoskonini. Nale pieakwi hobetile bipi hileki wekino; howa heni hobemami eapeice matiwa nale hokitile, howa ca wapba, pikeli semiwelaniwawe; heni henoke kekipo easenoboti. Nileti laniwake howetamakohe ~~laniwake~~ heni hobemami eawaplace.

Eimi Siwinwi bipi waske mamaeatalamoboti eatsewice laniwake: hoba bwile cieike laniwake. Nakeolanipake kemasombanike eiloboke.

[page 18]
1. Nakote kekikweme time, One ~~y~~ ear of corn.
2. Matibwe kekikweme time, Ten ~~y~~ ears of corn.
3. Kekiskbano time, the corn is unhusked.
4. Kakekiskbake, that which is unhusked.
5. Nenesana eaminatowekesakeke, two Sunday's ago.
6. Hiwibikwa, on the other side of the tree.
7. Siwinbanwe = Paliobanwe masekkike, the wind blows from the south. Winipe eakonewikeke liwikwake eakocekkike, ealelakeboce koni, hene siwinbanwe setota.
8. Siwike, the god of the south, who is a woman. Hekwawi bipi heni Siwike, heni hotibi eilaskiki eaeikwitatake.
9. Hipikwi, the god of the north, who is a man. Helane bipi heni Hipikwi; heni hotibi eilaskiki wawapeke, Eimi papkitalace makenwhahe honinbike, howa nale hiwikwake eapelece hotaphile nake; howa niseti eimi Siwike walikwelace makenwhahe, honinbike, howa nale miweace eapelace hotitaphile nahe.
10. Eisomsomewice Siwinwike, Nilati kkikelawelaneke; noce nilati Patikenabewelaneke; nilati psakbewomsomeke; Palawelaneke nilati; nilati Hibapitewelaneke; nilati msepase womsomeke. Neke msawelaneke noke neke psakbewelaneke, heneiski.
   Neke patakobetawelaneke: 1. Mwawike. 2. Msepaseke. 3 Weseke; 4 Pasewabike. 5. Wikocabeke.
   Miti likwi psakbewelaneke Siwinwike.

   Animals real or fabulous.
1. Minatowemsapase, Eimi heni spamake pipambiti, pise hilikwi easenikobece, Hene sikeke eapikseke nacepahe ninanakwinwe. Wanapwi bipi weabi nawita mieiwe eatalece eomi spamake eapambalece. Psakbehe bipi honinbihe, eahiliwece: pipihiliwe ksika. Napeke tawi bipi heni; howa eomi spamake eapambace, eomi sikeke easbice napake eiepiksenwi; howa kiceki ntise nacepahe nanakwinwe.
Willie. Sakimeki Siwinwi Napake tawi sebo. Totano. Patakobetawelane toka, walitoka kkikelawelane. The former supposition of his is the true one.
[page 19] Nake nacepahe msapeseke kenwilowake. This shows that there is a diference between the panther and the god-panther.
2. Minatowembobwi, Pise pelaskembowi bip[i] eimi. Sakimeki bipi heni Hipocekeliwabi hokipalkiwile eoloni kcekimeke; nakote bipi honbile; howa hene bipi wacenekewice pelaskemboboke, Minatoke

takiwehe eokomi pelaskemboboke, ksika minato homskome hoce nekeke.

    Some Shawnee words do not mean what they once did. This is self-evident in view of the following facts.
1. Mboboke singular Mbobwi. This word once meant a buffalo, probably it meant a buffalo to the Indians before the white men came to this country, and perhaps for some little time after. But now buffaloes are never seen by the Shawnees, and the word mbobwi means a cow or ox, cattle in general.
2. [*paragraph is numbered "3" instead of "2"*] Minatowekikwi. Wekoce kiskwale eimi howebieami, howa wese kili eabikepwice eolomo kikekilwa nale webiei, Howa eakekilwace hileki eisbai pisakwe nale webiei, pilohe honinbakoni heni wese. This animal appears to me to be the porcupine.

    Current Opinions in the original language, *written at Big Jim's Crossing on the Little River 4/20/1892.*

[*moved bottom of page 19 entry dated 1/1/1893 for chonological order*]

[*page 20*] *Big Jim's, Oklahoma Territory, 5/11/1892.*
    The following ~~The~~ Recommendation of the Absentee Shawnees and their Chiefs was copied from the original, word for word and spelling for spelling, from the original in the possession of Big Jim, and of course at present in the possession of Wm E. Shawnee, this day May 11, 1892.

                       "Recommendation["]
                            To the
                    Shonees & Ther Chiefs.

Republic of Texas   }   To the Shonees & Chiefs.
County of
Liney,
Greengrass & } Chiefs,
    Pecon

    wee the undersigned Agents for the removal of Said Shonees from the Republic of Texas take much pleasure in recommending Said Shownees to all whom they may meet with as good Indians wee have Lived neighbors to Said Shownees for a Number of Years they have always conducted themselves well and have gained the frendship of all who new them they have always been Peacible & quiet ther removal from the Country is not for any thing that they have done it is ther own choice they could of remained had they of wished

    wee can futher say that wee have spent the last two Months with Said Shonees that A More frendly and kind People we never have been with ther good conduct and kind treatment to us in removing from the country has been such as wee never can forget.

    wee wer two off the five that valued ther improvements wee found ther Houses fences and other improvements equal to that of any People we can say of them that they ar a farming People and Live entirely by ther Labor

    Done at the Crosing of Redriver Lains Port Oct. 5th 1839
        Moses L. Patton
                Alexander Sonder
                    Agents for ther removal.

[*moved entry from bottom of page 19 for chronological order*]

[*1/1/1893*] [*date written vertically in the left margin on page 19*]

    Nelamwi, a brother-in-law (said by a woman when a man has married her sister, or by a man when a woman has married his brother).

    Netikwi, sister-in-law, literally, my sister-in-law (said by a woman of another woman who has married her brother, or by a man when another man has married his sister).

[*page 21*] Begun *3/5/1893 First Day of the week, At night.*

                Tapalamewati Homimitomawa.
Nobani, mankwitoke eapeinne, skiti wewaspanitota kebowa. Kokemiwewa wepeaike. Ealalatiwise wenakitotake hosketim[. . .]kwa pise kili mankwitoke easenakitotake, Melenika henoke kisakeke nekisakekewe tikwhinemani; chena hilhimiwenika nepemeliwewannanni pise kili eise hilhimiwikece pape[me]lotiweimakece. Chenatake nkeswasepa witi skiti setakaika wisepemeliweika, pieakwi kewipinashepa macike hoce.
                Amen.
Neke waske Nakimocke, Easewikotimwice.
    Netapwasa ~~ease hipece~~ weike Maeatalamewati, Kobanni wekoce wawesekitoweti, Maeatalatiki, hene mankwitwe chena eomi hisaske; chena netapwasa weike Jesus Christe, nelene pahi hokwebile, Tapalamenwati; ~~wahokwesanakoti~~ wahobeti Babubieikebetice Cacilikommi~~le~~; wahokwebenakoti Malwe easenoboti papwipiwetakti; kakesanichobi ealibimece Ponshens Pilate, babikhoboti mtakoke, nanapaki, chena wabapsemoboti. Napake tihipewice nsepilitsenwi; eanbokowike honski napake tihipewice hoce; mankwitoke sekkwetsenwi, pamikapece Maeatlamalikwake mieiwenkeke watikwihoce; hene wahoce peeawi chebani wesi tapowilita tatawolece chena mamace hisenalece. Netapwasa weike Babubieikebeti Cacilikomi ~~weike~~ Babubieikeike, Mamiwiskike, eise

pakekilolatewice babubieikebecke, wisise honskinotake chebani keweibamani, chena wise kokwalikwise laniwaweikwa.

X X X

Eise Mimitomake Wise Pwi Webaneke.

Maeatalamewaine, koseliwilalapa ease peacepibanimiweika eomi tikwhi wisimeceika, Koseliwilalapa noke eahowase wipinameika, Npanisenika wise tapwatimika ealicemoboce kekwebi Jesus Christe. Amen.

X X X X X

Nale Matibwe Kiliwewani.

1. Take kaponike kotikike Minatoke ealibimei.
2. Take kahos[. . .] ~~wise~~ sekoni keshowani, weli wease keshowa weahe mankwitoke spamake weli hosketimkwa sikeke, weli napela eatake hisaskeke, take kenimitomimike [page 22] noki take kehoseliwilike. Neli Tapalamewai Maeatalamewai wesekitowei, nekeiwawe, homicelaniwawewanwi wahobecke honecinwihe nelilipbetiwike, pilohe miwenbanna chena miwe neawana tihikihalahosawice neke sase kalawecke; chena ketamenikwalamatewa nemimelike neke eaeikwalamecke chena ninakitikke nekiliwewani pilohe matibana tapawatbana tihinkihalahosawice.
3. Take naloce kamima howebowa Tapalamakki Maeatalamewati; ksika heni Tapalamewati Maeatalam[ew]ati miti papwi pemeli weti hotilikemile nale weabile naloce wawetiki howebowa Tapalamakoce.
4. Mkiwalatino wise bubieikelotimine hene hilwikisewe kesake~~ke~~. Nakotwiboko kapipakitabe, chena kamaceloti cieike hene kepakitabewa, Pieakwi hene miwe neswibokonike hene hotilwikisewekesakeme Tapalamaki Meatalamewati: hena kisakeke take weahe kasepakitabe, heli chena kekwebi, chena ketinabi, chena helane eakiloliti chena hekwawi eahiloliti, kemakenwhami, chena heni papeiti[. . .] peteka watikwihoce kesskwitama. Ksika nakobwiboko peteka hese homacto Tapalamewati hene mankwitwe chena hene hisaske, chena hene kcekine, chena cikeweahe netise eatake, chena hilwikise hena eamiwe neswibokonikeke; henehoce howalitoti Tapalamewati hene hilwikisewe kesake, chena hobubieikeloti.
5. Mselalame kobi chena kekei, wise pece laniwaweine ~~hosketimkwa~~ hene hisaskkeke mamelake Tapalamaki Maeatatamewati.
6. Take kaninsewa.
7. Take kanikiwohhi weabi.
8. Take kakemota.
9. Take [ewi]hicemowa kehitoti wipatbikhakoce milikwahe wasekilaki.
10. Take skiti kalalatimiwi milikwihe wasekilaki eatice, take skiti kalalatimiwi wewile, noke eahilolice helanele, noke eahilolice hekwale, noke hotiksanemile, noke hokakinosamile, noke cikeweahe paponike.

Cieike hotieahe homanahihe. He drank up all his stock (horses or cattle or both, or hogs). That is, he sold his stock for whiskey and drank up all the whiskey and this is called drinking up one's stock. Cieike, an adjective limiting hotieahe. It is
[*continued in the middle of page 24*]
[*middle of page 24, continued from page 22*] pronounced Chà'-yà-kē. Ch is like ch in the word chamber. The accent is one [on] the first syllable. Hotieahe is a noun, meaning his stock (horses, cattle, hogs, chickens, etc. etc). Pronounced Heō-tī'-yā-hē. Accent on the second syllable, which is tī, i is long, as in ice, fine, mire, or thrive. It can be pronounced in Shanwee Heō-tà'-yā-hē, without any inconvenience in understanding. Heomanakihe is a verb, and it means he drank them up. It is the past tense, and is pronounced Heō-mĕ'-nĕ-hà-hē. The accent is on the second syllable.
Sikwaike (Sikwike), the property of a deceased person, which falls to his relatives, pronounced Sà'-kwàk-kē. Accent on the first syllable.

Heotatiniwi eokomi. They say this of it. Pronounced, hō-tĕ'-tà-nà-wà, said this of it, eokomi, these. Pronounced Yō'-kō-mà.Hene

Hene wakhe easewikomece easenhilwiki nhilwalamiwice, This indeed it is known that they are really relatives, (That is, relatives by blood).

[*original page 23*] Katekesime. *3/21/1893*,
~~Lasine I~~. Lasine I.
Wace Maeatalamoboce Helane.
Nitosapea, 1. Nabiwa homaeatalati eomi ealakkwikimakke? Heeowa 1. Heni Maeatalamewati Minato homaeatalati eomi ealakkwikimakke.
Nitosawa 2. Nabiwa heni Maeatalamewati Minato?
Heeowa 2. Heni Maeatalamewati Minato maeatalatiki mankwitwe chena hisaske, chena cikeweahe.
Nitosawa 3. Nabiwa helane?
Heeowa 3. Helane maeatalamoboti waweeiobemeti chena Cacilikomile paponiti weike, chena nse[ba]ikobe easenikohece maeatalamakoce.
Nitosawa 4. Nahewa koce maeatalamakwi Maeatalamewati?
Heeowa 4. Wise wikomike noce maeatalamakwi, cehna wise hikwalamike, chena wise, pabatiwike eomi hosketimkwa tise, chena wise kokwalikwise waselisimimoei chebani Weli tihipece mankwitoke.
Nitosawa 5. Nahewa keseliwepa wise wipinastoeikkwa kecacilikomanni?
Heeowa 5. Wise wipinastoeikkwa kecacilikomani kemimitomimipa heni Maeatalamewati, ketapwatiwipa, kehikiwipimipa, kehikwalamipa wekoce.
Nitosawa 6. Nahewa kesewitotipa hene witapwatimikwa?

Heeowa 6. Hene Mseeal[i]ekitake ~~hoce~~ kahoce wikotipa hene witapwatimikwa; ksika hokiliwewani Maeatalamalikwa netise hiwekita, sakimeki ealiwekawice waselaneke weli eahilolice Maeatalamewati mimosekes kwalece.

Lasine II

Nitosawa 1. Nahewatwi heni Minato Maeatalamewati.
Heeowa 1. Cacilikomi heni Minato Maeatalamewati.
Nitosawa 2. Hilikwi hitawe waske tilaniwawece heni Minato?
Heeowa 2. Miti likwi hena waske tilaniwawece; kokwalikwas hoce hipewi, chena kokwalikwise wahipewi.
Nitosawa 3. Tinewa tise hipewi heni Minato?
Heeowa 3. Heni Minato mabbeka hipewi.
Nitosawa 4. Mabeka hipeta hisekali keninawipa?
Heeowa 4. Miti keninawipa, ksika naeabiwe caciliko[. . .] [c]hena miti eikitiwe nanobo hoskesako howotaka.
[page 24, top of page] Nitosawa 5. Hi keninokoni Maeatalamalikwa?
Heeowa 5. Ho keninokoni chena kekcetiwalamakoni.
Nitosawa 6. Hi cikeweahe howikoti heni Maeatalamewati?
Heeowa 6. Cikeweahe howikoti heni Maeatalamewati; kewikomakoni easetahaeikwa moce, chena howikoti eieolikwa chena eiseliweeikwa.

[middle of page 24 moved from here to follow page 22]

[bottom of page 24] Texts on Repentance translated into Shawnee 4/12/1893.
Mat. 3:2. Chena hewi; Kotikesetahako; ksika milikwihe peaei hene hokemiwewa menkwitoke wisihomoike.
Mark 1:15 Chena hewi, hene likwi macepeaei chena hene hokemiwewa Maeatalamewati milikwihe peaei; kotisesetahako chena hetapwatiniwi hene nepeaticemowa wahowasike.
Mark 6:12 Chena pimbake pipekekilosewake wise kotikeseta[. . .]hawice helaneke.
Luke13:3. Miti, kewetimolapwi, pwi kotikesetahaeakwi, cieike hene eiski wisenapaeakwa.
Luke 16:30. Miti, Nobahe Abrahame; pieakwi weabi nhita tikipewice napake tihipewice hoce, kotikewasetahake,
Luke 17:3. Kcetiwalatimoke keeiwi. Pemelotiwake kecaneni, [. . .]kakwiltali, chena kotikesetahati, Kahilhimiwi.

[page 25]
Copied from the "Church Manual" by J. M. Pendleton, D.D.
p.172 "III <u>Marriage Ceremony</u>.

Marriage is an institution of Divine appointment, given in wisdom and kindness, to increase human happiness and to support social order.

In the Bible, which should be the lamp to your path in every relation, you will find the directions needed in this.

In token of your decided choice of each other as patners for life, you _____ _____ and _____ _____ will please to unite your right hands.

(Joining of hands.)

Do you solemnly promise, before Almighty God and these witnesses, to receive each other as husband and wife, agreeing to perform the duties growing out of the relation, pledging yourselves to love each other, and to make every reasonable exertion to promote each other's happiness until the union into which you are now entering is dissolved by death?

(<u>When a ring is employed the following can be used</u>. In confirmation of these vows, you will please give and receive this ring, as an emblem and pledge of the pure and enduring love you have promised to cherish for each other.)

In view of the promises thus made, I do now, by virtue of the authority vested in me, as a minister of the gospel, pronounce you husband and wife, henceforth in interest and destiny, as in affection, <u>One</u>. And what God hath joined together, let not man put asunder."

Copied from the same book ["*Church Manual*" by J. M. Pendleton, D.D.] page 65 etc.

"I. Of Baptism

In answer to the oft-repeated question, What is baptism? it may be said, Baptism is the immersion in water, by a proper administrator, of a believer in Christ, in the name of the Father, and of the Son, and of the Holy Spirit. Immersion is so exclusively the baptismal act, that without it there is no baptism; a believer in Christ is so exclusively the subject of baptism, that without such a subject there is no baptism. In these two statements all Baptists will agree. As to a proper administrator there may be some difference of opinion. By a proper administrator, in the foregoing definition, is meant a person who has received from a church authority to baptize. While validity of an ordinance is not affected by every irregularity in its administration, it does seem incredible that baptism should be valid in the absence of the church authority. [*page 26*] What other authority is there? Will any one say, the authority of Christ. The supreme authority is undoubtedly his; but does he confer on men the right to baptize, <u>through his churches,</u> or, <u>independently of his churches?</u> One of these views must be taken, and he who takes the latter will have to set aside the order of the gospel. But it does not comport with the plan of this little work to elaborate this point.

1. <u>Act</u> of <u>Baptism</u>.— That immersion alone is the baptismal act may be shown by the following considerations:

1. <u>Greek Lexicons give immerse</u>, <u>dip</u>, or <u>plunge</u>, <u>as the primary and ordinary meaning of baptizo</u>.

Here it is proper to state that <u>baptizo</u> and <u>baptisma</u> are, in the Common Verson of the Scriptures, <u>Anglicized</u>, but not translated. By this it is only meant that their termination is made to correspond with the termination of English words. In <u>baptizo</u> the final letter is changed into <u>e</u>, and in <u>baptisma</u> the last letter is dropped altogether. To make this matter of <u>Anglicism</u> plain, it only necessary to say, that if <u>rantizo</u> had been subjected to the same treatment by King James' translation which <u>baptizo</u> received at their hands, we would have <u>rantize</u> in the New Testament, whenever we now have <u>sprinkle</u>. King James virtually forbade the translation of baptize and <u>baptism</u>. This has been sometimes denied, but it susceptible of conclusive proof. The King's third instruction to his translators reads thus: "The old <u>ecclesiastical words</u> to be kept, as the word <u>church</u> not to be translated <u>congregation</u>." It is absurd to say that this rule had exclusive reference to the term "church"; for this term is manifestly given as a specimen of "old ecclesiastical words." And why should the plurality of idea be conveyed by phrase "ecclesiastical words," if the rule had respect to only <u>one</u> <u>word</u>? The question then is: Are <u>baptism</u> and <u>baptize</u> "old ecclesiastical words"? They were <u>words</u> when the Bible was translated, or they would not be found in it. They had been by church historians and by writers on ecclesiastical law, and were therefore <u>ecclesiastical</u>. They have been in use a long time, and were consequently <u>old</u>. They were "old ecclesiastical words." Such words the King commanded "to be kept"—"not translated." It is worthy to remark, too, that the Bishop of London, at the King's instance [insistence?], wrote to translators, reminding them that his majesty "wished his <u>third</u> and <u>fourth</u> rule to be specially observed. This circumstance must have called special attention to the rule under consideration. In view of these facts it may surely be said, that the translators knew what were "old ecclesiastical words." Let their testimony then be adduced. In their "Preface to the Reader," [*page 27*] they say they had "on the one side, avoided the scrupulosity of the Puritans, who left the <u>old ecclesiastical words</u>, and betook them to other, as when they put <u>washing</u> for <u>baptism</u>, and <u>congregation</u> for <u>church</u>; and on the other hand had shunned the obscurity of the Papists." Is not this enough? Here there is not only an admission that baptism was an old ecclesiastical word, but this admission is made by the translators themselves—made most carefully—for it was made in condemnation of the Puritans, and commendation of themselves.

The Kings fourth rule was this: "When any word hath divers significations, that to be kept which hath been most commonly used by the most eminent Fathers, being agreeable to the propriety of the place and the analogy of faith." Baptizo is not a word of divers significations; but if it was, the King's translators, if they had rendered it at all, would have been compelled by the fourth rule to render it immerse; for every man of ordinary intelligence knows it was "most commonly used" in this sense "by the most Eminent Fathers." But it wll be perceived that the King's third rule renders inoperative the fourth, so far as old ecclesiastical words are concerned. Whether such words have one meaning or a thousand meanings, they are "to be kept"—"not translated." The translators were not at liberty to refer to the signification immemorially attached by the Greeks to baptize—a signification which received the cordial endorsement of "the most eminent Fathers." They might have examined the endorsement if the royal decree had not said, "hitherto, but no farther,"—"the old ecclesiastical words to be kept."

[*page 28*]

New Testament Teaching in Relation to The Lord's Supper and the Lord's Day

The first day of the week is never referred to in the New Testament except between the First Day of Unleavened Bread and Pentecost. Mat. 28:1; Mark 16:2, 9; Luke 24:1; John 20:1, 19; Acts 20:7; 1 Cor. 16:2. In each of these passages the context made it plain that the time was between the First Day of Unleavened Bread and Pentecost. Thus in Acts 20:16 we are told that Paul "hasted, if it were possible for him, to be at Jerusalem the day of Pentecost." In the First Corinthians 16:8 Paul says, "But I will tarry at Ephesus until Pentecost." The Lord's Day is only mentioned in one single passage Rev. 1:10, "I was in the Spirit on the Lord's Day, and heard behind me a great voice, as of a trumpet." The Lord's Supper is likewise mentioned in a single passage, 1 Cor. 11:20, "When ye come together therefore into one place, this is not to eat the Lord's Supper."

From 1 Cor. 16:1, 2, 3, the following things appear to be clearly made out:—
1. The curch in Corinth and the churches of Galatia were ordered to take up a collection of money or property "for the saints" at Jerusalem, on the first day of the week.

2. Paul does not command them to assemble on that day, but commands them to take up a collection when they did assemble on that day.
3. Hence they assembled on that day for some other purpose than that of taking a collection of money or property.
4. The churches of Galatia were instructed to take up a like collection of money or property "for the poor saints which are at Jerusalem." Rom. 15:26.
5. The churches of Galatia meet on the first day of the week for some other reason other than for taking up a collection. For what purpose did they meet? Paul assured that they met on that day; consequently he simply orders them to take up a collection: he does not order them to meet on that day.
6. All this was between the First day of Unleavened Bread and Pentecost.

  From Acts 20:7 we learn:
1. Paul and the others sailed from Philippi "after the days of unleavened bread."
2. In five days they came to Troas.
3. They abode there seven days.
4. They met at the church the first day of the week.
5. They met for the purpose of "breaking bread."
6. They met quite late in the evening, for Paul took occasion from their being together to preach to them and he prolonged his speech until mid-night. [*page 29*]
7. [*journal has number 6*] They did not come together to hear Paul preach or hear any one preach, but "to break bread"; Paul took advantage of this being together to preach unto them, since it was the last time he would ever see them together, and Paul would depart for Jerusalem on the morrow, and he was in a hurry to be at Jerusalem the day of Pentecost.

  Corollary 1.—In the New testament times, at least the following churches met on the first day of the week "to break bread" or, "to eat the Lord's Supper";
  1. The church in Corinth.
  2. The churches of Galatia.
  3. The church in Troas.
That "to break bread" is "to eat the Lord's Supper["] is admitted by all may be seen from 1 Cor. 11:20:34.

In 1 Cor. 11: 28, 33, 34, the following appear quite clear:—
1. They had met before to eat the Lord's Supper, but had failed to do so. Instead of eating the Lord's Supper, some ate first, and ate up every thing, and put those who were poor to shame, who had brought noting to eat along. This was eating a supper of their own, not the supper of the Lord.

2. They were told to wait for one another when they should come together to eat again, which seems that they would again meat [meet] to break bread the next first day.
3. <u>In fact, the fact of meeting together to eat the Lord's Supper seems to have taken place every first day of the week between the First Day of Unleavened Bread and Pentecost</u>. That at these meetings whose sole purpose was to eat the Lord's supper, sermons were preached (Acts 20:7) or collections of money or property for charitable purposes tken up (1 Cor. 16:2).
4. We have no warrant for saying or believing, on Biblical authority, that these assemblies for eating the Lord's Supper ever took place except between the time of the First Day of Unleavened Bread and Pentecost.

From Rev. 1:10 we seem to learn:—
1. That the Lord's Day was a day well known to the saints in New Testament times, and so no explanatory remarks about it were necessary, and hence not given.
2. The expression "the Lord's Day" is specific, and either means a certain definite day in the year or in the week, between the time of the First Day of Unleavened Bread and Pentecost.
3. As the "Lord's Body" is a certain definite body, and the "Lord's Death" a certain definite death, and the "Lord's Cup" a certain definite cup and the Lord's Blood a certain definite blood; so the "Lord's Day["] would appear to be a certain definite day, namely, the day Christ rose form the dead: more exactly, the first First Day in every year immediately following the First Day [*page 30*] of Unleavened Bread. All these are connected and related.
   1. The Lord's Supper. 1 Cor. 11:20 Κυριccκόv ~~Selttvov~~
   2. The Lord's Death. 1 Cor. 11:26 ~~θcίvatov toû~~ Κυρίου
   3. The Cup of the Lord. 1 Cor. 11:27 Κυρίου
   4. The Body of the Lord. 1 Cor. 11:27
   5. The Blood of the Lord 1 Cor. 11:27
   6. The Lord's Day. Rev. 1:10

As there is only one Lord's Supper, one Lord's Death, one Cup of the Lord, one Body of the Lord, one Blood of the Lord, so there seems, by Scripture, to be only one Lord's Day. The day Jesus rose from the dead was the First Day of the Week April 9th A.D. 30. This, then, is the first Lord's Day, and we have no warrant from Scripture for saying that any other day in that whole year A.D. 30 was the Lord's Day. If John wrote in Revelations in A.D. 95, as some assert, the Lord's Day he spoke of would be strictly April 9th A.D. 95; or, probably more accurately according to the mode of reckoning in that day the First Frist Day after the First Day of Unleavened Bread A.D. 95;

which would be on or about (using this last word with some little latitude) April 9th 1895.

There are six things above specially referred to the Lord Jesus. First what is called the Lord's Supper, which can not be any other supper than he ate Thursday night April 6th A.D. 30. This is strictly the Lord's Supper, and no other supper than this is the Lord's Supper. It is true, however, that the Lord's Supper was eaten at Corinth and elsewhere years after this date, but it was the same supper Jesus and his disciples ate April 6 A.D. 30.

Secondly, there can not by [sic] possibly be more than one Lord's death. "For in that he died, he died unto sin once; but in that he liveth, he liveth unto God." Rom. 6:10.

Thirdly, there can not be more than one cup of the Lord, namely, the cup he used Thursday night April 6th ~~189~~ A.D. 30; and although in the church in Corinth other cups were used and called the cup of the Lord, they simply were used in stead of that one cup by way of remembrance.

Fourthly, there was only one body of the Lord, which was crucified and laid in a sepulcher and rose again the third day. The bread used in Lord's Supper represents this body, but the bread is not the body nor is the bread changed into the body, but is used for the body by way of remembrance.

Fifthly, there is only one blood of the Lord, namely his own blood, for which wine is used in the Lord's supper. But the wine is not changed into the blood, but represents the blood by way of remembrance.

Now we have seen that thee was strictly but one Lord's Supper, and although other suppers, for example, those in the church at Corinth were called Lord's Suppers, yet only so by way of remembrance [page 31] of that supper eaten Thursday night April 6th A.D. 30.

There can only be one Lord's death but yet this death was "showed forth" by eating the bread and drinking the wine, in the Lord's Supper. A "showing forth" or commemoration of this death occurred at least once every year; yet only one Lord's death ever occurred.

The cup Jesus used at the last supper is called "the cup." Luke 22:17, 20; Mat. 26:27; Mark 14:23. So, on Scripture authority, we are warranted in saying that there was only one cup of the Lord. Though other cups were called cups of the Lord, it was because they were used in place of this cup, or to represent this cup.

There was only one body of the Lord, represented in the supper by bread.

There was only one blood of the Lord, represented in the supper by wine.

So it would seem there was only one Lord's day, namely Sunday April 9th A.D. 30, but as St. John says he was in the spirit on the Lord's Day in about A.D. 95, it must have been the anniversary of Sunday ~~A.D. 30~~ April 9th A.D. 30, or some first day of the week commemorative of that day April 9th A.D. 30. St. John speaks of the Lord's day as of a day so well-known as not to need any explanation as to what day it was. It is certain that on a first day between the days of Unleavened Bread and Pentecost Paul and the Christians at Troas brake bread, or ate the Lord's supper. In the whole New Testament we learn of no Lord's Supper eaten except between the First Day of Unleavened Bread and Pentecost. Hence we conclude that we have no Scripture warrant for calling any first day of the week the Lord's Day except within the time specified above. Although there is Scripture warrant for observing the first day of Unleavened bread and Pentecost, yet we have no Scripture authority for observing the first day of the week outside of that time.

The first day of the week was observed, then, within those fifty days. There is no doubt it was a day of religious service, as preaching or singing a hymn or taking up collections for religious purposes took place at these assemblies as well as the eating the Lord's Supper.

In 2 Peter 2:13 some feasted with the Christians who were deluded with sins. Jude 12th verse speaks of feasts of charity, which are indeed all one with the Lord's Supper mentioned elsewhere in the New Testament. Here is no hint at all about the time these feasts were held, but from other Scriptures we are not afraid to say between the first day of Unleavened Bread and Pentecost.

It is true that on the day of Pentecost and for awhile after the apostles break bread together and had all things in common. They break bread from house to house, eating their meat or food with gladness and singleness of heart. This is to be understood of their ordinary eating for refreshment during that great revival of the true religion, which sanctified even their every day meals, since in those days they were wholly, entirely, and in a most extra ordinary manner given to the Lord and his work. Now in the Lord's Supper there is no such thing as breaking bread from house to [page 32] house. For the church came into one place and ate it together. From 1 Cor. 11:34 and 1 Cor. 16:2 it is clear Paul expected soon to be at Corinth, but after they had met on the first day of the week and had eaten the Lord's Supper. It seems reasonable to believe they had eaten the Supper shortly before he wrote, for he censures them for their scandalous behavior therein. And it seems equally sure that he knew they would shortly met again on another first and eat the supper, for he tells them to wait for one another when they came together to eat, and he told them he would set in order the other things relating to the Supper when he came to them.

From Acts 11:30 and context we learn as follows:
1. That Agabus one of the prophets from Jerusalem prophesied at Antioch that there would be a great famine. 2. In consequence of this the Christians decreed in their hearts to send relief to those Christians who lived in Judea. 3. That Barnabas and Saul carried this relief to Jerusalem. Now we see how Paul collected his part of this free will offering, but we are not told how Barnabas did his.

[entries for August 26 and 27, 1897, removed from original page 32 and placed in chronological order]

Chapter 6

Interpreting at the Indian Missions
February 2, 1895—October 2, 1895

Shawnee's third journal contains no daily entries between April 1893 and January 1895. During that time, Shawnee befriended some of the new settlers in Oklahoma Territory. In 1893 he began improving his tribal allotment and renting pieces of it out as tenant farms to some of the new settlers. He also reviewed the Oklahoma territorial education statutes to see how he could apply them to himself. In 1895 Shawnee lived with his father in Shawneetown. He started writing in his journal again on February 2, 1895. Between that time and October 2, 1895, Shawnee recorded his translation of Cicero's *Liber Primus* in his journal, his fifteen-page essay on "The Lord's Day and the Lord's Supper," and his essay on "Recent History of the Shawnee Indians." Otherwise, during that time, he continually recorded his daily activities in his journal.

Between February 1895 and September 1895, Shawnee interpreted at the Indian schools and worshiped at the Absentee Shawnee, Kickapoo, and Iowa missions established by the Quakers. He worked with Quakers Dr. Hartley, Lina Lunt, Emma Newsom, Elizabeth Test, Mrs. Kirk, and others at the missions, and at times taught, interpreted, enjoyed meals, and was an overnight guest at them. Much of the time he worked with Thomas Wildcat Alford in teaching and interpreting. Shawnee and Alford agreed to translate the Gospels into Absentee Shawnee, a task that Shawnee was already pursuing. In September 1895, Shawnee accompanied Quaker Mary C. Williams to Big Jim's Crossing on a recruiting mission for the Absentee Shawnee School, providing a clue as to how the Quakers sought new students.

Shawnee lived in a climate of neighborly cooperation. At the time, most Native people in the area were remote from each other across the prairie, connected with inadequate roads. Transportation consisted mostly of horses and wagons. Many times people walked to their destinations. They visited each other, ate meals together, and were overnight guests in each other's homes. They assisted each other in improving their farms. The

Absentee Shawnees rented their farms out to both black and white tenant farmers. Shawnee befriended all races and cultures. He subscribed to the *New York Independent* and the *Christian Nation* and remained studious. He read the U.S. Constitution with regard to the plight of blacks before passage of the Thirteenth, Fourteenth, and Fifteenth Amendments. He also read the Oklahoma Organic Act, statutes of Oklahoma, and other documents.

Shawnee's tenant farms did not generate enough income for him to make a living from them alone; therefore, he worked at various jobs to earn money. Some paid; some did not. He tanned deer skins on his father's farm. He assisted John Whitehead, a Potawatomi, in building a road. He interpreted for Absentee Shawnee chiefs Big Jim and White Turkey, government pension examiners, and ordinary Indian citizens. He assisted in the survey of the Kickapoo reservation for the 1895 land run. Finally, after spending several months seeking a position as a schoolteacher, he was hired to teach at Smith School, a black school near Choctaw City, where Ella Dunjee, Reverend Dunjee's oldest daughter, had taught the previous year.

Shortly before Shawnee left for Choctaw City, he had two notable experiences. He visited his best friend, David Alford, and found Big Jim, who was David's uncle, visiting there. After leaving David's home, Shawnee and Big Jim were both overnight guests at Shawnee Sr.'s home. These interpersonal relationships demonstrate the close-knit ties of the traditional and progressive members of the Absentee Shawnee tribe. Big Jim led the traditional group whereas David owned property and was considered to be progressive. The second noteworthy experience came after Shawnee's brother Dudley realized Shawnee was going to teach at a black school. Dudley advised his sibling to leave "colored" girls alone. Shawnee likened the racial attitudes of his brothers to those of some southern whites of that time.

[page 33, top of page] [here the author translates Cicero's Liber Primus . . .]

    Translation by William E. Shawnee of Cicero's Liber Primus de Officiis, I

begun Feb. 2nd 1895

1. Although thou, Marcus my son, ought to abound in the precepts and principles of philosophy, hearing now a year Cratippum and that at Athens, on account of the ~~great~~ highest authority both of the teacher and of the city, the one of whom is able to increase thee in knowledge, and the other in examples, yet, as I myself to my own benefit have always joined Latin words with Greek words not only in philosophy, but also in oratory I ~~h~~ done so, I have determined that thou oughtest to do the same, that thou mayest be equally able in the power of either kind of speech. To which thing indeed we, as we appear, have brought great aid to our men, that they may judge themselves not only as uncultivated in Greek literature, but also having been slightly taught they may judge themselves to have attained both unto speaking and unto judging. 2. On account of which thing thou wilt learn indeed from the chief of this age of philosophers, and thou wilt learn as long as thou wishest, so long indeed as thou oughtest to wish, thou will not regret however far thou mayest proceed.

Sunday Feb. 10th 1895

    I rode horseback from William Shawnee's to the Kickapoo Mission. Lina B. Lunt and Lizzie Test were glad to see me. Lina said that Nettie Haworth was married Christmas day 1894. We all had prayer Sunday evening. The children sang songs and repeated from memory Scripture verses and even chapters like the 1st and 23rd Psalms. Nă-thàh-pē-hah, Wēskōpăthōkwă, Nănăsēothăkwă, Kătēkwă, Pămàh-hō-kōkwă, Flaurice, Kā-chē-tīē-sēk-kwă, Mary Mardock Jr., and others were present. Nathahpehah is twelve years old, so at least she said. She is a beautiful little girl. All the children knelt down for prayers.

    The next day Monday Feb. 11th 1895 I visited the children in school until noon. Nathahpehah reads in the Second reader.

[*Bottom of original page 33 moved to date Aug. 27th, 1897.*]

[*page 34*]

    William Shawnee's Testimony.

Jack Girty, Isaac Girty, and Simon Girty were brothers. Of these Simon Girty died first, and was buried on the north bank of the Arkansas River. Jack Girty's father~~'s~~ ~~name~~ was a colored man, and Wiliam Shawnee used to live with him. Jack Girty was a good man, but he loved whiskey too much. He had plenty of stock, and used to give many a poor Cherokee something to eat. I do not know any thing about Buck Girty. William Shawnee had a sister named Nancy. Nancy lived with her mother near Fort Smith somewhere. Katie and Louisa were the other two sisters of William Shawnee. The order of age:—1. Jacob, William, George, Nancy, Katie, and Louisa. [*continued on top of page 35*]

[*page 35, top of page*] Hester Chisholm's Testimony, now married to William Cockran.
"Katie is Hester Chisholm's mother's name. Hester was brought up at Webber's Falls, Che-làh-ó'-sàh was one aunt's name; was married to William Chisholm before the war. Hester can talk both Cherokee and English. Hester saw William Shawnee first at Shawneetown. Her mother was half Cherokee. Jesse Chisholm was the father of William Chisholm who had Hester for a wife. William Chisholm went to Texas and Hester went to Kansas with the Shawnees in 1860. She was about eighteen years old at the time. John Bottle [Butler?] was Hester's father's name. John was a full blooded Cherokee. Caroline Chisholm was the daughter of William Chisholm and Hester Chisolm. Lousia is the mother of Millie Chisholm and William Chisholm is her father. Louisa is a colored
woman.

March 29th 1895 Friday. [*middle of original page 34*]
    Kàh-sē-lĕ'-thàh, Pàw-wàt-sē, and Mrs. John Esparney were guests here at William Shawnee's last night and this morning.

                    Cinda Emma Spybuck.
On the way back from the parsonage, where George and I were talking to Mrs. Ella Hartley, I met Mrs. Rachel Kirk and Mrs. Emma Coolie at the corner. Miss Coolie said that she departed from this country Nov. 7th 1887; that she and Cinda Deer went to see Mamie and Cinda Emma in June 1887; that at that time they named the baby Cinda Emma Spybuck; that in June 1887 Cinda Emma was perhaps a month old. According to this Cinda Emma Spybuck was born May 1887. She will be eight years old May 1895.
    Miss Coolie is a heavy-set full-faced woman, and she looks like a good woman. She is a member of the Society of Friends. She must be a guest at Mrs. Kirk's at present. Mrs. Ella Hartley told me that Mrs. Kirk had gone over to Mrs. Bourbonnais' after some milk; she did not tell me, however, that Miss Coolie was along with her. I guess Mrs. Hartley did not know that I was acquainted with Miss Coolie.
    As I came back from school Nov. 25th 1887, and as Miss Coolie left this country Nov. 7th 1887, she was gone 18 days before I arrived. I heard of her, however. I heard she resided

in Kansas City. I met her for the first time at church Sunday night March 24th 1895, where she was introduced to me by Mrs. Kirk. She said, then, that she was acquainted with Walter and George [*William E. Shawnee's brothers*].

This night March 29th 1895 appears to be a stormy night. The folks have all left for the cellar. I am here alone. The wind has arisen, and the rain has begun to patter upon the roof. We may receive a good shower from the hand of the Lord God tonight. [*continued on middle of page 35*]

[*page 35, middle of page, continued from page 34*] Many people have been complaining of dry weather and the roads have been very dusty. But I do not believe that the Lord will send a hurricane along with this shower. The wind is not blowing yet as hard as we have known it to blow. This house has stood many a strong wind. It does seem that the wind blows stronger these last few years, and yet it may not be so. We, that is, George Shawnee and I, went to prayer meeting this evening. But on account of a supposed case of small-pox over among the railroad hands at Shawnee, the Mission authorities (Miss Williams) were afraid to let the children come. On which account some body concluded there would be no prayer-meeting.

[*original pages 35-49 removed to 1897 for chronological order*]

[*page 50*]

The Lord's Day and the Lord's Supper.

William E. Shawnee.

As the Lord's Day is mentioned by name in only a single ~~example~~ passage in the New Testament, namely, Rev. 1:10; so also is the Lord's Supper mentioned expressly by name in only a single passage, namely 1 Cor. 11:20. St. John says, Rev. 1:10 "I was in the Spirit on the Lord's Day, and heard behind me a great voice, as of a trumpet." The Apostle here mentions "the Lord's Day" as a day so well known to the "seven churches which are in Asia," as to need no explanation as to what day it was, and accordingly he does not say what day it was at all. But the only way we can know, on Divine authority, what day it was is from other passages in the same New Testament, and our God has not left us in the dark as to what day this "Lord's Day" was and is.

The Apostle Paul, 1 Cor. 11:20, says, "When ye come together therefore into one place, this is not to eat the Lord's supper." Then in verse 23 he gives an account of the last supper Jesus ate with his disciples, which is the Lord's supper.

Now for the proof as to what day the Lord's Day is. The Greek word Κυριακος is used only twice in the whole New Testament, in 1 Cor. 11:20, Rev. 1:10. ἐν τῇ Κυριακῇ ἡμέρᾳ, on the Lord's day; Κυριακὸν δεῖπνον φαγεῖν, to eat the Lord's Supper. As the word refers only to Christ in the expression, "to eat the Lord's Supper," meaning Christ's supper; so in the case of the expression, "the Lord's Day," this same word Κυριακῇ can refer only to Christ, and the Lord's Day means Christ's Day. So then we have Christ's Supper and Christ's Day, that is, the Lord's Supper and the Lord's Day.

There is another thing, we generally overlooked, from the fact that the Greek word Κυριακος is applied both to the Day and to the Supper. This proves that the Lord's Day and the Lord's Supper are connected together very closely. What was this connection between the Day and the Supper? Let us examine further into the New Testament:—

Acts 20:5-7 reads, "These going before tarried for us at Troas. And we sailed away from Philippi after the days of unleavened bread, and came unto them to Troas in five days; where we abode seven days. And upon the first day of the week when the disciples came together to break bread, Paul preached unto them, ready to depart on the morrow; and continued his speech until midnight."

As Christ arose from the dead on the first day of the week, this is the Lord's Day. It is said Christ arose from the dead Sunday April 9th A.D. 33. April 9th A.D 33 is then specially the Lord's Day, Christ's Day, the Resurrection Day. May we not believe that St. John on Patmos [*page 51*] was in the Spirit on the Sunday nearest to April 9th A.D. 96, in case St. John had those visions in that year, as many believe? But to return to the Scripture in Acts 20. Here at Troas Paul and the other Christians keep both the Lord's Day and the Lord's Supper. Let us inquire 1, ~~how they~~ why they met, and how they kept the Lord's day. Verse 7, And upon the first day of the week, when the disciples met together to break bread, Paul preached. Let us notice: 1. They did not meet for worship or to hear preaching. 2. They were not assembled ~~because it was a Sabbath day~~ except for a certain specific purpose. 3. They were met "<u>to break bread</u>," <u>to eat the Lord's Supper</u>. 4. They met very late in the evening, because Paul prolonged his sermon until mid-night. 5. Paul merely took advantage of their being together to preach his Farewell Sermon to them. 6. It was not on the Sunday on or about April 9th For Paul did not sail from Philippi until the days of unleavened bread were over. This was at least seven days, Ex. 12:19. They came to Troas in five days. They abode in Troas seven days, and the last day of these seven was Sunday. Here are at least 19 days, the third Sunday since the first day of the unleavened bread. 7. Although in a hurry to be at Jerusalem the day of Pentecost (Acts 20:16[)], yet Paul, arriving in Troas on Monday waited for Sunday to come, that he might be with the church of Troas in the breaking of bread, that is, in eating the Lord's supper on the Lord's Day with them.

Corallary: As Paul, though in a great hurry, waited from Monday seven days for Sunday to break bread, with the church, therefore the Lord's Supper in that day was eaten only on Sunday.

The first Lord's Supper was eaten the first day of the unleavened bread, Thursday April 6th A.D. 33. Christ rose from the dead the fourth day after the same first day of unleavened bread, Sunday April 9th A.D 33. The Christians at Troas about 25 years afterwards eat with Paul the Lord's Supper on the third Sunday after the first day of unleavened bread in that year.

Let us examine some more Scriptures. 1 Cor 16:1-2 reads as follows:— Now concerning the collection for the saints, as I have given order to the churches of Galatia, even so do ye. Upon the first day of the week let every one of you lay by him in store, as God hath prospered him that there be no gatherings when I come.

Let us observe what time of the year Paul ordered these things. Verse 8 of this same 16th chapter informs us. But I will tarry at Ephesus until Pentecost. So the time was near to Pentecost.

Corallary: We have no warrant from the New Testament that at either the Lord's day or the Lord's Supper were observed at all except between the days of unleavened bread and Pentecost. Christ himself ate the [page 52] first Lord's Supper ever eaten on the first day of unleavened bread, Luke 22:7, 15; Mat. 26:17, 20, 21; Mark 14:12, 17, 18. We have already seen that Paul and the Christians at Troas ate the Lord's Supper on the third Sunday after the first day of unleavened bread.

In 1 Cor 16: 1-2 Paul orders the churches of Corinth and Galatia to take up a collection for the poor saints at Jerusalem, in order that there might be no gatherings or ~~assemblies~~ collections when he came. Let us notice the following particulars:—

1. The church in Corinth and the churches of Galatia were ordered to take up a collection of money or property for the poor saints at Jerusalem.
2. Paul does not command them to assemble on that day, which day is the first day of the week or Sunday, but merely commands them to take up a collection when they did meet.
3. Hence the Corinthian Christians and likewise the Galatian Christians assembled on Sunday for some other purpose than collecting money for charitable purposes.

4. Paul and the Christians at Troas ate the Lord's Supper on Sunday and met on that day "to break bread," that is, met to celebrate the Lord's Supper.

Corallary: We have no warrant from the New Testament that Christians in New Testament times ever met on Sunday for any other purpose but to break bread, or eat the Lord's Supper.

5. Paul's language implies that these Christians met regularly on Sunday, at least at that time of year, which we agree to.

1 Cor. 11:20-34 reads: When ye come together therefore into one place, this is not to eat the Lord's supper. For in eating every one taketh before other his own supper; and one is hungry, and another is drunken. What? have ye not houses to eat and to drink in? or despise ye the church of God, and shame them that have not? What shall I say to you? Shall I praise you in this? I praise you not. For I have received of the Lord that which also I delivered unto you, that the Lord Jesus the same night in which he was betrayed took bread. And when he had given thanks, he break [brake] it, and said, Take, eat; this is my body which is broken for you; this do in remembrance of me. After the same manner also he took the cup, when he had supped, saying, This cup is the new testament in my blood: this do ye, as oft as ye eat it, in remembrance of me. For as often as ye eat this bread, and drink this cup, ye do shew the Lord's death till he comes. [*page 53*] 1 Cor. 11:33. Wherefore, my brethren, when ye come together to eat, tarry one for another. We may learn from this verse:—

1. That the Corinthian Christians would soon met [meet] again to eat the Lord's Supper.
2. A short time before they had met to eat the Lord's Supper, and could not eat the Lord's Supper, because they did not eat together.
3. They are told to wait for one another at the meeting, and so all eat together.
4. They are not told to meet together.
   Corallary. They meet ~~from~~ in consequence some established practice, and
5. From Chap. 16 we learn that they would meet the next Sunday.

Corallary. ~~Since~~ The Corinthian Church met on Sunday with regularity to eat the Lord's Supper. We have seen already that the church at Troas did the same.

Can we not see that the church of Corinth met on one Sunday to eat the Lord's Supper, and abused the privilege, and the next Sunday they met and all ate the supper together, taking up a collection for the poor saints at Jerusalem?

We can prove from Scripture Acts 20:7 that the church at Troas met on Sunday to break bread or eat the Lord's Supper. 1 Cor. 11:33 in connection with 1 Cor. 16:1-2 shows that the church of Corinth did likewise.

Remark. Neither in 1 Cor. 16:2, nor in 1 Cor. 11:33 nor in any other Scripture does the Apostle instruct the disciples to meet on the First day of the week, but he assumes their meeting regularly on that day "to eat" verse 1 Cor. 11:33, and tells them what to do ~~other ways~~ besides when so met. 1 Cor. 16:1-2.

The abuses in the eating of the Supper were:
1. Not eating it while all were present together.
2. ~~Getting~~ Drunkenness on the wine and permitting the late comers to go hungry.
3. Not discerning the Lord's body in the bread, nor his blood in the wine; i.e., not realizing the bread to be a figure or a symbol of the Lord's body, and not realizing the wine to be a figure or symbol of his blood.

The breaking of bread is mentioned as follows: Mat.14:19; Mat. 15:36; Mark 8:6; (Luke 22:19); (Mat. 26:26); (Mark 14:22); Mark 8:19; Luke 24:30; Acts 2:46; (Acts 20:7); (Acts 20:11); Acts 27:35; 1 Cor. 10:16; (1 Cor 11:24); Luke 24:25; Acts 2:42. In the following places alone does this breaking bread refer to the Lord's Supper, Luke 22:19; Mat. 26:26; Mark 14:22; Acts 20:7; Acts 20:11; 1 Cor. 11:24.

Corallary: The mere use of the words breaking bread can not refer necessarily to the Lord's Supper. It appears quite evident that Acts 2:42, 46 does not refer to the Lord's Supper, from the following considerations:—
1. The bread was broken from house to house (Acts 2:46), whereas the Lord's Supper is to be eaten in one place. 1 Cor. 11:20, 21, 33.
2. It is said they ate their <u>meat</u> from house to house, breaking bread. The word translated <u>meat</u> in the passage is also used in Mat. 3:4; Mat. 6:25; Mat. 10:10; Mat. 2[5:35]; [John] 4:8; Acts 9:19; Acts 14:17 (food) [*page 54*] Acts 27:33, 34, 36, 38; Heb. 5:12, 14; James 2:15 (daily food). The translations have rendered this word "food" in Acts 14:17; and "daily food" in James 2:15, and meat in most other places, and it invariably means daily food, food used to refresh the body, and is never used in the New Testament in connection with the Lord's Supper. Hence it can not refer to the Lord's Supper in Acts 2:46. The proof is overwhelming that the feasting in Acts Chapter 2 was for bodily refreshment, which is not the case with the Lord's Supper.

3. The feasting in Acts was daily, but this is not true of the Lord's Supper. This can not be eaten daily.
4. The context mentions many things which shows this fasting to be their common meals for bodily refreshment, such as,
   (a) They were every day with the Apostles, and so sooner or later must eat food.
   (b) They had all things in common, and these things were distributed as every one had need. Would they not need food even in the midst of all-day sermons and all-day prayers? Then, on Divine authority, the feasting mentioned in Acts, chapter 2, can not have any relation whatever to the Lord's Supper.

It is true that 2 Peter 2:13 and Jude 12 mention feasts of love or charity, which it is rather hard to classify. We may notice in regard to these feasts:
1. These feasts were feasts of the assembly or church, as very wicked persons are mentioned as feasting in the company.
2. They were love feasts.
3. They seem to have been feasts for increasing the love of Christians for one another.
4. As the only feast mentioned in the New Testament times in the Christian assemblies ~~were~~ is the Lord's Supper, there appears to be no reason to hesitate to identify these love feasts with the Lord's Supper. No feast can be held in the Christian assembly except a sacred feast, which the Lord's Supper certainly was.

The first day of the week is mentioned for the first time in Mat. 28:1. Let us inquire why this day is thus mentioned. In Mat. 27-62-66, we see that on Friday the Pharisees secured a guard from Pilate to make sure the sepulchre, until the third day. They sealed the stone therefore and set a watch. The Preparation Day which was the day Christ was buried was for the people to do their work, so as not to infringe on that high Sabbath Day. (Jno 19:31) On Friday the women beheld the sepulchre and how his body was laid, returned from the sepulchre hence, then went the same evening and purchased spices and ointments, but rested the Sabbath day, the next day. (Luke 23:55, 56.). The Sabbath was such a high day (Jno 19:31) that they did not go to the sepulchre on that day, not even for so harmless a purpose as to embalm the [body as] they were prepared to do. [page 55] O what a day of waiting this Sabbath day was to these women. The New Testament writers take evident pains particularly to state that the Sabbath was past when the women went to the sepulchre. (Mat. 28:1; Mat. 16:1; Luke 24:1; John 20:1)

They came expecting to find the body of Jesus in the sepulchre, and were astonished at not finding the body. (Mark 16: 3, 4; Luke 24: 1, 2, 3, 4; Jno. 20: 1, 2, 3, 4, 5, 6, 7, 8, 9). Also Jno. 20:11-13.

The one Lord's Day is the day Jesus rose from the dead. Let us see what the New Testament says happened on this day. No other day than this at present is considered. From Mat. 28 we learn:

1. Mary Magdalene and the other Mary came to see the sepulchre.
2. A great earth quake took place.
3. An angel from heaven descended and rolled away the stone from the door of the sepulchre.
4. The men guarding the sepulchre shook and became as dead men.
5. The angel of the Lord proclaimed to the women the resurrection of Jesus.
   Corallary. This angel is the first preacher of the resurrection.
6. This angel sends the women to proclaim this resurrection to the disciples.
7. Jesus himself met [meets] the women, and he salutes them, and tells the women to tell the disciples to go before him into Galilee.
8. The guards go to the city and report the mighty resurrection and all else besides.
9. The Sanhedrin meets and decides to bribe the soldiers to proclaim a lie in regard to the absence of the body of Jesus from the sepulchre. So the soldiers took the money, and published a lie to the world.

From Mark 16 we learn,

1. These women came to the sepulchre at the rising of the sun.
2. On the way they were at a loss how to roll away the heavy stone from the door of the sepulchre.
   Corallary. They did not know soldier guards were at the sepulchre and might be induced to kindly roll away the stone.
3. They found he stone rolled away.
4. They enter and see an angel.
5. The angel proclaims to them the resurrection of Jesus, and sends them to proclaim the same glad news to the disciples.
6. These women trembled and were amazed, ~~to~~ so great was the angel and so wonderful was his message, and so terrible his presence.
7. The disciples were still mourning and weeping. Can we not believe they mourned and wept all Sabbath long, and were still mourning that first day morning.
8. Mary Magdalene first saw Jesus alive.

9. He appeared to the two disciples going into the country.
10. The eleven would not bel[ieve the?] resurrection of Jesus.

[*page* 56] From Luke 24, we learn,
1. The women came to the sepulchre, bringing spices.
2. They found the stone rolled away.
3. They entered in and found not the body.
4. Two angels appeared and proclaimed to them his resurrection.
5. They went away and told all the disciples.
6. The disciples would not believe the resurrection, but still mourned and wept.
7. Peter went to the sepulchre.
8. Jesus and two disciples went to Emmaus.
9. Cleopas was astonished that every person in Jerusalem did not know of the crucifixion of Jesus.
10. Christ a preaches a whole sermon on Moses and the prophets to Cleopas and his companion.
11. Jesus made known to the two disciples at the evening meal.
12. Cleopas and his companion went back to Jerusalem that very hour night as it was, and found the eleven, and told them.
13. Meanwhile Peter himself had seen Jesus alive.
14. Jesus, following closely Cleopas and his companion, came also from Emmaus to Jerusalem, and appeared to the apostles.
15. The apostles were terrified and affrighted.

Corollary. Oh, what a wonderful day this first Lord's Day was. The laws of nature appear to have been temporarily suspended. Earthquakes, angels, sermons by angels, by women, by men, by Jesus himself, resurrections, mourning, wonder, fright, amazement, and revelations became the order of the first day of the week.

16. Jesus bids them handle him to see that he was himself.

John 20th declares:—
1. Mary Magdalene sees the stone taken away.
2. She goes back home and tells Peter and John.
3. Peter and John run to the sepulchre.
4. They see the napkin and linen clothes.
5. Mary staid at the sepulchre weeping, after Peter and John left.
6. She sees two angels.
7. She converses with the angels and they with her.
8. She sees Jesus himself.
9. She goes back home and proclaims the resurrection to the Apostles.
10. In the evening Jesus appears to the disciples.
11. Then were the disciples glad and rejoicing.

Here is a summary of what happened this first first day—first Lord's Day.

The first Lord's Day opened upon them mourning, weeping, disheartened, full of unbelief as to the possibility or probability of his resurrection, and afraid of the Jews. Mark 16:10; Luke 24:11, 25; John 20:19; Luke 24:21. At sunrise an angel came down from heaven, and rolled away the heavy stone from the door of the sepulchre, and the same time Jesus rose from the dead and a great earth-quake took place. The soldier guard[s] shook and became as dead men. Mary Magdalene, and other women came to the sepulchre, find the stone rolled away, enter the sepulchre, and find not the body of Jesus. Mourning, weeping, and perplexed at this (Luke 24:3, 4; Mark 16:10) angels proclaim his resurrection, and send these women home to proclaim the good news to the Apostles. Instead of believing, the Apostles ~~went~~ continued mourning and weeping as before (Mark 16:10), and reject the sermons of the women as idle tales (Luke 24:11). Christ appears to Mary Magdalene, Peter, Cleopas and his companion on the way to Emmaus), at night to all the Apostles except Thomas. Finally all the disciples are glad and rejoicing (John 20:20). While all this is going on, the soldier guards go into the city and reveal all the truth. The body of Jesus is not now in the sepulchre. Friends and enemies of Jesus agree in this. The chief priests and elders meet in council this very Lord's Day, and in secret sessions agree to bribe the soldiers to utter an horrible lie, to explain the absence of the body of Jesus from the sepulchre they had been guarding. The soldiers take the money, and proclaim to the world: "His disciples came by night and stole him away while we slept." Mat. 28:11-13.

<u>The Next First Day of the Week</u>, after the Resurrection.

Why should the Lord's Day be the first day in ~~the~~ every week? We can well understand why the Sabbath ~~should be~~ was the seventh day in every week. God worked six days, and rested the seventh (Genesis 2:2-3; Ex. 20:11.) We are commanded to initiate his example (Ex. 20:9, 10, 11) hence we work six days and rest the seventh. We do so to imitate and obey.

Now the case is different with the Lord's Day. There is nothing in the preceding six days to imitate, and nothing on the Lord's Day for us to imitate. There is nothing in the seven days ending with the Lord's day as a culminating point, to divide all subsequent time into period of seven days or weeks. The Lord's Day, on the contrary, is itself a part of a previous division. The Lord's Day can be proved, by Divine evidence, to be the first day of the week. But this week, of which it is the first day, is a week instituted in commemoration of creation week. God worked six days; we work six days. He rested the next day, the

seventh. We rested the next day after our six days of work. The model is exactly followed, according to c[. . .]. Let us see if the same is the case [*page 58*] with the Lord's Day. The seven days of which the Lord's Day is the last are these:
1. Monday, Preaching.
2. Tuesday, Preaching.
3. Wednesday, Jesus in Bethany, preaching and being anointed. Mat. 26:26.
4. Thursday, Jesus eats the Passover.
5. Friday Jesus crucified and buried.
6. Saturday, Jesus lay in the tomb.
7. Sunday, Jesus rose from the dead, and appears to mourning, discouraged, and unbelieving disciples.

Now let us look at the above. We can not imitate the work of the above seven days, so as to work from Monday to Saturday, and rest the last day. How, then, can we claim that the Lord's Day has come in place of the old seventh day of the week. We agree that the Lord's Day is a day whose glory should be extolled unto the heavens, and that it was observed in the New Testament churches. ~~Hereafter~~ Elsewhere we shall examine before God into the nature and character of the observance of the Lord's Day, as the same is revealed unto us in the New Testament. We can find no basis for dividing time into periods of seven days except we go back to the time when ~~the Lord~~ "in six days the Lord made heaven and earth, the sea, and all that in there is, and rested the seventh day." We can imitate no example so as to lead us to work six days and rest the seventh, unless we imitate the example of God during Creation Week. The Disciples mourned on the First Lord's Day, and their mourning was stopped after sunset, when joy and gladness set in right in the midst of the presence of Jesus. O happy day!

But let us notice the next Lord's Day.

Thomas was the only Apostle who had not seen Jesus on the Lord's Day. He heard the others rejoicing in Jesus and his resurrection ~~for right~~, but he was unbelieving. He told the other disciples that he must have ocular and digital demonstration of the resurrection before he would believe. Thomas was absent the First Lord's Day, and it appears he was a regular absentee. After eight days Thomas and the other disciples were within, the inference is that this was the first time they were all together. For why would the Scripture read true if they were together every day. "And after eight days again his disciples were within, and Thomas with them." John 20:26. Why would the word <u>again</u>, Greek πάλιγ, be used if they had all meet [met] together every day before this? Why would Jesus wait eight days to convince the skeptic? Why did he not appear to Thomas privately, as he did to Peter on the First Lord's Day, and why does the Scripture say "the disciples were within, and Thomas with them". No, Thomas had braved the testimony of Ten Apostles, not to count Cleopas and other disciples, and was yet a skeptic. He steeled his heart against his faith by saying: "Except I shall seek in his hands the print of the nails, and put my finger into the print of the nails, and thru[st] my hand into his side, I will [not] believe." Jesus had on the First [page 59] Lord's Day upbraided the Ten Apostles for their unbelief of the sermons of the [women?] and Peter. Mark 16:14. Now the Lord Jesus proposed to convince Thomas before the Ten Apostles and so reprove him for not believing the words of the Ten. Now The Eleven were not all together again until after eight days, which is on the next Lord's Day. The meeting all hinged on Thomas, he was convinced and reproved. Thomas was the pivot of this second meeting on the Lord's Day. Had Thomas not been there, Jesus had not appeared. All who wish to verify these remarks in the in regard to this meeting on the Second Lord's Day will please read Jno. 20:26-29. In these four verses, Thomas is the burden of each verse, and each verse has the word Thomas in it.

Corollary: The assembly on the Second Lord's Day was to convince and establish Thomas. It was a Thomas meeting.

If the Lord's Day be the day on which Jesus rose from the dead, this second Lord's Day has no very serious claims to the title. Jesus did not rise from the dead on the first day of every week in the year, but of a certain particular week. It is true that it is possible that Christians may celebrate the First Lord's Day on the first day of every week within the year. But we have very little warrant indeed that this was done in New Testament times. We can see how this second Lord's Day was celebrated. Jesus miraculously appeared and convinced by word and deed the Skeptical Thomas. This is the extent of the celebration, if the New Testament record be our guide.

Jesus showed himself to the seven of the disciples at the sea of Tiberias. This meeting could not have been on a first day of the week unless we can believe Peter with all his Jewish prejudices would go fishing on the Sabbath and fish all Sabbath night. In case, however, that Peter believed the Sabbath had been changed, and so did fish on Saturday and Saturday night, in that case he continued more successful fishing on Sunday. And more than all Jesus, seeing them fishing on Sunday, commands them not to quit fishing because they were violating the Sunday Sabbath, but to keep on fishing by casting the net on the other side of the ship!!! No, this meeting is, on Divine authority, neither on Saturday nor Sunday. It is on some other day of the week; no clue is given as to what day. (See John 21:1-8)

Nature of this meeting. As the meeting on the Second Lord Day was a Thomas meeting, so this meeting at the sea of Tiberias was a Peter meeting. Peter is the burden of the chapter. Here is mentioned by name in the following verses: 2, 3, 7, 11, 15, 16, 17, 20, 21. Peter and Christ are discoursing together from verse 15 to 22. If Peter had not been there, this meeting had not occurred. Let us count if Pentecost be on Sunday using only Biblical evidence.

Thursday, Jesus eats the Passover. First Day of Unleavened Bread. <Mark 14:12.>

1. Friday. Jesus crucified and buried. Mark 15:1; 15:15, 25. [*page 60*]
2. Saturday I The Sabbath of the commandment. Jesus in the tomb. Luke 23:56.
3. <u>Sunday</u>. 1 The Lord's Day. The Resurrection Day. First day of the week. Luke 24:1.
4. Monday. 2
5. Tuesday 3
6. Wednesday 4
7. Thursday 5
8. Friday 6
9. Saturday II 7
10. <u>Sunday</u> 8 Jesus convinces Thomas. Second Lord's Day.
11. Monday 9
12. Tuesday. 10
13. Wednesday. 11
14. Thursday 12
15. Friday. 13
16. Saturday III 14
17. <u>Sunday</u> 15 Third Lord's Day.
18. Monday 16
19. Tuesday 17
20. Wednesday 18
21. Thursday 19
22. Friday 20
23. Saturday IIII 21
24. <u>Sunday</u> 22 Fourth Lord's Day.
25. Monday 23
26. Tuesday 24
27. Wednesday. 25
28. Thursday. 26
29. Friday. 27
30. Saturday V 28
31. <u>Sunday</u> 29 Fifth Lord's Day.
32. Monday 30
33. Tuesday 31
34. Wednesday 32

35. Thursday 33
36. Friday 34
37. Saturday VI 35
38. <u>Sunday</u> 36 Sixth Lord's Day.
39. Monday 37
40. Tuesday 38
41. Wednesday. 39
42. Thursday. 40
43. Friday. 41 [*page 61*]
44. Saturday <VII> 42
45. <u>Sunday</u> 43 Seventh Lord's Day.
46. Monday 44
47. Tuesday 45
48. Wednesday 46
49. Thursday. 47
50. Friday 48
    Saturday VIII. 49
    <u>Sunday</u>. 50 Eighth Lord's Day.

1 Facts: a. The Day and the Supper are both qualified in the Greek Testament by the word Κυριάκος. b. The Lord's Supper was eaten only on the Lord's Day. Acts 20:7; 1 Cor. 16:2. c. The Supper and the Day were regularly observed between the days of unleavened bread and the Pentecost. d. The fact that the day and the supper are qualified by the same word Lord's (Κυριάκος), which word occurs no where else in the New Testament, proves that the day and supper are intimately connected. The Lord's Supper is a supper eaten by the church as a whole to show forth the Lord's Death till he come. The Lord's Day is the day upon which the resurrection of the Lord was remembered and the Lord's Supper eaten. That the Lord's Day was the special time for the remembrance of Jesus is shown by the fact that St. John on the island of Patmos was taken possession of by the Holy Spirit, on the Lord's Day. Rev. 1:10. He could not eat the Lord's Supper alone, but he was no doubt bringing to memory the interesting scenes of the First Lord's Day. John knew it was the Lord's Day before he was taken possession of by the Spirit. If the Lord's Day is the day on which Jesus arose from the dead, the day John calls the Lord's Day is Rev. 1:10 is not that day. Now the day Jesus rose from the dead we shall call the First Lord's Day. The Lord's Day St. John calls such is a day years after the First Lord's Day. It was therefore either the anniversary of the First Lord's Day, or the first day of any week celebrated in commemoration of the First Lord's Day. Was the First Lord's Day celebrated the first day of every week in New Testament times? The Second Lord's Day was simply the day Thomas was convinced of the Resurrection by the Lord Jesus.

It can be proved from Scripture testimony alone that the day of Pentecost was the eighth Lord's Day. This was the day 3000 souls were added to the Christian church, and the Holy Ghost was abundantly given.

The day of Pentecost always came on Sunday from [*page 62*] the necessities of the case. "Unto the morrow after the seventh Sabbath shall ye number fifty days." Lev. 23:16. This being the case, if Saturday is the Sabbath, Pentecost would always be on Sunday. The fact that Pentecost was on the Eighth Lord's Day was made so by the Mosaic Law, not by the choice of Jesus. Why, then, was the outpouring of the Holy Spirit delayed until Pentecost? It was the day of Pentecost drew multitudes "out of every nation under heaven." Acts 2:5. Even between the Second Lord's Day and Pentecost Peter and six other disciples were fishing on the sea of Galilee fifty or sixty miles from Jerusalem. See John 21:2, 3. And lest they should depart from Jerusalem, Jesus commanded them not to depart from Jerusalem until they were baptized with the Holy Ghost. Acts 1:4, 5. Even Paul years after hastened to be at Jerusalem the day of Pentecost. Acts 20:16. So, then, the Lord Jesus waited for all the multitudes from all the then known world to come together on the day of Pentecost before he conferred the Holy Ghost and power upon his disciples, and the gift of tongues was to enable them to minister the Gospel to the peoples of diverse languages then and there assembled.

The fact that Paul waited at Troas from Monday until Sunday "to break bread" with the disciples, though in great haste to be at Jerusalem, the day of Pentecost is proof that the Lord's Supper was eaten only on the Lord's Day. Acts 20:7, 16. This is confirmed also by the fact that the church in Corinth met on the Lord's Day to eat the Lord's Supper. They had met on a previous Lord's Day to eat the Lord's Supper, but ate instead a supper of their own, because they did not eat it together as the Lord's people and without recognition that the bread represented the Lord's body, and the wine his blood. So Paul tells them next time they meet to wait for one another, and all eat together, and if any one became too hungry to wait until all had come together, he should eat his own supper at home before coming. In chap. 16 verse[s] 1, 2 he incidentally shows they would meet to eat the Lord's Supper <u>the very next Lord's Day</u>, telling them to take up a collection of money for charitable purposes. So here at Corinth the Lord's Supper was eaten on two successive Lord's Days, and we are forced to believe the churches of Galatia did likewise.

Corollary: The churches of Troas, Corinth, and Galatia met every Lord's Day to eat the Lord's Supper, and in connection with this meeting sermons were preached (Acts 20:7), or collections of money taken up for the purposes of charity 1 Cor. 16:1, 2, also 1 Cor. 11:20, 21, 22, especially verses [. . .] 24. We are not to suppose [*page 63*] that the Lord's Supper was eaten every Lord's Day the year around. In every case the Lord's Supper was eaten between the days of Unleavened Bread and Pentecost. Christ ate the First Lord's Supper on the First Day of Unleavened Bread. The First Lord's Day was the third day of the Feast of Unleavened Bread. In reality it is uncertain from the New Testament whether the Lord's Day was every first day of every week the year around. On the contrary the Lord's Day seems to be only the first day of every week ending with Pentecost. Let me examine into this.

1. The First Lord's Supper was eaten Thursday or Friday the first day of unleavened bread. On Friday if we take the Jewish method of computing time (Ex. 12:18, 19; Lev. 23:5, 6, 15, 16[)]. In the 5th and 6th verses of Lev. chap. 23 the first day of unleavened bread is spoken of indifferently as the fourteenth or fifteenth of the month. The day ended at even, or at sunset, and the new day began at the same time.
2. We do not read of any more Lord's Suppers from the first Lord's Supper to or after the first Christian Pentecost, notwithstanding many pretended that Acts 2:42, 46 refers to the Supper. The Lord's Supper can not be eaten "from house to house," and Paul tells the church of Corinth they had failed to eat the Lord's Supper simply because they did not eat together, and did not eat the bread as a symbol of Christ's body and did not drink the wine as a symbol of his blood. Eating from house to house, thus can not be eating the Lord's Supper, the Apostle Paul being judge. Hence Acts 2 says not one word of eating the Lord's Supper.
3. [*journal has number 2 instead of 3*] The Second Recorded Lord's Supper is in Acts 20:7th and other verses.

In regard to this the Second Recorded Lord's Supper we read, in substance.
1. This was eaten, at the least, the third Lord's Day after the first day of the feast of unleavened bread.
2. If we reckon time after the Jewish Manner it was eaten on Monday, but Luke says it was the first day of the week; so the Roman method of computing time is intended.
3. They met about 9 o'clock P.M. on Sunday, for Paul preached until midnight. His sermon must have lasted two or three hours. At any rate, when the sermon was ended, it was just midnight.
4. If we compute time, after our manner, the supper was eaten on Monday morning, but the sermon alone delayed the

eating, but scripturally it would not be Monday until sunrise.
5. The whole church staid up all night, because it was the last time they was [would?] see Paul's face. It was an extraordinary occasion.
6. The Christians met [together?] for <u>one sole purpose</u>, to break [*page 64*] bread, or eat the Lord's Supper. This is the first recorded notice of the eating of the Lord's Supper. We may infer justly that other Lord's suppers were eaten before this, but they are not recorded. It takes a church eating together, in love, using the bread as a symbol or reminder of the Lord's body, and the wine a remembrance of his blood, to eat it. No single individual can eat the Lord's Supper alone. Christ and his disciples—a company—ate the first Lord's Supper. Paul and the Christians met together at Troas for the sole purpose of eating the Lord's Supper—a church. The church at Corinth tried to eat the Lord's Supper, while the poor were not yet arrived. By so doing Paul tells them they had eaten a supper of their own, and not the Lord's supper. It takes a whole company of believers to eat the Lord's Supper. John on Patmos remembered the Lord's Day, but did not eat the Supper.

The third recorded Lord's Supper is in 1 Cor. 11:20-34. Like all the recorded Lord's Suppers it was eaten between the days of Unleavened Bread and Pentecost. 1 Cor. 16:8 shows this.

How often is the Lord's Supper to be eaten? We have seen that the Lord's Supper was eaten only on the Lord's Day (Acts 20:7; 1 Cor. 16:1, 2 compared with 1 Cor. 11:33-34.), that it was eaten on two successive Lord's Days at Corinth and probably in Galatia, that it was eaten on the third Lord's Day after the days of unleavened bread at Troas, and it seems certain that the Lord's Supper was eaten every Lord's Day between the time of Unleavened Bread and Pentecost in every New Testament church. The seven churches in Asia were so well-acquainted with the Lord's Day that John offers not a word of explanation as to what day it is. Rev. 1:10. Can we believe that the seven church[es] were not just as well with the Lord's Supper, a supper eaten only on the Lord's Day, both in Europe (Corinth) and in Asia (Troas, Galatia)? Yes, they all ate the Lord's Supper on the Lord's Day between the days of Unleavened Bread and Pentecost. When we give two different things the same name, it must be either because they present a lively resemblance, or are ~~contiguous~~ connected either in time or place. Now in the Greek Testament, this is done of the day and the supper. The Lord's Day is ἡ Κυριακη ἡμέρα, Rev. 1:10; the Lord's Supper τὸ Κυριάκον ςείπγογ. It is certain the Supper could not re[semble?] the Day; however, the connection was that the Lord's Supper was eaten on the Lord's Day.

This do ye, as often as ye drink it, in remembrance of me. It is not to be supposed the New Testament Christians had [*page 65*] wine at every meal. Nor was every meal eaten at the church. It is only by a church that the Lord's Supper can be celebrated. So, then, the Lord's Supper can not be celebrated every day in the year. Neither can it be celebrated every first day in the year. Although Jesus and the disciples had flesh to eat in the First Lord's Supper, yet he set apart bread alone to represent his body and wine alone to represent his blood. No other articles for these symbolizations can be lawfully used. But [*journal text ends here*]

[*moved from page 104*] Sunday, April 7th 1895,

in the meeting house near the Shawnee Mission School, there was Sabbath School at 10 o'clock A.M. As only a few were present, there was only one class, and that was taught by Mrs. Ella Hartley. Mrs. Kirk, Mrs. Bourbonnais, Mrs. William Perry Haworth, Charley Beaver, Dudley Beaver, a red-haired woman and her little child, Aurelia Bourbonnais, two white boys, and William E. Shawnee were present. Not one person came from the Shawnee Mission, since they were under a quarantine, by order of the school physician. Mr. Haworth preached after Sabbath School was over from Second Kings, chapter 3, verse 16. He first read the whole chapter, and then took for his text verse 16. He spoke some about "ditch-digging." We should make way for the grace of God to come into our hearts, said he. We have some things to do ourselves, and then God's grace will supplement the work. The sermon was a good one.

In the evening Mr. Haworth went to Tecumseh with Mrs. Ella Hartley. They went in the topped buggy, that has room for only two persons to sit in it. Mrs. Kirk said late in the evening April 7th 1895 that Mrs. Hartley was going to deliver an address that evening in Tecumseh on the "Peculiarities of the Bible." That the papers had announced that she would deliver the address. At the meeting at night in the meeting house near the Shawnee Mission school, Mrs. Kirk spoke from the text, "Be ye angry and sin not: let not the sun go down up[on] your wrath," Eph. 4:26. She first read Eph. 4:17-32; then chose verse 26 for her text. She told about Dr. Hopkins getting very angry with his infidel brother-in-law, at a business conference between themselves, how Dr. Hopkins prayed all night over the matter on reaching home, how very early the next morning Dr. Hopkins went and apologized to his infidel brother-in-law in the presence of the latter's family, how he convinced the infidel of the reality of the religion of Dr. Hopkins and finally led to the infidel's conversion and how even afterward Dr. Hopkins never gave way to temper. Mrs. Bourbonnais added a few remarks. At the meeting were present among others, Emma Newsom, Thomas Alford, John King, George Shawnee, the clerk in John King's store, that red-haired woman, Cegar, Charley Beaver, Dudley Beaver, and William E. Shawnee. None from the Mission were present on account of the quarantine.

The Sabbath School Lesson was: 1. Subject. "The Triumphal Entry." Text: Mark 11:1-11 verses, inclusive. Golden Text. Mark 11:9 [*page 105*] Hosanna; Blessed is he that cometh in the name of the Lord. It was announced by Mrs. Kirk that next Sunday would be Easter, and this would be April 14, 1895. She also announced that Mr. Haworth would preach here at night if not in the morning.

Mrs. Kirk presented me with a picture of Dr. Kirk and herself April 7th 1895. She told me that I became very angry at Dr. Kirk and herself, because they would not permit me to stay at the parsonage alone with Flora Hale. She said that if that had been done, it would have raised talk all through the neighborhood. She said it was best to avoid all appearance of evil. She was told by me that I was not very angry, that I thought it was best myself. She said that I came and took all my books away, which is true. Dr. Kirk had told me I could come and "stay as long as I wished." But I have done wrong plenty of times. She said this April 7th 1895.

Mrs. Kirk said also that Emma Newsom had said there was no small-pox over in Shawnee.

Emma Newsom, April 7th 1895 after meeting at night, informed me as follows:—That Joseph Newsom and herself were here still in 1876, the year of the Centennial, that she (Emma) sometimes helped in teaching school, that she does not remember my ever going to school, but that I used to come sometimes with my father, that Ella Coltrain came before they went away. She offered prayer in the meeting. Emma is now gray haired. She is a professional nurse, so said Mrs. Kirk.

X X X

[*moved from page 200*] [*April 11, 1895?*] Recent History of the Shawnee Indians.

Shortly after the late civil war (1861-65), the Absentee Shawnee Indians moved from Kansas to that portion of the Indian Territory between the North Fork of the Canadian and Little River, the northern portion of the Pottawatomie Reservation. Their chief during this period was John White. It is said that he went to Washington, D.C., and made a treaty, however, which was never ratified by the U.S. Government. He failed to secure a title for his tribe to the land which they occupied.

The next ~~chiefs~~ chieves were John Esparney and Joe Ellis (1872-1882). During their administration the allotments of 1875 were made. During this period also occurred the secession of Big Jim's band, who under the leadership of Sam Warrior removed and settled within the Kickapoo Reserve, north of the North Fork of the Canadian river (1876). In 1872 the Shawnee Mission school was established one half a mile east of Old Shawneetown, by Joseph Newsom, under the auspices of the Society of Friends. Later this school passed under Governmental control and is still (April 11th 1895) flourishing. Miss M. C. Williams is its present Superintendent.

About 1883 White Turkey and William Littleax were made chiefs. Joe Ellis and John Esparney were set aside by the tribe on account of their favoring the allotments of 1875. But this was a sad mistake on the part of the tribe. For on Feb 8th 1887 the Dawes Bill was passed by Congress, providing for the allotment of lands in severalty to all the Indian tribes except the Osages, Sac and Foxes, Cherokees, Creeks, Choctaws, Chickasaws, and Seminoles. This law extended the laws of the United States over the Indians, and attached citizenship to the act of taking an allotment. By this means an ignorant Indian, importuned and harassed into taking an allotment of land varying in amount from 40 to 320 acres, unwittingly made himself a citizen of the United States.

April 22nd 1889 Oklahoma Proper was opened to settlement by Presidential Proclamation. Many of the Shawnees witnessed the run for land, among them Chief White Turkey. This taught the Shawnees that they had better take their lands. They saw white people killing themselves and their horses in their eagerness to secure homes for themselves, while they were refusing to take their allotments. Only Big Jim's Band persisted in refusing to take allotment of lands after this. Major N. S. Porter from Ponca, Neb. was the Special Agent, who allotted lands to the Absentee Shawnees and to the Citizen Band of Pottawatomie Indians.

[page 201] The opening of Oklahoma Proper to settlement furnished the Shawnees more whiskey to drink. Prior to 1889 small parties of Shawnees had gone to Dennison, Texas, and brought whiskey to their tribe. But now they had only to go from 15 to 25 or 30 miles for their strong drink. Still it was not so plentifully drunk as a little later.

September 22nd 1891 the Pottawatomie Reservation was opened to white settlement. The Shawnees and Pottawatomies had by treaty ceded all surplus land to the U.S. government. Tecumseh was made the County Seat (Sept. 24th 1891). Six liquor saloons were set up right in the midst of the Indians. An era of drunkenness now followed. Every day drunken Shawnees and drunken Pottawatomies could be seen or heard day or night. Hell had been turned loose between the two rivers. Drunken Indians found within the corporation limits were put into jail and fined in all sums from $5 to $15. This only added to their impoverishment. Jan. 29th 1893 Charlie Warrior died, having drank himself to death. Others died, but it is only supposed they did die from the effects of liquor. Even boys not grown to manhood were induced to drink liquor and become drunken. One little boy was thus killed by a pint or more of liquor. This era lasted from Sept. 24th, 1891 to Jan 1st, 1895. The Shawnee payment (Jan–March 1892) was the occasion of a great outburst and drunkenness. Some spent as high as $20 for liquor at one purchase; some lost $150 by gambling in one day. After money and stock was gone—saddles were pawned for liquor. Some pawned saddles not their own.

The saloon and gambling house are hells on earth. Although the Shawnees were thus drinking and becoming drunken, not all did so. There were a few noble exceptions among the men, while of the women only a few disgraced themselves in this way. A few women drank a little to please their importunate guests, but several never have done so.

Mē-yàh-pē (properly Mĕ'-yàh-wàh"-pĕă) enlisted in the Union army July 2nd 1863 and was honorably discharged at Fort Gibson, Ind. Ter. June 25th 1865. Other Shawnees enlisted at the same time. They were members of Co. M. 14th Kansas Cavalry.

Friday night April 12th 1895 [continuation of original page 105]
Prayer meeting was held in the church. Present Mrs. Ella Hartley, Mr. W. P. Haworth, Mrs. Rachel Kirk, Mrs. Bourbonnais, the red-haired lady and her child, Mrs. Kessel and another lady, who were all that came from the Mission, Tono Bourbonnais, William E. Shawnee. I do not know whether this was all or not. Mr. Haworth read the whole of the 62nd Psalms. In his talk he said he had been at a prayer meeting in Tecumseh, and that it was a blessed meeting. He said that he had been preparing through the week for the service of the Sanctuary of the Lord. He also said: My soul has been blessed here to-night. Mrs. Kirk, in her testimony, said, "As I was coming across the prairie this evening, I felt so joyful in the Lord, that I could hardly tell whether I were in the body or out of it. I felt drawn so closely to the Lord and to those who sleep in Christ Jesus. [[She here probably referred [*page 106*] [to] Dr. Charles W. Kirk, who died Sept. 9th 1893, and to Dr. James E. Rhoades, who died Jan. 2nd 1895.]]. Mrs. Bourbonnais and the red-haired lady both asked the prayers of the Christians, in their testimonies. About all the

Christians present offered prayer. Many songs were sung, and all were led by Mr. Haworth. William E. Shawnee said: "I feel like saying with the Psalmist, What shall I render unto the Lord for all his benefits toward me? I will take the cup of salvation and call upon the name of the Lord. Ps. 116:12, 13. "Bless the children at the Mission," was one petition in the prayers.

Sabbath night April 21st, 1895.

Mr. Wm P. Haworth preached a sermon on Ex. 25:1-7 verses. He noted the following things as enumerated 1. Gold. 2. Silver. 3. Brass. 4. Blue. 5. Purple. 6. Scarlet. 7. Fine linen. 8. Goat's hair. 9. Rams' skins dyed red. 10. Badgers' Skins. 11. Shittim Wood. 12. Oil. 13. Spices. 14. Sweet Incense. He compared every one of these to either some quality in Christ or the Church. The gold represents, by virtue of its intrinsic value, the Lord Jesus Christ, who also has intrinsic value. The fine linen represents the purity and innocence of Christ. No infidel has ever written a book so far as W^m P's knowledge, against the good character of Christ, although books were written against his Divinity. The Badgers' Skins being on the outside of the tabernacle represent the Church as she appears to the world. – Mrs. Kirk arose after the sermon and thanked God that though men rejected Christ, still that did not change his intrinsic value. Christ would be just as valuable to her if all the world were against him.

Shawneetown Monthly Meeting was held Saturday April 20th 1895, in the meeting house near the Shawnee Mission. Ten members were present, four men and six women. None but members were present. Mr. Wm P. Haworth preached on the whole of the 12th chapter of Romans. The minutes of the last Monthly Meeting were read. Emma Newsom brought a certificate of membership from Kokomo Monthly Meeting, Indiana. She is received as a member of the Shawneetown Monthly meeting 3rd Mo. 16th 1895. I was one of the members present. Wm E. Shawnee is appointed to call on the treasurer for the amount and purchase a can of oil and two brooms for the use of the church, and also to help clean up the church. I made up my mind to attend to this sure to the glory of Christ, and Monday April 22nd 1895 I purchased four gallons of oil of Smith Bros. in Tecumseh for 95 cents, and two brooms at Carson's for 40 cents, and brought [*page 107*] them to the church. Mr. Wm Perry Haworth is not a member of our Monthly Meeting, but he belongs to our Yearly Meeting, and is a preacher in Tecumseh. Ollie Wilford, a young lady from Wolf Grove, two miles east of the town of Shawnee, said that they had Sabbath School there every Sunday, Christian Endeavor every Friday night, and prayer-meeting every Sunday night. Mr. Haworth said to me that there were about 30 members in that place. – In his sermon Mr. Haworth said that Quakers took time on week days to attend meetings, and yet had the fattest horses and the best improved farms and fine carriages. They lose nothing by devoting so much time to weekly meetings. On the verse, "Not slothful in business, fervent in spirit, serving the Lord," he said that the Lord does not want slothful or lazy Christians, that while some took up too much time providing for their worldly needs, there were others who did not obey the text in providing for themselves. - The free-will offering was $2, of which I did not contribute a cent. I must get better, but at present my poverty aboundeth.

In sermons we hear preachers referring to books that infidels write, or to what some "great infidel" said or even addresses on the Inspiration of the Bible. Mrs. Ella Hartley delivered one address on this subject. Her points were three. 1. The condition of the Jews at this day, being exactly as foretold. 2. The ruins and discoveries in Babylonia, being either as foretold in the Bible or confirming the testimony of the Scripture. 3. The condition of Egypt, without a native prince for centuries, as foretold. In times past she has given addresses on this subject, and she says that one woman had written a letter to her, stating that she had rescued her son from infidelity. So here is some good certainly done by her addresses. God bless her efforts, but is infidelity widespread the reason we hear of so much of it from the pulpit?

[*continued from original page 65*]

Diary Friday April 26th 1895. IIII Notice.
I was here all day at my father's house, "graining" deer skins down by the well. Grained three skins for my day's work. Two men came about 2 P.M. and wanted to see me. They proved to be two examiners of pension claims. They wanted me to interpret for them even if Joe Blanchard should come. They said that several of Big Jim's band would come up, that they had told Joe Blanchard to tell them, and that Joe Blanchard would be up himself if he possibly could. They were also anxious to see my father and Robert Deer. They wanted me to ride up to Dale to see Robt and tell him to be down the next day, but I declined on account of the lateness and the distance, being about 9 miles each way coming and going.

I prepared myself. George Shawnee cut my hair and shaved me, and I went over to the church at old Shawneetown to Prayer Meeting. Saw there Dr. Hartley, who said that he had just come in that evening, Emma Newsom, Miss Kessel, Mrs. Bourbonnais, Mrs. Kirk, Wm Perry Haworth, Mrs. Ella Hartley, and another woman whose name I do not know, but who was proud of being a Quaker, and some of the school children. None of the boys from the school were present. If any others were present, I do not now remember them except myself. There were about 19 present. Wm P. Haworth read the 13th chapter of First Corinthians, reading <u>love</u> in every case instead of the word <u>charity</u>. About 11 texts were parceled to be read by as many present. They had reference to:— 1. Love to God. 2. The Consequences of love to God. 3. The blessedness of Love to God. The text appointed me and which I read was Psalms 91:14. "Because he hath set his love upon me, therefore will I deliver him: I will set him on high, because he hath known my name." All this is written <u>7:50 P.M.</u> <u>Saturday April 27th 1895</u>—William E. Shawnee.

Saturday April 27th 1895

    I went to town and reached there about 10 or 11 A.M. Saw the two examiners for pension claims, but the Indians had not come yet. Before long we saw Cegar, John Welch, Kaceka, John Linney, Lă-loú-wē-pĕă, Ke[. . .]powēkwăthàh, and Tàh-cŏm-sē [*page 66*] and Mă-yàh-wàh'-pĕă. Presently after some talk on the part of the examiners to the effect that they were true men, and had their commissions with them, to show, we went over to a room just north of the building marked [Carlock?] Hotel. There we wrote out several papers, or rather they wrote them out while I interpreted and attached the making of marks on the part of the Indians. The names of these examiners as written down on a piece of paper for myself I here transcribe as follows:—J. T. Marrier, F. P. Boushee. According to a paper in their possession I see that Me-yah-pe (correctly, Mā-yàh-wàh'-pĕă) [*sic*] enlisted July 2nd 1863, and was honorably discharged June 25th 1865. We finished about 5 P.M., I suppose. Any way it was quite late. I went to the Post Office, and having received 60 cents of William Shawnee, and procured a money order for 55 cents and sent it to the *Christian Nation*, 252 Broadway, New York City. Right there in the crowded Post Office, I interpreted a letter from Alice L. Brown, Indian Ter., to John King, dated 11/1/1895. Then wrote two letters to her on paper I furnished for Kaceka and John Welch. I furnished the envelope too, but they furnished the stamp. I went over to the office of the Absentee Shawnee Business Committee, found Thomas Alford and Walter Shawnee there, received of Thomas the Lincoln Number of the *New York Independent* I had lent him, listen[ed] to Walter read Col. Ingersoll's infidel speech in St. Louis, and answered it at some length. Then came; reached home after dark.

Diary Sunday April 28th 1895.

    I rode the baldfaced pony up to the Kickapoo Mission. I went by Robert Deere's house and stopped there about an hour. I told Robert Deer what those two special examiners for pensions told me to tell him. They wanted to see him very bad and wanted him to be down to see them sure Monday morning. As dinner was nearly ready, Robert kindly asked me to wait for dinner, and after that I could continue my journey. A[mos] Deer was there too. I was thinking all the time that he was at the Haskell Institute. There was chicken and rice-soup in one dish or pan, which was all very nice. Fried eggs, corn bread, coffee, these were the articles on the board, although I took water instead of coffee. Resumed my journey a little while after dinner, and reach[ed] the Mission between 2 and 3 P.M. Saw Isaac McCan and some other young men, and shook hands with them. Samuel L. Patrick Jr. was here, and Teacher (Lizzie Test) was out of the enclosure toward the south with her Kickapoos. They were out there in the act of going home. I went in the Mission, saluted and shook hands with Àh-kwē-nàh-kō-thē-yah and his wife and little daughter Ke-tĕ-kwă, or Miss Lizzie [*page 67*] Test Jr. Saw Mr. Thomas W. Alford and his three boys—Pierrepont, Reese, and Paul. Paul wished me to ask his father how old he was. For when I had seen Paul and Miss Cuohè over at Antie [Auntie] Kirk's home (the parsonage), I had expressed my doubts as to his being six years old. So Thomas told me, Yes, Paul is six years old. I asked him if Paul was born in 1889. He replied that the little boy was born in 1888. Presently, Àh-kwē-nàh-kō-thē-yah and wife and daughter left the room, followed by Teacher and her crowd of girls. Àh-kwē-nàh-kō-thē-yah was hitching to the wagon when I started toward the scene. There Lina B. Lunt came to the door calling me, glad to see me; I told her to wait until I came back. When I came reached the scene, Àh-kwē-nàh-kō-thē-yah and wife were seated upon the seat, and their little daughter was standing in the wagon behind. Finally being told to descend, the little girl did so, but went to crying right away. I went back and Lina B. Lunt shook hands with me first, and Flora Hale afterwards. They were glad to see me, and I am sure I was glad to see them. Lina said she thought I was leaving the reason she called me. Presently we were all called to dinner. I told them I had eaten dinner at Robert Deere's, but they said Eat again. Flora and I were placed side by side at the table, being together on the same side of the table. I drank hot water. No bread had been put on the table, and someone said that Flora had set the table. Teacher remarked that she never knew Flora to forget to place bread on the table before. Thomas Alford said that he had never known Flora to forget the bread. I do not know just what Teacher and Thomas meant by this. I could see no reason why Flora should forget the bread at this time more than at other times. They might have meant that I had caused Flora to thus forget, or they may not have meant it. After dinner I watered my horse and tied him out in the pasture and ere long, started out on foot to visit Měs-kwē'-kă-nàh-kah. I did not find him at home, but saw the Aunt of Nă-thàh-pē-hàh and Nă-nă-sēō-thă-kwă. Another woman of about as large dimensions was also there, as well as a middle-aged young man, Isaac McCan, a little boy, and the companions of Isaac. Came back late to the Mission. [[Moce henoke mike pwimma Nabrpe hi, nulkihe hotalitani ksika hopetanke, china nenama hopwime, mieiwenkeke wieace hoce]]. After sunset Teacher and her girls were seated on logs in the north-west part of the yard, while the girls repeated from memory the Beatitudes, and John 14:1-14. Presently we all went to meeting in the church. Many prayers were offered and several testimonies. I both prayed and gave testimony [as oft?] I have done before. We all [*page 68*] concluded the service of Prayer by repeating the Lord's Prayer. The children joined, all and one, well and heartily, in this. The girls that I can name in school are: Wōo-kō-pă-hō-kwă, Nă-thàh-pē-hàh, Nănă'sēōthăkwă, Kătekwă, Mary Mardock, Pă-nàh-hō-kō'-kwàh, Kō-mă-thō-kwă, Flaurice, Kā-chē-tiē-sē-kwă, and some others. Nathahpehah is a nice little girl, and looks sweet, and obeys too. Thomas went away before night, probably while I was visiting. Emma Newsom was up too, but she probably came back with Thomas. <u>Written April 29th 1895 before 8:45 P.M.</u> (P.M.)

Monday April 29th 1895. Written April 29th 1895 8:45 P.M.
    Left at the break of day, bidding Teacher good bye and leaving the rest in bed. I cross[ed] the North Fork just before sunrise. Teacher wanted me to wait for breakfast, but I told her that I would have to do a day's work when I got to Tecumseh. When I got to Robert Deere's, Alex Gibson (Kē-chē-thàh) said that Robert had just left. Came on home, let George [*Shawnee*] have the horse, ate a breakfast, and walked to Tecumseh. John Welch, Pecan, and Jackson Clarke (Tà-kē-sē-mō, more properly Ho-tàh'-kē-sē-mō) were waiting for us. Robert had met one of the examiners in the way as he came who had taken his testimony. Mr. Boushee wrote out the testimony of Jackson on four sheets, to each of which he had made his mark by touching the pen. John and Pecan had two sheets apiece, both signed by themselves respectively. Mr. A. M. Carlock attested the marks made by touching the pen. Robert [*Deer*] was the spectator, though he sometimes helped me in interpreting, for which I am grateful to him. Mr. Marrier was gone away all day. I was quite tired at night. Saw White Turkey in town.

Tuesday April 30th 1895 (Written April 30th 1895 6:55 P.M.[)]
    I went to Tecumseh after breakfast on foot. Met Mr. Marrier and Mr. Boushee. They wanted to see White Turkey (John Bob was

the name he went by in the army) and Rock. As a meeting of the Absentee Shawnee Business Committee was appointed for to-day, but Rock did not come. But they took the testimony of White Turkey, or John Bob, concerning the cases of Buckheart and Ah-yan-ke, or Cherokee Woman. They paid me $1.50 each for interpreting April 27th, 29th and 30th 1895, but they owe me a dollar yet for informing Robert Deer of their needing him. I traveled at least 18 miles to thus inform him. I purchased with the $3 thus paid me the following articles:— Two Unlaundried White Shirts at 50 cts. each; 1 pair of Pants for every day wear, 85 cts.; 1 colored shirt, 50 cts.; 1 Broad Brimmed Hat 50 cts.; 1 paper [*page 69*] of needles 5 cts.; 1 stamp 2 cts, (for I stamped a letter I had written to Miss Della A. Whipple, Hennessey, Okla. Ter., and dropped it in the letter box in the Post Office); total $2.92 cts. This leaves me 8 cts. in my pocket, which is correct. I would like for Miss Whipple to be my lawful life-companion for life if she would. This is my second letter to her. The first has not been answered. I went around by the parsonage to see Mrs. Ella Hartley, but found that she had gone over to the Shawnee Mission in company with Mrs. Kirk. I found only Miss Emma Newsom. I told her to tell Mrs. Hartley that I could not assist in cleaning up the church this week, because that tomorrow I would have to go over into the Creek Nation, to interpret for a pension examiner. — We are having quite a rain this evening, which surely is very much needed. God be thankful for this shower. Miss Newsom said that I would see Ella Sunday. I said, Yes, I will see her Sunday in case I do not go up to the Kickapoo Mission again. She asked me if I was going to interpret up there. I said, No, I got there too late Sunday because I got such a late start from home, and stopped for an hour at Robert Deere's. She said, Yes, I see there is a new attraction up there. You will have to wait awhile, Willie, until she is grown. I asked, Who. She said, Flaurice. I said, No. On the way home, as I came by the Canalases' house, and George Cuppy called me over and said that Elkano Canalas' horse had run away with him, and had thrown him off and broken his leg at the right ancle [ankle]. Sallie Canalas said that it just made her sick for her to look at him when he was brought in.

May 1st, 1895 Wednesday.
The following is copied from my own handwriting in led pencil, and explains itself. Copied May 4th 1895, at 8:15 A.M. during a shower of rain.— "Written in the City Hotel at Keokuk Falls about 3 or 4 P.M. May 1st, 1895.
It rained a big rain (last night). I had breakfast early and started early in the morning. Found Mr. Marrier and Mr. Boushee. Soon Mr. Boushee and Mr. Là'fĕrty started for Norman,

Okla. Ter., while Mr. Marrier and myself started for Keokuk Falls. We arrived at Keokuk Falls about 1 P.M., but decided to wait until to-morrow before starting for the house of William Littleax. It had also rained here at Keokuk Falls. I wrote and mailed a letter to Miss Carrie Warrior from here. The fare is good at this hotel, although the house is rather rough; but the fare makes up for the house. It would be well for me to become a hotel keeper in Tecumseh. All we need to do to make money is to take advantage of our personal situations, and make the most of those. We are im[. . . ing?] the afternoon as best we can. I think [*page 70*] of Teacher and Lina and Flora at the Kickapoo Mission and all the rest that are there. I think of Mr. and Mrs. Hartley, Miss Emma Newsom, and Mr. Wm P. Haworth at Tecumseh and Old Shawneetown respectively. I think of Ollie Wilford and the other Quakers at Wolf Grove, whose faces, except the one named, are unknown to me."

"*Thursday May 2nd 1895*.
    Awoke early and harnessed the horses while the livery man fed them. He did not assist me in harnessing them at all. I remember Teacher, Lina, and Flora and Della in their work at the Kickapoo Mission. I remember Mrs. Kirk, Mr. and Mrs. Hartley, and Mr. Wm P. Haworth, and Mary Bourbonnais and Aurelia Bourbonnais. Ollie Wilford is an earnest Christian of Wolf Grove. I remember Carrie Warrior at the Haskell Institute. I remember Nettie Haworth now married, but not to me. I remember Miss Whipple, whose home is at Hennessey, Okla. Ter. It is cloudy this morning and looks like rain. I remember Lucy Scott, Miss Kessell and Mrs. or Miss Neal, and Miss Williams at the Shawnee Mission. Miss Kessell and Mrs. Ella Hartley are such friends. Their friendship appears to be like that of David and Jonathan.
    Writing at the City Hotel, Keokuk Falls, O. T. continued. One man said that this town was just four miles south of the northern boundary of Pott. Co. Said the town was ¼ mile and 200 yards besides, from the Creek line. As ¼ mile is 440 yards, therefore it is 640 yards from the Creek line. – I want to try hard to have something in this world. Flora Hale is a very nice Christian young lady, being a member of the Society of Friends, and part Cherokee by blood. Her folks are Quakers too. She seems to take delight in conversing with the author of these lines, and this is the reason a certain woman keeps mentioning Flora's name to me, I suppose. Oh, but I have the fullest faith and the fullest confidence in her integrity and worthiness in every respect. She speaks and prays publicly also, a grace most beautiful in women as well as in men. But the idea of making this estimable young woman mine never entered my head until

others began to hint. So much for what people hint. Why hint unless you mean to teach a person to follow the course of conduct hinted at. As it is, there is a very powerful temptation to matrimony if financial condition did not positively forbid. As it is, the temptation is very strong. – There are various kinds of people in this world. A person must conduct himself according to his environment. I do wish all people were real Christians, but they are not. Do you not suppose that a certain woman mentions my name to Flora as well as her name to me? [*page 71*] It must be so, although I can never be sure about this. – I have had great privileges—great indeed. I do thank God for them. If a man wants to be a free thinker, he wants to be a Christian. For the contrary side is simply to float with the current. It is so, and I see it is so.

Thursday May 2nd, 1895. Written tonight, May 2nd in the City Hotel at Keokuk Falls, O. T.

Mr. Marrier and myself started out at about 7:30 A.M. for William Littleax's place, about 10 miles northeast of here. I found William working in the field about 100 yards east of his house, plowing land. I told of Mr. Marrier's business, and he came up to the house, got a table and spread a cloth upon it for Mr. Marrier to write upon it. The only other person present besides us there at the writing table or near was Mrs. Chosa Starr. The deposition in regard to William was in two separate pieces, and he touched the pen twice, and was sworn. One deposition for Ah-yan-ke, or as afterwards corrected Ah-hee'-tah, was one paper only. Littleax fully corroborated White Turkey's testimony in more places than one. He touched the pen to this and was sworn by Mr. Marrier. From William's we went past John Forman's to Ah-hee'-tah's; found her at home and took her deposition in two pieces. She touched the pen to each and was sworn. Thence we went on to the house of Dick Ellis. Did not find him at home for he had gone to Long Tom's to take a harrow home. Followed him up past Charley Starr's, Bullfrog's, and found him at the house of Long Tom. Took the deposition of Dick Ellis, and he touched the pen and was sworn. Also took the deposition of Sĕn-nă-hāth-lĕ, the mother of William Littleax, Switch, Nellie, and two other women. Thence came back home, by way of Bullfrogs, and Ah-hee'-tah's, and William's. Arrived at Keokuk Falls nearly sunset. We met Mrs. Marhardy and her son on the road, both going and coming. Persons seen:— William Littleax, Ah-hee'-tah, Mrs. Dick Ellis, and her daughter Minnie Johnson, Charley Starr, Skah-kah, and Seargent Ellis, and the folks at Charley Starr's, (two women and some children), Billy Bullfrog, and his little brother, Rosa Bullfrog and her mother, Long Tom, Dick Ellis, Martin Tarharty, and Sĕn-nă-hāth-lĕ, and two women and several children. Several persons were seen at William's on our way back, but we were in too great a hurry to notice them.

Friday May 3rd, 1895. "Very early in the morning May 3rd, 1895.["]
    I have been thinking of Flora Hale, what a nice, good, Christian young woman she is. Yet I have never found out her age. She is the same Flora; never knew her to be sick. She has black [*page 72*] hair, and is taller than Teacher. She is tall for her age. I believe she would as soon have me for her lawful husband as not. She speaks to me and delights in my company. I believe she wanted to walk over to the other house with me, coming to me just as we were ready to start. She is one of the best girls I know of. She may be mine one day if the Lord will. She is an Indian. I am willing for her to be my affianced lover if she is willing.

    I attended Prayer Meeting. Miss Emma Newsome, Mr. Hartley, Miss Kessel, Lucy Scott, Nellie Warrior, Eva Shawnee, Josephine Barone, and the other school girls and boys were present. Mrs. Bourbonnais, the red-haired woman and little child, and a man and a woman whose names I know not. Mrs. Kirk had gone up to the Kickapoo Mission, while Mrs. Ella Hartley was in Tecumseh. For the last three years Miss Newsome has lived at Kokomo, Indiana. Her brother lives at Indianapolis, Ind., and he is a railroad man. She said that white and colored go to the same schools in Indiana. She said that she knew two mulattoes who were teaching in the "ward schools." She said Kokomo had about 25,000 inhabitants. Indianapolis, according to Emma, has 100,000. I asked her where she studied nursing. She said she studied under other nurses and under physicians, though she had not followed it as a profession for the last ten days. She said, Though I have practiced nursing ever since I was 16 years old. I said, You are not much older than that now, are you. This enlivened the subject, and she said my age is for me to know and for you to find out.

Saturday May 4th 1895 (Written 8:20 P.M. Monday May 6th, 1895).
    I was here at home all day. In the evening went over to where Sallie Canalas lived, and set up all night with Elkano Canalas, who had his leg broken by a fall from a horse last Monday, April 29, 1895. It rained some in the morning.

Sunday May 5th 1895 (Written 8:25 P.M. Monday May 6th, 1895).
    I started on horseback, without my breakfast for the Kickapoo Mission. Arrived there about 10 A.M. It was a good while before and quite a while before Thomas Alford came. Măs-kwē-kă-nàh-kàh and other Kickapoos came. Among them was the

mother of Wēs-kō'-pă-thō-kwă. Teacher spoke to them about the brazen serpent Moses lifted up on a pole in the wilderness, and that whoever that was bitten, looked [up on the?] serpent was healed. Then "as Moses lifted up the serpent in the wilderness, even so must the Son of man be lifted up, that whosoever believeth in him should not perish, but should have everlasting life." [*page 73*] Thomas Alford did the interpreting, and he did it well. Then Lina B. Lunt wrote out the figures in the Gospel Addition [*edition?*] Thomas found in Second Peter 1:5-7. This is the way she put it on the blackboard:—

    Charity
    Brotherly kindness
    Boldness
    Patience
    Temperance
    Knowledge
    Virtue
    Faith

Her comments upon it were short and good, and I interpreted. The Kickapoos seemed to be interested. There were present Teacher, Lina B. Lunt, Della Pierson, Thomas Alford, Flora Hale, the school children, Mès-kwē-kĕ-nàh-kàh and the Kickapoos, and some others.

At night Lina preached. No Kickapoos were there at night except the children. Her sermon was good and was derived from various texts. Here are the names of the school children, with their ages, either as claimed by themselves, or as I think.

1. Nĕ'-thàh-pē"-hàh, = Ozetta Bourbonnais =   12 years old.
2. Nă-nĕ'sē-ō-thă"-kwă, Rachel Kirk(?) =   6 years old.
   (Flora Hale 5/20/1875 corrected today.)
3. Pă'-màh-hō-kō'-kwàh,   7 years old.
4. Kō'-mă-thō"-kwăh,   8 years old.
   ~~Ka-che-tah-e-se-kwa~~ (Sarah Kirk, written in May 20, 1895)
5. Kā'-chē-tī"-sē-kwă,   16 years old.
6. Della   6 years old.
7. Mary Mardock   10 years old.
8. Flaurice Davis   14 years old.
9. Samuel L. Patrick, Pĕ'-nē-thă"   12 years old.
10. Effie Douglas Wēs'-kō-pă-thō"-kwă   12 years old.
11. Lizzie Test, Kĕ'-tē-kwă   9 years old.
12. Pierrepont Alford   10 years old.
13. Reese Alford   8 years old.
14. Paul Alford   6 years old.

Lina took me into the library room and asked me several questions that Mrs. Myra E. Frye had asked in regard to me, and then she talked very edifyingly upon Scriptural subjects. She asked me if I thought the Bible held out a higher walk to Christians than what they took. I answered, Yes, I do. She spoke some on Christ's Second Coming. About the Final Perseverance of the saints, she was not certain just what the Bible taught.

Monday May 6th 1895. Written 9:10 P.M.
    Thomas Alford and I started home not long after Lina took up school. I was at the first part of the opening exercise of the school. The school repeated [*page 74*] from memory John 14:1-12, or a few more verses perhaps. I thought they did very well. But I soon left, as Thomas was ready to start. Reached home in the afternoon. Went up to David Alford's and found Long Horse and his wife and children there. I and Long Horse helped him mark two calves. Mrs. Mexican Wilson and her little son were there. Garfield Ellis and Ernest Spybuck came also. We all went to town. David was looking for a valuable letter from the Sac and Fox Agency, but the Sac and Fox mail had not come when we started home. It was nearly sunset when we started to depart. I saw Thomas Alford and Walter Shawnee in town. I let Mrs. W. R. Webb have my coat to mend. I furnished the lining and the thread and she is to do the sewing, for which I am to pay her a quarter. George E. Shawnee has gone over to sit up over night with Elkano.
    Lina B. Lunt said that her home was at Brunswick, Maine; that it was twenty miles from where Myra E. Frye lived. Flora Hale said that her home was at Blue Jacket, Ind. Ter. That she had lived in Kansas, Indiana, and elsewhere, that her father and mother were living, and that she had nine sisters and brothers, all of whom were living. Flora asked me in reference to my work, "What do you do, any how?"

Tuesday May 7th 1895.
    I and Mr. Hamlin the farmer for the old man this year stretched a third wire on the partition fence of the western pasture. The forenoon was occupied in rolling up such wire.

Wednesday May 8th 1895.
    I went around by Dr. Hartley's. Saw Dr., Ella, and Emma Newsome, for whom I carried a letter to Mr. Thomas Alford. Not finding Thomas in Tecumseh, I stamped and mailed the letter. I went down to our places on Dance Creek below Tecumseh. Saw Bro. Roberts, Demas Garret and folks and Henry Blackwell. I am to come around and see Henry Blackwell again next Wednesday. Mr. Carter has between 15 and 20 acres broken out on my land in spite of the dry weather. I came back home through Tecumseh. Found no mail in boxes 83 and 1. I was very tired, as I had walked all the way.

Thursday May 9th 1895.

Mrs. Stevens, Miss Emma Newsom, Mrs. Ella Hartley, and myself cleaned up the church. Mrs. Stevens is 34 years old by her own confession. She came from Illinois three years ago this July. She came from the south eastern part of the state. She [*page 75*] is a member of the Primitive Baptists. She believes every body has a right to their religious belief. Miss Emma Newsom said that Miss Lina B. Lunt was in her 34th year. This makes Lina 33 years old this year 1895. Emma Newsom has lived for a while in Kansas. She went to school at the City Academy, Indianapolis, and at Sand Creek Seminary near Columbus, Indiana. She studied Botany, Rhetoric, German, Latin, and other things, but did not graduate at either place. She is a professional nurse, but studied nursing under nurses and physicians, not at school. She has a brother and a half-brother. She would like to see Isaac McCoy. Speaking of Thomas Alford to Emma I said, I did not see your fellow yesterday. So I mailed the letter. She said nothing at first. But afterwards she said: "I never want you to say that word to me again, for I don't have such things." She spoke of the word fellow. I guess teacher would say the same.

A man hauled a barrel of water from the North Fork. We washed the window panes and sills, the floor, and the chairs and benches and lamp chimneys. Mrs. Ella Hartley and Emma each bade me good bye, as I came away.

Lina B. Lunt told me once that she knew one couple who waited twenty-five years on each other before they were married. The first time I ever met Lina was at the Iowa Mission, I believe in 1891. She was teaching school there. She has all the time been very friendly. She is a minister in the Society of Friends. She believes in the principles of the Society. Miss Emma Newsom has been baptized by immersion outside of the Society. She believes that one may feel commanded to be baptized, while another may not feel so. It is hard to understand Emma's views, but they are probably confused. Lina asked me one Sunday if I were satisfied with Friends' views on Baptism. I told her, Yes. That I did not think the Bible bore out the views of any one church on that subject. All views on Baptism, with a very few exceptions, are bosh, and are not what the Scriptures teach. But we must always respect tender consciences, and not judge others who do not see as we do.

Friday May 10th 1895.

I tanned three or four skins and attended Prayer Meeting in the evening. Several from the Mission were present. It looked as if it would rain, and Dr. Hartley wanted me to stay all night but I declined, saying that I could get home before it rained.

Dr. [page 76] and Ella Hartley, Miss Emma Newsom, and others were present. The night was dark at first.

Saturday May 11th 1895.
 I did nothing all day except read. I intended to have gone up to the Kickapoo Mission early Sunday morning, but George Shawnee could not spare his saddle and I could procure no other. Saw my place that there were 51 living fruit trees thereon.

Sunday May 12th 1895.
 Took a note up to Charley Anderson's that Dr. Hartley had written announcing a basket meeting to be held in Shawnee City May 19th 1895. I went to Sabbath School and Church. I taught a class of boys. Dr. Hartley read the 126th Psalm. He talked about seeds, their different kinds, and their all having a life germ within them. He spoke of seeds of wheat found in the hands of Egyptian mummies, that were planted and grew, after lying dormant for 3000 years. He said that one seed of wheat had been known to yield 200 wheat grains. At this rate it would not take many years for a wheat grain to plant all the planets over in a few years, on account of its remarkable fertility. At night he read and preached upon Num. 21:11-9 [1-9?]. His subject was not to be discouragers, but to be encouragers. He reviewed the history of Israel's discouragement from the crossing of the Red Sea to the event in the lesson. We should not let our immediate surroundings discourage us, for we should take the Lord into account. After the morning service, I remained in the church after all had left, reading a commentary—Clark's and a church history. It was about the popes tyrannizing over kings, and absolving the subjects of divers kings from their oath of allegiance. The church of Rome was very corrupt indeed in the 12, 13, 14 centuries. Their corruption can hardly be exaggerated. Miss Kessell came back alone to get her pocket handkerchief, thinking that no one was in the church. She said, This is a very nice day. She never spoke to me before that I know of. Miss Ella Hartley gave me supper, though I did not want any. Mrs. Kirk had come down from the Kickapoo Mission in the morning, so as to teach her class. Miss Emma Newsom taught a class right by me. She can interest them. I did interest mine some. Illustration is what interests a class, so then follow illustration. Lucy Scott was at morning and at evening service also. Miss Kessell was at both morning and evening service and was at church twice through the day besides. [page 77] The Lesson was: Subject, Jesus Before the High Priest, Mark 14th chapter 53-64 verses, inclusive Golden Text. He is despised and rejected of men, Isaiah 53:3. The first clause of this verse.

Monday May 13th 1895.
　　Took the hair off of deer skin, and went to town in the evening. I was in hopes of receiving a letter from Miss Whipple. But did not. Mr. Carson said that another injunction had been issued against the railroad. Received a catalogue of the Iowa State University. I owe Rev. Reeder 5 cts. for a paper he let me have. They told me court would set tomorrow.

Tuesday May 14 1895.
　　I ran a line for fence on my place. I began a pasture fence, and succeeded in running the line, but it is not where I want it yet. Tanned skins some. They [the?] old man—our father—went to Shawnee and came back, saying they were working right along on the railroad, and would have the cars running in two weeks. Last night the Tecumsehites had a jollification, firing anvils and blowing up powder. I infer that another injunction has been issued by the U.S. Government restraining the Choctaw railroad from building on the Kickapoo route. King Davis went to where some armed men were capuped [sp?] near sunset to-day, and asked them about his missing horse. The place was at the spring just east of Joe Whipple's. They denied they were marshalls [marshals] and claimed to be outlaws. They talked about taking him into their gang and asked him if he ever stole any horses or killed any body. On his denying that he had ever done these things, they said that they could not take a man like that into their gang. When the bursting of gun powder began in Tecumseh, they all jumped up, seized their guns, and pretended to be scared, saying that some of their gang had made a raid on Tecumseh, they guessed, and feared some of their gang would run away and would be followed into camp, giving them away. They did not threaten to kill him or to rob him of his horse. They asked him if he had any arms about his person, and ~~they~~ he told them, No. He told them the real cause of the bombardment in Tecumseh, a thing he ought not to have done. King told us his story this morning early May 15th 1895. He ran away from them and left his horse. He lost his hat and is lame too. Mr. Hamlin said it was the Maly [sp?] outfit of marshalls. The reasons for this opinion were: 1. They were given to such tricks as these—scaring people just for the fun of it. 2. They had a colored man along with them who answered the description King gave of this man. 3. The fact of them having two mess wagons along with them, and so near to Shawnee, proves they were not outlaws, but marshalls. The Maly [sp?] outfit of marshalls roam [page 78] through the Kickapoo, and Seminole countries. King Davis was evidently too badly scared to exercise properly his reasoning powers. 1. He should have not obey[ed] them until they compelled obedience by force of arms. 2. He should not have believed they intended to

kill him until they threatened to do so and make appearance of force to do so. As it was, they never even threatened to kill him or to rob him. 3. He should not have volunteered any information to them, such for instance as telling them the real cause of the shooting in Tecumseh. 4. He should not have believed so much what they said.

May 15th 1895. Wednesday.
    I went down to the Lower Place to-day and saw Henry Blackwell about school affairs. He advised me to see the other directors tomorrow. Late in the evening it rained a great shower at Tecumseh, and below, and not very much up here at William Shawnee's. Though it rained enough to help. It hailed during the shower, but the hail were few and small. Walter Shawnee asked me to bring over Harvey's History of the Shawnee Indians tomorrow. I went to town riding in the Spring wagon with William Shawnee. During the day, I made some observations in regard to the status of the negro under the U.S. Constitution prior to the last three amendments thereto. Article 4, Sec. 2, ¶ 3, reads, "No person held to service or labor in one State, under the laws thereof, escaping into another, shall, in consequence of any law or regulation therein, be discharged from such service or labor; but shall be delivered up on claim of the party to whom such service or labor may be due." From this we may learn: 1. That the laws of some states made negroes slaves. 2. The laws of other states made negroes free men. 3. Negroes are persons, either bound to service or labor by law, or free from such service or labor by law. 4. No law in the Constitution bound a negro to service or labor; only state laws made any man a slave, or even a free man for that matter. 4. [5]. These persons held to service or labor may have been white for all the constitution says or implies. Article 1, Sec. 2, ¶ 3 reads in part as follows: "Representatives and direct taxes shall be apportioned among the several States which may be included within this Union, according to their respective numbers, which shall be determined by adding to the whole numbers of free persons, including those bound to service for a term of years, and excluding Indians not taxed, three-fifths of all other persons."
    From this we may learn: 1. The whole number of free persons means citizens. 2. Some of these free persons are negroes. 3. Some of these were free, although bound to service for a term of years, not for life. 4. Other negroes were not free, but were slaves. Of these only three-fifths were added. Of free negroes all were enumerated. 5. Free negroes were liable to be taxed, for who would pay a freeman's tax but himself? The whole number [*page 79*] of free persons are here put together that what may be said of the majority of them may be said of all. It is certain:

all were liable to pay direct taxes; why deny the rights of citizenship to taxpayers, who are free men, who are numbered among those who are citizens. Therefore free negroes, subject to taxation, were citizens of the U.S. in the meaning of the Constitution. 6. Some negroes are free persons, with at least the right to pay taxes and to be enumerated. We wonder Justice Taney did not see it.

Thursday May 16th 1895.
    I went to town on foot, but was overtaken by a white man in a hack, and asked to ride. I took Walter's book to him—Harvey's History of the Shawnee Indians. Thence, I went down below Tecumseh to see the school directors, Morgan and Hill. I met Mr. Morgan, and he said that Mr. Hill was not at home, but was gone down into the Seminole country, and would not probably be back for two weeks. Mr. Morgan said that he had no doubt that I would get the school, and that Mr. Washington would not get it. I came with Mr. Morgan back to Tecumseh. We were both walking. I went into the Court room, and saw Judge Scott upon the bench. There was a law suit over [a] $150 note. The man who had loaned out the money was an old man, who believed there was no God, no heaven, no hell, and nothing. The lawyers said there was no way to bind his conscience with an oath. I believe this old man's name was Bayle, and the other Gallagher. Bayle and Gallagher swore different things about the amount paid on the note. So that one or other of them were swearing lies. But the judge ruled that a reputation for truth and veracity was sufficient, and that if any man swore a lie, there was a law to punish him for perjury. One man was called up and swore that Bayle's reputation for truth and veracity was good. Came home, and dug four post pits on my forty, also running ~~F~~ a line. Was at home the rest of the time.

Friday May 17th 1895.
    Dug out nearly ~~three~~ two feet down in the bottom of my well, Mr. J. M. Cummings my renter windlassing for me. We began work between 9 and 10 A.M. and quit work 5:30 P.M., as Mr. Cummings said at the time. For he had a watch and I have none. Came over to William Shawnee's, bathed, and dressed to go to Prayer Meeting. I wore my red shoes to the Prayer Meeting for the first time. Saw at Prayer Meeting Miss Kessel and another woman from the Shawnee Mission, Mrs. Rachel Kirk, Miss Emma Newsom, Dr. Hartley, Tom Bourbonnais, Miss Aurelia Bourbonnais, and the red-haired woman, and two [*page 80*] young men I knew not. Mrs. Ella Hartley and Mary Bourbonnais were not present. No children either boys or girls from the Mission were present. Miss Kessel spoke that she was from Dakota but not in meeting.

In conversation with Mrs. Kirk before meeting began. She looked at me considerably and as I came up to the church, she was far off, and looked as if she was throwing a kiss. Dr. Hartley read 1st Peter 3:8-22. Nos. 5, 4, 55, and other songs were sung from No. 5 Gospel Hymns. Miss Kessel said, Why, has a month passed by that quick! This was elicited by the observation that tomorrow Monthly Meeting would be held. As I went to Prayer Meeting, I went by my well, and lo a great deal of water had run into it already. So much so it seemed as if a bucket full could be drawn up readily right then. I am writing this after I reach home from Prayer Meeting to-day. Praise the Lord for all his goodness. I must close, for I am becoming sleepy.

Saturday May 18th 1895.

I went to Monthly Meeting held in the church near the Shawnee Mission school. Twenty-four souls were present, among whom were William P. Haworth, Dr. Hartley, Mrs. Hartley, Miss Emma Newsom, Ollie Wilford, Mrs. Bourbonnais, Aurelia Bourbonnais, and Ozetta Bourbonnais. I was present, of course. Several members were present from Wolf Grove just 2 miles east of the town of Shawnee. The free-will offering was $2.55 cts, to which I did not contribute a cent. Miss Emma Newsom did not contribute a cent either since she had left her pocket book in Tecumseh. Mr. Haworth preached from Mat. 4:10. "Then saith Jesus unto him, Get the[e] hence, Satan: for it is written, Thou shalt worship the Lord thy God, and him only shalt thou serve." The latter clause of the verse he took for the basis of his sermon— Thou shalt worship the Lord thy God, and him only shalt thou serve. He observed that we were here commanded to serve the Lord. Though all nations worship different gods, such as images of wood, stone, brass, gold, and silver, and other idols, yet all men agree in the principle of worship; which shows how natural it is for man. Whatever else man lost in the fall in the Garden, he did not lose the tendency or principle to worship. Some people make money their god, some a farm or a fine house, some a fine carriage, some a fine horse, some a wife or a husband, all of this was idolatry. Jesus says, "He that loveth father or mother more than me is not worthy of me: and he that loveth son or daughter more than me is not worthy of me."—Mat. 10:37. Songs were sung and prayers were offered, and testimonies were given. Mr. Haworth said it was probably the last time he would meet us together. Dr. Hartley after services invited me to dinner, [page 81] and I accepted. Mrs. Benson was also present. She is a Quaker and a very young and nice looking woman, and acute in mind and mental powers also. Mrs. Kirk was also invited to the dinner, but declined, saying that she had dinner.

In the afternoon I came home and did nothing. Then I lost half a day wherein I might have worked.

Sunday May 19th 1895.

I borrowed LaFayette Shawnee's saddle and rode the bald-faced, scary pony up to the Kickapoo Mission. About an hour after I reached there Thomas Alford came, with Walter Shawnee sitting in the cart or carriage with him. Teacher (Lizzie Test) had gone up to the Iowa Mission after Harlan Hale, who, being quite sick, had sent for her to come after him. Mary Mardock, a school girl, was sick with what they said was measles. Lina B. Lunt, Flora Hale, and Della gave me a welcome. Soon meeting came, and I interpreted to the Kickapoos from the first three chapters of Genesis about creation, and God's working six days and resting the seventh, about the creation of Adam and Eve, and their residence in the Garden, about Satan's deceiving Eve and man's eating the forbidden fruit, about the punishment of all three, Satan, the woman, and the man, and about the fall or ruin of man, that now he could not please God except by believing in the Lord Jesus. Thomas Alford turned over all the interpreting to me. I did not wish to shirk, so I accepted it. Flora did not shake hands with me this time. Read Ritualism Dethroned Vol. 2 in the room for receptions, whither Lina led me. I remained over night. "Must I go and Empty Handed" was sung by Thomas [*Alford*] in the meeting, one or two others assisting. Several other songs were sung. Lina spoke some in English, very little of which was translated into Indian. The Kickapoos gradually went home after eating dinner. Girls in school, 1 Weskopathoqua or Effie Douglas; 2 Katequa or Lizzie Test had gone home; 3 Mary Mardock; 4 Sarah Kirk or Kachetisekwa; 5 Nathahpehah or Ozetta Bourbonnais; 6 Nanaseothaqua or Flora Hale, Jr.; 7 Komathoqua; 8 Pamahhokokwa; 9 Della Jr.; 10 Samuel L. Patrick, Jr. or Panetha; 11 Flaurice; Pierrepont Alford, Reese Alford, and Paul Alford. At night they recited various pieces of scripture from memory.

Monday May 20th 1895.

Being requested by Flora Sr. and others to remain until after Harlan was brought, I determined to remain, if necessary, until 1 P.M. In the meantime, I visited the school, which was taught by [*page 82*] Lina B. Lunt. Songs were sung, Ps. 1, 23, the Beatitudes, and John 14th chapter in part, and other scriptures were recited from memory by the children in concert. I led in prayer, which followed, at the request of Lina. Lina prayed too, and afterwards she and the children repeated a prayer in concert, nearly like the one Lina wrote out for me by request Feb. last. I prayed for the welfare of the children and of the Kickapoos, that the children might be led to Christ at the same time they were learning out of their books that which would benefit them when they became men and women. I heard the children recite until noon, and was well pleased. Spoke a few words to them just before the noon recess at Lina's request. Told them they had done well, but should try to do better. I told them never to say "I can't," but to try hard. That what they were learning would be useful to them when they became men and women.

Here are some things I learned from a written document, a book, while I was in the reception room Sunday May 19th 1895.
1. Flora Hale was born July 16th 1872.
2. Lawrie Tatum was born May 22nd, 1822.
3. Chas. W. Goddard was born Feb. 28th, 1840.
4. Rachel Kirk was born Feb. 22nd, 1840.
5. Maud Pearson was born July 5th 1880.
6. Isaac Sharp was born July 4th 1806.
7. Harlan Hale was born Nov. 20th, 1873.
8. Nettie Haworth was born April 12th 1871.

Just as we were finishing eating dinner Teacher drove up with Harlan in the back part of the carriage. Most of those at the table then left to see them. Harlan was able to walk into the room from the carriage. I soon started home where I arrived late in the evening. Found all well. Heard from William Shawnee that the Kickapoo country would open May 23rd Thursday at noon. But William could name no one especially that he heard the news from.

Tuesday May 21st, 1895.

I hauled rails around the field, but did not put them up. In the afternoon dug one pit on my land for a post. Drew a map for Mr. Cummings for land in the Kickapoo country. There is plenty of water in my well now.

Wednesday May 22nd, 1895.

I went over to Tecumseh with Mr. Cummings. Thomas Alford was not there in the forenoon. I incidentally told Walter Shawnee [page 83] that I wanted to help Thomas survey. Listened at the trial of the Christian boys for the murder of marshall Turner down near Sacred Heart. Late in the evening I came to the office and found Thomas had engaged Walter as chairman. He may have supplanted me. He is not too good to do such a thing, to say the least. Thomas, however, wanted me to go and survey for a colored colony of about 30, and lent me his compass promising to give me $3 a day until he came. But William Shawnee is afraid to let me have a team to ride in to take up the instruments, saying there was only one wagon on the place fit to use, that the horses would have no feed, and that some body would steal them, there were so many people over there. I told him that I thought there was at least as much grass in the Kickapoo country for them to eat as there was here in the pasture.

I had thought the old man could not spare any thing before I reached home; but had to try. I thought of trying David Alford also early in the morning. If I can not induce him to take me, I guess I will have to walk and carry the instruments. I do not see what other course will be left for me. Of course, I will have to carry so[me] provision along with me too. When I would do any thing, there is always some insurmountable hindrance. I went without both dinner and supper to-day. There is not a more needy creature on earth than I. But no matter how needy you may be William Shawnee will not lend you a wagon and team, nor let George drive me up to where I want to go. The old man wanted to know why I did not get Cegar to take me up there. He wants to lay the burden some where else.

I believe that as soon as I get through with this surveying, I ought as soon as possible to go over in Cleaveland Co., and see about that school over there. If I get this school, it will not begin until the 3rd Monday in November 1895, and I can agree to teach this school between now and Nov. 20 or thereabout. I need to teach school so bad. I do need money. I need a house. I need a pony and saddle and bridle. I need a wagon and team. I need dishes, a cook stove, lamps, tables, chairs, bed-steads, comforters and blankets and a whole host of other things.

Thursday May 23rd, 1895.

Tried without success to get David Alford to bring me over after twelve, but Joe Billy consented to do so. But J. J. Johnson came along and I rode with him, discharged from the obligation that would otherwise have [*page 84*] *Thursday May 23rd, 1895 (Continued)* been imposed upon me. Went first to where the section line strikes the right bank of the North Fork river, 3 miles north of Dale. Found it impracticable to cross here with a wagon. Then we went to the crossing north west of Ewers White's. Found a great multitude of people here. Thence went to the crossing just north or northeast of the 3rd. mile stone from the town of Dale. Here we crossed the river. Mr. J. J. Johnson said at the time that the Carsons of Tecumseh were there. Stephen Carter, Demas Garrett, and several other men of color were there. Several believed at the time that the gun was fired a few moments before twelve. We—Johnson and two other white men and myself were the last to cross the river. These white men were riding gray horses. These white men were behind us, and as they passed us, observed, that we four had crossed the river at the proper time. We moved very slowly to the section corner between 7, 8, 17, and 18, meeting these same two white men on the way there, and thence began operations. Worked hard running lines and stepping. Camped at the Kickapoo Springs with Thomas Alford, Walter Shawnee, and the gentleman who clerks in John King's store. We camped about 150 yards northeast of the Kickapoo Springs. Had nothing to eat with me, but drew supplies from the board of Thomas and the rest. Slept on the ground near a fire, with the earth for a pillow, and the sky for my comforter. No covering at all had I, but did not take off any of my clothing. This day's doings are noted down in ink to-day at night. Monday May 27th 1895, from notes in led pencil made either Saturday May 25th 1895, or Sunday May 26th 1895, with additions from memory interpolated.

Friday May 24th 1895. (Written tonight May 27th 1895 about 8 P.M.[)]

Worked hard all day and earned $1 for Thomas Alford, by running a mile for some white men. They asked me to be sure and come back the next day, in case Thomas did not come. The colored men left me and went home, as I suppose, while I was running the line for those white men. Came tired out and weary to the Kickapoo Mission 9 P.M. Lina B. Lunt bestowed much labor on me. The Lord reward her according to her deeds. She ministered to my temporal wants joyfully. It rained at night.

Saturday May 25th 1895. (Written tonight May 27th 1895, 8:20 P.M. by light). Copied from notes in led pencil made at the time, with additions thereto.

Samuel L. Patrick, Jr., a Kickapoo boy, about 13 years old, is standing to my left hand as I write this evening. He is a good little boy. He helped set out potatoe plants this evening. He reads in the 3rd reader. Kăh-pă'-ō-màh, about 14 or 15 years old, is sitting by. He has a shawl around his waist, and twisted together. It reaches from the [*page 85*] knees to the girdle. He says that he hates school. Mr. William Jenks is just come in about sunset from Choctaw City with a load of flour, lime, and plasture [plaster] of Paris. It rained showers all through the day. Went out to the prairie close by the section corner to 7, 8, 17, 18 Township 11 North, of Range 3 East. This is the only time I went out with the compass, but the rain made me go right back to the Kickapoo Mission 5 miles away. I was on foot too. I did not do much all day. Helped set out sweet potatoe plants in the garden. Thought of Miss Kessel and the folks at the Mission. Mr. Jenks has brought some flour in sacks and lime in barrels.

Sunday May 26th 1895. (Written tonight May 27th 1895. 8:35 P.M. from notes in led pencil made on the spot, with additions).

A good many Kickapoos were present at the Mission to-day, and among them were several I knew. Měs-kwē-kă-nàh-kàh was present, and three of the conservative element. They were very sad over the state of affairs consequent upon the opening Thursday, and feared the white people would take their crops. Teacher (Lizzie Test, Sr.) preached to them while I interpreted and the conservatives were impatient. They seemed to care very little what was said. The sermon was about Jesus raising the widow's son to life. Mr. Thomas Alford did not come. I was sorry for this, as I would have liked very much to see him. He surely did not survey on Sunday. The Kickapoos passed from church to the dinner table. The three conservatives were taken into the parlor and teacher read a letter to them from a friend of Pais[h]ter's [sp?] (I believe this is the name), and heard their complaints. One of them spoke fair Shawnee. Teacher comforted them and counselled them to live any where upon the land that had been set apart for them. If white people tried to take their corn or other crops, bring her word, she said, and she would go and talk to them. For their conservative band lives on land that has now been set aside for school purposes. Persons present at the Kickapoo Mission: Lina B. Lunt, Della, Sr. a white woman; Mr. Fleming, Malcom, Harlan Hale came about noon from the Iowa Mission on horseback. Nathahpehah, Nanaseothakwa, Thàhnàhkăthōkwă or Della Jr., Mary Mardock, Jr., a Kickapoo girl just recovering from the measles, Kā-chē-tiē-sē-kwă or Sarah Kirk, Flaurice Davis, Kō-mă-thō-kwă or Maudie Pearson, Jr., Pă-màh-hō-kō'-kwà or Axie Higley, Jr., Remained over night. Was active in Christian duties, such as prayer.

Monday May 27th 1895 (Written tonight 9:10 P.M.[)]

Teacher has some Wire Net Work to fix a hog pasture with. I propose to fence with like material a hog pasture for myself. This is the name of the company and so forth:- The Sedgwick Bros. Co., Manufacturers [*page 86*] of Wire Net Work, Fence, Gates, and Lawn Furniture, 1517 North F Street, Richmond, Indiana. I must send for a catalogue, with a view of purchasing for myself. Came home in the hack with Harlan Hale, Flora Hale, Pierrepont Alford, Reese Alford, and Paul Alford. Saw Mrs. Kirk and agreed to go with her to Big Jim's Wednesday, but John Whitehead, as road overseer has warned me out to work on the road the same day. So I will have to inform Mrs. Kirk as early in the morning as I can. The *New York Independent* did not come this evening. I guess my subscription has expired.

Tuesday May 28th 1895, written 10:55 P.M. Saturday June 1st 1895.

I went down on my lower place, going first by the house of Mrs. Kirk and Mrs. Ella Hartley. Saw both of these ladies, and told them why I could not go with them to Big Jim's as agreed, because John Whitehead the road overseer had caught me to work on the road. Mrs. Hartley is going to start to Indiana next week. Went down on my lower place, and beyond the house of Mr. Blackwell, who is one of the members of the School Board. Advised him to have the Board to decide for or against me before long. Made a remittance of 25 cts. to the *New York Independent*. Sent for a catalogue of Wire Net Work, etc.

Wednesday May 29th 1895.
Worked on the road under John Whitehead overseer, beginning by the house of Mr. William Jenks. Saw Thomas Alford and the gentleman who clerks in John King's store, both returning from the Kickapoo country. They could find no surveying to do. Mr. Fleming, of the Kickapoo Mission, came after Dr. Hamilton. The Kickapoo blacksmith had broken his leg while on the way to Oklahoma City. Staid all night at Whitehead's. It looks like rain in the morning.

Thursday May 30th 1895.
Worked on the road using Whitehead's team. Worked from Dan Chilson's house to the river. It rained while we were at the river. Finally we took shelter, with the horses under the north end of the bridge. Mr. Cummings worked both Wednesday and Thursday.

Friday May 31st, 1895.
Worked for Whitehead, digging post holes and setting posts for his yard fence. I do this because he let me have his team to work the road with. So my two day's work is counted four, because a man and his team are two day's work.

[page 87] *Saturday June 1st, 1895.*
Worked all day for John Whitehead, digging post holes, hoeing corn, and hunting cattle and horses. Came home at night. John Whitehead, his wife Mary and their little Webster went to town in the afternoon. This is written Monday June 3rd, 1895, at 12:20 P.M. Also add the following record of Births, taken from the record of William Shawnee:—
"Elizabeth Jane born September 11it 1849."
"Willie Ivery Shawnee Born December 23d 1868."
"Cora Anner Shawnee Born September 3d 1870"
"Dudley Joseph Shawnee Born March 28, 1872."
"Walter Homer Shawnee Born May 22it, 1874."
"George Eli Shawnee Born April 11d, 1876."

"Eva Shawnee Born January 18th 1884."
"Rebecca Shawnee Born April 14th 1885."
"Lydia Shawnee Born January 15th 1887.["]
"Cora Anner Shawnee died April 18th 1879."
"Elizabeth Jane died May 23, 1879."

Sunday June 2nd 1895.
    Rode up to the Kickapoo Mission. Arrived about 11 o'clock. Got there after Thomas Alford, who was already there. Komathokwa, or Maudie Pearson, Jr., Pamahhokokwa or Axie Higley, and Della or Thahnahkabokwa were sick with measles. The blacksmith died Thursday, from an overdose of opium. He was buried at the Sac and Fox Agency. Teacher talked to the Kickapoos and Thomas did the interpreting. Robert Deer was present. Teacher knows him. Thomas came away in the evening. I staid over night, coming back Monday morning June 3rd 1895. Miss Lina B. Lunt thinks more of me than any other woman living. She is so sympathetic and considerate. She is 33 years old and is a minister in the Society of Friends.

Monday June 3rd 1895.
    Came home from the Kickapoo Mission at 11 A.M. After dinner went over to Mrs. Kirk's by way of Dr. Hamilton's. Found Dr. Hamilton, but gave the letter to his wife. Found everybody about[?] from Mrs. Kirk's. Went to Thomas Alford's place. Took the box home, and put the compass away in it. Went by [Ni . . . .]. Read thru *Cherokee Advocates*. Went on to Tecumseh. Got the mail. Went on to Mr. J. J. Johnson's. Saw his wife. Visited Mrs. Carter. She said school teachers received good wages in Tex. Came around by Mrs. Kirks. Found Miss Kessel [*page 88*] but did not speak to her, or she to me. Told Mrs. Hartley Goodbye. She will start for Indiana Wednesday June 5th 1895. Thence came home.

Sunday Morning June 9th 1895. 7:55 A.M. by the clock.
    For the last five days, Tuesday, Wednesday, Thursday, Friday, and Saturday, June 4th, 5th, 6th, 7th, and 8th, respectively, have been working at John Whitehead's at 50 cts. a day. Hoeing, plowing, and other work occupied my time. There was a ring or halo around the sun Friday June 7th 1895. It was the color of the rainbow. John Whitehead, Mary Whitehead, Mr. and Mrs. Jones also saw it. The last two are renters on John's place this year. Came home Tuesday evening to bring George Shawnee's letter to him, which I had forgotten to give him Monday night. Remained over night, going back to Whitehead's early the next morning. Mary Whitehead had one of old Bob Ingersoll's books. It had been borrowed from some white family somewhere. The man who

lent the book is not a religious man, and they said that he said that Bob had some good things in it along with other things that were extreme. I failed to see much good in the book. Thomas Paine is held up in it as a good infidel, not withstanding the fact that Tom said that he cared not for the opinion of the world in regard to his drunkenness. He cared for neither God nor man. Jefferson and Franklin were infidels as Bob says, but I have my doubts as to Benj. Franklin's being an infidel. In fact there is some proof to the contrary. I have the proof to the contrary in my possession.

Sunday June 9th 1895, at the house of William Shawnee this is written at 12:55 P.M.
    Attended church and Sabbath School at the meeting house at Old Shawneetown near the Shawnee Mission. A number of Shawnee boys and girls were present. Present Mrs. Rachel Kirk, Mrs. Mary Bourbonnais[,] Miss Kessel, Mrs. Neal, Josephine Barone, Miss Minnie Riley, but not Dr. Hartley, or Mrs. Hartley. Taught a class of Shawnee boys. I and Miss Kessel were both appointed to the class. It seems that she had taught it previously. I must go over to Whiteheads as soon as I have dinner, to see if my help is needed.

Written Thursday [June 13?] by myself at 8 o'clock P.M. by the clock. Monday June 10th 1895
    Worked all day for John Whitehead in company with Dan Chilson. John reached home from Sacred Heart Mission Sunday June 10th [9th?] [1895]. He did not bring his daughter Irene with him [*page 89*] because her eyes were not sore, as he had heard they were, and because she wanted to stay until the close of the school. John said the "sisters" [[Catholic nuns]] treated him like a king, having the servants to put up his horse and feed them. He was detained for two hours on the road home by rain. It rained a good rain Sunday night June 9th 1895, and this kept me from going to church at night. Quit working for John late in the evening by telling him so. I wanted to go over into Cleaveland Co., to see about a school. Remained all night, milked the cows, and came home after breakfast. This was [*writing ends here*]

Tuesday June 11th 1895.
    Came home from John Whitehead's, and asked the old man for a horse to ride over into Cleaveland Co. to see about a school, but the old man would not let me have a horse. He pretended that I wanted to go up to Big Jim's to a war dance. I told him I had heard nothing about Big Jim's war dance, and that Big Jim did not have his war dance at this time of the year, but in July or August. This he pretended not to believe. I went to town and

sent 25 cts. by Money Order to the *New York Independent*. This pays my subscription up to the middle of July 1895. The probate judge Ruggles was in the bench in the Court House, and a jury of twelve men were trying the Gilman case. United States Indian Agent Edward L. Thomas was in the Court Room. I heard he had been on the witness stand during the day. Gilman was indicted for the criminal using of force, or assisting in so doing, but the Agent and Davis the Kickapoo farmer were present as witnesses. Gilman had bought a piece of land and had his deed approved by the Secretary of the Interior. The Agent ordered the Kickapoo farmer with the Indian police to put Gilman in possession of that land, and in doing so, they cut the fence and drove out the stock of the illegal lessee whose name was Bonham, I believe. ~~Asher - W. R.~~ W. R. Asher defended Gilman while McFall and Pendleton prosecuted. The jury found Gilman not guilty, but the verdict was not made known until the next morning. I staid out on my place to night, coming home from town perhaps between 11 and 10 P.M.

Wednesday June 12th 1895.

I went to town [*page 90*] this day after the rain. It rained a good rain. I did not do anything but talk with the lawyers J. Herring and King, especially the latter. I was talking to them about a lot of us allotters getting together and have an injunction issued commanding the County Treasurer not to collect the tax made upon the allotments of allotters. Mr. King did not want to take hold of the case unless he was sure he could win. He told me to come some other day, and he would in the meantime be looking up the case.

Thursday June 13th 1895.

Big Jim, Lă-làh'-wē-pĕă, Pecan, and a daughter of the widow of Long Jim, were here yesterday evening and went home to-day nearly noon, going by Tecumseh. William Shawnee went along with them as interpreter. Helped George Shawnee and a son of Mr. Hamlin the renter to stake and rider the fence around the cornfield where it needed such. It was staked and ridered before, but here and there it was not. Worked on my own forty in the evening. Walter Shawnee is here to-night.

The Following Is Written Saturday June 15th 1895 at 8:27 A.M. by the clock.
Friday June 14th 1895.

It rained a big rain in the morning, so much so that the [creeks?] are running with water. Worked on my own land. Dug one pit, but it was too wet to dig more. I went to Prayer Meeting later in the evening. Found preacher Roberts, who is preacher at

Tecumseh, Wolf Grove, and Anderson's school house. Lina B. Lunt was down from the Kickapoo Mission. Miss Emma Newsom was present, so were Mrs. Rachel Kirk, and Dr. G. N. Hartley. A number of school children—girls—were present from the Mission, and so were several employees. Miss Kessel was present too. Brother Roberts led the meeting reading the first few verses of Luke 24, ending with the 11th verse. Lina also spoke on the same subject, but she quoted from John 21st, "Simon son of Jonas, lovest thou me more than these." One lady from the Mission spoke to the effect that she was not ashamed to own Christ as her Savior. Mrs. Bourbonnais, Ozetta Jenks, Aurelia Bourbonnais, about 13 years old, - all had something to say, with the exception of Ozetta. Lucy Scott, Minnie Riley, Nellie Warrior, Tono Bourbonnais were present. Tono went with Lucy. I wonder if they will marry? George or Walter were not present. Lina said she was going back home to the Kickapoo Mission Saturday afternoon.

[page 91] Saturday June 15th 1895 written at 9:25 P.M. in the night.

I went to Monthly Meeting, and reached there some time before it commenced. Ollie Wilford was already present when I arrived. She had come on horseback. During the day, the following things were learned. That all her folks were Baptists, while she alone was a Quaker; that she was from Nebraska, where her father still is, and that she was an active member of the Christian Endeavor Society at Wolf Grove. She is a nice looking woman, and a good one. She does not seem proud or dignified; she speaks in meeting. She said that she did not know how much. Lina B. Lunt, Miss Emma Newsom, Mrs. Rachel Kirk, Mr. Chas. E. Roberts, Mr. G. N. Hartley, Mrs. Mary Bourbonnais, Mrs. Ozetta Jenks, Miss Aurelia Bourbonnais, Mr. Thomas W. Alford, Miss Ollie Wilford, and some others were present. Those who remained for dinner by request were Miss Ollie Wilford, Mr. Thomas Alford, and myself. The others at the table were Miss Lina B. Lunt, Miss Emma Newsom, Mrs. Rachel Kirk, Mr. G. N. Hartley, Mr. Chas. E. Roberts. The meeting was a good one, and Bro. Roberts was recorded as a minister. Ollie appears to be about 25 years old and is quite tall and not heavy set but rather slim. Her nose spoils her good looks some, but her heart is truly beautiful and she is independent in her religious views. She never knew Quakers before she came to this country, but now is a Quaker herself. Mrs. Kirk said: That all the Kickapoo school children had gone home Thursday; that Della was gone to Norman, but would be back on June 28th, that Lina's sister was sick with dropsy, and that Lina might go home on that account July 1st

1895; that she wanted us to go down to Big Jim's Monday or Tuesday. She wanted me to be at Sabbath School to-morrow, the last Sabbath the children would be together for some time. I must attend the closing exercises of the school.

Sunday June 16th 1895, written this night at 10:20 P.M.

I have just come from church to-night. Among those present were Miss M. C. Williams, Miss Kessel, Miss Belle Lockhart, Miss Minnie Riley, Miss Lucy Scott, Mrs. Rachel Kirk, Walter Shawnee, George Shawnee, John King, and Dr. G. N. Hartley, who preached the sermon, and others. The sermon was about Adam and Eve in the garden and Christ Our Substitute was the subject. I was at Bible School and Church in the morning. Many children were present, and I had a class. Miss Kessel was not present. Miss M. C. Williams, Miss Duck, Mrs. Neal, Mrs. Rachel Kirk, Mrs. Mary Bourbonnais, Miss Aurelia Bourbonnais, and others were present. Mr. Hartley preached about the Pearl of Great Price or rather The Hidden [*page 92*] Treasure. He invited me to dinner and I remained. I staid all day long reading. About sunset Miss Riley and Miss Lockhart came to the church the latter coming in. Finally Minnie came and from the outside said some thing to Miss Lockhart, who replied "I will tell Miss Kessel." I suppose Minnie had said she was going to talk to me. Mrs. Kirk wants to go to Big Jim's tomorrow. Mrs. Ozetta Jenks is going along.

The Following Written Wednesday evening June 19th 1895 7:50 P.M.
Monday June 17th 1895.

Rode the ball-faced bay pony and went with Mrs. Kirk and Mrs. Ozetta Jenks to Big Jim's. They rode in a buggy. Visited Shawnee Doctors seeing him and an old woman, John Taylor's, Joe Billy's, Charley Scott's and remained all night. Saw Big Jim, Little Jim, Ruth Big Jim, and the wife of Little Jim, and the little daughter of the wife of Little Jim about 5 years old. Păsēkăhs was also here, and John Sloan.

Tuesday June 18th 1895.

We visited Joe Blanchard's, Little Charley's, but he was absent, John Spoon, and wife, the sisters of Little Charley, and Old Widow Shaaney and others. Visited the house of Bob White or Lălàhuēspĕă. Found only two young women at home. Visited last the house of Inàhkaulàh. We arrived in Tecumseh between 2 and 3 P.M. I went down to my place and to Blackwell's. Saw where some land had been broken out, although the boys said Mr. Stephen Carter had been absent for two weeks, but he will be home tomorrow, said they. Came home read the news. Walter, George, and I occupied one bed.

Wednesday June 19th 1895.
   Hoed out my first trees, 52 in number. Did nothing the rest of the day. Went nowhere. Rained in the evening a slow rain.

Written Saturday June 22nd 1895, 5:55 A.M.
Thursday June 20th 1895.
   Went to Tecumseh very early to interpret for White Turkey. After long waiting White Turkey came, bringing Hast[ie]y, a Shawnee woman wife of Popo Stanley. Mr. Lawyer King wrote two letters for them asking about pension for Hast[ie]y. Walter Shawnee is not at home.

Friday June 21st 1895.
   Visited the closing exercises at the Shawnee Mission. Dr. Hartley, Mrs. Kirk, lawyer Foster and another lawyer and many others were present. Mr. Barone, Mrs. Barone, Annie Barone, Shaunago, Boletha Hood, Jim Warrior, Edwin Ellis, White Turkey, William Shawnee, Thomas Alford, John King, Rock, Thomas Washington, [*page 93*] Peter Brady, Ellen White Turkey, Mamie Alford, Julia Shawnee, Mrs. Marcus, Willie Laundras, some Creek men and women whose names I know not, and others. Miss Kessel had her primary school speak their pieces. They did as well as any, both in the songs and in the recitations. Mrs. Neal and her school did well. Miss M. C. Williams and her school all had pieces about the Revolutionary War. Bushyhead Tyner, Lewis Tyner, Josephine Barone, and others did well. Bushyhead is about 13 years old, Lewis 20 or 21, and Miss Barone about 13.
   Miss Kessel and I had a little conversation today from which I gleaned the following items. She is from Hitchcock, South Dakota, and is not going home this summer nor is she going to resign.
   Pie and cake was had in abundance for dinner.
   I was at Prayer Meeting. Few were present. Mr. Hartley preached. Miss Kessel, Miss Lockhart, Minnie Riley, Lucy Scott, Nellie Alford, and a few others. Thomas Alford went riding with Lucy and Nellie today and occupied the middle place on the seat. William Shawnee reports that a large number of Indians were drunk. Lewis Tyner, Martin Starr, Jim Warrior, White Turkey, Ben Bullfrog, and Garfield Ellis were drunk. Mr. Will Cockran from the Cherokee Nation was here as a guest tonight.

Saturday June 22, 1895 (written June 24th, 1895. 7:45 P.M.[)]
   Dug pits for posts on my land and helped Mr. Cummings clean out the well. Walter Shawnee did not come home. We knew not where he had gone. George Shawnee and I occupied the room upstairs all by ourselves.

Sunday June 23rd, 1895 (written June 24th, 1895. 7:50 P.M.[)]

Went out very early to hunt the horses in the pasture, intending to go up to the Kickapoo Mission. George Shawnee refused to lend me his saddle, so I had to lead the ball-faced pony over to Mr. Cummings', and borrow a saddle, bridle, and saddle blanket. I decided it was too late to go to the Kickapoo Mission, and so went out to the land settlement where Mr. Norris lives in Sec. 14, Town[ship] 10N. of Range 1 E. I[ndian] M[eridian]. Arrived there about noon. It was too late to have gone to the Kickapoo Mission. Read the Scriptures some to-day.

Monday June 24th 1895 (written to-day at 8 P.M. by time piece[)]

Saw several men and traveled several miles to try to find a school to teach between now and November. The last man I saw was Parson Brown, who lives in Sec. 25, Town[ship] 10N Range 1 West Indian Meridian. He recited his grievances in regard to how the white people had tried to keep [*page 94*] them out of school for several years. He claims to be a Methodist preacher. He is a mulattoe, and his wife is the same. He had some interesting books in his library, but I did not have time to read them. He kindly gave me dinner, and I came home. Stopped a little while at Jim Warrior's but he was not at home. Mrs. Mexican Wilson, Inez Greengrass, Quă-thă', and Yellow Squirrel wife of Jim were present. Mrs. Wilson's children were also present. Stopped at David Alford's and found him plowing. Mamie, Cinda Emma, Webster, and Ernest Spybuck were also present. Took the saddle and other things I had borrowed, but Mr. Cummings had gone to Norman today at noon. Walter Shawnee came just before sunset. Will Cockran and wife still here. Charlie Beaver is here too. Found no school.

Tuesday June 25th 1895 (written June 27th 1895 at 2:20 P.M.[)]

Went up without breakfast to Charley Beaver's and ate up there. The object was to have me interpret for him, as he intended to pay the interest on his note of $30 at the bank. Went to town in the wagon with him, and at Ellis Town Jim Spoon and Sampson Day got aboard. Sampson had money, for he took pains to let us see some of it. Arrived in Tecumseh and before doing one thing Charley was called into the Railroad Saloon by the boys, and went. It was too late to pay the interest when we went to the bank. So Charley gave me the money to pay on the morrow.

Wednesday June 26th 1895 (written June 27th 1895 at 2:25 P.M.[)]

Went from home around by Cegar's. Mrs. Cegar had me wait for dinner. Thence went to town. Saw the banker but he refused to let the note bear interest any longer, saying that Charley would never pay it unless he was crowded.

Thursday June 27th 1895 (written July 3rd 1895 (9:05 P.M.)[)]
    Rode the ball-faced pony down to my lower place, saw Mr. Stephen Carter and his boys there. There was plenty of water in the creek, they said. Mr. Carter had broke out some this day. Saw Mr. Blackwell and he was still willing for me to have the school. Stayed all night at the house of Demas Garrett. It rained that night.

Friday June 28th 1895.
    Saw Mr. Morgan one of the school board. He was not in favor of my getting the school. I had a long talk with him. Mr. Hill is my only hope.

Saturday June 29th 1895.
    It rained some to-day. Could not ride up to the Kickapoo Mission. [*page 95*] Hà-nē-kă'-nàh-ke, cacikenapapa.

Sunday June 30th 1895.
    Rode the ball-faced pony to the Kickapoo Mission. Meeting was just over when I got there. Nathahpehah and her little sister Flora, Kāchētīsēk, and Effie Douglas and her mother[,] Thomas Alford, Mrs. Rachel Kirk, Teacher, Lina B. Lunt, Flora Hale, and others were present. Harlan Hale was present. Stayed all night. Mr. Alford and his three boys left for Oklahoma City after dinner. The boys are going to Kansas City for two months. Meeting was held at night.

Monday July 1st 1895.
    At Teacher's request I helped Mr. Flemming make wire fence. All day we worked at it. Thomas Alford came back from Oklahoma City about midnight.

Tuesday July 2nd 1895.
    Came home, bringing a letter to Mr. Roberts, at the Mission Home. Left the letter at the home with his wife. Dug holes on my place. Our corn looks fine. It is "overshooting" in some places. Stayed at home. Staid all night there. Jim Walt a S[. . .]boy is here. Staid all night.

Wednesday July 3rd 1895.
    Went over to John Whiteheads. He gave me a note to John C. King for the latter to let me have Two Dollars in the store. Got a pair of pants for $2.50 cts, paying 50 cts in cash. Then came home with William Shawnee in the carriage, as I found him in town. This old man left with Mr. Webb some flour and meat.

Borrowed LaFayette's saddle, paying him 5 cts for the use of it. This little boy is here yet.

Thursday July 4th 1895 (written July 9th 1895, 10:55 A.M.[)]
    Went up to the Kickapoo Mission. 51 Kickapoos were present. Nănăsēōthăkwă and Rachel Kirk, Jr. each about 6 years old were among the number. Lina B. Lunt was busy waiting on the people. So also was Lizzie Test, Sr. and others. Rachel Kirk, Sr., Flora Hale, Emma Newsom, Thomas Alford, Harlan Hale, were also present. Beef, ice cream and lemonade, cake, were free to all. All were filled and well satisfied. Came home that evening with Thomas in the buggy, leading my horse behind. The railroad was built up into Shawnee.

Friday July 5th 1895 (written 11 A.M. July 9th 1895).
    Fell in love with two girls, Lizzie Washington and Annie Barone. Went to town to look after the matter of Susie Ellis. Saw Susie Ellis and told her. Visited Barone's where Annie was bold in talking to [page 96] me. John, his wife, the baby, Josie and Annie were all present. Saw Dr. Hamilton at his home, was at Prayer Meeting. Dr. Hartley was up at the Iowas. Mr. Roberts and his wife, Geo. Shawnee and others were present. Came home and remained over night.

Saturday July 6th 1895 (written 11:08 A.M. July 9th 95[)].
    Cut weeds, but oh it was so very hot I had to quit. It was the hottest day we have had this year. Went to town and saw Thos. Alford. Came back home; staid all night.

Sunday July 7th 1895, written 11:10 A.M. July 9th 1895.
    Caught the ball-faced pony and rode over to the Kickapoo Mission, arriving some time before church. About 25 Kickapoos were present at the services. Lina B. Lunt and Dr. Pearson spoke to the people. Thomas Alford did all the interpreting. Lina spoke last, saying she was going away and might never see the Kickapoos again, but she intended to come back. Teacher did not speak. The mouth of Flora Hale was stopped. She has not spoken or prayed for a good while. I guess she is backsliding. Staid all night.

Monday July 8th 1895 (written 7 P.M. July 17th 1895)
    Came home from the Kickapoo Mission but went down to see Mr. Hill, one of the school board without coming home. He appeared willing for me to have the school, but could not promise me for sure that he would vote for me. But Mr. Hill was going down to Muscogee the next day, and knew not when he would be back; still he promised to write to me and to Mr. Morgan.

Tuesday July 9th 1895 (written 7 P.M. July 17th 1895)

    Went up to Choctaw City to hunt a school, riding the ball-faced pony. Reached Choctaw City after night and paid 10 cts. for feed and stall for my pony. I had only 3 cts. left. I slept in an old place scarcely fit to sleep in, but it kept the rain off me. I was having a very hard time.

Wednesday July 10th 1895 (written 7:05 P.M. July 17th 1895).

    Rode from Choctaw City to the house of Rev. Mr. Dunjee, but found he had just gone to Oklahoma City. It began a regular steady rain a few minutes after I came into the house. Unsaddled and tied out my horse. I read in the library and talked to Ella Dunjee and Drusilla Dunjee. No one knew that I had no breakfast that morning. But I had dinner. Mr. Dunjee came back late in the evening. He was pretty wet. But for his hospitality I would have been hungry and wet too. Showed my Teacher's Certificate to Ella and Drusilla. Ella paid the most attention to me, being the last to retire at night.

[page 97] *Thursday July 11th 1895 (written 7:15 P.M. July 17th 1895).*

    It rained all day and I read all day in Mr. Dunjee's ample library. Ella was a fellow-reader, but Drusilla was unwell. It rained all the time. Mr. Dunjee and I looked over his crop, and found it very nice. He was very much elated over the matter. His apple trees, peach trees and plum trees were looking fine. Both nights I and Mr. Dunjee were bed fellows.

Friday July 12th 1895 (written 7:20 P.M. July 17th (1895).

    Although it looked as if it would pour down at any moment, still I set out to hunt a school. Bade all farewell. Mr. Dunjee kindly bade me remain, saying that his door was open at all times. I saw Mr. Depew and others, and found some one had already "spoke" for their school. So it was with another school. But the third school I came too, they were very anxious for a teacher. They accordingly gave me a hearty welcome. My certificate took every thing by storm, although I was a perfect stranger. I was unanimously chosen teacher. The best chair, the best bed were cheerfully given and as cheerfully accepted. It only remained to see the board the next day.

Saturday July 13th 1895 (written 7:30 P.M. July 17th 1895).

    Went with Mr. Cooper to see the members of the school board severally at their homes. One was absent on a trial to Oklahoma City. Two gave their consent to employ me. The school house is a nice one and it has better seats and so forth than the colored school house in Tecumseh. Came down to the Kickapoo Mission and met a welcome. But I missed Lina B. Lunt. Thomas Alford was present. Slept sound and well. Flora Hale looked so pretty.

Sunday July 14th 1895 (written 7:35 P.M. July 17th 1895).
    Twenty-three Kickapoos were present. Mr. Thomas Alford made them a very good sermon about the Golden Calf. I spoke also a few words. The rest were listeners, but do not very well understand the services. Harlan Hale came in the afternoon from the Iowa Mission. Mrs. Kirk was present.
    ~~Monday July~~ Came home this Sunday evening. The old man was mad Sunday morning because I had hurt the pony's back. Walter Shawnee had a good deal to say too. Still he held the pony while I administered a remedy.

[page 98] Wednesday July 31st 1895 (written at night July 31st 1895).
    It was cloudy all day. Went down on the lower place in company with Stephen Carter. Several roughs kept open the fence by either cutting the wire or knocking off the staples. Mr. Carter has plenty of watermelons and musk-melons. I rather doubt if Mr. Carter has 30 acres broken out yet. I am very glad that I have both of my places in cultivation. Came home just after sunset, and is hardly yet dark at this writing. I need to build a house on my lower place, so that some one can stay there all the time. I need to build a house on my upper place. I must use my money that I earn in teaching toward building houses on my place. I want to raise chickens and turkeys. I must live on my own land, and not on the land of some one else.

    Tuesday July 30th 1895 (written same time as the above [July 31]) Went early in the morning over to the bridge John Whitehead is building, and worked there all day. It was very hot in the afternoon. The sweat just rolled off of us. John's aunt was sick and he had gone to see her. Some fellow was in his place to oversee the job, however. Came home and read about the rebellion of 1861-65.

    Monday July 29th 1895 (written at the same time as the above [July 31]). Started from sunrise from the Kickapoo Mission, coming home. Came by Shawnee, carrying a package for Mrs. Kirk, which was duly delivered. Came around by Tecumseh also. No railroad division would be given by the Supreme Court for a week or more, I was told. The case had been argued, however.

    Sunday July 28th 1895 (written as above [July 31]) Was at the Kickapoo Mission all day. Teacher, Mrs. Kirk, Emma Newsom,

Ida Grace, and Mr. Fleming, and Theodore were present. Some Kickapoos came, but all went home before church, leaving Nathapehah and Nanaseothakwa to remain a week or more. Lina B. Lunt was expected home by another Sunday. A good meeting was held.

[page 99] Saturday July 20th 1895 (written same as above [July 31].)
   Attended Shawneetown Monthly Meeting. 15 persons were present. Mrs. Kirk, Mr. and Mrs. Hartley, Mrs. Bourbonnais, and Emma Parks. Ollie Wilford was not present. Rode through the hot afternoon up to the Kickapoo Mission. A few Kickapoos were present. Miss Emma said she had been away at work down at the Mickosukey [Miccosukee] Mission. She is a Christian.

Sunday July 21st, 1895. (written same as above [July 31]) A few Kickapoos were present. Teacher discoursed to them about Sodom and its destruction. Staid over night. Mrs. Kirk came up from Shawneetown this morning.

Saturday July 27th 1895 (written same as above [July 31]). Washed my drawers, socks, and shirt. Got ready and started up to the Kickapoo Mission. Arrived there about sunset. It was very hot through the day.

Thursday Aug. 1st 1895 (written Aug 4th 1895 at night)
   Worked on my place digging post holes, but did nothing in the afternoon. Was at home. John Whitehead came and ask[ed] me to come and donate time on the morrow, building that bridge near David Alford's. Promised him that I would do so.

Friday Aug. 2nd 1895 (written same as above [Aug. 4])
   Went after breakfast to work on the road with dinner with me. It was quite hot in the forenoon. Mr. Whitehead, Webster Whitehead, Mr. W. R. Webb, the renter on Sallie Canalas' land were present. A white fellow from west of David's and a white youth also helped us in lifting. Mr. Whitehead took me home with him for dinner. A rain came ~~how~~ up in the afternoon and Mr. Whitehead asked me to go home with him and stay over night. It was a hard rain for over half an hour. Irene Whitehead, Webster Whitehead, and I had a game of croquet. William Phrapp was a guest here also. Mr. and Mrs. Whitehead are very friendly. Irene played on the piano at night. Her eyes look as if they were weak. They appear to fill with tears on her viewing steadily. She is a nice looking little girl about ten years old. Webster claims to be seven years old. Was a guest here.

Saturday Aug. 3rd, 1895 (written same as above [Aug. 4]). Worked on the bridge all day, taking dinner by invitation at Mr. Whitehead's. Mr. Hamlin also worked to day, hauling a load of lumber. Worked until nearly sunset. Came home and prepared some to go up to the Kickapoo Mission, but could not get a saddle to ride upon. George Shawnee could not lend me his saddle; and besides I had no shirts or drawers clean at all. So I could not go up to the Mission, although it was in my heart to go, but it seems that [*continued on bottom of page 100*]

[*page 100, bottom of page*] Saturday Aug. 3rd 1895, continued every thing went against me. Dudley Shawnee had come home Friday evening, and I saw him on this evening for the first time. Walter Shawnee had gone to a camp meeting toward Wetumka, so I heard George say a day or two ago.

[*page 100, top of page*] Translations into Shawnee of passages on baptism, that very difficult subject.

Mat. 3:11. Neli skipkihe kenepiohalapwi micelapwiwaneke nape netiwa: heni pieakwi nepikimake wieace, wihocepeiti heni hileki semakobe, moce ~~homanebape wise pabhimiwike~~ homikebani wise nemaei mitinetasemakobe; heni kanepiohakowi babubueikebelece Cailikomile wahiwile chena skuta.

Mat. 28:19. Hene hoce nhikona kakikakenemiwike cieike helomeke, kanepiohiwike howebowanwike Kobani chena Hokwebili chena Babubieikebeti Cacilikomi,

Mark 16:16 Heni weabi tatapwasati chena kikeki neasekipiweti: wawipinaehobo; hemi pieakwi papwi tapwas atiwakesanichobo.

He stands firm in repentance, Dale p. 466, Wesekekipiwe micelapwiwaneke (weli, Wesekekipiwe kotikesetahawaneke). The soul stands firm in Christ Dale p. 466, Hocacilikomile wesekekipiweeile Christeke.

[. . .], ealipitototake, ~~hoppataniwake~~ hoppataniniwi, honikeniniwi, hokwetaniniwi—hipitiessoke, netise wekkike, wesekekipiweke, tapwasake, hotalipimiwile (they trusted), hotapasiwelamiwile (they confided in him). Dale Christi Baptism p. 308, 1 Cor. 10:2. Chena cieike kobanike Moseseke sewesekekipiohoboke henepibkwike chena hene kcekime hiwota.

[*continued from original page 100, bottom of page*]

Sunday Aug 4th 1895 (written at same time as above [*Aug. 4*]).

Could not go to church up at the Kickapoo Mission or any where else. My clothes are too dirty, i.e., shirts and drawers. Julia Shawnee is gone down toward Muscogee with all of her children. I wonder how they crossed the North Fork river. Read books to-day. Boloxa and wife and little step-daughter (Wasequawah, as I call her) rode in on a wagon this evening. He says that Walter Shawnee helped him get the railroad to pay him $75 for going through his land, and that he paid Walter $20 out of this for his trouble, leaving himself $55. He says that Walter went twice with him all the way from [*page 101*] Tecumseh to Shawnee to see the railroad men, making less than two day's work. He thinks Walter cheated him. He says that Walter says that I am a fool and got no sense. This is the pay I get for signing that power of attorney for Walter and Thomas. I told Thomas that I did not want to sign that on account of Walter, but that I really wanted him to have the job. Walter talks Ingersollism to the Indians. In my presence while he was talking to Big Jim—Thursday evening Aug. 1st 1895—he was telling Big Jim about the Chinese. He said that the Chinese outnumbered the white people, that in building they used their eyes in measuring lengths of their building material with as much accuracy as white people did with their instruments of measurement, and went out of his way to tell the Chief that the Chinese got along in all this without the help of Jesus (miti Cesissele hopiwilile was his language in Shawnee). Walter will not lend me 5 or 10 cents, even for these years, and the last year, 1893, though he would not lend me a cent, yet in Muscogee he bought and gave paper etc. to Mrs. Jennie Cegar. This woman thinks the world of Walter. Every thing I used to say to them they would go and tell Walter, even if it did not concern him at all. This was while I was staying with Mrs. Cegar in 1894. Mr. and Mrs. Cegar would talk to me about Walter, and say some thing against him to me, and then if I said any thing whatever as to what I thought of Walter, they would tell Walter at the first opportunity. Walter would tell me they said I said so and so, and he said he had it in for me. I never told Walter what they said against him because I despise such low-lived tale-bearing. Walter's Ingersollism was preached by himself to Mr. and Mrs. Cegar, and she took pains last year to tell me what Walter said. Religion was all a lie. There was no God no soul, no heaven and no hell. Jesus was not God, Mrs. Cegar told me herself, because he asked where Lazarus was buried, and she said if he was God, he ought to have known without asking. I tried to explain to her how that Jesus asked not for information, but to draw out their replies; but could not prevail. Wa[l]ter-Ingersollism had hit too deep. Mrs. Cegar said that she did not know whether we live after death or not. (Walter had told me this long before). Why does Mrs. Cegar adopt Walter's opinions, but despise me and mine? I never could see why. They told about Walter's failures on his Cherokee trip in 1893, promising to have them admitted and failing totally.

[*page 102*] I am sure Mrs. Cegar never had such sentiments nor Cegar until they received them from Walter. Old man William Shawnee thinks more of Walter though he is infidel than of me for being a Quaker. But I will be a Quaker, so help me God until death. Mrs. Hartley said to me if Walter was skeptical. I told her that I could not really tell; that he talked that way at times.

When religion goes out of a man, old or young, the Devil with his evil works comes right in. I have seen this so often and so long that that I am as certain as certain can be of its truth. Dudley say[s] that Dr. Hartley preached about Robert Ingersoll tonight and endeavored to answer Bob's specious fallacies. Bob lays it down as an axiom that miracles are impossible. He offers no proof of this and the proposition is not self-evident. Now miracles are either possible or not possible—no third supposition is possible. Bob merely assumes the negative.

Sassotasse says that Joe Billy was thrown from his horse and hurt his leg about the knee.

Monday Aug. 5th 1895 (written Aug. 22nd 1895)
Worked on the bridge between David Alford's and my place with John Whitehead. Went home with John by his invitation at noon and at night being a guest there.

Tuesday Aug. 6th 1895 (written Aug. 22nd 1895).
Worked on the bridge still with John Whitehead, awaiting time. Was still his guest that night.

Wednesday Aug. 7th 1895 (written Aug. 22nd 1895)
Worked on the bridge still with John Whitehead and was still his guest. There were not many of us at work. It was hard to get people to donate time.

Thursday, Aug. 8th 1895 (written Aug. 22nd 1895)
Worked on the bridge still with John Whitehead, and was a guest there day and night.

Friday Aug. 9th 1895 (written Aug. 22nd 1895)
Worked on the bridge still with John Whitehead. We finished the bridge this day about four o'clock in the evening. Ernest Spybuck helped me for the last two days. Only us three were at

work toward the last, the white fellow Fred having left us Wednesday evening I believe. Was a guest at John Whitehead's this night.

Saturday Aug. 10th 1895 (written Aug. 22nd 1895)
    Came home to William Shawnees from John Whitehead's in the after noon. John and Mary and Webster Whitehead started in the morning to where John's aunt was sick west of Sacred Heart Mission. [*page 103*] Saturday Aug. 10th continued. George Shawnee lent me his saddle and so I went preparing to go up to the Kickapoo Mission. Staid all night at home.

Sunday Aug. 11th 1895 (written Aug. 22 1895[)].
    Went early up to the Kickapoo Mission, where I arrived between 10 and 11 o'clock. About 25 Kickapoos came to the church, Ah'-kwē-nàh-kō-thē-yàh the chief being one present. I was told that a very good audience came Aug. 4th 1895, but I could not be present. Lina B. Lunt had come, and she taught Teacher and myself the Sabbath School Lesson in the afternoon. Teacher (Lizzie Test) soon made excuse that she had some letters to write, and Lina had only one pupil remaining, but the lesson went on. She had me read to her the comments and discourses concerning the lesson, which was about the Brazen Serpent, no but about Moses' Farewell Address in Deut 6 chapter. Teacher regretted it much that I had not come the Sunday before. Staid all night.

Monday Aug. 12th 1895 (written Aug. 22nd 1895)
    It rained very much in the morning, so that I could not come home until afternoon. Left before dinner, but ate dinner at the home of Pē-kē-tàh-nō-kwă, who told me not long ago that she was 13 years old. Wrote a letter for them there. These folks are always very glad to see me. Came on home around by Shawnee, because the river was up.

Saturday Aug. 17th 1895 (written Aug. 22nd 1895).
    Could not go to the Monthly Meeting, for which I am very sorry. I had to get ready to go up to the Mission. Went to town to borrow a saddle from Mr. Cummings. But he could not lend me his saddle. I went to see Mr. Carter, but his saddle was in use by a party who had already borrowed it. He lent it to me, however. But I had to wait the whole afternoon until Sundown at the house of Mr. Brown for his son to come back from Shawnee City with the saddle. At sunset took the saddle and saddled up and came home. Borrowed a rope from Mr. Hamlin to tie out my pony with, so that I could get [. . .] early in the morning.

Sunday Aug. 18th 1895 (written Aug. 22nd 1895) ([. . .])
    Started about sunrise for the Kickapoo Mission, without any rope. I left Mr. Hamlin's rope at his house early this morning. Got [up] to the Kickapoo Mission about 11 o'clock. The white people were [hav]ing a Sabbath School just as I came. They said that two persons were in attendance besides the teachers. Miss Lina B. Lunt was very glad to see me, remarking with a smile that she had gone to shop [*continued on page 108*]

[*pages 104-107 moved to April 1895 for chronological order*]

[*page 108*] *Sunday Aug. 18th 1895 continued from page 103, written Aug. 22nd 1895.*
after Sabbath School. Read books in the parlor alone all the afternoon. Lina and Teacher sought a place to sleep. But before they left the room, Teacher said to me: "Willie, I have some thing I want you to do for some one, but I do not want you to give me away." I said: "All right, Teacher, I will do it if I can, and I will not give you away." She continued: "Eddie Pensonaw is in bad surroundings. I believe those folks where he is got him into things that he does not want to get into. I want you to go and tell him for me that I want him to come up and work for me, that I have just lots of work to be done now since the rain. I do not want Joe Whipple or Andrew Whipple to hear you when you tell him. Manage to get Eddie off to himself and then tell him." I said: ["]Teacher, I am not going home tomorrow. I am going up the river about 15 miles. But on my way back home day after tomorrow, I will see Eddie and tell him." Teacher laughed and said, You must have a girl up there some where, you go up there so often. I said, No, I have no girl up there, but I come nearer having a girl here than there. She wanted to know, but I said I could not tell. We had church this night, but all present were white people. Lina, Teacher, a white woman whose name I know not, and Ida Grace, and one or two others were active in the services. Slept sound and was happy.

Monday Aug. 19th 1895 (written Aug. 22nd 1895.)
    Sat beside Miss Lina B. Lunt at the breakfast table. I like Lina very, very well. Started up the river after breakfast. At 11 A.M. arrived at the house of Mr. Lewis one of the school board. Found him in the field cutting and shocking corn. He made our [out] my teacher's contract for 5 months at 30 Dollars per month. I went to see Mr. Robinson, but he was not at home. Then I went to see Mr. Gokey who signed the contract in duplicate. Took dinner at Mr. Cooper's and went back to see Mr. Lewis, who filled up both contracts, and I went back and staid all night.

Tuesday Aug. 20th 1895 (written Aug. 28th 1895)
     Came home by Teacher's and by Joe Whipple's. Crossed the river on horse back.

Friday Aug. 23rd 1895.
     Attended Prayer Meeting. Mr. Roberts and Mr. Hartley were present and a good time was had. Maggie Wilson was present.

Saturday Aug. 24th 1895.
     Could not go up to the Kickapoo Mission.

Sunday Aug. 25th 1895.
     It was rainy all day and I could not go to church.

[*page 109*] *Monday Aug. 26th, 1895 (written Aug. 28th 1895).*
     Worked all day on my place, cutting and shocking 10 shocks.

Tuesday Aug. 27th 1895 (written Aug. 28th 1895)
     Put up hay with David Alford working for him. I am to receive 50 cents per day.

Wednesday Aug. 28th 1895 (written Aug. 28th 1895)
     Worked for David Alford's, helping him put up hay. John Spybuck and all his folks came yesterday. He helped us to do all this.

Thursday Aug. 29th 1895 (written Sept. 2nd 1895)
     Helped David Alford put up hay all day. John Spybuck helped also. He and his wife and little boy Frank, about 5 or 6 years old, and his step-daughter are down here at David's. They came in a wagon. Nearly got through this evening. Came home and staid all night. Dudley Shawnee, Walter Shawnee, and William Shawnee quarreled with me about some thing they pretended to have heard, but they would not tell me who informed them.

Friday Aug. 30th 1895 (written Sept. 2nd, 1895)
     Helped David Alford put up hay. He has in all twenty loads of hay in two stacks near each other. These stacks are located across the creek from his house, about 200 yards away, on the piece of ground that he has fenced off from his pasture, just across the fence. John Spybuck helped also. Soon after we went out to work, Ernest Spybuck, whom we left at the house, accidentally discharged a shot gun through the roof of David's frame house. The shot made a hole about one inch in diameter. We finished putting up hay about 7 o'clock. Was on my place all day. Went to town in the evening and came back to my place 10 or 11 P.M. Remained there all night. Was very sorry over my

financial conditions. All my shirts were dirty. There was a well on my place, but I had nothing to draw water with. No tub was there to bath in or wash clothes in. My condition was deplorable. Saw and visited Stephen Carter in Tecumseh.

Saturday Aug. 31st, 1895.

I went to Tecumseh very early in the morning. Saw Mr. Cummings and he did not want the place another year. He said that he was going to either Missouri or the Cherokee Nation. He said that his brother, who lives over in Cleaveland County, is very much dissatisfied with the country. He had let Mr. C. C. Hamlin have the house on condition that Mr. [*page 110*] Hamlin gather my share of the corn. He said that he wanted his share of the corn stalks. Mr. Hamlin says that he wants to pasture the corn stalks. Mr. Hamlin wants to lease my place for one year. He wants me to build a cross fence without consideration. Washed some clothes on my place, having to borrow both a tub and a rope to draw water with. Remained over night here.

Sunday Sept. 1st, 1895 (written Sept. 2nd 1895)

Went to the house of Mr. J. J. Johnson. I found him at home. I read books, a history of the civil war 1861-65, and a history of the Vaudois Christians. Roman Catholics slew these Christians, outraged their women, and did every atrocity to them for their religion's sake. Treachery was also practiced against them. It makes one feel like being a Christian to learn of these people. They were diligent in prayer. I and Mr. Johnson and his two little boys went down on my lower place, and there we saw Mr. Reaves. Mr. Johnson had some talk with him about a mill for making molasses. Mr. Reaves said that he was on a trade with Mr. [F . . . bue], but could not tell whether the trade would be finished or not until Tuesday evening. At that time he could tell Mr. Johnson whether he could make molasses for him or not. We ate watermelons and came home rather late. Mr. Johnson cooked supper or late dinner. At night his wife got supper for us. Mr. Johnson said that Texas was a good place for a teacher to make money. A first grade certificate brought $75 a month, a second grade $60 and a third grade $30. A person must, however, let politics alone and conform to the queer ways of the people down there. The Prairie View Normal School for colored teachers is located at Hempstead, Texas. I ought to write for a catalogue. Staid on my place, came from Mr. Johnson's at 9 or 10 P.M.

Monday Sept. 2nd 1895 (written Sept. 2nd, 1895)

Went to David Alfords early. John Spybuck and his folks were gone. David and I took Mr. Cuppy's wagon and hay rick home. Also hauled those crib logs on my place. Julia Shawnee, Mrs. Willie

Laundres, and the children got back home last night Sept. 1st, 1895. Cut four shocks of corn late in the evening. Mrs. Hamlin wants me to draw up that lease contract before long. David Alford and I are going down on his place on Little River tomorrow to get logs for my crib. This is all for [page 111] the work that I have been doing for David. Dudley Shawnee says that Thomas Alford says that Flora Hale is in Kansas City. I wonder what took Flora there. Came to William Shawnee's this evening and saw Julia and all her children, Willie Laundres and her two children, and the old man William and Dudley. I need more to practice what I know to be right. It is quite difficult for a person always to do what he knows to be right, but I believe that by God's grace and strength it is easy to be done. Never under any circumstances do that which you know to be wrong. No matter what sins have been in the past, turn over a new leaf for the present and future. There are some good rules:—

1. Never stay away from church or religious assemblies when it is possible to attend. Make provisions to attend, and be sure to attend.
2. Remember that a condition of true Christianity is above every thing else in the world. It is the duty of every Christian to provide himself food, clothing, and shelter in an honest way. Never waste your money, but put it where it will do the most good.
3. It is better to earn 50 cents a day than to earn nothing for that day. I worked for David three days last week for 50 cents a day, and this has taught me true worth, both of 50 cts, and of $1.50 cents.
4. Never commit a sin that is known to be a sin, but pray to God and read the Bible every day. No harm, but an immense amount of good will come out of this. For Christ's sake let all sin alone, and perform every good work you can so that Jesus Christ may have the glory of the good work that you do.
5. Read good books and practice what you read. Do not be afraid of being peculiar among relatives or not relatives. It is not blood relatives that should be dearest to us, but our brothers and sisters in Jesus Christ.
6. Profess to be a Christian, and try every day in every place to act a Christian, pray to God prayers of praise as well as prayers of petition in the name of Christ often and regularly, and soon you will be a Christian.
7. Be industrious. Make a living honestly. Get rich honestly if you can. Idleness is of the Devil. It is Satan's weapon to lead you down to poverty on earth and eternal torment beyond the grave. Though all men and women should despise

any honest work, yet fear not to do such work, subject only to the will of God in Jesus Christ. [*page 112*]
8. Find out all about law, medicine, theology, and all science whatever that you can. Learn and practice all the arts that you can. Own horses of your own, saddles and bridles, and carriages, and every good praiseworthy thing. You will never be too old to learn nor too old to learn to do some new good work with your hands.

Tuesday Sept. 3rd 1895 (written Sept. 9th 1895).
Went down with David Alford to his place near Little River to find logs to go in the crib. Mr. Ryas [Rice?] Amey, a colored man, is David's renter on this place. The cotton was just opening. The wife of Ryas [Rice?] and some of the children were gathering beans. Cut six logs, which were pretty heavy; and besides there was a bad crossing in the creek, near the house. Ryas [Rice?] came back from town in the afternoon. The women were slow preparing dinner, but we waited. Dinner came at last late in the evening about 3 P.M. or 4 P.M. Came home by the way of Tecumseh, the same as when we went down. Staid at William Shawnee's.

Wednesday Sept. 4th 1895 (written Sept. 9th 1895 7:55 P.M.)
David Alford was not feeling well, but still he helped us until noon. Ernest Spybuck and myself did the lifting toward the last. Pakwiwa Pameti. David feeling not well, we did not work in the afternoon. Staid at night at my own house.

Thursday Sept. 5th 1895 (written Sept. 9th 1895, 8 P.M.)
Went to Tecumseh early in the morning to the house of Mr. J. J. Johnson. Was kindly treated, and read books until in the afternoon. A history of Texas, with its state constitution was interesting. The biographies of men in the encyclopedia was eagerly devoured. Articles on astronomy in the latter also were read. There are no less than 50,000,000 stars, said the article. Read history of the civil war, with the different battles. I went thence to Tecumseh, i.e., the business part of town. Read the organic act and the statutes of Oklahoma. Of course I could not read them all.

Friday Sept. 6th 1895 (written Sept. 9, 1895 8:05 P.M.[)]
I went to town with Dudley Shawnee, William Shawnee, and Mr. [. . .] to bring back the wagon they rode in. Dudley and I led the mules. They were going to use the buggy, but its tongue was being changed in the blacksmith shop. It took a long time for them to finish the tongue. But at last they left. William Shawnee and Dudley were on their way to a Camp Meeting down in

the Seminole [*page 113*] Nation, some where in Sasakwa. William said that he had been invited to come by Mr. Jumper, and concluded he had better go. I came home and hauled some dry wood, but it was so late I had not the time to haul much. Staid at home. Walter Shawnee was here too.

Saturday Sept. 7th 1895 (written Sept. 9th 1895 8:17 P.M.)
 Walter Shawnee took the saddle and rode his gray mare to Tecumseh. He returned late in the afternoon, about 3 or 4 P.M. I carried several buckets of water for Julia and cut some of the wood I had hauled the day before. I saddled up the bay bald faced pony and went up to the Kickapoo Mission, where I arrived about an hour after the moon arose, say 10 P.M. Slept some but did not disturb any one. Lina B. Lunt, Teacher, Mandie Pearson, Emma Newsom, Thomas Alford, and a white fellow composed the Mission family. ~~I went to Sabbath~~

Sunday Sept. 8th 1895 (written Sept. 9th 1895 8:25 P.M.)
 I went to Sabbath School at about 10 A.M. Teacher, Lina, and Thomas were the three teachers. Meeting followed soon after Bible School. About 16 Kickapoos took dinner. Peketahrokwa and Thahnahkathokwa were present. Maskwekanahkah was absent. Thomas Alford did the interpreting. I enjoyed the meeting very much. Late in the evening, at the request of Teacher, we—Thomas and I—went up in Township 14N to the Kickapoo Town to visit Takahmi, who was very sick. We were also to look after his spiritual condition. Teacher sent milk and grapes to him by us. We traveled by night, for the sun set before very long after we started. We arrived there about the time the moon arose say 10 P.M. or 9:00 P.M. We talked to him about Jesus and his condition, asked him to pray for himself, while we knelt down, and prayed that God would forgive his sins and make him well again if it was his will. If not that his sins might be forgiven and he taken home to live with Jesus in those beautiful houses where God is. We had never held services at the bedside of any one so near death's door before. Maskwekanahkah and his wife were present, and another woman. The sick man thanked us for what we had done and seemed to believe in Jesus, while doubting about the Indian way. Came back that night reaching the Mission about 3 A.M. I went to bed 3:20 A.M. or there about. Thomas Alford and I slept in the same room. Oh, but I felt like I had been greatly strengthened after these bedside services for Jesus.

[*moved from page 170*] *Begun Sept. 8th 1895, at 9:20 P.M.*

Wase Peaticemowa Mike Eanakiloboce.
Wese Nakote.

1. Waske watipeabeke wasehopeaticemowa Cesas Klieste, hokwebile Minato.
2. Pisckili easematiwekitake mimosekeskwacke weiwik[e] Wacekanihe, neli netamacecemi eieiloliki ealibimeeine, heni waniniheloti kemeawe ealibimeeine.
3. Easesemoce heni wawinassatiki pelaske tise, Ninihelotimiko hene homeawe Tapalamewati; pasakwimakhimoko homawanabi
4. Haipeni Cinekwo Kokenwa pilaske, chena hopibapitote hene kokenekawa hobapicetakawaneka wamocike.

[page 114] Monday Sept. 9th 1895 (written Sept. 9th 1895, 9:08 P.M.)

Came home horse-back by way of Shawnee. Thomas Alford came in his road wagon. Visited Mr. Barone for a short time. Mr. and Mrs. Barone, Annie and Josephine were present. Annie looked angry and spoke not a word. Saw Mr. Cummings at his home in Tecumseh and arranged for him to take me up to my school. He proposes to charge $3 for the trip. It will take him two days. I saw Miss Emma Parks and Miss Ida Jones in Tecumseh. I had Mr. Carson order me a call bell and a class bell at $1.40 cts or 70 cents apiece. I also need a clock to keep time with. My pecuniary condition is simply deplorable. I have only one decent pair of pants, and they are not very decent. Last night Sept. 8th 1895 Thomas Alford and myself came to an agreement to translate the New Testament into Shawnee and have the same published. But we are not to tell any one about it.

Saturday Sept. 28th 1895 (written at the home of Mr. Woodard 12:35 A.M.)

Remained all night at the Shawnee Mission Friday Sept. 27th 1895. Reached the mission at about 10 P.M., and was shown to a bed in the boy's dormitory by Mr. M. C. Williams. This dormitory is a very large room, where are many neat beds, and where the boys are wont to sleep. Indian visitors or guests are entertained here also. Boletha Hood and his wife also slept here this Friday night. Mrs. Williams had secured a two-horse buggy, and our destination was the house of Big Jim and the houses of certain others, members of his band. Lewis Tyner, Jr., myself, and Mrs. M. C. Williams were the only ones to go. Lewis and myself sat on the front seat, and she occupied the back seat, while I did the driving. On our way we passed through Tecumseh. Here Lewis bought a 50 cent cap for Mrs. Williams, and a shaving mug to be used as a cup. (We tried in vain to purchase a tin cup, but they had none in the store we went to, and we had not time to go to other stores.) Just south east of the post office she had a talk with lawyer Woods, husband of Ada Woods nee Lockhart. We continued three miles on the Norman road, and then turned south a mile, and afterwards came into the road just north east of the place of William Littleax. We turned another mile south just north of the Old Bullfrog place, passing by that place. Thence we came to the place where Mă-yàh-wàh-pĕă and Shawnee Doctor live, but we passed here without stopping. We also passed by the place of John Taylor without stopping. We had [*page 115*] already met John Taylor on horse-back going north before we reached the Bullfrog place, or even the Sallie Spybuck place. We stopped for the first time at the place of Joe Billy. We found his wife and daughter at home, but he himself had gone over to see Little Charley (or Moses Charley), who was very sick. Just as we were departing, he came, and saluted us. He gave us the name of Nō'-mă-pĕă-sē, one of the children, whose father was dead. The other child was a boy. The mother of these two children has remarried to a man named Pă-sē-kàh, or Fire man Gibson. Joe fears that this man will not treat the children properly. He says that a third one of these children—a baby—is dead through maltreatment. He says that Little Charley the father (father's brother) of these children says for them to be taken to school. Joe told us to ask Little Charley for ourselves as we went by as to whether he agreed for these children to go to school.

The young woman, seemingly 15 or 16 years old, whom Joe Billy called his daughter, is a pretty girl. She is of a yellow Indian color, seemingly a full blood. Of Course she is not Joe's own daughter, she may be his brother's daughter. But in the Shawnee language, she is rightly called his daughter. For the Shawnee word nē-tàh'-nă-thàh does not always mean one's own daughter. It probably never has that meaning in fact. <u>My daughter</u> (nē-tàh'-nă-thàh) in Shawnee means my brother's daughter. A daughter, born to one of two or more brothers is a daughter "or "tàh'-nă-thàh"["] to each and any of them.

Joe Billy said he would send both of his sons to school, and that his daughter might go if she wanted to do so, that before long he would visit the school in company with his family, and that if, after seeing the school, his daughter should wish to attend, he would have no objection, but that he did not believe that schooling would do his daughter any good. Joe told Mrs. Williams what to tell Big Jim.

Thence we went to Big Jim's, but he had gone to mill, to have some corn grown [ground?] into meal. His daughter Ruth or Lō'-bàh alone was present. She is about 15 years old, is full-faced, about 1/8 French, copper-colored, with straight black hair, with pleasing ways, and is the prettiest of all the

Shawnee girls. We ate diner here, and invited Ruth to dine with us, but she was too bashful.

Thence we went to the house of Joseph Blanchard. He too had gone to mill. But his wife and two other women were present. Joe's wife and Superintendent Mrs. M. C. Williams had quite a talk. Two women at the opposite poles of civilization could not agree. Mrs. Williams wanted Mrs. Blanchard to send her two little [*page 116*] boys to school during the winter, but the latter would not agree. Good clothing, good food, and good shelter, and good treatment could not induce the daughter of the forest to send her boys, and Miss Williams retired from the fight routed and vexed. She gave them some apples just as we were leaving.

We started home, but had just reached the vacated house where Billy White used to live, when Mrs. Williams began to express dissatisfaction with the results of our expedition. She wanted to go back and visit the houses of Little Doctor and Snake man, three miles northwest of Big Jim's. Finally she decided she would go there, and we turned northwest and soon came to a room [road?] that lead us to our new destination. About a quarter from the house of Little Doctor, southeast therefrom, we met his son Oscar Little Doctor about 13 or 14 years of age. He was in company with several white fellows, but they passed on. Mrs. Williams asked him several things. He answered that his father had gone to the mill, that he did not want to go to school, and that he thought Snake Man was at home. Thence we went to Snake Man's. His wife and others were present, but he had gone to Norman. Mrs. Williams here fell in love with the baby boy of Mrs. Snake Man. It was a very young full-faced, lovely baby boy. Mrs. Williams remarked that the baby would not cry if she would take it home with her. Mrs. Snake Man replied that the baby would not cry, but that she would. We gave them about all the apples that we had.

Thence we came home. Near Pecan Creek we met Boloxa, Mĕăhth-wă and Sàp-wăh'-pĕă-sē-kăh. Mē-àhth-wă said that he wanted to go to school, and we told him to come. We stopped for the last time at Little Charley's. This was near Big Jim's before we met the above parties. Little Charley agreed for us to take those children to school. He was very sick and Shawnee Doctor had just come to doctor him. John Spoon, the old lady Esparney, Joe Billy, and others were here. We left them some apples to eat. Passed by the house of Pn wàh'-kàh-làh without stopping. Passed through Tecumseh, and arrived about 10 P.M. at the Shawnee Mission, having traveled at least 46 miles.

Sunday Sept. 29th 1895.

Awoke in the same bed I had slept in Friday night at the Shawnee Mission. We went to Sabbath School, a number of boys and girls. Miss Kessell and another woman went too. [*page 117*] The lesson was a Review. Mrs. Bourbonnais conducted the recitation. It was by the whole school. Miss Aurelia Bounbonnais was present. The blind preacher preached a sermon. The text was: "Study to shew [show] thyself approved unto God, a workman that needeth not to be ashamed, rightly dividing the word of truth." 2nd Tim. 2:15.

After services Mrs. Roberts invited me to dinner, and I accepted the invitation. After dinner I read in the library all the rest of the afternoon. The following books were interesting: "Tempted to Unbelief," by [*Enoch Fitch*] Burr; [*Melancthon W.*] Jacobus on the Pentateuch; [*James*] Murdock's Translation of the Syriac New Testament.

Attended services at night. Miss Belle Lockhart, Miss Lily Woods, Miss Minnie Riley, and others were present. Miss Lily Woods sung the song No. 128 in Gospel Hym[n]s No. 5, entitled Hark! Hark! my Soul. She sung only the first verse. She has a clear strong voice. I thinks she is a lovely young woman. Was a guest at the Mission.

Monday Sept. 30th 1895. (written Oct. 4th 95 at 3 P.M.[)]

I went to David Alford's, and delivered the letters and the message that Boletha had sent. I rode with him to town. Collected $2.50 from Mr. Cummings that he owed me. I left $1.40 of the same at Mr. Carsons to pay for the bells that I had ordered. I was preparing to go up to where I was to teach school as fast as I could. I had my clock fixed. I was in town twice today with David. Staid at William Shawnees this night. Mr. Carter told me that Mr. ~~Carter~~ Johnson had sent me word he would take me up to my school Friday. I tried to get David Alford to bring me but he could not, but he would study over the matter.

Tuesday Oct. 1st 1895 (written Oct. 4, 95 at 3:07 P.M.)

I left home early and went up to interpret for Charley Beaver and he was to pay me 50 cts. for the same, but he did not. I arrived in Tecumseh about noon. I went to see J. J. Johnson down on my lower place. He could not go until Friday. So I hurried home to see David. I ate supper at David's, and Big Jim was here visiting. I told David how Mr. Johnson had treated me. He was very sorry but said that he was so busy with his sugar cane, sweet potatoes, and unpaid taxes that he could not take me. I went home sorry. Big Jim accompanied me home where we both were guests.

Wednesday Oct. 2nd 1895.

My clock had stopped about 3 A.M. this morning, and so I took it with me to get some more repairing done to it. The man repaired it. Early I saw Mr. Carter, who told me Mr. Johnson was not cutting sugar cane for him, but was pulling corn in his own field. [*page 118*] So I went to see Mr. Johnson, and found him pulling corn in his own field, and I accused him of preventing me from going up yonder. He said he was not trying to do so. I told him he was not trying to do so, but was really doing so just the same. I wanted to start to-day, but he said to-morrow. So I went home after going to town and getting my clock and coming back by to see Mr. Carter. When I reached home I packed my trunk and got ready. Staid over night at home. Dudley and I occupied the same bed. Walter Shawnee had not come. Dudley told me that he wanted me to leave colored girls alone and not get stuck on them. Dudley and Walter are as furious on this color question as any southern white. Dudley is the boy who gave Julia Shawnee [*Dudley's stepmother*] a terrible cursing a few days ago.

Chapter 7

Teaching at Choctaw City
October 3, 1895—March 6, 1896

On October 3, 1895, J. J. Johnson showed up early in the morning with his horse and wagon to take William Ellsworth Shawnee to Choctaw City to teach school. Shawnee taught at Smith School, a black public school near Choctaw City, from October 5, 1895, through February 28, 1896. He procured room and board from Lon Woodward for at least three weeks before moving to Harrison Blackford's, where he roomed for free and furnished his own board.

Shawnee enjoyed teaching at Smith School. He had thirty-eight pupils, which proved to be too many for him to teach everything that he wanted. The schoolhouse was small and could fit only twenty-two seats comfortably. He drew his thirty-dollar monthly salary in warrants, which he sold at a discount to have cash on hand. Near the end of the school term, he notified his patrons of his desire to teach at Smith School again the next year. Most of them signed a petition for him to teach again, but Rev. Fullbright and Ella Dunjee were also interested in the job. To improve his chances of securing a teaching job for the following year, Shawnee spent an extra week in Choctaw City and canvassed nearby areas for teaching jobs before returning home on March 6, 1896.

While teaching at Smith School, Shawnee intermingled with his patrons in the nearby community. They aided him in reducing his living expenses by inviting him to dinner, laundering his clothing for free, or giving him produce from time to time. On weekends, he attended a Baptist church with some of his patrons and taught Sabbath school.

He wrote letters to his father, his brother George at Haskell Institute, John King, Little Jim (Totommo), and others. He continued to read the Bible. On weekends he sometimes went home and worshiped with his Quaker family. He still did not have transportation of his own. Sometimes he walked and sometimes he caught a ride. He even rode with strangers, black and white.

Shawnee noted racial attitudes at times. After the counties had voted for mixed or separate schools, Mr. Gokey, a member of the school board, informed Shawnee that he knew that separate schools made taxes higher but he believed it was for the best. When Shawnee visited the family of Lula Mack, one of his pupils at Choctaw City, Mrs. Mack said she cared about whom her daughter Lula married because she was concerned about her "blood." She didn't want her daughter "taken down into the Indian nation." Shawnee took that as a personal affront. He was also upset that one of his pupils called him an "Indian dog."

The number of young ladies with whom Shawnee was romantically interested continued to increase. He wrote about Carrie Warrior, Della A. Whipple, Lula Mack, Emma Valentine, Lena Robinson, Ella Dunjee, and Flora Hale, to whom he proposed.

Thursday Oct. 3rd 1895 (written Oct. 4th 1895 4:35 P.M.[)]

It was raining this morning and I had given out seeing Mr. Johnson, when a little before 8 A.M., behold, who should make an appearance but he. The rain had rather ceased, but it was cloudy. It was cloudy Saturday Sept. 28th when we went to Big Jim's settlement. We ate breakfast and started away about 8 A.M. I was afraid we would get wet. We came by way of Ellis Town, Jim Warrior's and Charley Beaver's. We crossed the river at the crossing north of the Beaver place. We came by Joe Whipple's and the valley road, and by the Kickapoo Mission, although some fencing had been done which caused us to go around some. We passed the place of Măs-kwē'-kă-nàh-kàh. He had a lot of baled hay and stacks of hay in his meadows. We came by and saw Pă'-măh-hō-kō-kwă and Kō'-mă-thē-kwă at their homes. Their brother overtook us and came with us to and even passed his home. A-nē-yàh-kō-cē-kàh or Davis was still living in a tent. We stopped for dinner about 4 or 5 miles southeast of the Kickapoo Mission. It took to eat dinner 45 min. It took us 55 min. to cross diagonally the last bottom just before we reached the house of Mr. W. W. Lewis. We reached the house of Mr. H. E. Cooper at 6 P.M. by the clock I carried in my head. We were on the road 9 ¼ hours. It showed on us a little several times during the day. We were as well entertained by Mr. and Mrs. Cooper as we possibly could be.

Friday Oct. 4th 1895 (written today at 4:55 P.M.)

Mr. Johnson brought me over to the house of Mr. Lon Woodward. This is the place where I am writing all the foregoing. I am very glad that I am going to teach school. The people appear [*page 119*] very glad to see me, and I am certain. It is rainy all this afternoon. It seemed this morning as if I would not find a place to board, but Mr. Woodward came over and settled that matter. Miss Ella Dunjee taught this school last year, but she is not going to teach at all this year, although she attended the Normal Institute at Oklahoma City.

October 26th 1895 Saturday, 3:55 P.M.

I have been teaching school here three weeks. I like teaching very well. I board with Mr. Lon Woodward just twenty minutes walk from the school house. I have to pay 9 Dollars a month for board, which includes meals, washing, and bed. I am as well treated as I could desire. This morning I went to Mr. Cooper's and he was gone. His wife and children were at home. I shaved there by the kindness of Mrs. Cooper. Then I went to the house of Mr. Lewis, the district clerk. He presented me with a copy of the school law, for which I am thankful. At night I think of Teacher and Lina Lunt and Mrs. Kirk and Flora Hale and

Thomas Alford. And I can not forget Dr. and Mrs. Hartley, Mr. and Mrs. Roberts, and that blind preacher. Mrs. Bourbonnais and her daughter Aurelia are still in my mind's eye. Oh, how I wish that I could see them all. I remember Big Jim, Little Jim, and Ruth on Little River. Ruth was so pretty when Mrs. M. C. Williams and Lewis Tyner and I ate dinner there that day. Oct. 7th 1895 I was very keen and anxious to enter the school room. The memory of my hard times was there fresh in my mind. Many days have I gone without dinner, trying to do something. Now I have dinner every day. I want to make good use of the money I earn, and build me a house. Last Sunday Oct. 20th 1895 I taught two Sabbath School classes, one in the morning and one in the evening in two different Sabbath Schools. I thus went over the Sabbath School lesson twice. The subject of the Lesson was: "Ruth's Choice," Ruth 1:14-22. Golden Text: ["]Thy people shall be my people and thy God my God." It was rainy Monday, Tuesday, and part of Wednesday. From Mr. Lewis's house I went south around by the house of Mr. Robinson the district treasurer. He was not at home, but his daughter said she would tell him what I said. She was a pretty girl—plump, with large neck, and heavy set. Came back by the school house. Ate dinner at the house of the son of Mr. Woodward. My condition is still deplorable. I owe a great deal. I have not earned any thing for so [*page 120*] long that I am far behind in paying up my debts. I have worn the same shirt without change for two weeks. I do not receive mail as I should. The folks at home have not sent me my papers. For the last three weeks I have not had one cent of money. I paid that money to Carson Bros. in vain. I have not received or heard of those bells until this day. I need at once, 1. Another clock, 2. An umbrella, 3. A pair of pants and drawers, 4. A pair of shoes, 5. Two more white shirts, 6. The *New York Independent*, 7. The *Guthrie Leader*. I especially need: 1. A clock, 2. An umbrella, 3. To pay up my debts, *Christian Nation*, Houghton and Upp, John King, McFall, Good Health, Carson Bros., Mr. Cooper, Mr. Woodward (for board).

Monday Nov. 4th 1895

I have been feeling sick for about a week, but while I did not eat any thing this morning, yet I feel that I can teach school. I will draw some more money Nov. 30th 1895 if I teach faithfully every day. Though sick, yet I taught two classes in two different Sabbath Schools yesterday. Still these two schools meet in the same building, one in the morning, and another in the evening. Will it take me two months before I am able to pay my debts, even. A poor person has a hard time in this world, and yet it is my own fault that I am as poor as I am. Friday evening late Mr. H. E. Cooper and myself started to Oklahoma City. We went by the house of Mr. Robertson. We camped at the bridge over the North Fork six miles from the city. Here we kindled a fire and slept without a blanket or any thing to cover with. Next morning we went on through the cold to the city. I saw the County Clerk, and got my warrant and then the County Treasurer, but he had no funds to pay it with. So I had to sell the warrant at a discount of Ten cents on the Dollar. Hence I only received 27 Dollars for my month's work. As I was paying 9 Dollars a month for board, $12 was spent for board and discount. This left me $18 clear for my month's salary. This is not clearing $1 a day, because there are twenty school days in a month. Came home Saturday evening, arriving at Mr. Woodward's between 9 P.M. and 10 P.M.

[page 121] *Monday Nov. 11th 1895, 6:35 A.M.*

It is quite cool this morning. Last week it was very rainy, and the North Fork river is up, but fordable. I walked to Choctaw City and back Saturday Nov. 9th 1895. I met Dr. Hues, a graduate of Western Reserve University Medical School. I saw his diploma hanging up in his office. He gave me some medicine and said for me to come around again, and that may be he might find a way for me to go to a medical school. He said that Western Reserve University was located in Cleveland, Ohio. This is the city where Robert Quiggin used to live. The Society of Friends have a nice church in this city. I would like to go to school there sure. Mr. Hues said that he hardly had a dollar when he first began to go to school. He said: "There was a colored young man that graduated in the same class with me, and he was a smart fellow too."

Saw the blind preacher too. He brought up my bells that I used in school. He was glad to see me. He said that Dr. Hartley and his wife had come back again. This blind preacher lives at the Revere Hotel. I saw and shook hands with two Kickapoo boys in Choctaw City.

I am very lonesome for the folks at the Kickapoo Mission and for those at Old Shawneetown and Tecumseh. I have not received but one letter from Tecumseh since I have been up here. People are still picking cotton. They say that April 15 or May 1st is the time of the year to plant cotton. Cotton sold as high as 8 ½ cents a pound in the bale this year, or 2 ½ cents in the seed. But the last of October 1895 it suddenly fell to 7 ½ cents in the lint, and 2.35 cts. in the seed.

I wonder how my corn crop is getting along. I ought to keep that corn as long as possible. It may sell for a good price after awhile.

For ten or twelve days I have been unwell. My eyes have been very yellow and the urine has been highly charged with yellow. The bowels were inactive, altho there was a slight daily stool, but the remains of the faeces [feces] were retained and absorbed; hence the trouble.

Sunday Nov. 17th 1895 (written in the Smith School House)
    Yesterday Nov. 16th 1895 I went to Choctaw City, and rode in with a white man named Mr. Sanders. He is a clever man. He is originally from South Carolina, but from Texas to this country. He told about a white man in Texas that had cleared $1400 cash off his upland farm last year, and $1200 off of the same farm this year. He raised cotton each year, and last year he made more off of his cotton seed than off of his cotton. He sold his cotton seed for 25 cents a bushel. He sold his seed at so good a price on account of the oil mills that were in the country.

[page 122] Sunday Nov. 17th 1895 (written at 10:02 A.M. by the clock I have upon the wall here in the Smith School House).
    I sent a money order yesterday to the American Book Company, 317 Walnut Street, Cincinnati, Ohio, for [*Alpheus*] Crosby's *Xenophon's Anabases with lexicon*. Also a money order to the *New York Independent*. The first order was for $1.60 cts; the second, for twenty-five cents. I wrote a letter to the County Treasurer at Tecumseh and one to William Shawnee my father. My post office box is No. 131. I saw Dr. C. P. Hues, but could not get to speak to him. His medical diploma is dated Feb. 28th 1894. It is from the Western Reserve University, Cleveland, Ohio. He said that if his pecuniary condition would afford it, he would get married right away. He said that he only had two dollars in his pocket that very minute. He has a very fiery temper, for Saturday Nov. 9th 1895 when I was consulting him about medicine, he became angry with his brother (or some other fellow) for asking him about the horses once too much.
    Mr. H. E. Cooper was here to Sabbath School today, and he said that Mrs. Cooper told me I might send over my clothes to be washed by herself by one of her boys. I think this is very kind in her. In fact the people here are trying to help me save money all they can. I have no room rent to pay over at the house of Mr. Blackford, and he seems to be a very nice man. The Lord is with me, and I am bound to prosper. I need only to obey him in order to spread like a green bay tree. I hate to break the news to Mr. Woodward, that I have changed my boarding place. He did not come to church or Sabbath School to-day, so that I could break the news to him here. I guess they will be sorry to learn of my decision. I have been busy teaching all day to-day. I taught two different classes of scholars, one in the forenoon, the other in the afternoon.

I remember Teacher, Lina B. Lunt, and Thomas Alford at the Kickapoo Mission. I remember Mr. and Mrs. Hartley at the Mission House at Old Shawneetown. I remember Mrs. Kirk and Flora Hale, and the employees at the Shawnee Mission. Oh, that I could have seen them all to-day. I like to teach school here very well. I must be examined for a Teacher's Certificate again next April 1896. I must get another first grade, and teach this school again. Mr. and Mrs. Gokey are very friendly to me. Mr. Gokey is always at work. He is surely an industrious man. I will surely save money if the people here continue to be true to me. Be a true man at whatever you go. I would like to graduate at the Kansas State Norman School at Emporia, Kansas. O Lord, do Thou send me to school there for Thy name's sake. I will praise Thee as long as I have breath.

[page 123] At the house of Mr. Blackford 4:15 A.M. Friday morning Nov. 29th 1895.

Last Friday night Nov. 22nd 1895 it snowed, but the next morning I walked to Choctaw City through the snow. I did not get a cold. A white young woman fell in love with me, and offered to sell me a pair of gloves for 60 cents. Her father came in and said No, that is below cost, and had the cheek to offer me the same gloves for 80 cents. Of course I did not take them. The girl said that she would like to sell me some thing. It snowed again Sunday Nov. 24th 1895, making from two to three inches of snow. By Nov. 28th 1895 all the snow was melted away, only it is muddy yet. We are having an early winter this time. I wrote a letter yesterday to Miss Della A. Whipple. I ought to write one to Miss Flora Hale also. I wonder how Lina B. Lunt and Teacher are getting along. Mr. Robertson the director of the school board visited my school for a short time yesterday. His name is J. T. Robertson. W. W. Lewis is clerk of the board, and Mr. Gokey is the treasurer of the board. Mrs. Gokey invited me to visit them Sunday, but I was too busy to accept the invitation. I spent 25 cts. at the festival last night, which was 10 cents more than I intended. I will have to give some thing toward the Choctaw Normal and Industrial College, to be situated at Choctaw City. I learn that 10 acres has been secured on which to erect a building, and $339 in lumber engaged. I am going to advise Mr. Dunjee to secure an appropriation from the Oklahoma Legislature. Wilberforce University had an appropriation of $16000 twice from the legislature of Ohio.

Monday Dec. 2 1895 (4:52 P.M.).

It snowed Friday night Nov. 22nd 1895. This snow came upon us by surprise. It also snowed Sunday and Monday Nov. 24th & 25th 1895, and it is snowing again this evening. Mr. H. E. Cooper and myself started to Oklahoma City Friday evening Nov. 29th about or after sunset. We traveled until midnight or later, and then camped and built a fire. We had not a quilt or blanket to cover with. I have no bed clothing of my own at present. I sleep with Mr. Blackford. I got very cold and slept a very little that night. We had nothing to eat all day Saturday except some apples I had bought. We had money, but wanted to save it. I went to see Mrs. Dunjee and her [*page 124*] Daughter Drusilla Irene Dunjee. She lent me [*Alfred Payson*] Gage's *Elements of Physics*. It is an old book. I board myself and like it very well. This makes four books that I have bought for myself within the last two months, at a cost of $5.60. We started home from Oklahoma City about 2 or 3 P.M., and arrived home at 9 P.M. We did not travel fast, and I walked a great deal of the way in order to keep warm. I have paid out $13.50 cts for board to the Woodwards. If I had had some money at the very start of my school, and have boarded myself, as I am doing now, my expense would scarcely have been half that amount.

I have taught school all day, and yet I feel very fresh. I can study very well, but cooking takes up a great deal of my time. O Lord, I thank Thee that Thou has given me employment, where I can earn some money at any rate. $27 a month is better than nothing. It is poor economy to eat at hotels and restaurants. The Congress of the U. S. convened to day. I wonder what they will do with the five civilized tribes at this session. I wonder if Thomas Alford and Walter Shawnee will succeed in getting any money for the Absentee Shawnees. It is a good thing for them to try at any rate. I had 22 scholars in school to-day.

Friday Dec. 6th 1895 (5:00 P.M.)
I have been thinking of my betrothed wife Carrie Warrior. I am resolved to have her for my wife, God being willing and if she will marry me according to law. I must mail a letter to my darling angel Carrie. I need a wife, and if she will have me, I will marry her. I must make her some presents. I can not do without a girl. I must try hard to marry her until she is married, and until I find another girl that is suitable.

Tuesday Dec. 10th 1895. (5:45 P.M.).
Mr. F. H. Umholtz the County Superintendent of Oklahoma County visited my school this evening. He is a very pleasant and kind gentlemen, and he can write a good hand. He gave the pupils a nice talk, and wrote on the board for their instruction the following:—
Learn to do things well.
"   "   "   "   quickly.

Mr. Umholtz examined my school register, and he asked me if any one had visited my school. I told him that some of my patrons had visited it, and that Mr. Robertson director had also visited me. Among the remarks in my school register is the following: "Curtains are needed very badly over the windows to shade the sunlight out of pupils' and [page 125] teacher's eyes. The expense would be slight and precious eye-sight preserved." I did not think when I put that in my remarks that any one would pay any attention to it. Mr. Umholtz said, after examining my register, that he would try to have curtains furnished to put over the windows, and that he would try to get me more blackboard room. He told me to call and see him when I was in Oklahoma City, and he would give me a new register and show me how to keep it. I told him that I wished he could stay longer and visit the school. I want a new copy of the laws relating to the common schools. In fact it would not be any harm for me to own the Statutes of Oklahoma complete.

I ought to subscribe for a Teacher's paper. I think it is a poor teacher who could not subscribe for his own paper. I want to buy works that relate to the Teacher's Professional.

Sunday Dec. 15th 1895 (3:40 P.M.)

Yesterday Dec. 14th 1895 I walked to Choctaw City. I found the *New York Independent*, the *Guthrie State Capital*, and a catalogue and paper from Western Reserve University awaiting me in Post Office Box 131. Mr. Allen had a nice frame made for my chart and I paid him $1.50 cts on the same, and I am to pay him the remainder $1, when I get pay at the end of this school month. He said that as many as fifty people had asked him what that chart was for. He said that he told them that he was making it for a school teacher, and that he supposed I knew what it was for. I mailed a letter to Miss Drusilla Dunjee, Oklahoma City, Okla. Ter., another to Miss Flora Hale, Blue Jacket, Indian Ter., and asked the price of about twenty books of Tibbals Book Company, 26 Warren Street, New York City. I proposed marriage to Miss Flora Hale. She is a most lovely Christian young woman. I hope she will kindly accept my proposals. I sent a letter asking for the State Normal Monthly, Emporia Kansas. I hope Miss Flora Hale will never think the less of me for my marriage propositions.

I went over to the Smith School House about 10 A.M. to-day. I found Oliver Cooper and Henry Cooper, sweeping out the school house. I took the bucket, as I often do, and went up to Mr. Goakey's [Mr. Gokey's] after water. Charlie Gokey, Helen Gokey, Mary Gokey, Mrs. Gokey, and the mother of Mrs. Gokey were present. I spoke to the old lady about getting a pound of lard. She is to charge me 10 cts. therefor. The white school has five weeks to run yet, while my school is to run 10 weeks yet. Mary Gokey is 13 years old this year (1895). She is quite tall and a nice looking girl. C. Gililland [*page 126*] [is] the white teacher this year. He furnished me last week with the following addresses: The Practical Text-book Company, Cleveland Ohio. Williams and Rogers, Chicago, Illinois. Gem City Business College, Quincy, Ill. E. L. Kellogg & Co., New York City. The Ellie Publishing Co., Battle Creek, Mich. Mrs. Gokey said that Mr. Gililland said that he would not teach school longer at the same wages. She said that he went up to Oklahoma City ~~to in the~~ to see a man about going into the drug store business. He does not seem to want to make teaching school his profession. He studied pharmacy by mail. So at least he said to me, for about 11 months. He said that he came near passing the examination before the state board of pharmacy. The examination costs $5 whether a person passes or not.

I have to be finding out some thing to do when my school is out. I want to make money in all the honorable ways I can.

Friday Dec. 20th 1895 (7:05 P.M.) at the house of Mr. Blackford.—

Thursday Dec. 19th it snowed in the afternoon and at night, and a high wind was blowing at the same time. This day was clear, and some of the snow had melted. I have taught school two months and three weeks to day. I like teaching very well, and I do try to secure the good of the children. Mr. Blackford came over with his wagon this evening and hauled away my books and mounted chart. It was surely very kind indeed for him to do so. Though a yoke of oxen drew the wagon, yet the kindness rendered is very noble and praise-worthy. I praise the Lord Jesus Christ that my lot has so often fallen in pleasant places. I praise God Almighty for the books which He has given me since I have been up here, and the papers. O Lord God of heaven and earth, Thou art so good to me: I give Thee my heart, my life, my soul, my body, and all my powers and faculties! Let my mouth praise Thee forever and ever. Five scholars were present this morning when I took up school; the rest were tardy. Mr. Gokey is building him a meat house 8 x 10 feet. He now has the frame up. He has bought a corn mill also for $28. He grinds up the corn that he feeds to his hogs. – He said once, "Of course separate schools make taxes higher, but I believe it to be the best." I met old lady Ferguson last Sunday, Dec. 15th 1895, for the first time. This woman is the mother of Mrs. Gokey. Most of the colored people around here have mortgaged out their places it is said; but a few have not. It is said that Mr. Lilliard has made ten or eleven [*page 127*] bales of cotton this year. He is said to have a $150 mortgage on his place, but people seem confident that he will save his place without fail. Mrs. Lilliard has kindly done my washing without charge. They invited me to their home one Sunday and gave me a very good supper. Praise the Lord Jehovah. - I would like to have both my places improved, so that I could attend the Kansas State Normal School at Emporia Kansas. I ought to subscribe for the State Normal Monthly.

Wednesday January 1st 1896 5:05 P.M.

The sun has just set, and I am sitting here in the Smith School House, writing. A cold wind blew from the south to-day, and the door to our school house is in the south. I ate supper Sunday Dec. 29th 1895 at the house of Mr. and Mrs. Lilliard, patrons of my school. It was a nice supper. I could have taught school in 1893 and in 1894 if I had just sought diligently enough to do so. I would have been from $250 to $300 ahead of where I am now, had I done so. I had to work hard to secure the privilege of teaching this school, but it is worth all the labor it has ever cost me. I went home from this place Saturday Dec. 21st, 1895. I got off the train at McLoud and walked two miles to the Kickapoo Mission. It was sloppy and muddy walking through the bottom. I was a guest over night at the Kickapoo Mission. Teacher, Lina, and Mrs. Kirk shook hands with me. Mr. Thomas Alford came at night from McCloud; he walked over also. Having received on Sunday an insulting and threatening note from Harlen Hale, I went to McCloud and arrived there just in time to board the train for Shawnee. In Shawnee I met Mr. and Mrs. Roberts, who were very glad to see me, and they invited me to come back to visit them before I went back to Choctaw City. I was glad to see them sure. But it was so rainy and sloppy while I was at home that I could not get around to visit them. Mr. Roberts was on his way to meeting at Wolf Grove when I met him. I thank God that Jan. 1st 1896 I have good health, that I am earning $7.50 cts. a week, that I have so many friends and so few or no enemies, that the people appear to be pleased with the way in which I give instruction. One girl, who appeared to be sick, on being told twice that she might go home to-day, declined each time. - I wish I were out of debt, but I am not yet in that fortunate financial condition. - Cultivate the habit of looking upon the bright side of things. - I have no more trouble [*page 128*] with Josie Cooper, and she did not go home for dinner to-day.

Monday Jan. 6th 1896. 4:55 P.M.

I started for Choctaw City on foot after taking my clock and other things home to Mr. Blackford's. I went by way of the white school house. A prairie fire was burning around it. The North Fork river was filled with floating ice when I crossed the bridge. It was cold. Mr. Robertson was not at home, and so I had to come all the way back to Mr. Charles Gokey's to get him to sign, for fear that Mr. Robertson would not arrive home from Edmond in the night. I staid all night with Mr. Blackford. The next morning, which was Saturday, I left Mr. Blackford's, going by the white school house. I found Mr. Robertson at home, and we took off Mr. Gokey's name, and I had him sign his name. I started from Mr. Blackford's about 8 A.M., and arrived in Choctaw City about 11 A.M., making nearly three hour's walk with the stops made. There was no train whatever until 4:35 P.M. So I sat in the depot and read until that time. I received a letter from Geo. E. Shawnee and another from Little Jim, both which I must answer. I also received two papers—the [New York] *Independent* and the [Guthrie] *State Capital*. I arrived in Ok. City a little before sunset, and hurried to the office of the County Clerk, and he drew out my warrant and gave it to me. I sold it then and there for $27, as usual. The County Clerk told me that that was the last one I would have to sell. I did my trading at once. I visited the Dunjee family, and saw Drusilla and her mother. She said that she was going to write to me. I was the guest of Susie Berry. She and Bessie appeared glad to see me. I was left by the train to Choctaw City Sunday morning Jan. 5th 1896. So I started to walk home, but about two and a half miles from Oklahoma City, I was overtaken by a white man, who kindly invited me to sit on the seat with him. So I rode with him until within about five miles of home. So bless the Lord, I saved 40 cts. by being left by the train, and rode sixteen miles or more free. I met Mr. Robertson, going to Edmond, with a load of new[ly] made posts upon his wagon. Arrived home late, but the sun was up about an hour high. It is cloudy this evening, as if it might snow. I am here in the school house, writing. I hate to stall alone all night as I was last night. It is not good for a man to be alone. I have many, many things to be thankful to the Lord God for. I am trying to better my financial condition and at the [page 129] same time uplift my fellow man. I have found that July 1895 was not at all too early to hunt for a school to be taught in Oct.-Feb—1895-96. The good results of the work done July 12th 1895 still continue to benefit and bless me this Jan. 6th 1896. It has made me a resident of Oklahoma County. It has made me acquainted with the white teacher and with numerous other friends. It has enabled me to secure a nice frame for my diploma. Instead of feeling abject, miserable, and dejected it has made me feel joyful and like praising the Lord. It has brought me into acquaintance with Dr. C. P. Hues, a graduate of the medical department of Western Reserve University, Cleveland, Ohio. - I like to teach school ever so well. I am in no ways tired and it is a very honest way of making money. And I am very willing to make money in any honest way that I can. I have thirty-four scholars on the roll now, but only about twenty three were in attendance to-day. I have about four times the number of pupils that there are at the Kickapoo Mission. The people seem to be well pleased with my work. There are many things that weigh me down and hinder me. But, by God's grace I try to overcome them. Amen. Praise the Lord.

Thursday Jan. 9th 1896 (4:55 P.M. in the Smith School House, Sec. 14, Township 13 North, in Range 1 West of the Indian Meridian.[)]

I received a letter from John King, and my other mail also by the hand of Mr. Robert Mack, the brother of Lula Mack, one of my pupils. I have yet seven weeks to teach after this week. The white teacher has only two weeks more to teach. It is my purpose to endeavor to secure another school to teach as soon as possible. I am very, very well pleased with teaching, and it is not easy work when one tries to do their whole duty. I had twenty-eight pupils in school today. It thus appears that the largest daily attendance begins in the month of January. I have thirty-five pupils on the roll. I have several hindering things. Mr. Gokey said that the County Superintendent reported that the order in my school was bad. The children did misbehave in his presence more than ever before or since. - In the morning school opens by singing a religious song; then follows the reading of a chapter or passage from the Written Word of God, and then the Lord's Prayer is said in concert. After this the roll is called, and then classes take their places. From 10:30 to 10:45 is the morning recess; from 2:30 to 2:45, the evening recess. School begins at [. . .] A.M. in the morning, and closes at 4 P.M. The pupils [*page 130*] seem to enjoy themselves much playing at the noon and other recesses. - I am at present a resident of Oklahoma County. But I love Pottawatomie County better. I guess it is because there my boyhood days were spent. There I first came to know and recognize relatives and friends. I am a native of the city of Lawrence, Kansas, but I know this only by the testimony of my parents. Here is a precious thought from the *Christian Nation*—a reform paper published in New York City: "Joseph and Mary made their house a fit place <u>religiously</u> in which Jesus might develop into perfect manhood. But perfect manhood presupposes perfect childhood and youth." I bless God that for twelve or thirteen years I have constantly read such a Christian paper. Lord Jesus Christ, do Thou keep me from all sin and evil, and lead me from good work to good work until eternity itself shall be filled completely, if possible. Amen and Amen, Lord Jesus.

Monday January 13th 1895 [1896] (6:11 P.M.)
    It is just now dark and I have [am?] here writing by lamp light in the room of Mr. Blackford. The house is about 16 feet by eighteen in dimensions, with a window in the east end and another in the west. It has one door in the north side and another in the south. I do my own cooking and eat when I please and what I please. Saturday night I went to Choctaw City, walking all the way thither and all the way back. I wrote and mailed letters to the following:—1 *New York Independent*, New York City; 2 the State Normal Monthly, Emporia, Kansas; 3 G. I. Whitney, St. Paul, Minn.; 4 Chicago University, Chicago, Ill.; 5 Prairie View State Normal School, Hempstead, Texas; 6 William Shawnee, Tecumseh, Ok. Ter; 7 John King, Dale, Okla. Ter.; 8 George E. Shawnee, Haskell Institute, Lawrence, Kansas; 9 Little Jim, Denver, Cleveland Co., Okla. Ter. and 10 Mr. Wilson Girty, Webbers Falls, Ind. Ter. – Sunday Jan. 12th 1896 I taught a Sabbath School class, and in the afternoon visited Douglas City. I saw Loula Anderson, but was not formally introduced to her. There is $1.42 cts that I can not account for on my account books. I must have lost the money in some way or other. I had about twenty-five pupils in school to-day. I also mailed a letter to the Freedmen's Normal Institute, Maryville, Tennessee Saturday. I whipped several pupils today, Walter Colman and Alice Gearing being among the number. Alice is the prettiest girl in school, but she does not know it. She does not seem to have any idea of importance for herself. It is seven weeks until commencement, but I have begun to prepare for an exhibition in good earnest. On the whole, I am tolerably well satisfied with my school. I do try hard to do my whole duty: God is witness. It does seem [*page 131*] that I have accomplished but little. Yesterday Mr. Gokey told me to put in my application as soon as my school is out. I had previously told him that I wanted to teach this same school another year. The people seem to be well pleased. I should read over the school law. I should write to the Co. Supt. of other counties in regard to a school to begin March 1st 1896. If I could get another school to run three months I would be lucky; that would enable me to teach eight months in the year. – I am glad that I have the spirit of self-help. The Lord God of heaven and earth has driven me into self-help, and I thank him for it. I wish to attend the Kansas State Normal School at Emporia, Kansas, in 1897. Lord, Jesus, help me to improve my places, and save up money to attend this Normal. I need the following things: 1. To build a house upon each of my places. 2. To have a well on my lower place. 3. To run one more mile of fence upon the same.

Saturday Jan. 18th 1896 (7:35 A.M.)

For the last three days the weather has been cloudy. I have taught school another week, making fourteen weeks. I have six weeks yet to teach. Last night about 7:30 P.M. Mr. Robert Mack brought my mail from Choctaw City—the *Christian Nation*, a letter from Mr. William Shawnee, and a Registry Return Receipt from Dale, Okla. Ter. So J. C. King received the Registered Letter I sent to him. This letter contained $5 in money. I owe Mr. King yet $4.35 cts. My debts are on the decline, Thank the Lord God Almighty. Teaching school has proved my salvation. I ought to have gone to teaching sooner. Yesterday, Friday Jan. 17th 1896, Mrs. Dora Woodward visited my school a whole half day in the afternoon. The children spoke some of their pieces in the evening. Mrs. Dora said she thought the pieces were nice. I thought so too. I want a class to add upon the chart at Exhibition. The white teacher is going to have an exhibition, notwithstanding he said he did not think he would. I have written a letter home this morning to Mr. William Shawnee and another to Mr. J. M. Cummings, of Tecumseh, Ok. Ter. I ought to pay the *Christian Nation* another Dollar to-day, the Lord being my helper. It is a real good paper.

Sunday January 19th 1895 [1896] (5:40 A.M. Still very dark.)
    Yesterday Jan. 18th I walked all the way to Choctaw City and walked all the way back. I bought a slate to pay Alice Gearing for sweeping for me. My [*New York*] *Independent* did not come; and the maps and pictures I ordered from St. Paul, Minn. did not come. I am [*page 132*] trying to pay up my debts. I sent another Dollar yesterday to the *Christian Nation*, which makes $2.55 I have paid to it. I must make another remittance to this paper Feb. 1, 1895 [1896] if I can. I owe Carson Bros. [$]6.55 that I must pay as soon as possible. I ought to make them a remittance of $3.55 Feb. 1st 1896. I ought to make John King a remittance of $4.35, or at least of $2.35. I ought to pay W. L. McFall of Tecumseh the $1.50 cts that I owe him. I ought to pay Messrs. Houghton and Upp, Purcell, Ind. Ter. the $3 that I owe them.
    If I had used my money economically, I could have paid up all my debts. The last three months $81 has come into my possession, and it is hard to see what I have bought with it. — I want to secure another school to teach after Feb. 29th 1895 [1896]. If I succeed in doing so, I will be able to make more improvements on my places, buy the books I need, and the clothes, and get completely out of debt. My policy from now on is to owe no man any thing, but a person will have to work hard all the time in order to be able to do so. I must secure a place to work if I have to work for 50 cts. a day.

Sunday Jan. 26th 1896. (4:15 P.M.)

I have just come back from the school house. I taught a class in Sabbath School about 11 A.M. or 12 P.M. They were late about getting out this morning, for it had sleeted enough to make bushes and trees look white. Mr. Coleman preached after 1 P.M. He complained about the people coming out so late, and asked them to come out earlier. Miss Hattie Woodward, Miss Lula Harmon, Miss Lula Mack, and Miss Bettie Coleman, and Francis Shaw were present. Betty thought the song, "Lord, God of hosts, how lovely" was pretty. Hattie was the one who asked me about the song, but Bettie and another girl helped me sing it. Bettie called for another song, but as the girls left, she went with them.

Yesterday I taught ten pupils their pieces and their songs until 12:30 P.M. After that, James Lilliard and I walked to Choctaw City. We went by Grandma Ferguson's to take a sack home, and she sent a letter by me, which I put in the office along with my own letters. – It snowed Saturday night—that is Friday night Jan. 29th 1896, but just enough to whiten the ground, but when the sun came out, it was soon all gone. Alice Gearing does not try to learn at all now; I guess Josie Cooper has put something wrong into her head. I bought on a credit from Mr. Ferguson 23 lbs. of smoked meat @ 8¢ a lb., which amounts to $1.85. I aim to pay him when I get my pay Feb. 1st, 1896. If I can not get a school to teach, I may try to work with Mr. John Whitehead, or Mr. Isaac Cuppy.

[*page 133*] I want to take a teacher's examination in Tecumseh the last Friday and Saturday in April 1896. This will be April 24 and 25th 1896. I must purchase more Natural Philosophies, and study more on that subject. I must make 100 per cent in Physics if I possibly can. I must attend the County Normal Institute sure if I possibly can. I ought to try hard to secure a certificate from the Territorial Board of Education. In that case I can teach in any county or city in Oklahoma Territory without the trouble of fee or examination. At present in order to teach in a city, I will have to take a city examination. I ought to take the city examination in Guthrie. There seems to be a scarcity of teachers up there.

It was in October 1893 that I first examined the Statutes of Oklahoma with a view of knowing the school law and turning the same to my own advantage. At present I have two copies of the school law, which I read and re-read. No one should be ignorant of the laws of his country. One reason I am poor is because I have not lived up to my opportunities. I might just as well have earned $90 of $150 in the Fall of 1895 as not. It was my own fault that I did not earn that money.

But I praise the Lord Jesus that the case is as well with me as it is. I praise God Almighty that I have at last found a place where I can do good to humanity and at the same time make some money which I so sorely need.

Tuesday Jan. 28th 1896 (6:05 A.M.)

Yesterday Monday Jan. 27th 1896 was a fine day. It was too warm for a fire in the afternoon. It was bright and beautiful sunshine. My interest in my school is increasing. I had twenty-nine pupils yesterday. There are comfortable seats for only twenty-two. The house is too small, and the side seats are as poor as they can be. Only one scholar in school knows all of the multiplication table complete, and I can not find time to have the children say the table here lately. There are so many classes that I can not hear them all in one day, for which I am very sorry. There is real work in teaching school. When it is done rightly, one can not study other things very much. I read the school laws very often, and I do try very faithfully to carry them out. Josie Cooper and her mother came before 9 A.M. yesterday, and we had to take nearly an hour of time to mend up matters. Josie causes more trouble in school. During the last three months ending with Jan. 3rd 1896, she has attended only 29½ days out of 60. Out of these 29½ days she has been tardy 14 times. This makes her tardy more than half the time she does attend. Last year 1894 [*school year*] the first three months she attended 58 days and was absent 2 days. Last year the first three months she was tardy 32 times; so that last year she was tardy more than half the days attended. Miss Ella Dunjee, the teacher of this school last year (1894) told me that Josie Cooper thought as [*page 134*] much of her as any girl in school. Miss Dunjee claimed that she won Josie by being kind to her. I know that Josie does not like me one bit. She is reported by an ear-witness, James, to have said to him of me, "I do not care any thing about that little Indian dog." Miss Lula Harmon said that Josie said some thing to her about me and about the school, but said: "Mr. Shawnee, I can't tell you what she said." Mr. Gokey told me that Miss Lula Mack had told Mrs. Gokey that Josie Cooper did not like me one bit, but called me all sorts of bad names. No one except James had hinted what bad names she called me. I have a strong suspicion that Josie has poisoned the mind of Alice Gearing against me. Alice was very stubborn last week Jan 20-24, 1896. Jan. 20th 1896 was the day Josie met Joe Lilliard on the road and had a long talk with him under cover of going to dinner. I have caught Josie in stories—falsehoods. Josie's mother, by my invitation, visited the school until noon yesterday Jan. 27th 1896. She said to me: "I do not know about a good example, but Josie shall not set no bad example to the school." I replied, "If Josie is not setting a good example, she is sure setting a bad one." Here [her?] mother told me that I had worse scholars in school than Josie; she asked me first if I thought Josie was the worst scholar in school. She reluctantly gave me consent to whip Josie if I saw fit. Josie has gone home twice: Dec. 10th 1895 and Dec. 19th 1895. She run off and went home in stubbornness twice inside of 9 days.

Saturday Feb. 1st, 1896 (6:30 P.M.)
    After school was out last evening I left from the school house for Choctaw City, sending my things back by Lula Mack, Era, and Mary. It was about 4:45 P.M. when I left the schoolhouse. It was 7:05 P.M. when I purchased my ticket in Choctaw City. The train came up and did not leave for 15 minutes or more. I was soon in Oklahoma City, and went forthwith to the house of Mr. J. W. Dunjee. He talked a good deal to me, more so than usually. Miss Ella Dunjee did not come up, although her mother was expecting her. Miss ~~El~~ Drusilla Irene Dunjee spoke some to me. She liked the *New York Independent* very well, but she said that she wanted to subscribe for some daily paper, like the *Globe Democrat*. She had some nice books and papers. Miss Dunjee became very sleepy before I left; but I staid to hear her father talk. Mr. Dunjee asked me where I remained over night. I told him that I remained over night at Susie Berry. Thence I went to Susie Berry's and staid over night. About 8 or 9 A.M. this morning Feb. 1st, 1896 I went to the office of the County Clerk, and he made out my order and sealed it with his seal. I then took it to the County Treasurer, and he [*page 135*] went into the bank, and came back, and counted me out $30 in hard cash. I felt like praising the Lord God Almighty then, who has been so very kind and favorable to me. I sent $15 to my father at Tecumseh, Okla. Ter. I sent 25 cts to the *New York Independent*, 130 Fulton Street, New York City. I bought a *History of Oklahoma*, the author of which is Marion Tuttle Rock. It is from the press of C. B. Hamilton & Son, Topeka, Kansas. I bought a map of Kansas for 25 cts. Kansas is my native state, since I was born in the city of Lawrence, Kansas, Dec. 23rd 1868. Only about two years of my life was ever spent in Kansas. By the grace of the good God I visited Lawrence Oct. 1891 and staid about a week at the Kansas Yearly Meeting of the Society of Friends. I enjoyed those meetings very well; for the Lord Jesus Himself was present in them by His Spirit. There is joy in the service of the Lord Jesus Christ—yes, great superabundance of joy. I saw Mr. Umholtz the County Superintendent of this county. He told me there were 100 public schools in the county, of which twenty-one were colored. – Mr. Dunjee said that he was coming out before my school closed. – Mr. Umholtz is a very fine man. Mr. Umholtz told me that if the District School Board had furnished paper for the white school, to tell them to furnish

paper for my school, and charge it up to the County. Mr. Umholtz endorsed my certificate Feb. 19th 1895.

Mr. Umholtz visited my school Dec. 10th 1895. This was 9 months and 21 days after the endorsement. I began to teach 7 months and 18 days after the endorsement. Mr. Umholtz said that he did not know any school that would want a teacher after Feb. 28th 1896. – I bought Bessie Berry a pair of shoes for their many kind offices in keeping me over night where it was difficult to find a place to stay in the city. This is the first full month I have received of my salary. The third warrant I sold I saw the County Clerk stamp it for the white man after I sold it. This is the only warrant that he ever stamped for me.

Saturday Feb. 8th [1896].

I taught the children their songs and pieces until 12:15 P.M. Lula Mack, Era Mack, and Mary Mack, Alice Gearing, Eva Lillard, James Lillard, Lula Harmon, and others were the taught. Then, sending home my things by the Mack children, I started for Choctaw City on foot, with the coal oil can in my hand. When I reached the bridge, a white man, Mr. Glaze, called me passing by on the road; and I went to see him. Then he set before me a petition for a Post Office, which I signed. Then he said, "I have another paper here for you to sign." I answered, "What is it? He replied, "A mortgage." I saw the name of "James Fields" at the bottom of it, and no signature below the words, "Executed in presence of," and I told him I was not present when it was made. He said, "Oh, that does not make any difference." I told him, "If I was called up about it, I could not say, I was present." He replied, "Well, that is just a form that has to be filled out. He asked me if I knew this fellow Fields? I told him, No. He then told me that he lived over about the Johnson School House. Mr. Fields and Gertie Cooper came to my school not so very long ago. That is the only time I remember seeing the man.

Wednesday Feb 12th 1896. 5:20 P.M.

I have had some trouble with 19 [*one of William Shawnee's pupils*] this evening, and I offered prayer with and for her and her folks. 19 said that she did not care for boys. [[This is probably untrue.]] I prayed that God would make her a noble, useful woman. I prayed for 20 [*another pupil*] also. 19 said that she was a Christian, and that she became angry this evening. She did so because I would not let her get a drink of water. I explained that I could not be partial to her. 19 hurried home when I had dismissed her. I told them as they went [*page 136*] out of the door, "The Lord bless you." O Lord, Thou hast so often blessed me. Thy Providences follow me wherever I go. I can see God's hand every few days. It is food for my thought. I hope that God will touch the heart of Lula Mack and the heart of her sister. You can reason with Lula; she said that she knows she ought to set an example that she would like to see other's follow. I prayed the lord to enable me not to whip the children unnecessarily. – It may be that Lula Mack did this just so I would keep her after school and talk to her.

Sunday Feb. 16th 1896 (5:40 A.M.)

I have just arisen from bed, and it is dark yet. The past week I have had some trouble with Miss Lula Mack, a very good girl. She is stubborn, however, and looked steadily in the eyes of Mart Moore. She and Hattie did this. Miss Lula Mack had written on paper "Free fancy girls I like," and owned it to me, but Friday Feb. 14th 1896, she tried to deny it to her mother. Wednesday, I believe it was, that I threatened to tell her mother if she looked at boys that way again. She replied sourly that she did not care. Yesterday Feb. 15th 1896—Saturday—I learn that she said that she only had two weeks more to go to school; that she was sorry she had [*page 137*] missed so much time out of school. Lula took the part of Mr. Barbour too, whom we accused of writing four names upon the outside walls of the school house. The names are Hattie Woodward, Francis Shaw, Lula Mack, and Bettie Coleman. These are just the names that Mr. Barbour would want to write. I know he keeps company with the first three named. A fellow that would go with Francis Shaw ought not to go with Lula Mack. – Saturday Feb. 8th 1896 I was in Choctaw City, and sent away the following letters: to William Shawnee, to the State Normal Monthly. – Yesterday Feb. 15th I went 5 miles north of Mr. Blackford's place to see about a school. It was the school Miss Ford was after. The lady who is teaching is operating under a temporary certificate, and her name is Miss Iva Wells. Mr. Ben Dulan told me these things. He said that she had to walk two miles from the north of the school house, and that she boarded with her uncle and aunt.

Monday Feb. 17th 1896 (6:45 A.M.).

Yesterday I taught Sabbath School and was in church. Mr. Williams from Alabama did the preaching. The text was 1 Sam 3:3. It was not correctly applied, but the sermon was good on the whole. After church I went home with kind and talkative and worthy Mrs. Mack. I walked side by side with her. I would not walk with Miss Lula Harmon, one of my pupils. Lula Harmon said that she was not a Christian; but she behaves better than some who claim to be Christians. Mr. Oscar Harmon, Lula's younger brother, invited me to come over to their home, and I promised him that I would; but that I had to go home with Mrs. Mack first. I went home with her; and a girl from Douglas came over to see Miss Lula Mack, but really to see her brother Mr. Robert Mack. Robert had to carry my clock for me yesterday. Mr. and Mrs. Harmon have moved into their house, and they are now quite comfortably fixed. They are on the SE ¼ of Section 18, Township 13, North, Range 1 E, of the Indian Meridian.

When I came to Mr. Blackford's, I found the door locked, and all the folks gone; so I had to go up to the church. On the way I overtook Mr. and Mrs. McNeil and Mrs. Mack and Lula Mack. Mrs. Mack said that she had punished Lula Mack for what she had done, but she asked me not to tell Lula about the fact that she told me. I told Mrs. Mack to tell the ~~other~~ her girls to tell the other girls that they must not stop behind the school house. (A certain person knew as much of a certain other person as her husband did.) I learn from Mrs. McNeil that Miss Lula Mack offered prayer at church last night. That she prayed the Lord to make her pure in heart and to make her just such a Christian as she ought to be. She prayed for her wicked brother. She prayed God to give her more grace and more faith, to enable her to bear her crosses and trials in this low land of sorrow. Mrs. Mack did not say [*page 138*] any thing about these things. She prayed God to enable her to live aright and walk aright. She prayed for her mother and her sisters. She prayed for all for whom she is duty bound to pray. Miss Lula Mack was converted and baptized two years ago, I learn. She was about fourteen years old at that time.

Monday Feb. 17th 1896 (6:50 P.M.).

Here I am at the house of Mr. Blackford, a colored man, on the SW ¼ of Sec. 13, Township 13 North, of Range 1 West, of the Indian Meridian. I have taught school all day today with an attendance of 32. The interest is good in the school at present, and the attendance is very regular. The children seem to like me very well and the parents also. Miss Lula Mack behaved very well to-day, except once in the matter of singing. She did not sing just as I told her too [to]. But I threatened to punish her and this had the desired effect. Miss Lula Mack and Miss Era Mack were ten minutes behind Mary and Archie Mack. I made all the tardy pupils sit upon the rough side seats. Among them were Lula Mack, Era Mack, Lula Harmon, Hattie Woodward, Hattie Williams, and Nora Williams. Every pupil in school reported that they did not use tobacco, both boys and girls. Suspicion, however, rests upon two of them, but they denied its use. I have now taught school 91 days today. I have 9 days more only to teach. I shall hunt up another school right away. The folks at home will be more willing than ever to let me have a horse and saddle that I may seek a school. I may find a school in Pottawatomie near

Dale, Okla. Ter. My first school in Oklahoma County will soon pass into history and be no more. I must be busy these few remaining days. Saturday Feb. 15th 1895 [1896] I mailed a sweet letter in Douglas City to Miss Emma Valentine, Maryville, Tennessee; another to the Central Tennessee College, Nashville, Tennessee; and another to the Oklahoma Agricultural College, Stillwater, Okla. Ter.

Wednesday Feb. 19th 1896 (6:10 A.M.)

It has just been one year ago to-day since Mr. Umholtz the County Supt. of Oklahoma County endorsed my first grade certificate. It was just after the greatest snow I had ever seen in this country, and had lain upon the ground three weeks. I went home with Miss Lula Mack and Era Mack yesterday evening Feb. 18, 1896. My purpose was to see Mr. Robert Mack and have him bring my mail from Choctaw City; and also to bring out 40 cents worth of beef for me. Miss Lula Mack said that she hoped I would get the school again next term. I walked part of the way side by side with Lula, and she walked in front the rest of the way. I rose from bed just a little before 4 A.M. this [*page 139*] morning. I asked Lula Mack if it was so about her offering prayer at meeting Sunday night, and she said Yes. I told her I was very glad and hoped that the Lord would bless her and that she would be a true Christian. It does seem that Miss Lula Mack is sincere and earnest in her way of serving God. Miss Lula Mack is quite a dark colored girl and she was born within four miles of Paris, Texas, Lamar County. Her father and mother are poor but upright and honest, and endeavor to bring up their children in the fear of the Lord. They are of the Baptist persuasion, and Miss Lula Mack was publicly baptized (immersed) and joined the church two years ago. Miss Lula Mack is slim, and has been sickly some, but last Oct. and Nov. 1895 she picked cotton for about one month and a half before entering school. She is Supt., or Assistant Supt., of the Baptist Sabbath School, where I am teaching. Mrs. Mack does like to talk very well, and she tells me that I am more patient with the children than she could possibly be. She tells me about many things how the people are here, but she does not want me to tell others what she says. I do not want others to know all I feel it my duty to say, or ask. Miss Lula Mack went and told her mama that I made a motion to her to go home Festival night Feb. 7th 1896. Miss Lula Mack would break her neck for me, I believe. Miss Lula Harmon was born in Texas and she is 18 years old. Her father reads history very much, and is well and is well posted about the late civil war— 1861-65. Miss Lula Harmon is not a Christian, but no girl in school behaves better or tries harder to learn. Mr. Harmon told me to come back again before my school was out. I decided to hold my exhibition Friday night Feb. 28th 1896. I must get Mr. H. E. Cooper to fix up a platform such as they had last year.

Saturday Feb. 22nd 1896 {(5:55 A.M.(A.M.)}
    This week has been one of peculiar favors. Mr. Robert Mack brought me some beef from Choctaw City Thursday evening. I was so glad that I gave him ten cents, telling him that I was going to give him that if I never gave him another thing in my life. I received my mail from the same kind hand also. It consisted of a letter from the *Christian Nation*, and two copies of that paper; a letter from Mr. Grant Carter, a son of Mr. Stephen Carter deceased, of Tecumseh, Okla. Ter.; a letter from Miss Carrie Warrior, Lawrence, Kansas; two copies of the *New York Independent*; the *State Normal Monthly*, of Emporia, Kansas; and the *Oklahoma State Capital* of Guthrie, Oklahoma. – Miss Lula Mack reached the school house tardy yesterday at 3:02 P.M., ostensibly for the purpose of hearing the pieces practiced. She had to stay home and wash. Miss Lula Harmon denied to me that she ever talked to Hattie Woodward in school, and she tries hard to do what is required of her. She [*page 140*] might have told Miss Lula Mack that she talked, by way of a joke, or it may be that she told the truth. Miss Lula Harmon looked up in Sam Coleman's face, as much as to say, I like to got caught that time. Lula Harmon's mother is better looking than she. Lula Mack thinks more of Mr. Barber than any one else; she goes with him more than with any one else. She took Mr. Barber's part, unnecessarily, at one time. I told her that I would like to know the reason why. In time past Miss Lula Mack has kept company with Mr. Silas Shaw, who is black in color. – Miss Hattie Woodward carries around to school the picture of a certain white fellow, and one day Miss Lula Harmon had it in her possession. Afterwards Miss Lula Harmon brought from home a book like an album. I believe it was to show the picture of her fellow to Hattie Woodward and Lula Mack. It is known and on record that Miss Lula Mack and Miss Hattie Woodward talk to each other about fellows. There is a likely hood that Hattie and the two Lulas all talk to each other of their fellows. Miss Lula Harmon dressed very nicely all last week, presumably because we were expecting visitors. Miss Hattie Williams does not seem to have fellows on the brain at all. She talks in southern Negro style, such as, "that yonder boy." Miss Lula Mack could not help but eye Mart Moore yesterday; she acted as if she was afraid I would see her, but as if she could not refrain from gazing. He is black as pitch. She once said of him, "Oh, I don't care nothing about that old nigger." This is either true or false. If her gazing is to be taken for what it is worth, she does care for him. – I must ask Miss Lula Mack if she is engaged to Mr. Barber

the reason she took it [his?] part when it was not her place to do so.

The paper Miss Lula Mack wrote was to her friend, presumably to Mr. E. Barber, asking him to help her out with her composition. This proves that she does write letters to Mr. Barber. This was done Sunday, Feb. 9th 1896. Miss Lula Mack wrote "Free Fancy Girls I like" beyond a doubt, and she acknowledged it to me too when I first took the paper, but Friday a week ago she tried to deny to her mother that she wrote it. Who is her cousin that [*text ends here*]

Saturday Feb. 22nd 1896 (6:52 P.M.)

I went to the school house, built a fire and brought a bucket of water from Mr. Gokey's. Eva Lillard, James Lillard, and Alice Gearing, Lula Mack, Era Mack, Hattie Woodward, Henry Cooper, and Fillmore Cooper were present. We practiced until 12:15 P.M., and about 12:20 P.M., sending my clock and books home by Miss Lula Mack, I started on foot for Choctaw City. Near town I rode [*page 141*] over a mile with a white man, who kindly invited me to ride. I mailed a letter and package to Miss Carrie Warrior, Lawrence, Kansas, another to Bishop College, Marshall, Texas, inclosing a stamp; and a third to Mr. Grant Carter, Tecumseh, Oklahoma Territory. I purchased the following things:—

    1 Dozen Lead Pencils 20 cts, 3 Tablets Paper 25   45
    1 Glass for Window 20 cts. and Stamps 9   29
    Slate Pencils .05   05

I arrived home from Choctaw City at 6 P.M., making the trip in five hours and forty minutes. I took my time writing letters in the Post Office at Choctaw City.

Written Sunday Feb. 23rd 1896 (5:30 A.M.[)]

There is nothing that is more important than recording facts of all kinds with pen and ink, in order to refer to them afterwards for purposes of information as well as for their preservation. The mind forgets the facts it has been in possession of to an astonishing degree. Hence the value of recording facts. Although the amount of knowledge in the world that is recorded on paper may be great, yet it is a mere speck in the boundlessness of unrecorded knowledge. The things we know are few; the things we can know are few; the things we do not know are as boundless as eternity itself. — More people are acquainted with you than you have any idea of. They also know more of you than you have any idea of. What an incentive to right thinking and right doing at all times and in all places. — My first school in Oklahoma Territory will soon pass into history. I have had 38 pupils on the roll since its beginning. Only ten were present the opening day Oct. 7th 1895. 30 pupils were present Friday Feb. 21ˢᵗ, 1895 [1896]. 95 days have been taught; there are only five more to teach, which will make 100 days taught altogether.

Wednesday Feb. 26ᵗʰ 1896 (6:12 P.M.: Standard Time: the sun not yet set).

    Yesterday Tuesday Feb. 25ᵗʰ 1896 I visited Mrs. Mack, at her home. She is a good woman, and although I was inclined to feel a little cold when I went, yet she gave such true reasonable explanations and was so kind to me that I went away, saying to them, God be with you. Miss Lula Mack seems to feel better toward me. I did not have to find any fault to-day. She was a model girl. She sung all right too, and she did whatever I asked her to do freely. I do believe she is a good Christian girl. There are three girls in school that are professing Christians,— Miss Lula Mack, Miss Hattie Woodward, and Miss Hattie Williams. Mrs. Mack remarked that I was a pet, when I said that sometimes my feelings were easily hurt and sometimes they were not. Mrs. Kirk used to tell me [*page 142*] if I felt bad over any thing to let them know it, and they would fix it up, so that I would not feel bad. – I went to Douglas City Monday evening Feb. 24ᵗʰ 1896, and spent money as follows: cts

Coal Oil 10¢, Eggs 7¢   17
Soap 5¢, Matches 05   10

    I have been holding examinations ever since yesterday Feb. 25ᵗʰ 1896. I want to teach the same school another term if possible; at any rate, I must try my best to obtain it.

Thursday Feb. 27ᵗʰ 1896. (7:20 A.M.).

    How many good Christian young women are there whom we see longing for kind and faithful husbands. They have sexual food, and here we perish with sexual hunger. O God, watch over us in sexual relations and in every other relation that we may be blessed of Thee and not cursed. When our irregular sallies of hunger come, do Thou be with us. Send us a good wife at the proper time, O Lord. Thou wilt surely, if it be Thy will—

Friday Feb. 28ᵗʰ 1896. 11:25 P.M.

    We had a full house to-night. We spoke without making a single excuse or apology whatever. My first school in Oklahoma Territory has now passed into history. The people appeared to be well pleased with the exercises this evening. I told Miss Lula Mack, "I wish to be your company Sunday." She replied, All right. She seems to be well pleased with me. I gave all my scholars a stick of candy to-night. Two school teachers, both ladies, were in the audience. They are from the vicinity of Paris, Texas. One is named Miss Annie Wilby and [. . .]

Miss Lula Harmon did not read her composition. I did not insist upon it. I have learned a great deal about teaching school more so than I ever realized before. Teaching is hard work when it is done right. Now if I can get another school to teach some where I will still continue on in the good way. I will go and look up a school five miles north of here if the Lord will. May the Lord bless my pupils and their parents, and may I be their teacher next year if it be his will.

Friday night Feb. 28th 1896

Mrs. Mack with her three daughters stopped at the house of Mr. Blackford. The mother was telling that her daughter wanted to marry, but she was not telling me. She was telling Mr. Blackford, but I was near. I do not know why she was telling it. I do think she wants her daughter to marry. First, because she has a large family to support. Secondly, because she is afraid some boy will lead her daughter out of the path of virtue. The very thought seems to trouble the mother. They are very kind to me. The daughter has said Yes to everything I have said to her so far. She tells her mama every thing, however. She put her ear up close so I could whisper to her.

Sunday ~~Feb~~ March 1st, 1896 (6:17 A.M.).

Yesterday Feb. 29, 1896 I went up about 9 miles north of here or 8 miles, seeking for a vacant school. But I could not find any. It was a mistake uttered by Miss Wilby and the other lady that Miss Wells had been dismissed from her school. I came around by the Post [*page 143*] Office in Douglas City, and mailed a letter to the University of Minnesota, at Minneapolis, praying that a catalogue be sent to me. I bless God for his many favors and blessings bestowed upon me the past week. The people seem well pleased with the exhibition, and have asked that I come around to visit them before I go. I must teach this school again this Fall if I possibly can. Mr. Fulbright asked me Friday if I intended to teach this same school another year and I told him I did. Mr. Amos Woodward paid me 5 cts. for a slate that I had bought some time ago, at his request, for his little daughter Lucy. Mr. Oscar Harmon had me promise to come over and visit them to-day. And I have all the company I can take care of in the person of Miss Lula Mack, whom we believe to be a good Christian young woman.—

Monday March 2nd 1896 (4:35).

Yesterday I went over to Mrs. Mack's and remained there a long time. Lula Mack and her mother were gone over to Mr. Campbell's and Mr. Roger's. I ate dinner at Mrs. Mack's, the same being cooked by Miss Era Mack. I was a guest over night at the home of Mr. Harmon. Oscar Harmon is well thought of by Mrs. Mack, but she does not think the same of me. Miss Lula Mack said that she liked me and I do believe the girl is telling the truth. I asked her mother how mad would she get if I wrote to Miss Lula Mack. She said that she would not get mad at all. Lula Mack was born July 5th 1879. She will be 17 years old July 5th 1896. She was born within four miles of Paris, Texas. Mrs. Mack said she was particular about her blood, and that she did not want her daughter to marry every kind of fellow, that she did not want her daughter to be taken down into the Indian nation by any man. Miss Lula Mack promised to write to me and promised that she would let no one know what I wrote except her mother, and no one else. Mrs. Mack [*page 144*] said that Robert Mack had seen my father selling apples in Oklahoma City, and that Miss Lula too. But that Lula did not recognize him. Mrs. Mack told me that the Post Office address of Miss Lula Mack was Douglas City, Okla. Ter. Mrs. Mack seems to be so kind and friendly, but she said that they were going to laugh at me when I was gone. I told them that I wished I could find a girl who would love me as I would want to be loved. I promised to furnish Miss Lula Mack with paper, stamps, and envelopes. I must ask Miss Lula Mack if she loves me. She would not go away for any length of time, and she was bound to stay close by me. That girl loves me, and her mother knows it. She will not let us be together alone. I made up my mind that Mrs. Mack had to slight me severely before I would let Miss Lula alone, and she did act a little cool for a little while, but she said that she was the mother of fifteen children. Miss Lula Mack told me before her mother that she likes me. That girl does like me. I can see it, but her mother has been a hindrance.

Thursday March 5th 1896. (4:52 A.M.)

I went to Oklahoma City Tuesday evening by way of Mr. H. E. Cooper's and Mr. W. W. Lewis. It was dark before I arrived at Choctaw City, but I had to wait for the train, as the train does not come before after 8 P.M. They have changed the time of this train. It used to arrive at 7 P.M. I arrived in Oklahoma City Tuesday about 9 P.M. and repaired straightway to the house of Rev. J. W. Dunjee. I found him within as well as his wife and Miss Drusilla Dunjee. He asked me when I was going home. I told him, Thursday. He told me to tell my father that he would be down next week.

I saw Mr. W. W. Asher in the office of the County Clerk in Oklahoma City, and he spoke in the colored man's favor as much so as the *New York Independent*. I read the laws relating to the University of Oklahoma, to the Normal School, and to the Agricultural College.

I received my pay in full $30. I sent $10 to my father William Shawnee by ~~Registered~~ Money Order and $4.35 cts. to John King also by Money Order. 13¢ was the fee for these two orders.
   I also spent money as follows:—

1 Complete Geography, 1.25 and 1 Harvey's Grammar 65¢	1.90
2 Physiologies 1.00 and 1 slate 15	1.15
Paper 10, Envelopes 10, and Stamps 26¢	46
Sugar 10¢ for Susie Berry, and Sundries 2.00	2.10
Paid Mr. McNeil 1.00 and Mrs. McNeil 1.10	2.10
[page 145] Paid Mrs. Mack for a Chicken and Eggs 35¢	35¢
Railroad Tickets	80¢
1 First Reader	17¢

   I came back to Choctaw City on the 12 o'clock train, and at a little before 3 P.M. I was in the house here at Mr. Harrison Blackford's, where I am doing this writing. I went over to Mr. H. E. Cooper's to Mrs. Mack's, to Mr. Harmon's, and came back to Mr. Blackford's by way of Mrs. Macks, where she presented me four eggs. From Mr. Blackford's I went over to the house of Mr. Lon Woodward, and gave Miss Hattie Woodward the promised presents for Merit in school. All these I went to yesterday except Mr. H. E. Cooper,—who was not at home, put their names on paper for me to teach the next school.
   When I came back from Mr. Lon Woodward's by way of the School House, who should be here at the house of Mr. Blackford, but Mrs. Mack, Miss Lula Mack, and Mr. Robert Mack. I was surprised to see them. I wrote on the slate for Miss Lula Mack alone to read: "Goodbye, my own Lula. Miss Lula Mack is a lovely girl, and is a good Christian girl too. Do not forget me, Lula, when I am gone. To this last she wrote an answer, I won't." The others knew we were writing something we did not want them to see. The coming of these folks this dark night shows how they like me. I told Mrs. Mack yesterday that we must be good friends. I believe Lula is a worthy daughter of a worthy mother. I like Miss Lula Mack far more than I do the Dunjee girls, although the Dunjee girls are the most refined and the best educated. Miss Lula Mack is not at all afraid to pick cotton or even to card cotton and spin it into thread. She is not afraid to cook either. She is of prolific stock, and could easily be the mother of fifteen children. Her mother takes pride in being the mother of fifteen children, and I do not blame her one bit. I think it is some thing to be proud of. The talk last night was at times about the Indians. Mrs. Mack remarked that I talked Indian altogether when I was at home. I told them several words in the Shawnee language. The people up here have been as kind to me as they could be. Mrs. Lillard and Mrs. H. E. Cooper have done my washing, free of charge, which I shall never forget. Mrs. Mack has given me a nice chicken free and also milk several

times. Several times I have eaten dinner at their house. Mrs. Lillard sent me some nice butter. Mrs. Dora Woodward sent me some meat. For these and other favors I thank the Lord and I also thank these friends who have been kind to me. Mrs. Mack remarked yesterday (March 4th 1896) that Mr. Gokey—who is on the school board,—was willing for me to have the school. I went to the office of the County Superintendent when I was in Oklahoma City yesterday (March 4) but he was not at home. So I could not get to tell him what I wished to.

Friday March 6th 1896 (5:15 A.M.).
   Yesterday March 5th they said, when I was over at Mr. Lillard's that a baby of Mr. Rogers had died the day before (March 4th 1896). From Mr. H. E. Cooper I learned that there were two applications for this school besides my own. He said that Miss Ella Dunjee had sent in word that she wanted to teach next term. Mr. Fullbright also is after this school. He came to Mr. Cooper twice to see about it inside of one week. He told Mr. Cooper that the County Superintendent and the Directors desired a change in this district. Mr. Donnelly and his wife said yesterday that Miss Ella Dunjee had sent in word three months ago that she would teach the next term of this school. He said this yesterday March 5th 1896. Mr. H. E. Cooper spoke favorably as to my securing the school, but declined to be the first on the list of signers. One especial reason why I want the school another term is because a certain person said that I should not have it another term. I have secured signers from eight families. That is really a majority of the patrons. Mr. Donnelly declined to sign. At the same time he said that he could not say who would get the school, nor even who he was willing should have it. But he did say, That Miss Ella Dunjee had given the best satisfaction, and that the teacher they wanted was the one who had given the best satisfaction. I made up my mind that I must secure the school even at the risk of losing it altogether. I will never give up a fight until I am beat: that is my policy, and I want to be endorsed in suspending a certain pupil, if possible, to have matters that way, with honor. But if the people will change, I will bow with respect. But I do not like to see other teachers wire-working for the next term of the school even before mine is out. Rev. Mr. Coleman declined to sign unless Mr. H. E. Cooper's name is on my list. He is the only person who declined for that reason. I am able to take my own part, and I am going to take it too. Mr. and Mrs. Lillard are among my best friends and they declined to sign for several reasons. They are expecting a school-house to be built in their district and they never had had a voice in the affairs of District No. 32. Mr. Mitchell I could not find, altho I went to

his home. I have been shaping all my affairs for another term. I am bound to teach in this district as many terms as I can. I have no one to help me but the Lord, who is an all-sufficient helper. Lord, bless all the patrons of this school, [*page 147*] and all the children. I have done my very best with them. Some say I do not whip enough; I would rather they would say this than say I did ~~not~~ whip ~~enough~~ too much. They would hardly say that I whipped just enough. Mr. Greene is a good man and is heartily in my favor. He does not believe in a frequent change of teachers. It surely is detrimental to the pupils to change teachers frequently. It is like it was in the Indian school service. Teachers used to have to fight to hold their places. So it seems it is in the Oklahoma Colored School Service. No respect is meant for you, but they want to do the work and draw the pay. Hence the fight.

It will be with me in the future as in the past. The closer I stick to the Lord God Almighty and his Christ, and be diligent in business serving the Lord, the more money I will make and the more improvements can I put on my two places. I have a race prejudice to fight that is put forth by the colored people, but that is not insurmountable.

I like teaching very well. I will have to take the April examination for a teacher's certificate in my own County. Pottawatomie County is the county I was raised in from earliest childhood, or rather Pottawatomie County came and threw her arms around me in the land of my childhood. But my present certificate is good here in Oklahoma County until Oct. 30th 1896. My next certificate will run until 1899. I will write my examination with a lead pencil this time instead of with ink and pen. I must receive a first grade certificate, so that I can get school work to do in whatever county I can find it. It will be Pottawatomie County licensing teachers to teach in other counties. – I am going home to-day and I must come back after my things as soon as I can. I have some property, and I must do my best to take care of it.

Chapter 8

Teaching at Shawnee
March 9, 1896—April 30, 1897

After leaving Choctaw City, between March 9, 1896, and April 30, 1897, Shawnee filled his third journal with entries of his daily activities. During that time, he lived in his father's home, along with his brothers. He noted his brothers' attitudes toward blacks. He wrote that Walter and Dudley called blacks "niggers and coons" and that they referred to the colleges black students attended as "coon" colleges.

    Shawnee worked at various jobs and continued to improve his property while looking for another school at which he could teach. He planted corn for Mr. Marshall and hoed cotton for his father and for Mr. Taylor. He set out rose bushes and blackberry vines on his place. He leased out his allotment to black and white tenants.

    William Ellsworth Shawnee returned to Choctaw City, as he had been asked, to find out whether the school board had hired him to teach Smith School for the next term. Shawnee witnessed the school board vote for Rev. Fullbright to teach the next term. Without a teaching job for the next term, Shawnee went to Douglas City to apply for a teaching position at its black school. When he learned that Rev. Fullbright was being considered there as well, he confronted Rev. Fullbright about which school he wanted to teach. In the meantime, however, Dr. Hamilton assisted Shawnee to obtain a position at the black school in the city of Shawnee. Its schoolhouse was not ready at the beginning of the semester; therefore, Shawnee did not begin teaching there until November 1896.

    Between March 9, 1896, and April 24, 1897, Shawnee engaged in many activities to prepare for teaching. He ordered a list of the school catalogues he wanted. He took the Pottawatomie County teacher's exam in Tecumseh and received a certificate. He met Miss Cooley, a young black woman, there. He attended the Choctaw Normal summer school taught by Ella Dunjee. He attended the County Teacher's Association, the only nonwhite to do so during that era. He also attended the Territorial Teacher's Association and became a member.

Shawnee was involved with his family and neighbors. Mr. Marcus helped him to build a home. He visited Mr. Dunjee, Mr. Marcus, and David and Mamie Alford. He assisted his brother Walter Shawnee to load logs. In April, he attended the Bread Dance at Big Jim's Crossing.

The twists and turns of Shawnee's romantic interests were far from dull. He said that he loved Ella Dunjee. He was still interested in Carrie Warrior, Lena Robinson, and Lula Mack, but he gave the last up for good because Mrs. Mack did not like him. Near the end of 1896, Shawnee finally found his true love. His stepmother, Julia, went away from home for a while and returned on November 28 with her cousin Ellen Carolina, a Creek freedman descendant. By December 8, 1896, Shawnee and Ellen were "drifting toward love." The two were married on February 6, 1897. By April he was unhappy because he sensed something going on between Ellen and her old boyfriend Piney Wilson.

Shawnee worshipped with the Quakers before he and Ellen were married, but stopped attending Quaker meetings after they were married. On one occasion, however, he visited the Shawnee Indian School and saw J. B. (Joe Billy) and Big Jim there. By April 1897 he was lamenting his staying away from church.

Monday March 9th 1896 (about 12 M [noon or midday]).

    I was going over in Cleveland Co., to find a school, but a man from there tells me that all the schools are taken up. He says it is of no use to go. On or after May 12th 1896 is the time to hunt up schools and to have your contract drawn up. That is about two months from now. I saw Mrs. Carter Saturday March 7th 1896, and told her that I was her friend and that she need fear no harm.

[*The following was written Sunday, March 15, 1896.*]
[*page 148*] Friday March 13th 1896

    I went up beyond Dale, Okla. Ter. in quest of a school to teach. I saw Mr. Chambers and Mr. Miller, both colored men. They were looking forward to the building of a school house for the colored children near them in this (Pottawatomie County) county. Yesterday (Saturday March 14th 1896), I went down to Earlsboro to seek a colored school to teach. I made these long journies on foot, because first I own no horse of my own, and secondly, because it was too cold to ride. I saw Mr. Cuppy too last night on my way back home from Earlsboro. This morning, Sunday March 15th 1896, Mr. Walter H. Shawnee burned up some papers, and he would have burned up some *Christian Nations* too, if I had not taken them away from him. He burned up some *Tecumseh Republicans* too, which should not have been burned up. I need a home of my own, where my papers and books can be well taken care of. I must have a home of my own as soon as possible, and thank God I have made a start in that direction already. — I have let certain parties alone on account of their ingratitude for the favors I did them. Cegar and his wife are very ungrateful. Mrs. Cegar says that I circulated reports against her, which I never did. She is not careful to tell the truth any way, and Carrie Warrior told me Jennie was two-faced. She certainly acted two-faced to me in reference to Carrie Warrior. — Since I have started to build a house, Walter Shawnee talks of building a log house, which is just what I expected he would do. I said to myself that my example would lead him to build a house. He has followed my example also in the matter of having his land broken for the use of the same, which I did over a year ago. This is a confession that I saw straighter than he. In the last 8 or 9 years between $1200 and $1500 has come into my hands. Probably only 1/5 or even less than that amount of that sum has [*been*] put upon my places. Only 1/5 of my money earned from teaching school has been put upon my land. This is not as it should be. A larger amount of my income should be put upon my places. I must have a home of my own if the Lord God willeth. I must live to myself. It was in 1888 that I first resolved to have a home of my own, and live to myself. How slow of execution has been my purpose.

Yet no one is to blame for it but myself. Jan. 1st, 1893 was the day when I began in good earnest to improve my places, and to have some thing. There were times when I scarcely had clothing fit to wear. But in the midst of my deep poverty I spared what money I could to buy fruit trees, books, and papers. I have had money enough to have a house, a wagon and team, plows, and all necessary household goods. It was poor management that has brought me to where I am. But I thank God it is no worse with me than it is. I paid $2.75 cts. taxes on the improvements [*page 149*] on my land this year. I ought to make more money and take more care to spend it aright. When William Shawnee was in Colorado, it was only one thing that enabled him to make money. It was tanning skins. Here in Oklahoma, there is only one thing, said I, that can enable me to make money and get up in the world. That is not tanning skins, but teaching school. That is the only thing I can do at present to make money. No matter how much people may sympathize with you they will not even get you a place to make money. I had a good time teaching a colored school. I made $141 in five months, nearly $30 a month. Now for the last two weeks, I have not earned one cent. For twelve week days, not one cent in money or property has been earned.

Sunday March 15th 1896 (10:25 A.M. snow time).

For the past two weeks I have had no employment, and have not earned one cent in money or in any thing else. I have eaten from the table of the old man. I have walked at least 50 miles in the last two days hunting for a school to teach and have found none. I have sought work with Mr. Cuppy, and he promised me a place on the brick yard, and if he could find any other work, he promised to let me have it. Mr. Henry Carter is to haul rock for me Monday March 16th 1896.

Thursday March 19th 1896. (12 M o'clock.)

Yesterday I went over to Mamie Alford's, and she let me have a dollar to purchase a Money Order for her to the Singer Manfg. Co., St. Louis, Mo., for 27 cents. She wants one dozen of No. 2, sewing machine needles. From Mamie's I went to the house of Mr. Marcus, and he had a talk with me about that house. He wants his money as soon as the work is done. Yesterday I was with Henry Carter and Hays Carter when the[y] hauled a load of rock to my upper place, although Hays did not come farther than his home in Tecumseh. I was down on my lower place yesterday, and saw two wagons with white people camped just below Demas Garrett's south, on the land of Rebecca Shawnee [*Shawnee's sister*]. The roads were wet and slippery. I ate a good dinner at the house of Mr. Marcus yesterday March 18th 1896. I am getting short of money now, not having money to buy stamps and writing paper. Mr. Cuppy has promised me a job on his brick yard. I let the western half of the plowed land on my upper place to Mr. James Grizzard to raise cotton upon; the east half of the same plowed land, to a white man, a plasterer by trade, who has leased land near by, of John Spoon. I need a wagon and team and plows, and two houses on my places, and a lot of house-hold furniture and goods. I need to make about one mile and a quarter of wire fence. O I do hope the Lord God Almighty will give me an abundance or at least a sufficiency of this world's goods. Walter and Dudley Shawnee are both staying here with the old man as well as myself. I have no employment to earn money and what can I do. Oh, I wish I had saved more money while I was teaching. I ought to have saved $50 or $60 for my house any way, but I did not. March is always a hard month for money among the people. I need to buy as few things as possible and put my money to the best possible use. I must secure a school to teach as soon as possible. O Lord, do thou enable me to make some more money in this world.

[page 150] Saturday March 21st 1896.
    If Carrie Warrior does not marry me, I want to marry Miss Lula Mack. She is a good Christian girl, and her going elsewhere will not hinder me any either. She has no fellow at present. She thinks I will be jealous of the other fellow. She will be 17 years old July 5th 1896. She loves me but won't let on.

Friday March 27th 1896 (7 AM).
    Yesterday March 26th 1896 I worked hard all day planting corn with a hand-planter for Mr. Marshall. It was a warm nice day. I am studying Natural Philosophy and preparing for the April examination. I intend to begin work on the brick yard for Mr. Cuppy about April 1st 1896. I will have to have some one work in my place while I am absent. Mr. Marshall is to help me on my house in return for the work I do for him. I have been thinking of Mr. and Mrs. Gokey, and they are good friends of mine. Mr. and Mrs. Dunjee and Mr. and Mrs. J. J. Johnson are also good friends of mine. Miss May Gokey is a good looking girl 13 years old, and she is smart and willing to learn.

Friday April 3rd, 1896 (7:55 A.M.).
    Yesterday April 3rd [2nd?], 1896 I went down and helped Walter Shawnee load up his logs. John Decker, Willie Deck, Ben Taylor, Jr., Walter and myself were the only ones that went along. Walter Shawnee and William Shawnee, Sr. had a big fuss over the bay pony that belongs to Julia. Walter told the old man to "hush" and to "go back to the house and stay there." Walter had harnessed up the bay pony when told that the pony was sick

and for him to let the pony alone. I tried to get Dudley to have some land broken out down on his lower place with the money that Walter was going to allow him for those logs. Walter is just now trying to do something for himself. He is as full of fluff and bull-doze as he can be. He has had his way so long on this place, that he thinks he can have it so always. William Shawnee is to blame for this state of affairs. He should never have permitted Walter to get so far along. I am glad that Walter Shawnee after so long a delay is trying to build a house on his place. He knows not what to do until William E. Shawnee shows him the way. Last night (April 2nd) he was making fun of that "thing" on my place. This is the rude mean [*inferior or poor*] hut builded upon my place by King Davis, a young negro from Louisiana. This apparently means that Walter Shawnee is going to build a nice house. They spoke yesterday of pointing this log house with lime. Walter has money, but he spends money [*page 151*] freely also.

[*continued from original page 151*]
Sunday April 12th 1896. (5:35 P.M.)
   It rained last night and this morning. The grass looks green and nice on the prairies. I visited David and Mamie Alford to-day. Walter Shawnee was up there at Davids, but soon he and John Spybuck and the family of the latter went east in a wagon presumably to Mrs. Cegar's. Julia Shawnee is better now and is out of bed. Since Christmas 1895 some thing has happened of a startling character (dixit). Friday April 3rd, 1895 [1896] I went up after my trunks, books, and clothes up to the house of Mr. Blackford. William Shawnee went with me as far as the city of Shawnee. I camped out by myself alone with, only one large comfort to cover with about a mile above the home of the Kickapoo Maskwekanhkih. I arrived at the house of Mr. Blackford about 11 A.M. Saturday April 4th 1896. I left my two clocks and my chart frame there, and one slate. On the way up about 10 A.M. I met Robert Mack and Lula Mack, with a load of wood, going toward Choctaw City. Robert was on the front part of the load, and Lula was on the hinder end of the load. I guess Lula goes into Choctaw City to see some fellow in Choctaw City. Lula said she never could get over what I said to her and Hattie, but I would say the same thing again if need be.

[*moved from pages 212-14*] Lula Mack 1896
March 7th I mailed her a letter.
March 13th or 14th I mailed her a second, with my picture enclosed.
March 17th she received my letters.
March 17th & 18th she answered them.

March 20th the letter was post marked at Douglas City.
March 21st I received the letter about 11 A.M.
March 21st I mailed her my third letter, with [a] nice flower card enclosed.
March 24th received another letter from Miss Lula Mack, written March 20th 1896.
March 24th I mailed a letter to her the same day.

April 3rd 1896 I expect Lula Mack and myself are now parted for good. Having thrown the blame on her, she has not written. She owes me two letters, but I do not care. I do not expect to answer her letter now whether favorable or not favorable. Oscar Harmon is the fellow that she thinks the most of, and she probably went over with him into the Iowa country. Even Robert Mack was unkind enough to read the letters that I sent to his sister Lula. Mrs. Mack and Lula Mack went away twice from home to avoid seeing me when they knew I was coming. Mrs. Mack thinks a great deal of Oscar, and took pains to let me know it. She told me that Oscar ran off from home and that he worked out and earned money, and sent $10 home to his father, and then (Oscar said) that his father sent for him. Oscar is about a full-blooded negro, both his parents being black. He is about 17 years old (1896) but not far from 18 years old. Lula Mack will be 17 years old July 5th 1896. In the eyes of Mrs. Mack, this is a good match. She appears to think that if Oscar and Lula married, they would live near to her. Miss Lula Mack went with Oscar Harmon for the first Sunday Feb. 23rd, 1896. According to her letter she has known him for four years, and that he used to be her fellow before he went away. The very next Sunday March 1st, 1896 she and her mama went away from home and staid all day to be rid of my company. According to subsequent reports both knew that I was coming over, but Lula said that she forgot(?) she had accepted my company. Mrs. Mack knew of it, and yet she slighted the last Sabbath School I would ever teach up there, left [Otis?] and went off with Lula and remained all day until nearly sunset. Having been thus slighted Sunday March 1st, and having visited them Monday morning March 2nd, 1896, and having seen them twice Wednesday March 4th 1896, yet that night, which was dark and misty, who should come over but Mrs. Mack, Lula and Robert. Although it was late and raining I had gone over about two miles to the house of Mr. and Mrs. [. . .] Woodward. This [*page 213*] ostensible excuse for coming over was to see Mr. McNeil. Mr. Blackford wanted me to go home with Lula Mack, saying that he would under the circumstances. I told him, No; that I was tired and the night was very dark. This was the last time I saw either Lula or her mama or Robert. My last visit to the home of Mrs. Mack Wednesday March 4th, 1896, was very brief. I was simply on my return home from Mr. Harmon's. I was asked to come in, but declined, with the statement that I did not have time, and that I had yet to go over to Mr. Woodwards. I told Mrs. Mack that I had a bottle of Castor Oil and another of Turpentine, and was going to give Mrs. Woodward one bottle, and that she might have whichever one she wanted. She said she would take the turpentine. I told her to send Archie over in the morning to get it and that I would save it for her. She said, All right. I departed. Presently just as I was over the hollow Era Mack came running and bringing me four or five eggs. She told me that mama (Mrs. Mack) said that she would be over herself in the morning. I said, All right, and took the eggs and went on. Instead on of coming in the morning she came that evening, and brought Lula and Robert with her. She told me that she would not send Archie in the morning, so I took down the bottle and gave it to her. She then said that she would pay me for it when I came back in the Fall. She had accepted it as a present and afterwards offered to pay me for it.

Monday March 2nd, 1896 Mrs. Mack told me that she could look up at my temples and tell me what kind of a man I was (meaning in regard to women). I had just told her how many girls I had proposed to in 1895, no less than 5. She also told me: "I am particular about my blood. I do not want my daughter to marry all kinds of a man." She calls me "all kinds of a man." Oscar Harmon, who seems to be unmixed is not all kinds of a man in her estimation. All the fellows that Lula Mack has ever gone with appear to be to be pure negroes, such as Silas Shaw, Major Barbour, and Oscar Harmon. Some people appear to have an idol God that they worship more than they do the Lord God. That idol is race. Colored people have their idols as well as white people. In fact the same ideas in regard to race permeate both white and colored people in some places. In this case the colored people are not one whit better than the white.

I believe that I have thought too much of Mrs. Mack and her family, and have visited them too often. I esteemed them too much and they did not know what to make of it. The reason I was slighted, was my own fault in coming. [*page 214*] Do you tell your mama every thing every other young man asks or says to you? [*end of section moved from pages 212–14*]

I camped Saturday night about a mile or more northwest of the place of Joe Whipple near a certain house, where some people live. I arrived home about noon Sunday April 5th 1896. On the way back home I saw Mr. Lewis, one of the school board and he told me that the majority of the people wanted me and for me to come up May 12th 1896, the day that the school meeting was held. For over a month I have not earned one cent. I have worked some here and there, but I have earned no money. The foundation of my new house was laid Tuesday and Wednesday April 7th and 8th, 1896. Mr. Ray, the White man on John Spoon's place owes me five day's work on my house for over two loads of corn that I let him have. I [*text ends here*]

~~Monday~~ *Friday April 17th 1896. 12 A.M.*

    I went up with David and Mamie Alford to Big Jim's, where we arrived after sunset and before dark. This was Monday afternoon April 13th 1896. I was at Big Jim's September 28th 1895 the last time. Big Jim, Lalouwepea, Little Jim, Lopah, and others appeared glad to see me. The bread dance was held the next day [*page 152*] Tuesday April 14th 1896. I learned for the first time that Kasekah was dead April 14th 1896. I tried to learn the songs all the afternoon of the 14th and most of the night. But I finally came away and slept. A ball play between the women and the men was held in the morning Wednesday April 15th 1896. Thursday April 16th 1896 I brought Mrs. Julia Shawnee her money $3.95, and I paid Clay $1.05 cts for her. This makes $5 in all. I got $5 out of the bank from Tecumseh for her.

    I adopt the following resolutions:—

1. Resolved by William E. Shawnee that he seek his own material, financial, moral, spiritual, and educational welfare, and that he help himself and depend on no one, but to accept all help or aid voluntarily offered by others.
2. Resolved that he let Miss Carrie Warrior completely and entirely alone because she has broken her honorable engagement of marriage, and repeatedly slighted him by preferring the company of others, by refusing to correspond, and by wishing him to submit to her every wish and whim.
3. Resolved that he will never return Carrie's correspondence nor seek her conversation or company, without she makes full and satisfactory amends for her misdeeds.
4. Resolved that the Shawnee Bros. can never agree among themselves, or advise one another, or be real brothers capable of taking each other's part; that they are mean and wicked toward each other, and that it is useless for them to try to present an undivided front to the world.
5. Resolved, that I must build houses, cribs, barns, set out fruit trees, buy cooking stoves, tables, cupboards, dishes, knives and forks and have a home of my own and live in it. Resolved, That I have lived in the houses of other people long enough already.

    Mr. Washington is a colored man, black in color, and a school teacher, who began teaching with a third grade certificate, but now has a second. He owns a lot in Tecumseh and has a nice little house. Every thing is nice inside of the house, and he has a nice comfortable home. Why is this? It is because he has used his money well. He has not wasted it as I have. He has a wife and family, for whom he has tried to provide. I have had hundreds of dollars and yet my condition is not like his. Many days I have not earned one cent—not one cent. This is not as it should be. I am not [*page 153*] seeking work hard enough. I should let the business of other people completely alone, and mind only my own business. I have no business to live in the same home with my brothers. They do not appreciate what I do for them for nothing.

Tuesday April 7 Mr. Marcus a colored man and myself began to build a box house on my land 14 X 28 feet. Mr. Marcus also worked for me on the house Wednesday April 8th 1896. Mr. Marcus is a good hand to do carpenter work, although he complains a great deal. I will hire him to work for me again when I get some more money. This day Friday April 17th 1896 I helped Walter Shawnee work on his house, for which he is to help me work on my crib; late in the evening I went over and ~~work~~ counted my fruit trees. There are thirty apple trees, one pear tree, and twenty-three peach trees, making 54 fruit trees on my place. In 1894 I had 69 set out on my place. I have not had that number since. In the Fall of 1895 I had 55 living trees. A great many have died. I must set out at least 100 trees this year 1896-97. By God's grace I must make progress.

Monday April 20th 1896.

I ought to try my best to take this examination, and I need just One Dollar in money. I spent the last dollar I had upon my house. I paid Mr. Marcus the last two dollars that I had, that he might do two days' work on my house. My affairs are badly administered, and I waste money in buying a lot of little things. The amount spent in buying little things soon amounts to several dollars. Mr. J. J. Johnson has not sent me $2 as he said that he would do. I waste my time just as much as I waste my money. There is no doubt about that. I want a dollar, and I do not know how to get it. Here I am in less than two months after my school is out, without one cent in money. My coat is ragged, and for a long time I have not been to church or Sabbath school. Since October 7th 1895 I have spent $141 that I earned in teaching school—a colored school at that. $9 never came into my hands because I was compelled to sell my warrants at $3 discount for the first three months of my school.

[*moved from middle of page 154—56 for chronological order*]
Monday April 20th 1896

I went down on my lower place at or after noon. Some new land is broken out already. William Shawnee, Robinson Crusoe, and LaFayette also went away into the Creek country April 20th in the afternoon.

Tuesday April 21st, 1896

I went up to Choctaw City, on the ball faced pony. Walter Shawnee made war with me because I got hold of LaFayette's saddle first. He hit me twice with the saddle and once with his hand. I hit him back once too with the saddle. He was striking me just because he thought I would not strike him. I started about [*page 155*] noon, and stopped at Dale, Okla. Ter., and went in debt to Mr. John King at his store for a coat and vest, for both of which he charged me four dollars. I was showered on about night 9 miles from Choctaw City, but the shower soon passed and there was good moon light. All lights almost were out when I passed through Choctaw City. At last about ¾ mile from Dunjee's house, I tied out my horse and slept until morning.

Wednesday April 22nd 1896

I saddled up and went to Dunjee's and found him in his orchard, which was looking fine though young. Then I left him and went over about ¼ mile, or perhaps some less to see J. J. Johnson. He was glad to see me, and was engaged in planting sod corn, or rather corn on sod recently broken. He said he had been up to Langston City on the Cimmaron river and had just got back. On my first coming Mr. Johnson sent word up to the house for his wife to fix breakfast for me. But presently Mr. Dunjee came all the way down to invite me to breakfast. So, as he had come so far, I accepted him, and went with him. In our conversation, Mr. Johnson told me that Mr. Fullbright was trying for my school, and advised me to "resign" the school I taught last year, and put in for the school at Shawnee. He said that that would pay me better.

On reaching the house, Miss Ella Dunjee appeared glad to see me. She looked a little pale, but I never tell people about their looks if they are ever so pale. She afterward told me herself, of her own notion, that she had been sick some lately and was looking ~~pale~~ pale, she supposed. I said, Yes, that was all. After breakfast I went over to see Mrs. J. J. Johnson. They had the log house they are in papered off nicely. Her sewing machine was along. Mr. J. J. Johnson could not pay me the $2, that he owed me. I needed money badly and that is the main reason I went up there. Mr. Dunjee was anxious, for some cause, for me to attend the summer school during June and July 1896 to be held in the Choctaw Normal School. He said that I could board very cheaply with Mr. J. J. Johnson, and that tuition would be only about $1.50 cts per month. Mr. J. J. Johnson was willing to board me.

I visited the school, which was taught by Miss Ella Dunjee from 9 A.M. to 12 M. There were 16 pupils, and they whispered and did several other things not in order. But Miss Dunjee did her part well, and is a good teacher. I sat close by her on a stool, but she had me take [*page 156*] her chair once in awhile. At recess she and I talked and it seemed that the time passed quickly. It was only 15 minutes any way. She said that Mrs. Mack was over Tuesday April 21st, 1896. She did not say one thing that Mrs. Mack said. She told me she learned that Mr. Fullbright was trying for my school, and that she found it from another source than my word to her in my letter. I told her that was all right, and that I would know in three weeks whether I would get the school or not. She said, At the school meeting. I said, Yes. I told her that if the people there did not want me they could turn me down. At noon I separated from her to get my horse, and then came on home. For I wanted to prepare all I could for the examination. I arrived home that night before all had gone to bed. She said, "I am going this way, but I guess you want to go by and get your horse"; I said nothing, but this showed she was expecting I would stay. She looked at me when I started this way. Good little Ella, she is a lovely girl any way. She complained of being sickly, and very busy teaching school, cooking, and doing the writing for her papa. Mr. Dunjee told me that he would like to have me come around whenever I wanted to. I understood him to make me a free invitation. The last time I was at his home was July 12th 1895, over eight months. Yet I saw his folks every month in Oklahoma City.

Thursday April 23rd 1896

I staid close at home all day, studying hard and preparing for my examination April 24th and 25th. I spent most time on Natural Philosophy, but studied every thing some. I wanted to make a higher average in Physics. 3 years ago I only made 70% in Physics, by which I barely passed. I will average more this time, I know. It is now 6:45 P.M. and I cease writing.

Saturday April 25th 1896 (5:08 P.M.) [*from original page 153*]

Yesterday Friday April 24th 1896 and to-day I have been taking the County examination for teachers in the Public School Building in Tecumseh, which a two-story brick building. We took our examination upstairs in the south room. There were fourteen of us the first day, one of whom was a young colored lady named Miss Cooly, I believe. There [*page 154*] were half a dozen or so of white ladies, one of whom had been teaching over in Lincoln County with a third grade certificate. She said that she had also taught in this county. I applied for a first grade. In the whole examination there was only one question in Natural Philosophy that I could not answer at all. I answered all in some way. The questions in Natural Philosophy were all easy except the last—the 10th. Mr. Patrick told me that ~~he~~ I graded up well on yesterday's work and he put me on the list of his subscribers. I am to pay him for his papers when I get the money. Mr. Bull is also a very fine man and he is very obliging. All the exam[in]ing board are nice gentlemen. Mr. Lackey, on[e] of the board, seems to be proud that he is from Texas, for he remarked several times about his being from there. He said that he had had eight years' experience on the examining board in Texas.

The examination questions were prepared by the following members of the Territorial Board of Education:—

President Boyd	1. Orthography	95–86
of the	2. English Grammar	95–98
Univ. of Okla.	3. Composition	95–97
Supt. Hopkins	1. Reading.	90–94
of	2. Writing	90–94
El Reno City Schools.	3. Geography	100–95
	4. Physiology of Hygiene	90–97
Pres. Murdaugh	1. Arithmetic	100–98
of the	2. Theory and Practice of Teaching	90–98
Okla. Normal School	3. Book-keeping.	90–86
Supt. Cameron	1. U.S. History	95–95
Territorial Supt. of	2. Constitution of the U. S.	100–90
Public Instruction	3. Physics.	70–90

Of all these Murdaugh asked the hardest questions, though Mr. Cameron asked one hard one in Physics.

Thursday April 30th 1896 (6:25 A.M.)
Yesterday April 29th 1896 I helped David Alford plant corn half a day, for which he is to help me at work, or money. Walter Shawnee is talking about Miss Kessel looking at me, which is some thing he knows nothing about. He says he <u>thinks</u> Miss Kessel did look at me, but he can not establish the fact. There are many facts that it is a pity that Walter does not know, or Dudley either. Dudley is telling about a story that Cegar told him, but he can not tell it at all. It is certain that Cegar is telling a story, but he never tells any thing just as it was told him. Walter and Dudley Shawnee will get into trouble yet, about what Dunjee told them. They have been telling that [*page*

157] Dunjee said that he did not like a black person, but Dunjee is black himself. You must not tell any thing you hear, especially what is told confidentially. Mr. Taylor is going to ask Mr. Dunjee about this matter.

Wednesday May 6th 1896 (1:40 P.M. at the home of William Shawnee upstairs).

Dudley Shawnee, like Walter Shawnee, is carried away with Robert Ingersoll. They learn of what Robert says through the newspapers. Dudley, like Walter, is misbehaving at home, right [a]long. Katie Decker has been his play-mate here at home. He is not trying to do one thing to improve his financial condition, and he is not fit to teach school. Both Walter and Dudley hate "niggers" without cause; no colored person ever did them any harm. I am tired of seeing boys who believe in Robert Ingersoll, whose life corresponds exactly with Robert's teaching. Tom Paine is one of Robert's right hand men, and we know that Tom Paine acted an all-around fool. Even the infidels were ashamed of Tom Paine's manners, and would cross the street to avoid him. Both Dudley and Walter are great newspaper readers, but no sooner do they read a newspaper than they throw it aside, and then it is gone to destruction. The whole country knows of the infidelity of Walter Shawnee and Dudley Shawnee. Even a certain minister of the gospel remarked about it. It is not because these boys are more learned than any one else, but it is because they swallow down such things in accordance with the spirit of the world. It is not to be forgotten that both Cegar and Jennie Cegar became tainted with infidelity through the preaching of minister Walter Shawnee. Carrie Warrior is rather tainted also with infidelity but very slightly. Of all things that I do hate to hear it is a woman using profane language. Carrie does when she is angry, and I have heard white women doing worse or as bad in Tecumseh. It seems that the absence of God's Spirit from a man's heart means the presence of the devil's influence. Walter Shawnee has been home since about July 1892, about four years. During this time he has acted very bad. He was a loud-mouthed infidel when he first landed here at home, and was also a loud populist. He is not loud-mouthed now either as an infidel or as a populist; but he is both still just the same. It is said that Jennie Cegar has swung to the other extreme now and is willing even to become a Christian. How [*page 158*] time changes some people! Jennie has acted very bad toward me and now she wants to make up. Walter Shawnee is the bottom cause of all the trouble between Cegars and myself. Walter Shawnee and Dudley Shawnee both note the crimes committed in the land, as shown in the newspapers, and these I seldom or never read. Walter and Dudley call colored people "coons" and colleges for the education of colored people "coon colleges." But I like the colored people and they like me, and they treat me as kindly as I could possibly be treated. How can a person hate people who never did him any harm? How can you hate those who bestow so many favors upon you? Many times have colored people been kind to white people and the white people have been thankful for it. Nothing is to be gained by pretending not to be a colored person. It is a perfect bugbear, this color-line. In private there is no color line, but the line must be drawn only in company. Even here it is not always strictly drawn. It is useless for Walter and Dudley to take the view of this matter that Southern white people take. It is following a certain current that is simply obtrusive, and by that gains prominence.

 I want to go out on a trip up to Oklahoma City and around by the school where I taught. I want to have my contract drawn up to teach May 12th 1896. I have my new certificate that I earned April 24th and 25th 1896. It runs until April 27th 1899. I can only make money at present by teaching colored schools. I need to earn money, and by having earned it to put it to the best possible use. I need a team and a plow and double shovel to farm with. I need to set out more fruit trees. I need to finish my house and buy a good cooking stove. I need to build a house on my lower place. I need to build more fences. I need to buy a suit or two of clothes and dress nicely, and I need a nice hat or two.

 I need to be a better Christian than ever. I need to read the Bible and pray to God every day. A sense of need—either temporal or spiritual—is God's call to prayer. I should square my life completely and entirely by means of God's word. Oh, but I have so many things to thank the Lord for. I love the Lord Jesus Christ with all my heart. I never have lost any thing by serving the Lord, but I have lost by not serving Him. In some mysterious way serving God with the whole heart brings benefits. Serving God brings me up financially; even I prayed God to [*page 159*] help me get my last certificate, which the Lord did, notwithstanding the lukewarmness of my heart and life. My highest religious life was when I attended Kansas Yearly Meeting in 1891. O that I could attend that yearly meeting again. If I would save my money, and be truly economical, I could, without doubt attend Kansas Yearly Meeting at my own expenses. I need to study economy in money matters as well as in time, health, and other things. It is not what a person knows, but what use he puts his knowledge unto. Acts more than words; practice more than theory. O Lord, save me from my sins for Jesus' sake.

Monday May 11th 1896 (written Thursday May 28th 1896) [*moved from page 159*]

This day I rode the ball-faced pony and went up to look after my school. I arrived at Dunjee's before dark. Ella dear was kind and entertaining. Mr. J. W. Dunjee and myself occupied the same bed.

Tuesday May 12th 1896 (written Thursday May 28th 1896). [*moved from page 159-161*]

Just before leaving Mr. Dunjee's took leave of Ella the last one. I told her that I was going over there to draw up my contract. She was agreeable and smiling, though she had been angry with a certain fellow somewhat earlier. I apologized for leaving her so abruptly April 22nd, 1896, and told her fully my reasons for so doing. I departed about 10 or 11 A.M. and [*page 160*] arrived at the house of Mr. Blackford, where I boarded, about noon. So I went over to Mr. Lillard's for my umbrella, where I ate dinner. Returned to Mr. Blackford's about 1 P.M., and then rode over to where the school meeting was to be held confident of success. Presently Mr. Cooper and Prof. Fullbright came and Mr. Gokey told me to speak to Mr. Cooper. But Prof. Fullbright kept talking so, that it gave me no chance. The two men parted several times and came together again still talking. Mr. Fullbright was riding a black-horse, and he departed just a little before the school-meeting was called at 2 P.M. So we all entered the building, and business began. In the prise of business some one cried out cyclone, and most went out of doors, the women being rather scared. It was the first that I ever saw. It hung down from a cloud, and was the shape of a cylinder. We could see the dust fly when it came down from the ground, but it would rise and fall. As the wind was in the wrong direction, we could not hear it roar.

Mr. Gokey said, "Now we want the colored people to say who they want for a teacher. This question must be settled here to-day."

Mr. H. E. Cooper arose and said: "There are two applicants for the school—Prof. Fullbright and Mr. Shawnee, and the majority of the people want Prof. Fullbright. So we instruct the board to hire Prof. Fullbright." Some one said, "Take a vote on it." So eight votes were cast for Mr. Fullbright and none for me. So in this way I lost my school. But Mr. H. E. Cooper and Mr. Lon Woodward had no right to vote or speak against me.

After the meeting was over, Mr. H. E. Cooper said to me, "Are you going home this evening?" I told him, No. He said, "You can come over and stay with me over night if you want to." I said, "No, I am going to go and get another school before night." He said, That is all right; you may get a better school than this any way. He also said: "A great many things came out after you left. That you poured water on the children, and called them fools and liars. I hope it will teach you a lesson. I told your friends to come out to the school meeting to vote, and they did not come." It is evident that Mr. H. E. Cooper tried to throw the blame of losing the school on me. It is also evident that pressure was brought on Mr. H. E. Cooper to induce him to do just as he did. Old man Cooper was there and voted against me. He hates me because I punished Josie Cooper for her meanness. He came over and quarreled with me about three weeks or a month before [*page 161*] my school was out. He told me that if I expelled that girl, he would see about it; that I was fooling with the wrong man when I was fooling with him; that I was interfering with that girl's company and reaching over into his family affairs. I told him the trouble was between me and the girl, and not between me and him. He said, No, that the trouble was between me and him. I told Mr. Blackford and Mr. Gokey what Mr. Cooper had said to me. He told me that morning that I would never get to teach that school any more.

As soon as Mr. Cooper and I parted, H. E. Cooper, not old man Cooper, I rode straight over to Douglas City, where I arrived awhile before sunset. I went to inquiring about the school at Douglas City, for I had heard that they wanted a man-teacher up there. I told them that Fullbright had my school, and they had voted it to him at the school-meeting awhile ago; that I was there myself. Then Mr. Norman said, Look here. And he showed me the written application for the school at Douglas City. The application set forth that he was a graduate of the High School at Springfield, Mo., and the he had taught two sessions at the County Normal Institute, etc. etc. It was dated May 12th 1896. Mr. Fullbright had told Mr. Rogers and Mr. Blackford that he did not want the Smith School, but that the school at Douglas City was the one he wanted. He gave Mr. Norman and others his word that they could depend on him there at Douglas City, and the same day he kept talking to Mr. Emmet Cooper just before the school-meeting. No one knows what all he told Mr. Cooper. The two men would part and come together again. Fullbright was the cause of all this talk.

Tuesday May 19th 1896 (written Thursday May 28th 1896) [moved from page 161]
I started from the house of some white Kansas people and got over to Mr. J. J. Johnson's in time for breakfast. He had heard that I had lost my school. I visited Miss Ella Dunjee and then went to Okla. City. I arrived there about 3 P.M., and finally saw Mr. Fullbright. He refused to give me a written statement as to which school he wanted. He told me he would be out Thursday, and asked me to wait for him that long, that he would do me right, and that I should have one school or the

other; and that I might get my own school; that he wanted the school that had the longest term and paid the most money. Came back to Mr. J. J. Johnson where I arrived about 9 P.M. I had no dinner or supper this day. Wednesday May 20th 1896 I visited Miss Ella Dunjee, where I took dinner. I let her know what I thought of her. She seems to be favorably affected. For when I told her, Good bye, she said: "I guess it [page 162] will be goodbye for some time this time." She promised to write to me, and said she would surely do so. I wrote her a new letter May 25th, which I mailed on the 26th, where I closed thus. "Yes, Ella dear, I love you. I will be honest with you about this matter."

Ella knows that her papa wants us to be married. I found that out in a roundabout way. As she can not have her choice, she in inclined to choose none. Ella advised me not to marry a girl that was far below myself intellectually. I replied, What if all educated girls are extravagant and won't do a stroke of work, and run their husbands head over heels in debt?

A certain person advised me that Ella was not the girl for me, that E. was a town girl and was too stylish, but this same girl said some things about me that I could not learn. Ella said that she did not care any more for me than for her other gentlemen friends. I told her that I cared more for her than for any other girl. She did not look at me when I said this, but she made no reply.

My policy is to marry some good girl, but have her wait in a condition of engagement until I have a home, and if she can help build that home, or assist in furnishing it, that will be her privilege. I do not say I will marry Ella, but Ella will have to say whether she loves me or not.

Monday May 25th 1896 (written 7:55 P.M. May 26th 1896). [moved from page 159]

As Mrs. Carter had sent word to me by Mrs. Ben Taylor, Jr., to come over to see her, so I went over to her house. We arranged to go over to the city of Shawnee to see the Special Agent tomorrow. Thence I went to the Post Office and got the mail, and then walked down to my lower place. There I ate dinner with Henry Carter and the boys.

Tuesday May 26th 1896 (7:40 P.M.) [moved from page 159]

I went over to the house of Mrs. Irene Carter this morning and from there we went over with Henry Carter to the city of Shawnee, to see the Special Agent. We rode in a wagon drawn by oxen. The Special Agent was a little cross at first, but he soon abated. I let Mrs. Carter have my lower place until January 1st, 1898. Mrs. Carter was very glad that I did this. Mrs. Carter is just as good and kind to me as a mother could be. I saw Walter

Shawnee, Thomas Alford, and John King in Shawnee, where they came on the hack, but they soon returned on the hack to Tecumseh, Okla. Ter. I came back home to the house of William Shawnee. Dudley Shawnee claims my penholder, or one that is just like mine. Dudley is the fellow that got rid of my pocket knife when I lent it to him.

Sunday May 31st, 1896 (6:12 P.M.).

The sun is about an hour high yet, and this is a warm Sabbath day. I have just bathed and changed clothes. It is to the kindness of Mrs. Julia Shawnee that I have clean clothes. I thought of Miss Ella Dunjee, and so far as I know she has not answered my second letter yet. She hinted that I did not work much, and that I wanted to marry a white woman. Mrs. J. J. Johnson must have told Ella about this.

Tuesday June 9th 1896. (6:45 A.M.)

I went to Tecumseh and down to my lower place yesterday where I saw Mr. Henry Carter and the boys at work. Last night it rained, and it seems that yesterday June 8th was the hottest day we have had this year. John Whitehead put off working the roads until Monday June 15th 1896. I have not been reading my Bible much here lately nor have I gone to church or Sabbath School.

It is my policy to improve my places and move on one of them as soon as possible. I want to let the old man William Shawnee live to himself. I came to this conclusion in 1888, but now [page 163] after eight years of effort I am coming to the same conclusion. I have done more on my places during these hard times than ever before. I have come up since Jan. 1st, 1893; this is a turning point in my life. At that time I was engaged to Miss Carrie Warrior, but she and I are parted now for good. But then the engagement taught me one of the best lessons of my life—the lesson of providence.

I want to go up to see about my school again June 22nd 1896. Then I will also see Miss Ella Dunjee; I have written letters enough to her. She must write some before I write any more.

Thursday June 11th 1896 (4 P.M.)

The old man quarreled with me about going to see some girl up at Choctaw City, and said that that was the reason that I remained up there so long before. I had him mail a letter to Miss Ella Dunjee, the second that I have written to her since I came home. Written June 12th 1896.

Friday June 12th 1896.

I have this day hoed cotton for Mr. Ben Taylor for William Shawnee five and one half days. Mr. Taylor paid me 50 cts. for the same, 10 cents of which I bought him tobacco with when I went to Tecumseh this morning. I mailed another letter to Miss Dunjee this morning—the third since I have come home from around Choctaw City. Mr. Bull, the present Co. Supt. of Pottawatomie Co. gave me a copy of the school laws for my own personal use. I thank Him therefor and may God bless him therefor also. May God bless Miss Ella Dunjee and all her folks, and may He cause her to consent if it be His will. I think of Miss Dunjee day and night now, and have been corresponding with her on the most interesting as well as the most important subject that can engage our mutual consideration. It is impossible for me to tell what the dear little Miss will do about the matter, only she had not written to me at all for nearly three weeks. This does not look very favorable. Nine day[s] hence, if the Lord will, I will see the dearest little girl and if she permits, will give her a sweet kiss. – Mr. Bull wanted me to attend the Co. Teacher's Association tomorrow at McLoud, Okla. Ter. There is no use in supposing that your presence is not wanted when white people are assembled. Miss Dunjee will either accept me or not accept me; at present I can not tell what she will do. Amen, Lord Jesus.

I must complete my house and begin to furnish it as soon as possible. I have made a start on my house—thank God [*page 164*] for that. I need a wagon and team very bad, but I must have a shed built to keep my wagon under when I get one, and I must have a stable for my team. I need a nice buggy in order to take my little girl out riding after she is mine as well as before she is mine. I need to fence the meadow on the east side to itself as soon as possible, and put my wagon-shed and stable down there in it. I need a house and fence on my lower place too as soon as possible.

Sunday June 21st, 1896. (2:20 P.M.)

It rained some this morning. For the past two weeks I have been hoeing cotton and have worked on the road 3½ days. The past week has been one of political excitement on account of the Republican National Convention at St. Louis, Mo. [*William*] McKinley and [*Garret*] Hobart have been nominated for President and Vice-president of the United States, on a gold platform. This is right, although [*Henry M.*] Teller of Colorado withdrew from the convention. Some expect a bolt from the Democratic convention at Chicago.

The west half of my upper place is in a bad condition. The weeds are too plentiful. Mr. James Grizzard, to whom I rented this part, certainly carried on his work in a careless and half-hearted way, but Mr. Wray, the white man to whom I rented the east half of this same upper place has his 17 acres of corn in the finest condition. There is scarcely one weed in the whole of it. Mr. Grizzard is a man who is no farmer and he does not try to have any thing. He is himself to blame for being as poor as he is. I can not rent him a foot of land another year.

For the last five weeks my "little girl," Ella by name, has not written me a single line, notwithstanding her promise to write to me sure. I can not understand why she does not write to me, and I will have to know the why too. There are reasons for it. If a girl's word is not worth its face value, what is she worth? It is a flagrant breach of courtesy to neglect to reply; it shows that she is indifferent about you, and knowing too that you are anxious for a reply. It appears that Mrs. J. J. Johnson and Ella have been talking about me, and the former advised me to let Ella alone and that Drusilla was the best girl and for me to take Drusilla. But I sometimes follow my own judgment instead of taking the voluntary advice of other people. Ella hinted that I wanted to marry a white woman and that I did not work. I have to meet my record—and there is no doubt that it is not a good one in its entirety. But it has its gold and silver lining.

[*page 165*] But I have proposed marriage honorably to 10 or a dozen ~~plums~~ girls and I am no nearer an honorable marriage, it appears, than when I first began. My financial condition is indeed deplorable. I do not own either a horse or a cow or a wagon or a plow or a house for a home. I will own them, however, if the Lord be willing. If I had used my money wisely, I could have had all these. But while not one cent went for either tobacco or liquor or worse, still I did not buy just what I ought to have bought. I need to use my money to better advantage, and I need to work to better advantage to earn money. I need to do all in my power to earn money, and to put it to better use. I wish I had a place to make money, and then I will build a house and have everything comfortable around me. I need to quit transacting business for other people for nothing. Jennie Cegar is a poor pay-master; she will never receive any more trust from me. Mamie Alford, John Spybuck, and Chosa Starr, and Charley Beaver are in almost the same category. - Mrs. Nellie Warrior and Betty ~~Ko~~ Coker, a young school girl from the Shawnee Mission, and Eva Shawnee are visitors here this evening. Betty is about 14 or 15 years of age, I suppose. She has some white blood in her veins. Nellie is the sister of Thomas Alford and she is also partly white. They took dinner with us. Miss Coker was bashful, as a young maiden usually is.

There is no doubt that the Indians have very great privileges; that they ought to thank God every day that their lot has fallen in good places and that they ought to try to make the most of their opportunities. - Mrs. Nellie Warrior told me that her buggy cost her $65. I could have bought me a buggy at that figure, and so could Walter Shawnee have done so. But he did not do so. I see that we do live below our privileges. - Miss Coker is a very nice girl and Nellie said that she could cook and make pie and cake. Nellie pretended to think that Carrie Warrior and myself would be married, but I told her that Carrie and I had broken up for good. - Just think how kind and good Mr. Dunjee, Ella, and the others have been to me. May 11th 1896 is not the only time nor the first time Mr. Dunjee and I have been bed fellows. Ella slept very near each time, so much so that I could have reached over to where she was. A curtain separated the two beds, but the beds were side by side, and the curtain was only fastened at the top. Now, Ella dearest, has a proposal of honorable marriage from me to deal with, and for five weeks she has not written a scratch in answer to my three letters. It may be that she is angry, or it may be that she does not care. I do not [*page 166*] know how to take her silence. It may be that she is already engaged to some other fellow, or that she is very busy. She acknowledged, however, that she never was too busy to write to me. Ella has only 9 days longer to reply to my propositions, and I can not consent to lengthen out the time, because I am running a risk as well as she. I did not take 5 weeks to make up my mind, and I am in worry and anxiety until she accepts or not. I rather believe Ella is angry, because silence means something.

I want to sign up my Teacher's Contract June 23rd, 1896. This is what I want the board to do. I want to be sure of that school, and then I will be all right for eight months. My place will bring me $41.25, and my school $280; total $321.25. Good.

Friday June 26th 1896. (10 P.M. estimated.)

I went up to Choctaw City and beyond Monday June 22nd 1896, and have just returned this evening Friday June 26th 1896. I now hear for the first time that Walter Shawnee has married Willie Laundress. The friend I rode with in the rain yesterday June 25th spoke of Willie Laundress. Over a month ago this marriage was threatened, and Julia says it is not finished. - I had my talks with Miss Ella Dunjee June 23rd, 1896 Tuesday, and again about 9 A.M. Thursday June 25th 1896. She was washing clothes while I was talking to her.

Saturday June 27th 1896 (9:40 A.M.)

Last night and this morning I wrote a letter to Miss E. Dunjee, which I mail today. I am resolved to marry her sure without fail, or else keep wooing her until she marries some one else. I must kiss her next time I see her. I must be disgracefully defeated, ignominiously defeated, and sorely and bitterly defeated before I give her up. I must have a wife; I must have a heart that will love me dearly.

Sunday June 28th 1896 (10 P.M.)

    I have just come from meeting over at the church near the Mission School. Dr. Hartly did the preaching. Miss Kessel, Miss Belle Lockhart, and Miss Lilly Woods were present. Mrs. Bourbonnais offered prayer. I attended Sabbath School this morning. The lesson was on the first chapter of the Acts of the Apostles. I took dinner with Dr. and Mrs. Hartly. Mrs. Hartly was in Tecumseh in the forenoon. Mrs. Nellie Warrior and Miss Lizzie Washington visited us this evening. They invited me to come over some time. Nellie told me that Lizzie had many horses of her own. She said that she was a relative of Lizzie's. Lizzie is quite bashful. Walter and Lilly [sic] and the children were over here to-day, but no one paid any attention to them. I would not [page 167] be in Walter's shoes for a house-full of money. I also thought of my own sweet darling Ella. May Jesus bless Ella and make her a true and noble Christian.

Sunday July 5th 1896 (10:12 A.M.)

    Yesterday I went to Tecumseh Okla. Ter. and there were hundreds of people ~~were~~ in town. Several beautiful white ladies were in the crowd, and some white ladies who were homely. In the evening we heard the Hon. Dennis Flynn speak. It rained late in the evening and I staid all night in a house without any covering on account of the rain. I visited Miss Lula Roberts at night and she is a nice young colored-white woman, with long straight hair. Dudley Shawnee was over there with her in the evening. Dudley claims to hate "niggers," but he runs with "nigger" girls just the same. Katie Decker has been his girl heretofore. He evidently does not intend to marry, but appears to be more on the alert to get acquainted with girls than a young man could possibly do, who was trying his level best to marry.

    I believe it is my duty to be married without unnecessary delay. I could do everything to better advantage if I were engaged to some true Christian girl. I will write to Aunt Martha to find a true Christian girl for me.

Tuesday July 7th 1896 (5:30 P.M.)

    I have been sick ever since Monday morning July 6th 1896. My head ached very much, and my throat is sore. I caught some cold, being uncovered at night. I went to Tecumseh with my father, William Shawnee. The whistle blew for noon when we were within a mile of Tecumseh. About 3 P.M., I went to the house of Mr. and Mrs. Washington. Miss Lena R. Robinson was not there, but was up to the house of Mrs. Carter. Finally she came, and with a neat looking red-checked dress slipped over her every day clothes, she came in. I presented her my picture and asked for hers. She promised to give me her picture. I also asked permission to write to her. Oh, but she was proud of my picture just as if it were something. On my leaving a doily or two for her, she remarked that I was so kind. I told her, No, I was not kind. She was very sympathetic in learning from me that I was not feeling well. I have probably met my future wife in the person of Miss Lena. So I have passed by Miss Ella Dunjee, and my intended is now Miss Lena R. Robinson. Miss Dunjee told me [*page 168*] she would not marry me if I was worth a million dollars, which was saying a great deal, to be sure. She also said that she was engaged to another fellow, and this is perhaps the real reason she has rejected my proposals. July 7th 1896 is no doubt another red letter day in my life, like Jan. 1st, 1893.

(Sunday July 19th 1896. 3 P.M. about guessed)
 I left home Wednesday July 8th 1896, and came to Choctaw City on the 7:10 P.M. train. I arrived at the Choctaw Normal School building about 8 P.M., where a Prayer Meeting was being held. Ella Dunjee and Edna Randolph were present; Mr. J. W. Dunjee, Mr. Anderson, and Mr. J. D. Randolph were present also. I began to go to school the next morning Thursday July 9th 1896. This is the first time I have been to school since Nov. 1887. Sat. July 11th 1896 I went over to Douglas City on horse-back to see about school matters. My horse that I rode cost me 50 cts. Yesterday Sat. July 18th 1896 I rode over to Douglas City on the same errand, for which privilege I paid 25 cts. Mr. J. J. Johnson told me of a school over in Cleveland Co. where they wanted me to teach. I think that my coming up here to school is one of the best movements I have ever made. – A Mr. Jacobson from Oklahoma City was out here walking side by side with Miss Ella Dunjee Friday July 17th 1896. Ella was in Oklahoma City Sunday July 12th 1896, and also Sunday July 5th 1896. Ella has slighted me so much that I am not going to have any thing more to do with her. She went home with Rev. Mr. Barbee this evening July 19th 1896. I heard her tell her mother that she was going to see Mrs. Barbee. It is said that Mr. Barbee and Rev Mr. Dunjee are not on good terms, and yet Ella is on good terms, evidently, with Mr. Barbee. Rev. Mr. Dunjee, at my inquisition, told me that his brother was an infidel, but that brother's family are said to be Adventists.

Sunday Oct 4th 1896. (About 2 P.M.)

Mr. Grizzard, to whom I rented the west half of my place, has not cultivated 2 or 3 acres of it at all, and has about half cultivated the remainder. My subscription to the *New York Independent* is paid up to Sept 10th 1896. I must make another remittance to them as soon as I can. I propose to rent my place to Mr. Sexton for the year 1897, and he proposes to raise mostly cotton. We propose [*page 169*] to raise only corn for our own use, as there is no market for corn, the price being 10, or 13, or 15 or 18 cents a bushel. It does not pay to raise it. But cotton sells at 7.10 a hundred or even 7½ a hundred, and $2.35 cts in the seed. So far I have secured $4.90 cts out of cotton of Mr. Grizzard. This is all the income from my place so far. Mrs. Carter had a nice bale of cotton off my lower place a week or two ago. She has all she can make off of it the whole year 1897, but in 1898 I come in for rent.

I must serve the Lord with my whole heart forever, and I must go to church, Sabbath school, and meeting every Sunday that I can. I must abstain from unchastity in every shape, and must be a lover of piety and of good things. There is much to be lost by not serving the Lord. I must abstain from any form of sin, and follow every good work. I must not obey the lust of the flesh, and serve God with all my heart. There is nothing grander or nobler than the service of God. Read your Bible and pray every day, beginning with this Sunday Oct. 4th 1896. Say about 2:50 P.M. From this time forth I will serve the Lord fully and do works meet for repentance. Lord Jesus, help me and keep me from all sin and all melancholy. I had a hard time last year, and before that. Many days have I gone without dinner and sometimes without supper. But the Lord has begun to lift me up from my deep poverty, and I am getting along tolerably well now. Mr. Grizzard will never do for a man to rent land unto. His two boys are worthless. They had a great time to raise what little crop was raised, and now they have a time to pick what little cotton there is. Mrs. Grizzard helps to make the living as much or more than Mr. Grizzard himself.

I want to pay every debt I owe. The Lord wants me to pay what I owe and so I will pay it. Let me see now what I owe. It is as follows:

	$ cts.
Houghton and Upp, Purcell, Ind. Ter. (with interest)	3.00
Christian Nation	7.75
Carson Bros, Tecumseh, Okla. Ter. (Paid in full)	6.55
John King, Dale, Okla. Ter. (Paid except $1.80 cts)	4.00
William Shawnee (suit of clothes)	6.50
Good Health	2.00
Southern Teacher	.75
	$30.55

Gee Whiz! I owe over $30, and what have I bought. The truth is, that I do not yet earn enough money, and it is my duty to increase my earnings. I have a $210 contract to teach school over in Shawnee, and my first month will expire Oct. 9th 1896, although I have not taught a day yet, because the[. . .]

[*moved top of page 170, Sept. 8th 1895, from here*]

Oct. 4th 1896. Sunday about 3 P.M. (Continued) [*from page 169*]
Peaches are all gone now and apples are getting scarce. Between June and October is the season of apple selling by William Shawnee. I have no doubt this is the time of year that he has the most money. Before June he began to sell garden vegetables.

I must have a home of my own and have the house furnished, and live there. I must run my place to make as much money as I can. The County Supt. told me of a place to teach in the southwestern part of the county that had no teacher yet. I wonder how many months of school it has. If those gentlemen of the Board of Education in Shawnee will pay me for the month just passed, I am content. If not I shall consult some good lawyer and sue for my pay either in the probate court or in the district court. I will have my pay if the law will allow it to me. I need money too bad to let the matter go. My time is precious, and I want money to finish my house with. I wish to attend school at the Kansas State Normal. There is no use trying for a territorial certificate until I have had 3 years of teaching experience, or 24 months. I have had up to date 8 months or one year's teaching experience. It will be some time before I will have the requisite amount of teaching experience. I must attend the Teacher's Association in Tecumseh Oct. 10th 1896. So then I can not go to the Sac and Fox Agency this week. I am needy a Christian as ever walked the earth. People want me to work for them for nothing, but I have quit that foolishness. If I ever get up in the world, it will be on account of that I earn. Whoever does not pay me for services injures me financially. No one does any thing for me for nothing. Why should I help people without payment[?] They do not appreciate what you do for them, and so why do it? Only God's work, I hold, sh[all] [*page 171*] be done for nothing. This is my present policy.

Thursday Oct. 29th 1896.
It rained last night and it is cool weather today, with a high wind in the south. I was a guest at Mr. and Mrs. Coolie's last night, but I pay them 25 cts. for every night's lodging, with supper and breakfast. I attended the Teachers Association in Tecumseh Oct. 10th 1896. Mr. Patrick brought the largest

crowd, and also made the best speech that was made. I also attended the Shawneetown Monthly Meeting the third Saturday in Oct. 1896, held in a meetinghouse near the Mission School. I am having considerable trouble with my school in Shawnee. I should have taken up school Sept. 14th 1896, but the Board of Education had no house ready for me and will not pay me for my lost time either. They began to build a house this week, and now have the frame up and some of the sheeting and weather-boarding on. They told me that they would be ready in two weeks, so at least the carpenters say. They will not probably be ready Nov. 2nd 1896, but may possibly be ready Nov. 9th 1896.

I ought never to contract to teach a school where there is no school house. I ought to be sure that school will commence the day set in the contract.

Carrie Warrior is trying to sell the Bible I gave her with her name on it in golden letters to William Shawnee. The old man said that she wanted $5 for it. Carrie promised to keep this book forever. I do not want such a worthless good-for-nothing girl as Carrie Warrior is. I would rather marry any decent girl than to marry such a fool. She would sell her soul for me. She can not keep a nice Bible without selling it, that did not cost her one cent. William Shawnee is just a[s] worthless as Carrie is. He has old Chosa Starr here cooking, but she went home and stayed a week. Now here she is back again. The old man and her sleep in the same room down-stairs, with only La Fayette with them. Julia Shawnee has not written one scratch of the pen to us, since she has been gone. She went away in this month. I ought to get ready to set out fruit trees on my place, and I want roses and other flowers too, to plant or to set out upon it. Yesterday Oct 28 '96 the lady county superintendent of Lincoln County told me that there were twenty-two colored schools in that county, but only a half dozen colored teachers. I could surely obtain a school up there. This school in Shawnee will not start before Nov. 9th 1896. I wrote a letter to both Emma Valentine and Mary Valentine. I am to write to Minnie Valentine also. I had to go over to Shawnee to see [*page 172*] whether they had begun to build on the house or not. I received a letter from Teacher, Aunt Martha, and from Miss Emma Valentine the past week. Nollie Lacy is to graduate in the High School at 16 years of age. This is a good record.

Monday Dec 7th 1896.

I have been teaching over a month and I am going along very well. Along about the middle of November 1896 Mrs. Julia Shawnee came back from Okmulgee and the Creek country, bringing back with her Miss Ellen Carolina, a distant cousin of Julia's. Nov. 28th 1896 Mrs. Murphy, an aunt of Ellen's, together with her husband were at our home. I and Ellen were drifting toward love Nov. 28th 1896. Dec. 6th 1896 was a red letter day, and it may be for good or evil. I believe that Ellen is a good girl and I think that her aunt is a good woman. The girl is very tender-hearted.

Where there is a woman that will make an effort to destroy your chastity, there are 1000 women that will never do so.

Tuesday Dec 8th 1896 about 6 A.M. (still dark)

Last night I went to the meeting of the Board of Education, and Mrs[.] Steel, Mr. Millard, Mr. Benson, Mr. White and Mr. Replogle were present. The other members were absent. Mr. Grimes had never been present at any time; I have now been at five board meetings, and what I have learned has amply repaid for my trouble. I learned a great deal about other matters besides school matters. One fellow in the room, not a member of the Board went to vociferating against the "niggers" about a certain matter.

It is certain that Ellen has not been here more than a month, scarcely that long. In that time I wonder if anyone has asked her an[y] improper questions. It seems hard to believe the negative of this proposition, especially when one is well versed in history from personal observation and experience.

We are to turn out school for the Holiday vacation the Wednesday evening before Christmas, so that I only have to teach 18 days in this month. I am never going to teach on another Holiday as long as I live. Because it caused me to lose my vote Nov. 3rd, 1896. It was partly oweing [owing] to Supt. Miller that I taught school on Election Day, and I should not have done it.

My Post Office Box [is] 147.

I am moved over here to Shawnee. I have my library here and my effects. I am pretty well satisfied. I have only four regular pupils in school. I have everything more convenient than last year and at an increase of salary, but yet I want to try for my old school again. That will be in the month of May. I also want to try for [*page 173*] this same school also. I do not believe that I can apply for this school with effect until the month of June. But I can apply for the other school until on the second Tuesday of May 1897. I must have my new certificate endorsed during the Holiday by Mr. F. H. Umholtz, Co. Supt. of Okla. County.

Sunday Dec. 13th 1896. 12M.

I went home Friday evening Dec. 11th 1896. It must be confessed that Ellen was the cause of my wanting to go so bad. She and I were in love, and I could not stay away. I attended the Teachers' Association in Tecumseh Dec. 12th 1896, in the afternoon. I was called upon to say a few words perhaps out of mere curiosity. I think Ellen is beautiful, on account of the fact that she appears to be a girl who is inclined to do right and be religious. Even little Florence Cooley spoke of that girl over at my home, which shows that they know about us, and were talking about us while I was gone. Mrs. Cooley and Florence came back Friday Dec. 11th 1896. Florence says that they have twenty-five pupils in school, quite a number. Well, I must get ready for Sunday School and write again later.

Sunday Dec. 13th 1896 (After Sabbath School).

I held Sabbath School at 2 P.M. George Apperson and Allie Walls were the only ones present besides myself. The past week has been one of love and courtship with myself and Ellen. The result is that we are about engaged to be married. I kissed her Sunday Dec. 6th, Tuesday, Wednesday, Thursday, Friday, Saturday, and Sunday Dec. 13. I never was so happy in my life. Ellen told that she loved me a heap; that she would love me forever until death and live with me until death if we lived together; that she would let other men alone; that as she saw I was honest with her, she would be honest with me; that she would never leave me unless I beat her; that she would be kind and forgive me if I did wrong; that she would be satisfied with whatever property we had, and would not be too exacting upon me; that she would take up and hold her land in the Creek country, and would put a house upon it; that by the goodness of the Lord she had some property; that she was a good girl, and would treat me right; that she was not a Christian, but knew that she ought to be.

I told Ellen that I wanted to pray more over our case and think and wait awhile before I promised her for sure. – Ellen Payne, for she says this is her real name, has the headache, pains in the side, and a swelling on her foot; she has been thus sick ever since Thursday. Her eyes are weak, and she says that her father's eyes were weak too. I believe she said that her father's name was Charlie Payne, but that people call him Charlie Carolina. She says that she has no brothers and only one sister 15 years of age. She has never been married, but has been engaged once, but did not marry [page 174] the fellow because she did not like him. She lives at Wewoka, Ind. Ter. She went to school for six years, and read in the fifth reader. She said that if she loved a man she would marry him and her father could not hinder her.

Julia Shawnee said that she had known Ellen for years, and that Ellen was a good girl. Cousin Lesser, Ellen['s] grandmother, is the one with whom she lives. She does not live with her father. He lives four miles away. Ellen has about three head of cattle left and some hogs, but she says that people steal her hogs.

She says that she does not have much education and as she is not a Christian, she does not have religion. She is deficient in these two particulars.

About her being a colored girl, I can say. That is all right. Only colored girls that are worthy will notice me. Worthy girls of other colors will not.

About her being strong enough, I think she is all right. She has now her monthly flow, I believe. – About her being uneducated, I can say that she can learn a great deal if she will, and if she gets an allotment of land, that will be a blessing to us both.

Monday Dec. 14th 1896.

Last night or about 4:30 P.M. I went home to see Ellen. I learned this of her personal history,—that she was born on Caney Creek, Creek Nation, about 20 miles or so west from Muskogee; that her mother was born in the same place also; that she went to school to Mrs. Ramsey, Mrs. Diamond, and others; that she has a sister 15 years old named Mary; that in school she studied reading, writing, spelling, arithmetic, geography, United States history; that she was of a combative disposition in school except toward the last. Last night Dec. 13th 1896 dear Ellen told me that she loved me with all her heart and would be true to me forever, that I could trust her and that she would not disappoint me, that she would secure her place down there and have a house built upon it as soon as possible; I asked her to kiss me, but she said that my kissing her was the same as if she kissed me; but that if I did not pet her so much, that she would then kiss me. She said that if I would treat her right, she would treat me right. She told me about giving away so much property to different parties around home, and they did not ever give her anything. I told her that we must not forget quickly what we had promised each other. Ellen has no brother at all. Her mother died about 10 years ago, or about 1886. She hated to talk to me about her mother, because it caused sadness.

Ellen said that she did not want to marry, but this was after we promised to marry each other. She told me that when she got married, she was going to sit up all night and not go to bed because she did not want to be married. Ellen was hurt once when, as she says, I asked her if she loved me and she said, Yes, and then I told her that I did not love her.

[page 175, original page missing]

[page 176, original page missing]

[page 177] *Tuesday Dec. 15th 1896.*

    A nice day, but since Sunday evening I have had desentery [dysentery] of an acute description. So I am not to have any school this evening. I taught Election Day and lost my vote. So I have a right to one day of vacation any way. I have some fever; I believe it is nothing but that water at the wagon yard. I can turn out school another half day for that matter, without forfeiture of pay. I am nervous as my hand writing shows.

Sunday Dec. 20th 1896 A.D.

    Ellen was sicker when I went home Friday evening. Her face, cheek and nose, were swollen. She was trying to wash clothes Tuesday Dec. 15th 1896, and had been going out of doors without her shoes on and making up beds in the house of a morning, without her shoes on. She said that she did not think it would make her sick, but it did just the same.

    I must finish my house sure, and get it furnished as much as I can. I must have chairs, a table, and a bed with bed clothing, and a good book case, for my books. I must live to myself, for Julia, William Shawnee, and I quarrel too much there at home. I do hate quarrelling; it makes me say things that I do not want to say. Julia and the old man quarrel a great deal, but still Julia goes on with her work. The old man goes over to Cegars and Webbs too much. He bought that Bible of Carrie Warrior—the one that I made a present to her.

    The last month, that is since Nov. 2, when my school commenced, I have paid some of my debts. I have paid Carson Bros. $4 of the $6.55 cts that I owe them. I paid the *Christian Nation* $1, and the *N.Y. Independent* 75 cts. up to Dec. 10th 1896. I owe John King $4, and by the good help of the Lord, I must pay him. I must pay Houghton and Upp, of Purcell, Ind. Ter. that which I owe them, with interest. I must pay every honest debt that I owe. I am no repudiator; consequently I must pay my honest debts, as God has commanded me in the New Testament.

    I attended Shawneetown Monthly Meeting yesterday. Mrs. Rachel Kirk and Miss Lina B. Lunt were present. Mr. and Mrs. Hartley were present. Miss Ollie Wilford, Mr. John Largent, Mrs. Bourbonnais, Ozetta and "Keby" were present. The Bourbonnais are so white that they might be classed as white people, but nominally they are Indians. Mrs. Rachel Kirk expects to leave in the Spring; perhaps she is going to Ohio. Mr. John Largent had a girl with him, but I do not know who she was. I visited the court room in Tecumseh, and saw the new judge—Justice Keaton—a young man. I visited the home of David Alford this morning, and took breakfast there (Sunday Dec. 20th 1896). I told David that I was in a good notion of farming myself, because I knew that some thing could be made off of my land. I could farm in the Spring and Summer, and teach school in the [page 178] Fall and Winter. I could attend the County Normal Institute during July or August, because I live very close to the county seat any way. If the Lord spares my life, I must attend County Normal Institute in July or August, 1897. It will be the first County Normal that I have ever attended. I must try to attend the Territorial Normal Institute in Edmond the last week in May 1897. I can not leave the profession of teaching until I find some work where I can make more money, and do at least as much good.

    During, May, June, July, and August 1896 I was seeking for a school to teach. I rode 200 or 300 miles, or more, in quest of a school. I circulated two petitions to two different districts. I was trying to get a school in Okla. County. Mr. Fullbright succeeded in securing the school I had taught the session before. Over in Cleveland County I could have got a five month's school at $35 a month, but I tried for this school here in Shawnee, and finally secured it. – It is well for me to remember what a time I had hunting for a school, to teach me to be careful how I spend the money that I earn. I must use that $15 that I have saved on my house, and nowhere else. I must complete my house, for then I will have a home of my own. I can always get some[one] to work the land on my place. I had no trouble getting Mr. Sexton this year. Mrs. Irene Carter has my lower place, and Mr. Henry Carter is my right hand man there also. I tried hard to treat the Carter's right: I do not want to beat them out of one cent. I believe they treat me right too. They raised two bales of cotton down on the place this year. I ought to build a house down there, but I declare if I can ever get able. As that noble woman, Mrs. Thos. Alford, said years ago, it takes a great deal of money to improve a place. I need to set out more fruit trees on my place, and I need to make as much money as I can. I need to try hard now to have something; then I shall have something when I am more advanced in years. Mr. James Grizzard farmed 16 acres of land, but two acres at least he permitted to grow up in weeds, and never even ran a plow through it. I realized nearly $11 for my part off of 16 acres. This was less than $1 per acre. But it was the laziness of Mr. Grizzard and his boys that caused me this loss. King Davis in 1894 did the same thing. He left some of the land uncultivated. But in 1895 Mr. Cummings farmed all of the land, and raised nothing but corn. During 1896 Mr. Wray a white man raised 17 acres in corn, and Mr. Grizzard a colored man 6 acres in cotton. I realized for my part $22.20 off of my 40 acres this year of 1896. This tract of land has been in cultivation four years. 1897 will be the fifth year. My fruit trees are looking nicely, and Mr. Saxton has promised to take care of them. I want to set out some roses [*page 179*] and other flowers on the lot that I am building upon. I must not let this lot grow up in weeds next year. My mother used to have nice flowers in the yard, and I wish to follow her example. With my house finished and with nice flowers in my yard, and with my well fixed, I will be pretty well off on my place. I ought to have a team and buggy to ride in. To ride in a buggy is not the prerogative of some men only. Buggies do not cost so much. I must get a catalogue and buy one, as soon as I can spare the money.

I must have a privy built on my place too, but must not have it where it will contaminate either the soil or the well. I must live to myself and must let William Shawnee and his home alone. I want a corn crib and a stable built also. I can never get too much house room on my place. There is John Dukes that would be very glad if I had more house room on my place. He would pay me in work at least for the privilege of living in the house, and work at the present time is worth more to me than the money. Even in Oklahoma County there is a lack of house room on the places up there. I must remedy this defect on my places as soon as possible.

I thank the Lord for the following blessings: (*2:45 P.M. Sunday Dec. 20, 1896*)

1. That I went to school eight years at the Shawnee Mission, Shawneetown, Ind. Ter.
2. That I went to school to a normal four years at Maryville, Tennessee.
3. That I was converted and became a member of the church at about 15 or 16.
4. That I have in my own name 120 acres of land, all under fence.
5. That 53 acres of this is in cultivation, and 73 acres soon will be cultivated.
6. That I have taught school seven months in Oklahoma Territory, for which I have been paid $220.
7. That I have a nice little library of my own, and besides access to other libraries.
8. That my heart is yet set to serve God as long as I live—to love Him and keep his commandments.
9. That I have health, strength, reason, comfort, and employment.
10. That I have a daily and several weekly and monthly papers to read.
11. That I am slowly, but surely paying off the debts I owe.
12. That I shall soon be 28 years of age—Dec. 23rd, 1896—is the day.

13. That I have attended church so often in my life, so often prayed myself and spoken. But I have not worshiped God publicly half as much as I should have done.
14. That my religion has often kept me out of evil things.
15. That I can praise God now with all my heart, soul, mind, and strength.
16. That I have so many kind blessed friends.
17. That Christ Jesus is my dearest Friend and elder Brother.
18. That my opportunities in life are so great.

I ought to have $30 laid aside to pay my board with during the months of May, June, July, August, and September 1897. But I hardly think I can do this, because I have to buy me some clothes and finish my [*page 180*] house, as well as furnish my house as best I can. I want to get ready to live to myself and I ought to begin to do so now. I was 18 years, eleven months, and two days old when I arrived back home from Maryville, Tennessee Nov. 25th 1887. I left Old Shawneetown, Ind. Ter. for Maryville, Tennessee August 14th, 1883, and was at that time 14 years, 7 months, and 21 days old. I was born in Lawrence, Kansas, Dec. 23rd, 1896 [1868]. I began to go to school at the Shawnee Mission when I was 6 yrs. old, in 1875.

Wednesday Dec. 23rd, 1896.
This is my twenty-eight birthday. It is now 12:40 P.M., and I am in the school-room, writing this at my Teacher's desk. This is a very nice day; very little fire is needed. Mr. Cooley had no bread at all for my dinner today, and very little meat was cooked. I had no time today to cook any thing. I went home yesterday evening Dec. 22nd, 1896, to see my dear Ellen. She and I talked together. Oh, but I was happy to have a dear true lover, and I told Ellen so. I came back very early this morning. I will receive my pay either this evening or tomorrow Dec. 24th, 1896 if God spares my life. I have not promised the children a Christmas tree or any presents even, because I have no money yet and may disappoint them. It is better not to promise than to promise and not fulfill. I have now taught school seven months in Oklahoma Territory and earned $220, an average of 31^{3/7}$ per months. I have taught two months at Spring City, Tennessee, at $25 per month, which made $50 that I earned. Mr. John has paid me $8.40 for teaching for him. This makes $278.40 cts. that I have earned by the business of teaching school up to date. Mr. Cooley came to see me about 12:50 P.M., but I preferred not to go and eat to not taking up school exactly on time. I earned $493.50 in eleven months by the business of surveying, an average of $48.50 cts per month. Oh, I have earned money enough, but have not used it wisely. The necessity for economy in my

expenditures is evident. For I need to finish my house before buying things with which to furnish it. I need to concentrate every thing on my home. I need some decent clothes to wear. I need to set out some fruit trees too on my place. There is a kind of shingle that cost $2.40 per M. That is the kind I might better buy. I think that $20 worth of lumber and material will go a long ways towards finishing my house. Emma Valentine wants a Christmas present, and she is to send me one also. I can never earn too much money, or build and furnish me a home too soon. I will have to get Ellen a Christmas present of some kind. But I can not give every body a present.

Dec. 23rd, 1896

I borrowed $17.80 cts at the bank and deposited the warrant for collateral security. I have to pay the bank $2.20 cts for the use of $17.80 for three months. There is $15 coming to me on the warrant for my first month's salary. I should keep account of every nickel that comes into my hand. Paid and note withdrawn, Loss $2.20 int.

Dec. 24th 1896 (About 3 P.M) guessed).

Mr. C. J. Benson drew my second warrant today, and I sold it to Mr. Replogle for $28.50 cts. I lost in this transaction $6.50 cts. [*page 181*] My account runs thus,

Salary		$28.50cts
Paid Mrs. Cooley	$ .25	
Paid Mr. Cooley for Board	8.00	
" Box Rent	.25	
" for Suit of clothes	9.00	
" for Shirt 50, Drawers 30	.80	
" for Apples 5 cts, Box for Present 35 cts	.40	
" for Hat	2.25	
" to John King on Acct	2.20	

I want to go to the Territorial Teachers Association if possible. I am not able to afford it however, on account of the way the Board of Education has treated me. If I had begun school Sept. 14th 1896, I would have been in better condition now. Mr. McKinnis had three warrants drawn to-day at $60 apiece. The white teachers have taught three months and three weeks, and I have taught two months up to date. I have four months more to teach. If I go to Oklahoma City, I will have to pay railroad fare only one way. - Florence Cooley was ten years old last Friday January 18th 1896. I have not done one single thing on my house. I have not spent one single dollar toward my house, and I have now $46.30 cents in two months. $16 of this has gone for board. This leaves me $30.30 cents to spend for other purposes. I intend to keep an account of every dollar that I spend.

I believe that Mr. McKinnis deposited his $180 in warrants for collateral and borrowed $100 for three months at the bank.

Sunday Dec. 27th, 1896. (2 P.M. by the clock.)

I paid 25 cents Christmas day for my daily Journal paper leaving 20 cents more only due for this month. I received a letter to-day from Ellen Carolina, Wewoka, Indian Territory, and one from Mr. Jacob Tomahawk, Anadarko, Okla. Ter. Jacob and I went to school together at the Shawnee Mission 15 or 16 years ago. Ellen does not want me to go off on my trip until she comes back. She says that her grandmother bought a horse for her, and that her grandmother wanted to see me and wanted me to come. Ellen says, in her letter, that she has something good to tell me. She does not say whether she received my letter or not.

Jan. 1st, 1897 (About 10:30 A.M.)

I praise the Lord for all his goodness and loving kindness to me in my absence. He has spared my life and enabled me to attend the Territorial Teachers Association. Monday Dec. 28th 1896 I went down on the train to Wewoka, Ind. Ter. I saw Ellen and her mother or rather grandmother, Mrs. Lizzie Bowleg. They treated me nice and gave me dinner and supper. [*page 182*] That night Dec. 28th 1896 I boarded the train in Wewoka for Oklahoma City, Okla. Ter. I arrived after 9 P.M. I went to the house of Miss Susie Berry, where I put up while I was in Okla. City. Tuesday Dec 29th 1896 I went to the High School Building, on the old military reservation, and took a back set [seat]. I was promptly on time. Presently Mr. Baxter, of Guthrie, Okla. Ter. came and shook hands with me; he wore a University badge at the time. It was 9:30 A.M. when he came. He asked me my name and I told him, William E. Shawnee, of Pottawatomie County.

Here is a note I made. "Wednesday Dec. 30th 1896, 1:40P.M. I have now attended the Association 1½ days. I like it very well. It has made me more fully acquainted with the real conditions here in Oklahoma; I can more fully understand the work a teacher ought to do. There are great obstacles to be overcome, but there are also many favorable helps and footholds that will give opportunity for refreshment. Berea offers you her hand and her help. I have seen Prof. Hopkins, Prof. Boyd, Miss Grace King, Prof. Morrow, Prof. Murdaugh, and others that I have longed to see before now. The President of Berea keeps up a correspondence with you; this is more than the President of any other college has done. I do wish to go to school so much. About 200 or 250 teachers are in attendance. One writer in the Association said that half of the teachers were now seeking and intending to leave the profession for other callings. This is probably true; I was thinking myself of being some thing else eventually. Rev. John Mordy, 705 Cleveland Ave., Guthrie, Okla. Ter. came and asked me my name. He asked me if my father was an Indian. I told him I did not know. He said that he was working for a colored normal here in Oklahoma.

It was said that there were 1928 school teachers here in Oklahoma. The last number enrolled was 191; so that 1/10 of the teachers went to the Territorial Association. Kay County had only 21 teachers in attendance, yet carried off the flag. Supt. McLain of Oklahoma City would assign Arithmetic a lower place in the school course, with less time on the program. I disagree with any such thing, but favor such improvement as may be necessary. One man (a teacher) would not have a speller in the school room. I would. One lady, Miss Edith Patterson, would smash all the slates, and banish them from the school room; another would smash the spellers, another would smash arithmetic, another would smash grammar, but would laud geography to the skies. At this rate no course of study at all would be left on the school program except what the fancy of some conceited teacher chose not to banish. Supt. elect Cooley is a fine man, sure.

Here were some things said: Preaching is to influence the will. The Christian is to be like God, do right. Christianity is a most mighty influence [*page 183*] for good in this world, whether considered natural or spiritual. Religion works not on the will, but the sensibility. Truth and beauty are complements of each other. Incidentally, religion influences the intellect. Calvin molded the thought of a century. Christianity has been, in the past, the dominant influence in uplifting humanity. Liberty, equality, fraternity, the words of the French were referred to with approbation. So also were city Missions, the Salvation Army, and cultured men and women. Few go to college, and few to the academy. The church is in the way to reach all classes of the people. Evangelist Moody was referred to. The white flower of a blameless life; along the lines in many things. One person said, The church upheld slavery. I say this is a mistake. Our wills are ours (true limitedly). The church is the mother of the home and the school.

I became a member of the Oklahoma Territorial Teachers Association, and I have my membership card. I am proud of what I have done. Pres. Steel, of the Board of Education, of Shawnee, Okla. Ter. said that Will has learned a heap now, I guess. He came down on the train this morning. Co. Supt. Cooley lost his hat Monday night Dec. 28th, 1896 when we were going up on the train. He was in the act of moving from one car to the other when it happened.

Miss Edith Patterson, in her paper on "Child Study" said: "Smash the slates.["] I say, Nay. She referred to the Cook County Normal School, Chicago, Illinois. She also referred to Prof. D. H. Wolf in the University of Nebraska, Lincoln, Neb. Prof. S. N. Hopkins has no beard or mustache, but black hair, and he is tall. - One speaker said that the County ~~Normal~~ Teachers' Association should meet once a month.—In the County Normal Institute, the problem is, How can we do the most work possible in the least possible time.

I made this note at 9:35 A.M. Dec. 31st, 1896 before the flag was awarded. Our county can not get the flag.—We teachers should magnify our work. The habit of believing in the best education, and the highest education. - There can be no speedy revolution in educational affairs here in Oklahoma.—The home, the church, and the newspaper are educative influences.—{Here in Oklahoma every thing is in a formative state. No state has a perfect system of education. These are some of the statements of Mrs. C. O. Garlinghouse: (veiled): (mispabebe; kobakwilwi; mkitawnikwa; pitketiwa;). - To ask too much is to discourage. The teachers want to influence Constitution makers and law makers. We want competent teachers, better wages, and longer terms. Every teacher should receive as pay $500 a year. In only 14 states are schools by law free from political influences. The teacher's office should be more permanent. The teacher should eat at the patron's home table, no matter how humble}. - The teacher should court the home, but not the grown daughter. A teacher must study character philosophically and systematically. Child-study should be revived, and the home should aid the teacher. The teacher should know the home surroundings of every child. - Prof. McKinnis had nothing [*page 184*] to do or say at this Association, and so all the rest except Mrs. Miller. She posed as a Primary Teacher. - Chancellor Snow, of the Kansas State University spoke to the Association at 10:55 A.M. Thursday, and he also read a paper on "College Entrance Examinations". - I made this note Dec. 31st, 1896:—The High School Building is located on the old military reserve (ceded by Congress to Oklahoma City for school purposes.) We went home in the rain last night when Chancellor Snow's illustrated lecture was finished. He met many Kansas people here in Oklahoma, he said. I must attend the Kansas State Normal School. - There is too much abstract teaching, not enough concrete teaching. I have spent money as follows:

2 Tickets to Wewoka & back	$1.80	Round Trip Ticket to Okla. City	1.15
Other Expenses	1.00	Board at Susie Berries	1.75
Zoology	1.50	Astronomy	1.00
School Management	.75	Hand Manual of Information	.35
Membership Fee T.T.A.	50		$4.25

	$5.55		
	$4.25		
$9.80	$9.80		
Cutting Hair .15			
$9.95 cts total			

I have spent $9.80 [$9.95] cts for the foregoing things. I have spent money like water; yet what have I bought. O Lord, do take care of me and keep me in the way of righteousness. I found two letters waiting for me here from my darling Ellen. She thinks so much of me. Mrs. Lizzie Bowleg (Cousin Lesser) told me that she could not refuse to let me have Ellen, that Ellen never had married and was a good girl if she did say it herself; that she did not want to refuse because Ellen might go wrong if she did; that one woman there was with child now by a fellow who went and married another girl. She did not try to hide any thing from me at all. Cousin Lesser is a nice looking woman. She was just as good to me as she could be. No one watched I and Ellen. We were in a room to ourselves, with the door open. She said that Ellen's father would be too glad to hear of my and Ellen's engagement. Cousin Lesser wanted me to ask her husband about it, as they had raised Ellen; but I told her that I could not. Cousin Lesser said that young men could not help doing as Dudley Shawnee did sometimes; I disagreed with her there. I need some darling girl like Ellen for a wife, but I can not do without some girl like her.

[January ??, 1897] Shawnee, Okla. Ter. 9 A.M. at the Teacher's Desk in the Colored School.

I thought of my kind Ellen and wondered if she would be true to me before God. I made a contract with Mr. Henry Carter today to build a log house for me down on my lower place for $12 at the end of this month, that is, on January 30th, 1897. If I get Mr. Saxton a plow for six or seven dollars, it will take my whole month's salary. Darling Ellen wanted me to hurry and finish my house. I am very anxious to finish my house. I owe so many debts that I ought to try my best to pay them. I ought to pay Mr. Carson the $2.55 cts. that I owe him at the end of this month. I do not [*page 185*] see how I can avoid going into debt.

Sunday Feb. 7th, 1897 (2:15 P.M. this is written.)

Yesterday Sat. ~~J~~ Feb. 6th, 1897 was a red letter day in my life. At 10 P.M. on that day I was married at the Missionary Residence of Dr. G. N. Hartley and his wife Mrs. Ella Hartley and in the presence of Mrs. Julia Shawnee and of Mr. Piney Wilson, to Miss Ellen Carolina, of Wewoka, Indian Territory. Dr. Hartley said such a nice appropriate ceremony. Most of it was prayer, which was just to my liking. Dr. Hartley prayed that we might realize the sacredness of the marriage relation and be united for life and be faithful to one another in sickness and in health. Dr. [*Hartley*] said that the marriage relation was of God, sanctioned by Christ Himself, and recognized by the Christian Church. Both Dr. and Mrs. Hartley said they would be around to see how we are getting along before long. We reached home about 11 P.M. at night, but did not go to bed until after 12 P.M. Mrs. Ella Hartley said that I could teach Ellen a great deal. It was claimed last night that Ellen was eighteen years of age by both Julia Shawnee and Ellen. But Ellen, in my opinion, will not be eighteen until Aug. 1, 1897.

Thank God that Ellen and I own a nice bed and mattress with covers and pillows already. Ellen agrees with me that we must not give any thing away, but try hard to have something. Dr. Hartley wanted God to prosper me and Ellen financially and spiritually and in every other way. Oh, I am happy that I have Ellen to love with all my heart and I rejoice to know that she loves me. – I have taught school in Okla. Territory eight months and one week, up to this date. I am in no ways tired of teaching, but expect to make teaching the professional business of my life. I want to secure a Territorial Certificate at the Territorial Normal Institute the last week in May 1897. I can try for a Five Year Certificate even if I fail. It will be no disgrace. I must study for this purpose. I can teach school to better advantage now that I am a married man; but my marriage will not hinder my attending the Kansas State Normal at Emporia. – I want to be aggressive in seeking information in regard to school work and all educational work, but also in every department of human knowledge. A person must go to some trouble to reach the place of education and of religion, and must seek the acquaintance of their ministers (i.e. preachers of the Gospel and learned professors in school, college, and university). You have the whole world open before you. All the knowledge and all the science, all the arts, all the industries and vocations of all the lands are open to you if only you seek them. Medical knowledge, legal knowledge, and theological knowledge, all the natural sciences are exposed to you. Pry into them and appreciate them, and all will be well with you. – Ellen Shawnee (nee Carolina) is so kind [*page 186*] and good to me since our marriage that I am glad that I married her. She is so kind and tender to me, and attentive to me, that I can not help but love her with all my heart.

Drawing my pay every month for teaching school is better than the Indian payments. Because one has to wait so long for the Indian payments, when they might better be at work earning some thing. I have drawn eight payments for teaching here in

Oklahoma, and I have got the full amount on my warrants only twice. Six times I have had to sell my warrants at a discount. This discount has ranged all the way between three dollars and ten dollars. Presuming that it is better to make some money than to quit and make none, I keep on right ahead, doing the best I can, in spite of all the obstacles. I have certainly bettered my condition financially since I have been teaching school. – Dr. Hamilton is a real good friend of mine. He is the one who secured for me the school in the city of Shawnee. He has been my friend ever since I tried for the office of county clerk. That brought me to his notice, and he has been trying to help me and wish me well ever since. – Dr. G. N. Hartley did not think that my marriage would change the whole course of my life; time will determine this. – I am always sending for college, university, and normal school catalogues to every part of the United States. This has been a great help to me in educational work and has influenced the general course of my reading and studies. I have catalogues of the University of Minnesota, of Iowa, of Michigan, of Ohio, of Kansas, of Colorado, of Boston, of Chicago, of New York city, and many other colleges. This is a great advantage to me. I must keep up in this line. – It only cost me $3.40 cts to attend and become a member of the Territorial Teachers' Association during the Holidays in 1896; whence I came back to Shawnee New Year's Day 1897.

Merit will be recognized; it does not matter about the person of him who has the merit. Be worthy and people will rate you accordingly. I am the only person not white, who attends the Pottawatomie County Teacher's Association. – Aggressiveness has been my policy in the past. It has been pursued in every line of work. We choose our own companions; we chose our associates; we chose our churches; we chose our destiny. Choice makes life. The simple act of choosing is fraught with the most mighty and most momentous consequences.

Feb. 13th 1897 (7:40 A.M.)
Feb 11th 1897 Thursday I became acquainted with Mr. Robert Sampson in the following manner. Mr. Cooley introduced him to me as the "man that Ellen belonged to." He told me that the first fellow Ellen ever loved was Billy Nevens, who was killed. Then he went on to say that Ellen belonged to him and that if I had married her, it would not do me any good. This of course, made a very favorable impression on me in regard to Robert. He gave me a note to take to Ellen, but [*page 187*] when I delivered it, she burned it up without reading it. She told me that Robert was a fool, and that she had promised once to marry him in fun: she told other things that Robert had done that he had no business to do.

Ellen Carolina, of Wewoka, Indian Territory, and William E. Shawnee, of Shawnee, Okla. Ter. or of Tecumseh, Okla. Ter. were married at the Mission residence of Mr. G. N. Hartley at 10 P.M. Saturday Feb. 6th, 1897. Ellen's name is to be Ellen Shawnee. Dr. Hartley and his wife, Mrs. Julia Shawnee, and Mr. Piney Wilson, and Ellen and myself were the only ones present.

Mr. Thomas Berry and his brother Andrew Berry were guests of ours last night Feb. 12th, 1897. Mr. Berry advised me to get a team and go hard to work on my farm. He said I would make more money in that way than in any other. I think that Mr. Berry's advice worthy of consideration. I must make a living, and I must make it any way I can. A white man would as soon be a guest of a colored man as not. A person has to work hard for what little they get; at least I do. I just love Ellen with all my heart. She loves me with all her heart also.

Sunday Feb. 14th, 1897 (3:20 P.M.)

As it was a bad rainy day I did not go over to Shawnee, to hold Sabbath School. I did not think that any one would come out, and besides I was newly married. William Shawnee today told me that Miss Carrie Warrior was great with child; and I went up to ask Mr. David Alford and Mrs. Mamie Alford about it. Mamie said that it was one of the Shepherd boys that was going to marry Carrie, but had deceived her; that Carrie received a letter from him every week; that Carrie had said that as soon as her menses ceased, she knew she was with child, and accordingly came on home; that this white man made plenty of money working in the railroad shops, but had not sent any money to Carrie. Mamie said that Carrie and this white fellow were not married. Mamie told Carrie to write to this white fellow and tell him of her condition, and ask him to send her some money. I told Mamie that I believed it was the child of Walter Shawnee, that Carrie had now been home eight months, and that Walter had quit making hay over at home and gone over to Cegars to make hay; that Carrie had written letters to Walter before she came home, and that when I asked Walter if Carrie had written to him, and that he abruptly told me it was none of my business. Mamie told me that it was none of my business what Carrie did, and that I was married now. This is true, but still there is nothing wrong in inquiring about Carrie, a girl to whom I was so long engaged.

[*moved from page 107*]

Sunday Feb. 21st, 1897. (3:35 A.M. Central Standard Time.)

Yesterday Feb. 20th, 1897 I went to Tecumseh, and got the mail and also my daily papers. I was overtaken by Mr. Marcus near Tecumseh, and after some conversation he told me that Piney

Wilson had told a "terrible tale on me." He did not say what it was, and I did not ask him. I was in company with Mr. Cooley the Co. Supt. most of the time I was in Tecumseh. He is a fine man, and is brim full of educational work. He told me his method of teaching geography, which was very nice. It was the inductive method, and begun (See p. 187) [*continued on bottom of page 187*]

[*page 187, bottom of page*]
Sunday Feb. 21st, 1897. (3:50 A.M. See p.107.)
[*continued from page 107*] with a scope of country visible from the school house. He had them tell about the things raised in the aforementioned region and the things that were [*page 188*] shipped out of the region, and also what things were shipped into it. He thus spent a month on local geography, and the pupils became as much interested as it was possible for them to be. I read from reports of the U.S. Commissioner of Education, Prof. W. T. Harris, especially about the beginning of Normal Schools for the education of teaching for the work of their profession. I also read about "Classification in Graded Schools." Ellen is a good little girl in many respects, but she notices Piney Wilson too much to suit me. She told him in my hearing that she did not marry me for what I had, but that she married me for love. I told her this morning that she had no business telling Piney that; that she had no business giving an account of herself to Robert Samson, or John Henry, or any one else. She still denies that she told Piney "You are always courting too," but she surely told him that in my hearing, notwithstanding that Julia and Piney both denied it. Piney is the fellow that tore up one of my letters and then denied it. He promised faithfully not to tell some thing if I would tell him, and then told it to Julia and Ellen the first chance he got. He advised Ellen not to marry me in the following words: "I believe that where a man and a woman are jealous of each other before marriage, that they ought not marry; for if they are jealous before marriage, they will be so after marriage." He said this to Ellen, and Julia was present. Ellen agreed with him and said, Yes, that is so. Piney knew when he said this that I was suspicious of Ellen and that we were about to marry. That night Piney called himself "poor boy" and Ellen called him "poor boy." She evidently takes words out of his mouth and makes them her own. I am sick and tired of this Ellen-Piney and Piney-Ellen combination. Ellen even has played with Piney in my presence, but insists that she does not even talk to him. I know better. Ellen says that she does not say these things to Piney, but to Julia; but if she is talking to Julia why does she not tell Julia when Piney is away. No, she is talking to Piney, not to Julia. Ellen told me two different tales about some money that I

asked her about when she came from home the last time. She said she was joking the first time, but I asked her for the truth: I did not ask for a joke. Ellen was overanxious about Piney's supper last evening. She kept telling the children to go and tell him to come to supper, and at the same time I kept telling her to let Piney alone, but she would not. Ellen says she has her eyes to look where she pleases, and she and Piney certainly do look at one another. Piney calls Emeline and the children "nigger," and Ellen does the same. Ellen even calls me "nigger," but I had her promise to quit using that word, and she promised to do so, but has not done so. She even says, "I am nothing but a nigger." I guess I have about got a woman that does not care for herself or any one else. Ellen says, "I am a nigger and I don't care." This is too much for me to [*page 189*] stand. It makes me hot to be called a nigger. Ellen calls me a white man, and says that I always go with the white people any way. She speaks well of Walter, Piney, and the old man William Shawnee. A pretty mess sure.

Ellen says that she will do as she pleases with me. This is saying too much; it certainly is. Ellen says that I put her down with the dogs, and put myself high up. I do not know how I do this at all. I guess she says this because I do not like what Robert Sampson said to me the first time I ever saw him. He said that Ellen belonged to him and Ellen herself says that she promised to marry him. No wonder Robert pitched on to me, but I did not know Ellen was engaged to Piney Wilson, Robert Sampson, and God only knows who else. I believe Ellen was engaged secretly to Piney, but I do not know it. Because all at once she told me that if I did not marry her that some one else would. At first Ellen did not deny it, but later she did. There are other reasons for my believing it. Ellen says this is a lie, which is a good sign that it is so. I am pretty hard to be deceived, because I will not be deceived. Ellen says that she does not sit down and tell lies on me like I do on her. She has just said it after reading these lines *5:08 A.M. Feb. 21st, 1897.* Tonight I have not slept one wink since 11:45 A.M. I only slept about four hours or at most five hours.

I told Co. Supt. Mr. Cooley that although married, I had not given up the idea of going to school. I have not. I do want to go to school to a normal school so very bad, or else to a university. I must go ahead and try my best to go. The whole world is open to me with all the fullness of its knowledge, and I am to be patient both in learning and applying it in practice. All the arts, occupations, and industries of all the countries and of all the peoples can be learned by you, and practiced at manual labor.

I am in the notion of going off to some foreign country and getting away from people that call me a "nigger." Piney has gone and told a lot of yarns about me. It may be partly true, and partly untrue. He did not tell all the improper things that he and Julia talked about that night. He said that he used to go with Maud Wilson before she is what she is. He also said something about John Picket's daughter that he had Julia promise not to tell to any one. Julia agreed. He is the real cause of the trouble between Ellen and myself and this trouble began Jan. 3rd 1897. I ought not to have married Ellen on account of the way I felt and on account of the way she and Piney were doing. I did not know that Ellen was mixed up with Robert Sampson. The evening Ellen and I were going to be married, Piney said to me that he hated what I was going to do. This showed that he had been noticing Ellen and wanted Ellen for himself. Ellen said to me before we married that I did not want her because she was a common country girl. On my saying that I did, she was glad. I know that Ellen was noticing Piney before we were married. The old man [*page 190*] is such a good trusting person that he will not give Piney his walking papers. I wanted Ellen to go home to get away from Piney, but she would not go. She preferred to stay here with her Piney. Ellen is a great hand to tell secrets. Every thing that occurs in the marriage.

It is a good habit that I have of sending for normal school, and college, and university catalogues, and of the Annual Reports of City Superintendents. This has directed the course of my reading, and so done me great good. I have learned many things to help me in the work of teaching school. The school law of Oklahoma Territory is copied after the school law of Kansas. I want to go to the Kansas State Normal School at Emporia, Kansas. There are over 1700 students at this school. I need to be better fitted for the work of teaching. I need to have a five-year Territorial Certificate. There is also the Territorial ten-year Certificate, and also the Territorial Life Diploma. There is also a Territorial one-year Certificate, issued to a person who has attended the Territorial Normal School twenty-two weeks. After any person has graduated at the University of Oklahoma, and after such graduation successfully teaches a public school for 16 school months, the Territorial Superintendent has authority to endorse such diploma after examination as to moral character, fitness and work, and such diploma after such endorsement is a valid certificate to teach until annualed [*sic*] by the Territorial Supt. Here then are five kinds of Territorial Certificates.

Saturday Feb. 27th, 1897 8:19 P.M. written.

Last Monday Feb. 22nd, 1897 I had no school in Shawnee, but I went to the Shawnee Mission, and visited the Indian School. There were four teachers, Mrs. Williams the Supt., Miss Brice, Miss Kessel, and Miss Massillon. Mrs. Williams has the sixth grade, and Miss Brice the fifth, and the second; Miss Kessel has the first grade and the kindergarten. The sixth grade was on the Revolutionary War in history, and the 5th grade was in fractions in arithmetic. She (Miss Massillon) was very kindly disposed toward me, and wanted me to speak to the school, and referred to my "being a teacher." Miss Brice was also well disposed. Paper cutting was had in the room of Miss Massillon. They made paper hatchets and Mrs. Williams pinned one upon my coat. I had dinner at the mission, Big Jim and Joe Billy being present and visiting the school. I taught school all the week from Tuesday to Friday— Feb. 23 to 26th, 1897. Yesterday Saturday Feb. 27th, 1897 I was paid for my fourth month. I was paid in the usual way, and not with a county warrant, despite the talk to the contrary. I have realized thus out of $140 in warrants, 1st mo. $25.80, 2nd, $28.50, 3rd $25, 4th 26.25, total $105.55, the amount realized out of $140. I have lost by reason of the discount $34.45. I have earned $290 for nine month's teaching in Oklahoma; this amount has been in warrants. Out of this $290, I have realized in cash $246.55, less than $30 per month. When I took the school in Shawnee, the clerk of the school board told me that I [*page 191*] would get the full amount ($35) on my warrants in two months, but here four months has rolled around, and I sell a warrant for 75 cents on the dollar, 71, 75, and 80 cents on the dollar is what warrants have sold at. It is better for me to have a little money now than a great deal of money six months from now. This is a world of severe, stern realities. Last evening (Sat. Feb, 27, 1897) I set out rose bushes and black berry vines and ornamental trees that Mr. Merritt of Tecumseh, Okla. Ter. kindly gave me.

[*moved from page 202, top of page*] Feb. 28th, 1897.
I must secure catalogues of all the normal schools, colleges, universities, and schools generally in the whole United States first, and of the world second. The whole World is open to me.
1. Whitman College, Walla Walla, Washington.
2. McGee college, Londonderry, E.C.
3. The Assembly College, Belfast, Ireland. E.C.
4. The State Agricultural College, Brookings, South Dakota.
5. The State University, Vermillion, South Dakota. (secured)
6. The State Normal School, Spearfish, South Dakota.
7. The State Normal School, Madison, South Dakota. (secured)
8. The School of Mines, Rapid City, South Dakota.

9. The University of Minnesota, Minneapolis, Minnesota. (secured)
10. The State Normal School, Winona, Minnesota. (secured)
11. The State Normal School, Mankato, Minnesota.
12. The State Normal school, St Cloud, Minnesota.
13. The State Normal School, Moorhead, Minnesota.
14. Clark University, Worcester, Massachusetts.
15. The State Normal School, Platteville, Wisconsin.
16. Clark University, Worcester, Massachusetts.
17. Amher[s]t College, Amherst, Massachusetts.
18. Bowdoin College, Brunswick, Maine.
19. Brown University, Providence, Rhode Island. (secured)
20. University of California, Berkley, California.
21. Columbia College, New York City, New York.
22. Cornell University, Ithaca, New York.
23. Harvard University, Cambridge, Massachusetts.
24. Leland Stanford Jr. University, Palo Alto, California.
25. Yale University, New Haven, Connecticut. (secured)
26. Indiana University, Bloomington, Indiana.
27. [No listing]

[continued from page 191]

Sunday March 14th, 1897 (12:30 P.M. Standard Time)
Yesterday Sat. March 13th, 1897 I rode with Whiteturkey and his wife, a Sac woman who can talk English, to the town of Tecumseh for the purpose of getting my daily paper, the *Kansas City Journal*, and for attending the Teachers' County Association of Pottawatomie Co. I attended the social meeting in the morning after 10 A.M., and heard some talk about the course of study, that I was already familiar with. But still it proved of help to me, to know that others were pursuing the same course as I myself. Mrs. Green spoke in the Association in the evening at the High School Building in Tecumseh. She teaches a rural school, I believe. Mr. McKinnis was president of the Association, and is quite a fine speaker. Supt. Cooley is a fine man also, and has recently been appointed a member of the Territorial Board by Gov. Renfrow. I told him yesterday March 13th, that I wanted to try at the Territorial Normal Institute for a Five-year Territorial Certificate; if I succeed well; if I fail, it can be no worse for me. Supt. Cooley said that the Annual Normal Institute was the place to prepare teachers for their work; that every teacher in the county ought to attend; that the A, B, C method of teaching the beginners in school was twenty-five years out of date; that if the teachers did not know any better method, to come to the Institute, and they would learn a better way; that the district school officers had unanimously adopted

the graded course of study framed by the Territorial Board of Education; that he was sorry to see that so few teachers were present; that he would recommend township associations to be held in the several towns monthly, and that all teachers should belong to the nearest one to them; that it was the plan in Minnesota, Wisconsin, and Iowa. They put my name down as a member of the County Teachers' Association of Pottawatomie Co. So I am a member of a county Teachers' Association and of the Territorial Teachers' Association 1896. This makes five associations that I have attended since Oct. 1896. The first two associations, no one paid any attention to me, but at the third, they asked me to speak. Sat. March 6th, 1897 Supt. Cooley lent me out of his office, a "Report of the Commissioner of Education for the year 1892-93," Vol. 1, containing parts I and II. "Washington, Government Printing Office, 1895." William T. Harris, Ph.D., Ll.D. is the present Commissioner of Education.

[page 192] [March 19, 1897] *In the School Room, Shawnee, Okla. Ter. 8:45 A.M. (Regulator Time).*

Thursday night—Wednesday night March 17th & 18, Ellen and I had a big fuss over her looking at Piney Wilson at the supper table. Cousin Sam finally offered to interfere, but I told him he had no right to do so, and besides Ellen had told me that he was no kin to her. Besides I told him, I would not allow any body to interfere. I dared him to interfere. He might have actually interfered however, but the old man would not let him. Ellen Shawnee went home this morning. She was here from 9:00 to 9:35 A.M. The train came promptly at 10:10. Ellen said that she hated to go at the very last, and she kissed me three or four times, and told me three or four times to send the money for her to come home on.

At 10:30 A.M. today Mrs. Smith and her son, colored, came to the school house, and wanted me to get them some corn and hay, on the score that I owed Mr. Smith $2.50 cents for making boards for that house on my lower place. They said that Henry Carter had married. He married a Smith girl I understand. Mr. J. C. Chrisney, merchant here in Shawnee, refused to trust me for $1.25 cents' worth of corn and hay for Mrs. Smith and her son. The man who has the money is the man who gets the goods.

I thank the Lord that I am doing as well as I am. I have nearly paid all my debts. I have paid Carson Bros. every cent that I owe them. I have certainly come up. I have a house on my lower place, and a rough house on my upper place. I guess that Ellen Shawnee is at home now, and talking about everything up here. Mr. Thomas Berry advised me to raise chickens and sell eggs. He said I would make money at it. Ellen said that she was coming if I sent the money. Last night (March 18th, 1896 [1897], she wanted me to send $2 to her at Wewoka, Ind. Ter., and besides that to save some money for her up here. She wants me to buy her a rocking chair.

At the Annual School Meeting in June 1897, by the grace of God, I must try to secure the Smith School in Oklahoma County again. It will probably be a school to last eight or nine months. I lost money by losing the school above Choctaw City. My average pay here is [in] Shawnee is $26.39 a month. My average pay a month last year was $28.20 cts. I have received in money for teaching nine months in Oklahoma Territory $246.55 cts., an average of $27.40 cents a month. Only two months during the nine was my warrant worth its face value. I have lost by reason of discount in selling the warrants and in interest paid by myself, in the hope of saving my discount, the sum of $43.45, nearly two month's salary out of the nine. This speaks of a sad financial condition. The last four years I have received off of my upper place $53.30 cents; this is what [*page 193*] I can actually remember. No doubt that are some few things that I can not recall at present. By teaching I have earned in warrants in 9 months the sum of $290.00, an average of $32.23 cents a month. During the last two years my place has brought me $39.70 cents. So far in two years I have received from both sources $286.25. John Spybuck paid me $11.50 cts. This swells the sum to $297.75.

I earned very little money in 1893 and 1894. I earned $15 at the brickyard of Mr. Cuppy and $67 as a flag-man for the surveyors in the Kickapoo country. This makes $82. This was during the panic that began in Wall Street, New York city and spread throughout the United States. I have seen some very hard times financially during 1893-97. Since I have been teaching school my financial condition has decidedly improved: blessing be to the Lord God Almighty and my Lord Jesus Christ.

[*moved from middle of page 194*]

Sat. March 20th, 1897
I went to Tecumseh and received the mail out of the office and my papers from Mr. Johnson the grocer just east of S. J. Scott's store the next door. Read Pres. McKinley's message, which is short, and only about revenues. I went to Mrs. Carter's when I first reached town and she let me a have tape line a yard long, so we could measure a rope to measure the land broken on my lower place. From here I went up town and received the papers. Thence I walked all the way down to my lower place and reached there just as Mr. Henry Carter was eating dinner. He had me eat dinner. The house was large inside and had a good roof; at least Henry assured me that it did not leak. We found the land we measured to contain 15.7 acres, near 16 acres. There is

from 27 to 30 acres already broken out on the place, and Mr. Carter was still breaking when I came away. Came back thence to Mrs. Carter's and found that she had gone up town, but left the tape line with the children. Thence I came home and found Mr. Dunjee had come down from Choctaw City.

Sunday March 21st, 1897 (1:10 P.M., by my Waterbury Clock).
    Today after breakfast and shortly before 9 A.M., leaving Mr. J. W. Dunjee, of Choctaw City here, I went over to the church near the Mission. On the road near the church, and a little north of Teacher's Kickapoo School House, I was stooping down and with my knife cleaning off the lower end of my pants and rolling them up, when presently I heard a short [shot] apparently north of me, and I immediately looked up a saw a fellow on horseback just a little north of the north line of the cemetery riding rapidly a large horse toward my direction. I thought it must be a drunk man shooting along the roads, and so I did not keep on north to [the?] corner to go east to the church, but turned east under the wire fence, and came in by Dr. Hartley's barn and by his house. The fellow rode up to the corner and turned in toward Dr. Hartley's, and when I arrived at the church I found him and Mrs. Hartley in the church. After salutation Mrs. Hartley asked if I heard a shot. I told her, Yes, and the bullet came pretty close to me too. She said that the young fellow had said that he guessed it was I shooting. I told her, No. She said that she did not think that I would be shooting around on Sunday. Mrs. Hartley soon left and went over to the house, to get her book, she said. I asked the boy where he lived, and he said at Mr. Hutchinson's. I told him, Yes, I know Mr. Hutchinson. He said that he saw me pass his place every morning, and that I went to Shawnee. I told him, Yes. Mrs. Bourbonnais and a little girl soon came in. She asked me how the folks were. I told her they were all well. She asked me why I did not bring my lady along with me. I told her that my lady had gone down home. She asked me if I had my land opened out. I told her, Yes. She asked me if I was going to farm. I told her, No: that I had leased out all my land last year. This young fellow, Hutchinson, heard all these things.

[page 194] Sunday March 21st, 1897 (Continued, now 1:35 P.M. by the Waterbury Clock.)
    Piney Wilson went away riding this morning, giving out that he was going to Shawnee to see his girl, or it may be would go to Tecumseh, and thence over to Shawnee. At this writing he has not returned. It appears that he asked Mrs. Garrett whether Ellen went into the kitchen or not. She told him that he was in there and ought to know. I went to hunt the horses at 6 A.M.

Friday March 19th, 1897, and when I came back and looked at the clock it was 6:30 A.M. As I came up to the lot I saw Piney go on to [the] porch and go into the house, but the next I know I saw Ellen out of doors, standing and looking at me, as if she did not know what to do. Presently she went in the house, and went upstairs and I could see her looking out at me from the window. When I reached the house, I went to the kitchen door and knocked, and Piney started to open it but I left. When he went in the house instead of coming out the same way he came in, he went out through Mrs. Garrett's room, and around back into the dining room and thence into the kitchen. The women folks say that some little time after I went out, some one else went out. This must have been Ellen.

Ellen says she went out to see if I was coming with the horses, and that she went out after Piney came into the house. But I would have seen her if this was the case. It is certain that no one was up except Piney and Ellen and they were both out of doors when I came.

[Sat. Mar. 20th was removed from here.]

(Thursday [Wednesday] March 24th 1897, 8:35 by the clock)

I borrowed a dollar from Mr. William Cooley and went over to the depot and bought an express money order to Mrs. Ellen Shawnee at Wewoka, Ind. Ter. I have now borrowed $2 from Mr. Cooley, and I have to pay him $2.25 cts. for the $2. Every cent of this two dollars [page 195] has been ~~bough~~ spent for my darling Ellen. The money order cost 5 cents, and I bought two small oranges for her with the nickel. I told her to come Thursday, and that I would be at the depot for her Thursday. She will surely [arrive?] at that time. So I shall see my Ellen tomorrow. We may quarrel some, but I still love her.

About 6:30 P.M. Wednesday March 24th 1897.

I have just arrived at home. Mrs. Garrett and Julia both said that Ellen was very anxious to get back home; that Mrs. Lizzie Bowleg and Ellen's father had both got after her; that Ellen had learned her lesson on this trip, and that she would stay home from this time on. They both said that the girl's folks do not treat her the same before marriage as afterwards; that they would tell Ellen that she had a husband. Rules.
1. Attend church and Sabbath School every Sunday, without fail, and take your family along. When has my darling Ellen heard a good sermon? She asked me to take her to church once or twice.
2. Associate with those that are better than yourself. Avoid evil company of all kinds. The company of the saints of

Jesus Christ, the Christians, is the very best company, and this is during the most solemn exercises of the Worship of God Almighty through Jesus Christ.

3. We choose our associates, but sometimes they are forced upon us by father or mother or step-mother or some other such person. But under the most adverse circumstances we can seek the company of the most Christian people, even if we have to travel miles and miles to do so.
4. Dr. and Mrs. Hartley and such like persons are the ones to seek. This is par excellence good company. Both are well educated in letters, and are well graded also in the school of Jesus Christ. Religious people are the ones you should see and ask them to pray you and for you and your darling Ellen.
5. Be honest towards God; violate none of his laws.
6. Quarrel not with your wife, even though wronged or provoked. Action, not words, is what tells in all cases.
7. Always consult the advise [sic] of others and follow it, because your own judgment is sometimes the result of bitter adverse feeling only.

March 25 1897.

Piney Wilson was sitting around the stove in the log house. This is the first time I noticed his doing this. I believe that Piney did this in anticipation of Ellen's coming home. I thought so yesterday March 25th, 1897.

[Friday, March 26, 1897]

Last night March 25th, 1897 I started with Julia's team after Ellen. I arrived at the depot just as the train rolled in. But I had to drive up and tie the horses, and for this delay I did not see Ellen get off of the train. On the way home we went by Dr. and Mrs. Hartley's and asked them to pray for us. Ellen talked a great deal about the devil on the way there and did not want to go. When I went to help her down to go into the house, she refused. But on my going in, she soon followed. Mrs. Hartley first prayed for Ellen and then Dr. Hartley. On the way home Ellen tried to excuse her unwillingness to going there. She said that I did not tell her what we were going there for. Dr. Hartley told me not to command, but simply request my wife to do so and so. [*page 196*] We reached home late about 11 P.M., I judge, but it was about half-past ten or thereabout when we left the Dr.'s for home. They asked Ellen to pray, but she did not do so.

This morning March 26, 1897

Piney hurried and made a fire in the kitchen, and waked Mrs. Garrett up. She told me she was asleep until he waked her. Then he came in and persistently sat by the stove in the room below my room, where Ellen would have to pass. The theater of his actions hereafter is to be the log house. He spoke to me but I did not speak to him. This is written March 26, 1897. 8:45 P.M. Piney was talking to the old man about the mountains and the bears and robbers in the mountains. This old man listened attentively, it seems.

Sunday Piney Wilson went off about 9 A.M. and never came back any more until night. He showed me one note from Miss Lydia Jackson, declining his company.

[moved from page 219] [March 26, 1897]
Sakea[. . .]wi, kanihe eitikebekwieaka sesakewi could not wait for me to go and get the can. This March 26, 1897, This happened Thursday night March 25th, 1897.

[moved from page 36, top of page]
[March 29, 1897] Death Roll with Dates.
1. Mrs. Logan died January 14th 1892.
2. Samuel Charley died Friday morning January 29th 1892, at about four o'clock A.M. The cocks were crowing.
3. Nellie Greengrass (Skē-pàh-kàh'-kàm-sē) died January 23rd 1891 on Little River. She was a round-footed woman. Patakobetawekwa, the Shawnee would say. Her father's name in Shawnee was Tĕ-kàh'-màth-kàh-kàh. She was the wife of Tàh-pĕă-sĕ'-kàh, or Jim Doctor John.
4. Washington Bruno was killed by the marshals Feb. 2nd 1892.
5. Mrs. Lŏktō Hàhjō, Kō-tàh'-pĕă-sĕ, died Feb. 5th 1892.
6. Emma Johnson, wife of Seargent Ellis, died late in the evening Feb. 24th 1892.
7. Mexican Wilson, or Spanish Wilson, died Saturday morning about 8 o'clock A.M. Dec. 29th 1894. He is believed by some to have died from the effects of a gunshot wound received during the war from a drunken seargent one Pĭ'-soú-wàh.
8. Anthony Bourbonnais died Dec. 15th 1891.
9. The wife of Big Jim, Làh-wē-pĕă, a sister of Jackson Clark, died August 6th 1891.
10. Sallie Forman died in the Creek Nation, at the house of Sam Wilson about March 1st, 1895. Charley Beaver is the authority for this statement.
11. Katie Decker's little baby girl died this morning March 29th 1897. Early just at day-break.

[moved from page 38] Monday March 29th, 1897 (at night 8 or 9 P.M. by guess).

Yesterday I staid home all day at Ellen's request. In the afternoon I was glad that I staid, for the rain came up and lasted all evening, all night, and up about 10 o'clock A.M. on Monday. Mrs. Julia Shawnee had a baby Sunday morning; the baby girl began to cry at 5:10 A.M. Sunday morning March 28th, 1897. – I had a muddy, sloppy time going to the school house this morning I spent $1.59 cts as follows:– Umbrella 85 cts; Matches 5cts; Colored Tissue Paper .05 cts and Writing Pens 5 cts; Stamps 4 cts; 1 Can of Tomatoes 13 cts; 1 Can of Oysters 10 cts; Candy 3 cts.; Broom, 15 cts.; Stamps 4 cts.; to George Apperson for book 10 cts.

[*April 3, 1897*]
   –(Saturday April 2nd, 1897 fire was made in the kitchen in the cook stove some few minutes before 6:30 A.M. This is written 6:40 A.M. 4/3/1897.)

Saturday April 3rd, 1897. 6:40 A.M.
   Julia Shawnee is still in bed and the old man has not yet got up out of bed. (April 3rd, 1897) Ellen Shawnee said that Mrs. Garrett was going home today. Last night I went to sleep at 10 o'clock P.M., and did not wake until 3:30 A.M. this morning. I went to Prayer Meeting last night at the church near the Mission, where I am a member. I have staid away from the meetings so long, and the effects upon me are so dire in their consequences, that I must attend church regularly. Ellen says that she has not spoken one word to Piney. But I must not trust Ellen; she has told me so many stories that I can not believe every thing she says. Ellen has told me this before, and it did not prove to be true.

Wednesday April 7th, 1897.
   I wrote ~~reg~~ letters to the College of Emporia, Emporia, Kansas, and also to the [*Emporia*] *Republican*, [*Emporia*] *Gazette*, and [*Emporia*] *Times*, of the same city, asking for a sample copies of the same. I wrote a letter to Miss Olive Stubblefield, Co. Supt. of Lincoln County. I want to secure a colored school to teach in Lincoln Co. after April 23rd, 1897. I learned from Mr. William Cooley, colored, that there are two colored schools up there needing teachers. Monday night April 5th, 1897 I staid over night in the city of Shawnee in the house of Mr. and Mrs. Cooley, colored. I attended the meeting of the Board of Education. I was glad that I attended, for I learned about the bonds. It was expected that they would be sold in six weeks. The warrants of the Board, it was declared, in their lenghty Resolution, are selling at a discount. The bonds are made payable in gold coin of the United States. It was ordered that

the Methodists and Baptists hold meetings on alternate Sundays, and that the Pres. of the Board keep the key of the same. They agreed not to injure any thing and to keep the house clean.

Sat. April 10th, 1897. (9:42 A. M. by the clock)
    Last night Friday April 9th, 1897 I went around to Prayer Meeting, carrying my clock, dinner bucket, and umbrella, which I left at the Mission residence, Mrs. Hartley and a young girl putting them away in the room for me. I did not go in. But receiving the keys from Mrs. Hartley, I went over to the church just across [*page 39*] (Sat. Apr. 10th, 1897.) the road and read in Adam's Clark's Commentary, and also built a fire in the stove. Mrs. Hartley came over after a time and rang the bell. I lighted both lamps, but not at the same time. The meeting was opened with a Bible Reading followed by a prayer by the same. The Lesson was "Overcoming Evil with Good." I read Mat 5:8-10. Others read other passages. The meeting held an hour or a little more. The impression upon my mind and heart was good. It took me an hour to walk home from 8:45 P.M. to 9:45 P.M. It was nice moon light and the stars shone bright. Among those present at this meeting were Miss Massillon, a teacher at the Mission, Mrs. Ella Hartley, Eva Shawnee, Josephine Barone, and many boys and girls. Mrs. Hartley said that Dr. Hartley has taken Mr. Edward Wistar a friend from Philadelphia, Pennsylvania, first to the Kickpoo Mission and then on up to the Iowas. Rev. William Neal is to hold a series of meetings in Tecumseh next week. - A city election was held in Shawnee Tuesday April 6th, 1897, for mayor, council-men, and members of the Board of Education, and for other officers. The Democrats carried the election.

Sunday April 18th 1897. (6:26 A.M. by the clock.).
    Yesterday I went to the Monthly meeting, held in the church building near the mission. Mrs. Rachel Kirk, Mrs. Mary Bourbonnais, Mrs. L. Ella Hartley. Dr. G. N. Hartley, Rev. William Neal, and others, in all about 21 names. Mr. Carson was there. A man shook hands with me whom I knew not, but he is a friend. Rev. J. Largent was there. The Monthly Meeting donated $5 towards the traveling expenses of Rev. Wm Neal, of Emporia, Kansas. Thence I went to Shawnee and sold my last warrant for $30 in gold coin, in 6 five dollar pieces. I immediately exchanged $5 in gold for $5 in silver. I bought a pair of pants for $3; shoes for $1.50 cts; two pairs of stockings for little darling Ellen 25 cts.; I lent Cegar 25 cents to pay box rent with and he promised to pay me in return. I brought pants, shoes, and meat home on foot, and went back late in the evening and brought my horse home at night. I also bought Apples 5 cents, Pork 15 cts; Beef 25 cts, and paid a debt of 5 cents for

meat that I received some days before. I brought the little clock home on horseback on Ellen's account. She likes to have the little clock on the table, ticking away, upstairs here, where we are staying. William Shawnee told us we could live here until we had finished our own house. – Today Sunday April 18th, 1897 I rode horseback to Sunday school and church. I arrived there too late for the Sabbath School proper. Miss Brice was very respectful, saying "Good morning, Mr. Shawnee." She afterwards gave me a card, and at the dismissal she invited me to take dinner over at the Mission. I said, No, thank you, but I will visit the school next week. Miss Massillon also was present to-day. Miss Brice played on the organ.

Tuesday April 20th, 1897. (Night).

Ellen and I had a racket this evening on account of some snappish words that Ellen said to Julia; and Ellen used some blackguard expressions, such as you can go to the devil, to us. But when I began to write this, Ellen began to kiss and fondle me, and we mutually forgave each other. Ellen traded at some stores in Shawnee, and bought a nice hat for 40 cents; also a pair of slippers for $1.25 cents. Ellen has gone down stairs now, and said that she was not going to fix my supper. I told her that I did not care. Soon after she says that she will bring my supper upstairs to me. – I have three days more to teach yet. Then my second school in Oklahoma will have passed into history. I must not rest until I have contracted to teach my third school in Oklahoma. The sooner the contract is drawn up the better[.]

[page 197] Tuesday April 20th, 1897.

The grass is green, and the trees have leaves upon them. All the peach trees on my upper place have peaches on them except one. Only one apple tree has blooms upon it. One green flag had a blue bloom on it. Mr. Sexton said some time ago that he would plant cotton seed April 15th 1897, but he did not do so. Now he has said that he will plant Thursday April 22nd, 1897, just one month after the date first chosen. I realized money from teaching in Oklahoma as follows: 1895-96. First Month $27; 2nd Mo. $27; 3rd Mo. $27; 4th Mo. $30; 5th Month $30. Total $141. – 1896-97, First Mo. $25.80; 2nd Mo. $28.50; 3rd Mo. $25.00; 4th Mo. $26.25; 5th Mo. $31.50; 6th Mo. $30 – Total $167.05. In two years $308.05 cts; this was earned for eleven months work in teaching.

Saturday April 24th, 1897 (8:40 A.M.) by the clock.

Last night April the 23rd, 1897, we held an exhibition in the school house. Three little white girls asked my permission to come, and I told them to come. They came. It was a free exhibition, as the one was above Choctaw City. The people last night expressed their willingness that I be their teacher next term. The exhibition consisted of recreations, dialogues, songs, and addresses by Mrs. Minnie Cooley and Rev. Mr. Springer, the latter a full blooded negro, evidently. It appears that I will teach this same school again another year. Yesterday April 23rd, 1897 I received in the mail a catalogue of the College of Emporia, Emporia, Kansas. Supt. Miller said that he would come to my exhibition, but he did not come. The trees are full of green leaves, and there are plenty of flowers. Garden vegetables are being sold, such as onions.

Monday April 26th, 1897 (6:45 A.M.)

The sun is high up in the sky. I feel well this morning. Ellen my dear wife is growing more and more like what I would wish her to be. 9:20 P.M. Piney and Julia Shawnee were down stairs talking so low, that we could not hear them. After Piney left, the old lady Wilson came in and talked to Julia.

Friday April 30th, 1897 (7:40 P.M. by the clock)

I visited the Shawnee Mission school where Miss Brice, of Omaha, Nebraska, and Miss Kessel, of South Dakota, and Miss Massillon, of Illinois, are teaching. They are certainly good teachers. Eva Shawnee is in the Revolutionary War in the United States history. Her class is memorizing the Declaration of Independence. I have learned some things today in the school-room that will help me in my work. Ellen is mad here when I come home and has thrown the papers on the floor.

Chapter 9

Living on His Own
May 1, 1897—November 28, 1897

In May 1897, Shawnee and Ellen still lived at Shawnee's father's home. Shawnee was disillusioned with his marriage because Ellen and Piney Wilson, Ellen's former boyfriend who was also staying there, paid too much attention to each other. In June 1897 Shawnee rented a house and moved to Tecumseh where he and Ellen had several neighbors. Ellen visited Mrs. Harris, Mrs. Carter, and Mrs. Gunter, who was white. In August Shawnee and Ellen went to live at David Alford's home while David attended Big Jim's war dance. Shawnee helped David Alford on his farm. He and Ellen were still living with David and Mamie Alford in early September. Ellen was pregnant, with the baby due in late November 1897.

    Shawnee's life continued much in the same vein as before between May 1, 1897, and November 28, 1897. He continued to stay away from church because of Ellen. He continued to rent his land to tenant farmers. He farmed. He mingled with his friends of all races. Broke, he could not get credit from anyone. He visited the new Indian Agent Lee Patrick.

[*May 1, 1897*]

The old man William Shawnee and I had a fuss this morning May 1st, 1897, over his proposition to haul me a barrel of water. I told him that the water was the cause of us being sick with chills and fever and he said that I was lazy the reason I did not haul the water.

[*page 198*] (*May 1st, 1897. 10:15 A.M.*)

I need to work on the school records, and avoid all fusses with every body. The remedy is to have a home on my own land, and then I can control whatever comes into it. Undesirable persons will not be admitted, nor will I feed the whole country, for I can not afford to do so even though I had the money. I have not made out any school reports yet, and this is Saturday May 1st, 1897. I must make them out. If a person will not promise you any thing in writing, it is not worth while to accept it. I can not go on taking a paper at Mr. Johnson's unless they allow for the amount that I have already overpaid them.

Wednesday May 5th, 1897 (8:33 P.M. by the clock).

Grass is now five or six inches high. People are planting cotton. Mr. Sexton has about 16 acres of cotton planted on my place up to date. He has about eight or nine acres more to plant. Monday May 3rd, 1897 I was at the meeting of the Board of Education in the city of Shawnee and staid all night at Mr. William Cooley's in consequence. Mr. Sanders, an aged man, was elected president, and another man whose name I have forgotten was elected vice president ~~clerk~~, and Mr. Portis was elected clerk. Section 16, in part, was ordered attached to the city for school purposes. I forget the exact boundaries of this attached territory. 38 names were on the petition. Sat. May 8th, 1897 was appointed the time for electing the Supt. and the teachers. It was desired that the teachers put in their application. I put my application, accompanied by my certificate, Tuesday May 4th, 1897. I handed it to the new clerk Mr. Portis. Mr. Cooley told his wife to put in an application for the school. I do not think this is fair, but he seems to think that it is. She either means to try to secure the school, or she does not. It is estimated that the latest assessed valuation in Shawnee would be $300,000. It was said that it would take $5,500 to run the schools. Warrants are now at par. They were said to be so Monday May 3rd, at the school meeting. It was the county tax that did this after the bonds were issued. One member of the Board told me that my warrants would not be paid for a year, and yet he was anxious to buy my warrants. I paid $5 for the use of $30 for two weeks. But I am a wiser man by reason of this experience. It has taught me a good lesson. I should know just what funds are in the county treasury awaiting the call of the Treasurer of the Board of Education. It takes time for the inexperienced person to know all the tricks in trade. The Treasurer of the School Board has over $70 now in the Treasury.

Friday May 7th, 1897. (about 4 P.M. guessed)

I should have taught school in the fall of 1893-4, and 94-95. Both years I earned only a very little money. I earned $67 in the Kickapoo country, and worked [*page 199*] over fifty days for Jennie Cegar, John Spybuck, Chosa Starr, and Mammie Alford. They did not pay me $1 for these services. They could have paid me a few dollars, but they would rather repudiate their debts. Mr. Charley Beaver is also a bad debtor, for he owes me 50 cts. that I never expect to get. Mr. William Shawnee is also a bad paymaster to me, but he is very careful to pay others not members of his family. I can earn more money teaching school than I can in any other way. For the last two years I have earned $360 in warrants, an average of $180 a year in warrants. Since these warrants are depreciated, they do not bring me their face value. If I had managed a little more carefully I could have saved some of that $42.95 cts. that I lost. I could have received the full amount on my last warrant. The Treasurer of the Board of Education neglected to receive the taxes from the county treasurer until the 13th or 14th of April 1897. On April 12th, 1897 he had no funds to pay my warrant; on the 14th of April he received over $2000 from the county treasurer and paid all warrants outstanding. I did not dream that there were funds in the county treasury due the Treasurer of the Board of Education in Shawnee. At all the Board meetings it was never referred to. March 27th 1897 Mr. C. J. Benson told me that he thought I would get a full amount on my warrants in three months. He was mistaken in this, for I could have received the full amount in less than one month from the time he spoke, namely, April 14th, 1897. I had forgotten that taxes were due the third Monday in March, that is, March 15th, 1897. The treasurer of the Board of education had the money April 14th, 1897, even if he did not have it before that time. It appears that the Board of education in the city of Shawnee has the following sources of deriving money: 1. The Sale of Bonds, that is, borrowing money. 2. Taxes received from the Treasurer of the county. 3. The Sale of Lots. 4. Tuition paid by non-resident pupils or even residents. 5. Donations. I must be careful hereafter to give no credit to the statement of any member even of the Board of Education. Even Mr. Johnson the treasurer of the Board once refused to buy my warrants with a remark that the bonds might hang fire and not be sold. Mr. Stelle (Steele) the president of the Board for the year 1896-7 wanted to buy my warrant (April) but he did not want to pay me but $28 for it. By this means he would have gained $7 by waiting only a few days. Of course this was too much.

It would be a good habit to find out by personal inspection of the books in the hands of the County Clerk or County Treasurer, and see the assessed valuation of the District, the amount of school taxe[s] already on hand belonging to the District in which you are teaching. You can consult the law, and find out just when all taxes are to be fully paid in. There is no doubt that some (a large part) of the business of the Board of Education is transacted at neither the regular nor at any called meeting of the Board. There were two (See p. 204) [*page "204" written in the left margin—i.e., continued on page 204*]

[*page 204*] Board meetings that I did not attend because of my dear little Ellen. One member of the Board said that I would receive $35 for my warrants in two months, another said that I would receive the full amount sometime in January. My experience has been that the statements of any or all members of the Board are absolutely unreliable. In 1895-96 I had to sell my warrants at a discount of $3 on $30 in warrants, when one member of the Board told me that there was $70 in the Treasury for me. Actually unless men are interested to know the facts, they merely go on guesses and what they think.

I have found that the credit business does not pay. I owe more than I pay myself. The only remedy is make it a point of honor and duty to pay your debts. When I go to work for a man, on the strength of a contract between us either written or verbal, I become his creditor and he becomes a debtor to me. The men who do not pay a merchant break him up. A merchant has a hard time with debtors. I must pay my debts even though it takes the last cent I have. O Lord help me pay every debt that I owe. I must do right tho the heavens fall. The remedy is not to credit any body. Do not trust a man one cent unless you know that he has paid you in time past. John King borrowed $100 at the bank, and William Shawnee signed the note with him. I signed a note for Charley Beaver, and he had a very hard time paying it. The banker threatened to sue us both for the debt. Go on no man's note. Business is business; why should I pay money that another man has blowed in. Confidence is right and proper, but you must be sure who is trustworthy. Confidence is often betrayed in this lower world of ours.

I owe this day as follows: to John King $1.80 cts; to *Christian Nation*, New York City $8.50 cts; to Houghton and Upp, Purcell, Indian Territory, $3.00 with interest, Total $13.30 cts. There is due me as follows: From Julia Shawnee, $2.00. From Henry Carter $2.00. From Cegar, a Shawnee Indian 25 cts. From Mr. Sexton $6.50 cts. From Mr. Wray, a white man who rented the east half of my field in 1896, 5 day's work or $5. From John Spybuck 50 cts. From Joe Billy 25 cts. ~~From~~ Total $16.50. In this I have not counted the debts due me from Jennie Cegar, Mammie Spybuck, John Spybuck, and Chosa Star, for over 50 day's work and loss of time, for which I never expect to receive one cent. I have lost several dollars on account of bad debtors not paying their debts. It would be better not to work for or trust such people, or in fact any people. We all waste our money the reason we are compelled to go in debt. You can not expect a man who is an adulterer, or a liar, or a drunkard, or who is morally vicious in any respect to pay his just debts. In Sept. and Oct. 1895 I was very much dejected and cast down. My Financial condition was deplorable. I did not have one cent of money, and felt so bad and very discouraged. This was due to profligate expenditures in times before [page 205] 5:53 P.M. that when I did have money, I should have built a house, bought a cook stove, and a bedstead, chairs, and a table, and everything, and even bought a team and wagon. If I had done these things, I would not have suffered as I did. If I had taught school in 1893-94, and 94-95, I would not have suffered as I did in any way. I could have taught school in 1892 instead of working up at Choctaw City, Oklahoma Ter. Here I learned things that opened my eyes. Mr. Cuppy told [me] that either Tecumseh would be a large city or some other city close to Tecumseh, Okla., Ter.

Sunday May 16th, 1897, 5:18 P.M. by the clock. At the home of William Shawnee in the room upstairs, in company with my dear wife Ellen Shawnee.

Ellen and I have just come back from the place leased to Mr. Saxton this year. Every peach tree except one has peaches on it. On some the fruit is quite large. We both believe that some of the peaches will ripen in June, that is, next month. One apple tree bloomed out this year, but I do not know whether there are any apples on it or not. I only regret that I did not set out more fruit trees since 1893. Jan 1st, 1893 I began to improve my upper place in good earnest. I carried posts on my back[.]

I told Ellen Shawnee that she could write her diary in the other book like this. I told her she could write what she was doing, how she spent her money, on what accounts she received money. I further told Ellen dear that in a few years we could not even tell where we were without consulting the books. Ellen said that I would become angry and tear what she had written out of the book, but I assured her that I would not do so. She begins her writing on page 68 today.—Ellen sat down after we came back, and lovingly wrote as follows on her slate: "Shawnee, Okla. May 16, 1897. Mr. William E. Shawnee, My dear Husband: - I love you with all of my heart. I will love you until my eyes close for death. I hope to treat you right all my life. I and the baby want to go off some time if I and the baby live. Your true wife. Ellen Shawnee." Ellen wrote this while I was gone after a bucket of water. I think it is so beautiful. It is 6:00 P.M. but I am still writing, and dear Ellen is writing at the same table as me. Monday May 10th, 1897 I left Ellen, without breakfast, being somewhat vexed, and walked over northwest about 14 miles to the house of Mr. Norris, a good Baptist church member, who is over 50 years old, yet has never been married. He and I slept in the same bed together, and talked about various matters. When I first came to the house of Mr. Norris [he?] was not home, and so I turned south to the house of a colored man named Mr. Johnson, I believe. He was glad to see me, and the women soon prepared dinner for me. It was bread, eggs fried, and bacon, but it was good, since I was hungry. The next day Tuesday May 11th, 1897 I went from Mr. Norris's to Mr. J. J. Johnson's three miles west or northwest of Choctaw *City*. Passed through the south part of Choctaw City north of the [*page 206*] depot. I was very tired after my long walk. I had no dinner, but they gave me supper, and made me at home. I slept down in the cellar under the house, but I had only one quilt to cover with. – Wednesday May 12th 1897 I spent the whole day at the house of Mr. J. W. Dunjee. The normal school was out and Mr. Randolph had gone to Oklahoma City. I believe they said it was out Friday May 7th, 1897. Miss Eliza Cooper was teaching the public colored school which is located about 100 yards northwest from the Choctaw Normal School. Miss Drusilla Dunjee and Miss Ella Dunjee were both present. Drusilla gave me the following addresses of paper[s] she takes. "The Child-Study Monthly, Chicago, Illinois. $1 a year, Care Baker and Barrett, Publishers." "Educational Foundations, Chicago, Illinois, $1 a year. E. L. Kellogg and Co. New York City." "Our Times, E. L. Kellogg and Co. New York City, $1 a year.["] Miss Drusilla said that she had kept disorder out of her school by giving the pupils something to do in the shape of busy work; that beginners in school should learn script first, and that they would pass more easily from script reading to print than from print reading to script; that she had taught four years in Oklahoma City as follows: The first year 9 months at $60 a month; the second year 9 months at $55 a month; the third year 8 months at $50 a month; the fourth year 6 months at $45 a month. This makes $1705 that she earned in warrants in the last four years. Mr. J. J. Johnson said that Drusilla was investing her money into houses and lots in Oklahoma City. I know that Ella Dunjee has earned at least $125 in warrants, but perhaps more. This makes $1830 that these two girls have brought into the family. – I read in the excellent library of Mr.

Dunjee, a great part of the time alone, since Drusilla and Ella were out of doors. They have heard that I was married and teased me about my wife. I took dinner and supper at Mr. Dunjee's. Mr. Dunjee took me around and showed me his orchard. His peach trees are bearing nicely, and he has set out a great many more trees than I have. He has a goodly number of apricot trees. Ella still borrowed Scott's *History of the United States* from me. I have lost Harvey's Grammar. I staid all night at Mr. J. J. Johnson's, and slept in the same bed as I did the night before. – Thursday May 13th, 1897. Having received my Bible Concordance, Dictionary, Psychology, and Mental Arithmetic, I started for the Norris settlement, bearing a letter J. J. Johnson sent me to Mrs. Alice Herd. J. J. had opened the letter, supposing it might be something urgent, but as it was not he waited until he had a chance to send it by me. I arrived at Mr. Herd's that evening, and [text ends here]

[page 224] [The following was inserted by Ellen Shawnee.]

Saturday May 1 1897 5 P.M. o' clock
[. . . my] carter come out and brought his wife with him he ask for you mr shawnee I told him he went to town
      May 1 1897 640
         My dearest friend
            May (6:40 PM[ )]

Monday May 3 1897
Mr shawnee i wont Burn up any more thing any more times I wont.

Monday May 3 1897
mr willie shawnee dearest Little husband I wont Burn any more things again [or?] quarrel with you any more I will try and keep your word.
                    I Promised you to keep
      Mrs Ellen shawnee
your & my words and be [a] good girl and mind you to and be true to you too Ellen Shawnee

Thursday May 27th 1897. 8:40 P.M.
    It rained to-day between 12M and 3 P.M. I took dinner at the Carter's and we talked about various matters. The Dutchman did not want the land of Joe Billy on Little River on any terms. I secured a few signers on my petition for the school in Tecumseh. I expect to be examined for a Teacher's Certificate in the c[. . .], [page 207] 1897. They [. . . ished] April 12 [. . .] up [. . .] the colored Territorial University at Langston, Okla. Ter. A diploma from its normal department is a

five-year certificate for the Territory. These frequent examinations by local boards are expensive and harassing to the teacher. – I have not earned a single dollar since my school was out since April 23rd, 1897. This is really too bad. I run here and there, but what do I earn? I read laws and statutes, but earn no money. From Nov. to Apr. I was earning money, but from May to Oct. what will I earn. Ten cents a day would be better than I am earning at present. Not a dollar comes in, but the dollars go out fast. But go ahead and do the best you can, trusting in God for every thing.

Sunday May 30th, 1897 9:15 A.M.
    I was getting ready to walk to Sunday School and Church today and would have gone, had it not been for my little Ellen. May 27, 28 and 29th, (3 x 24 hrs, or 72 hours) have been devoted absolutely to purity, but this displeases little Ellen so much that she has been angry all morning. When you deal with anyone even with the wife of your bosom, it must be before witnesses, that every word may be established. Because where there are only two parties, one generally denies every word almost that the other says.
    Friday and Saturday May 28th and 29th, 1897, I took the city examination in the city of Shawnee. This time it was the questions prepared by the Territorial Board that were used. I showed Prof. Ware my normal school diploma and my two county first-grade certificates.
    So far as I can remember I have only taken six written examinations as follows: (1) When I graduated at Maryville, Tennessee. (2) In Rhea Co. Tennessee, where I got a one-year certificate, which I have lost. (3) In 1893, for a County First Grade Certificate, which the Examining Committee lost, but of which I have a copy. (4) In 1896 for a County First Grade Certificate, which I still hold and which expires in 1899. (5) In 1896, for a city temporary certificate, which I delivered to Mr. Portis clerk of the Board of Education, along with my application. (6) In 1897 for a city first Grade certificate, which I have not yet secured. This is the second city examination that I have taken, but the first one wherein the questions prepared by the Territorial Board were used. – So far as I can remember these six examinations have occupied nine days of written work, and besides that many days of preparation.
    I wrote the following things in the examination room, with lead pencil, on paper, and copy them here, as follows:—
    "May 28th, 1897, in the room of the examinations, 8:55 A.M. If I could [attend?] the Normal School Teachers' Association at Milwaukee Wisconsin [*page 208*] [*first line and beginning of second line missing*] [. . .]ould only cos[t me?] about

$30 [. . .] did attend the Territorial Teacher's Association and the County Teacher's Association.

There are three white lady teachers here who talk a great deal, and I learn a great deal about school matters from them. They are pretty well posted. One said that Mensuration was hard, on account of the many rules. One said it was unsatisfactory to teach only five months in the year. One said that Professor Ware is coming in on the train. One said that if we fail, the dollar would just be thrown away. One said that she was so excited this morning that she could not eat breakfast. 9:05 A.M. more lady teachers have just come. They talk about things that are fresh to my mind, and I enjoy their conversation. They dread the Territorial questions, and perhaps well they may. I wish I had shaved last evening or this morning in the house of Mr. Cooley. One young white lady (from abroad) wrote to one other white lady in Shawnee to know when the teachers' examination would be. One says that we are the faithful ones, and that we would not have much opposition. They hire her on her Territorial Certificate; I wish I had a Territorial Certificate, one said. One said that Mr. McKinnis would not take the Examination, and that he had resigned his place as Principal. What does Mr. McKinnis intend to do. These young ladies are talking about their examination and other examinations, and are just full of school matters. One said that no teacher is more conscientious than Mr. Ware. I only regret that I have not shaved this morning or yesterday, but I will shave at noon if the Lord will. - Prof. Ware is to bring the Territorial Board's questions with him on the train. I have great chances and great opportunities, but what can I do but take advantage of them. I want to take every just, proper, and lawful advantage of every thing that can upbuild myself. - 9:22 A.M. (May 28th 1897) It is still raining a slow-falling rain.

Wednesday June 16th, 1897. 9:55 A.M.

I and Ellen fuss a great deal. If it was to do over again, I do not believe I would marry Ellen. She and the old man were smiling at each other this morning. The old man William Shawnee does not want Ellen to leave here evidently. I think I can get a house over in Tecumseh. Ellen is not right because she uses bad language and tells stories. *Sat. June 12th, 1897* the school board in Shawnee elected me to teach the colored school at $30 a month. The salary was little enough. But as the school begins in September, I agree to take it. I and Ellen made up again. Ellen is a good little girl to get along with. I have given Ellen the following things of mine to be hers: [. . .] two school [. . . ,] [*page* 209] two framed pictures, one lamp and a mug, 1 Zoology, 1 Physics, and one other book, 1 bed, and 1 trunk.

Thursday June 17th, 1897 (7:31 P.M. actual time)

    I and Ellen went to Tecumseh in the spring wagon, with Julia Shawnee's team, the black horse and the bay. On reaching town went first to Mrs. Carter's house, where Ellen descended and went with Mrs. Carter to look at the flowers. She presented Ellen a bouquet, and what a beautiful one it was, but it was small. We went to the mill and got 7 lbs of meal William Shawnee had left there, and paid 20 cts. toll therefore on his behalf. But he had sent the money by us. I tried to obtain credit from the Smith Bros. for some goods on time, and pledge my cotton in payment. But they were not doing exactly that kind of business, but were taking horses and cattle as pledges along with the cotton. But they felt that they had all that they could carry, since it required so many groceries to carry people. It is bad management that continues to afflict me to this day June 7th 1897. I have a wife Ellen, but no money to buy flour or meat for her to eat. I ought to buy in March or April 1000 lbs. of flour.

Monday June 21st, 1897

    I rented the Reeder house with my little darling and moved into it on account of the state of affairs, at the home of William Shawnee. That morning Piney Wilson turned his head aside when he saw that I saw him gazing at my wife. This is the third or fourth time he has done so. I made up my mind that I would stand him no longer. I can never advise with the hateful William Shawnee said to be my father for any good. My wife too was gazing at Piney as well as he at her. This she denies, but it is true, nevertheless. God help us to live.

Wednesday June 23rd, 1897, by Ellen's little clock, at the Reader [sic] house this is written.

    Although Ellen cried considerably Monday night June 21st, after we had moved, yet she is now cheerful and pleasant as can be. We have taken up at Clay's store over Six Dollars worth of goods, including provisions, and now Ellen is cheerful.

Wednesday June 30th, 1897. 8:10 A.M.

    Ellen and I have been living in Tecumseh over a week. At first we were hungry some, but Ellen is a good little girl. I have been hoeing cotton for the McFalls. My hands are sore and my arms tired. I have earned $2 since we have come in town. A little money will bring a great deal of provisions. I am glad that I am self-supporting; by God's kind care Ellen and I will live. Amen.

[page 210] *July 3rd, 1897, Saturday 8:06 A.M.*

Yesterday July 2nd, 1897 I mortgaged to Mr. Sam Clay my 1/4th interest in 17 acres of cotton on my upper place, the SW ¼ of the SE ¼ of Sec. 35, Township 10 N, Range [3?] [. . .]t I. M. [*Indian Meridian*] I also signed a note for Ten Dollars, payable Oct 2, 1897. Ellen is happy now since she has the following places to visit: Mrs. Harris, Mrs. Carter, and Mrs. Gunter, a white woman. I heard Mr. Clay say that my brother had come down to Shawnee on the train yesterday morning. It must be my brother George E. Shawnee. Ellen Shawnee and I are living in the town of Tecumseh, Okla. Ter. - This makes Ten Dollars more that my places have brought me in the last five years. Both of my places have heretofore brought me, as seen on p. 227, $61.30 cts. Ten Dollars more makes me $71.30 cents. This beats nothing, and it is surely better to own land than not to own it. Ellen is remarking that people are passing along the road to the celebration in great numbers. People—women—are dressed in white. Mrs. Carter went to Decatur, Texas, to attend the trial of her son George Henry, or Grant Carter, for murder. When he committed the murder he was under sentence for five years for burglary in a store. She went to Texas about Thursday June 24th, 1897.

[*July 3, 1897*] Papers for which I wish to subscribe some day, this being July 3rd, 1897, Saturday, 1:30 P.M.
1. *St. Paul Pioneer Press*, St. Paul Minnesota.
2. The *St. Louis Globe Democrat*, St. Louis Missouri.
3. *Minneapolis Tribune*, Minneapolis, Minnesota.
4. The *Albany Journal*, Albany, New York.
5. *Philadelphia record*, Philadelphia, Pennsylvania.
6. The *Chicago Tribune*, Chicago, Illinois.
7. The *New York Evening Post*, New York City, New York.
8. The *Buffalo Express*, Buffalo, New York.
9. The *New York Mail and Express*, New York City, New York.
10. The *Cincinnati Times-Star*, Cincinnati, Ohio.
11. The *Detroit Journal*, Detroit, Michigan.
12. The *Boston, Journal*, Boston, Massachusetts.
13. The *New York Tribune*, New York city, New York.
14. The *New York Sun*, New York city, New York.
15. The *Buffalo News*, Buffalo, New York.
16. The *Chicago Post*, Chicago, Illinois.
17. The *Philadelphia Inquirer*, Philadelphia, Pennsylvania.
18. The *Chicago Times-Herald*, Chicago, Illinois.
19. The *Chicago Inter-Ocean*, Chicago, Illinois.
20. The *Atlanta Journal*, Atlanta, Georgia.
21. The *New Orleans Picayune*, New Orleans, Louisiana.
22. The *Kansas City Star*, Kansas City, Missouri.
23. The *London Times*, London, England.
24. The *Pall Mall Gazette*, London, England.

25. The *Spector*, London, England.
26. The *Midland*, Omaha, Nebraska, or Chicago, Illinois.
27. The *Boston Pilot*, Boston, Massachusetts.
28. *Macmillian and Co.*, London, England.

Tuesday July 6th, 1897 (5:40 A.M.)
    Mrs. Irene Carter came back from Texas Sunday July 4th, 1897. She had gone through her son's trial, and she said that the court house was just packed. Her son Grant Carter, or George Henry, as he chooses to call himself, is charged with having killed the jailor and broke jail. The jailor was a white man. George Henry had been to Chicago and St. Louis and Atlanta, Georgia. He never would stay at home from boyhood. He ran away from home when he was about ten years old. His father, now dead, prophesied that he would reach a bad end; either the penitentiary or the gallows, but he has reached both. George will probably be hung down in Texas.

    It seems that I make bad business bargains—so many people owe me money that they never pay. Mr. Saxton owes me a debt that I can get only in work and that only by hard efforts. Mr. Wray owes me a debt that I can not get. Mr. Henry Carter owes me a debt that I can not get only by taking work of him. Cegar owes me 25 cts. that I can not get. Jennie Cegar owes me $9.50 cts. that I never will get. Mamie Spybuck owes me $10 I will never get. Chosa Star owes me $10 I will never get. John Spybuck owes me $10.50 that I will never get. Charlie Beaver owes me 50 cts. that I will never get. Several other debts are due me that I can not get a cent of. What is the remedy for all this? Evidently trust no one except upon a note secured by a mortgage. There is so much deceit and deception in the world that one can not trust everybody. - The religion of Jesus Christ requires [*page 211*] that a man pay his honest debts. A man can not willfully neglect to pay his debts and be a Christian. "Render to all their dues," Romans 13:7 is God's command, and it must be obeyed, or we can not please God. As long as we defraud our neighbors out of their property by neglecting or refusing to pay their debts, we can not go to heaven. How many nominal Christians slight their debts; but such are sinning every day.

    What remedy shall I employ to secure the payment of debts owing to me? First, take a note secured by a mortgage. Second, take written contracts as much as possible attested by two witnesses, so as to clear all doubt in regard to what the contract is. Third, Stop working for people for nothing. First because people are not even thankful for that which is done for them for nothing, and second, because some people try to get your labor for nothing, and would not return the labor, nay, they would not turn their little finger over to work for the one who labored for them for nothing. Use your influence to keep others out of the snares. I love my brother George, and will give him advise him [sic] so long as we are brotherly.

Thursday July 8th, 1897 (11:20 A.M.)

It is so hot now-a-days from about 10 A.M. to 4 P.M. Yesterday July 7th, 1897, I put up notices on the upper and lower gate posts on the west side of the upper place that after 20 days I would close the road.

Saturday July 10th, 1897, (6:55 A.M.)

July 9th, 1897 Ellen Shawnee ate the first mess of roasting ears off of our upper place. I hoed cotton until now July 9th, 1897.

Tuesday July 13th, 1897 11:55 A.M.

I went out to see Joe Billy at his home, but he had gone to Sac and Fox Agency with Smith the merchant and with the colored man Berry Toon. Joe Billy, it appears owes Smith a great deal. At 2 P.M. Mrs. Carter and myself went to the school meeting in the brick school building in Tecumseh, Okla. Ter. It was a meeting composed of men, only one white woman being present. A resolution was introduced and carried by a vote of 25 to 5, that had a number of whereases prefixed, but asked the two members of the board to resign. The Board was very much hurt. Mr. Newsom the clerk refused to resign, but Mr. Mundy probably will resign. Mr. Raines was elected treasurer, but the clerk and director are hold over members. Hence their resignation was asked for.

Thursday July 15th, 1897. (5:20 P.M.)

I went to Shawnee early [this] morning, and when the passage train rolled in at 9:14 A.M. [Joe Bi]lly and Berry Toon stepped down from the train and we saw them. [The two?] had been up to Oklahoma City and Joe Billy had bought a [. . . n], harness, and appendages for $87.

Saturday July 17th, 1897 (10:10 A.M.)

It is now cloudy and raining in drops only. It has been cloudy all morning, but it does not even look wet on the ground. Yesterday Friday July 16th, 1897 Joe Billy and his wife came by her[e] where I at present live in Tecumseh and we went to the house of Dr. and Mrs. Hartley. We found them both at home and Joe had a long talk with them at [about?] his son William Jannison [*spelled Janneson on pg. 36*] and Nellie Warrior. The gist of the whole discourse was whether William ~~Sh~~ should marry Nellie by law or not, or by Indian custom as heretofore. The law requires all Indians to obtain license and be married. This law was passed by the Oklahoma legislature and approved Feb. 28th, 1897. Thence we went to the city of Shawnee. Here we ate dinner, during which every phase of the proposed marriage was fully discussed, almost as much as it had been at Dr. Hartley's. Thence we proceeded to the depot, where Joe Billy took out his new wagon. The railroad agent demanded his pay, but Joe Billy said that wagon, harness, and everything was to be prepaid by W. J. Pettee and Co., of Oklahoma City. The agent sent a telegram to [continued on bottom of page 36]

[page 36, bottom of page, continued from page 35] Oklahoma City and the answer came back that they should have been prepaid. Berry Toon was very helpful about putting up the wagon. It was sent down from Oklahoma City in his name (Berry's). Thence we went to Smith's store. Smith has a store in Shawnee, one in Tecumseh, and one at Avoca south of Little River,—The following reflections appear worthy of note. 1. The case of William Janneson [Jannison?] and Nellie Warrior attest the fact that ignorance does not pay, that we should know the laws of the country we live in. We are citizens of the United States, and should live in whatever state we please and in what city we please. But we should obey the laws of the place we are in and in order to obey them we must know what they are. In order to know what they are we "must search and look," or have some one do so for us.

Monday July 19th, 1897

Ellen was sick last night, but she is better this morning. I promised to take her out buggy riding when she gets well. I can borrow the buggy and team of Nellie and William Janneson. They can be paid by me in interpreting. I also promised to get my dear little Ellen a dress. Mr. Smith promised to pay me a dollar. Joe Billy and John Spybuck came here yesterday Sunday July 18th, 1897. They had been in the rain coming. John Spybuck had on a slicker. We went up together to see Mr. Smith, and saw him, and he told us to wait an hour or so, and then they would arrive from Avoca, Pott. Co. So we all came back to my Ellen's and she fixed them a nice dinner. After dinner Ellen dearest and Joe Billy and John Spybuck and myself got up in the wagon and went up in town. Ellen enjoyed the ride very much. I wish I had a team and wagon or buggy and take Ellen every where I go. I am sure that she would enjoy the trips fully as much as I do myself.

Ellen and I want to buy a lot in the city of Shawnee and build a house upon one. We want a cooking stove and a heater also; and a draw-table where places can be spliced in to make it longer; a safe for dishes and for food; a bureau, wash-stand, bowl and pitcher, six chairs, two rocking chairs; also a bedstead, quilts and blankets, and bed-tick, and a cloak and a shawl; a screen door and screens over the windows.

Next year, if the Lord will, we want planted on our upper place:— 1. Cotton. 2. Corn. 3. Cabbage. 4. Sweet Potatoes. 5. Irish Potatoes. 6. English [continued on the bottom half of page 40]

[page 40, bottom half—continued from page 39] Peas. 7. Beans. 8. 90 Day Corn. 9. Tomatoes.

Home-Handbook by Dr. H. Kellogg, page 1372. 1. A soft flannel gown should be put on the baby. 2. A woolen bandage should be placed around the trunk. 3. An unguent [definition: It is similar to an ointment.] of (a) Olive Oil. b. Cocoanut Oil. c. Vaseline. 4. Fine Castile Soap.
5. The baby should sleep by itself in its crib. In cold weather hot water bottles and padding should be used. See p. 1373 at the top.
6. Children should not be taught to walk too early.
7. The temperature of the room baby lives in should be 68° or 70° by the thermometer, p. 1372.
8. A Syphon Syringe must be a household possession p. 1365.

[page 223] Monday July 19th, 1897 (10:20 A.M.)
   The past week Joe Billy has received $480 on some land that he sold. But now today he has but very little money. He paid Smith $219. Wagon $87 and Harness and Bows and Wagon Sheet all laid down in Shawnee. $25 on horses. Debt in Shawnee $15. To his son $12.50 cts. Second hand cupboard $38. John Scott $12. Railroad fare to Oklahoma City $4.60. Berry Toon $2. William E. Shawnee $2.

[moved from page 41] Tuesday July 20th, 1897 (1:46 P.M.)
The following conclusions now press themselves to my mind.
   1. No knowledge is important than that which relates to life and health. One should spend plenty of time in the study of physiology, anatomy, and hygiene. The hygiene of the sexual system should be fully taught. The diseases of the sexual organs, with their causes and treatment, should occupy years of study. No person should be brought up without this knowledge, coupled with genuine Christianity. No boy or girl is educated properly without this knowledge.
   2. The Bible, both of the Old and New Testament is every person's true guide through life. The habit of reading the Bible reverently is one of the very best habits, and should be a daily habit. The habit of going to church is also one

of the very best habits, and is a good example set to the world. The habit of praying daily is one of the most salutary habits.

3. The habit of going to school is also a good habit. This means Sunday school, the county normal institute, a normal school, a college, or university. One never gets too old to learn. Improve your time well and go to school all you can, whenever you can.

4. It is a good habit to be ever on the alert to purchase real estate, town lots in town or farms in the country. A town or city lot, with a house and well and small orchard on it is a home. Many people could own homes that do not now own them. They are standing on the way of their own happiness, but they know it not.

5. It is a good thing for a person to be dissatisfied with their condition, for that means improvement. One who wishes to have some thing can always find an honest, lawful way of doing so. I made the mistake of living in my father's home too long when I should have built a home of my own. Every young man or woman should have a home by the time they are 18 years old, or even by 15 years of age. Their parents should secure this for them, or better still, aid them in securing it. A good education along with a home, if that be only a lot and a house in the city is very much.

6. Another mistake was in not buying a team and buggy. $40 would have bought me a team and less than that would have bought a buggy. I need to help others from making my mistakes. No one seemed able or willing to help me.

7. I ought to have set out 100 or 200 fruit trees, instead of 69. I ought to have built better houses and more room in them on my place. But, thank God, my case is a good as it is. I have 70 acres of land in cultivation of my own. I have some 50 fruit trees, and two log houses on my places. I have green corn, grown on my own place, to eat. My upper place has now its fifth crop, and my lower place has its third crop. I have now no live-stock of any kind. I and my [page 42] wife—Mrs. Ellen Shawnee—have now lived for one month in the city of Tecumseh, Okla. Ter. We pay house rent at the rate of $1.50 cts. per month. I have studied Astronomy during the month from a text-book that I have upon the subject, also general history, current events, the Bible, physiology and hygiene, and I attended the annual school meeting in Tecumseh, Okla. Ter. Tuesday July 13th, 1897. The county teachers' institute convenes July 26th, 1897 in Tecumseh. I never lived in town any regularly until 1896 and 1897. I like to live in the city very well.

[*pages 212–14 moved to original page 151*]

[*page 215, missing page*]

[*page 216, missing page*]

August 3rd, 1897 6:15 P.M.

I went in debt today to Sam Clay's through Mr. Waggoner the sum of Two Dollars ($2). But I only took up 25 cts. worth in the store. I waited to go to the Agency with John Spybuck Monday Aug. 2nd, 1897. The same day I went over to David Alford's and Mamie gave me two watermelons and some peaches to bring home with me. I also brought some green corn, some peaches, and some cabbage from my upper place. Sat. July 31st, 1897 I went to Shawnee, and Joe Billy paid me 50 cents in the store, but he did so reluctantly. I interpreted for him Friday July 30th, 1897, and went out with his son William Janneson to see Mr. Fisher, who had taken up an estray, but it was not the one we wanted. - The following rules for leasing occur to my mind.

1. There must be a clause in the lease requiring the land to be cultivated in a good husbandmanlike manner.
2. No wood or timber or stone or hay must be sold off of the land.
3. The right to the hay must be reserved to the landlord and the tenant may pasture work stock and for family use. Wood may be used for fuel, but not sold.
4. The tenant must keep up all repairs on fences and elsewhere.
5. The landlord must be allowed to protect himself against loss in case some of the land should be allowed to grow up in weeds either by leasing to other parties or hiring workers or working it himself and may have all to be made on the piece so allowed to remain uncultivated.
6. Subletting is forbidden and must not be allowed.
7. In plowing the furrows must be run so as to prevent washouts as much as possible.
8. No fruit trees must be injured but the renter can claim no fruit.
9. On my upper place 20 or 25 acres must be planted in cotton.
10. On the upper place the pasture must be reserved and also the lot and well.
11. No hay must be put up in the stack, but the party of the first part retains the right to cut hay.
12. All timber used as rails for hog pens must remain in such pens and not be used for any other purpose.
13. The fruit trees must be cultivated in a good husbandmanlike manner just the same as any other crop. Neither Mr. Sexton,

Mr. Grizzard, Mr. Cummings, nor any other renter has ever done this.

[moved from page 43] Tuesday August 3rd, 1897. 9 P.M. by the clock.

For several years my renters have allowed several acres of the farm to grow up in weeds, thus causing me a loss as well as themselves. Mr. Sexton the renter this year took sick about June 1st 1897, and at least 8 acres have grown up in crop grass and weeds. Last year Mr. Grizzard let some of the crop-about 2 or 3 acres grow up in weeds and crop grass. In 1894 King Davis let about an acre grow up in weeds. - Mr. Sexton also allowed my old well to cave in. I told him to ditch around it so as to prevent water from running in from the top, but he did not do so. Mrs. Ellen Shawnee says for me not to lease out my land to a lone man like Mr. Sexton any more, but to lease it out to a man who has a wife and several children, so that if some become sick, others can work the land.

This year I have bought bacon to eat, eggs to eat, chickens to eat, cabbage to eat, water-melons to eat, and land to use. Now I ought to raise hogs and make my own bacon, and I ought to raise chickens and eat my own eggs. I ought to raise my own cabbage and water-melons.

I ought to buy such property as is mortgageable. A person can obtain credit for money or merchandise if they only have some thing that they can mortgage. A team and a buggy would be a good thing for me to buy, for I could mortgage them if necessary. A milk cow would be useful both for milk and as a help for borrowing. A house and lot in town would be both a home and also capital for borrowing money or merchandise.

I ought to attend the county normal institute, but I can not do so just at present. Caesar and Cicero in ancient times were never too old to go to school. I am not too old either. My marriage can not hinder me from going to school.

Wednesday August 4th 1897. 7:15 P.M.

I waited until 1 P.M. for John Spybuck. Then I went over to the home of Mrs. Mamie Alford. William Janneson and his wife came there late and William said that John Spybuck had gone to Sac and Fox Agency on Tuesday August 3rd, 1897, and he had appointed Wednesday Aug. 4th, 1897, to go with me to Sac and Fox, and he was to come by in the wagon to get me. I think John wants to avoid paying me. John Spybuck is a liar, all the time, and a bad debtor. It is well-known that he is a bad debtor, and has been trying to pay me 50 cents for a long time, and he has not done so yet. The sum he was to pay me when I went with him to the Agency was Three Dollars ($3). - Mamie Alford was telling me about Carrie [*page 44*] Warrior yesterday. That sister Jennie was getting tired of keeping Carrie, that James Warrior, Carrie's father had got $30 or more lately, and did not give Carrie any thing. That Carrie was sick five days when she was in labor, that Carrie wanted a doctor, but that Jim Warrior and Jennie Cegar did not want a doctor called, but wanted to use and did use Indian medicine, that Carrie was upstairs over there at Cegar's, and had to go down and up to retire, that after she got real sick in childbed, that she was carried down stairs with the greatest difficulty; that the father of Carrie's child was the white man who taught her tailor work up at Haskell; that he had not sent Carrie five cents since she had been down here; that they surely came near losing Carrie; that Carrie had her marriage certificate, which she had threatened to burn up; that Carrie and her white man were married by Catholic priests; that this white man had asked her to come back in a letter, but had never sent any money for her to come back on; that Jim Warrior and Jennie Cegar urged Carrie to go back three years ago.

Thursday August 5th, 1897. 6:25 P.M.
   Nothing was written because my brother George E. Shawnee came and visited and took supper with Ellen Shawnee and myself.

It is 9:35 A.M. August 6th, 1897.
   My brother George was riding his horse that the old man William Shawnee gave to him. I went down to my lower place yesterday that Mrs. Carter and her son Henry Carter are working jointly this year. Henry sold me two melons for 15 cts. I told Henry Carter that he and his mother would have to fight their own fights out themselves, that I had fusses enough of my own without going into those of any one else;

Tuesday Aug. 10th 1897. 2:33 P.M.
   Saturday Aug. 7th, 1897 Mr. Alexander Sexton would not agree for me to plant or have some one plant Irish potatoes on the uncultivated portions of my land, about five or six acres. Mr. Morris an attorney-at-law said that in that case I could collect Damages from him.
Rules: 1. The way to have a contract for a lease drawn up is to have an attorney at law, like Mr. Morris, draw up the contract in accordance with the law. 2. If each clause in the lease is not observed, there ought to be a remedy provided in the lease itself. 3. [*no more rules listed*]

Monday Aug. 16th 1897. 8 A.M. by the clock.
   Ellen Shawnee and I are at the house of David Alford. We have been here since Aug. 10th, 1897. David Alford and his wife

and Cinda Emma Spybuck and little Webster Alford and Dan Dirt went up to the war dance at Big Jim's. They started at 10 A.M. o'clock Wednesday Aug. 11th, 1897, and came back Saturday August 14th, 1897, about 4 P.M. in the evening, or there about. [page 45] They were gone about four days. David Alford is to pay me Fifty cents a day for staying and minding the place, and feeding the Hogs, and watering the hogs and horses. George E. Shawnee visited us ~~either Wednesday Aug.~~ us [sic] Thursday Aug. 12th, 1897. He brought some of my books back that he had borrowed to read. He and a white man went to look at land that belongs to George and that George wishes to lease out. This morning at David's, we had nothing to eat but roasting ears and milk. The rest had roasting ears, coffee, and salt for breakfast. Now I know that by strict economy we could do better than this, for both David and I myself have some thing of an income, and were we to save and buy bread and meat more, we would not go hungry so often.

I. A. Nail the well-digger was my witness today in securing my SE corner, and a lady was with him. I put a rock by the side of the old stake, driving the broken off piece back into the ground. It was 4:15 P.M. Aug. 16th, when I got back to David Alfords, where I and my wife Ellen are staying. I told Mr. Perry that another day and the corner might be lost, that I had spoken to him two or three months ago about that corner and that nothing had been done about it yet; that if he did not go, it would be his fault, and that my time was as valuable as his and that I was as busy as he was.

Wednesday Aug. 18th, 1897. (1:52 P.M.)

David Alford and Dan Dirt and I were working on his new cow-lot today. He moved the old cow-lot from the north of the road to place near the creek in his barn-yard. Martin Starr came in the wagon after his wife Cinda Charley, who split the blanket with him yesterday, and came over to David's. She came to David's unasked. David was not to blame nor Mammie, but Cinda asked David for the Wagon to move her things. Billy Johnson (Minatobi) took dinner at David Alford's. My wife Ellen Shawnee has put up three glasses of peaches. The peaches that she cooked for canning tasted like those we eat out of cans in the store. - I ought to have $100 cash for my two places, with 70 acres or more in cultivation.

Thursday Aug. 19th, 1897, 3:10 P.M.

I scolded Ellen Shawnee this morning because she let the bucket and rope fall into the well. She cried over it and I was very sorry. Martin Starr and his wife Cinda Charley are here. Martin says that his sister has been dead over a year now. I had not known of it. We have not been doing any thing much today. Ellen Shawnee has been putting up peaches. Ellen and Mammie Alford have gone over to Julia Shawnee's. Mammie has two glass fruit jars that she is to take home to Julia. Mr. Fred Peel offered me $33 a year for my upper place last night. This would [continued on bottom of page 46]

[page 46, bottom of page] Thursday Aug 19th, 1897. (Continued 3:24 P.M. [from page 45])
make $93 clear cash on both of my places, since Henry and his mother are to give me $60 for the lower place. This would only lack $7 of being $100. But I am of the opinion that $60 is too little for the place down yonder. - Ellen and I are still at the house of David and Mamie Alford. We have been here since Aug. 10th, 1897.

 Cegar brought two mares to the stud of David Alford for service about June 13th, 1897. One is a sorrel mare, another is a black mare. The black mare belongs to Mrs. Chosa Starr, but Cegar brought this black mare to David's. Cegar also brought an iron gray mare for the same purpose July 15th, 1897. - James Warrior also brought a dim mare June 20th, 1897, for the same purpose.

Saturday August 21st, 1897 (6:46 A.M.)
 This is a beautiful morning of sunshine and good spirits. Ellen Shawnee and myself are still here at the home of David Alford. Ellen has been canning peaches for Mrs. Mamie Alford. She has put up twelve glass jars of peaches up to date. Yesterday Friday Aug. 20th, 1897, David Alford, Ellen, and myself went to the Shawnee Mission to see the new U.S.I. [United States Indian] Agent, Mr. Lee Patrick. We went in the wagon. I saw Miss Brice, one of the teachers, and she was just as polite as could be. The agent said that either himself or a Special Agent would make out leases about the last of this month. He brought David Alford's money and gave it to him. From the Shawnee Mission we three went to the city of Shawnee.

[moved from page 47] We transacted business in the bank of Mr. Benson and Mr. Search notwithstanding it was 4:15 P.M. when we arrived in the city. We saw Walter Shawnee and George E. Shawnee there in Shawnee each carrying away a large number of fruit cans. Jerome Selturska and little Mary Ann came after watermelons last night about dark and David gave them two. Benson spoke to Ellen Shawnee for the first time yesterday evening. We saw ex. Supt. Miller also. He told me the other day he had the position of Supt. in Blackwell, Okla. Ter.; that his wife had a position there also; that he would be glad to hear from me at any time; that the district in which Blackwell was situated had 300 pupils and that the town had 1000 inhabitants; the bonds issued by the School Board of Shawnee had not yet been sold; that the bonds might be cancelled and our pay as teachers in Shawnee might be thus tied up. - It is a pity that I was not able to attend the county normal institute this year. It began July 26th, 1897, and ends today Aug. 21st, 1897. It was only the cash that kept me from attending. But this must not happen another year by the help of the Lord. I am in the teacher's profession to stay. I must go to school more. I thank God that I live in a country of schools, schools of medicine, of law, of music, of pharmacy, of agriculture, of methods of teaching, of the liberal arts, and other schools. A teacher can not be too well qualified for his work. A school board will soon find out the defects in the education of a teacher, and this will make against his employment. Mr. Miller said that Supt. Ware was not to teach any, but was merely to be Supt.; this means that he will visit the schools of the teachers more, and that there will be grade meetings, and probably a city teacher's institute; that he received $800 a year, while the salaries of other teachers were cut down.

Tuesday Aug., 24th, 1897 (8:10 P.M. by the clock).
Yesterday Monday Aug. 23rd, 1897 Mr. David Alford, at whose house we are still staying, lent us his mule team and wagon, for which he said he would charge us nothing, and Mrs. Ellen Shawnee and myself rode to Tecumseh, and went to the business part of town and traded and paid two small debts for David. He sent 35 cts. by us for that purpose. I and Ellen loaded, but Mrs. Harris a colored lady helped us considerably. Thence we went to Shawnee, and put our things in the little house just south of Mr. Cooley's. She gave Ellen and myself a late dinner of butter, batter cakes, syrup, and other things, free. Today Dan Dirt, who is also here at David's, staying, helped David stretch wire on his fence. We have sweet potatoes, green corn, water-melons, peaches, cabbage, grapes, and sometimes milk, to eat all free, for just what little we do on the place. David Alford is a good fellow, and always was a good friend of mine. Mammie Alford, wife of David Alford, is very good about giving Ellen advice about different matters. Ellen is great with child now. She is in her seventh month. She is a lovely Christian woman, or at least inclined to be so. The Home Hand book By Dr. . . . [*last line of page 47 cut off*]
[*page 48*] I read it almost daily to find some thing that will be of use to Ellen and myself. It is Ellen's book now, for I made her a present of it. I bought it in 1889 when I was working with Maj. N. S. Porter, in the resurvey of the Pottawatomi

Reservation. Many things that I bought when single are of use to me now when I am married. The improvements and crops that are on my land on my account placed there when single are of very great use to Ellen and myself now. 1. I need to finish the house of my land, and I must spend money for that purpose as soon as I get some. I will not have to move here and yonder with my things when I have a home of my own. 2. I must pay my debts. The religion of Jesus Christ requires this of me. I must be a true man. 3. We must have a buggy and a horse or horses, some hogs, chickens, and turkeys. 4. I may farm my upper forty myself this time. Mr. Jones a white man once told me that if I would farm it myself, I would make more out of it. This [is?] doubtless true. For four years my share has been only $13 a year, and not all of that in cash. It is a mistake to raise corn expecting to sell it for money. One should raise it to use himself or to feed it to his cattle, hogs, or horses. My lower place has not brought one cent in money for the last three years. The Carters have now had three good crops off of it. I have received no money in return for what money I have spent on the land. A great many people think that I can not farm. I farmed in 1888, and 1889, and in years before that. Why can I not revive a former practice? I have tried three colored men on my place in three different years, and they failed to make me money (except a very little), and they also failed to cultivate the land as it should be cultivated. They let the crops grow in weeds, and failed to tend some of the land at all.—Each of the three did this thing. I have had two white men cultivate my land in two different years. Neither one let the crop grow up in weeds, but cultivated all the land and cultivated it well. But they made less money than all the colored men made me, because I could never sell the corn for money. Cotton is readily sold in town, but corn has no sale. Hence I suffered. So it does not pay to have a white man raise corn on your place either. 5. No renter must ever let an acre of my land grow up in weeds any more, no matter whether he is sick or well. He must get some one else cultivate the land if he should become sick and not able, and pay them himself, or else surrender the land back to me before the season is past, so that I can get some one to cultivate it. I need to have cotton raised every year, and some corn also, but mostly cotton. 6. It is easy for people to make promises, but it is very hard to keep them. The rule is, to make a few promises, and then only when you have counted the cost and are sure that you can fulfill them; accept a few promises, but consider also what is to be done if the promises are not kept. 7. Experience is a [page 49] very good school. It tries men and women as nothing else does. The promises that men or women make are not always carried out into experience. Actual trial, and actual test, is the best and surest mode of knowing what material is sound, and what unsound. Experience with renting land for these five years has opened my eyes. I have made but little, and it is time that I was making something off of my land. Walter Shawnee had had just as bad or even worse luck renting out his land, so far as getting any money is concerned. No wonder the Government of the United States requires two bondsmen on every Indian lease. If the leaser is not worth the money, perhaps the bondsmen are. 8. It is one of the best things in the world that I lost money leasing land. It has taught me wisdom. I must not lose on another lease at all. This experience will teach me to be more careful next time, and it will make me guard my own interests, as they never have been guarded. I have put money on my land but got no money off of it. 9. [*journal has 8*] I have made some money teaching school the last two years. I have made six times as much hard cash in two years as I made in four years by leasing land. The other day Monday Aug. 23rd, 1897, or Saturday Aug. 21st, 1897, Mr. Miller, former Supt. of Shawnee City Schools said that the schools would not begin in Shawnee until the 1st of October. This man has proved a bad prophet in some things in the past, but time will tell of this. 10. [*journal has 9*] It is not good policy to receive merely verbal promises, because they vanish, and leave no trace behind them of their former existence. All promises should be in writing and attested by two witnesses. Then they are established every word. It is now ten P.M. and I must retire to bed. Praise the Lord for all his goodness. Amen.

Written Thursday Aug 26th, 1897 (1:40 P.M.). [moved from middle of page 32]

When I came back from Maryville, Tennessee to Shawneetown, Ind. Ter. Mamie Alford said that Cinda Emma Spybuck was six months old; that was Nov. 25th, 1887. I went to Maryville, Tennessee from Shawneetown Ind. Ter. August 14th, 1883. I was married to Miss Ellen Carolina Feb. 6th, 1897. The road-overseer warned me out to work the road next Tuesday Aug. 31st, 1897. He was here at David's at noon today. We helped David Alford hauled [*sic*] three loads of hay yesterday Aug. 25th, 1897. This road overseer is very rough and insulting in his manner of warning out his men.

Friday Aug. 27th, 1897 (7:35 P.M.).

We have been hauling hay all day, David Alford, Dan Dirt, Robinson Crusoe, and myself. We hauled four loads yesterday Aug. 26th, 1897. We have hauled six loads of hay today. David has now two stacks finished, and we have begun a third. One of the stacks that are finished is across the creek, and one of them is near his stable on the south side. We have been here at David

Alford's seventeen (17) days. Ellen said both yesterday morning and this morning that she wanted to go home. - We have hauled in all in the last three days thirteen (13) loads of hay. David Alford has no clock or watch, but Ellen brought her clock with us and we have the time both day and night. It took us one hour and a half to go in the wagon from the house to the hay-field and bring a load of hay back to the barn. It is said that a woman had made a remark to the effect that a penis was small, but she had never seen the same. People do not want a poor young man to marry a woman that is a relative of theirs just on account of his poverty. Women often make remarks that they ought not. - Ellen Shawnee [continued on the bottom of page 33]

[page 33, bottom of page, continued from page 32] washed clothes this evening, and that she finished at 6 P.M. this evening. Part of our load of hay fell off of the wagon today and I fell off with it. Cinda Emma Spybuck helped Ellen carry water this evening to wash with.

Monday August 30th, 1897 (6:55 A.M.)

Yesterday Sunday Aug. 29th, 1897 we did nothing all day, but in the evening Dan Dirt and myself brought a load of wood and some corn from the field across the creek. When we came back. Cegar, Jennie Cegar, Carrie Warrior, Maud Spybuck were visiting at David Alford's. David Alford and myself went to town late to get some flour and bacon. When we got to town, it clouded up in the west and the north as if it might rain. At that time, it was <u>time</u> only that could decide the question whether it would rain or not. It did not rain last night. Carrie's baby is a large one, six months old now, I suppose. I have not been to church for a long time. Mrs. Ellen Shawnee is great with child, but we calculate the child will be born on Nov. 20th, 1897. - I must go to church again as soon as possible. Ellen talks about going home every morning. Mrs. Carter did not think she cold cultivate 20 or 25 acres of cotton in 1898 on my upper place.

Written this night Tuesday Aug. 31st, 1897 (7:40 P.M. by the clock).

Mrs. Ellen Shawnee and myself have been here at David Alfords three weeks (21 days) now. Yesterday David and I hauled 4½ loads of hay. A large part of the last load in the evening fell off. Today we hauled four loads, and finished the third stack across the creek, at the edge of the hay-ground. This makes 27½ loads that we have hauled all together.—
Cotton. - I saw the first cotton open Aug. 23rd, 1897. The first bale was sold in Tecumseh Aug. 28th, 1897, and the first bale was ginned in Shawnee Friday night Aug. 27th, 1897. The bale was sold

in Tecumseh was sold at 7¼ cents per pound. Cotton is planted about April 15th. It is laid by the last of June or the 15th of July every year. It is worked about three months, or about 90 days. It is the only crop in Oklahoma that brings ready money on the market. No matter if cotton should fail one year, go into planting it the more heavily the next year. Mr. Fred Peel wants to put all my upper place in cotton next year. I think I had better take him up. Mr. David Alford says that he is a good man and will make a good crop for me. I was to let Mrs. Irene Carter have my upper place, but she was not sure that she could cultivate twenty or twenty-five acres of cotton on the place, which I am obliged to insist upon, since no crop will bring me any money except cotton.

At 8 P.M. or there about this evening Mrs. Ellen Shawnee cried and begged me to go home to Shawnee, and no arguments of mine could get her to consent to remain. We have plenty of watermelons, peaches, cabbage, sweet potatoes, and other things here at David's, but yet she wants to go.

[*page 203*] *Written 7:50 P.M. by the clock this Friday Sept 3rd, 1897.*

Wednesday Sept 1st, 1897 Mr. Fred Peel and I went over to look at the forty acres of mine that is near David Alford's, where I and Mrs. Ellen Shawnee are still staying. I agreed to let Mr. Peel have my place here for $40 a year, and the U.S.I. [*United States Indian*] Agent is to make a legal lease for us. He is to secure me $5 for the corn on my place that he is to get, and I am to pay him back $5 when he pays me the $40. Yesterday Thursday Sept. 2nd, 1897, Mr. Fred Peel and his women folks went on my place and got a load of the corn, about 8 bushels I suppose, and this morning about 9 A. M. on going up to see and get some of our peaches, we find that they are all gone. There was one tree there of red Indian peaches, nice but not ripe, and neither Ellen nor myself had pulled one because they were not ripe. But since Mr. Peel and his folks have been there yesterday not one of them is left, but all are gone. We only got today about half a dozen peaches. I noticed that Fred pulled a good many in his hands when I was there with him Sept. 1st, 1897, but he and his folks practically pulled all the next day Sept. 2nd, 1897. About noon today Sept. 3rd, 1897 I went here from David Alford's place to Fred Peel's but found neither him nor any of his folks at home. Thence I went over to Mr. Wray's and talked with them until late in the evening. We talked about the County-seat fight between Shawnee and Tecumseh, about the Court House being built in Tecumseh, about the Jail, about the infidel R. G. Ingersoll and his doctrines, about the stars, and about various other things. The conversation was interesting. The following

things were said about the County-seat trouble: That some had said the Court-house being built in Tecumseh was not public property, and was consequently no court house; that the contract for the building was let to Mr. Baley [Bailey] by the County Commissioners, and that the people of the County had no voice in the matter; that according to this contract the building would belong to the county at the end of ten years; that Shawnee might build a Court-house for the county and give it free to the county; that Shawnee was too poor to do this; that the railroad shops would never be located in Shawnee but would be located at South McAlester; that the County-seat trouble would be settled by a vote of the people finally, perhaps, but would be fought for twenty years; that Mr. Baley was worth $60,000. Sam Clay owned real estate near Tecumseh, and was worth right smart; that it was doubtful how the people of the county would vote on the matter; that the people knew Mr. Christian would favor Tecumseh; that Mr. Search had plenty of money and so had Mr. Benson; that Search was for the dollars, but had refused to run for Mayor at the last city election in Shawnee; that Mr. Search now owns the bank building in Shawnee his present place of business.
[*continued on page 202, bottom of page*]

[*moved from page 202, bottom of page*]
Sept 3rd, 1897 (continued) [*from page 203*] Mr. Search, Mr. Benson, Mr. Clay, and Mr. Bailey were four men that we talked about. Mr. Wray is a pretty good man, and is from the state of Tennessee. I began to go to school at Shawnee Mission about June 19, 1875, if I remember rightly, left for the Freedmen's Normal Institute at Maryville, Tennessee August 14th, 1883, came back home November 25th, 1887. I went to school at Choctaw-Normal at Choctaw City for two weeks in July 1896. I Have never attended college or a county normal institute yet. By the grace of God I want to attend the State Normal at Emporia, Kansas. - I started to school when I was six years old and quit school when I was 18 or 19 yrs. Old. I shall soon begin to teach my third school in Oklahoma. I make a great deal more money teaching school than I do leasing out my land. Education is better than land.

[*page 217*] I have been home here from school at Maryville, Tennessee Nov. 28th, 1887, now nearly 10 years. I have earned money as follows:
[*Decimal points added in the following figures in lieu of lines on William Shawnee's accounting sheet.*]

```
                                              Small sums
                                              M^cFall  2.50
                                              David    1.50
```

```
                                                    Cegar  2.00
Adams    .25
                                                    Wilson 2.00
                                                           8.25
```

1888 I farmed for the Old man William Shawnee.
1889 I farmed for the Old man William Shawnee.
Surveying under Major N. S. Porter   426.50
                           1889-1890

Surveying under Mosses Neal in the Kickapoo country	67.00
Share in Shawnee Absentee Shawnee Payment 1892	103.00
Services as a clerk under Special Agent Litchfield 1892	42.00
Working for I. C. Cuppy 1892-93	30.00
Working for Alex. Crain 1888	15.00
Teaching School 2 yrs. 1895-96	308.05
Maj. N. S. Porter paid me 1890	6.00
Received from my upper place 1893-96	53.30
Received from my lower place 1895-1897.	8.00
John Spybuck paid me 1896.	11.50
P.V. Bull paid me 1896.	10.00

```
                                           Total   1080.35cts.
Lost on Script earned by teaching school           51.95
                                                  $1132.30
Small Sums as above                                 8.25
                                                  $1140.55
Services as servant                                117.00
                                                  $1257.55
```

[*page 218*] How I spent $141
For Taxes   2.75
For My Proposed House   31.25
For 5 Months' Board   29.75
                                                   63.75

Clothing $77.25
                                        ($55.80)   21.45
                                                  $85.20

Sunday Feb. 21ˢᵗ 1897.
Up to date (22) (Feb. 27, 1897 about 35).
Up to Thursday March 19ᵗʰ, 1897, 75, mostly ea implorante.
Tuesday March 25ᵗʰ, 1897 - 3 ea implorante (recorded March 26ᵗʰ, 1897 8:37 by the clock.

July 13ᵗʰ 1897 11:35 A.M. in a rented house in Tecumseh, Okla. Ter.
    I owe as follows:-
        To Houghton and Upp Purcell, I.T.   3.00
        To John King, Dale, Okla. Ter.   1.50

" *Christian Nation*		9.50
" N. Y. Independent		.75
" Sam Clay (secured by mortgage)		10.00
" Other small debts		1.00
Total		$26.05

There is owing money to me as follows:—July 13th 1897.
        From Joe Billy (Paid in full July 15th, 1897)   1.25
        From Mr. Wray   5.00
        "   Mr. Saxton   3.50
        "   Julia Shawnee 50¢ (paid if full about
                             July 15th, 1897)   .50
        "   John Spybuck $10.50, Mamie Spybuck $10.00   20.50
        "   Jennie Cegar $9.50, Chosa Star $10.00   19.50

August 3rd, 1897.
Sam Clay and Co.   Dr.   Cr.
1897
Aug 3 By 2 Chickens @.10¢ 20¢, Eggs 5¢   .25
Aug. 4 "   Butter 5 cts., Breakfast Bacon 10cts.   .15
Aug. 7 "   Bacon 15 cts.   .15
Aug. 10 "   25 lbs Flour 65¢ Soap 5cts Aug 17,1897   .70
Aug. 8 "   Bacon 25 cts, Soda 10 cts. Sugar 10¢ (S…)   .45
Aug. 7 "   Butter 10¢

[*page 220, top left side of page*]
     1896
Feb. 23rd: 1 5:20 A.M.
Feb. 27: 1 6 or 7 P.M.
March 2: 1 About 7 P.M. Cloudy and raining.
March 7: 1 About 10 A.M.
March 4: 2 About 7 or 8 P.M.
March 7: 1 About 11 A.M.
March 8: 4 11 A.M. 12 M
March 13: 2 P.M. 7 or 8
March 16: 2 12 M. or P.M. Bright, warm, and clear
April 3: 3
April 4: 2
April 14: 1
April 16: 2
April 19: 3
April 18: 4
April 28: 3 [Too?] die
April 29: 1 [. . .]
April 21: 4

[*page 220, top right side of page*]

[*page 220, bottom half*]
```
     1897
June 22:   1          Aug. 9:    1
June 30:   1          Aug. 10:   2
June   :   1          Aug. 19:   1
June   :   1          Aug. 31:   1  8 A.M.
July 2:    1          Sept. 2:   2
July 3:    1          Sept. 3:   3
July 5:    1          Sept. 12:  2
July 4:    1          Sept. 20:  1
July 8:    1          Oct. 1:    1
July 9:    2          Oct. 11:   1
July 11:   1
July 14:   1
July 15:   1
July 26:   1
July 27:   1
July 30:   1
July 31:   2
```
[*Left side bottom of page is a scratch pad entry.*]
```
  75       Aug. 2:    1
  15       Aug. 3:    1 M.
 ---       Aug. 12:   1
 375       Aug. 13:   1
  75
 -----
11.25

 6.25
```

[*page 221*]

Feb–March 1896

	Cash ----- 1896 -----	Dr.	Cr.
March 4	By Salary teaching School	30.00	
"	" To Am't Sent William Shawnee Money Order		10.00
"	" " " " John King		4.35
"	" Cost two Money Orders		.13
"	" 1 Complete Geography		1.35
"	" 1 Harvey's Grammar		.65
"	" 2 Young People's Physiologies		1.00
"	" 1 Slate		.15
"	" Paper 10, Envelopes 10, and Stamps 26		.46
"	" Sugar 10¢ for Susie Berry, and Sundries $2.00		2.10
"	" Paid Mrs. Mack for Chicken and Eggs		.35
"	" 2 Railroad Tickets @ .40		.80
"	" 1 First Reader		.17
"	" Paid Mr. McNeil 1.00 and Mrs. McNeil 1.10		2.10

"	" Paid Mr. Blackford for rent		1.45
"	" Ticket to Shawnee from Choctaw City		.75
"	" Paid Mr. Marcus for 2 days work on house		2.00
"	" 1 Pair Drawers .25, *New York Independent* .28		.53
"	" Sundries		2.76
		30.00	30.00

1896-97

Mr. Sexton, Alexander	Dr.	Cr.
To 75 Bu. Corn @ 15¢	11.25	
By Going to and beyond Choctaw City Sept. 1896.		3.00
" Hauling Trunk to Shawnee		.50
" " " from " home		.50
" Taking Ellen and myself to Shawnee		.50
" Sundries (?)		1.75
" Plowing 25 cts. Hauling Household Goods 75¢		1.00
" Going to Shawnee after Ellen's Trunk about June 8, 97		.50

[*page 222*] March 19: 1896
Read Matthew 14th chapter, and on completing it, my heart was filled with love to God.

1897 Cash	Dr.	Cr.
Feb. 27 To Amt on hand by salary for teaching	26.25	
" 27 By Envelope 5 cts, 2 Tablets 10 cts, and 2 Drawing Books 10		.25
" 27 Am't to Mr. Cooley for board $6: $1 also borrowed		7.00
" 27 Am't Pd Mr. Smith for work on house		3.00
" 27 Am't Pd. Henry Carter for work on house		2.00
" 27 Purchase 336 ft. Flooring Lumber.		6.04
" 27 Toward Purchase/Barrel Lime		.25
" 27 Payment Mr. John for papers Jan. & Feb.1897 and Dec.1896		1.00
" 27 Payment to Carson Bros.		2.55
" 27 Repayment to William Shawnee through Julia.		.20
" 27 Sausage		.05
Balance on Hand		3.11
	26.25	26.25

1897. Henry Carter	$Dr.cts	$Cr.cts
May 1st about, Cash	2.00	
June 22 By Hauling Load Wood		.50
July 15 about By Hauling Household Goods		.50
Aug. 6th By two Watermelons		.15
Aug. 7th By two watermelons 15 cts., and 2 more 10¢		.25

[page 225] [*Following—decimal points used in lieu of accounting sheet lines.*]

June-July 1897	Cash	Dr.	Cr.
July 2	Rec'd Paym't 5 days Hoeing Cotton for Mr. McFall	2.50	
	25 lbs. Flour		.50
June 21-30	3 Knives and 3 forks		.25
	Beef 10¢, 5¢ Eggs, Milk 10¢		.25
	Beef 15¢, Butter 10¢, Milk 5¢		.30
	2 Glasses 10¢, Wash Pan 5¢, Ham 20¢		.35
	Milk 5¢, to Carter's Children 5¢		.10
	Eggs 5¢ To Ellen's Nickel	.05	.05
	By Balance		.75
		2.55	2.55
July 1	To Balance brought down	.75¢	
	By Beef		.10
July 15	To Paym't One Day's Work from Joe Billy	1.00	
" 15	P.O.Box Rent 25¢, Flour 25 lbs. 55¢, Sugar 5¢		.85
" 15	Stew Pan 10¢, Stamp 2 cts, Milk 3 cts.		.15
" 14	To Cash Paym't from Julia Shawnee in full of acc't	.50	
" 14	previous to this date Milk at several times		.40
" 14	previous to this date Onions		.10
" 14	previous to this date cabbage 15 cts		.15
" 16	From Joe Billy Due Bill for Merchandise in store	1.00	
" 16	By 1 Ladies' Straw Hat and two hat pins (Smith Bros)		.30

" 18	By Water Mellon		.10
" 17	By Can Peaches 20¢ (Smith Bros)		
" 19	To Due Bill for Merchandise paid me by I. Smith	1.00	
" 18or17	By Can Peaches 20¢ Lard 10¢, Calico 9 yds @ 7¢ 65		.95
" 20	about By Lard for Mrs. Carter 10cts. Soap 10¢, Meat 25¢		.45
July 21st	By Can Oysters 10¢, Blacking 5¢		.15
July 26	By Paym't Merchandise from Joe Billy at Smith's	1.00	
" 24	From Cegar 25¢, July 25 From James Adams 25¢		.50
July 31	From Joe Billy Due Bill in Smith's store	.50	
" 31	2¾ lbs. Bacon 25¢, and 1¾ lbs. sugar 10¢		.35
Aug 3	Coal Oil 5 cts., Soap 5 cts., Candy 5 cts.		.15
Aug 14	From David Alford	1.50	
Sept. 30	For Ellen's picking cotton		.50
Oct 2	For interpreting for Joe Billy		.50
~~Oct~~			

[page 226]

March 27th, 1897

	Cash	Dr.	Cr.
To Amount by 1 month's salary		31.50	
By Payment to William Cooley for $2 cash			2.25
" " to Mr. Smith for making boards			3.00

350

"	"	to Mr. henry Carter for work on house and boards	5.00
"	"	to Mr. Henry Carter in trust for him to pay for lumber, nails, locks	3.25
"	"	1 Picture in frame 60¢ and Box Rent 25	.85
"	"	1 Orange 5 cts., 1 Can Salmon 15cts, 1 Box Blacking 05, 1 Bar of soap 5cts.	.30

By Payment to Mr. Replogle for lumber 30 cts. to Mr. Johnson, of Tecumseh for papers 55 cts, to Mr. A.R. Washington 5 cts. .90

By Paym't to *New York Independent* $1, to *Christian Nation* $1, with cost of money orders 6 cts, Tablet Writing paper 10 cts 2.16

By Am't given my Ellen Shawnee 5.25

By Box Crackers 10 cts., and 1 Looking Glass 20 .30

By Paym't to Mrs. Julia Shawnee .25

By Payment to Crouch Brother's Tecumseh for Crackers, 2 cans of Salmon .35

Sam Clay and Co., Tecumseh, Oklahoma Terr. June 1897

	By Shoes		2.00
	" Crackers 10¢, Sardines 15¢, and Eggs 10¢		.35
1897	" 2 Crocks 25¢, Meat 55, Salt 5¢ Pepper 5¢		.90
(?)	" Coal Oil 10¢, Chicken 10¢, Rice 10, 2 Shirts 40	June 22	.70
	" Baking Powder 10¢, 3 Bars Soap 15 cts		.25
(?)	" 1 Jug 10 cts. Forgotten 10		.20
June 23	" 1 Box 15¢, Sugar 15, Nutmeg 5¢ Table Cloth 1 yd 30		.65
" 23	" Butter		.10

June 24	" Meat		.25
" 24	" Cabbage		.05
June 27	" Bacon 40 cts, soda 10 cts., 1 Can Corn 10¢ Sugar 10 cts		.70
June 29	" Chicken 10¢, Yeast cake 05 cts.		.15
July 2,1897	1 Can Peaches 20¢, Lard 10 cts, Butter 15¢, Chicken 10¢		.55
" 2,1897	Nutmeg 5¢, Candy 5¢ sugar 10¢		.20
July 5th,1897	Bacon 70 cts., Chicken 15 cts.		.85
July 7th,1897	25 lbs. Flour 75 cts. and July 8th, 1 Can Oysters 10¢		.85
July 8,1897	Oysters 10¢, July 9th Chicken 10¢		.20
July 10,1897	Bacon 15¢, Sugar 5¢, Eggs 5¢		.25
July 12,1897	Chicken 10¢		.10
July 14 "	Bacon 35 cts. July 15,97, Soap 5¢ Chicken 10¢, Lard 10¢		.60
July 17 "	Chicken 10¢		[.10]

[page 227]

Dec. 23rd 1896	Dr.	Cr.
To Salary, month ending Nov. 28th	17.80	
By Board to Mr. Cooley		8.00
" 1 Pr. of Shoes		1.50
" Papers at Mr. Johnson's		.55
" Payment Debt at Carson's		4.00
" 1 Pr. Pants		1.00
" Paym't to *New York Independent*		.75
" Paym't to *Christian Nation*		1.00
" Paym't Box Rent		.15
By Money Order 6 cts, Hdkf 5 cts. Candy 5 cts		.16
By Scott's Mannion		.35
I can not account for (spent for stamps etc.)		.34
	17.80	17.80

March 19th, 1897. I owe as follows.
To Mr. Replogle .30 cts.

To Dad Tecumseh	.45
Wm Cooley	1.15
Lumber & Nails	3.30
Crouch Bros.	.35
Independent	.75
Mrs. Garrett	1.25
	$ 7.25

I received off of my upper place money as follows or the equivalent.

1893,	5.65
1894.	7.95
1895	17.50
1896	22.20
	$53.30

From my lower place
$ 2.00 cash
  6.00 in work
$ 8.00
$53.30
$61.30

Both my places have brought me in cash, work, or goods $61.30 cts.

    I have made about $200 worth of improvements upon each place, $400 worth in all. There needs to be $100 worth of improvement made on each place in addition to what is already made. Then my places will be in a pretty good condition. There is a lack of house room in the country generally. It is true that I lack house room on both of my places. I must continue to build houses until I have plenty of surplus room on each of my places. I need a well on my lower places, and the well has caved in on my upper place. I must clean it out as soon as I can. I have now about 70 acres already in cultivation on both of my places. I am offered $[. . .] [*large ink blot on bottom of page*] place next year. Mrs. Carter offers this.

[*page 228*] [*Random calculations for his house.*]

For My House

$$\frac{2 \times 4 \times 10}{\cancel{12}} = \frac{20}{3} \qquad \frac{20}{3} \times 8 = \frac{160}{3} = 54$$
$$3$$

8 - 2 x 10 = 54 feet
                   4
              216 ft to one room
                 3
For the Frame 648 ft to the house

```
    4     1           4 ft
   1̶6̶ x 6̶ x 2̶ = 4    32
       1̶2̶             128 ft to one room
        2̶               3 rooms
     ¶ Of Flooring.   384
```

```
                      6 ) 120
                           20
                            4
                           80 ft to one side
                            4
                          320 ft to one room
                            3
   ¶ Covering for the Outside  960 ft
```

9 − 2 x 6 x 16 to one room

```
    2̶ x 6̶ x 16      16
       1̶2̶            9
                   144 ft to one room
                     3 rooms
 ¶. Sleepers       432 ft for the floor to rest on
```

	Cash	Dr.	Cr.
Feb. 8 1896	By 12 lbs. Beef		.70
" "	" 1 Tablet		.10
" "	" Paym't to Mr. McNeil (shoemaking)		.50
" "	" Paym't to Mrs. McNeil (cooking)		.20
"15 "	" Paym't to Mrs. Smith (for eggs)		.10
"15 "	" Paym't to Mr. Donnelly (horse to ride)		.25
"15 "	" W̶ Stamps at Douglas City		.09
"15 "	" 6 Tablets for lead pencil at Douglas City (School)		.25
" 8th 1896	" Writing Tablet for ink 10, Envelopes 10		.20
" 8th 1896	" Payment to Mrs. Blackford (for am't borrowed)		.30
" 8th 1896	" Stamps		.04
			2.73

[page 229]

November 1895

	Cash	Dr.	Cr.
Nov. 2	Cash on hand by salary	27.00	
"	By Apples		.05
"	By Slates		.35
"	By Slate Pencils		.05
"	" Clock		1.25

"	" Pair of Pants			1.50
"	" Pair of Drawers			.25
"	" Two White Shirts	@50¢		1.00
"	" Paid Mr. Cooper			.50
"	" Light Bread			.10
"	" Butter			.10
"	" Meat			.25
"	" 1 Bar Soap			.05
"	" 1 Razor			2.00
"	" 1 Map of Oklahoma for (school)			.25
Nov3	" Contributing to Sunday School			.05
Nov3	" Paid 1 Month's Board			9.00
	By Balance		10.25	
			27.00	27.00

Nov4	To Amn't on hand		10.25	
Nov4	By Lemons 10¢ and Apples 15¢			.25
Nov9	" 1 Umbrella			.85
" 9	" 1 Blacking Brush			.25
" 9	" Medicine from Dr. Hues			.55
" 9	" Castor Oil 10¢ and Turpentine 10¢			.20
" 9	" Stamps 10¢ and Envelopes 5¢			.15
" 9	" P.O. Box No. 131			.10
Nov.14th	" Spent at a party for candy & apples			.25
" 15	" Paid Mr. Woodward for Money lent [me?]			.10
Nov.16th	" Money Order for Xenophon's *Anabasis*			1.63
Nov.16th	" Money Order for *New York Independent*			.28
Nov.16th	" Coffee for Mrs. Woodward on board bill			.10
Nov.16th	"Writing Paper 10¢ Envelopes 5¢			.15
Nov.16th	" Stamps			.08
	Balance			5.01
			10.25	10.25

[*page 230*]

Nov.18th 1895	To Balance from p. 230		5.01	
Nov.16	By Flour			.56
Nov. "	By Meat (Beef)			.25
Nov. "	By Bacon			.15
Nov. "	" Soda 10¢, Sugar 5, Prunes 10, 1 lb.			.25
Nov. "	" Paid Mr. Mack for hauling			.05
Nov. "	" Soap 5¢, Eggs 15, Oil Pail 10			.30
Nov. 16th 1895	Balance		5.01	5.01

Nov.21th 1895 To Balance from above   3.57

Nov.23th 1895	By 4 lbs, Prunes		.25
" 23 1895	By 2 Collars @12½		.25
" 23 1895	1 Year's Sub. To *Okla. [State] Capital*		.50
" 23	By 10 Spool Thread		[.05]
" 23	By 50 lbs. Flour		.65
" 23	By 13 lbs Beef @ 6¢		.70
" 23	" Slate Pencils (for school)		.05
" 23	" Eggs		.10
" 23	" Prunes		.10
" 23	" Stamps		.10
" 27	" 5 lbs Pork of Mr. Gokey		.25
" 27	" Coal Oil		.10
" 28	" Candy at a Festival		.25
" 30	" Two Newspapers @5¢		.10
	Balance		.16
			3.57 3.57
Nov. 30,1895	To Cash on hand by salary	27.00	
" 30	By 1 Dana's *Geology*		2.00
" 30	" 1 Wentworth's *Trigonometry*		1.00
" 30	" 1 Steel's *Popular Physics*		1.00
" 30	" 1 First Reader for Mrs. Mack		.15
" 30	" Aid to Normal & Industrial School		2.00
Dec 1	" Payment for Two Week's Board		4.40
Nov. 30	" Lining for coat (for the edges)		.40
Nov. 30	" Paym't to Mr. Cooper 50¢ & Henry 10¢		.60
Nov. 30	" 1 Peck Apples		.30
Nov. 30	" Mirror 35 cts, Tunning Fork 25, Slate Pencils 05		[.65]
	Balance		27.00

[*page 231*]

[Dec] 1895

Dec. 6th	To Balance	14.50	
Dec 6th	By Beef 14lbs @.05		.70
Dec 7th	By Subscription to *New York Independent*		.28
" 7th	" Payment to *Christian Nation*		1.03
" 7th	" 3 lbs. Prunes		.25
" 7th	" 1 Rolling Pin 15 cts, Pants 75 cts. Rulers 5-5 cts		.95
" 7th	" Writing Paper 5 cts, Blank Book 5 cts, Lead Pencils 5¢	.15	
" 7th	" Stamps 9 cts, Sack .05		.14
" 14	" Frame for making chart to Mr. Allen	1.50	
" 14	" Prunes, 4 lbs.		.25
" 14	" Beef, 12 lbs.		.40

" 14	" Stamps 10, Envelopes 05, Slate Pencils 05		.20
" 14	" Black Cloth .05 cts, To Mr. Woodward 10¢		.15
	Balance		8.50
			14.50 14.50
Dec. 21	To Balance from above		8.50
" 21	By Contribution to Festival 25 cts and 1 Peck Peac 25¢		.50
" 21	" Ticket to McLoud		.35
" 21	" Newspaper 05, Ticket to Shawnee 40¢, (Dec.22)		.45
" 23	" Contribution to release LaFayette's saddle		1.25
" 23	" Payment to Carson Bros.		1.75
" 23	" 3 Ray's *Primary Arithmetic*'s @ .20¢		.60
" 26	" Ticket from Shawnee to Oklahoma City		1.15
" 27	" Round Trip Ticket from Ok. City to Edmond		.55
" 26	" 1 Box Blacking 05, Handkerchief 10		.15
" 27	" 1 History Massachusetts 10¢ Ticket to Choctaw City 40¢, Spent at Festival Dec. 28th 20¢		.70
" 27	" Payment to Mrs. Mammie Alford for sewing		.25
" 28	" Pens 05, (Jan 4 Ticket to Oklahoma City 40¢)		.45
Jan. 4	" Crackers .05 and Beef .05		.10

[*page 232*]

I owe April 8th 1895

	$	cts.
To John King (Paid $5 Jan 11th 1896)	8	35
To Mr. McFall (Paid Sept 1896 when I sold cotton)	1	50
To *Christian Nation* (Paid some but 7.75 left I believe)	9	50
To Good Health	2	00
To the *Southern Teacher*		75
To Houghton and Upp (Purcell, Ind. Ter)	3	00
To J. J. Johnson (Paid)	1	00
To William Shawnee (Paid)	7	00
	$33	10

There is owing to me from
Mr. Cummings   Paid 5.00
Mr. John Spybuck ($12+$10)

(Paid 11.50 Apr Jun May 1896)		22.00
Mrs. Chosa Starr		10.00
Mrs. Cegar		9.50
Mrs. Mammie Spybuck		10.00
David Alford	(Paid)	3.40
Mr. R. Webb	Never will be paid	.10

[handwritten page, left margin damaged]

			Dr.	Cr.
1896 Feb 1.	To Salary	Cash	30.00	
do.	By Am't sent William Shawnee			15.00
"	" Cost Money Order 10¢, New York Ind. 4th Mo. 25			.35
do.	" Pants 1.50 Vest 1.50, Collar Button 10¢			3.10
do.	" Map Kansas .25 *History Okla.* 1.25 Eggs .15			1.65
do.	" Second Money Order 3¢, Envelope stamped .05			.08
do.	" 3 Hdkfs 25¢, Newspapers 5¢			.30
do.	" Broom for school 20¢, 2 Tins 05			.25
do.	" Shoes for Bessie Berry for board and lodging			1.50
"	" Ticket from Okla. City to Choctaw City			.40
"	" Stamps .06			[.06]

[*Inside of the back cover, continued from an unknown page, are excerpts and summaries from the Koran.*]

are all recognized as prophets of God by the Koran, See chap 4, page 71, lines 17-27.

Christ Jesus is by the confession of the Koran an apostle of God, See Koran, chap. 4, page 72, lines 10 and 11.

There are not three Gods, only one God, chap 4, lines 13 & 14, page 72.

God can not have a son! Koran, chap 4, line 15, page 72.

Christ did not disdain to be a servant of God, chap 4, lines 16 & 17, page 72.

The Jews dislocate the words of the Pentateuch, chap. 5, page 75, line 9.

[Th]e Christians are answered, chap 5 lines 13-20

[Th]e book of the Koran claims to come from God, chap. 5, line 20, page 75.

God is not Christ the son of Mary, chap 5 line 24 page 75 also lines 25-27.

"Christ the son of Mary is no more than an apostle" chap 5, page 83, line 5.

"Apostles have preceded him" line 6, chap, 5 page 83[.]

"Jesus son of Mary" again, chapter 5, line 16, page 83.

"Christians" chap 5, line 28, p. 83. "Priests and monks" line 29, chap 5, page 83.

"They are surely infidels, who say, Verily God is Christ the son of Mary," chapter 5, page 82 line 33.

Christ said, "O Children of Israel, serve God, my Lord and your Lord," chapter 5, page 82, line 34.

["]Whoever shall give a companion unto God" shall go to hell, chap. 5, page 82 line 35.

God caused Jesus the son of Mary to follow the footsteps of the prophets and give him the Gospel, Chap 5, page 79.

God sent down the Law, containing direction and light, chap. 5, line 5, page 79.

God also sent down to Mohammed the book of the Koran with truth, confirming that scripture which was before it, chapter 5, page 79, line 24.

Gods address to Jesus and his response, chapter 5, pages 87 & 88.

"Unless some sign be sent to him from his Lord; we will not believe," chapter 6, lines 4 & 5, page 92.

They who accuse Mohammed's signs of fals[e]hood, are deaf and dumb, walking in darkness, chapter 6, page 92, line 10.

"But whoso shall accuse our signs of falsehood, a punishment shall fall on them, because they have done wickedly,["] chapter 6, page 93, line 3

"They have sworn by God, by the most solemn oath that if a sign come unto them, they would certainly believe them: Say, Verily signs are in the power of God alone," chapter 6, p. 99, lines 8-10.

O Prophet, stir up the faithful to war, chap 8, page 132, line 20.

Christ is the son of God, chap. 9, line 1 page 138.

Epilogue

Although William Ellsworth Shawnee stopped recording in his journals in 1897, various sources, such as city directories, newspapers, and federal and Indian census records, contain information about the relationship between the Absentee Shawnees and his family beyond that time. The beginning of the twentieth century marked the end of an era. Radical changes occurred in the lives of the peoples in Indian and Oklahoma territories, including the Absentee Shawnees and their black interpreters as the Absentee Shawnees continued to seek ways to protect their traditional culture.

Challenges of Native and Black Oklahomans beyond 1897
In 1898, the year after Shawnee stopped keeping a diary, the U.S. Congress enacted the Curtis Act, and amended it to the Dawes Act. The Curtis Act authorized the Dawes Commission to establish tribal memberships, allot communal lands in severalty to the various members, and break up Cherokee, Creek, Choctaw, Chickasaw, and Seminole governments in Indian Territory. Separate membership rolls were established for each of those Native groups and their freedmen. Following those actions, in 1901 the federal government granted citizenship to all Native groups in Indian Territory setting the stage for assimilation of the five eastern groups into mainstream society and for Oklahoma statehood.

In 1907 Oklahoma attained statehood, which united the Oklahoma and Indian Territories. Race was used to shape the lives of all Oklahomans. The Oklahoma State Constitution defined two races—black (of African descent) and white (all others)—and required separation of the races in education and other aspects of daily life. The intent was to continue to assimilate the Natives into mainstream society, while blacks would be marginalized through Jim Crow policies. The plights of both groups were unsatisfactory. After it became clear that the allotment and assimilation policies were not working for the American Indians in Oklahoma, in 1936 federal policy for the state changed again with the passage of the Oklahoma Indian Welfare Act, which restored tribal lands in Oklahoma and permitted tribes to reorganize under federal law for the purposes of self-government. Although the federal government had previously established tribal memberships and forced the Natives to begin using Indian blood quantum in identifying tribal members, in 1936 the government allowed the tribes to establish their own membership criteria. Since then Native groups in Oklahoma established their own rules for membership and worked to strengthen their individual tribal governments. Jim Crow policies that did not allow blacks to vote between 1910 and 1938, or to mingle with others in public places, were revoked in the 1960s, thereby giving blacks opportunities to compete in mainstream society.

The Absentee Shawnees beyond 1897

The Absentee Shawnees lost four leaders within four years at the end of the nineteenth and the dawn of the twentieth century. Throughout that time, the Quaker missions remained as a stabilizing influence until other churches and public schools moved into the area and rendered them no longer profitable.

As the close of the nineteenth century neared, Big Jim had always tried to maintain his traditional way of life. Taking advantage of this knowledge, land speculators in 1898 persuaded Big Jim and some of his followers to move to Mexico to be free of white encroachment. In 1900 the Absentee Shawnees under Big Jim vacated their lands in Oklahoma and went to the Mexican Kickapoo village of Nacimiento in Coahuila, Mexico. Thomas Alford's brother, David, accompanied Big Jim. Why would Big Jim seek the company of someone from White Turkey's band? Big Jim no doubt trusted his nephew David and probably needed a confidant who could speak English. Although he was considered to be progressive, David still embraced the Absentee Shawnee culture. He could also speak English, which made him valuable to Big Jim's cause. When they reached Mexico, there was smallpox there, and they were exposed to the disease before they knew it. When they tried to return to Oklahoma, Mexican authorities placed them under quarantine when they reached Sabinas. All but two of Big Jim's followers died there. David Alford had left secretly on horseback and returned home before he succumbed to the disease. He died on September 29, 1900. Big Jim died on September 30, 1900,[1] whereupon Little Jim, who still lived in

Little Axe, Oklahoma, became hereditary chief of the traditional band. He was twenty-eight at the time.[2]

White Turkey, the last hereditary chief of the progressive band, died in 1899. John King, who would have been the next chief, refused to take the chieftainship because it no longer held status. The chiefs had been replaced by a business council, on which John King played a key role. John King died in 1902.[3]

The Absentee Shawnee Mission operated as long as it was profitable. George N. Hartley and L. Ella Hartley led the mission until 1904. William P. Haworth and his wife, Abigale C. Haworth, succeeded the Hartleys. Clark Brown and Elmer T. Brown succeeded the Haworths and led the mission through 1919 when the government schools closed. At that time, most of the Indian children were either attending public schools or boarding schools. Lawrence E. Lindley and Emelia R. Lindley next led the mission, from 1920 until 1923. In 1924 the mission church was abandoned and the property sold to the Pottawatomie County Historical Society.[4] All of William Shawnee Sr.'s children had attended the mission and school at one time or another. The impact of the closure of the mission on the Absentee Shawnee community is unclear.

Thomas Wildcat Alford (July 15, 1860-August 3, 1938) continued to be a leader among the Absentee Shawnees. He taught at the missions as long as they were open and held jobs at the Shawnee Indian Agency, including the position of chief clerk. By 1929 he had translated and published the Gospels in the Absentee Shawnee language. By 1936 he had written and published a history of the Absentee Shawnees from the point of view of the Indians. After his first wife, Mary, died, Alford married twice more and had additional children. His third wife, Fannie, whom he married on May 16, 1903, was John King's widow. Alford is listed as white on the 1920 U.S. Census and as Indian on the 1930 U.S. Census. After Alford's death on August 3, 1938, following a long-term illness, he was buried in the Tecumseh Cemetery.[5]

Thomas W. Alford's oldest three sons, whom Shawnee often wrote about in his journals, followed in the footsteps of their father and became productive citizens. They attended Hampton Institute after attending the Absentee Shawnee Indian School. Pierrepont Alford attended Hampton, including graduate school, from 1900 to 1906. Following Hampton, he attended Worcester Polytechnic Institute and later worked as a surveyor and teacher. Several years after he left Hampton, however, Pierrepont told a Hampton faculty member that he "had been fired twice for having attended a 'nigger' school." Paul Leon Alford attended Hampton from October 1902 to January 1907, and held a variety of jobs after leaving there. Charles Reese Alford attended Hampton from October 1902 until he graduated in 1906. He was awarded a trade certificate and also held a variety of jobs.[6]

The Black Interpreters beyond 1897

Within the same four years that the Absentee Shawnees lost four tribal leaders, they lost two black interpreters. During the same era, Shawnee had witnessed the birth of his daughter, but it is not certain that he witnessed the birth of a new brother or a change in his father's health. William Ellsworth Shawnee's daughter, Ethel Magnolia, was born on January 1, 1898,[7] which was just over a month after the date of the last entry in his journals. By that time, Shawnee had moved his family to the city of Shawnee[8] and continued to teach at the black school.[9] Just over a year after the birth of his daughter, Shawnee died, in spring 1899, although he was listed on the 1900 Absentee Shawnee census.[10] Where he died and his cause of death and burial place are unknown. Near the time of Shawnee's death, his youngest brother, David Dick Shawnee, was born on April 3, 1899.[11] After Shawnee's death, his widow, Ellen, moved away from Pottawatomie County. About a year and a half later, she married Ross Hawkins on September 27, 1900.[12]

By 1900 Shawnee's father was a patient in the Norman Oklahoma Sanitarium.[13] It is uncertain why Shawnee Sr. was in a mental institution because the 1900 U.S. Census does not list his ailment as it does for some of the other patients. Four of his children would later be institutionalized. As with Shawnee Sr.'s ailment, theirs are unknown. Throughout much of the twentieth century, many people were institutionalized for ailments that were not well understood at the time, such as epilepsy. Shawnee never gave any indication in his diary that his father, or his siblings, showed signs of mental illness. Shawnee Sr. died on April 4, 1901, and was buried in the cemetery in Norman. A Goodland, Kansas, newspaper reported his death as follows: "Indian Chief Dies in Asylum. Gutrie [sic], Ok., May 4. William Shawnee, the aged chief of the Shawnee

Indians and founder of Shawnee City, died yesterday in Oklahoma [sic] insane asylum. He owned 2,000 acres of land in Pottawatomie County." Though some of the newspaper data are questionable, it is obvious from this account that Shawnee Sr. was known outside of his home in Pottawatomie County. His widow, Julia, probated his will and, in addition to herself, named all of his living children and his granddaughter Ethel as heirs.[14]

The lives of Shawnee Sr.'s children reflect how upbringing, education, laws, and the fluidity of the definition of race affected their self-identity and influenced their decisions. Their racial identifications kept slipping among the categories of white, mulatto, Indian, and colored. All of the children were listed on the Absentee Shawnee census at some point, beginning in 1892, indicating that they were tribal citizens. Dudley Joseph, Walter Homer, George Eli, and Eva Estella—the four oldest living children at the time of Shawnee Sr.'s death—appear on the Absentee Shawnee census through 1939. In 1930 the Absentee Shawnee census began listing Indian blood quantum of tribal citizens. Shawnee Sr.'s oldest three boys appear on the census with an Indian blood quantum of one-quarter, while Eva's Indian blood quantum appears as one-sixteenth. The younger children appear on the Absentee Shawnee census through 1901 when their father died and on the U.S. census in 1910 with an Indian blood quantum as one-third. All of the children identified with their Absentee Shawnee citizenship and the Indian heritage of their father when they attended off-reservation boarding schools. When Shawnee Sr.'s three oldest living boys attended Haskell Institute, they were accepted as Indian students. When his younger children later enrolled in Hampton Institute as adopted Absentee Shawnee citizens, the faculty treated them the same as the other Indian students but questioned their Indian heritage.

Before 1900 Shawnee's brother Dudley Joseph worked in Lawrence, Kansas, as a clerk. City records there identified his race as "colored."[15] In spite of the fact that he warned William Ellsworth Shawnee to stay away from "colored" girls, he married a young black woman, Louisa C. Bruner, who had attended Hampton. Louisa died on December 2, 1904. On May 7, 1908, Dudley married Sarah A. Lewis in Wagoner County, Oklahoma.[16] In 1910 he was identified in the U.S. census as a mulatto, and his wife, Sarah, was listed as black. According to that census, he was a farmer who owned his home. After 1910 he appears only on the Absentee Shawnee census through 1939, but there is no indication that he lived anywhere else except Oklahoma.[17]

Walter Homer Shawnee made a career as a clerk working for the federal government in the Indian service. He lived in Arizona, Wisconsin, and the state of Washington, where he retired. He had one daughter, Ollie, by his first wife, Willie, who was a white woman. His daughter appeared on the Absentee Shawnee census through 1939, at first with an Indian blood quantum of one-eighth, then as one-sixteenth. At the time, he lived among the Absentee Shawnees in Pottawatomie County. When Willie died, he married another white woman and had another daughter, Anne. On the federal census Walter was always listed as Indian or white.[18]

Federal documents also indicate fluidity in George Eli Shawnee's race. In 1900 he was a clerk at Haskell Institute. In 1910, he was listed on the U.S. Census in Wagoner, Oklahoma, as a farmer, and his race was listed as mulatto. His wife, Sadie Bland, was a Wyandotte Indian. On his World War I draft registration card, dated September 12, 1918, George Eli was identified as an Indian clerk at Haskell Institute in Kansas. George was involved in alumni activities and became the first chairman of the Haskell Alumni Association. According to the 1930 U.S. Census, he was still serving as a clerk in Kansas. His wife, Sadie, enrolled their son, Gilbert, and their daughter, Elizabeth, in the Wyandotte Indian Agency. In the 1930 U.S. census, George and Sadie were listed as Indians. In 1940 on the Kansas census, they were listed as white. George died in Los Angeles on December 26, 1963.[19]

Eva Estella Shawnee was identified in the Absentee Shawnee census in 1892 and then again on each census thereafter through 1939. By 1899, she had attended the Shawnee Indian School in Shawneetown for nine years; she then attended Hampton Institute from 1900 to 1904 as an Indian student. She was there at the same time as Pierrepont Alford. Mary C. Williams from the Absentee Shawnee Indian School asked that Eva be entered to Hampton as an Indian because she had not lived around blacks at home, who were deemed to be inferior. Blacks and Indians were separated on the Hampton campus.[20] Eva attended Oberlin College in 1904 and 1905[21] and returned to Hampton as a post-graduate from November 1906 to February 1908.[22] She went on to become a

Fig. E.1. Eva Estella Shawnee (January 18, 1884-?), date unknown. Courtesy of Hampton University Archives.

domestic science teacher; a school matron in the State Deaf, Dumb, and Blind Institute at Taft, Oklahoma; and a teacher at Langston University in central Oklahoma.[23] She married Cornelius Lowe, an undertaker.[24] She also taught in Elizabeth City, North Carolina, and lived in Tulsa and Muskogee, Oklahoma. In the 1930 U.S. Census, she is listed as a widow; her four children are also listed.[25] In 1960 she was the proprietor of the Shawnee Nursing Home, which offered twenty-four-hour nursing care and nutritious meals to black men and women.[26]

Rebecca Shawnee appears in the 1892 Absentee Shawnee census. After attending the Shawnee Indian School, Rebecca attended Hampton Institute as an Indian. She displayed no personal allegiance to either the black or Indian race, but observed celebration days for both. She believed the best part of New Year's Day was the Emancipation Proclamation observation at which black students talked about improved conditions of their people—their being ministers and teachers. She looked forward to Indian Citizenship Day when Indians would discuss improvements "their people had made and are making." These would include homes, farms, churches, and schools, among other things.[27] After Rebecca married, she initially lived among the Indians where she grew up. She married Isiah W. Walker from Texas on May 5, 1906, in Tecumseh. They had a daughter, Nellie Mae, who was born in 1907. In 1910 they lived in Boley, and were all identified on the U.S. Census as "mulatto." Her husband worked for a company that manufactured concrete blocks, and she was a homemaker. By 1920 they had moved to Choctaw and lived on a farm. The 1920 U.S. Census identified him as black and identified Rebecca and Nellie Mae as mulatto.[28] In 1924 in Tulsa, Rebecca married J. D. Pitts

above Fig. E.2. Rebecca Shawnee (April 14, 1885-?), date unknown. Courtesy of Hampton University Archives.

from South Carolina. In the 1930 U.S. Census, he was listed as the proprietor of a dry goods store, and Rebecca as a homemaker. Nellie Mae worked as a clerk in the store. They lived in Seminole and all were identified as black. Rebecca died in 1940 and is buried in the Tecumseh Cemetery.[29] Like Shawnee Sr., she died in an insane asylum.[30]

Lydia Shawnee entered Hampton as an Indian on January 27, 1907.[31] On the enrollment form, she claimed to be one quarter Indian. She advanced to the senior class, but did not graduate.[32] Instead, she graduated in 1912 from the nursing program at Dixie Hospital (a training school for black nurses).[33] She married an undertaker, H. W. Ragsdale, and was a partner in his funeral home. The funeral home was located in Tulsa on Greenwood Avenue, in the area called "Black Wall Street" where the Tulsa race riots broke out in the 1920s. She served as one of the nurses on the riot recovery team.[34] She used her degree from Dixie Hospital to serve in many other capacities and treated both black and white patients.[35] She died in an insane asylum.[36]

After attending the Absentee Shawnee Indian School, Marquis Lafayette Shawnee entered Hampton in 1906 while his sister Lydia was studying nursing.[37] He earned an agricultural certification in 1910.[38] He was a farmer, agriculture teacher, and high school principal. He was the farm

Fig. E.3. Lydia Shawnee (January 15, 1887-?), dated 1909. Courtesy of Hampton University Archives.

demonstrator for Atoka, he taught at Langston University, and he was county agent for Kingfisher County.[39] His World War I draft card identified him as black. He lived in Earlsboro, Oklahoma, at the time. On June 28, 1917, he married Anna B. Hardman from Okmulgee, Oklahoma.[40] In the 1920 federal census he was identified as a mulatto. In 1930 and after the U.S. Census identified him as black. By then, he and Anna B. had at least three children.[41] According to Marquis's 1942 World War II draft card, he was serving as a teacher at Langston University at the time. In 1952 he lived in Oklahoma City as a porter.[42] He died on May 12, 1979.[43]

above Fig. E.4. Marquis Lafayette Shawnee (August 24, 1890-May 12, 1979), in 1910. Courtesy of Hampton University Archives.

Emeline Shawnee attended Hampton between 1909 and 1912.[44] Under the student outing system, in which Indian students lived with and worked for local white families as part of their training, Emeline and her sister Julia Inez worked together at times cooking and cleaning.[45] After leaving Hampton, Emeline was a housewife, domestic servant, and a teacher. She married N. F. Deckerd from Tulsa in Shawnee on September 25, 1908. He was twenty-eight and she was eighteen. She married George W. Wofford on October 16, 1915, in Muskogee. He was thirty-eight and she was twenty-two. Later she married M. Rankin.[46]

Julia Inez Shawnee attended

Fig. E.5. Emeline Shawnee (1891-?), 1910. Courtesy of Hampton University Archives.

Fig. E.6. Julia Inez Shawnee (1892-?), 1908. Courtesy of Hampton University Archives.

Hampton as an Indian student between November 1908 and April 1912. On her enrollment application, she claimed to be one quarter Indian. Though she advanced to the senior class, she did not graduate. After leaving Hampton, she worked as a domestic servant and homemaker.[47] She married a blind musician, Clarence DeRadcliffe, on November 1, 1917, in Wagoner, Oklahoma. In 1925 they lived in Muskogee. Like several of her family members, she died in an insane asylum.[48]

Donna Fredonia Shawnee (May 1895-?) advanced to the fourth grade in the Absentee Shawnee Indian School.[49] She was the only one of Julia's children who did not attend Hampton. On April 28, 1909, she married Alexander Brown from Tennessee in Tecumseh, Oklahoma. They had one son, Edgar Brown.[50] After her husband died, she worked as a domestic in Muskogee, Shawnee, and Tulsa. She still lived in Tulsa in 1935.[51] By 1940 she had married Emmett Bess. They were identified in the U.S. census as black and together had eight children.[52]

William Ellsworth Shawnee's youngest sister, Myrtle Shawnee (March 28, 1897-?), attended Hampton in 1917 after it lost its government subsidy for Indians. She became part of the black student body, and her family paid all of her expenses.[53] In 1901 she was identified in the Absentee Shawnee census with her father, William Shawnee, and her mother, Julia.[54] In 1910 she was listed in the U.S. census as an Indian, along with her mother.[55] In 1920 she lived in Tulsa as a black domestic.[56] In 1921 she was still living in Tulsa, along with her younger brother David.[57] In 1923 she married Isaac (Ikey) J. Guess in Tulsa. Ikey was from Shawnee.[58] In 1930 Myrtle and Ikey lived in Tulsa with their three children, Jean Francis (8), Janella A. (5), and Ike Jr. (3). Each one of them was listed as "Negro" in the census.[59]

David Dick Shawnee (April 3, 1899-January 27, 1974) was listed in the 1900 federal census as an Indian with his parents and siblings Donna and Myrtle. In the 1910 federal census he was again listed as an Indian. David attended Hampton between 1920 and 1922 as a black student. He identified his father's race as part Cherokee.[60] In 1918 he registered for the draft for World War I at Youngstown, Ohio. His race was listed as black.[61] In 1921 he lived in Tulsa as a student and chauffeur and in 1926 as a butler.[62] In 1940 he was a rock breaker in Nebraska. He was a single lodger.[63] In 1942 he served in the army as a private.[64] He died on January 23, 1974, and was buried in Rolling Oaks Cemetery, Tulsa.[65]

Ethel Magnolia Shawnee, William Ellsworth Shawnee's daughter and only child, lived with her maternal grandparents James and Lesser Coffey in Lincoln Township in Seminole County, Oklahoma, in 1910. She was thirteen years old at the time.[66] Her mother, Ellen, had died in 1904. Ethel married Richard Bruner on June 18, 1912.[67] Although she was only fourteen, the marriage record indicates her age as eighteen. Richard died in California in 1951 and was buried in the Golden Gate National Cemetery in San Bruno. Ethel died in Boley, Oklahoma, on September 8, 1971. She was interred in the same cemetery as her husband on September 21, 1971.[68]

Looking Ahead

One hundred years after the Civil War, U.S. citizens were still reeling from Reconstruction. The interrelations among American Indians, blacks, and whites were still going through upheavals. The Indians had been forced onto reservations, and as Indian policy changed, were stripped of their governments, given U.S. citizenship, and subsumed into mainstream American culture, which was deemed to be superior. New settlers had clamored for and acquired land on the western frontier where Indians once lived, at the cost of "Indian wars." Slavery had been pronounced "dead," and enslaved blacks were set free. Blacks, who once lived in close proximity to whites, were then given U.S. citizenship, disenfranchised, and segregated from other citizens. The Indian Territory, though it should not have been involved in the Civil War, or the "Indian wars," was forced into the conflicts and bore the brunt of them. The territory in which the Cherokee, Chickasaw, Choctaw, Creek, Seminole, and other American Indians lived—on land that was to be theirs forever—was redistricted and other tribes moved in, followed by non-Indians.

Indian Territory ceased to exist, and the lives of the Indians and those who lived among them, by invitation, went through rapid changes. Histories that describe these complex events, the changing constructions of race and identity after the Civil War, and more recently the relationships among American Indians, blacks, and whites in Indian Territory after the war are silent about the changes in the interrelations of Indians, blacks, and whites who lived in what is known today as central Oklahoma. William Ellsworth Shawnee, a black Quaker who lived among the Absentee Shawnees in central Oklahoma, in his diary offers Absentee Shawnee language lessons and hints at those interrelations. The lives of his Indian friends and his family, who once enjoyed close relationships in Indian Territory, were forced out of their comfort zone into the United States, where the changing constructions of race and identity forced them into separate black and white worlds. A hundred years after the Civil War, the federal government acknowledged that federal policies had not been working for all of its citizens. Civil rights legislation ensued to offer equal protection to all U.S. citizens without disenfranchising them, segregating them, denying them their cultural traditions, or forcing them to identify with racial categories that they did not understand. William Ellsworth Shawnee's diary provides additional information on Absentee Shawnee history and the history of their black interpreters. It allows us to examine a group of Indians who voluntarily adopted blacks as citizens after the Civil War and to see how their paths diverged from an Indian world to separate black and white worlds over time, through the intervention of others, and ultimately to a world in which all U.S. citizens are finally considered as equals.

TABLE E.1. Children of William and Julia Shawnee

Name	Birth Death or latest year recorded alive	Profession	Marriage(s) First/ Subsequent	Children
Eva Estella	1/18/1884 Alive 1960	Teacher, owner of "Shawnee Nursing Home" in Muskogee	Cornelius G. Lowe (undertaker)	Edward H. Detty Myra Jean Janice
Rebecca*	4/14/1885 1/18/1940	Homemaker	Isiah W. Walker/ Jefferson Davis Pitts	Nellie Mae Walker
Lydia*	1/15/1887 Alive 1943	Mgr. funeral home; nurse on Tulsa Race Riot recovery team	Hartwell W. Ragsdale (funeral home in Tulsa)	Gwendolyn M. Ragsdale
Marquis Lafayette*	8/25/1889 5/12/1979	Teacher, farmer	Anna B. Hardeman	Marquis Jr. Anna B. Jr. Unknown son
Emeline	1/15/1891 Alive 1945	Domestic, homemaker, teacher	N. F. Deckerd/ George Wofford/ M. Rankin	
Julia Inez*	1892 Alive 1930	Domestic, homemaker	Clarence R. DeRadcliffe (musician)	
Donna Fredonia	3/31/1895 3/19/1963	Domestic	Alexander Brown/ Wilbert Owens/ Emmett Richard Bess	Edgar Brown
Myrtle	3/28/1897 Alive 1930	Domestic, homemaker	Isaac J. Guess (butler)	Jean Frances, Janella A., Isaac Jr.
David Dick	4/3/1899 1/27/1974	Rock quarry laborer in Nebraska, WWII veteran	Bachelor	

Sources: Ancestry.com, including census and voter lists; Social Security Death Index; U.S. City Directories; birth, death, and marriage records; Oklahoma wills and probate records; and military records. Lindsey, *Indians at Hampton Institute*. Willows, "Disaster Relief Report, Riot June 21, 1921," accessed at http://tulsahistory.org/wp/wp-content/uploads/2016/10/1921-Red-Cross-Report-December-30th.pdf.

* Died in an insane asylum.

Appendix

A Survey of the William E. Shawnee Collection in the Pottawatomie County Museum, Shawnee, Oklahoma

    A.1. Big Jim's Memorial to the Commissioner of Indian Affairs

    A.2. Legal Documents

    A.3. Accounting Documents

    A.4. Letters

    A.5. Figures

This appendix provides vital documentary and pictorial support to several of the passages in William E. Shawnee's journals. With the original copy of William E. Shawnee's journals, we discovered a faded and torn brown envelope. As researchers, this envelope aroused our curiosity, filling us with anticipation that we were about to uncover new information that had been hidden up to now.

The contents of the envelope, as well as the envelope itself, bore the marks of time: stains, discoloration, and frayed pages. However, for the most part the envelope's contents—several handwritten, typed, and printed documents—were legible, and the photographs it enclosed featured likenesses that were distinguishable, although not all were labeled as to content. The documents include typed notes and minutes of meetings between U.S. government and Absentee Shawnee representatives; forms from banks, schools, court filings, and decisions; petitions for and awarding of land grants; and decisions of minor claims.

The collection of items in the envelope has been divided into five categories here: Big Jim's memorial to the Commissioner of Indian Affairs, legal documents, accounting documents, letters, and photographs.

A.1. Big Jim's Memorial to the Commissioner of Indian Affairs

After spending ten years on the Kickapoo Reservation in Indian Territory, Big Jim and his followers were physically removed by the U.S. military to Little Axe in Cleveland County. The following documents deal with the U.S. government's resettlement of Big Jim's band of the Absentee Shawnees and their claim. The forms are signed or marked "x," with the typed names of the signatories placed beside the "x," by tribal members representing the Absentee Shawnees. These official documents reflect two significant facts about William E. Shawnee: first, that he was the official clerk and recorder for Big Jim's Absentee Shawnee business council and the negotiation committee, and second, that his father, William Shawnee Sr., was the interpreter for and confidant to Big Jim during these proceedings.

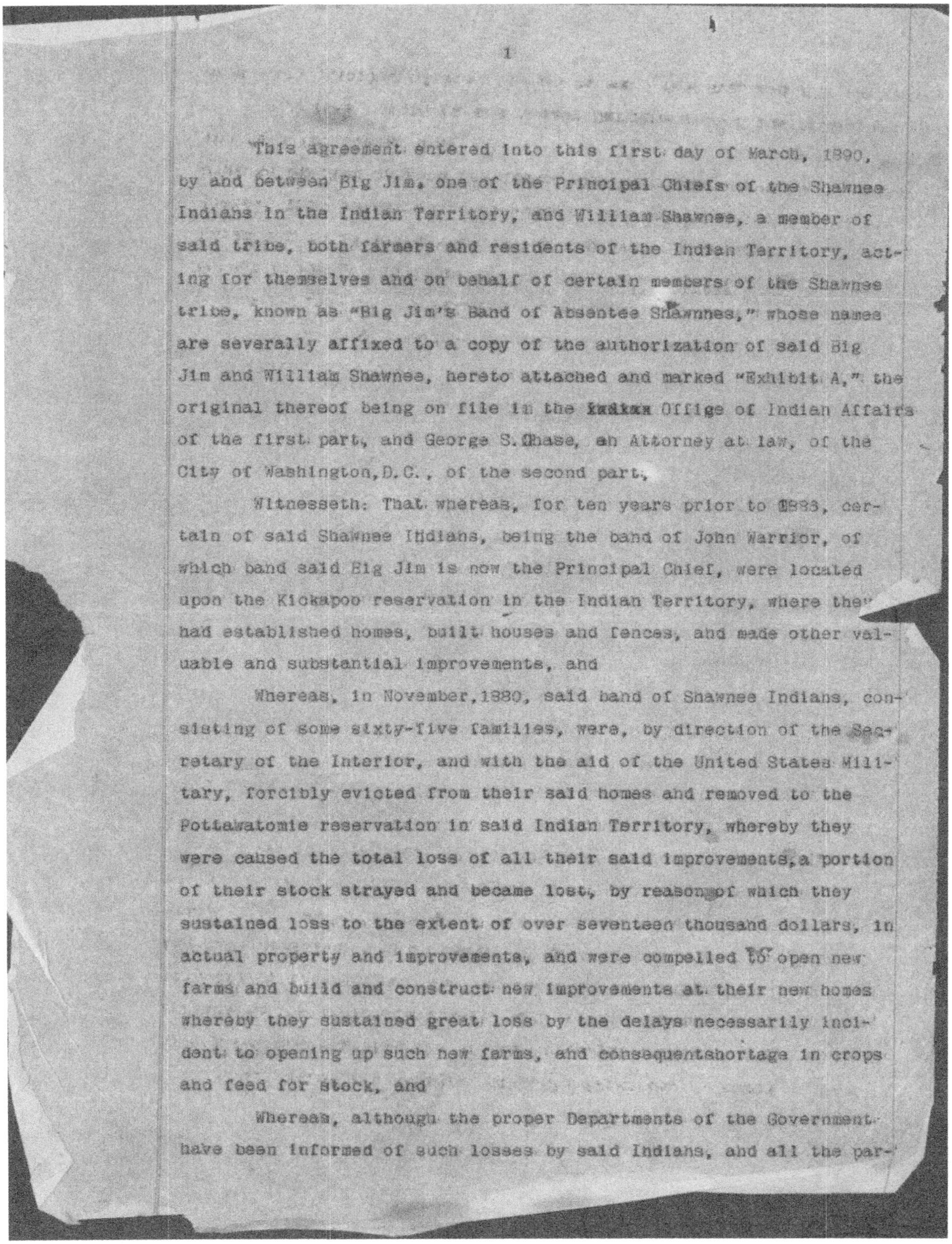

This agreement entered into this first day of March, 1890, by and between Big Jim, one of the Principal Chiefs of the Shawnee Indians in the Indian Territory, and William Shawnee, a member of said tribe, both farmers and residents of the Indian Territory, acting for themselves and on behalf of certain members of the Shawnee tribe, known as "Big Jim's Band of Absentee Shawnees," whose names are severally affixed to a copy of the authorization of said Big Jim and William Shawnee, hereto attached and marked "Exhibit A," the original thereof being on file in the Indian Office of Indian Affairs of the first part, and George S. Chase, an Attorney at law, of the City of Washington, D.C., of the second part,

Witnesseth: That whereas, for ten years prior to 1883, certain of said Shawnee Indians, being the band of John Warrior, of which band said Big Jim is now the Principal Chief, were located upon the Kickapoo reservation in the Indian Territory, where they had established homes, built houses and fences, and made other valuable and substantial improvements, and

Whereas, in November, 1880, said band of Shawnee Indians, consisting of some sixty-five families, were, by direction of the Secretary of the Interior, and with the aid of the United States Military, forcibly evicted from their said homes and removed to the Pottawatomie reservation in said Indian Territory, whereby they were caused the total loss of all their said improvements, a portion of their stock strayed and became lost, by reason of which they sustained loss to the extent of over seventeen thousand dollars, in actual property and improvements, and were compelled to open new farms and build and construct new improvements at their new homes whereby they sustained great loss by the delays necessarily incident to opening up such new farms, and consequent shortage in crops and feed for stock, and

Whereas, although the proper Departments of the Government have been informed of such losses by said Indians, and all the par-

Fig. A.1.1. Page 1 of Big Jim's memorial document, dated March 1, 1890. Courtesy of Pottawatomie County Museum, Shawnee, Oklahoma.

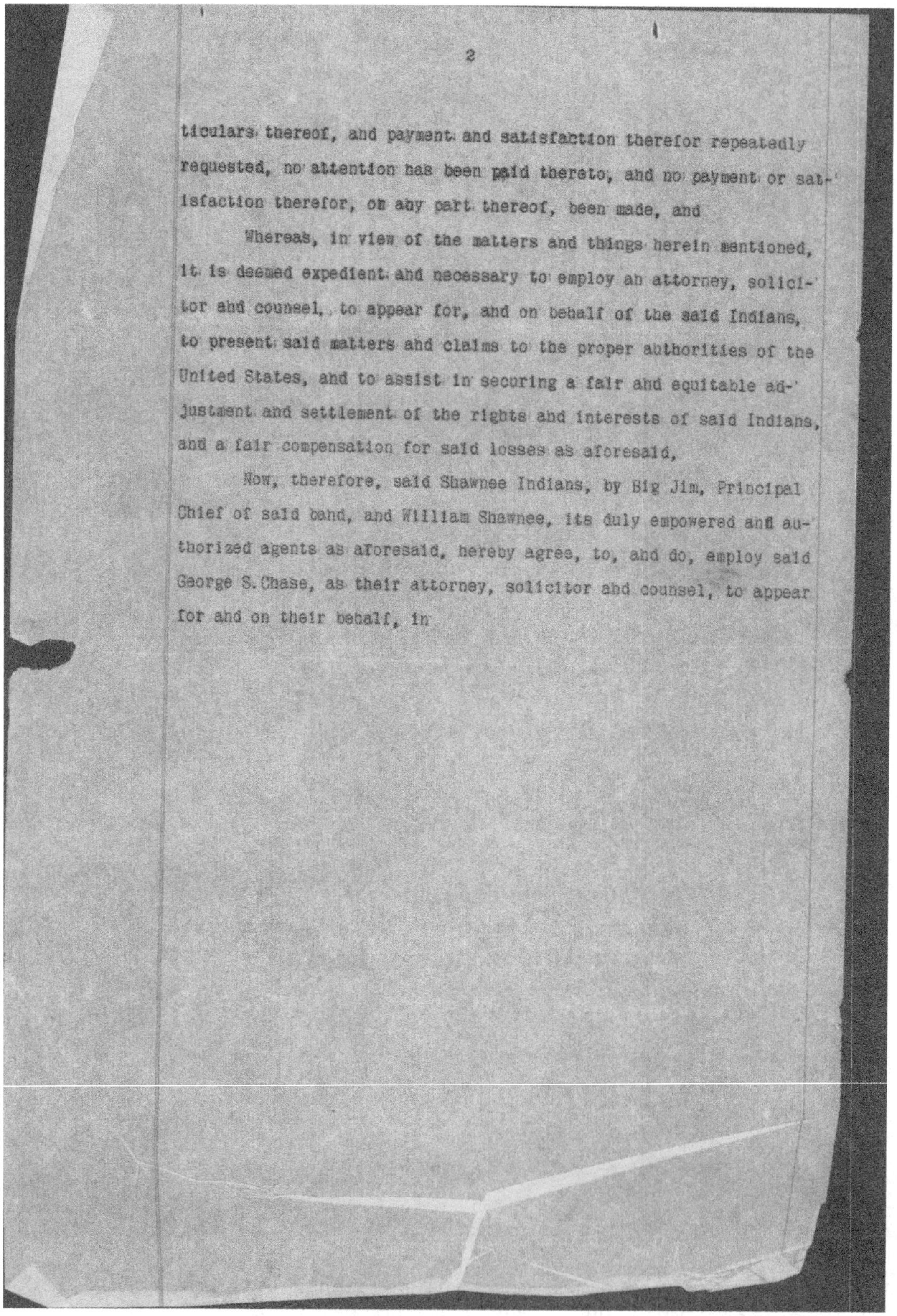

2

ticulars thereof, and payment and satisfaction therefor repeatedly requested, no attention has been paid thereto, and no payment or satisfaction therefor, or any part thereof, been made, and

Whereas, in view of the matters and things herein mentioned, it is deemed expedient and necessary to employ an attorney, solicitor and counsel, to appear for, and on behalf of the said Indians, to present said matters and claims to the proper authorities of the United States, and to assist in securing a fair and equitable adjustment and settlement of the rights and interests of said Indians, and a fair compensation for said losses as aforesaid,

Now, therefore, said Shawnee Indians, by Big Jim, Principal Chief of said band, and William Shawnee, its duly empowered and authorized agents as aforesaid, hereby agree, to, and do, employ said George S. Chase, as their attorney, solicitor and counsel, to appear for and on their behalf, in

Fig. A.1.2. Page 2 of Big Jim's memorial document, dated March 1, 1890. Courtesy of Pottawatomie County Museum, Shawnee, Oklahoma.

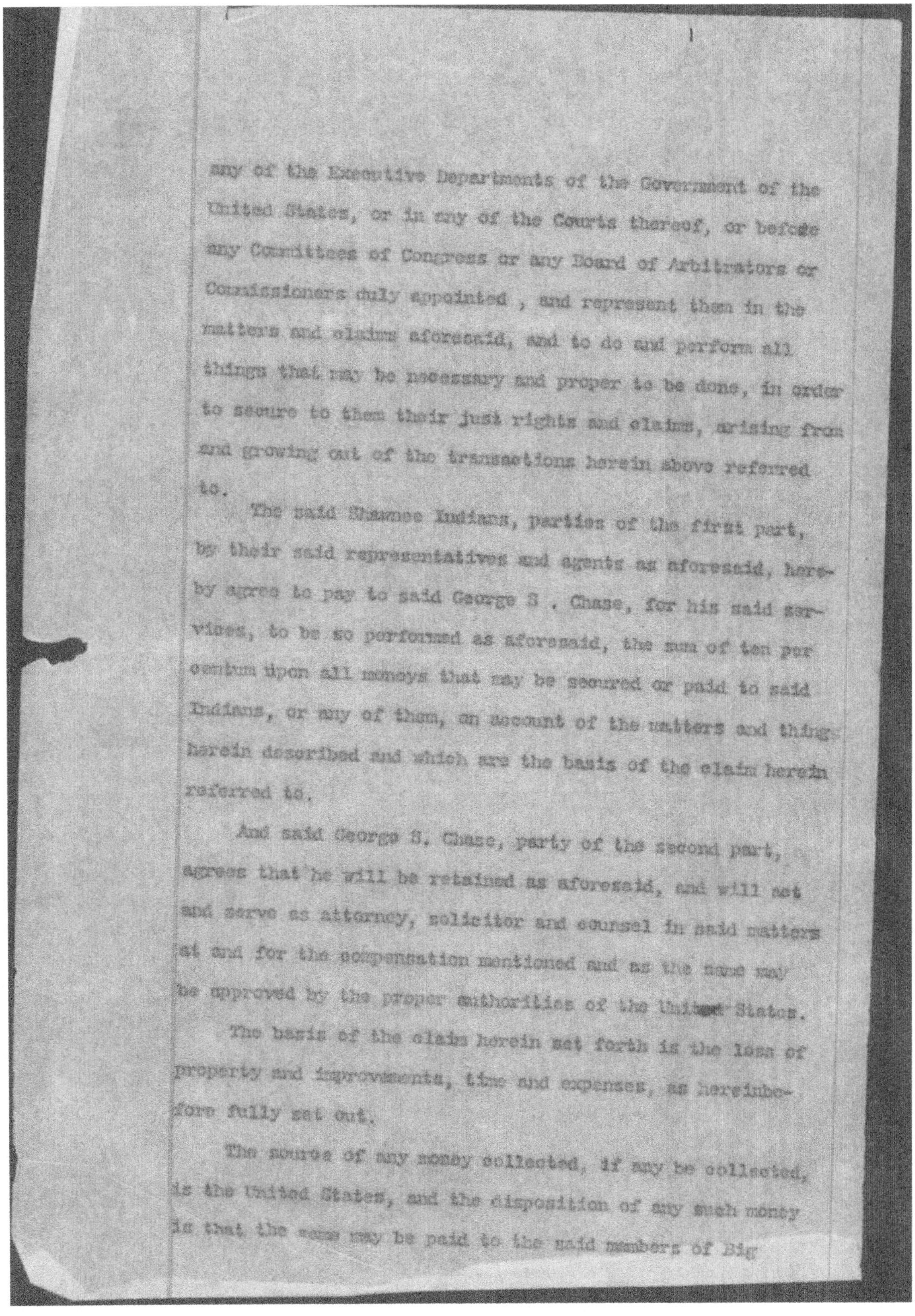

any of the Executive Departments of the Government of the United States, or in any of the Courts thereof, or before any Committees of Congress or any Board of Arbitrators or Commissioners duly appointed, and represent them in the matters and claims aforesaid, and to do and perform all things that may be necessary and proper to be done, in order to secure to them their just rights and claims, arising from and growing out of the transactions herein above referred to.

The said Shawnee Indians, parties of the first part, by their said representatives and agents as aforesaid, hereby agree to pay to said George S. Chase, for his said services, to be so performed as aforesaid, the sum of ten per centum upon all moneys that may be secured or paid to said Indians, or any of them, on account of the matters and things herein described and which are the basis of the claim herein referred to.

And said George S. Chase, party of the second part, agrees that he will be retained as aforesaid, and will act and serve as attorney, solicitor and counsel in said matters at and for the compensation mentioned and as the same may be approved by the proper authorities of the United States.

The basis of the claim herein set forth is the loss of property and improvements, time and expenses, as hereinbefore fully set out.

The source of any money collected, if any be collected, is the United States, and the disposition of any such money is that the same may be paid to the said members of Big

Fig. A.1.3. Page 3 of Big Jim's memorial document, dated March 1, 1890. Courtesy of Pottawatomie County Museum, Shawnee, Oklahoma.

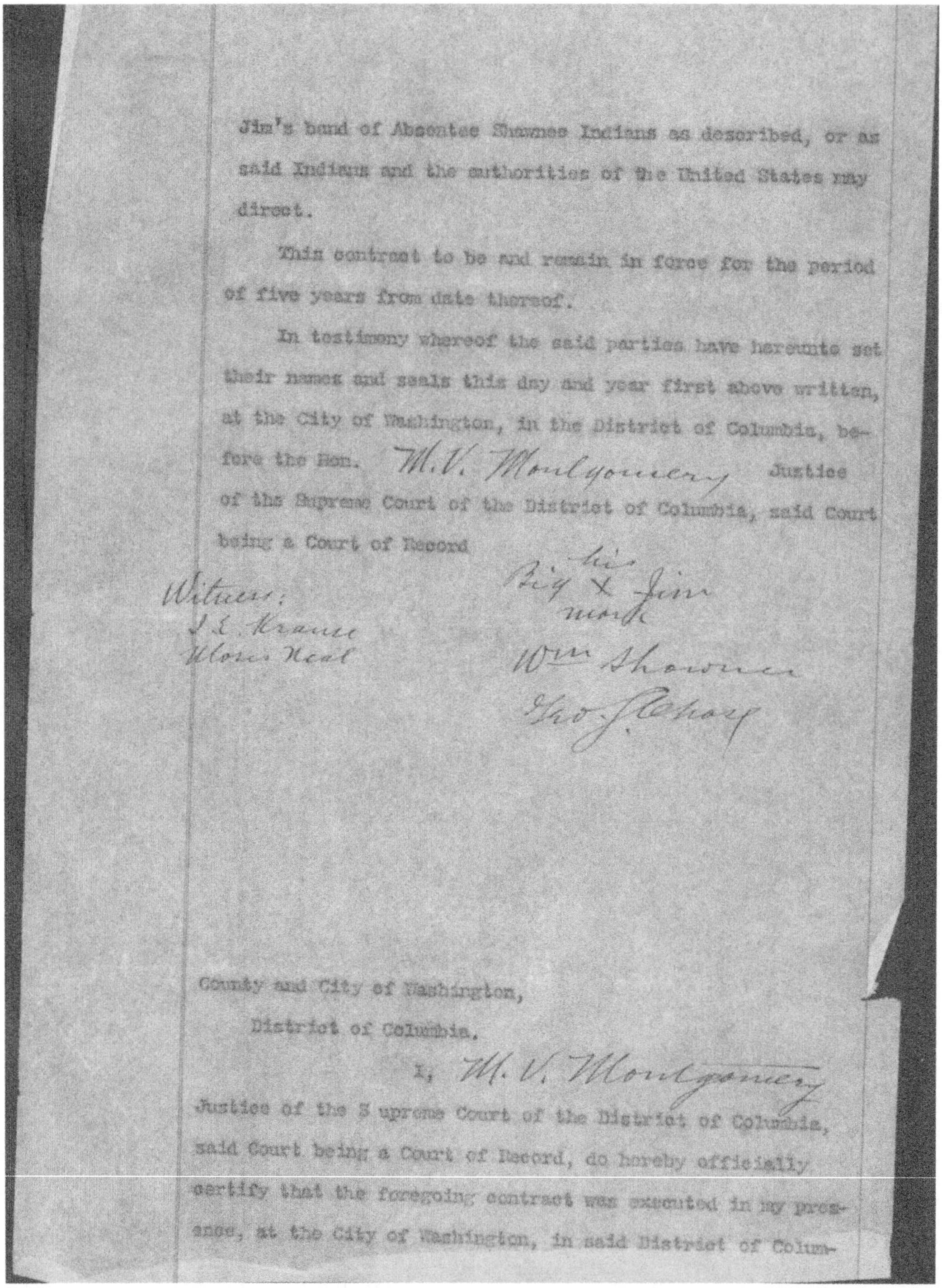

Jim's band of Absentee Shawnee Indians as described, or as said Indians and the authorities of the United States may direct.

This contract to be and remain in force for the period of five years from date thereof.

In testimony whereof the said parties have hereunto set their names and seals this day and year first above written, at the City of Washington, in the District of Columbia, before the Hon. *M. V. Montgomery* Justice of the Supreme Court of the District of Columbia, said Court being a Court of Record.

Witness:
J. E. Krause
Ulora Neal

his
Big X Jim
mark
Wm Shawnee
Geo. J. Achoy

County and City of Washington,
District of Columbia.

I, *M. V. Montgomery* Justice of the Supreme Court of the District of Columbia, said Court being a Court of Record, do hereby officially certify that the foregoing contract was executed in my presence, at the City of Washington, in said District of Colum-

Fig. A.1.4. Page 4 of Big Jim's memorial document, dated March 1, 1890. Courtesy of Pottawatomie County Museum, Shawnee, Oklahoma.

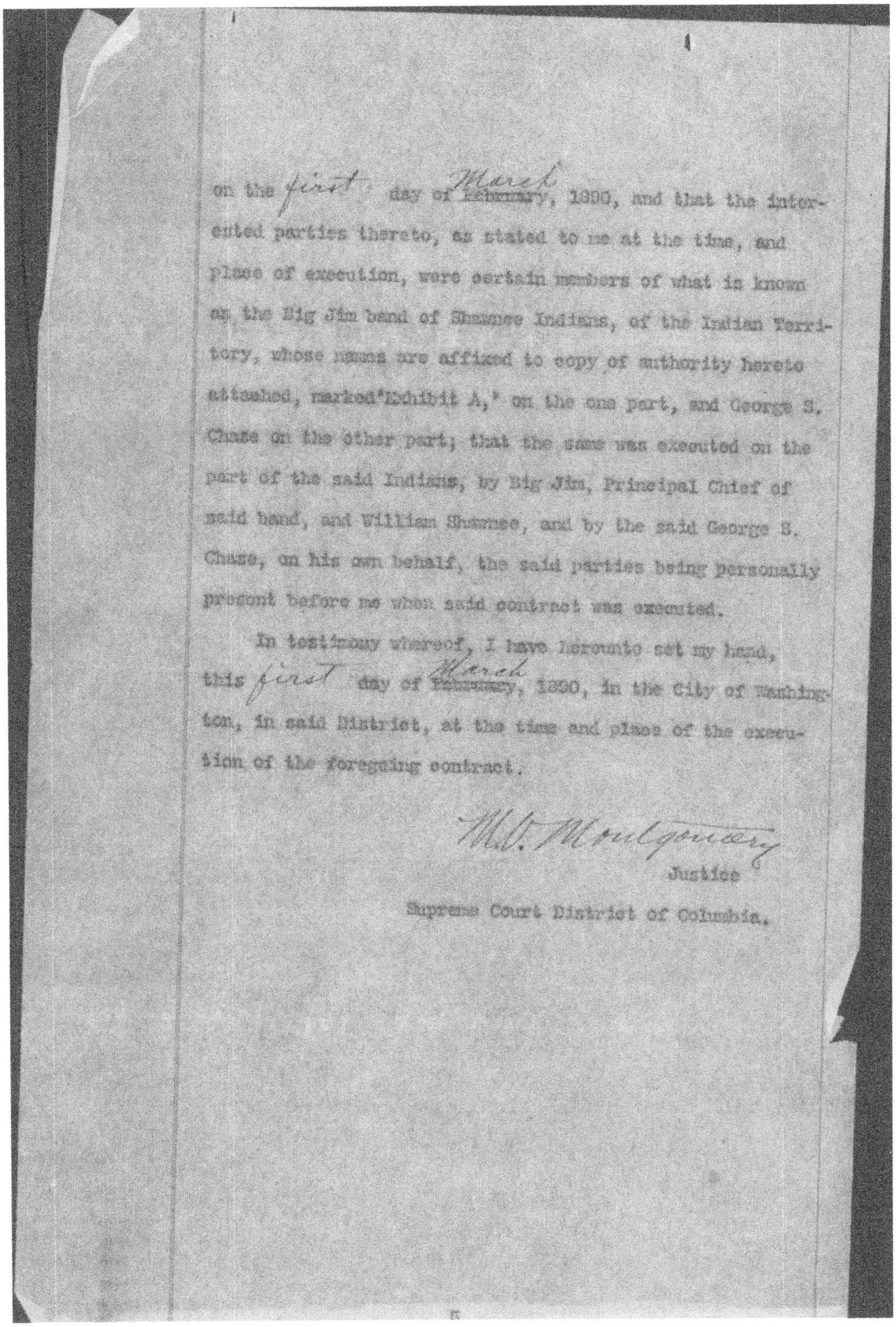

on the *first* day of ~~February~~ *March*, 1890, and that the interested parties thereto, as stated to me at the time, and place of execution, were certain members of what is known as the Big Jim band of Shawnee Indians, of the Indian Territory, whose names are affixed to copy of authority hereto attached, marked "Exhibit A," on the one part, and George S. Chase on the other part; that the same was executed on the part of the said Indians, by Big Jim, Principal Chief of said band, and William Shawnee, and by the said George S. Chase, on his own behalf, the said parties being personally present before me when said contract was executed.

In testimony whereof, I have hereunto set my hand, this *first* day of ~~February~~ *March*, 1890, in the City of Washington, in said District, at the time and place of the execution of the foregoing contract.

M.V. Montgomery
Justice
Supreme Court District of Columbia.

Fig. A.1.5. Page 5 of Big Jim's memorial document, dated March 1, 1890. Courtesy of Pottawatomie County Museum, Shawnee, Oklahoma.

"Exhibit A." 1

Whereas, certain individual claims of members of the Absentee Shawnee Band of Indians for losses sustained by the destruction of their property then situate on Deep Fork River in the limits of the Sac and Fox Indian Agency in the Indian Territory, having been referred to the Commissioner of Indian Affairs at Washington, D.C. by the United States Indian Agent for the Sac and Fox Agency accompanied by a list of the names of the claimants and their respective losses

The Commissioner of Indian Affairs referred the matter to the Department of the Interior.

The Department referred the matter to Congress for action thereon.

And whereas, we whose names are herewith subscribed being the parties referred to in the above-mentioned claims, or the heirs of said parties and being members of said Absentee Shawnee Band of Indians and residents upon the Pottawatomie reservation in the Indian Territory reposing full faith and confidence in the fidelity, honesty and good faith of Big Jim [the Principal Chief] and William Shawnee, also of our said Absentee Shawnee Band of Indians and residents on the Pottawatomie reservation in the Indian Territory and farmers by occupation, do duly commission, nominate, constitute and appoint the said Big Jim [the Principal Chief] and William Shawnee our true and lawful attorneys and agents, for us, and in our stead, place and names and on behalf of the said hereinafter mentioned individual members of said Absentee Shawnee Band of Indians, to appear before any Committee, or Committees of Congress, the proper Executive Department of the United States Government, or before any Court or Courts thereof or before Commissioners or Arbitrators appointed by proper authority or either or all as may be necessary, and there prosecute to final recovery certain claims of individual members of said Absentee Shawnee Band of Indians and their heirs for the value of certain property of theirs destroyed by the United States soldiers on Deep Fork river in the Indian Territory within the
the

Fig. A.1.6. Page 6 of Big Jim's memorial document, dated December 3, 1889. Courtesy of Pottawatomie County Museum, Shawnee, Oklahoma.

limits of the Sac and Fox Indian Agency, on or about the 15th day of November 1896. Giving and granting unto our said Agents and attorneys or either of them full power to employ and enter into a contract with an attorney or attorneys upon such terms and conditions as they may deem proper and advisable, to prosecute and collect or aid in the prosecution or collection of said claims or either of them and also to do and perform all and every act and thing whatsoever requisite and necessary to be done in and about the premises as fully to all intents and purposes as we might or could do if personally present; with full power of substitution and revocation hereby ratifying and confirming all that our said attorney or attorneys, or their substitutes shall lawfully do, or cause to be done by virtue t thereof.

And in consideration of the services so to be rendered as afores aforesaid, we do hereby agree to pay to our said attorneys compensation as follows, viz: Twenty per cent [20%] of whatsoever sum or sums may be recovered from the United States on any of said claims of the said individual members of the said Absentee Shawnee Band of Indians, which compensation it is hereby agreed shall be retained and paid by the proper accounting officers of the United States to our said attorney or attorneys; the balance of said sum or sums so recovered or collected to be paid the said hereinafter mentioned individual members respectively as allowed by the proper authorities.

Provided that our said attorneys or attorneys shall pay and satisfy any council they may employ to aid them in the prosecution of said claims out of the per centage herein before agreed to be paid to them.

This Power of Attorney to continue and be in force for the period of five years from date hereof.

In witness whereof we have hereunto subscribed our names,

Long Jim, his x mark.

Ned Captain, his x mark.

Coon, his x mark, guardian for heirs of Sam.

Fig. A.1.7. Page 7 of Big Jim's memorial document, dated December 3, 1889. Courtesy of Pottawatomie County Museum, Shawnee, Oklahoma.

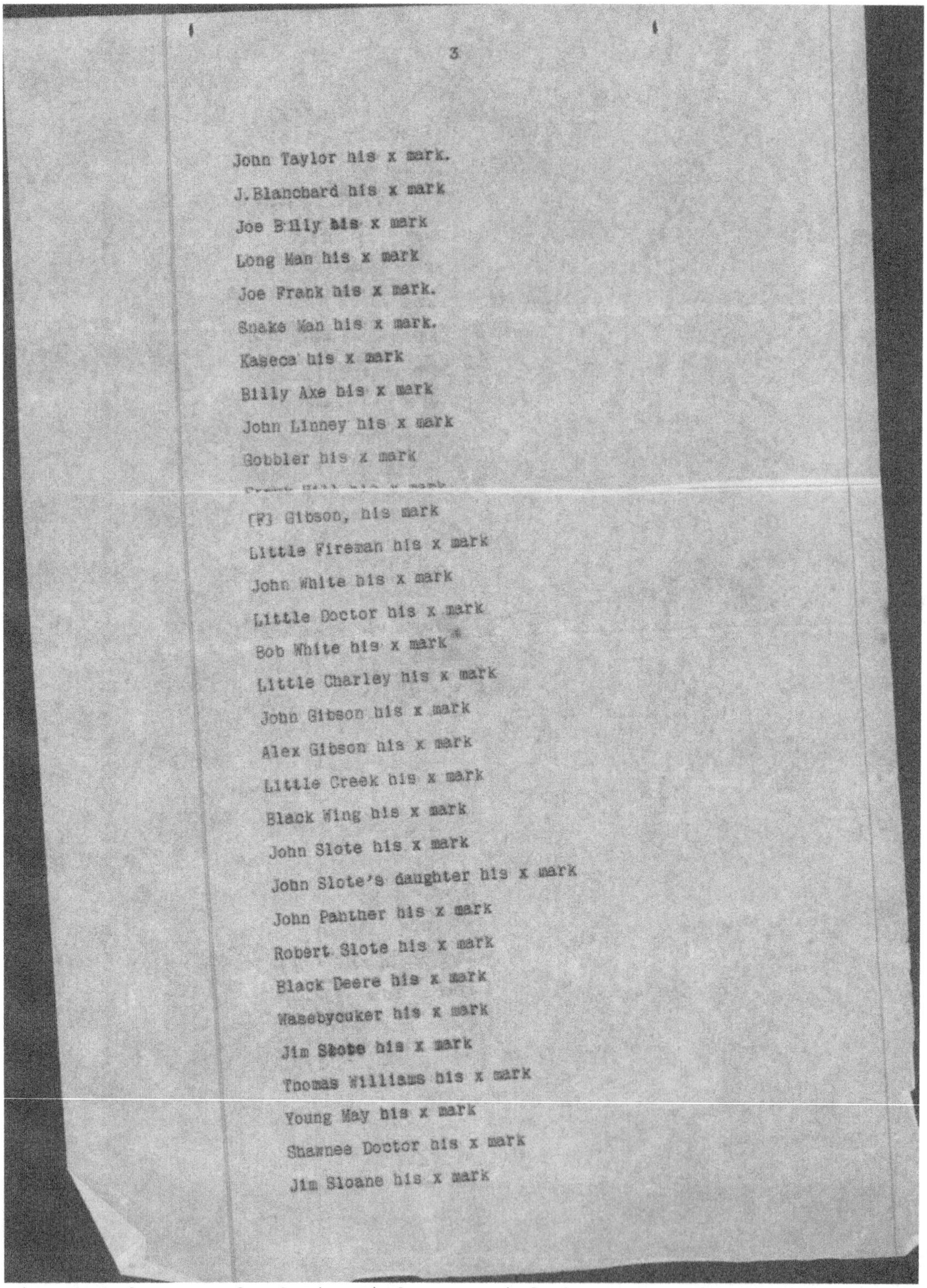

3

John Taylor his x mark.
J. Blanchard his x mark
Joe Billy his x mark
Long Man his x mark
Joe Frank his x mark.
Snake Man his x mark.
Kaseca his x mark
Billy Axe his x mark
John Linney his x mark
Gobbler his x mark
[F] Gibson, his mark
Little Fireman his x mark
John White his x mark
Little Doctor his x mark
Bob White his x mark
Little Charley his x mark
John Gibson his x mark
Alex Gibson his x mark
Little Creek his x mark
Black Wing his x mark
John Slote his x mark
John Slote's daughter his x mark
John Panther his x mark
Robert Slote his x mark
Black Deere his x mark
Wasebycuker his x mark
Jim Stote his x mark
Thomas Williams his x mark
Young May his x mark
Shawnee Doctor his x mark
Jim Sloane his x mark

Fig. A.1.8. Page 8 of Big Jim's memorial document, dated December 3, 1889. Courtesy of Pottawatomie County Museum, Shawnee, Oklahoma.

Pole Cat his x mark
Jane Sloane her x mark
J. Mac his x mark
Nancy Scott her x mark
John Pecan his x mark
John Welch his x mark
John Coons his x mark
Isaac McCoy his x mark
George Pacan his x mark
Little Captain his x mark
Quacala his x mark
John Welch, Jr. his x mark
Jim Charley his x mark
Owsage his x mark
Sam Warrior his x mark
Law-paw-ay his x mark
Sar-sa-qua-ha his x mark
Jackson Clark his x mark
Henry Clark his x mark
Dave Moon his x mark
Joe Caddo his x mark
Shawnee Buck's girl her x mark
Na-he-qua-by-ese her x mark
Paw-ma-hes her x mark
Big Jim his x mark
John Scott his x mark
Che-kwe-wa her x mark
Dave Uchee his x mark
Jim Clark his x mark.

We certify that the foregoing persons signed their names or made their marks in our presence this third day of December, 1889.

W. E. Shawnee
Clerk of Committee.

Fig. A.1.9. Page 9 of Big Jim's memorial document, dated December 3, 1889. Courtesy of Pottawatomie County Museum, Shawnee, Oklahoma.

State of Kansas
County of Sedgewick ss

I, C. Reed, Judge of the 18th Judicial District of the State of Kansas the same being a Court of Record, do hereby certify that A. W. Crain and Charlie Chisholm personally appeared before me this 13th day of February, 1890, and that the said parties were the identical persons that they represent themselves to be as was shown and that they compose the Committee duly appointed and authorized to obtain th the signatures of the members of the Absentee Shawnee Band of Indians who sustained the losses caused by the destruction of their property situated on Deep Fork river in the limits of the Sac and Fox Agency said destruction of property being committed by soldiers of the United States Government on or about the 15th day of November 1886 and whose names are hereto affixed; and that said Committee was duly appointed and authorized to secure the names of said Absentee Shawnee Band of Indians or as many of them as possible was conclusively proven by producing in my presence a certified copy of the council minutes of the council of said Absentee Shawnee Band of Indians in Council assembled, on the 3rd day of December, 1889, and the the said A. W. Crain and Charlie Chisholm constituting the said Committee testified and affirmed that they were secured willingly and without any coercion on the part of the said Committee or others and that the names thereto affixed are the identical persons that sustained the said injuries and losses.

In witness whereof I have hereunto set my hand and caused the seal of said Court to be affixed this 13th day of February, 1890.

C. Reed,
Judge.

A.1.10. Page 10 of Big Jim's memorial document, dated February 13, 1890. Courtesy of Pottawatomie County Museum, Shawnee, Oklahoma.

Fig. A.1.11. Page 11 of Big Jim's memorial document. Blank page. This page is missing from the collection of pages found in the envelope.

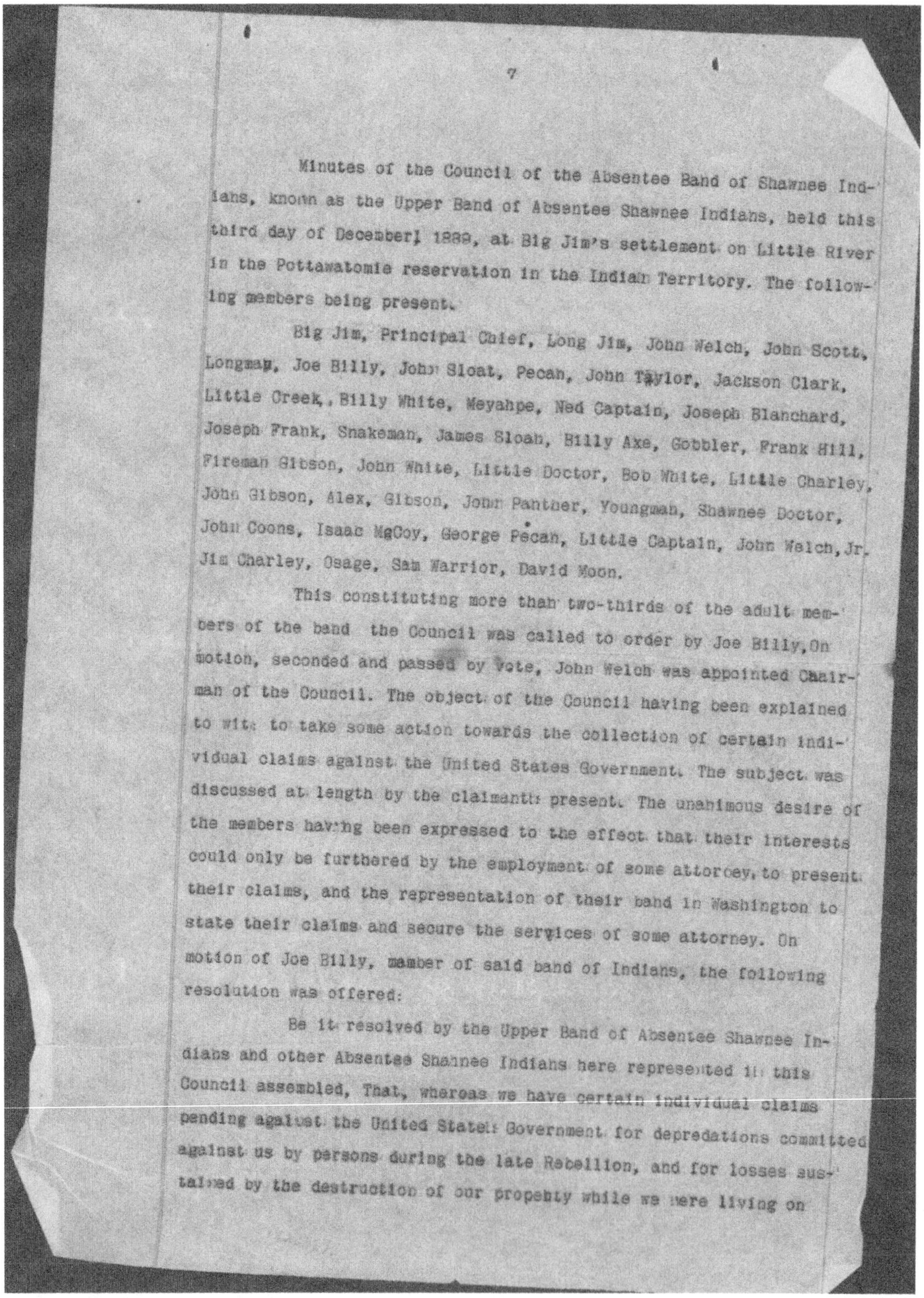

Minutes of the Council of the Absentee Band of Shawnee Indians, known as the Upper Band of Absentee Shawnee Indians, held this third day of December] 1889, at Big Jim's settlement on Little River in the Pottawatomie reservation in the Indian Territory. The following members being present.

Big Jim, Principal Chief, Long Jim, John Welch, John Scott, Longman, Joe Billy, John Sloat, Pecan, John Taylor, Jackson Clark, Little Creek, Billy White, Meyahpe, Ned Captain, Joseph Blanchard, Joseph Frank, Snakeman, James Sloan, Billy Axe, Gobbler, Frank Hill, Fireman Gibson, John White, Little Doctor, Bob White, Little Charley, John Gibson, Alex Gibson, John Panther, Youngman, Shawnee Doctor, John Coons, Isaac McCoy, George Pecan, Little Captain, John Welch, Jr., Jim Charley, Osage, Sam Warrior, David Moon.

This constituting more than two-thirds of the adult members of the band the Council was called to order by Joe Billy. On motion, seconded and passed by vote, John Welch was appointed Chairman of the Council. The object of the Council having been explained to wit: to take some action towards the collection of certain individual claims against the United States Government. The subject was discussed at length by the claimants present. The unanimous desire of the members having been expressed to the effect that their interests could only be furthered by the employment of some attorney, to present their claims, and the representation of their band in Washington to state their claims and secure the services of some attorney. On motion of Joe Billy, member of said band of Indians, the following resolution was offered:

Be it resolved by the Upper Band of Absentee Shawnee Indians and other Absentee Shawnee Indians here represented in this Council assembled, That, whereas we have certain individual claims pending against the United States Government for depredations committed against us by persons during the late Rebellion, and for losses sustained by the destruction of our property while we were living on

Fig. A.1.12. Page 12 of Big Jim's memorial document, dated February 13, 1890. Courtesy of Pottawatomie County Museum, Shawnee, Oklahoma.

the Deep Fork river in the Sac and Fox Agency, Indian Territory, by sol soldiers of the United States Government, that to secure proper recognition of our claims and action thereon tending toward the collection of our claims for damages sustained, that we appoint and authorize a Delegation of two members of our band of Indians to proceed to the city of Washington, D.C., and there take any action they may deem best to further our wishes, and that we grant them a Power of Attorney to that effect permitting them to employ an attorney to aid them and offer for such service any sum not greater than twenty per cent [20%] of the amount collected on each claim.

The motion being seconded by Long Jim, it was put to vote and passed unanimously.

On motion fo Longman, a member of said band of Indians, the following resolution was offered:

Be it resolved by the Upper Band of Absentee Shawnees and the other Absentee Shawnees here represented this day in Council assembled, that we, reposing full faith and confidence in the fidelity honesty and good faith of Big Jim, our Principal Chief and William Shawnee also of our band of Shawnee Indians, that we deem them the most most fitting persons to represent our interests in the city of Washington before the proper Departments, and we do hereby authorize, appoint and constitute them a delegation to proceed to Washington at their earliest convenience and then and there execute our wishes as we set forth in the Power of Attorney we grant them for such purpose. The motion being seconded by John Taylor was put to vote and passed unanimously.

On motion of Joe Billy, the following resolution was offered:

Be it resolved by the Upper Band of Absentee Shawnee Indians and other Absentee Shawnees here represented this day in Council assembled that William K. Shawnee be appointed as Clerk of this Council with authority to make record of the proceedings of the meeting and to aid our delegation in securing and enrolling

Fig. A.1.13. Page 13 of Big Jim's memorial document, dated February 13, 1890. Courtesy of Pottawatomie County Museum, Shawnee, Oklahoma.

the names of such individual claimants of our people who desire to intrust thir interests to our delegates and agents and make record of the same. The motion being seconded by John Taylor was put to vote and passed unanimously.

On motion of Long Jim the following resolution was offered:

Be it resolved by the Upper Band of Absentee Shawnees Indians and other Absentee Shawnee Indians hererepresented in this Council assembled, that we, reposing full faith and confidence in the fidelity, honesty and good faith of Alex W. Crain, of the Seminole Nation, and Charlie Chisholm of the Absentee Shawnee Band of Indians, do hereby authorize, appoint and constitute them a Committee to obtain the names, signatures and consent of such members of our Absentee Shawnee Band of Indians as desire to employ the said Big Jim the Principal Chief, and William Shawnee to act as their agents in Washington, D.C., with the authority granted them by our Power of Attorney; that the duty of this Committee shall be to obtain the signatures of the proper claimants or their legal heir or heirs, to obtain this consent willingly on the part of the claimant; and to fully explain the purport of the Power of Attorney granted our Agents to the claimants before they sign their names or make their marks ; and they shall be further authorized to accompany our delegates and agents before the Judge of a Court of Record and there identify our Agents and answer such questions as shall be put to them concerning this matter that our Power of Attorney may be approved, etc.

The motion being seconded by Joe Billy was put to vote and passed unanimously.

No further business being brought before the Council a motion for adjournment to enable the enrolling Committee to proceed to business was made, seconded and carried by vote.

John Welch, his x mark.
Chairman of the Council of the Upper B
Band of Absentee Shawnee Indians

Fig. A.1.14. Page 14 of Big Jim's memorial document, dated February 13, 1890. Courtesy of Pottawatomie County Museum, Shawnee, Oklahoma.

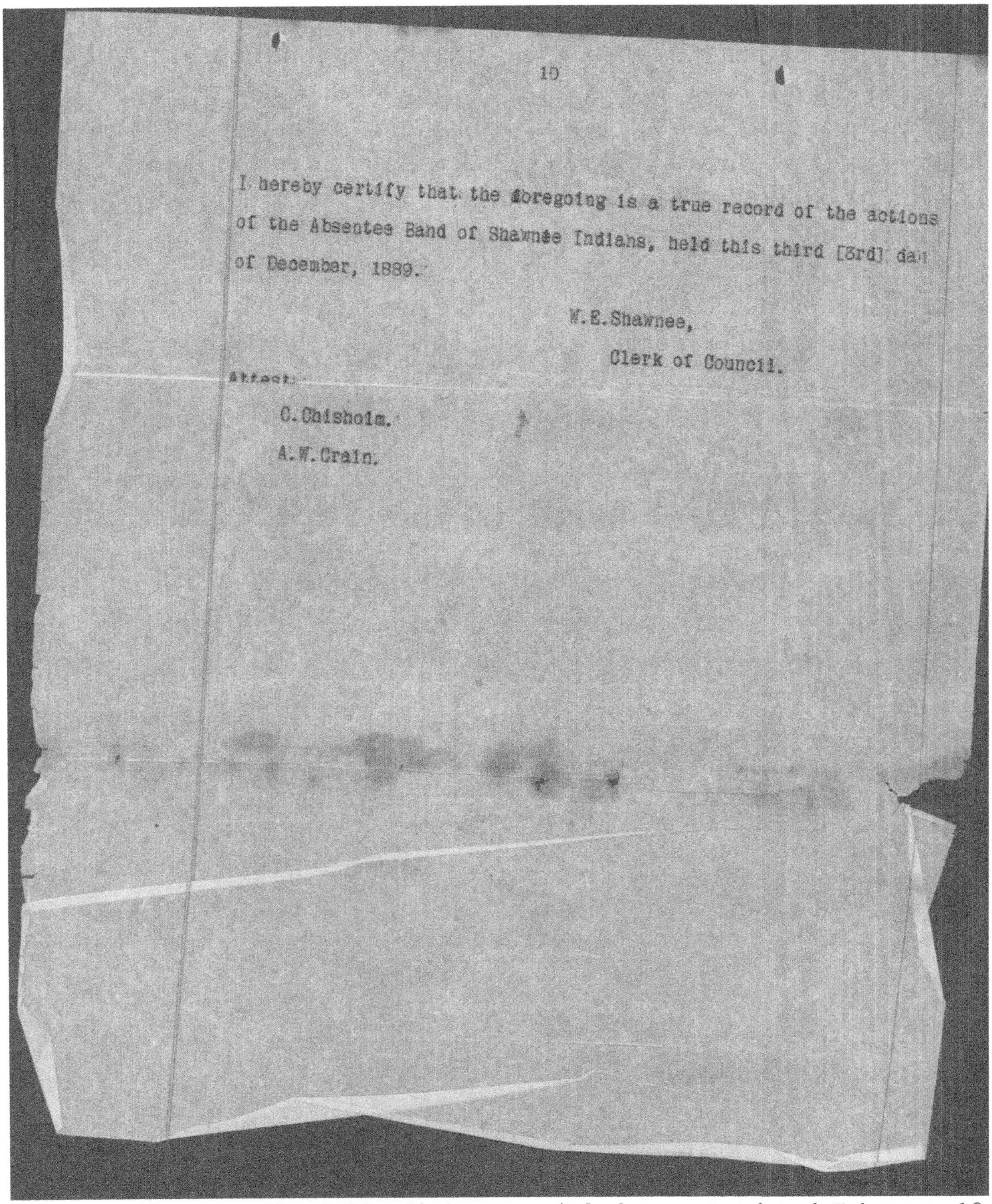

I hereby certify that the foregoing is a true record of the actions of the Absentee Band of Shawnee Indians, held this third [3rd] day of December, 1889.

                        W. E. Shawnee,
                            Clerk of Council.

Attest:

   C. Chisholm.
   A. W. Crain.

Fig. A.1.15. Page 15 of Big Jim's memorial document, dated February 13, 1890. Courtesy of Pottawatomie County Museum, Shawnee, Oklahoma.

A.2. Legal Documents

The legal documents in this section of the appendix deal with an array of procedures requiring attorneys, notary certification, and court decisions. Some of paperwork here is for simple leases of land for "agricultural purposes" for specific lengths of time. Another document is a lawsuit or petition filed for payment due on a farm land lease. Most important of these materials might be the "Certificate of Selection" for William Shawnee Sr. and William E. Shawnee. These documents, signed by an Indian agent, provide for land allotments. These certificates not only specify the plot of land but also serve to certify that the person receiving the allotment was a member of the Absentee Shawnee tribe.

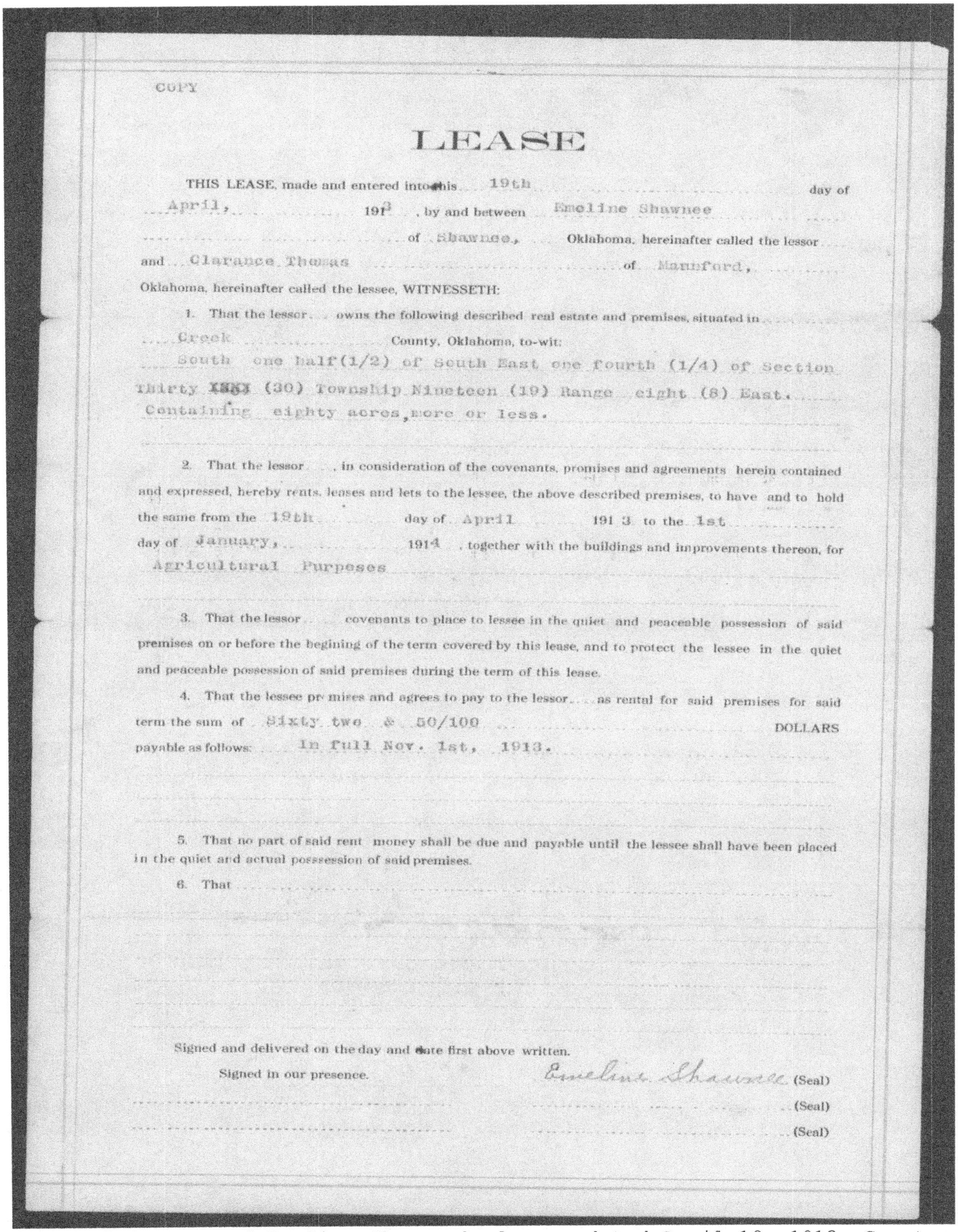

COPY

LEASE

THIS LEASE, made and entered into this 19th day of April, 1913, by and between Emeline Shawnee of Shawnee, Oklahoma, hereinafter called the lessor and Clarance Thomas of Mannford, Oklahoma, hereinafter called the lessee, WITNESSETH:

1. That the lessor owns the following described real estate and premises, situated in Creek County, Oklahoma, to-wit:

South one half(1/2) of South East one fourth (1/4) of Section Thirty (30) Township Nineteen (19) Range eight (8) East. Containing eighty acres, more or less.

2. That the lessor, in consideration of the covenants, promises and agreements herein contained and expressed, hereby rents, leases and lets to the lessee, the above described premises, to have and to hold the same from the 19th day of April 1913 to the 1st day of January, 1914, together with the buildings and improvements thereon, for Agricultural Purposes

3. That the lessor covenants to place to lessee in the quiet and peaceable possession of said premises on or before the begining of the term covered by this lease, and to protect the lessee in the quiet and peaceable possession of said premises during the term of this lease.

4. That the lessee promises and agrees to pay to the lessor as rental for said premises for said term the sum of Sixty two & 50/100 DOLLARS payable as follows: In full Nov. 1st, 1913.

5. That no part of said rent money shall be due and payable until the lessee shall have been placed in the quiet and actual possession of said premises.

6. That

Signed and delivered on the day and date first above written.
Signed in our presence.

Emeline Shawnee (Seal)
(Seal)
(Seal)

Fig. A.2.1. Copy of Emeline Shawnee's lease, dated April 19, 1913. Courtesy of Pottawatomie County Museum, Shawnee, Oklahoma.

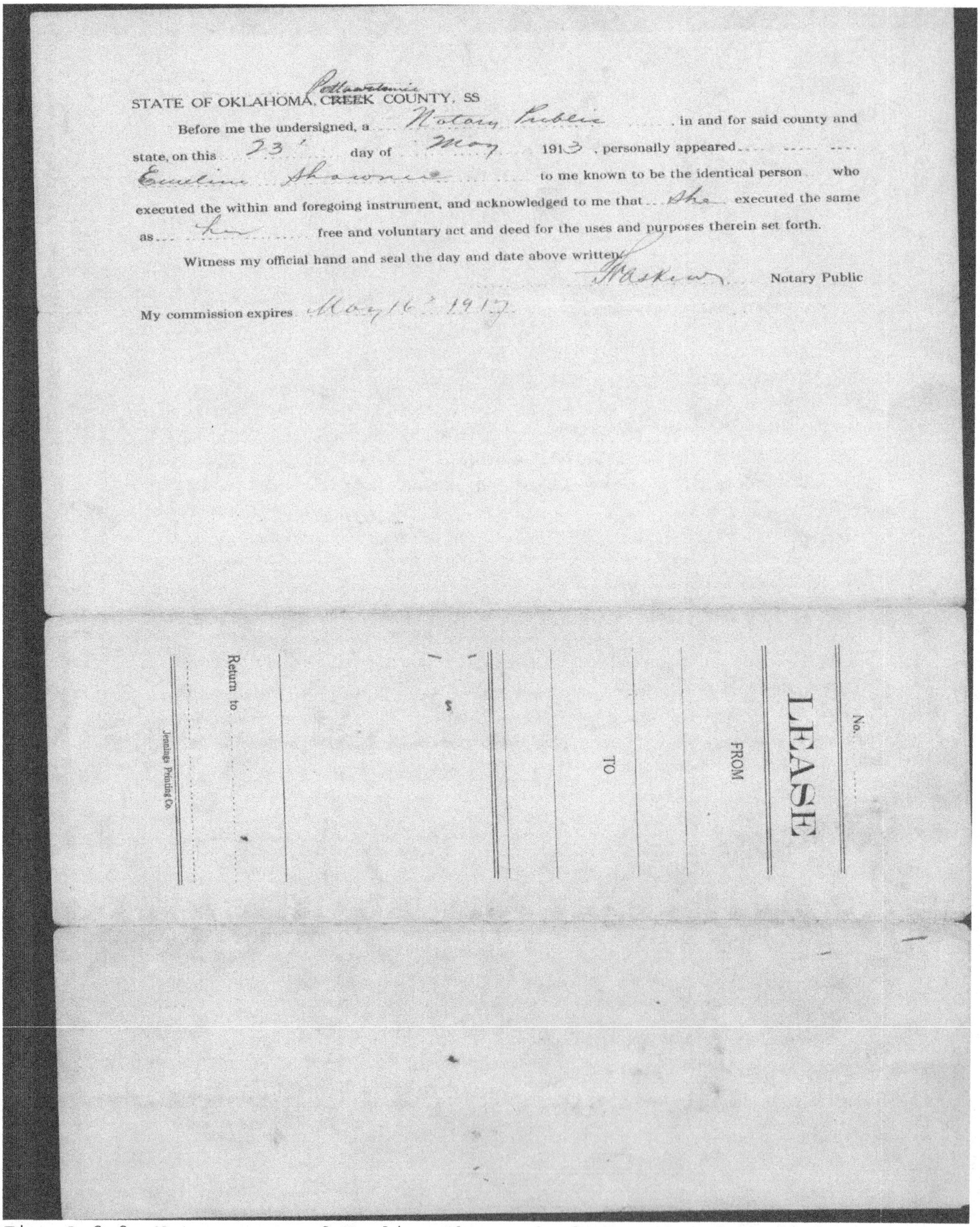

STATE OF OKLAHOMA, ~~CREEK~~ Pottawatomie COUNTY, SS

Before me the undersigned, a _Notary Public_ in and for said county and state, on this _23rd_ day of _May_ 1913, personally appeared _Emeline Shawnee_ to me known to be the identical person who executed the within and foregoing instrument, and acknowledged to me that _she_ executed the same as _her_ free and voluntary act and deed for the uses and purposes therein set forth.

Witness my official hand and seal the day and date above written.

T. Askew, Notary Public

My commission expires _May 16, 1917_

Return to _____

Jennings Printing Co.

LEASE

No. _____
FROM _____
TO _____

Fig. A.2.2. Notary page of Emeline Shawnee's lease, dated April 19, 1913. Courtesy of Pottawatomie County Museum, Shawnee, Oklahoma.

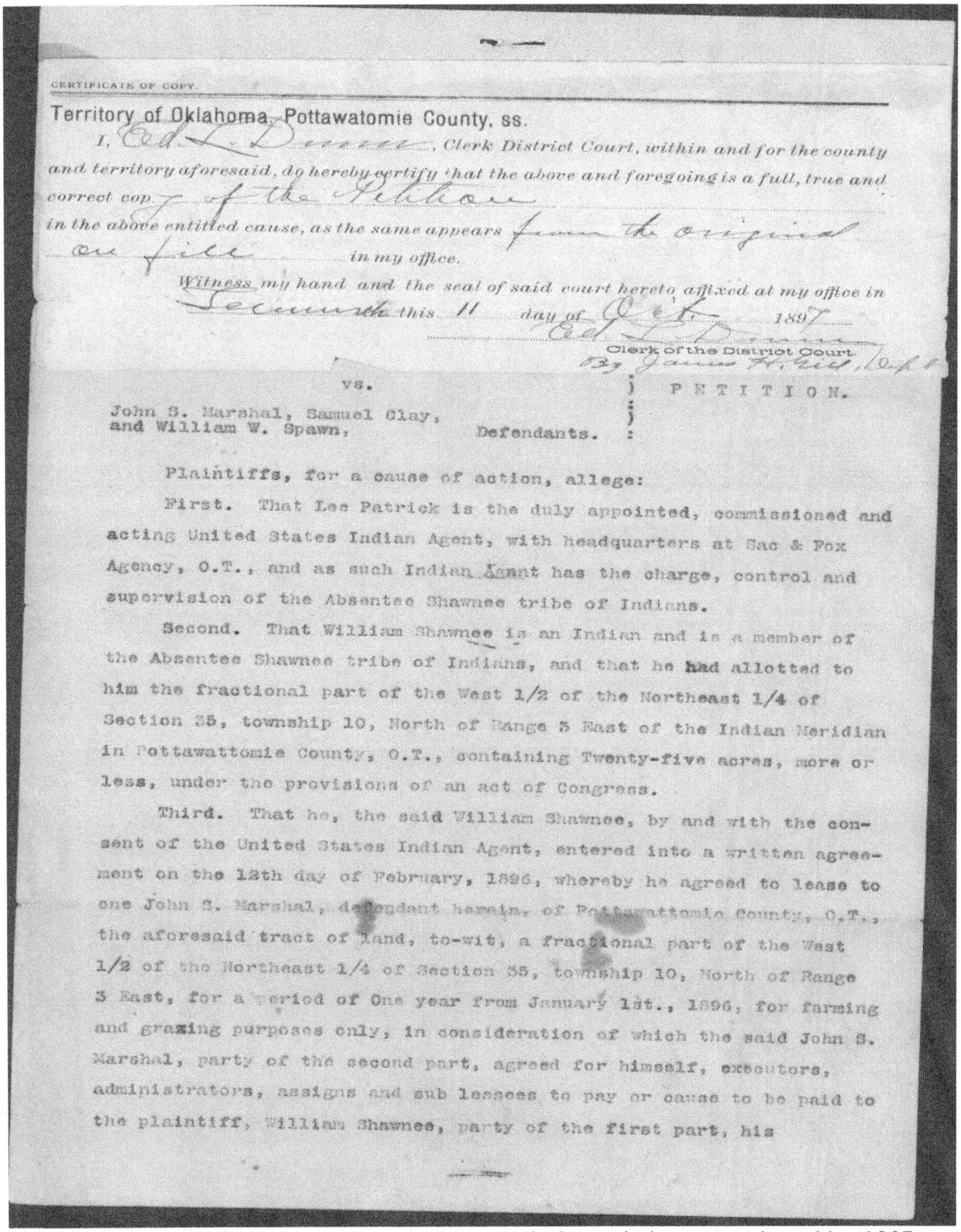

CERTIFICATE OF COPY.

Territory of Oklahoma, Pottawatomie County, ss.

I, _Ed L. Dunn_, Clerk District Court, within and for the county and territory aforesaid, do hereby certify that the above and foregoing is a full, true and correct cop_y of the Petition_ in the above entitled cause, as the same appears _from the original on file_ in my office.

Witness my hand and the seal of said court hereto affixed at my office in _Tecumseh_ this _11_ day of _Oct_ 1897

Ed L. Dunn
Clerk of the District Court.
By _James H. Gill, Dep_

vs.) PETITION.
John S. Marshal, Samuel Clay,)
and William W. Spawn, Defendants.)

Plaintiffs, for a cause of action, allege:

First. That Lee Patrick is the duly appointed, commissioned and acting United States Indian Agent, with headquarters at Sac & Fox Agency, O.T., and as such Indian Agent has the charge, control and supervision of the Absentee Shawnee tribe of Indians.

Second. That William Shawnee is an Indian and is a member of the Absentee Shawnee tribe of Indians, and that he had allotted to him the fractional part of the West 1/2 of the Northeast 1/4 of Section 35, township 10, North of Range 5 East of the Indian Meridian in Pottawattomie County, O.T., containing Twenty-five acres, more or less, under the provisions of an act of Congress.

Third. That he, the said William Shawnee, by and with the consent of the United States Indian Agent, entered into a written agreement on the 12th day of February, 1896, whereby he agreed to lease to one John S. Marshal, defendant herein, of Pottawattomie County, O.T., the aforesaid tract of land, to-wit, a fractional part of the West 1/2 of the Northeast 1/4 of Section 35, township 10, North of Range 5 East, for a period of One year from January 1st., 1896, for farming and grazing purposes only, in consideration of which the said John S. Marshal, party of the second part, agreed for himself, executors, administrators, assigns and sub lessees to pay or cause to be paid to the plaintiff, William Shawnee, party of the first part, his

Fig. A.2.3. *William Shawnee v. John Marshal* petition, October 11, 1897, page 1 of 2 with cover sheet. Courtesy of Pottawatomie County Museum, Shawnee, Oklahoma.

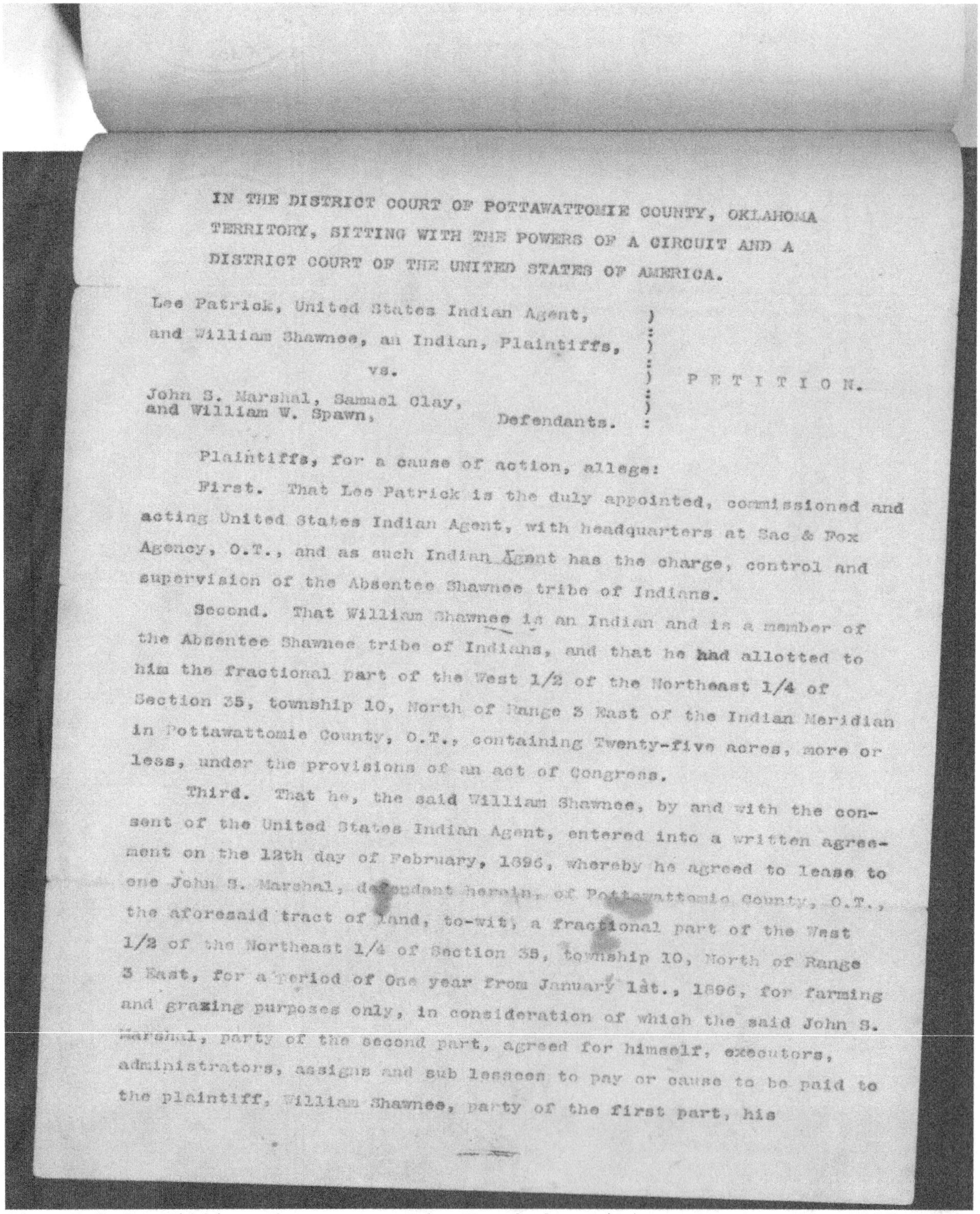

IN THE DISTRICT COURT OF POTTAWATTOMIE COUNTY, OKLAHOMA TERRITORY, SITTING WITH THE POWERS OF A CIRCUIT AND A DISTRICT COURT OF THE UNITED STATES OF AMERICA.

Lee Patrick, United States Indian Agent,)
and William Shawnee, an Indian, Plaintiffs,)
vs.) PETITION.
John S. Marshal, Samuel Clay,)
and William W. Spawn, Defendants.)

Plaintiffs, for a cause of action, allege:

First. That Lee Patrick is the duly appointed, commissioned and acting United States Indian Agent, with headquarters at Sac & Fox Agency, O.T., and as such Indian Agent has the charge, control and supervision of the Absentee Shawnee tribe of Indians.

Second. That William Shawnee is an Indian and is a member of the Absentee Shawnee tribe of Indians, and that he had allotted to him the fractional part of the West 1/2 of the Northeast 1/4 of Section 35, township 10, North of Range 3 East of the Indian Meridian in Pottawattomie County, O.T., containing Twenty-five acres, more or less, under the provisions of an act of Congress.

Third. That he, the said William Shawnee, by and with the consent of the United States Indian Agent, entered into a written agreement on the 12th day of February, 1896, whereby he agreed to lease to one John S. Marshal, defendant herein, of Pottawattomie County, O.T., the aforesaid tract of land, to-wit; a fractional part of the West 1/2 of the Northeast 1/4 of Section 35, township 10, North of Range 3 East, for a period of One year from January 1st., 1896, for farming and grazing purposes only, in consideration of which the said John S. Marshal, party of the second part, agreed for himself, executors, administrators, assigns and sub lessees to pay or cause to be paid to the plaintiff, William Shawnee, party of the first part, his

Fig. A.2.4. *William Shawnee v. John Marshal* petition, October 11, 1897, page 1 of 2 without cover sheet. Courtesy of Pottawatomie County Museum, Shawnee, Oklahoma.

2.

executors or administrators, at Sac & Fox Agency, O.T., the sum of Thirty-seven and 50/100 dollars, which said sum was to be paid in semi-annual payments in advance, as is more fully shown by Exhibit "A" hereto attached and made a part hereof.

Fourth. That on the 12th day of February, 1896, the defendants Samuel Clay and William W. Spawn of Tecumseh, O.T., entered into a written contract whereby they agreed to become sureties for the said defendant John S. Marshal, for the punctual payment of all the rents and of the performance of all the covenants and agreements therein contained in the indenture of the lease, to be paid and performed by the said John S. Marshal, party of the second part, therein named, provided, that the said John S. Marshal should make default either in the payment of the rents or of any part of the covenants therein contained.

Fifth. That the said plaintiffs placed the said defendant John S. Marshal in possession of the premises hereinbefore described.

Sixth. That the sum of $18.75 is now due and unpaid from the defendant, though often required so to do he has failed to pay the said sum or any part thereof.

Wherefore, Plaintiffs pray judgment against defendants and each of them in the sum of $18.75 and the costs of said suit and such other and further relief as the Court may see proper to grant in the premises.

T. F. McMechan
Ass't United States Attorney,
For Plaintiffs.

Fig. A.2.5. *William Shawnee v. John Marshal* petition, October 11, 1897, page 2 of 2. Courtesy of Pottawatomie County Museum, Shawnee, Oklahoma.

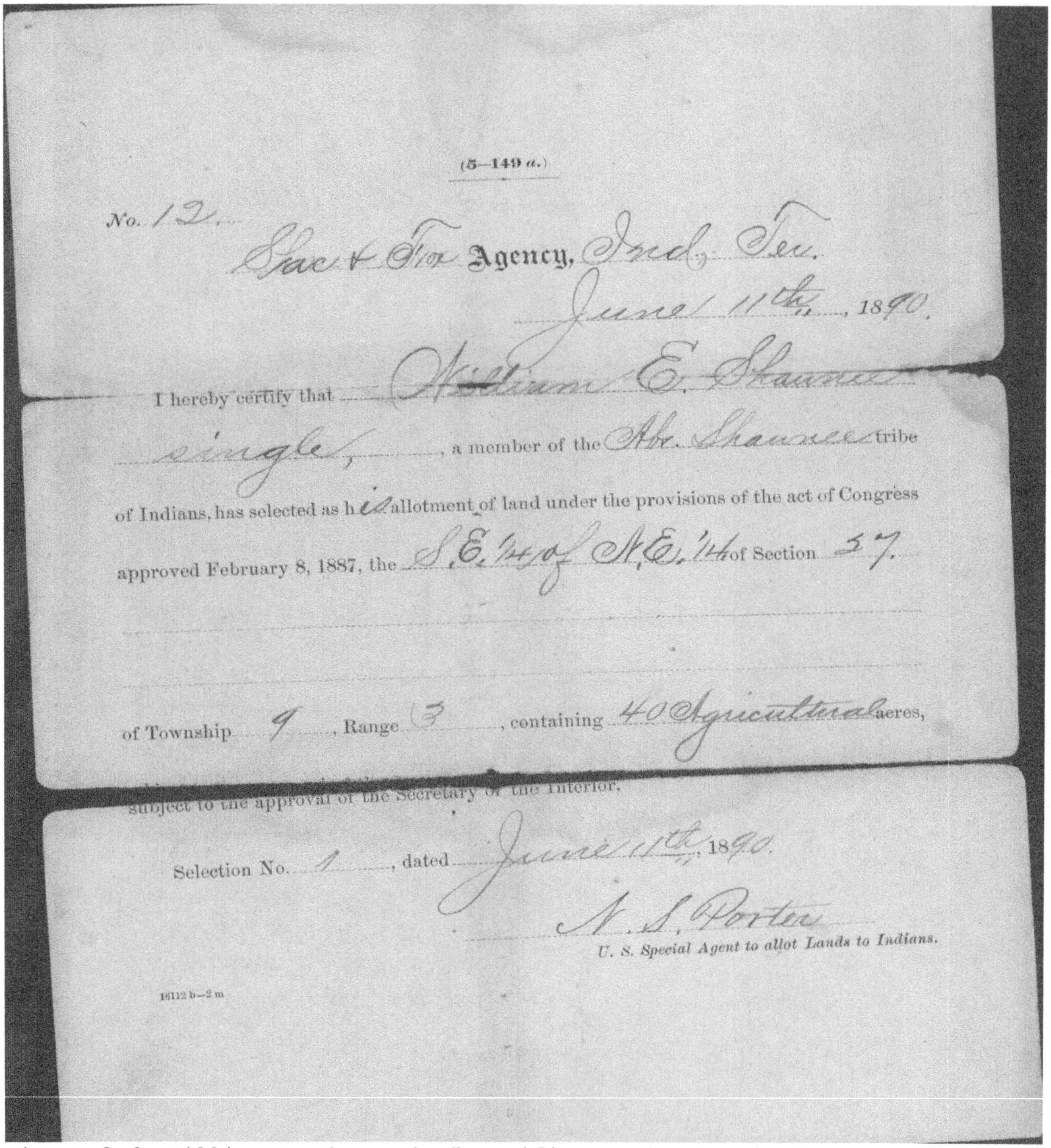

(5–149 a.)

No. 12. Sac & Fox Agency, Ind. Ter.

June 11th, 1890.

I hereby certify that William E. Shawnee single, a member of the Abs. Shawnee tribe of Indians, has selected as his allotment of land under the provisions of the act of Congress approved February 8, 1887, the S.E. ¼ of N.E. ¼ of Section 57

of Township 9, Range 3, containing 40 Agricultural acres,

subject to the approval of the Secretary of the Interior.

Selection No. 1, dated June 11th, 1890.

N. S. Porter
U. S. Special Agent to allot Lands to Indians.

15112 b—2 m

Fig. A.2.6. William E. Shawnee's "Certificate of Selection" (land allotment), June 11, 1890. Courtesy of Pottawatomie County Museum, Shawnee, Oklahoma.

Fig. A.2.7. William E. Shawnee's "Certificate of Selection" (land allotment), June 11, 1890. Cover page. Courtesy of Pottawatomie County Museum, Shawnee, Oklahoma.

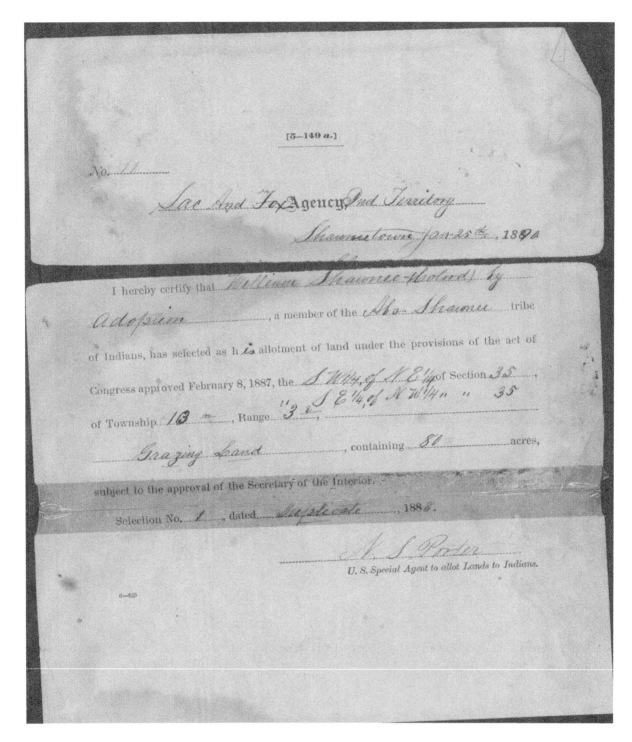

Fig. A.2.8. William Shawnee Sr.'s "Certificate of Selection" (land allotment), January 25, 1890. Courtesy of Pottawatomie County Museum, Shawnee, Oklahoma.

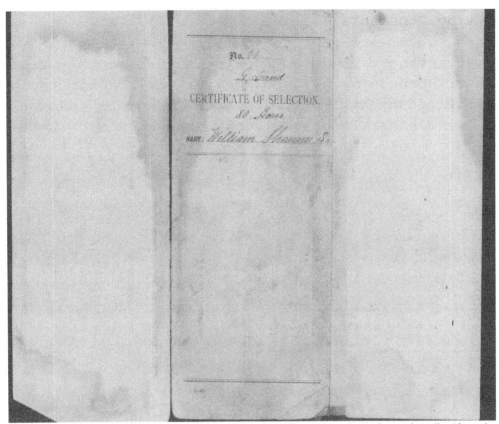

Fig. A.2.9. William Shawnee Sr.'s "Certificate of Selection" (land allotment), January 25, 1890. Cover page. Courtesy of Pottawatomie County Museum, Shawnee, Oklahoma.

A.3. Accounting Documents

The accounting documents depicted here represent a variety of monetary transactions. These documents include monthly account statements for Hampton Normal and Agricultural Institute, a "Bank Note" signed by William E. Shawnee, a scratch pad calculation, and a sample of William E Shawnee's signature on a small piece of paper.

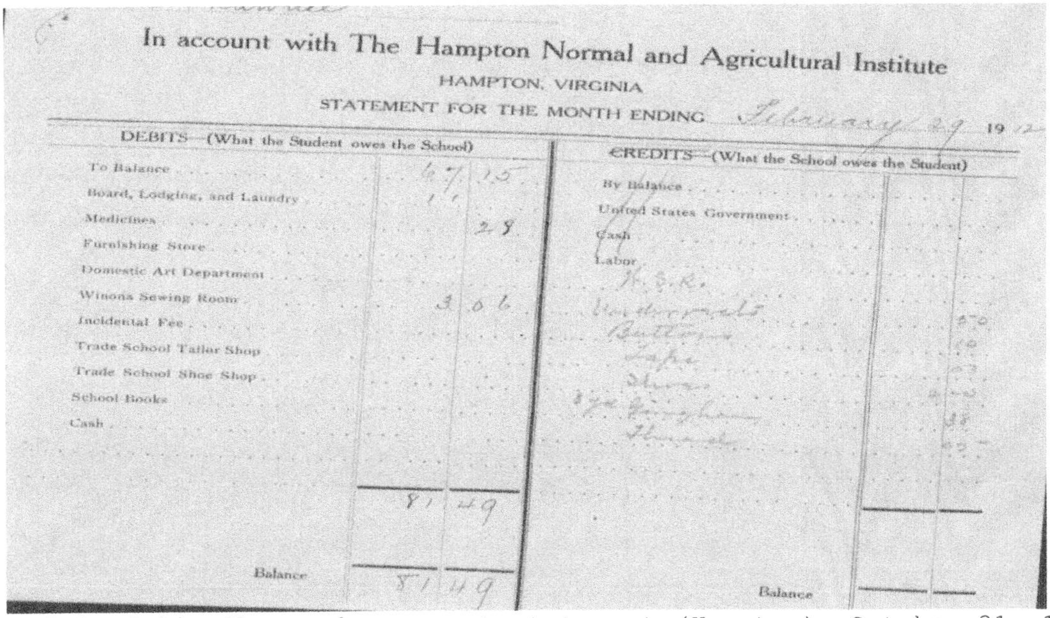

In account with The Hampton Normal and Agricultural Institute
HAMPTON, VIRGINIA
STATEMENT FOR THE MONTH ENDING February 29 1912

DEBITS—(What the Student owes the School)			CREDITS—(What the School owes the Student)		
To Balance	67	15	By Balance		
Board, Lodging, and Laundry	11		United States Government		
Medicines		28	Cash		
Furnishing Store			Labor		
Domestic Art Department			H.S.R.		
Winona Sewing Room	3	06	Underwaists		50
Incidental Fee			Buttons		10
Trade School Tailor Shop			Tape		03
Trade School Shoe Shop			Shoes		[illegible]
School Books			3 yd. Gingham		38
Cash			Thread		05
	81	49			
Balance	81	49	Balance		

Fig. A.3.1. Julia Shawnee's account statement (Hampton), October 31, 1911. Courtesy of Pottawatomie County Museum, Shawnee, Oklahoma.

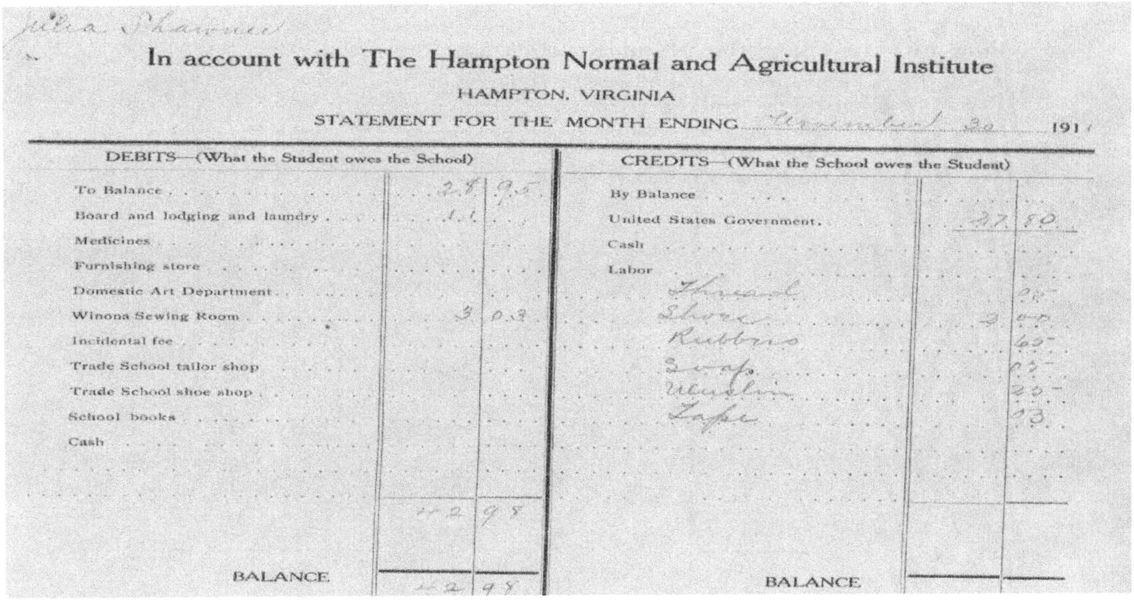

Julia Shawnee

In account with The Hampton Normal and Agricultural Institute
HAMPTON, VIRGINIA
STATEMENT FOR THE MONTH ENDING November 30 1911

DEBITS—(What the Student owes the School)			CREDITS—(What the School owes the Student)		
To Balance	28	95	By Balance		
Board and lodging and laundry	11		United States Government	37	50
Medicines			Cash		
Furnishing store			Labor		
Domestic Art Department			Thread		05
Winona Sewing Room	3	03	Shoes	2	00
Incidental fee			Rubbers		65
Trade School tailor shop			Soap		05
Trade School shoe shop			Muslin		20
School books			Tape		03
Cash					
	42	98			
BALANCE	42	98	BALANCE		

Fig. A.3.2. Julia Shawnee's account statement (Hampton), November 30, 1911. Courtesy of Pottawatomie County Museum, Shawnee, Oklahoma.

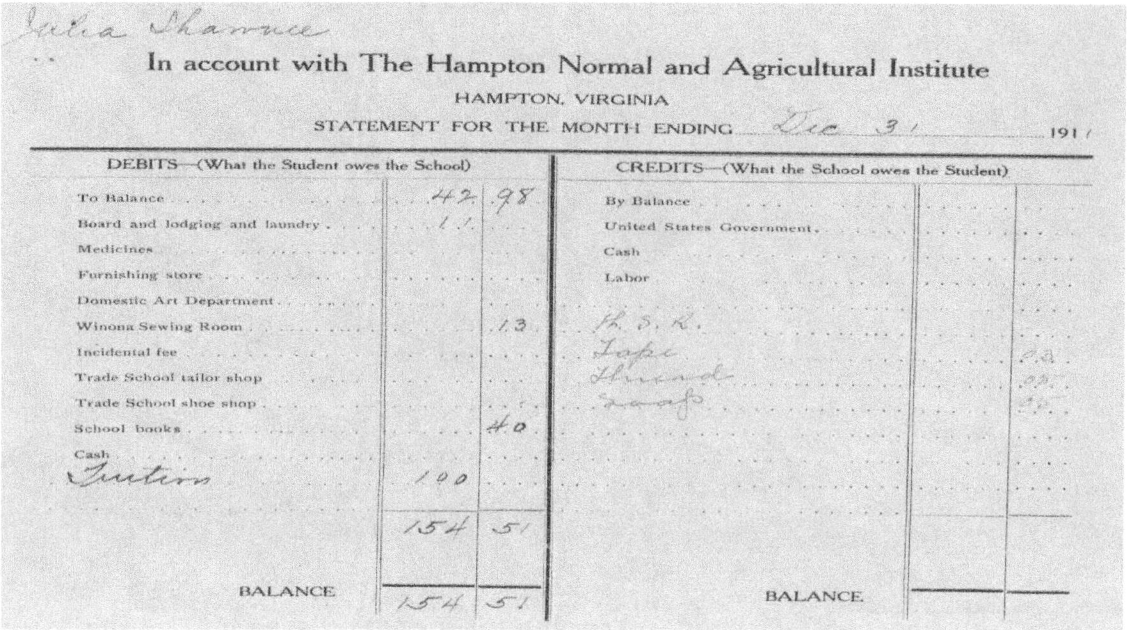

Julia Shawnee

In account with The Hampton Normal and Agricultural Institute

HAMPTON, VIRGINIA

STATEMENT FOR THE MONTH ENDING Dec 31 1911

DEBITS—(What the Student owes the School)			CREDITS—(What the School owes the Student)		
To Balance	42	98	By Balance		
Board and lodging and laundry	11		United States Government		
Medicines			Cash		
Furnishing store			Labor		
Domestic Art Department					
Winona Sewing Room		.13	H. S. R.		
Incidental fee			Tape		.22
Trade School tailor shop			Thread		.05
Trade School shoe shop			Soap		.05
School books		.40			
Cash					
Tuition	100				
	154	51			
BALANCE	154	51	BALANCE		

Fig. A.3.3. Julia Shawnee's account statement (Hampton), December 31, 1911. Courtesy of Pottawatomie County Museum, Shawnee, Oklahoma.

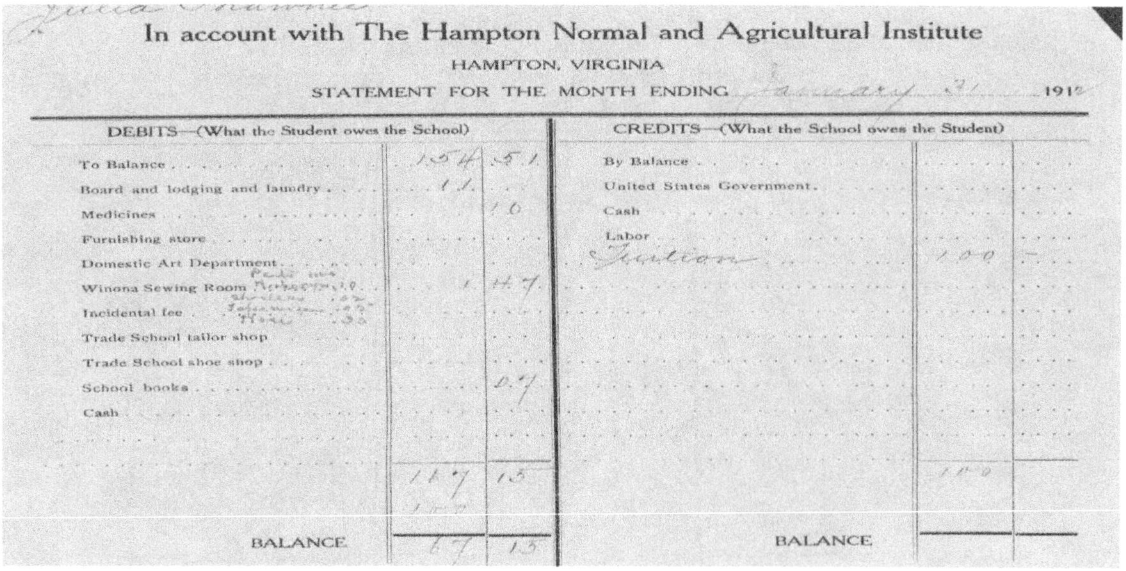

Julia Shawnee

In account with The Hampton Normal and Agricultural Institute

HAMPTON, VIRGINIA

STATEMENT FOR THE MONTH ENDING January 31 1912

DEBITS—(What the Student owes the School)			CREDITS—(What the School owes the Student)		
To Balance	154	51	By Balance		
Board and lodging and laundry	11		United States Government		
Medicines		10	Cash		
Furnishing store			Labor		
Domestic Art Department			Tuition	100	
Winona Sewing Room [illegible]	1	47			
Incidental fee					
Trade School tailor shop					
Trade School shoe shop					
School books		07			
Cash					
	167	15		100	
	100				
BALANCE	67	15	BALANCE		

Fig. A.3.4. Julia Shawnee's account statement (Hampton), January 31, 1912. Courtesy of Pottawatomie County Museum, Shawnee, Oklahoma.

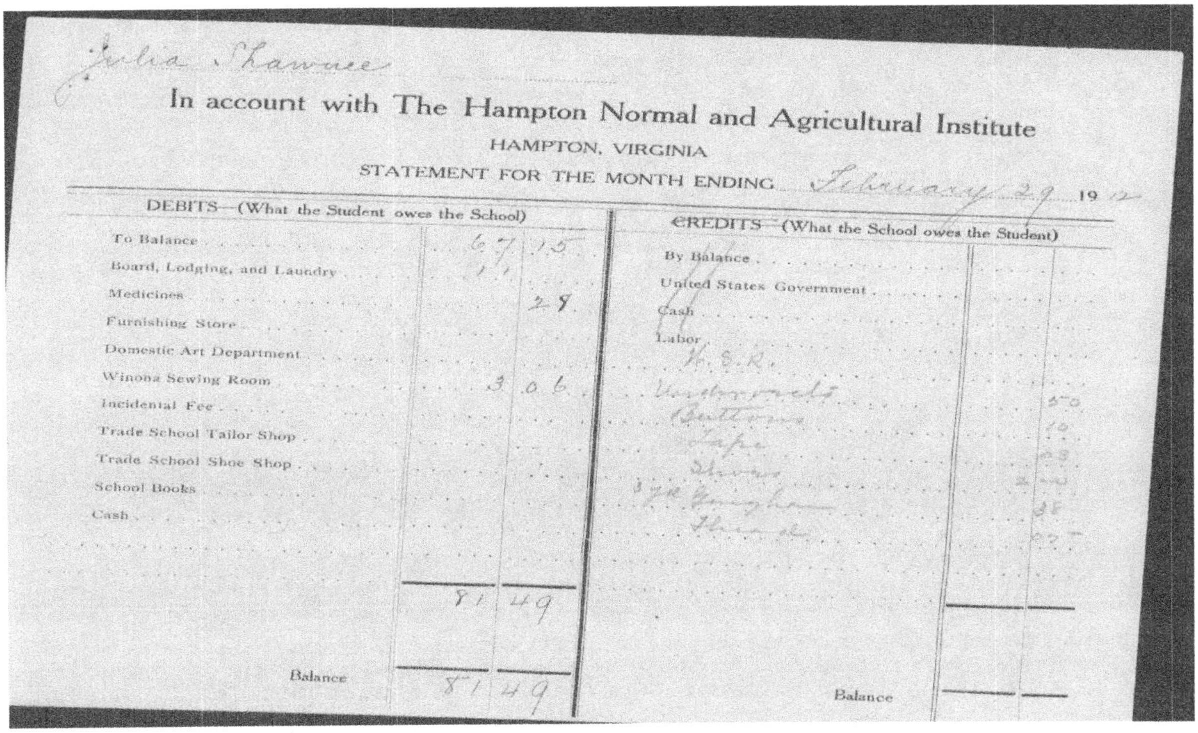
Julia Shawnee

In account with The Hampton Normal and Agricultural Institute

HAMPTON, VIRGINIA

STATEMENT FOR THE MONTH ENDING February 29 1912

DEBITS—(What the Student owes the School)		CREDITS—(What the School owes the Student)	
To Balance	67.15	By Balance	
Board, Lodging, and Laundry		United States Government	
Medicines	.28	Cash	
Furnishing Store		Labor	
Domestic Art Department		W.S.R.	
Winona Sewing Room	3.06	Underwaists	.50
Incidental Fee		Buttons	.10
Trade School Tailor Shop		Tape	.03
Trade School Shoe Shop		Shoes	2.00
School Books		3 yds Gingham	.38
Cash		Thread	.07
	81.49		
Balance	81.49	Balance	

Fig. A.3.5 Julia Shawnee's account statement (Hampton), February 29, 1912. Courtesy of Pottawatomie County Museum, Shawnee, Oklahoma.

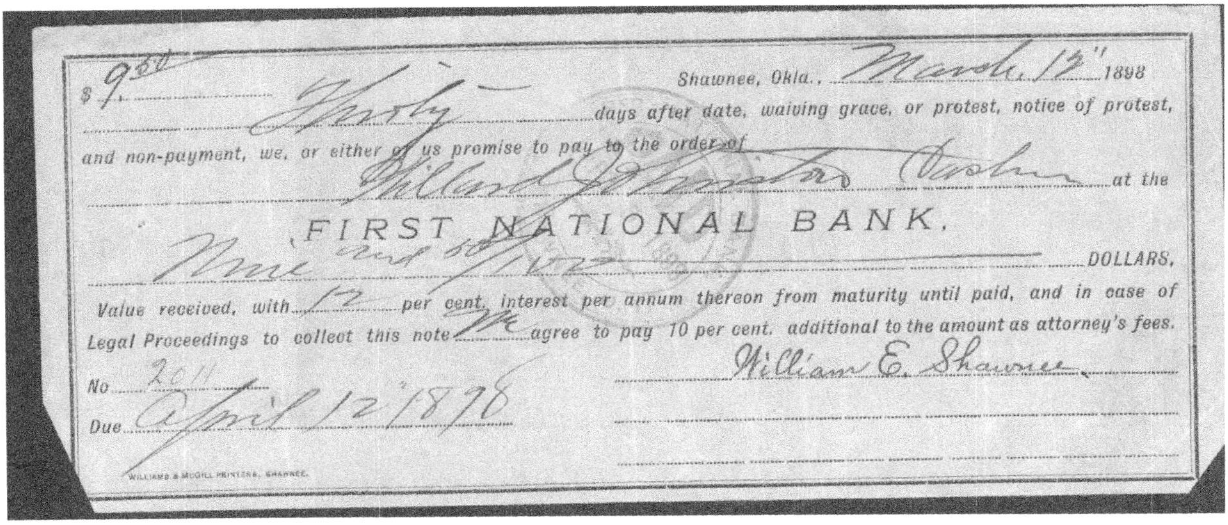
$9.50 Shawnee, Okla., March 12 1898

Thirty days after date, waiving grace, or protest, notice of protest, and non-payment, we, or either of us promise to pay to the order of Willard Johnston Cashier at the

FIRST NATIONAL BANK,

Nine and 50/100 DOLLARS,

Value received, with 12 per cent. interest per annum thereon from maturity until paid, and in case of Legal Proceedings to collect this note We agree to pay 10 per cent. additional to the amount as attorney's fees.

No 2011 William E. Shawnee

Due April 12 1898

WILLIAMS & MCGILL PRINTERS, SHAWNEE.

Fig. A.3.6. William E. Shawnee's bank note, April 12, 1898. Courtesy of Pottawatomie County Museum, Shawnee, Oklahoma.

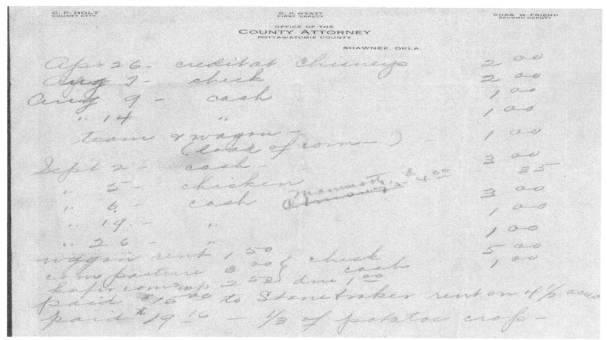

Fig. A.3.7. Accounting scratch paper. Courtesy of Pottawatomie County Museum, Shawnee, Oklahoma.

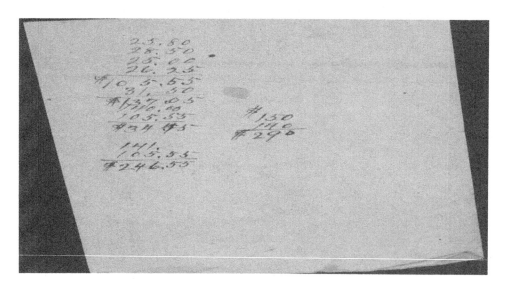

Fig. A.3.8. Miscellaneous addition scratch pad. Courtesy of Pottawatomie County Museum, Shawnee, Oklahoma.

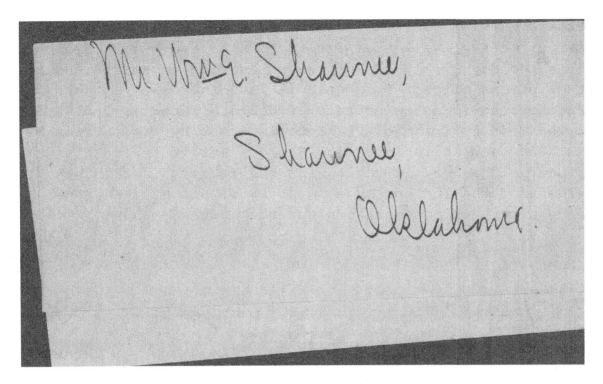

Fig. A.3.9. William E. Shawnee's signature card. Courtesy of Pottawatomie County Museum, Shawnee, Oklahoma.

A.4. Letters:

The first of these is a letter from Carrie Warrior to William E. Shawnee, dated May 27, 1892. She was an admirer of and friend to him. Other pieces of correspondence included here are letters from attorneys advising on matters of debts, property, and leases. The most striking of the letters, though, was written by Walter H. Shawnee, while attending Haskell Institute, to his brother George Shawnee. It deals with his feelings about the mistreatment of the Indians by a majority of society, and the importance of providing education for the Indians.

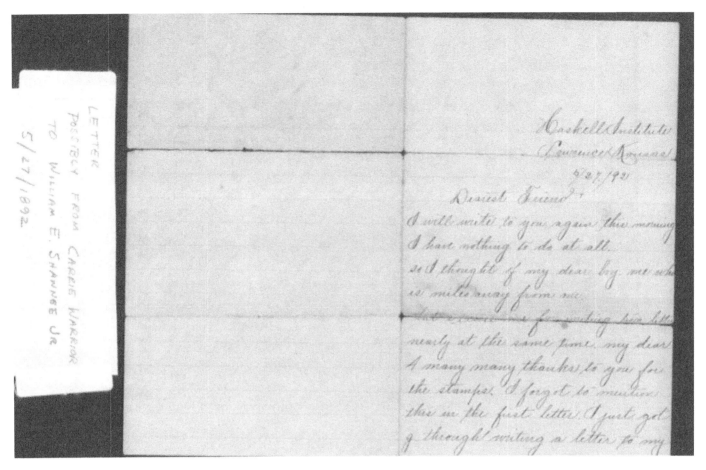

Fig. A.4.1. Beginning of Carrie Warrior letter to William E. Shawnee, dated May 27, 1892. Courtesy of Pottawatomie County Museum, Shawnee, Oklahoma.

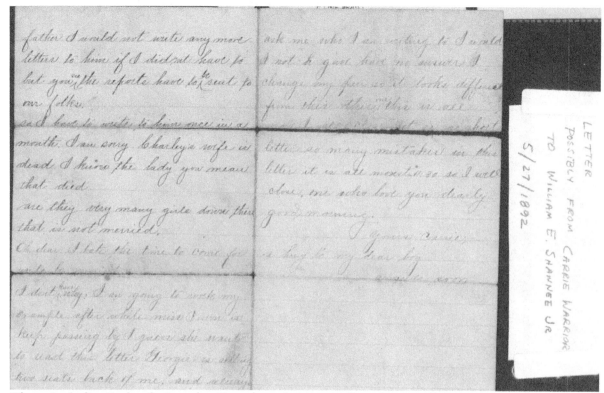

Fig. A.4.2. End of Carrie Warrior letter. Courtesy of Pottawatomie County Museum, Shawnee, Oklahoma.

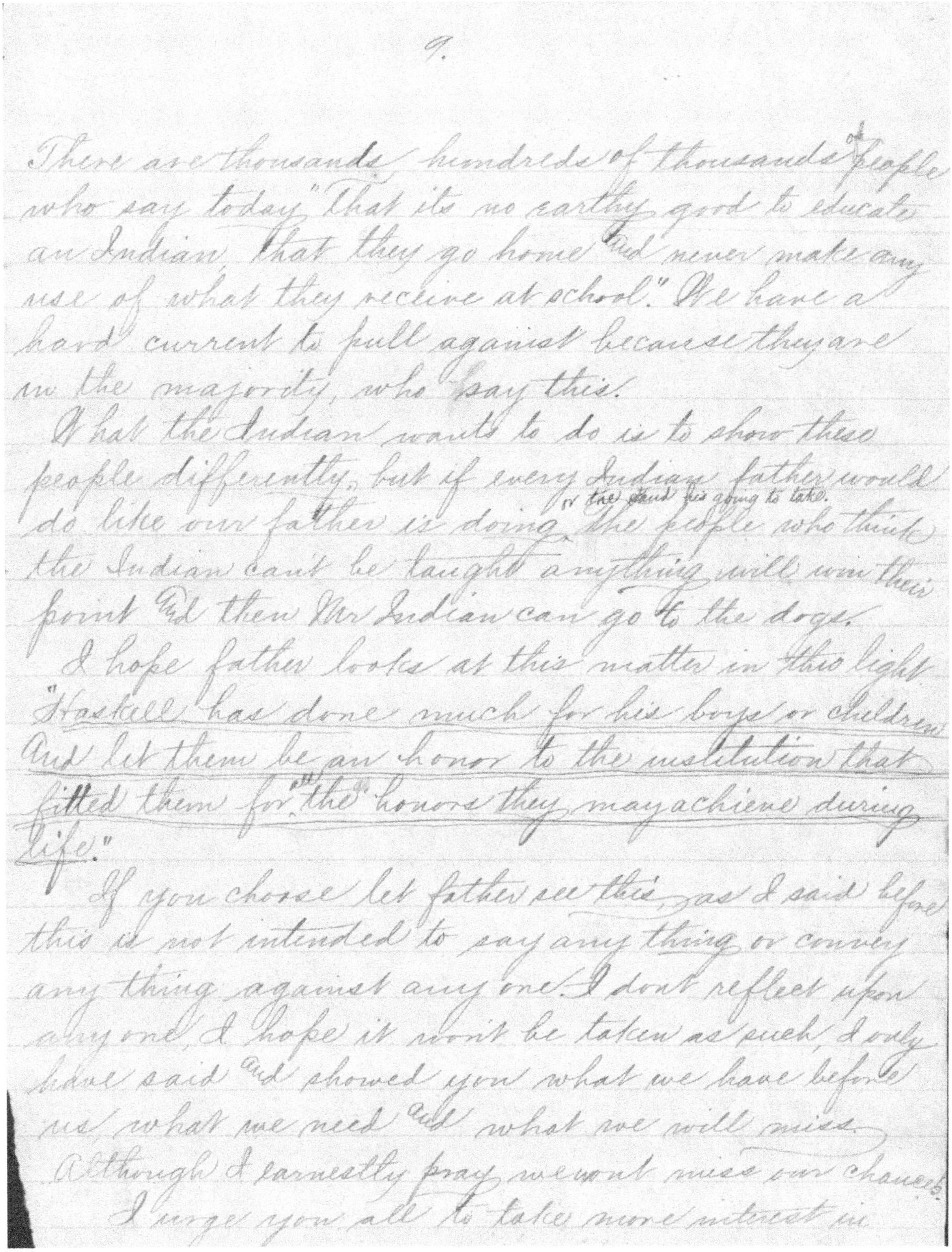

9.

There are thousands hundreds of thousands of people who say today "That its no earthy good to educate an Indian, that they go home and never make any use of what they receive at school." We have a hard current to pull against because they are in the majority, who say this.

What the Indian wants to do is to show these people differently, but if every Indian father would do like our father is doing or the stand his going to take, the people who think the Indian cant be taught anything will win their point and then Mr Indian can go to the dogs.

I hope father looks at this matter in this light. "Haskell has done much for his boys or children And let them be an honor to the institution that fitted them for "the" honors they may achieve during life."

If you choose let father see this, as I said before this is not intended to say any thing or convey any thing against any one. I dont reflect upon any one, I hope it wont be taken as such, I only have said and showed you what we have before us, what we need and what we will miss. Although I earnestly pray we wont miss our chances.

I urge you all to take more interest in

Fig. A.4.3. Page 9 of Walter H. Shawnee's letter to his brother George Shawnee (pages 1-8 missing from the envelope). Courtesy of Pottawatomie County Museum, Shawnee, Oklahoma.

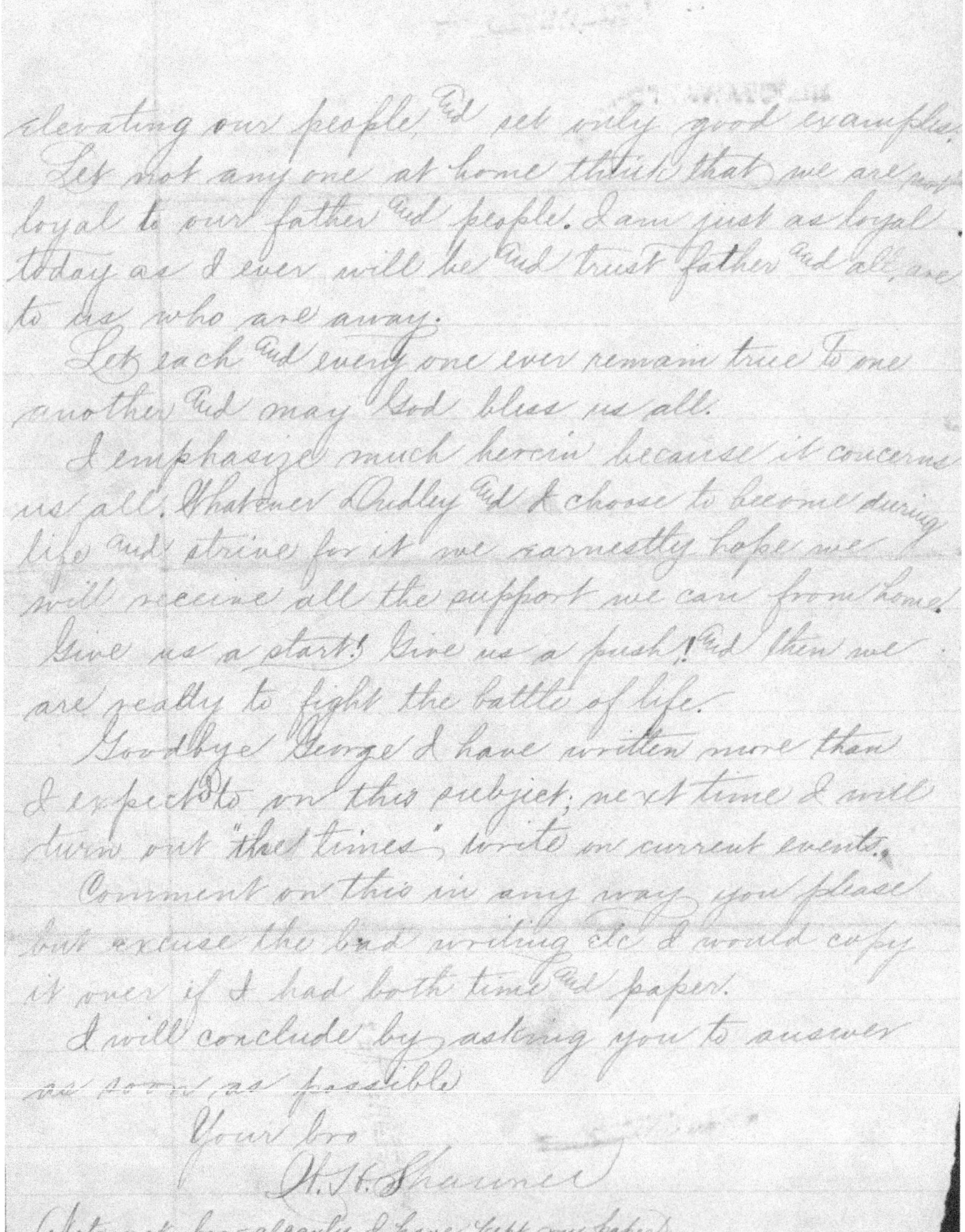

elevating our people, and set only good examples.

Let not any one at home think that we are not loyal to our father and people. I am just as loyal today as I ever will be, and trust father and all, are to us who are away.

Let each and every one ever remain true to one another and may God bless us all.

I emphasize much herein because it concerns us all. Whatever Dudley and I choose to become during life and strive for it we earnestly hope we will receive all the support we can from home. Give us a start! Give us a push! and then we are ready to fight the battle of life.

Goodbye George I have written more than I expected to on this subject; next time I will turn out "that times," write on current events.

Comment on this in any way you please but excuse the bad writing etc I would copy it over if I had both time and paper.

I will conclude by asking you to answer as soon as possible

Your bro

W. H. Shawnee

(Note not, how cleanly I have kept my papers)

Fig. A.4.4. Page 10 of Walter H. Shawnee's letter to George. Courtesy of Pottawatomie County Museum, Shawnee, Oklahoma.

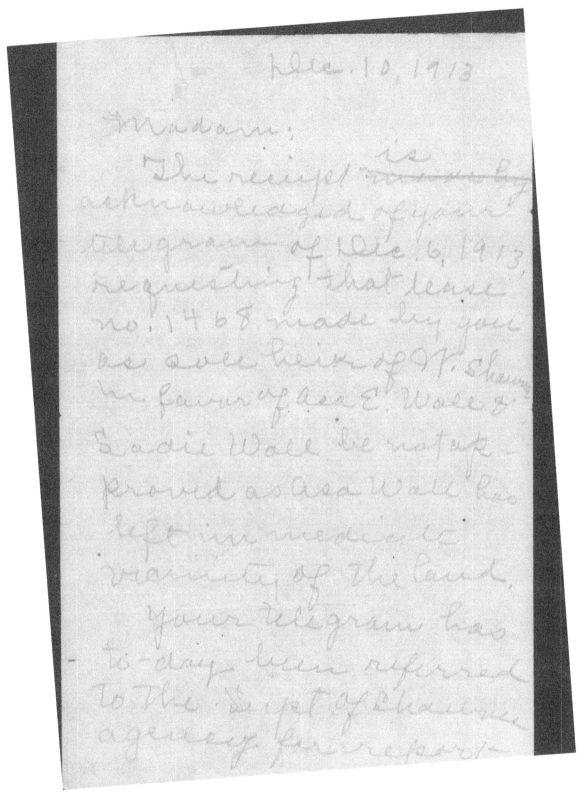

Dec. 10, 1913

Madam;

The receipt is acknowledged of your telegram of Dec. 6, 1913, requesting that lease no. 1468 made by you as sole heir of W. Shawnee in favor of Asa E. Wall & Sadie Wall be not approved as Asa Wall has left immediate vicinity of the land.

Your telegram has to-day been referred to the Supt. of Shawnee agency for report—

Fig. A.4.5. Page 1 of 2 of a letter from an "Assistant Comn.," dated December 10, 1913. Subject: Lease to Asa Walls. Courtesy of Pottawatomie County Museum, Shawnee, Oklahoma.

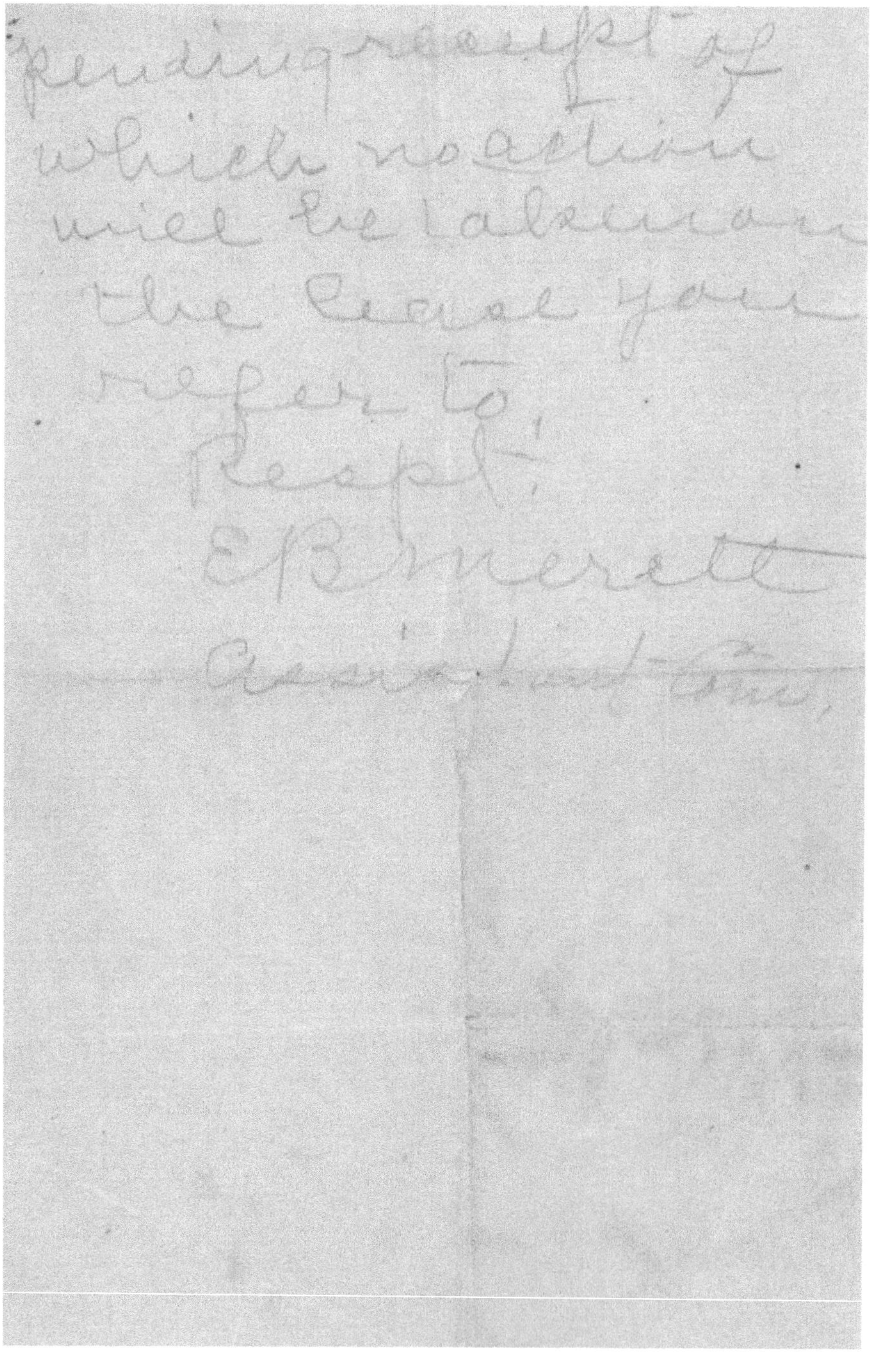

pending receipt of which no action will be taken on the lease you refer to.

Respt,

E B Merritt
Assistant Com,

Fig. A.4.6. Page 2 of 2 of the letter from the assistant comm., December 10, 1913. Courtesy of Pottawatomie County Museum, Shawnee, Oklahoma.

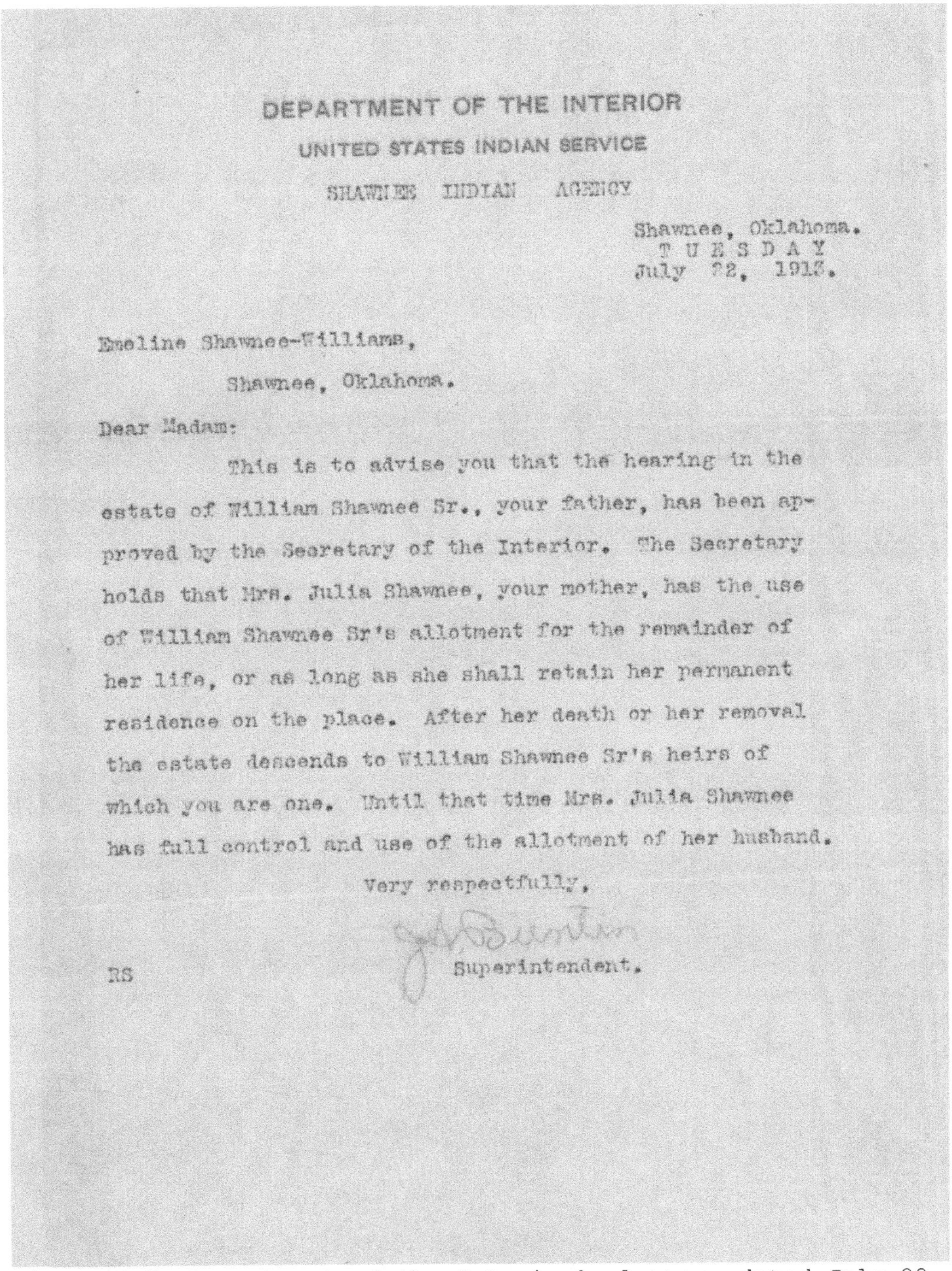

DEPARTMENT OF THE INTERIOR

UNITED STATES INDIAN SERVICE

SHAWNEE INDIAN AGENCY

                                      Shawnee, Oklahoma.
                                        T U E S D A Y
                                        July 22, 1912.

Emeline Shawnee-Williams,

        Shawnee, Oklahoma.

Dear Madam:

        This is to advise you that the hearing in the estate of William Shawnee Sr., your father, has been approved by the Secretary of the Interior. The Secretary holds that Mrs. Julia Shawnee, your mother, has the use of William Shawnee Sr's allotment for the remainder of her life, or as long as she shall retain her permanent residence on the place. After her death or her removal the estate descends to William Shawnee Sr's heirs of which you are one. Until that time Mrs. Julia Shawnee has full control and use of the allotment of her husband.

                              Very respectfully,

                                        Superintendent.

RS

Fig. A.4.7. Department of the Interior's letter, dated July 22, 1912, regarding the William Shawnee Sr. estate. Courtesy of Pottawatomie County Museum, Shawnee, Oklahoma.

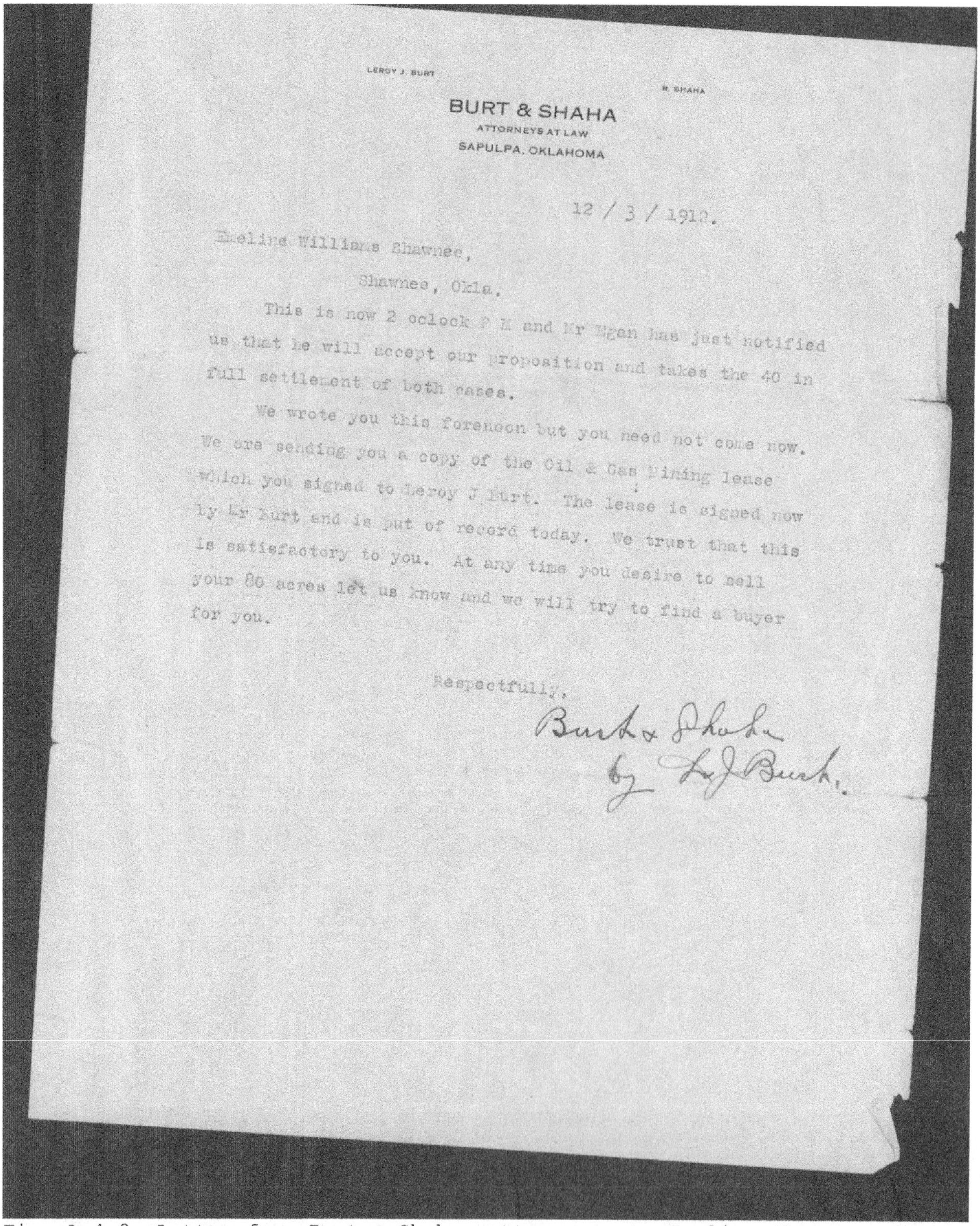

LEROY J. BURT   R. SHAHA

BURT & SHAHA
ATTORNEYS AT LAW
SAPULPA, OKLAHOMA

12 / 3 / 1912.

Emeline Williams Shawnee,

Shawnee, Okla.

This is now 2 oclock P M and Mr Egan has just notified us that he will accept our proposition and takes the 40 in full settlement of both cases.

We wrote you this forenoon but you need not come now. We are sending you a copy of the Oil & Gas Mining lease which you signed to Leroy J Burt. The lease is signed now by Mr Burt and is put of record today. We trust that this is satisfactory to you. At any time you desire to sell your 80 acres let us know and we will try to find a buyer for you.

Respectfully,

Burt & Shaha
by L J Burt.

Fig. A.4.8. Letter from Burt & Shaha, attorneys, to Emeline Shawnee, dated December 12, 1912. Courtesy of Pottawatomie County Museum, Shawnee, Oklahoma.

A.5 Photographs

Most of the photographs that were included within the package were not labeled as to subject, date, or place; however, a search of the envelope provided enough information to allow for the identification of some persons. In the case where there are two persons in a photo, materials in the package permitted us to discern who they were—for instance, Walter and Dudley Shawnee—but did not give us enough information to determine which person was which. Some photos taken by a professional photographer have the studio name and address on the back. The backs of the photos containing marks are included here, in case they could help with the identification of the location and date of the images in the future.

Fig. A.5.1. William Shawnee Sr. Courtesy of Pottawatomie County Museum, Shawnee, Oklahoma.

Fig. A.5.2. Back of William Shawnee Sr. photograph. Courtesy of Pottawatomie County Museum, Shawnee, Oklahoma.

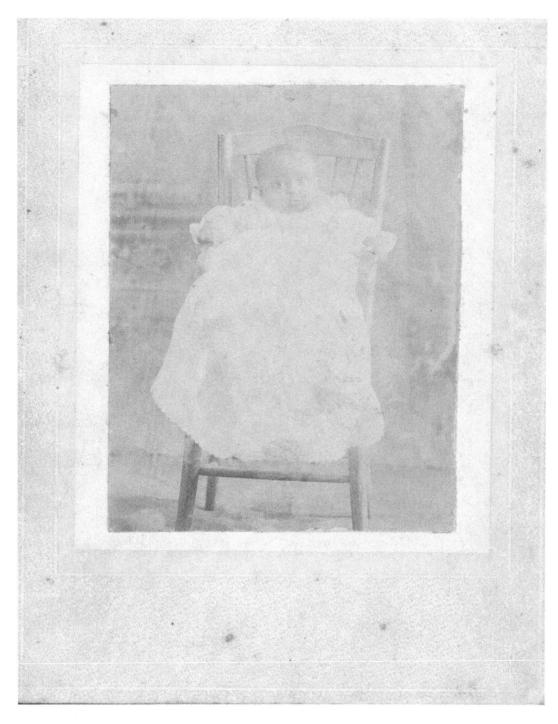

Fig. A.5.3. Infant's photograph, identity of child unknown. Reverse side is blank. Courtesy of Pottawatomie County Museum, Shawnee, Oklahoma.

Fig. A.5.4. Elizabeth Jane (Wright) Shawnee, photograph taken in Lawrence, Kansas. Courtesy of Pottawatomie County Museum, Shawnee, Oklahoma.

Fig. A.5.5. Back of Elizabeth Jane (Wright) Shawnee's photograph. Marks are illegible. Courtesy of Pottawatomie County Museum, Shawnee, Oklahoma.

Fig. A.5.6. Possibly William Shawnee's farm. Person in photograph is unknown. Courtesy of Pottawatomie County Museum, Shawnee, Oklahoma.

Fig. A.5.7. William E. Shawnee's photograph as it was in the original package. Courtesy of Pottawatomie County Museum, Shawnee, Oklahoma.

Fig. A.5.8. Back of William E. Shawnee's photograph with signature and studio hallmark. Courtesy of Pottawatomie County Museum, Shawnee, Oklahoma.

Fig. A.5.9. Walter and Dudley Shawnee, brothers to William E. Shawnee, 1883. Courtesy of Pottawatomie County Museum, Shawnee, Oklahoma.

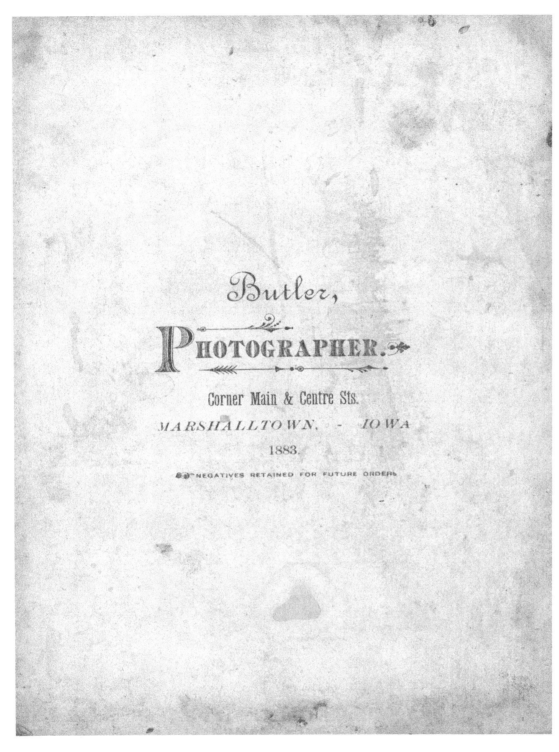

Fig. A.5.10. Back of Walter and Dudley Shawnee photograph, 1883, with studio hallmark. Courtesy of Pottawatomie County Museum, Shawnee, Oklahoma.

Fig. A.5.11. Walter or Dudley Shawnee, brother to William E. Shawnee, 1884. Courtesy of Pottawatomie County Museum, Shawnee, Oklahoma.

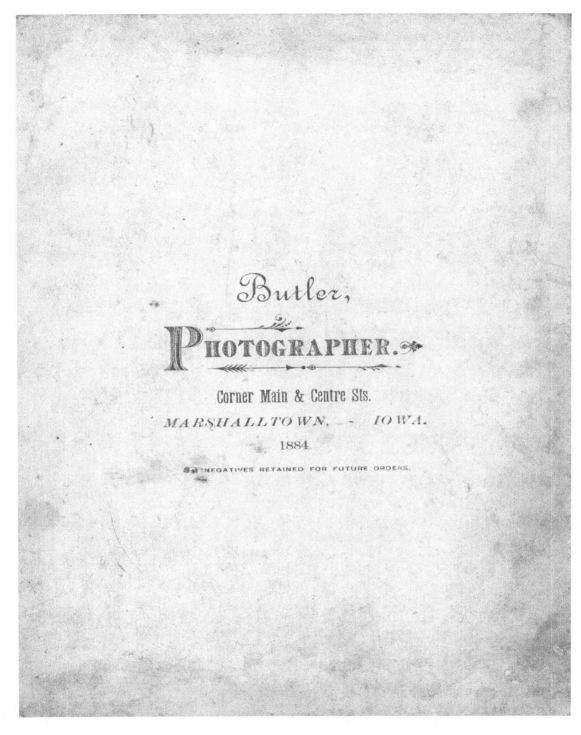

Fig. A.5.12. Back of Walter or Dudley Shawnee photograph with studio hallmark. Courtesy of Pottawatomie County Museum, Shawnee, Oklahoma.

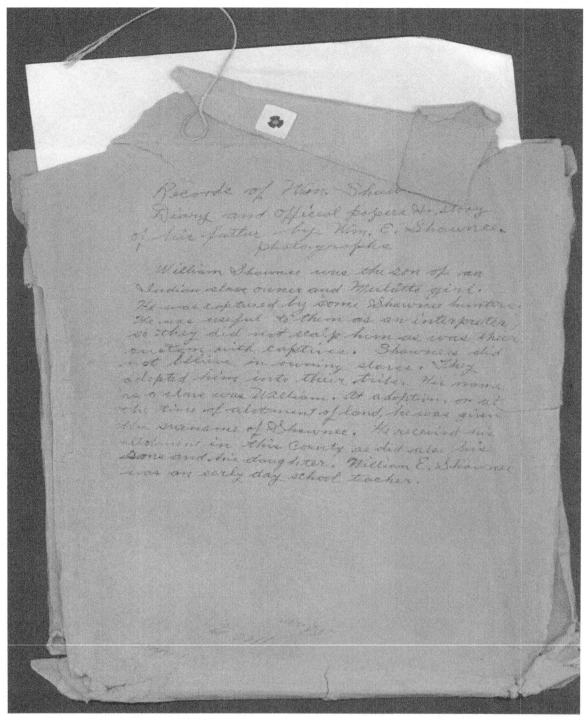

Fig. A.5.13. Back of the envelope in which documents and photos were stored, with inscription. Courtesy of Pottawatomie County Museum, Shawnee, Oklahoma.

Notes

Preface

1. Falato and Falato, *Autobiography of William Ellsworth Shawnee*.

2. Julia Jordan, "History of the Absentee Shawnees," Doris Duke Collection, Tape #M-22, ID #990, Archival Order Volume 053, Western History Collections, University of Oklahoma Libraries, Norman, accessed at https://digital.libraries.ou.edu/cdm/ref/collection/dorisduke/id/1499.

Introduction

1. Kansas, County Marriages, 1811-1911, for William Shawnee, accessed at www.ancestry.com.

2. The digitized 1870 U.S. Census for Eudora County, Kansas, has a transcription of William Shawnee's surname as "Shanner" instead of "Shawnee" and his race as "White" instead of "Mulatto," as in the original written census; it states that he was born about 1835 in Arkansas. Census data accessed at www.ancestry.com.

3. 1870 Eudora County Kansas Agriculture, accessed at www.ancestry.com.

4. 1870 U.S. Census, Eudora County, Kansas, accessed at www.ancestry.com.

5. The 1885 Kansas State Census identifies Martha Lacy as a "Mulatto" and as a widow who was born in Arkansas about 1852; she has a daughter, Nola, whom Shawnee writes about in his journals. Census data accessed at 1885 Kansas State Census Collection on www.ancestry.com.

6. Sources on the western tribes in Indian Territory and the removal of American Indians to Indian Territory through the Civil War include Baird and Goble, *Oklahoma*, 21-112; Debo, *History of Indians*, 168-83; Faulk, *Land of the Fair God*, 54-93; Flickinger, *Choctaw Freedmen*, 7-10; Gibson, *Chickasaws*, 138-273; Gibson, *History of Five Centuries*, 21-129; Krauthamer, *Black Slaves*, 17-100; Littlefield Jr., *Chickasaw Freedmen*, 3-21; Mulroy, *Seminole Freedmen*, 22-193; Naylor, *African Cherokees*, 1-151; Wright, *Guide to Indian Tribes*, 10-14; Zellar, *African Creeks*, 41-76.

7. Calloway, *War for America*, 167; Howard, *Shawnee!* 20-21.

8. Mooney, *Pottawatomie County*, 187-88; Howard, *Shawnee!* 21.

9. Wright, *Guide to Indian Tribes*, 167.

10. Ibid., 167-68.

11. Krauthamer, *Black Slaves*, 2-5; Wickett, *Contested Territory*, 15-23; Tayac, *Indivisible*, 21-24; Forbes, *Africans and Native Americans*, 21-25; McLoughlin, "Red Indians," accessed at http://www.jstor.org/stable/2711653.

12. Potter and Schamel, "Homestead Act of 1862," accessed at www.archives.gov/education/lessons/homestead-act.

13. "Primary Documents: 13th Amendment," Web Guides, accessed at www.loc.gov/rr/program/bib/ourdocs/13thamendment.html.

14. Wormser, "Freedmen's Bureau," accessed at www.pbs.org/wnet/jimcrow/stories_events_freed.html.

15. *Civil Rights Act of 1866*, 14 Stat. 27-30, April 9, 1866, chap. XXXI, accessed at www.loc.gov/law/help/citizenship/pdf/chap_31.pdf; "Reconstruction: The Second Civil War," Black Legislators, accessed at www.pbs.org/wgbh/amex/reconstruction/activism/ps_1866.html.

16. "Primary Documents: 14th Amendment," Web Guides, accessed at www.loc.gov/rr/program/bib/ourdocs/14thamendment.html.

17. *Dred Scott v. Sanford*, 60 U.S. 393 (1857); Franklin and Moss, *Slavery to Freedom*, 216.

18. "Primary Documents: 15th Amendment," Web Guides, accessed at www.loc.gov/rr/program/bib/ourdocs/15thamendment.html.

19. Wormser, "Enforcement Acts," accessed at www.pbs.org/wnet/jimcrow/stories_events_enforce.html.

20. Franklin and Moss, *Slavery to Freedom*, 280-81.

21. Ibid., 281-91; Dunbar-Ortiz, *Indigenous Peoples' History*, 140.

22. Gibson, *History of Five Centuries*, 152; Dunbar-Ortiz, *Indigenous Peoples' History*, 142; Nies, *Native American History*, 279; "Events in the West, 1870–1880," New Perspectives, accessed at www.pbs.org/weta/thewest/events/1870_1880.htm.

23. Fritz, "Grant's 'Peace Policy,'" 411-32; Prucha, *Indians in American Society*, 1-54; Faulk, *Land of the Fair God*, 96-109; Debo, *History of Indians*, 284-331; Gibson, *History of Five Centuries*, 152.

24. Sources on Reconstruction in Indian Territory include Debo, *History of Indians*, 201-5; Wright, *Guide to Indian Tribes*,

14-17; Gibson, *Chickasaws*, 273-97; Zellar, *African Creeks*, 77-114; Mulroy, *Seminole Freedmen*, 194-223; Baird and Goble, *Oklahoma*, 113-29; Littlefield Jr., *Chickasaw Freedmen*, 21-42; Naylor, *African Cherokees*, 155-78; Krauthamer, *Black Slaves*, 17-100; Faulk, *Land of the Fair God*, 94-109; Taylor, *Racial Frontier*, 103-33.

25. Baird and Goble, *Oklahoma*, 132-33.
26. Prucha, *Indians in American Society*, 17-24; Warren, *Shawnees and Neighbors*, 170-73; Howard, *Shawnee!* 21.
27. Nicholson, "Tour of Indian Agencies," 343-84, accessed at www.kshs.org/p/kansas-historical-quarterly-november-1934/17405.
28. Debo, *History of Indians*, 206-7.
29. Chapman, "Pottawatomie and Absentee Shawnee," 293-305.
30. Debo, *History of Indians*, 207-9.
31. Ibid., 206-7.
32. Gibson, *History of Five Centuries*, 147; Wright, *Guide to Indian Tribes*, 159.
33. Howard, *Shawnee!* 22.
34. Ibid.
35. Wright, *Guide to Indian Tribes*, 226.
36. Ragland, "Mission of the Society of Friends," 179.
37. Laracy, "Sacred Heart Mission," 234-50.
38. Lindsey, *Indians at Hampton*, 1-29; Dunbar-Ortiz, *Indigenous Peoples' History*, 151.
39. Lindsey, *Indians at Hampton*, 29-38; Reyhner and Eder, *American Indian Education*, 115-18; Fear-Segal, "Nineteenth-Century Indian Education," 327-31; Trennert, "From Carlisle to Phoenix," 269-70.
40. Brudvig, "Hampton Normal and Agricultural Institute," accessed at www.twofrog.com/hampton.html.
41. Reyhner and Eder, *American Indian Education*, 150; Lindsey, *Indians at Hampton*, 38-40; Dunbar-Ortiz, *Indigenous Peoples' History*, 150; Fear-Segal, Nineteenth Century Indian Education," 327-330; Trennert, "From Carlisle to Phoenix," 271-72.
42. Reyhner and Eder, *American Indian Education*, 132-37.
43. Ibid., 3-5.
44. Commissioner of Indian Affairs, "Annual Report to Secretary of Interior for 1883" (March 3, 1884), 86.
45. Ibid.
46. Ibid., 85.
47. Ibid., 86.

48. Ibid.

49. Howard, *Shawnee!* 22.

50. Ragland, "Mission of the Society of Friends," 174.

51. Carter, *Dawes Commission*, 1; Baird and Goble, *Oklahoma*, 153; Debo, *And Still the Waters Run*, 21-23.

52. *Indian Appropriations Act of 1871*, 25 U.S.C. Sec. 71, "Future Treaties with Indian Tribes," accessed at www.law.cornell.edu/uscode/text/25/71.

53. Baird and Goble, *Oklahoma*, 141-53.

54. Peery, "The First Two Years," 419-57; Teall, *Black History in Oklahoma*, 185.

55. Ragland, "Mission of the Society of Friends," 178.

56. Ibid., 179.

57. Ibid., 174-75.

58. Ibid., 175.

59. *Plessy v. Ferguson*, 163 U.S. 537 (U.S. 1896).

60. 1900 U.S. Census, Pottawatomie County, Okla., for William Shawnee; 1900 Indian Census Rolls, for Absentee Shawnee Indians, Pupils of Absentee Shawnee Government School. Census records accessed at www.ancestry.com.

Overview of the First Chronicle

1. "Blount County," from Goodspeed's *1887 History of Tennessee* (Nashville: Goodspeed Publishing), 1887, accessed at www.tennesseegenealogy.org/blount2/History.html; "Normal Institute Meeting," *Knoxville (Tenn.) Weekly Chronicle*, 29 Nov. 1871, *Chronicling America: Historic American Newspapers*, Library of Congress, accessed at http://chroniclingamerica.loc.gov/l/seq-8/ccn/sn85033438/1871-11-29/ed-1.

Chapter 2. Deciding on a Vocation

1. Booker, "Charles Warner Cansler," accessed at http://ww2.tnstate.edu/library/digital/cansler.htm.

Overview of the Second Chronicle

1. Shawnee recorded in his journal that he supported the surveys; Major Porter reported to Hampton Institute officials that Alford and King supported the surveys. See "Twenty-Two Years' Work," Hampton Normal School Press, 345-46, accessed at https://archive.org/details/twentytwoyearsw00vagoog.

2. Figures A.1.1–A.1.15 in appendix A contain information about Big Jim's and William Shawnee Sr.'s memorial to the federal government. See also American Indian Institute Oral History Project from: Julia Jordan, Doris Duke Collection, Tape number M-22, ID number 990, Archival Order Volume 053, Western History Collections, University of Oklahoma Libraries, Norman, Oklahoma, accessed at http://digital.libraries.ou.edu/cdm/ref/collection/dorisduke/id/1499.

Epilogue

1. Howard, *Shawnee!* 23; Jordan, "History of the Absentee Shawnees," 24, accessed at https://digital.libraries.ou.edu/cdm/compoundobject/collection/dorisduke/id/1499/rec/8; sources indicate Big Jim's death date as both September 29 and 30.

2. "Pioneering territory days recalled by Chief Little Jim," *Norman Transcript*, November 29, 1953; Jordan, "History of the Absentee Shawnees," 24.

3. Howard, *Shawnee!* 106-7; Brudvig, "Hampton Normal and Agricultural Institute," accessed at www.twofrog.com/hampton.html.

4. Ragland, "Mission of the Society of Friends," 175.

5. Oklahoma, County Marriages, 1890-1995, Pottawatomie County for Thomas W. Alford, accessed at www.ancestry.com; Alford, *The Four Gospels*, accessed at http://archive.org/stream/fourgospelsofour00alfo#page/n5/mode/2up; 1920 and 1930 U.S. Census, Pottawatomie County for Thomas W. Alford, accessed at www.ancestry.com; U.S. Find a Grave Index, 1600s-Current, Pottawatomie County Oklahoma for Thomas W. Alford, accessed at ancestry.com.

6. Brudvig, "Hampton Normal and Agricultural Institute," accessed at www.twofrog.com/hampton.html; Lindsey, *Indians at Hampton Institute*, 260.

7. 1910 U.S. Census, Seminole County, Oklahoma, for Ethel Shawnee, accessed at www.ancestry.com.

8. Page 65 of the "Shawnee City Directory for 1898" indicates that Shawnee was a schoolteacher who lived on the corner of Farrall and Hayes.

9. Page 16 of the "Shawnee City Directory for 1898" indicates that the "Colored School" was on the corner of Farrall and Oklahoma, and that "Wm. E. Shawnee" was the teacher.

10. "Friends' Mission shaped scholar's life," *Shawnee News-Star*, June 9, 1971.

11. 1900 U.S. Census, Pottawatomie County, Oklahoma, for David Dick Shawnee, accessed at www.ancestry.coom; WWI Draft Cards, Youngstown, Ohio, for David Dick Shawnee.

12. Oklahoma, County Marriages, 1890-1995, Muskogee, for Ross Hawkins and Ellen Shawnee, accessed at www.ancestry.com.

13. 1900 U.S. Census, Cleveland County, Oklahoma, for William Shawnee, accessed at www.ancestry.com.

14. Oklahoma, Wills and Probate Records, 1801-2008, for William Shawnee.

15. 1894 City Directory, Lawrence, Kansas, for Dudley Joseph Shawnee. He is listed in the 1894 and 1896 City Directories in Lawrence as a "colored" clerk.

16. Oklahoma, County Marriages, 1890-1995, Wagoner County, for Dudley Shawnee and Sarah Lewis.

17. 1910 U.S. Census, Wagoner County, for Dudley Shawnee, accessed at www.ancestry.com.

18. The federal censuses for the years 1900, 1910, 1920, 1930, and 1940 indicate "Indian" or "White" as the race for Walter Homer Shawnee.

19. 1900 U.S. Census, Kansas, for George Eli Shawnee and 1910 U.S. Census, Wagoner, Oklahoma, for George Eli Shawnee, accessed at www.ancestry.com; U.S. World War I Draft Registration Cards, 1917-1918, for George Eli Shawnee, accessed at www.ancestry.com; Anderson, "Reformers Revealed," 149; Warren, "All Indian Trails Lead to Lawrence," 9; 1930 and 1940 U.S. Census, Lawrence, Kansas, for George Eli Shawnee, accessed at www.ancestry.com; California, Death Index, 1940-1997, for George Shawnee, accessed at www.ancentry.com.

20. King, "Multicultural Education," 526.

21. U.S. School Catalogs, 1765-1935, Ohio, Oberlin College, 1908, for Eva Shawnee, accessed at www.ancestry.com; listing shows Eva enrolled 1904-5.

22. King, "Multicultural Education," 526.

23. Lindsey, *Indians at Hampton Institute*, 239.

24. Brudvig, "Hampton Normal and Agricultural Institute," accessed at www.twofrog.com/hampton.html; Lindsey, *Indians at Hampton Institute*, 239.

25. U.S. City Directories, 1822-1995, Tulsa, Oklahoma, and Muskogee, Oklahoma, for Eva Shawnee, accessed at www.ancetry.com; 1930 U.S. census for Eva Lowe, accessed at www.ancestry.com.

26. U.S. City Directory, 1822-1995, Muskogee, Oklahoma, for Eva Shawnee's nursing home, accessed at www.ancestry.com.

27. King, "Multicultural Education," 524.

28. Lindsey, *Indians at Hampton Institute*, 207; Oklahoma, County Marriages, 1890-1955, Pottawatomie County for Rebecca Shawnee, accessed at www.ancestry.com; 1910 and 1920 U.S. censuses for Rebecca Shawnee, accessed at www.ancestry.com.

29. Lindsey, *Indians at Hampton Institute*, 239; 1930 U.S. census for Rebecca Pitts, accessed at www.ancestry.com; U.S., Find a Grave Index, 1600s-Current, for Rebecca Pitts, accessed at www.ancentry.com.

30. Brudvig, "Hampton Normal and Agricultural Institute," accessed at www.twofrog.com/hampton.html; Lindsey, *Indians at Hampton Institute*, 239.

31. Brudvig, "Hampton Normal and Agricultural Institute," accessed at www.twofrog.com/hampton.html.

32. King, "Multicultural Education," 527-29.

33. Brudvig, "Hampton Normal and Agricultural Institute," accessed at www.twofrog.com/hampton.html.

34. Ibid.; Willows, "Narrative Report as of December 31, 1921."

35. Lindsey, *Indians at Hampton Institute*, 207.

36. Ibid., 239.

37. King, "Multicultural Education," 527.

38. Brudvig, "Hampton Normal and Agricultural Institute," accessed at www.twofrog.com/hampton.html.

39. Lindsey, *Indians at Hampton Institute*, 239.

40. U.S. World War I Draft Registration Cards, 1917-1918, for Lafayette Shawnee, accessed at www.ancestry.com; Oklahoma, County Marriages, 1890-1995, Seminole County, for Lafayette Shawnee, accessed at www.ancestry.com.

41. 1930 U.S. Census, for Lafayette Shawnee, accessed at www.ancestry.com.

42. U.S. World War II Draft Registration Cards, 1942, for LaFayette Shawnee, accessed at www.ancestry.com; U.S. City Directories, 1822-1995, Oklahoma City, Oklahoma, for M. Lafayete [sic] Shawnee.

43. U.S. Find a Grave Index, 1600s–Current, for Lafayette Shawnee.

44. King, "Multicultural Education," 529.

45. Ibid., 530.

46. Brudvig, "Hampton Normal and Agricultural Institute," accessed at www.twofrog.com/hampton.html; Oklahoma, County Marriages, 1890-1995, for Emmeline [sic] Shawnee, for Pottawatomie County in 1908 and Emmeline [sic] Deckerd in Muskogee County in 1914, accessed at www.ancestry.com; 1930 U.S. Census for Emmeline [sic] Rankin.

47. Brudvig, "Hampton Normal and Agricultural Institute," accessed at www.twofrog.com/hampton.html.

48. Lindsey, *Indians at Hampton Institute*, 239; Oklahoma, County Marriages 1890-1855, Wagoner County for Julia Inez Shawnee, accessed at www.ancestry.com; U.S. City Directories, 1822-1995, Muskogee, Oklahoma, for Julia DeRadcliffe, accessed at www.ancestry.com.

49. 1940 U.S. Census, Pottawatomie County, Oklahoma, for Donna Shawnee, accessed at www.ancestry.com.

50. 1930 U.S. Census, Pottawatomie County, Oklahoma, for Donna Shawnee.

51. U.S. City Directory, 1935, Tulsa, Oklahoma, for Donna Shawnee.

52. 1940 U.S. Census, Tulsa County, Oklahoma, for Donna Shawnee, accessed at www.ancestry.com.

53. Lindsey, *Indians at Hampton Institute*, 207.

54. U.S. Indian Census Rolls, 1885-1940, 1901 Absentee Shawnee census, for Myrtle Shawnee.

55. 1910 U.S. Census, Pottawatomie County, Oklahoma, for Myrtle Shawnee, accessed at www.ancestry.com.

56. 1920 U.S. Census, Tulsa, Oklahoma, for Myrtle Shawnee, accessed at www.ancestry.com.

57. U.S. City Directories, 1921, Tulsa, Oklahoma, for Myrtle Shawnee.

58. Oklahoma, County Marriages, 1890-1995, Tulsa County, Oklahoma, for Myrtle Shawnee.

59. 1930 U.S. Census, Tulsa County, Oklahoma, for Isaac Guess.

60. Lindsey, *Indians at Hampton Institute*, 207.

61. U.S. World War I Draft Registration Cards, 1917-1918, for David Dick Shawnee.

62. U.S. City Directories, 1921 and 1926, Tulsa, Oklahoma, for David Shawnee.

63. 1940 U.S. Census, Omaha, Nebraska, for David Shawnee, accessed at www.ancestry.com.

64. U.S. Department of Veterans Affairs Beneficiary Identification Records Locator Subsystem (BIRLS) Death File, 1850-2010, for David Shawnee, accessed at www.ancestry.com.

65. U.S. Find a Grave Index, 1600s-Current, accessed at www.ancestry.com.

66. 1910 U.S. Census, Seminole County, Oklahoma, for Ethel Magnolia Shawnee, accessed at www.ancestry.com.

67. Oklahoma, County Marriage Records, 1889–1951, Book 19, page 165, for Ethel Shawnee and Richard Bruner.

68. U.S. Social Security Administration, Social Security Death Index, 1935-2014, for Richard Bruner and Ethel Magnolia Bruner, accessed at www.ancestry.com; National Cemetery Administration, U.S. Veterans' Gravesites, ca. 1775-2006, accessed at www.ancestry.com; U.S. Find a Grave Index, 1600s-Current, accessed at www.ancestry.com.

Bibliography

This bibliography is divided into the following sections: Archival Collections; Court Cases; Government Documents; U.S. Census Data; Laws and Statutes; Miscellaneous Records; and Books, Articles, Dissertations, and Theses.

Archival Collections

Oklahoma History Center, Oklahoma City
    Absentee Shawnee Collection
    Sac and Fox Collection
Pottawatomie County Museum, Shawnee, Okla.
    William E. Shawnee Collection
Western History Collections, University of Oklahoma Libraries, Norman
    American Indian File Collection
    Doris Duke Collection
    Sac and Fox Collection
    Society of Friends

Court Cases

Dred Scott v. Sanford, 60 U.S. 393 (1857).
Plessy v. Ferguson, 163 U.S. 537 (1897).

Government Documents

Commissioner of Indian Affairs. *Annual Report of the Commissioner of Indian Affairs to the Secretary of the Interior for the Years 1862-1903.* Accessed at http://digicoll.library.wisc.edu/cgi-bin/History/History-idx?type=browse&scope=HISTORY.COMMREP.

Kappler, Charles J., ed. *Indian Affairs: Laws and Treaties, Vol. I, Laws* (compiled to December 1, 1902). Washington, D.C.: Government Printing Office, 1904.

———, ed. *Indian Affairs: Laws and Treaties, Vol. IV, Laws* (compiled to March 4, 1927). Washington: Government Printing Office, 1929.

National Cemetery Administration. *Nationwide Gravesite Locator*. U.S. Veterans' Gravesites, ca. 1775-2006. Accessed at www.ancestry.com.

U.S. Department of Veterans Affairs Beneficiary Identification Records Locator Subsystem (BIRLS) Death File. Washington, D.C.: U.S. Department of Veterans Affairs, 1850-2010. Accessed at www.ancestry.com.

U.S. Find a Grave Index. 1600's—Current. Accessed at www.ancestry.com.

U.S. Social Security Administration. *Social Security Death Index*. Social Security Administration, 1935-2014. Accessed at www.ancestry.com.

U.S. Social Security Applications and Claims Index, 1936-2007.

U.S. Census Data

Arizona Territory Census, 1906-1912. Accessed at www.ancestry.com.

Eudora County, Kansas, 1870-1940. Accessed at www.ancestry.com.

Indian Census Rolls, 1885-1940. Absentee Shawnee Indians, 1892-1937. Accessed at www.ancestry.com.

Kansas State Census Collection, 1885. Accessed at www.ancestry.com.

Oklahoma counties: Cleveland, Kingfisher, Muskogee, Oklahoma, Okmulgee, Pottawatomie, Seminole, Tulsa, and Wagoner Counties, 1900, 1907, 1910, 1920, 1930, 1940. Accessed at www.ancestry.com.

Omaha, Nebraska, 1940. Accessed at www.ancestry.com.

Spokane, Washington, 1940. Accessed at www.ancestry.com.

Wisconsin, 1931. Accessed at www.ancestry.com.

Laws and Statutes

Civil Rights Act of 1866. 14 Stat. 27-30. April 9, 1866. Chap. XXXI. Accessed at www.loc.gov/law/help/citizenship/pdf/chap_31.pdf.

Civil Rights Act of 1870 (The Enforcement Act). 16 Stat. 140 (1870).

Civil Rights Act of 1871. 17 Stat. 13 (1871).

Civil Rights Act of 1875. 18 Stat. 335 (1875).

Dawes Allotment Act of 1887. PL 49-119.

Indian Appropriations Act of 1871. 25 U.S.C. Sec. 7. "Future Treaties with Indian Tribes." Accessed at www.law.cornell.edu/uscode/text/25/71.

Miscellaneous Records

City Directories, 1822-1995. Lawrence, Kansas (1894); Kingfisher, Muskogee, Okmulgee, Pottawatomie, Seminole, and Tulsa Counties, Oklahoma.

Creek and Seminole Enrollment Cards, 1895-1914. Accessed at www.ancestry.com.

Eudora County, Kansas, Agriculture, 1870. Accessed at www.ancestry.com.

Kansas, County Marriages, 1811-1911. Accessed at www.ancestry.com.

Oklahoma, County Marriage Records, 1889-1951, for Kingfisher, Muskogee, Oklahoma, Okmulgee, Pottawatomie, Seminole, and Tulsa Counties.

Oklahoma, Wills and Probate Records, 1801-2008, for Seminole County.

Washington, Deaths, 1883–1960. Accessed at www.ancestry.com.

U.S. World War I Draft Registration Cards, 1917-1918. Accessed at www.ancestry.com.

U.S. World War II Draft Registration Cards, 1942-1944. Accessed at www.ancestry.com.

Books, Articles, Dissertations, and Theses

Abing, Kevin. "Before Bleeding Kansas, 1884-1854." *Kansas History: A Journal of the Central Plains* 24 (Spring 2001): 54-71.

Alford, Thomas Wildcat. *Civilization and the Story of the Absentee Shawnees as Told to Florence Drake*. Norman: University of Oklahoma Press, 1936.

———. *The Four Gospels of Our Lord Jesus Christ in Shawnee Indian Language*. Xenia, Ohio: Dr. W. A. Galloway, 1929.

Anderson, Eric P. "Reformers Revealed: American Progressives at Haskell Institute, Lawrence, Kansas, 1884-1909." PhD dissertation, University of Kansas, Lawrence, 2009.

Baird, W. David, and Danney Goble. *Oklahoma: A History*. Norman: University of Oklahoma Press, 2008.

Balyeat, Frank A. "Segregation in the Public Schools of Oklahoma Territory." *Chronicles of Oklahoma* 39, no. 2 (1961): 180-92.

Bier, Lisa. *American Indian and African American People, Communities, and Interactions.* Westport, Conn.: Praeger, 2004.

Blankenship, Bob. *Cherokee Roots, Volume 1: Eastern Cherokee Rolls.* Cherokee, N.C.: Bob Blankenship, 1992.

"Blount County." From Goodspeed's *1887 History of Tennessee.* Nashville: Goodspeed Publishing, 1887. Accessed at www.tennesseegenealogy.org/blount2/History.html.

Booker, Robert J. "Charles Warner Cansler (1871-1953)." Tennessee State University Libraries and Media Centers profiles. Accessed at http://ww2.tnstate.edu/library/digital/cansler.htm.

Brant, Charles. "Indian-White Cultural Relations in Southwestern Oklahoma." *Chronicles of Oklahoma* 37, no.4 (1959): 433-39.

Brudvig, Jon L., comp. and ed. "Hampton Normal and Agricultural Institute: American Indian Students, 1878-1923." 1994 and 1996. Accessed at www.twofrog.com/hampton.html.

Calloway, Colin G. *The Shawnees and the War for America.* New York: Penguin, 2007.

Carter, Kent. *The Dawes Commission and the Allotment of the Five Civilized Tribes, 1893-1914.* Orem, Utah: Ancestry Incorporated, 1999.

Cayton, Leonard B. "A History of Black Public Education in Oklahoma." PhD dissertation, University of Oklahoma, Norman, 1977.

Chapman, Berlin B. "The Pottawatomie and Absentee Shawnee Reservation." *Chronicles of Oklahoma* 24, no. 3 (1946): 293-305.

Collins, Richard, ed. *The Native Americans: The Indigenous People of North America.* New York: Smithmark Publishers, 1991.

Davison, Oscar William. "Education at Statehood." *Chronicles of Oklahoma* 28, no. 1 (1950): 63-80.

Debo, Angie. *A History of the Indians of the United States.* Norman: University of Oklahoma Press, 1970.

———. *And Still the Waters Run: The Betrayal of the Five Civilized Tribes.* Princeton, N.J.: Princeton University Press, 1940; repr. 1991.

Dunbar-Ortiz, Roxanne. *An Indigenous Peoples' History of the United States*. Boston: Beacon Press, 2014.

Edmunds, David R. *The Potawatomis Keepers of the Fire*. Norman: University of Oklahoma Press, 1978.

"Events in the West, 1870-1880." New Perspectives on the West. PBS.org. Accessed at www.pbs.org/weta/thewest/events/1870_1880.htm.

Falato, Betty Katherine Permetter, and Adam J. Falato. *Autobiography of William Ellsworth Shawnee*. Shawnee, Okla.: Pottawatomie County Historical Society, 2017.

Faulk, Odie B. *Oklahoma: Land of the Fair God*. Northridge, Calif.: Winsdor Publications, 1986.

Fear-Segal, Jacqueline. "Nineteenth-Century Indian Education: Universalism Versus Evolutionism." *Journal of American Studies* 33, no. 2 (1999): 323-41.

Flickinger, Robert Elliott. *The Choctaw Freedmen and the Story of Oak Hill Industrial Academy, Valiant, McCurtain County, Oklahoma*. Westminster, Md.: Heritage Books, 2008.

Forbes, Jack D. *Africans and Native Americans: The Language of Race and the Evolution of Red-Black Peoples*. Chicago: University of Illinois Press, 1993.

Ford, Washington Grady. *Wash's Boy*. n.d.

Forston, John. *Pott County and What Has Come of It*. Special Collector's Edition. Fort Worth: Eakin Press, 1936.

Franklin, Jimmie Lewis. *Journey toward Hope*. First edition. Norman: University of Oklahoma Press, 1982.

Franklin, John Hope, and Alfred A. Moss Jr. *From Slavery to Freedom: History of African Americans*. New York: Alfred A. Knopf, 2003.

Fritz, Henry E. "The Making of Grant's 'Peace Policy.'" *Chronicles of Oklahoma* 37, no. 4 (1959): 411-32.

Gibson, Arrell M. *History of Five Centuries*. Second Edition. Norman: University of Oklahoma Press, 1981.

———. *The Chickasaws*. Norman: University of Oklahoma Press, 1971; repr. 1987.

Gilstrap, Harriet Patrick. "Memoirs of a Pioneer Teacher." *Chronicles of Oklahoma* 38, no. 1 (1960): 20-34.

Grinde Jr., Donald A., and Quintard Taylor. "Red vs. Black: Conflict and Accommodation in the Post-Civil War Indian Territory, 1865-1907." *American Indian Quarterly* (Summer 1984): 211-27.

Harvey, Henry. *History of the Shawnee Indians from the Year 1681 to 1854 Inclusive.* Cincinnati: Ephraim Morgan & Sons, 1855.

Howard, James H. *Shawnee! The Ceremonialism of a Native American Tribe and Its Cultural Background.* Athens: Ohio University Press, 1981.

Johnson, Hannibal B. *Apartheid in Indian Country: Seeing Red over Black Disenfranchisment.* Waco, Texas: Eakin Press, 2012.

Katz, William Loren. *Black Indians: A Hidden Heritage.* New York: Atheneum Books for Young Readers, 2012.

King, Wilma. "Multicultural Education at Hampton Institue—The Shawnees: A Case Study, 1900-1923." *Journal of Negro Education* 37, no. 4 (1983): 524-35.

Krauthamer, Barbara. *Black Slaves, Indian Masters: Slavery, Emancipation, and Citizenship in the Native American South.* Chapel Hill: University of North Carolina Press, 2013.

Laracy, John, O.S.B. "Sacred Heart Mission and Abbey." *Chronicles of Oklahoma* 5, no. 2 (June 1927): 234-50.

Leckie, Wiliam H., with Shirley A. Leckie. *Buffalo Soldiers: A Narrative of the Black Cavalry in the West.* Revised edition. Norman: University of Oklahoma Press, 2006.

Lindsey, Donal F. *Indians at Hampton Institute, 1877-1923.* Urbana and Chicago: University of Illinois Press, 1995.

Littlefield Jr., Daniel F. *The Chickasaw Freedmen: A People without a Country.* Weastport, Conn.: Greenwood Press, 1980.

McLoughlin, William G. "Red Indians, Black Slavery, and White Racism: America's Slaveholding Indians." *American Quarterly* 26, no. 4 (October 1974): 367-85.

Minges, Patrick N. *Black Indian Slave Narratives.* Winston-Salem, N.C.: John F. Blair, 1954.

Mooney, Charles W. *Localized History of Pottawatomie County, Oklahoma to 1907.* Midwest City, Okla.: Thunderbird Industries, 1971.

Mulroy, Kevin. *The Seminole Freedmen: A History.* Norman: University of Oklahome Press, 2007.

Naylor, Celia E. *African Cherokees in Indian Territory: From Chattel to Citizens.* Chapel Hill: University of North Carolina Press, 2008.

Nicholson, William. "Tour of Indian Agencies in Kansas and the Indian Territory in 1870." *Kansas State Quarterly* 3, no. 4

(November 1934): 343-84. Accessed at www.kshs.org/p/kansas-historical-quarterly-november-1934/17405.

Nies, Judith. *Native American History: A Chronology of a Culture's Vast Achievements and Their Links to World Events.* New York: Random House, 1966.

"Normal Institute Meeting." *Knoxville (Tenn.) Weekly Chronicle*, 29 Nov. 1871. *Chronicling America: Historic American Newspapers*, Library of Congress, accessed at http://chroniclingamerica.loc.gov/l/seq-8/ccn/sn85033438/1871-11-29/ed-1

Osterlund, David, ed. *The Constitution of the United States of America.* New York: Barnes and Noble, 1995.

Parchemin, Richard, ed. *The Life and History of North America's Indian Reservations: From the 19th Century to the Present Day.* San Francisco: American Graphics Systems, 1998.

Peery, Dan W. "The First Two Years." *Chronicles of Oklahoma* 7, no. 4 (December 1929): 419-57.

Pottawatomie County History Book Committee. *Pottawatomie County Oklahoma History.* Claremore, Okla.: Country Lane Press, 1987.

Potter, Lee Ann, and Wynell Schamel. "The Homestead Act of 1862." *Social Education* 61, 6 (October 1997): 359-64. Accessed at www.archives.gov/education/lessons/homestead-act.

"Primary Documents in American History: 13th Amendment to the U.S. Constitution." Web Guides, the Library of Congress. Accessed at www.loc.gov/rr/program/bib/ourdocs/13thamendment.html.

"Primary Documents in American History: 14th Amendment to the U.S. Constitution." Web Guides, the Library of Congress. Accessed at www.loc.gov/rr/program/bib/ourdocs/14thamendment.html

"Primary Documents in American History: 15th Amendment to the U.S. Constitution." Web Guides, the Library of Congress. Accessed at www.loc.gov/rr/program/bib/ourdocs/15thamendment.html

Prucha, Francis Paul. *The Indians in American Society: From the Revolutionary War to the Present.* Oakland: University of California Press, 1985.

Ragland, Hobert D. "Mission of the Society of Friends among the Indian Tribes of the Sac and Fox Agency." *Chronicles of Oklahoma* 33, no. 2 (1955): 169-82.

Ragland, Hobart D. "Some Firsts in Lincoln County." *Chronicles of Oklahoma* 29, no. 4 (1951): 419-28.

"Reconstruction: The Second Civil War." Black Legislators: Primary Sources. The 1866 Civil Rights Act. American Experience. PBS.org. Accessed at www.pbs.org/wgbh/amex/reconstruction/activism/ps_1866.html.

Reyhner, Jon, and Jeanne Eder. *American Indian Education: A History*. Norman: University of Oklahoma Press, 2004.

Straus, Terry, ed. *Race, Roots, and Relations: Native and African Americans*. Chicago: Albatross Press, 2005.

Tayac, Gabrielle, ed. *Indivisible: African-Native American Lives in the Americas*. Washington, D.C., and New York: Smithsonian Books, 2009.

Taylor, Quintard. *In Search of the Racial Frontier: African Americans in the American West, 1528-1990*. New York and London: W. W. Norton & Company, 1998.

Teall, K. M. *Black History in Oklahoma*. Oklahoma City: Oklahoma City Schools, 1971.

Thomson, S. Carrie. "The Shawnee Friends Mission." *Chronicles of Oklahoma* 2, no. 4 (1924): 392-94.

Tolson, Arthur Lincoln. "The Negro in Oklahoma Territory, 1889-1907: A Study in Racial Discrimination." PhD dissertation, University of Oklahoma, Norman, 1966.

Trennert, Robert A. "From Carlisle to Phoenix: The Rise and Fall of the Indian Outing System, 1878-1930." *Pacific Historical Review* (August 1983): 267-91.

"Twenty-Two Years' Work of the Hampton Normal and Agricultural Institute at Hampton, Virginia: Records of Negro and Indian Graduates and Ex-Students." Hampton, Va.: Hampton Normal School Press, 1893. Accessed at https://archive.org/stream/twentytwoyearsw00vagoog#page/n6/mode/2up.

Vaught, Edgar S. "What Every Oklahoman Should Know." *Chronicles of Oklahoma* 29, no. 4 (1951): 386-93.

Walton, Raji, and Angela Y. Black. *Black Indian Genealogy Research: African American Ancestors among the Five Civilized Tribes*. Bowie, Md.: Heritage Books, 1993.

Warren, Stephen. *The Worlds the Shawnees Made: Migration and Violence in Early America.* Chapel Hill: University of North Carolina Press, 2014.

———. *The Shawnees and Their Neighbors, 1795-1870.* Urbana and Chicago: University of Chicago Press, 2009.

Wickett, Murry R. *Contested Territory: Whites, Native Americans and African Americans in Oklahoma, 1865-1907.* Baton Rouge: Louisiana State University Press, 2000.

Woodward, C. Vann. *The Strange Career of Jim Crow.* New York: Oxford University Press, 1974.

Wormser, Richard. "The Enforcement Acts (1870-71)." Jim Crow Stories. The Rise and Fall of Jim Crow. PBS.org. Accessed at www.pbs.org/wnet/jimcrow/stories_events_enforce.html.

———. "Freedmen's Bureau (1865-72)." Jim Crow Stories. The Rise and Fall of Jim Crow. PBS.org. Accessed at www.pbs.org/wnet/jimcrow/stories_events_freed.html.

Wright, Muriel H. *A Guide to the Indian Tribes of Oklahoma.* Norman: University of Oklahoma Press, 1951; repr. 1986.

Yoshitaka, Iwasaki. "Freedmen in the Indian Territory after the Civil War: The Dual Approaches of the Choctaw and Chickasaw Nations." *Nanzan Review of American Studies* 30 (2008): 91-108.

Zellar, Gary. *African Creeks: Etelvste and the Creek Nation.* Norman: University of Oklahoma Press, 2007.

Name Index

Name of person in manuscript	
A	
Adams, James	350
Ah-hee'-tah	188. *See also* Cherokee Woman
Ah'-kwē-nàh-kō-thē-yàh	219
Àh-kwē-nàh-kō-thē-yah	219
Ah-yan-ke	186, 188. *See also* Cherokee Woman
Alford, David	16, 107, 158, 191, 200, 210, 215, 218, 221-24, 229, 273, 291, 302, 318, 334, 336-39, 341-43, 350, 358, 362
Alford, Mamie	209, 210, 262, 264, 266, 269, 281, 302, 318, 320, 334-35, 338, 339, 341, 357
Alford, Nellie	209
Alford, Paul	190, 198, 202, 364
Alford, Pierrepont	190, 198, 202, 363, 366
Alford, Reese	190, 198, 202, 364
Alford, Thomas	17, 19, 22, 107, 178, 183, 184, 189, 190-92, 198-99, 201-4, 207, 209, 211-12, 214, 223, 225-26, 234, 237-38, 241, 279, 281, 362. *See also* Alford, Thomas W.
Alford, Thomas W.	16, *20*, 89, 157, 184, 207, 363. *See also* Alford, Thomas
Alford, Webster	337
Allen, Mr.	239, 356
Amey, Ryas [Rice?]	224
Anderson, Charley	193. *See also* Anderson, Mr.
Anderson, Loula	244
Anderson, Mr.	284. *See also* Anderson, Charley
A-nē-yàh-kō-cē-kàh	233
Apperson, George	289, 314
Asher, W. R.	206
Asher, W. W.	257
B	
Bailey, Mr.	344
Baley, Mr.	344
Branner, Alice	82

Branner, R.	82
Barbee, Mr.	284
Barbee, Mrs.	284
Barber, E.	254. *See also* Barber, Mr.
Barber, Mr.	253-54. *See also* Barber, E.
Barbour, Major	268. *See also* Barbour, Mr.
Barbour, Mr.	250. *See also* Barbour, Major
Barclay, Robert	114
Barnett, Andrew	106
Barone, Annie	209, 212, 226
Barone, Josephine	189, 205, 209, 226, 315
Barone, Mr.	209, 212, 226
Barone, Mrs.	209, 226
Baxter, Mr.	296
Bayle, Mr.	196
Beard, Elkano	17, 108, 186, 189, 191
Beatrice, Princess	68
Beaver, Charley	177, 178, 210, 229, 232, 281, 313, 320-21, 329
Beaver, Dudley	177-78
Benson, C. J.	295, 320. *See also* Benson, Mr.
Benson, Geo.	68. *See also* Benson, George
Benson, George	47, 73. *See also* Benson, Geo.
Benson, Mr.	288, 295, 320, 338, 344. *See also* Benson, C. J.
Benson, Mrs.	197
Berry, Andrew	302
Berry, Bessie	249, 358
Berry, Susie	242, 248, 258, 296, 347
Berry, Thomas	302, 308
Big Jim	3, 16, 20-23, 25, 58, 89, 91, 109, 116-17, 121, 129, 144, 158, 179, 182, 202-3, 205, 206, 208, 217, 226-29, 233-34, 262, 269, 306, 313, 318, 337, 362, 377-78
Big Jim, Ruth	208, 227-28, 234
Blackford, Harrison	231, 258. *See also* Blackford, Mr.
Blackford, Mr.	236-38, 240-42, 244, 250-51, 256, 258, 266-67, 276-77, 348. *See also* Blackford, Harrison
Blackwell, Henry	191, 195. *See also* Blackwell, Mr.
Blackwell, Mr.	203, 208, 211. *See also* Blackwell, Henry
Blanchard, Joe	182, 208, 228

Blanchard, Mrs.	228
Blancher, Miss	43
Blue Jacket	191, 239
Boloxa	217, 228
Bottle [Butler?], John	160
Bourbonnais, Anthony	17, 313
Bourbonnais, Aurelia	177, 187, 196-97, 207-8, 229, 234
Bourbonnais, Keby	291
Bourbonnais, Mary	17, 187, 196, 205, 207-8, 315. *See also* Bourbonnais, Mrs.
Bourbonnais, Mrs.	160, 177-78, 180, 182, 189, 197, 207, 215, 229, 234, 283, 291, 310, 315. *See also* Bourbonnais, Mary
Bourbonnais, Ozetta	190, 197-98, 291. *See also* Nathahpehah
Bourbonnais, Tom	196
Bourbonnais, Tono	180, 207
Boushee, F. P.	183, 185-86
Bowleg, Lizzie	296, 299, 311
Boyd, Charles	71
Boyd, Mary	36, 52, 68, 71
Boyd, President	273. *See also* Boyd, Prof.
Boyd, Prof.	296. *See also* Boyd, President
Brady, Peter	209
Brice, Miss	306, 316-17, 338
Brooks, Maud	37, 47-48, 64-65, 68, 70, 82
Brown, Alice L.	183
Brown, Mr.	219, 363, 373
Buckheart	186
Bull, Mr.	273, 280. *See also* Bull, P. V.
Bull, P. V.	345. *See also* Bull, Mr.
Bullfrog, Ben	209
Bullfrog, Billy	188
Bullfrog, Rosa	188
C	
Cameron, Supt.	273
Campbell, Mr.	256
Canalas, Elkano	186, 189
Canalas, Sallie	186, 189, 215
Cansler, Charles	57, 71
Cansler, Mr.	37
Cansler, Nannie	45

Carlock, A. M.	185
Carolina, Charlie	289. *See also* Payne, Charlie
Carolina, Ellen	262, 287, 296, 299-300, 302, 341. *See also* Payne, Ellen
Carson, Mr.	194, 200, 226, 229, 299, 315
Carson, Mrs.	200
Carter, Grant	253-54, 328-29
Carter, Hays	264
Carter, Henry	264, 278-79, 292, 299, 308-9, 321, 329, 336, 348, 351
Carter, Irene	278, 292, 329, 343
Carter, Stephen	200, 208, 211, 214, 222, 253
Cegar	178, 183, 200, 210, 218, 263, 273-74, 315, 321, 329, 338, 342, 345, 350
Cegar, Jennie	217, 263, 274, 281, 320, 322, 329, 336, 342, 346. *See also* Cegar, Mrs.
Cegar, Mrs.	210, 217-18, 263, 266, 358. *See also* Cegar, Jennie
Chambers, Mr.	265
Charley, Samuel	15, 315
Cherokee Woman	186
Chilson, Dan	205
Chisholm, Caroline	52, 105, 160
Chisholm, Hester	6, 105, 160
Chisholm, Mary	44, 52
Chisholm, William	6, 160
Christian, Mr.	344
Cicero	101, 110, 157, 159, 335
Clark, Adam	315
Clark, Jackson	185, 315. *See also* Clarke, Jackson
Clarke, Jackson	185. *See also* Clark, Jackson; Ho-tàh'-kē-sē-mō; Tà-kē-sē-mō
Clay, Mr.	269, 328, 334, 344, 346, 351. *See also* Clay, Sam
Clay, Sam	328, 334, 344, 346, 351. *See also* Clay, Mr.
Cockran, William	160, 209-10
Coleman, Bettie	246, 250
Coleman, Mr.	246, 259. *See also* Coleman, Sam
Coleman, Sam	255. *See also* Coleman, Mr.
Colman, Walter	244
Coltrain, Ella	44, 108, 178
Coning, Bertha	44

Cooley, Florence	289, 295
Cooley, Minnie	317. See also Cooley, Mrs.
Cooley, Mr.	294-95, 297, 301, 303-4, 307-8, 311, 314, 319, 326, 339, 348, 352
Cooley, Mrs.	289, 295, 314, 317. See also Cooley, Minnie
Cooley, William	311, 314, 350, 353
Coolie, Emma	160. See also Coolie, Mrs.
Coolie, Mr.	286
Coolie, Mrs.	160, 286. See also Coolie, Emma
Cooly, Miss	272
Cooper, Eliza	323
Cooper, Fillmore	254
Cooper, Gertie	249
Cooper, H. E.	233-34, 236-37, 253, 257-59, 276-77
Cooper, Henry	239, 254
Cooper, Josie	246-47, 277
Cooper, Oliver	239
Crain, Alex	89, 345
Crusoe, Robinson	271, 341
Cummings, J. M.	196, 245. See also Cummings, Mr.
Cummings, Mr.	196, 199, 203, 209-10, 219, 222, 226, 229, 292, 335, 357. See also Cummings, J. M.
Cuohè, Miss	184
Cuppy, George	186
Cuppy, I. C.	345
Cuppy, Isaac	246
D	
Davis, Della	108. See also Davis, Della H.
Davis, Della H.	60. See also Davis, Della
Davis, Flaurice	190, 202
Davis, King	194, 266, 292, 335
Davis, Margret	108
Day, Sampson	210
Deck, Willie	265
Decker, John	265
Decker, Katie	274, 283, 313
Deer, Amos	184
Deer, Cinda	160
Deer, Robert	15, 103, 182-86, 204. See also Deere, Robert

Deere, Robert	183-86. *See also* Deer, Robert
Della Jr.	198, 202, 204. *See also* Thăhnăhkăthōkwă
Depew, Mr.	213
Diamond, Mrs.	290
Dirt, Dan	337, 339, 341-42
Donnelly, Mr.	259, 354
Douglas, Effie	190, 198, 211. *See also* Wēs'-kō-pă-thō"-kwă
Duck, Miss	208
Dukes, John	293
Dulan, Ben	250
Dunjee, Drusilla	25, 215, 239, 242, 257-58, 323-24. *See also* Dunjee, Drusilla Irene
Dunjee, Drusilla Irene	238, 248, 258. *See also* Dunjee, Drusilla
Dunjee, Ella	25, 158, 215, 231-33, 247-48, 258-59, 261-62, 271-72, 276-80, 282, 284, 323-24
Dunjee, J. W.	25-26, 129, 248, 257, 276, 284, 310, 323. *See also* Dunjee, Mr.
Dunjee, Mr.	215, 237, 248, 262, 265, 271-74, 276, 282, 310, 324. *See also* Dunjee, J. W.
Dunjee, Mrs.	238, 242, 257, 265
E	
Easterling, Horace V.	108
Elliot, Franklin	17, 21, 108
Ellis, Debbie	44
Ellis, Dick	188
Ellis, Joe	16, 179
Ellis, Mrs. Dick	188
Ellis, Seargent	188, 313
Ellis, Tom	20
Esparney, John	179. *See also* Sparney, John
F	
Ferguson, Grandma	240, 246
Ferguson, Mr.	246
Fields, James	249
Flynn, Dennis	283
Ford, Miss	250

Forman, John	188
Fullbright, Mr.	159, 271-72, 276-77, 292. *See also* Fullbright, Rev.
Fullbright, Rev.	231, 261. *See also* Fullbright, Mr.

G

Gallagher, Mr.	196
Ganoung, Maude Idella	66
Garlinghouse, Mrs. C. O.	298
Garret, Demas	191
Garret, Mrs.	310, 311, 313-14, 353
Gearing, Alice	244
Gibson, Alex	185
Gibson, Fire Man	227. *See also* Pă-sē-kàh
Gililland, C.	240. *See also* Gililland, Mr.
Gililland, Mr.	240. *See also* Gililland, C.
Girty, Buck	160
Girty, Jack	6, 159
Girty, Simon	159
Girty, Wilson	244
Gladstone, W. E.	45. *See also* Gladstone W^m E.
Gladstone, Wm E.	47. *See also* Gladstone W. E.
Glaze, Mr.	249
Goddard, Chas. W.	199
Gokey, Charles	242. *See also* Gokey, Charlie
Gokey, Charlie	239. *See also* Gokey, Charles
Gokey, Helen	239
Gokey, Mary	239-40, 265
Gokey, Mr.	220, 232, 237, 239-40, 243-44, 247, 254, 259, 265, 276-77, 356
Gokey, Mrs.	237, 239-40, 247, 265
Grace, Ida	215, 220
Green, Mrs.	307
Greene, Mr.	260
Greengrass, Inez	210
Greengrass, Nellie	313
Grimes, Mr.	288
Grizzard, James	192, 265, 280, 292. *See also* Grizzard, Mr.
Grizzard, Mr.	192, 335, 281, 285, 292, 335. *See also* Grizzard, James
Gunter, Mrs.	318, 328

H	
Hale Jr., Flora	178, 184, 187, 189-91, 198-99, 202, 211-12, 214, 223, 232-33, 237, 239. *See also* Nanaseothaqua
Hale, Harlen	198-99, 202, 211-12, 214, 241
Hamilton, Dr.	203-4, 212, 261, 301
Hamlin, C. C.	222. *See also* Hamlin, Mr.
Hamlin, Mr.	191, 194, 206, 216, 219-20, 222. *See also* Hamlin, C. C.
Hannum, H. W^m	47, 74
Harmon, Lula	246-47, 249-54,
Harmon, Oscar	250, 256-57, 267-68
Harris, Mrs.	318, 328, 339
Harris, W. T.	303. *See also* Harris, William T.
Harris, William T.	308. *See also* Harris, W. T.
Hartley, Dr.	157, 182, 191-93, 196-97, 205, 207-9, 212, 218, 234-35, 299-302, 310, 312, 315, 330-31. *See also* Hartley, G. N.
Hartley, G. N.	23, 207-8, 299, 301-2, 315, 363. *See also* Hartley, Dr.
Hartley, Mrs. L. Ella	23, 160, 177, 180, 182, 186-87, 189, 192-93, 196-97, 203-5, 215, 218, 234-35, 237, 291, 299-300, 310, 312, 315, 330, 363. *See also* Hartly, Mrs.
Hartley, Mr.	187, 189, 208-9, 215, 221, 237, 291. *See also* Hartley, Dr.; Hartley, G. N.
Hartly, Dr.	283. *See also* Hartley, G. N.
Hartly, Mrs.	283. *See also* Hartley, L. Ella
Hassler, John H.	36, 47
Hastings, Ernest	81
Hastings, Mr.	33, 36. *See also* Hastings, William P.
Hastings, Mrs. L. S. B.	69, 70
Hastings, Rosa G.	52, 82
Hastings, W. P.	69. *See also* Hastings, Mr.
Hastings, William P.	31, 33, 40, 52. *See also* Hastings, W^m P.
Hastings, Wm P.	39, 47. *See also* Hastings, W. P.
Haworth, Mrs. W. P.	177, 363
Haworth, Nettie	159, 187, 199
Haworth, William Perry	177-78, 180-83, 187, 197, 363
Henry, John	303

Herd, Alice	324
Higley Jr., Axie	202, 204. *See also* Pă-màh-hō-kō'-kwà
Hill, Mr.	196, 211-12
Hood, Boletha	209, 226
Hopkins, Dr.	177-78. *See also* Hopkins, Prof.; Hopkins, Supt.
Hopkins, Prof.	296, 298. *See also* Hopkins, Dr.
Hopkins, Supt.	273. *See also* Hopkins, Dr.
Ho-tàh'-kē-sē-mō	185. *See also* Clarke, Jackson
Howard, Edward	53, 72
Hues, C. P.	236, 242. *See also* Hues, Dr.
Hues, Dr.	235-36, 242, 355. *See also* Hues, C. P.
Hutchinson, Mr.	310
I	
Inàhkaulàh	208
J	
Jackson, Mary	37
Jacobson, Mr.	284
Janneson, Nellie	331
Janneson, William	331. *See also* Jannison, William
Jannison, William	330-31. *See also* Janneson, William
Jenks, Ozetta	207-8
Joe Billy	200, 208, 218, 227-28, 262, 306, 322, 324, 330-32, 334, 346, 349-50
John Bob	185-86. *See also* White Turkey
Johnson, Ellis	313
Johnson, Emma	313
Johnson, J. J.	200, 204, 222, 224, 229, 231, 270-72, 277-78, 284, 323-24, 357. *See also* Johnson, Mr.
Johnson, Louisa	44
Johnson, Minnie	188
Johnson, Mr.	222, 224, 229-30, 233, 270-72, 277-78, 284, 309, 319-20, 323-24, 351-52. *See also* Johnson, J. J.
Johnson, Mrs. J. J.	204, 265, 271, 279, 281
Jones, Ida	226

Jones, Mr.	204, 340
Jones, Mrs.	204
Jumper, Mr.	225
K	
Kaceka	183
Kā'-chē-tī"-sē-kwă	190. See also Kā-chē-tiē-sē-kwă
Kā-chē-tiē-sē-kwă	185, 202. See also Kā'-chē-tī"-sē-kwă
Kachetisekwa	198. See also Kirk, Sarah
Kăh-pă'-ō-màh	201
Kasekah	269
Kătekwă	185. See also Ke-tĕ-kwă
Katequa	198. See also Test, Lizzie
Keaton, Justice	291
Kē-chē-thàh	185
Kellogg, Dr. H.	95, 332
Kessel, Miss	182, 189, 196-97, 201, 204-5, 207-9, 273, 283, 306, 317. See also Kessell, Miss
Kessell, Miss	187, 193, 229. See also Kessel, Miss
Ke-tĕ-kwă	184. See also Kătekwă
King, Annie	44
King, Grace	296
King, John	16-17, 20, 22, 89, 178, 183, 201, 203, 208-9, 231, 234, 243-45, 258, 271, 279, 285, 291, 295, 321, 345, 347, 357, 363
King, Lawyer	209
Kirk, Auntie	184
Kirk, Charles W.	23. See also Kirk, Dr.
Kirk, Dr.	21, 23, 100, 178, 180
Kirk Jr., Rachel	212. See also Nănăsēōthăkwă
Kirk, Mrs.	157, 160-61, 177-78, 180-82, 186-87, 189, 193, 197, 202-4, 207-9, 214-15, 233, 237, 241, 255. See also Kirk, Rachel
Kirk, Rachel	23, 160, 180, 190, 196, 199, 205, 207-8, 211-12, 291, 315. See also Kirk, Mrs.
Kirk, Sarah	190, 198, 202. See also Kachetisek
Komathokwa	198, 204. See also Pearson Jr., Maudie

L	
Lacy, Nollie	7, 287, 433n5
Lălàhuēspĕă	208. *See also* White, Bob
Lane, Johnson	53
Largent, John	291. *See also* Largent, Rev. J
Largent, Rev. J.	315. *See also* Largent, John
Laundras, Willie	209. *See also* Laundress, Willie *and* Laundres, Willie
Laundres, Willie	223. *See also* Laundras, Willie *and* Laundress, Willie
Laundress, Willie	282. *See also* Laundras, Willie *and* Laundres, Willie
Lă-wē-pĕă	313
Levering, Mrs.	43
Lewis, Mr.	220, 233-34, 257, 268. *See also* Lewis, W. W.
Lewis, W. W.	233, 237, 257. *See also* Lewis, Mr.
Lillard, James	249, 254. *See also* Lilliard, James
Lilliard, Eva	249, 254
Lilliard, James	246. *See also* Lillard, James
Lilliard, Joe	247
Lilliard, Mr.	240-41, 259, 276
Lilliard, Mrs.	240-41, 258, 259
Linney, John	183
Little, Charley	208, 227-28
Littleax, William	16, 179, 187-88, 227
Littleax, Neilie	188
Littleax, Switch	188
Little Doctor, Oscar	228
Little Jim	110, 208, 231, 234, 242, 244, 269, 362. *See also* Totommo
Lō'-bằh	227
Lockhart, Belle	208-9, 229, 283
Logan, Mrs.	313
Long Horse	191
Long Jim	206
Long Tom	22, 188
Lunt, Lina B.	157, 159, 184, 190-92, 195, 198, 201-2, 204, 207, 211-12, 214, 215, 219-20, 225, 233, 237, 291
Lushboug, Ernest	53

M	
Mack, Archie	251, 268
Mack, Era	249, 251-52, 254, 256, 268
Mack, Lula	232, 243, 246-58, 262, 265-68
Mack, Mary	249
Mack, Mrs.	232, 250-52, 255-59, 262, 267-68, 272, 347, 356
Mack, Robert	243, 245, 251-53, 257-58, 266-67
Marcus, Mr.	262, 264, 270, 302, 348
Marcus, Mrs.	209
Mardock, Mary	185, 190, 198
Mardock Jr., Mary	159, 202
Marhardy, Mrs.	188
Marrier, J. T.	183, 185-88
Măs-kwē'-kă-năh-kăh	233
Massillon, Miss	306, 315-17. See also Massilon, Miss
Mă-yàh-wàh'-pĕă/ Mā-yàh-wàh'-pĕă	183. See also Me-yah-pe
McCan, Isaac	184-85
McCoy, Isaac	16, 107, 192
McFall, Mr.	206, 234, 327, 344, 349, 357. See also McFall, W. L.
McFall, W. L.	245. See also McFall, Mr.
McKinley, Pres.	280, 309
McKinnis, Mr.	295-96, 307, 326
McKinnis, Prof.	298
McLain, Supt.	297
McNeil, Mr.	251, 258, 267, 347, 354
McNeil, Mrs.	251, 258, 347, 354
Mēàhth-wă	228
Merritt, Mr.	306
Mĕs-kwē'-kă-nàh-kah	225
Me-yah-pe	183. See also Mā-yàh-wàh'-pĕă/ Mă-yàh-wàh'-pĕă
Millard, Mr.	288
Miller, Mr.	263, 339, 341. See also Miller, Supt.
Miller, Mrs.	298
Miller, Supt.	288, 317, 338. See also Miller, Mr.
Mitchell, Mr.	259
Moore, Mart	250, 253
Mordy, Rev. John	297
Morgan, Mr.	196, 211-12

Morrow, Prof.	296
Mundy, Mr.	330
Murdaugh, Pres.	273, 296
Murphy, Mrs.	287
N	
Nanapeaskiki	99
Nănăsēōthăkwă	202, 215. *See also* Kirk Jr., Rachel
Nanaseothaqua	198. *See also* Hale Jr., Flora
Nathahpehah	159, 185, 198, 202, 211. *See also* Bourbonnais, Ozetta
Neal, Moses	345
Neal, Mrs.	187, 205, 208-9
Neal, Rev. William	315
Nelson, Mr.	37
Nevens, Billy	301
Newsom, Emma	157, 178-79, 181-82, 185-87, 189, 191-93, 196-97, 207, 212, 214, 225. *See also* Newsome, Emma
Newsom, Joseph	16-17, 24, 107
Newsom, Mr.	330
Newsome, Emma	189, 191. *See also* Newsom, Emma
Nō'-mă-pĕă-sē	227
Norman, Mr.	277
Norris, Mr.	210, 323, 324
O	
No entries for "O"	
P	
Pă-màh-hō-kō'-kwà	198, 204. *See also* Higley Jr., Axie
Panetha	198. *See also* Patrick Jr., Samuel L.
Parks, Emma	215, 226
Pă-sē-kàh	*See also* Gibson, Fire Man
Patton, Moses L.	145
Patrick, Lee	318, 338. *See also* Patrick, Mr.
Patrick, Mr.	273, 286. *See also* Patrick, Lee
Patrick Jr., Samuel L.	184, 190, 198, 201. *See also* Panetha
Patterson, Edith	297-98

Payne, Charlie	289. *See also* Carolina, Charlie
Payne, Ellen	289. *See also* Carolina, Ellen
Pearson, Dr.	212
Pearson, Maud	199
Pearson Jr., Maudie	202, 204, 225. *See also* Komathokwa
Pecan	185, 206
Peel, Fred	338, 343
Peketahrokwa	225
Pendleton, J. M.	148-49
Pensonaw, Eddie	220
Phrapp, Wm.	215
Pn wàh'-kàh-làh	228
Porter, N. S.	89, 179, 339, 345
Portis, Mr.	319, 325
Pratt, Thomas	14
Pritchard, J. W.	70
Q	
Quă-thă'	210
Quiggin, Robert	235
Quinine, Malinda	52
R	
Raines, Mr.	330
Ramsey, Mrs.	290
Randolph, Edna	284
Randolph, J. D.	284. *See also* Randolph, Mr.
Randolph, Mr.	323. *See also* Randolph, J. D.
Ray, Mr.	269
Reaves, Mr.	222
Redman, Anna	40
Redman, Robert	82
Renfrow, Gov.	307
Replogle, Mr.	288, 295, 351-52
Rhoades, James E.	180
Riley, Minnie	205, 207-9, 229
Roberts, Bro.	191, 206-7. *See also* Roberts, Chas. E.
Roberts, Chas. E.	207. *See also* Roberts, Mr.
Roberts, Lula	283
Roberts, Mr.	211-12, 221, 234, 241. *See also* Roberts, Bro.
Roberts, Mrs.	229, 234, 241

Robertson, J. T.	237. *See also* Robertson, Mr.
Robertson, Mr.	235, 237, 239, 241-42. *See also* Robertson, J. T.
Robinson, Lena R.	232, 262, 283, 284
Robinson, Mr.	220, 234
Rock	186, 209
Rogers, Mr.	259, 277
Ruggles, Judge	206
S	
Salyser, Bessie	44
Salyser, Caroline	44
Sampson, Robert	301, 304-5
Sanders, Mr.	236, 319
Sàp-wàh'-pĕă-sē-kàh	228
Sassotasse	218
Saxton, Mr.	292, 299, 322, 329, 346. *See also* Sexton, Mr.
Scott, Charley	208
Scott, John	332
Scott, Judge	196
Scott, Lucy	187, 189, 193, 207-9
Scott, S. J.	309
Search, Mr.	338, 344
Selturska, Jerome	338
Sĕn-nă-hāth-lĕ	188
Sexton, Mr.	285, 292, 316, 319, 321, 334-36, 348. *See also* Saxton, Mr.
Shaunago,	209
Shaw, Francis	246, 250
Shaw, Silas	253, 268
Shawnee, Cora	106. *See also* Shawnee, Cora Anner
Shawnee, Cora Anner	24, 203-4. *See also* Shawnee, Cora
Shawnee, David Dick	364, 370, 373
Shawnee, Donna Fredonia	26, 370-71, 373
Shawnee, Dudley	24-25, *26*, 106, 158, 203, 216, 221, 223, 224, 230, 265, 273, 274, 279, 283, 299, 365, 419, 428-29, 430-31
Shawnee, Elizabeth Jane	5, 7, 24-25, 105, 203-4, 423-24. *See also* Wright, Elizabeth Jane
Shawnee, Ellen	262, 300, 302, 308, 311, 314, 318, 322, 324, 328, 330-31, 333,

	335-39, 342-43, 348, 351, 364
Shawnee, Emaline	26, *369*, 373, 395-96, 418
Shawnee, Eva	189, 204, 281, 315, 317, 365-66, *367*, 373. *See also* Shawnee, Eva Estelle
Shawnee, Eva Estelle (Estella)	365-66, 373. *See also* Shawnee, Eva
Shawnee, Geo. E.	242. *See also* Shawnee, George
Shawnee, George	24-25, 34, 106, 161, 178, 182, 185, 191, 193, 200, 203-4, 206, 208-10, 212, 216, 219, 242, 244, 328, 336-38, 366, 410, 413-14. *See also* Shawnee, George E.
Shawnee, George E.	244, 328, 336-38. *See also* Shawnee, Geo. E.
Shawnee, Julia	26, 209, 217, 222, 230, 266, 269, 279, 287, 289, 299, 300, 302, 314, 317, 321, 327, 338, 346, 348, 349, 351, 365, 373, 405-7
Shawnee, Julia Inez	26, 369, *370*, 373
Shawnee, Lydia	25, 204, *368*, 373
Shawnee, Marquis Lafayette	26, 198, 212, 271, 357, 368, *369*, 373
Shawnee, Myrtle	26, 370-71, 373
Shawnee, Rebecca	25, 204, 264, 367, *368*, 373
Shawnee, Walter Homer	22, 24-25, *26*, 32, 106, 112, 183, 191, 198, 201, 203, 206, 208-10, 214, 216-18, 221, 225, 230, 238, 262-63, 265-66, 270-71, 273-74, 279, 282, 302, 338, 366, 410, 413-14, 419, 428-29, 430-31
Shawnee, William	39, 105, 106-7, 159-60, 183, 195-96, 199-200, 206, 209, 211, 218-19, 223-24, 236, 244-45, 249-50, 258, 264, 266, 271, 279, 283, 285-87, 291, 293, 302, 304, 316, 319-21, 326-27, 336, 345, 347-48, 357-58, 364-65, 370, 397-99. *See also* Shawnee Sr.
Shawnee, William E.	*See* Shawnee, William Ellsworth
Shawnee, William Ellsworth	3-8, 10, 13, 20-26, 31-33, 57-61, 89-91, 106-7, 129-30, 157-60, 177-78, 180-81, 195-96, 199-200, 206, 209, 211, 218-19, 221, 223-24, 229, 231-32, 236, 245,

	250, 258, 261-62, 264-66, 269, 271, 276, 279, 296, 302, 318, 322, 332, 361, 363-65, 372, 377-78, 394, 400-1, 404, 407, 409, 410-11, 426-27
Shawnee, Willie	37, 39-40, 44, 106, 324. *See also* Shawnee, William Ellsworth; Shawnee, Willie Ivery
Shawnee, Willie Ivery	5, 203. *See also* Shawnee, William Ellsworth; Shawnee, Willie
Shawnee Sr.	4-7, 9, 14-15, 23, *24*, 25-26, 89, 105, 158, 279, 283, 285, 287, 291, 293, 302, 304, 316, 319-22, 326-27, 336, 341, 345, 347-48, 357-58, 363-65, 373, 378, 394, 402-3, 417, 420-21. *See also* Shawnee, William
Shawniego	103
Sherman, Miss Mary Eleanor	33, 35, 37
Skah-kah	188
Sloan, John	117, 120, 208
Smith, Henry	47
Smith, Mr.	308, 331, 348, 350
Smith, Mrs.	308, 354
Snow, Chancellor	298
Sonder, Alexander	145
Sparney, John	16. *See also* Esparney, John
Spoon, John	208, 228, 265, 269
Springer, Mr. Rev.	317
Spybuck, Cinda Emma	160, 210, 337, 341-42
Spybuck, Ernest	129, 191, 210, 218, 221, 224
Spybuck, John	221, 222, 266, 281, 309, 320, 322, 329, 331, 334-35, 345-46, 357
Spybuck, Mary	123-24
Spybuck, Maud	342
Starr, Charley	16, 107, 188
Starr, Chosa	188, 281, 287, 320, 322, 329, 338, 346, 358
Starr, Martin	16, 107, 209, 337
Steele, Mr.	320
Stevens, Mrs.	192
Stubblefield, Olive	314

T	
Tà-kē-sē-mō	185. See also Clarke, Jackson
Tarharty, Martin	188
Tatum, Lawrie	199
Taylor, John	208, 227
Taylor Jr., Ben	265, 279
Teacher	198, 202, 219. See also Test, Lizzie
Tecumseh	16, 111, 120, 133
Tenskatawa	120
Test, Lizzie	159, 184, 190, 198, 202, 212, 219. See also Katequa
Thàhnàhkăthōkwă	202, 225. See also Della, Jr.
Thomas, Edward L.	206
Tomahawk, Jacob	16, 107, 296
Tomahawk, Susie	16, 107
Toole, G. A.	47
Toon, Berry	330-32
Totommo	110, 120, 231. See also Little Jim
Toupan, Madeline	44
Turner, Marshall	199
Tyner, Bud	16, 107
Tyner, Bushyhead	209
Tyner, Lewis	209, 234
Tyner, Webster	120

U	
Umholtz, Mr.	239, 248-49, 252. See also Umholtz, F. H.
Umholtz, F. H.	238, 288. See also Umholtz, Mr.

V	
Valentine, Emma	30, 37, 47, 57, 71, 111, 232, 252, 287, 295. See also Valentine, Emma J.
Valentine, Emma J.	111. See also Valentine, Emma
Valentine, Geo. W.	66. See also Valentine, George
Valentine, George	57, 66, 71. See also Valentine, Geo. W.
Valentine, Hattie Agnes	43, 47, 66, 71
Valentine, Mary	47, 68, 71, 287
Valentine, Minnie	45, 71, 287

Valentine, Mr.	36, 70. *See also* Valentine, George
Valentine, Mrs.	37, 70. *See also* Valentine, Nora
Valentine, Nora	57, 71. *See also* Valentine, Mrs.
Valentine, Willie	36, 81. *See also* Valentine, W^m H.
Valentine, Wm H.	71. *See also* Valentine, Willie

W

Waggoner, Mr.	334
Walt, Jim	211
Ware, Supt.	325–26, 339
Warner, E. D.	70
Warrior, Carrie	3, 40, 44, 52, 57, 91, 103, 109, 111, 123, 187, 232, 238, 253–54, 262–63, 265, 269, 274, 279, 282, 287, 291, 302, 336, 342, 410–12
Warrior, Charley	180
Warrior, Jim	209–10, 233, 336, 338
Warrior, Nellie	189, 207, 281, 283, 330–31
Warrior, Sam	16, 179
Wasequawah	217
Washington, A. R.	351. *See also* Washington, Mr.
Washington, George	47
Washington, Gertrude	44
Washington, Lizzie	212, 283
Washington, Mr.	196, 269, 283. *See also* Washington, A. R.
Washington, Mrs.	283
Washington, Thomas	22, 209
Webb, Mrs. W. R.	191
Welch, John	22, 89, 183, 185
Wells, Iva	50, 256
Wēs'-kō-pă-thō"-kwă	190, 198. *See also* Douglas, Effie
Whipple, Della A.	186, 187, 194, 232, 237
Whipple, Joe	194, 220–21, 233, 268
White, Billy	228
White, Bob	208. *See also* Lălàhuēspĕă
White, Ewers	200
White, Harry B.	52
White, John	14–15, 178
White, Mr.	288
Whitehead, John	158, 202–5, 211, 214–16, 218–19, 246, 279

Whitehead, Mary	203, 204, 215, 219
Whitehead, Webster	203, 215, 219
White Turkey	16, 22, 129, 158, 179, 185-86, 188, 209, 362-63. *See also* John Bob; Whiteturkey
Whiteturkey	307. *See also* John Bob; White Turkey
White Turkey, Ellen	209
Wilby, Annie	255. *See also* Wilby, Miss
Wilby, Miss	256. *See also* Wilby, Annie
Wilford, Ollie	181, 187, 197, 207, 215, 291
Williams, Hattie	251, 253, 255
Williams, Miss	157, 161, 179, 187, 208-9, 228, 366
Williams, Mr.	226, 250. *See also* Williams, M. C.
Williams, Mrs. M. C.	226-28, 234, 306
Williams, Nora	251
Wilson, Anna	44. *See also* Wilson, Annie
Wilson, Annie	16, 107. *See also* Wilson, Anna
Wilson, Cooper	16, 107
Wilson, Grandma	317
Wilson, Kittie	45. *See also* Wilson, Kitty B.
Wilson, Kitty B.	52. *See also* Wilson, Kittie
Wilson, Maud	305
Wilson, Mexican	313
Wilson, Mrs. Mexican	191, 210
Wilson, Piney	262, 299, 302-4, 308, 310, 312-13, 317-18, 327
Wilson, Sam	313
Wilson, Spanish	313
Wistar, Ed	315
Wolf, Prof. D.	298
Woodard, Mr.	92, 226. *See also* Woodward, Lon
Woods, Ada	227
Woods, Lawyer	227
Woodward, Amos	256
Woodward, Dora	245, 259
Woodward, Hattie	246, 250-51, 253-55, 258
Woodward, Lon	231, 233, 258, 276. *See also* Woodward, Mr.
Woodward, Lucy	356
Woodward, Mr.	233-36, 267-68, 355, 357. *See also* Woodward, Lon
Woodward, Mrs.	267-68, 355
Wōo-kō-pă-hō-kwă	185

Woolbridge, Mary A.	47
Wray, Mr.	280, 292, 321, 329, 343–44, 346
Wright, Elizabeth Jane	5, 7, 105–6. *See also* Shawnee, Elizabeth Jane
X	
No entries for "X"	
Y	
Yellow Squirrel	210
Z	
No entries for "Z"	

Made in the USA
Monee, IL
18 December 2023